THE CIVILIZATION OF THE AMERICAN INDIAN SERIES

INDIAN SURVIVAL IN
COLONIAL NICARAGUA

INDIAN SURVIVAL IN
COLONIAL NICARAGUA

By

Linda A. Newson

UNIVERSITY OF OKLAHOMA PRESS : NORMAN AND LONDON

The paper in this book meets the guidelines for permanence and durability of the Committee on Production Guidelines for Book Longevity of the Council on Library Resources, Inc.

Publication of this work has been made possible in part by a grant from the Andrew W. Mellon Foundation.

Library of Congress Cataloging-in-Publication Data

Newson, Linda A.
  Indian survival in colonial Nicaragua.
  (The Civilization of the American Indian series; v. 175)
  Bibliography: p. 429
  Includes index.
  1. Indians of Central America—Nicaragua—Cultural assimilation. 2. Indians, Treatment of—Nicaragua—History.   3. Indians of Central America—Nicaragua—History. I. Title. II. Series.
F1525.3.C84N48   1986   972.85'00497   86-40078
ISBN 0-8061-2008-8 (alk. paper)

Contents

PART SIX
Conclusion

Illustrations

TABLES

Preface

The colonial experiences of Indians in Latin America were infinite. While few groups survived the colonial period unchanged, the cultural and demographic changes they experienced varied considerably. Some groups became extinct at an early date, others experienced a sharp decline followed by a slow recovery, and still others continued to decline into the nineteenth century. As a geographer I have been interested in identifying regional variations in population trends during the colonial period and suggesting factors that may have been responsible for differences in the level of survival of Indian populations. Although this book is limited to a study of the colonial experiences of Indians in Nicaragua, I hope that it will contribute to an understanding of these wider patterns and processes.

The idea for this book, perhaps surprisingly, arose out of an earlier piece of research I conducted on the cultural and demographic changes experienced by Indians in the island of Trinidad during the Spanish colonial period. Even in that small island clear spatial variations in Indian survival emerged that seemed to be related to how Spanish activities were distributed and whether the Indians had been allocated in encomiendas or charged to the care of missionaries. Wider reading enabled me to develop more fully some of my ideas concerning the differential survival of Indian populations. These appear in summary form in the Introduction to this book and will not be elaborated here. At the same time I was eager to conduct an in-depth comparative study to test some of the ideas I had developed. It seemed desirable to choose two societies which were markedly different but which, for methodological and practical reasons, were administered by the same audiencia. Several alternatives were considered, but nowhere was the contrast between Indian groups at the time of the Spanish conquest as marked as it was in Nicaragua, where the lacustrine depression dividing the Pacific lowlands from the central highlands and the Mosquito coast effectively divided Mesoamerican chiefdoms from South American tribes. Furthermore, the regions they inhabited fell under the administration of not only one audienca but also the same governor. In 1972, when the study was initiated, Murdo MacLeod's *Spanish Central America* had not been published, and little was known about the colonial period in Nicaragua, so that a study of that country was seen to have added advantages.

Archival research was conducted in Central America in 1973 and

1978 with financial support from the Social Science Research Council, the Central Research Fund of the University of London, and the Sir Ernest Cassel Educational Trust. Without their support this study would have been impossible. Most of the research was conducted in the Archivo General de Centro America, in Guatemala City, the national archive in Nicaragua having been destroyed in the Managua earthquake in December, 1972, and access to the cathedral archive in León being denied. Further research was conducted in the Spanish archives in Seville and Madrid. In particular I would like to thank the Director of the Archivo General de Indias, Rosario Parra, and her staff for all the help they provided me during my many visits to Seville. I would also like to thank the many fellow researchers with whom I shared coffee, wine, and ideas on those occasions. Thanks are also due the secretarial and cartographic staff at King's College for the many hours they spent struggling with my difficult manuscript and maps. Finally thanks are due George Lovell, Rod Watson, and David Robinson for sharing with me the fascination of Indian demography and making the research for this book so enjoyable.

LINDA A. NEWSON

London

INDIAN SURVIVAL IN
COLONIAL NICARAGUA

Part One

INTRODUCTION

CHAPTER 1

Indian Survival in Colonial Spanish America

Although controversy reigns over the size of the Indian population on the eve of Spanish conquest, probably most scholars of historical demography could agree that the highlands of Middle America and the Andes possessed the largest Indian populations and that smaller numbers were to be found in the lowlands of South America. At the end of the colonial period the highlands still possessed substantial Indian populations, but in the tropical coastal lowlands and islands of the Caribbean they had disappeared and largely been replaced by black slaves; small numbers still remained outside European contact in the tropical forested lowlands, including the Amazon Basin, and in remote parts of the empire, such as southern Chile and Argentina, while the rest of Latin America was characterized by a mixture of Indians and mestizos. It might be supposed that the greater survival of Indian populations in the highlands was a function of the larger numbers that had existed there at the time of the Spanish conquest. This would assume that the degree of Indian depopulation (and subsequent recovery) was the same throughout the subcontinent. In attempting to estimate the aboriginal population of America, Dobyns has suggested that the Indian population declined by a ratio of between 25:1 and 20:1 from the time of Conquest to the population nadir, which in many regions was reached in the midseventeenth century.[1] Several authors, including Dobyns himself, have recognized that the scale of Indian depopulation varied from region to region, and a number have produced evidence of different depopulation ratios for different areas. Smith, working on the central Andes, found that between 1520–25 and 1571 the ratio of decline on the coast was a staggering 58:1, whereas in the highlands it was 3.4:1.[2] From population estimates for Peru provided by Cook, it appears that between 1570 and 1620 the general scale of depopulation was lower but that losses continued to be higher on the coast than in the highlands, where the ratios of decline were 2.8:1 and 1.7:1, respectively.[3] A similar difference in depopulation ratios between the coast and the highlands has been noted by Cook and Borah for central Mexico.[4] They have calculated that between 1532 and 1608 the depopulation ratio for the coast was about 26:1 and for the plateau area 13:1. In comparing Peru and central Mexico, it would appear that the decline in the Indian population in coastal Peru was far greater than that in coastal Mexico but that the decline in the Peruvian sierra was smaller than that on the Mexican plateau. Denevan agrees

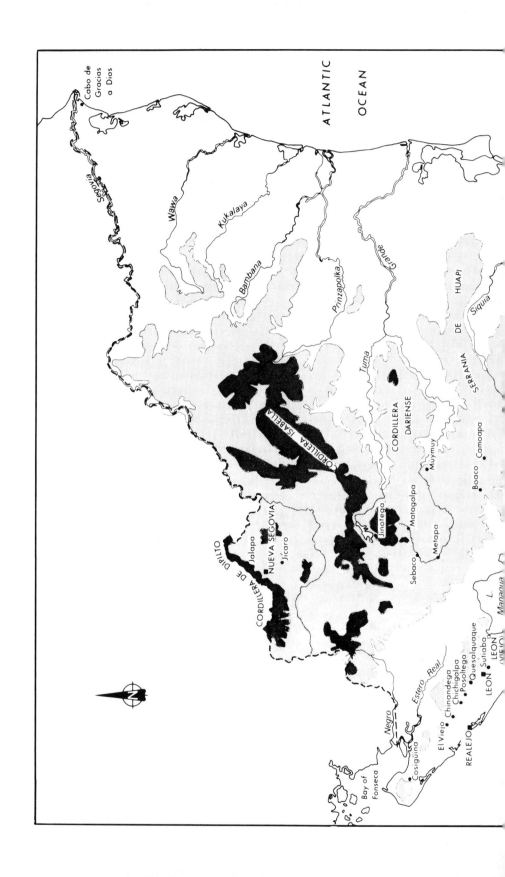

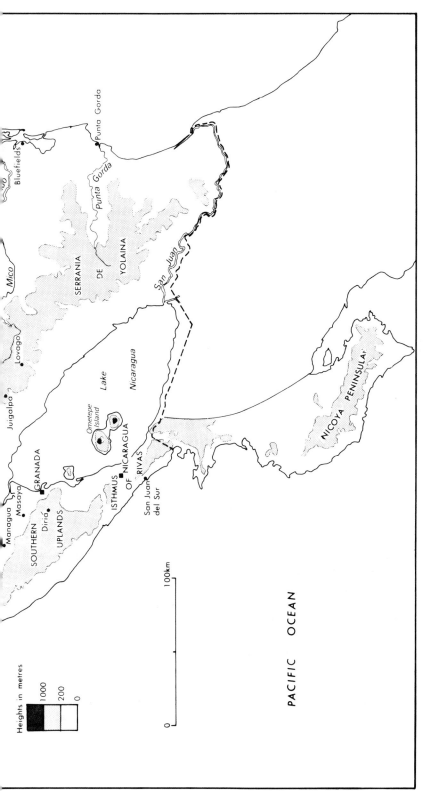

Fig. 1. Nicaragua and Nicoya

that Dobyns's depopulation ratios are too high for the highland areas but suggests that they are not high enough for the tropical lowlands, where, on the basis of research on the Indian population of the Llanos de Mojos, in northeastern Bolivia, he estimates that the depopulation ratio from contact to nadir was probably at least 35: 1.[5] It is also clear that Dobyns's depopulation ratio is too low for the islands and fringing mainland of the Caribbean, where the Indian population became almost extinct within a generation. Furthermore, within these broad areas there is evidence of local and regional variations in the levels of depopulation.[6]

Unfortunately little research has been conducted on the recovery of Indian populations in Spanish America, but it made a significant contribution to the survival of some Indian groups at the end of the colonial period; other Indian populations continued to decline throughout the colonial period until they became extinct or began to increase in the Independence period. The decline in the Indian population was halted first in Mexico, where from about the middle of the seventeenth century most areas began to register increases. The actual timing of the increase appears to have been varied from area to area, as does the rate of increase, which was affected by migratory movements.[7] In Central America the Indian population did not begin to increase until the end of the century,[8] while in Peru the recovery did not occur until the mideighteenth century.[9] In all these areas, therefore, the dramatic decline in the Indian population in the early colonial period was in part compensated for by a later recovery. Thus demographic trends during the colonial period cannot be inferred from a comparison of the size of the Indian population at the time of Spanish conquest and on the eve of Independence. There were considerable variations in the scale of depopulation and subsequent recovery, if it occurred at all, which combined to produce different levels of Indian survival at the end of the colonial period.[10]

Before passing on to examine possible explanations for these variations in Indian survival, it is desirable to define the terms "Indian" and "survival" as they will be used in this book. An Indian can be defined on the basis of race or culture. Before the fifteenth century human groups were relatively isolated so that it was easy to distinguish different genotypes, but subsequent miscegenation has made the differentiation of the races difficult. Since the seventeenth-century, Indians in Spanish America have generally been defined on the basis of their culture rather than their race.[11] A disadvantage of defining Indians on cultural criteria is that acculturation may occur without miscegenation so that in areas where non-Indian cultural traits predominate there is a danger of underestimating the proportion of the population which is Indian by biological descent.[12] However, to define Indian populations on racial criteria, such as cephalic indices or blood groups, is impossible on a large scale and in a historical context. Also there are few Indian villages where miscegenation has not penetrated and hence few Indians who might be described as biologically "pure." Although there is little choice, therefore, but to define Indians on cultural criteria, it has the advantage that in terms of the economic and social life of the Indians culture is more significant than race.

Superficially it might seem that defining survival would not constitute a problem. Nevertheless, Tannenbaum makes the point that "the greatest success story racially speaking, in America, is the mestizo,"[13] and it could be argued that the Indian has survived but in a different genetic and cultural form. This kind of survival is not considered here as survival, but it does not follow that those Indians who are considered to have survived have not experienced some degree of cultural, and to a lesser extent racial, change, for indeed they have. Nevertheless, large numbers of Indians, particularly those in the highlands of Latin America, retain many cultural traits dating from the pre-Columbian period which have weathered over five hundrd years of contact with nonindigenous peoples. The extent of their survival was even greater at the end of the colonial period.

At this point it is important to stress that what is being discussed here is cultural survival and not the survival of biological populations, for the two kinds of survival are not always compatible. Cultural survival may be defined as the persistence of a group's economy, sociopolitical organization, and ideology without change which would result in its transformation into a fundamentally different form. The adherence of a group to its culture may, however, conflict with the aim of biological survival. Wagley, for example, has shown in his study of two Tupí tribes in Brazil how the Tenetehara reached near extinction through the strict adherence to rules governing marriage, which were unworkable when the population declined following European contact, whereas the Tapirapé, whose social organization was more flexible, were able to survive.[14] To ensure biological survival, therefore, it may be necessary for the group to make cultural changes. These changes may involve the disintegration of its culture and the incorporation of its former practitioners into a new social group. Under Spanish colonial rule many indigenous cultures disappeared, and the surviving individuals were incorporated into newly established nation-states. This does not mean that their culture was always completely destroyed; as will be shown later, the culture of individuals and small groups survived with them, but the organizational structure of their cultures was transformed.

Alternatively, the biological survival of a proportion of the members of a society may be achieved without their incorporation into a new culture by internal transformation. For example, Guayakí horticulturalists in Paraguay were able to survive European contact by retreating into the interior forest areas, where they became hunters and gatherers.[15] Since the aims of cultural and biological survival may conflict, it is necessary to indicate that the aim of this book is to study variations in cultural survival. This will be done by examining the processes of cultural change, including changes in the size of Indian populations as defined on cultural criteria.

In attempting to explain spatial variations in the degree of Indian survival, two factors which are known to have contributed to the decline in the Indian population should be examined: disease and death resulting from the direct actions of conquistadors and colonists. There appears to be common agreement, at least among most recent writers on the historical demography of Latin America, that disease was a major factor in the decline of Indian populations.[16] The most notable killers were smallpox, measles, typhus, plague, yellow fever, and malaria. In the documentary record there are many accounts of the populations of villages and whole areas being reduced by one-third or one-half as a result of epidemics, particularly of smallpox and measles, and the devastating impact of these diseases on previously noninfected populations has been corroborated by historically more recent epidemics.[17]

It is a commonly held view that the greater decline of the Indian population of the tropical lowlands was due to yellow fever and malaria, which occur only in climates where the mean temperature is over 20°C, and possibly also due to the greater virulence of diseases in warmer climates.[18] There are several difficulties with these proposals. First, it seems likely that malaria and yellow fever, which require insect vectors for their propagation, were relatively late introductions to the New World. It is generally considered that malaria was introduced into the New World about the middle of the seventeenth century and that the first agreed epidemic of yellow fever occurred in Yucatán in 1648,[19] although a few would argue for its presence at an earlier date.[20] Hence the early decline in the Indian population cannot be attributed to these diseases. Second, although it is true that intestinal infections are more prevalent in the tropics and, although not contributing directly to the mortality rate, would have increased the susceptibility of Indians living there to more deadly diseases,[21] a number of other Old World diseases were equally if not more virulent in the cooler highlands. Smallpox and pneumonic plague thrive in cool, dry climates, where unhygenic conditions are often created which also encourage the spread of typhus.[22] Furthermore, the concentration of population in large nucleated settlements in the highlands would have enabled and facilitated the spread of disease, whereas in the tropical lowlands its spread would have been hindered by the dispersed character of the population and settlements.[23]

Despite these comments it is important to recognize that many tropical coasts earned early reputations for being unhealthy, and it may be that there were other tropical diseases, as yet unidentified, which may have contributed to the higher death rate in those areas. At present, however, there is insufficient evidence to conclude that the lower level of Indian survival in the tropical lowlands can be accounted for wholly in terms of the greater impact of disease. Indeed, although disease was clearly a major factor that contributed to the decline of Indian populations and later retarded their recovery, the pattern of its impact is likely to have been much more complex than is often suggested. The spread and impact of particular diseases would have depended not only on altitude and climate but on a variety of other factors, including the presence of vectors for transmitting the diseases, population density, the degree of interpersonal contact, subsistence patterns, sanitation, and immunity.[24]

Sixteenth-century observers blamed the rapid decline in the Indian population on the systematic killing, overwork, and ill-treatment of the Indians by conquistadors and colonists. There is no doubt that in the Caribbean islands the Black Legend was a reality which contributed significantly to the almost complete extinction of the Indians there. In addition many islands and the fringing mainland of the Caribbean as well as parts of Central America were depopulated as a result of the Indian slave trade. In 1542 the crown under pressure from the Dominicans and eager to protect the dwindling supply of labor promulgated the New Laws. Although they were often infringed, the New Laws did lead to an improvement in the treatment of the Indians to the extent that the aftermath of conquest on the South American mainland which occurred mainly after their introduction did not result in a repeat of the demographic disaster that had occurred in the islands. Thus this change in crown policy can in part account for differences in the decline of the Indian population in these broad areas, but it cannot account for regional variations within them. Nor can the regional variations be accounted for by the employment of different policies toward the Indians in different areas, since it was the crown's intention that laws and institutions formulated in Spain should apply uniformly to all parts of the empire. While laws might be interpreted differently by different administrators on the ground, officials were constantly changing, and it is doubtful that personnel in any one area interpreted the laws consistently in a manner that might account for a smaller or larger decline in the Indian population; any spatial variations in Spanish-Indian relations that emerge should therefore be interpreted as reactions to local conditions rather than as expressions of differences in government policy or in its interpretation by its officers.

It is suggested that the level of survival of particular Indian groups during the colonial period was a function of two factors:

1. The nature of human societies at the time of Spanish conquest and related to this the size of the Indian population. These influenced the type of institution used to control and exploit the Indians and the ability of the group to resist or adapt to changes brought about by Spanish conquest and colonization.

2. The existence and desirability of resources in the area inhabited by the group.

In conquest and colonization probably no other colonial power has been faced with such a variety of cultures: highly stratified agricultural states and chiefdoms existed in the highlands of Middle America and the Andes; egalitarian tribes subsisting on shifting cultivation supplemented by wild food resources inhabited the tropical lowlands; and hunters, fishers, and gatherers lived in northern Mexico, southern Chile, and Argentina. The Spaniards had two basic aims with respect to the Indians: to effect their conversion and "civilization" and to exploit them as sources of profit and labor for the benefit of colonists and the empire. Once the Indians had been conquered, three institutions could be employed to achieve these aims—the encomienda, the mission, and slavery—and the eventual adoption of one of them depended on the nature of the Indian societies the Spaniards encountered.[25]

The encomienda was a grant of Indians to an individual who, in return for providing the Indians with protection and instruction in the Catholic faith, could levy tribute from them in the form of goods or money and until 1549 could also demand labor services. Later in the sixteenth century labor was organized under the repartimiento, or mita, which required each Indian village to make available a quota of its tributary population for approved work for specified periods and wages. The encomienda and the repartimiento were later superseded in many areas by free labor. The encomienda and the repartimiento were considered appropriate for controlling and exploiting Indians in the highland states and chiefdoms of Middle America and the Andes for several reasons. First, these Indians had been subject to labor drafts and tribute payment in the pre-Columbian period, so that, although the systems by which they were exacted were modified, such demands were not considered extraordinary. Second, the hierarchical structure of these societies permitted the Spaniards to control and exploit large Indian populations through a relatively small number of native leaders; a closer means of control, such as slavery would have provided, was unnecessary.

The control and exploitation of tribes and bands could not be effected so easily by means of the same institutions. These Indians had not paid tribute or provided labor for extracommunal purposes in pre-Columbian times, so that no organizational structure existed for their exaction, and the task was made even more difficult by the lack of effective native leadership. Thus to impose the encomienda and the repartimiento would have required considerable managerial inputs. Since these Indians produced only small surpluses, if any, and could provide only small sources of labor, the Spaniards did not consider the task worthwhile. Instead, the initial conversion and civilization of tribal Indians was left to the missionaries, who could supply the closer form of supervision required. Theoretically after ten years mission settlements were to be handed over to the secular authorities and the Indians were to pay tribute and provide labor in the same way as those Indians who had been granted in encomiendas. In practice, however, they persisted much longer.

The nomadic hunters, fishers, and gatherers provided even less in terms of surpluses and sources of labor and were more difficult to control than were tribes, so that little effort was made to bring them under Spanish control. However, where the Spaniards exploited lands and minerals within their territories, often using imported labor, the Indians harassed their settlements, and the Spaniards responded by attempting to control them by enslavement or extermination. Indian slavery was forbidden from 1542, but it continued in remote parts of the empire, notably northern Mexico, southern Chile, and Argentina, where the Indians proved exceptionally difficult to control.

Thus, although there were some exceptions, there was a fairly high degree of correlation between the nature of Indian societies and the institutions and mechanisms used to control and exploit them. Inherent differences in these institutions and in the Indian groups they affected combined to produce different levels of cultural and demographic change, resulting in the greater survival of state and chiefdom groups as compared with tribes and bands.

The nature of Indian societies at the time of Spanish conquest influenced their level of survival in other ways. A number of authors have observed that contact is less disruptive and the conquered group more likely to survive when the two contacting cultures are similar.[26] In such instances the dominance of one group over another may be achieved by the transference of power at the highest level of organization or, as Steward terms it, level of sociocultural integration, whereas at lower levels there may be relatively little cultural change. Thus in the highland states of Middle America and the Andes the Spaniards could control the Indian population by modifying the indigenous state institutions, so that at lower levels of organization, such as the community or family level, the culture was able to survive relatively unchanged.[27] Where no form of state or supracommunity organization existed, then to control the native population the Spaniards were forced to make changes at the community or family level of organization, thereby removing the barriers to the rapid acculturation and racial assimilation of individuals. As a result the less complex societies, such as bands or tribes, were more vulnerable to changes brought about by Spanish conquest and colonization than were chiefdoms or states.

The adaptability of an Indian group to change is also related to its level of develolpment. More advanced societies are more adaptable, since they possess greater ranges of strategies that can be put into operation should circumstances change. Less advanced groups are often highly adapted to specific environments to the extent that any change in the environment in the form of ecological alteration or culture contact often results in the cultural or biological extinction of the group. As a result less advanced groups tend to resist cultural change.[28] Hence in Spanish America the more highly developed states displayed less resistance to Spanish control than did the less advanced groups, and particularly the bands who refused to submit to Spanish authority and waged constant war against the Spaniards throughout the colonial period. This is an alternative way of interpreting Benedict's distinction between the "submissiveness" of the "high cultures" and the "freedom-loving tribes" who resisted Spanish domination.[29]

The kind and degree of cultural and demographic change experienced by Indian groups during the colonial period was also related to the distribution of resources which attracted conquistadors and colonists, since it influenced the degree of contact between Indians and other races. Colonists settled in areas where there were mineral deposits or large, sedentary Indian populations that could be employed in the development of commercial agriculture. In these areas demands on Indian lands, labor, and production were greatest, and Indian communities in the vicinity experienced the greatest economic and social changes. The close contact between the races in those areas also provided the greatest opportunities for the ill-treatment and overwork of the Indians and for miscegenation; many authors have noted that miscegenation was most common in the cities, mines, and haciendas.[30] Conversely, the lack of resources and remoteness of an area from centers of economic activity generally encouraged Indian survival.[31]

Against this background this book examines the cultural and demographic changes experienced by Indian groups in Nicaragua during the colonial period. Nicaragua is a particularly good area in which to examine these ideas, since on the eve of Spanish conquest it was inhabited by Indian groups representative of two cultural types: chiefdoms and tribes. The borderline between the two cultural types fell along the lacustrine depression dividing the Pacific lowlands from the central highlands and Caribbean coast. This boundary not only was of local significance but also formed part of the major divide between the cultures of Mesoamerica and South America. These two cultural types and the resources of the country directly influenced the subsequent cultural and demographic history of the Indians during the colonial period.

The book is divided chronologically into four main sections at dates that were significant in terms of the cultural changes experienced by the Indians: Conquest, 1550, and 1720. Reasons for choosing the Conquest as a significant date are obvious, and 1550 is appropriate for it marked the effective introduction of the New Laws and the end of the Indian slave trade, which played such an important role in the early history of Nicaragua. The choice of 1720 is less obvious but was adopted for a number of reasons. First, it was the date of the abolition of the personal encomienda. Second, about this time Indian populations were beginning to register clear increases, although in some areas the increases had begun slightly earlier. Third, it marked the beginnings of the Bourbon reforms and attempts to revitalize the empire. MacLeod has also viewed this date as significant in terms of the socioeconomic history of Central America.[32]

Within each major section the character of Spanish colonization is described as a prelude to discussing the cultural and demographic changes experienced by the chiefdoms and tribes. This sequence is not meant to imply that the process of culture contact was unidirectional or that the Indians were passive recipients of Spanish culture, but it is considered preferable to describe the context in which the changes were occurring before discussing the character of the changes themselves. The discussion examines the nature of such institutions as the encomienda and the mission, which directly affected Indian communities, as well as the distribution of non-Indians and their economic activities. From the latter it is possible to identify the areas of most intense contact between Indians and other races and the level of demand placed on Indian communities in terms of land, labor, and production. Subsequently the cultural changes experienced by the chiefdoms and tribes are examined separately. In terms of the structure of the book, it might have been preferable to discuss the nature of Spanish colonization, including the institutions employed to control and exploit the Indians, separately for chiefdom and tribal groups, but their effects were not always limited to one group or the other. Hence, although the encomienda was the main institution that affected the chiefdoms, it was also introduced to the fringes of the tribal area. Moreover, many of the economic activities established by the Spaniards had influences outside the areas in which they were situated, particularly in the demands they made on Indian labor. Thus to discuss the character of Spanish colonization separately for chiefdoms and tribes would involve considerable repetition. Each major section concludes with

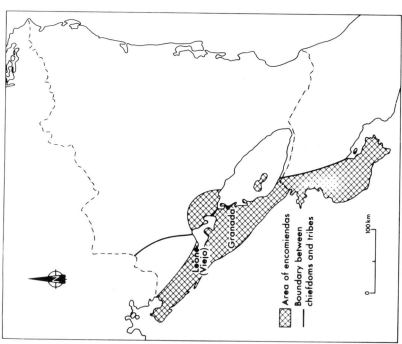

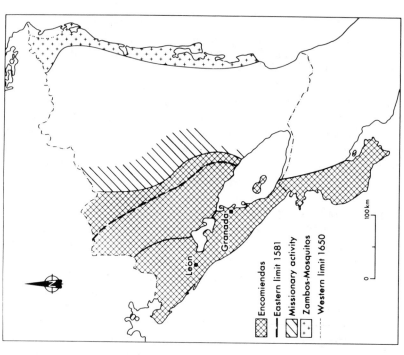

León
(Viejo)

Granada

Area of encomiendas

Boundary between
chiefdoms and tribes

0   100 km

León

Granada

Encomiendas

Eastern limit 1581

Missionary activity

Zambos-Mosquitos

Western limit 1650

0   100 km

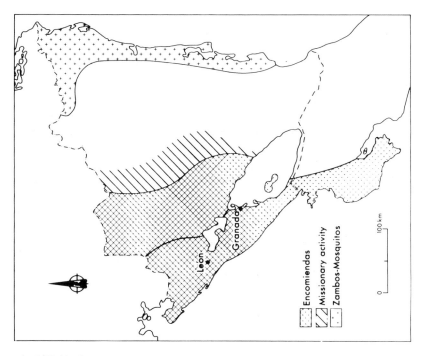

Fig. 2.
Zones of cultural influence.
Upper left, 1550;
upper right, 1550–1720;
right, 1720–1821.

a discussion of the demographic changes experienced by the two groups, the size of the Indian population being used as a surrogate measure of their survival. This is acceptable given that throughout most of the colonial period the Indian population was culturally defined.

The discussion of cultural changes experienced by Indians in Nicaragua is uneven. This is largely a reflection of the availability of documentary evidence, which in turn is related to the importance the Spaniards attached to the two Indian groups. The larger Indian populations found in the chiefdom area attracted conquistadors and colonists from an early date, and it was there that the Spanish centers of administration and economic activity developed. Thus from the time of the Conquest there are accounts of these groups by conquistadors, chroniclers, missionaries, and royal officials, among others. For most of the tribal area, however, there is a lack of evidence until the end of the sixteenth century, and even from then onward it is fragmentary compared with that for Pacific Nicaragua, although it does improve during the colonial period as the area came under European influence. Thus any reconstruction of Indian cultures in this area at the time of discovery has to rely mainly on the documentary evidence from the seventeenth and eighteenth centuries, before which time they undoubtedly experienced some degree of change as a result of intermittent and indirect contact with other cultures and races. Until more archaeological investigations have been conducted in this area, there is no alternative but to rely on the inadequate documentary evidence available. The analysis of cultural changes experienced by the tribal groups is made even more difficult by the variety of cultural influences to which they were exposed. Although the civilization and conversion of tribal Indians were largely left to the missionary orders, on the western fringes of the area Indian communities were brought under Spanish administration and allocated in encomiendas. The picture is complicated even further by the settlement of the English on the Mosquito Coast and by the emergence of a mixed race known as the Zambo-Mosquito, who gradually extended their influence over the tribal groups from the east. Because of the variety of cultural influences on Indians in the tribal area the discussion of cultural changes experienced by them after 1550 is divided into four sections: tributary Indian villages, the missions, Indians outside Spanish control, and residents on the Mosquito Coast. The last category poses a problem in assessing Indian survival, because the Indians living on the Mosquito Coast contributed to the emergence of the Zambo-Mosquito. As a mixed racial group the Zambo-Mosquito cannot be classified as Indian any more than can mestizos, but there were considerable variations within the group, and those who inhabited the Nicaraguan part of the coast were more "Indian" in race and culture. Nevertheless, the culture of the Zambo-Mosquito in Nicaragua changed so substantially during the eighteenth century as a result of contact with the English that, although today they are known as Miskito Indians, they are not included here among Indian survivors at the end of the colonial period.

Part Two

NICARAGUA ON THE EVE OF SPANISH CONQUEST

CHAPTER 2

Indian Cultures and Their Environments

The Indians of Latin America have been classified on the basis of archaeological, historical, linguistic, and cultural evidence, but in most instances the Indians of Nicaragua and Nicoya have been divided into two major groups: those who had strong relationships with and possessed characteristics common to Indians in Mesoamerica, and those who had greater affiliations with Indians in South America.

The first major attempt to classify Indian cultures in recent years was made by Cooper in 1942. He proposed a division of South American cultures into three types: sierral, selval, and marginal.[1] This classification was modified in 1946 by Steward, who added a fourth category called the Circum-Caribbean and Sub-Andean type, to give the developmental sequence of Marginal, Tropical Forest, Circum-Caribbean and Sub-Andean, and Andean cultures.[2] The Circum-Caribbean culture was considered to be the foundation on which the Andean civilizations were built and was characterized by the presence of large sedentary farming communities, which were socially stratified, possessed some form of political organization, and had a priest-temple-idol complex.[3]

According to Steward, the origin of this cultural type was in the Andean area, and from there it spread to Central America, Colombia, Venezuela, and the Antilles. As it spread into the tropical forested lowlands, it introduced new technologies, but it failed to maintain any of its sociopolitical, religious, and material elaborations. Hence the Tropical-Forest type was derivative from the Circum-Caribbean type and was characterized by smaller villages formed by unstratified groups, whose economy was based to a greater degree on wild-food resources and whose religion was based on shamanistic practices.[4] Under this fourfold typology the whole of Central America was classified as Circum-Caribbean.[5]

A more recent analysis of cultural traits by Chapman using historical evidence has suggested that the tribes of eastern Honduras and Nicaragua should be classified as Tropical Forest cultures, since much of the cultural elaboration to be found there is the result of post-Conquest acculturation.[6] She also rejects the proposed origin of the Tropical Forest cultures as derivative of Circum-Caribbean cultures and suggests that the Tropical Forest cultures in Central America originated from a "sweet manioc culture" which developed in northwest South America before and independent of any Circum-Caribbean culture. She suggests that the former was introduced to the area by Chibchan peoples a few thousand years before the Christian Era.[7]

In 1959, Steward modified his typology of South American cultures and changed the names of the types to give an indication of their characteristics; thus the Tropical Forest type was renamed Tropical Forest Farmers, and the Circum-Caribbean type was called Theocratic and Militaristic Chiefdoms. He also recognized the presence of Tropical Forest peoples in Central America by indicating that northern and eastern Honduras was inhabited by Tropical Forest Farmers.[8]

The distinction between Mesoamerican cultures and those with South American affiliations was effectively made by Kirchhoff when he defined Mesoamerica on a cultural-linguistic basis, including within it Pacific Nicaragua and Nicoya.[9] Kirchhoff's eastern boundary of Mesoamerica was defined more precisely by Stone using archeological, historical, and ethnological evidence, although she admitted that the boundary was difficult to define exactly because of the natural blending of cultures at the margins of culture areas and the presence of cultural outliers and inliers within the two major culture areas.[10] This view has been echoed by Baudez, who maintains that there was no sharp break between Mesoamerican cultures and other Central American cultures. He also notes that, although the cultures of the Pacific region possessed many traits characteristic of Mesoamerica, they were essentially marginal to the Mesoamerican civilization. As such he prefers to talk of a zone of Mesoamerican tradition and a zone of South American tradition.[11] Accepting his arguments, I employ these terms in the following discussion, although the boundary between the two zones has been redrawn on the basis of my interpretation of historical documents in conjunction with published archaeological and linguistic sources.

A precise cultural boundary is difficult to define not only because of the complex culture history of the region but also because of the inadequacies of the source material. Archaeological investigations, particularly in Nicaragua, have been limited, while the documentary record for the contact period is very fragmentary. The main sources of evidence are the documents written by early conquistadors, officials, and missionaries. In addition, there are a number of published accounts by Spaniards who had some experience of life in Central America, for example, Gonzalo Fernández de Oviedo y Valdés, Pascual de Andagoya, Juan de Torquemada, Girolamo Benzoni, and Alonso Ponce. These accounts contain useful information on the region though not always about the Indian population that inhabited it.[12]

Other accounts include the works of official chroniclers, such as Pedro Martyr D'Anghera, Juan López de Velasco and Antonio de Herrera y Tordesillas, who, although they never visited Central America, in their official capacities had immediate access to the early reports from the New World and could interview some of the conquistadors personally.[13]

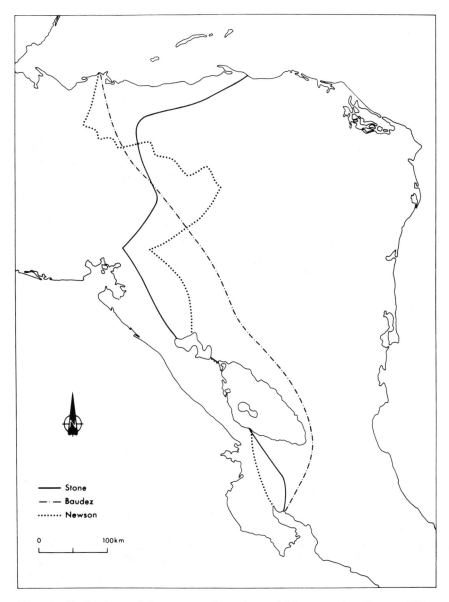

Fig. 3. Projections of the eastern boundary of Mesoamerica (Stone, "The Eastern Frontier," p. 119; Baudez, *Central America,* inside cover).

Many of the authors of secondary accounts copied indiscriminately, and sometimes incorrectly, from each other and from the documents to which they had access, and their works must be used with care.

In the early sixteenth century Oviedo recorded that four languages were spoken by Indians in Nicaragua—Chorotega, Chondal, Orotiña, and "Nicaragua, which is the same as they speak in Mexico."[14] López de Gómara, on the other hand, distinguished five Indian languages—Coribici, Chortega, Chondal, Orotiña, and Mejicano,[15] as did the *oidor licenciado* García de Palacio, who recorded that the following languages were spoken: Pipil Corrupta, Mangue, Maribio, Potón, and Chontal.[16] Since that time recent research has identified a number of other languages that were spoken at the time of the Spanish conquest. From this evidence it is clear that the cultural-linguistic groups that were found in the Mesoamerican zone were the Chorotega, the Maribio, the Pipil, the Nicarao, and the Nahuatl, all of whom have their linguistic origins toward the north, whereas the South American zone was inhabited by the Sumu, the Matagalpa, and the Rama, whose affiliations are toward the south. Nevertheless, there were colonies of Nahuatl traders in the South American zone and outliers of Ulua Indians belonging to the Sumu cultural-linguistic group in the Mesoamerican zone.

THE MESOAMERICAN ZONE

At the time of the Spanish conquest several Indian groups of Mesoamerican origin inhabited western Nicaragua and possessed colonies in the South American zone. Probably all of these groups arrived during the Christian Era, but they formed several distinct migrations. The first migrants to Central America from the north appear to have been the Chorotega, and they were closely followed by the Maribio. About the same time the Nahuat-Pipil were also arriving in the area. Later the Nicarao migrated to Nicaragua, and finally Nahuatl trading groups established colonies in the area. The precise origin and date of the migration of each group will be discussed separately. Each belongs to one of two major linguistic stocks: Oto-Mangue and Uto-Azteca. The Chorotega and possibly the Maribio belong to the former, and the rest to the latter.

The Oto-Manguean Stock

THE CHOROTEGA

The Chorotega probably represent the first definitely identifiable migration from the north into Central America.[17] On the basis of informa-

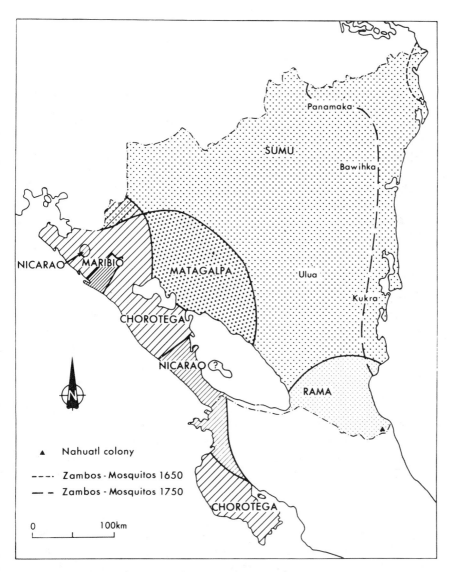

Fig. 4. Indian cultures on the eve of the Spanish Conquest.

tion collected from old Indian informants Torquemada relates that the
Chorotega migrated south from Soconusco (Chiapas) at the same time
as the Nicarao as a result of oppression by the Olmec.[18] He distin-
guishes the Chorotega from the Nicarao by saying that the former lived
in the mountains inland whereas the latter lived on the coast. When
these groups arrived in Choluteca, an old man prophesied that the

Chorotega would settle on the Pacific coast and would establish a good port near the island of Chira in the Gulf of Nicoya. The Nicarao, on the other hand, would settle on a lake in which there was an island with two mountains. Following the prophecy, the Chorotega continued south and established themselves in western Nicaragua and Nicoya, displacing the Corobici who were living there.[19] Although Torquemada specifically states that the Chorotega and the Nicarao left Soconusco together, he also refers to the Chorotega as those "who went first" ("que iban en la delantera"). The later arrival of the Nicarao is also suggested by the fact that they had to fight the Chorotega to gain possession of the lands they finally occupied on the Isthmus of Rivas.

Archaeological evidence also supports the later arrival of the Nicarao, and this evidence will be discussed later. Although it seems probable that the Chorotega did arrive in Nicaragua before the Nicarao, it is not certain by what period of time they preceded them. Although it will be shown that the date of the departure from Soconusco described by Torquemada was probably about A.D. 800, it is assumed that this date referred to the last migration before the Spanish conquest, which was that of the Nicarao.[20] Chapman suggests that the Chorotega arrived slightly before the Nicarao in the ninth and tenth centuries.[21]

Archaeological evidence supports the arrival of the Chorotega in Nicaragua and Nicoya about A.D. 800. The Chorotega have been associated with Nicoya Polychrome wares, particularly those belonging to the Papagayo group, which exhibit influences from Mesoamerican cultures, including the Maya, with whom the Chorotega came into contact during their migration south. These pottery types have been dated at between A.D. 800 and 1200, and they are particularly abundant in Nicoya.[22]

The Chorotega belonged to the Oto-Manguean linguistic stock, but their language was known by different names in different areas.[23] Mangue was spoken on the Pacific coastal plain, and two forms existed, called Nagrandan and Dirian. Choluteca was spoken on the shores of the Bay of Fonseca and Orotiña in the Nicoya Peninsula.[24] In the sixteenth century the Chorotega were living around the Bay of Fonseca, in an area often referred to as Chorotega Malalaca or Chorotega Malaca.[25] In 1586, Friar Alonso Ponce noted that Mangue was spoken in Nicomongoya and Nacarahego in Choluteca, and it is possible that it may have been spoken farther west, in present El Salvador.[26] The Chorotega were also established around León and Granada, and in 1586 the following towns were described as Mangue-speaking: Sutiaba, Mabiti, Nagarote, Matiare, Nindirí, and Masaya.[27] Although at the same time Managua was described as Nahua-speaking, Oviedo recorded that the Indians living there spoke Chorotega.[28] Since both accounts are considered to be fairly reliable, it is likely that both languages were spoken there, the Mexican language having been introduced after the Conquest, when it was used as a lingua franca throughout Central America.[29]

Squier divided the Chorotega into two factions called the Dirian and the Nagrandan.[30] The Dirian occupied the southern part of the area lying between the northern extremity of Lake Nicaragua, the Tipitapa River and the southern half of the Lake Managua to the Pacific. This area included the towns of Granada—the former Indian town of Jalteba—Masaya, Managua, Tipitapa, Diriomo, and Diriamba. To the north along the northern shore of Lake Managua and on the plain of León to the Pacific were the Nagrandan, whose main town was León. According to Levy, just before the Spanish conquest these two groups had fought a war and remained bitter enemies.[31] Although the Chorotega formerly occupied the greater part of the coastal plain from the Bay of Fonseca to Nicoya, as a result of the arrival of the Nicarao in Nicaragua and their final establishment on the Isthmus of Rivas, the Chorotegan groups around León and Granada were separated from those living in Nicoya.[32]

THE MARIBIO

As a result of the political upheavals taking place in Cholula in the seventh and eighth centuries another Indian group, known in western Mexico as the Tlapaneca-Yopi, also migrated south. They closely followed the Chorotega to western Nicaragua, where they were known as Maribio and later Sutiaba.[33] Linguistically the Maribio are thought to have belonged to the Hokan-Sioux stock, although more recently Kaufman has suggested that they also belonged to the Oto-Manguean stock.[34]

In 1586, Friar Alonso Ponce's secretary recorded that Maribio was spoken on the Pacific coast of Nicaragua in the towns of Mazatega, Chichigalpa, Posoltega, Posolteguilla, and Chinandega, but the inhabitants of Sutiaba itself were described as Mangue-speaking.[35] This is likely to have been an error; a census five years previously had recorded that Maribio was spoken throughout the province of Sutiaba, which included the towns of San Pedro, Soyatega, Posolteguilla, Xiquilapa, Ayatega, Cindegapipil, Panaltega, and Distanguis, although Mexicana Corrupta was apparently used as a lingua franca throughout the area.[36]

Between Chinandega and Sutiaba was the town of Yacacoyaua (or Yacacoyagua), where, according to Ponce's secretary, the Indians spoke Tacacho. The character and origin of this language are unknown, but the fact that in 1581 the languages spoken there were recorded as Chontal and Mexicana Corrupta suggests that it was probably a remnant of a formerly more widespread language spoken by the early inhabitants of western Nicaragua.[37]

The Uto-Aztecan Stock

Central America was at various times influenced by the migration of Nahua-speaking peoples into the area. There appear to have been three major migrations: two early migrations of people who spoke Nahuat, and a later one of Aztec traders who spoke a more recent dialect known as Nahuatl.[38] The first Nahuat-speaking peoples to arrive in Central America were known as the Pipil, and they probably arrived during the ninth and tenth centuries A.D., about the same time as the Chorotega.[39] The other Nahuat-speaking group to enter the area were the Nicarao, who finally settled in Nicaragua about A.D. 1200. Finally Aztec traders began to establish colonies in the area between the fourteenth and sixteenth centuries.

Although these migrations were distinct, the documentary record is sometimes confusing with respect to the languages that were spoken by these groups. Many documents merely describe the language spoken as "Mexicana" or "Pipil," which could refer to any one of the three groups. Sometimes, however, the terms "Mexicana Corrupta" or "Pipil Corrupta" were used. These terms refer to Nahuat dialects, which were held in contempt by later Nahuatl speakers. Francisco Vázquez refers to "Mexicana Corrupta or Pipil (as we would say the language of children or that spoken by those of little intelligence)."[40] Similarly, in the early sixteenth century the language spoken by Indians living in the vicinity of Granada was described as "the same as that of Mexicano in its sound, although coarse and rustic."[41] A further problem is that Nahuatl was used as a lingua franca in the early colonial period, so that its distribution appears wider than it was in pre-Columbian times.[42]

For the same reason place-name evidence is also unreliable. While some villages with Mexican names may indeed have been inhabited by Mexicans in the pre-Columbian period, others were given those names during the early colonial period.[43] Furthermore, there is little archaeological evidence for the presence of Mexican cultures in Central America, because Mexicans tended to adopt the culture of the Indians they met in the course of their migrations.[44] Thus any attempt at describing the distribution of Mexican groups at the time of Conquest must be based on historical accounts however difficult they might be to interpret.

THE NAHUAT-PIPIL

The Pipil

Although all Nahuat-speaking peoples in Central America were known as Pipil, the term is used here to refer to the descendants of the early migration(s) to distinguish them from the other Nahuat-Pipil group, the Nicarao.

It is possible that at the time of the Spanish conquest the Pipil were living in an area south and east of the Bay of Fonseca. When Ponce visited the area in 1586, the Indians of El Viejo were described as speaking "Mexicana Corrupta and they call it Naual, and those who speak it Nahuatlatos."[45] At the same time Indians speaking "Naual" were living in the neighboring village of Chinandega and between Matiare and Managua. Since the dialect was described as Nahual, and this is generally regarded as an old dialect, these people could have been descendants of early Pipil migrants. However, Oviedo's description of the town of El Viejo and the culture of the Indians living there suggests that more likely they constituted an outlier of the Nicarao.[46] Nevertheless, the fact that in 1586 other Nahual-speaking Indians were living in the Bay of Fonseca at Ciuatepetl and that those at Olomega near Zomoto (probably present-day Somotillo) had recently moved to El Viejo suggests that they may have been descendants of early Pipil migrants who had formerly lived farther north.[47]

The Nicarao

The migration of the Nicarao to Central America can be reconstructed from the oral traditions of Indians that were recorded by early chroniclers. The interviews of Friar Francisco Bobadilla with Nicarao Indians in 1528 were recorded by Oviedo in his *Historia general y natural de las Indias,*[48] while Torquemada in his *Monarquía indiana* provides a more detailed account of the migration constructed from information collected from aged Indian informants.[49] Friar Bobadilla established that the Nicarao had come from Ticomega and Maguatega, whereas Torquemada recorded that they had arrived in Soconusco from Anahuac. Lehmann has attempted to resolve this apparent conflict in the accounts by suggesting that the two settlements referred to by Friar Bobadilla were in the Cholula Valley, which was one of the oldest and most important religious centers of Anahuac.[50]

The date of the migration of the Nicarao south from Cholula and their establishment in Nicaragua cannot be stated definitely. One of Torquemada's informants said that the migration took place "avra siete u ocho edades o vidas de viejos" ("seven or eight ages or lives of old men ago").[51] Thompson, Jiménez Moreno, and Chapman believe that the life of an old man was equivalent to 104 years, which would mean that the migration occurred between 728 and 832 years before 1528, when the information was recorded. This would place the migration of the Nicarao at about A.D. 800, and it is assumed that the date refers to their departure from Soconusco, so that they probably left their original home in Chololua in the seventh or eighth centuries A.D. It is assumed that the date refers to their departure from Soconusco, since Torquemada's infor-

mants specifically stated that the cause of the migration had been oppression by the Olmec and the date 800 coincides with the time the
Olmec were becoming aggressive.[52]

Lothrop suggests that the migration of the Nicarao from Cholula occurred later, between the end of the ninth century and the end of the
eleventh century, the Nicarao arriving in Nicaragua at the beginning of
the fifteenth century. He reaches this date by calculating the age of an
old man at fifty to seventy years and by assuming that the date of departure referred to their departure from Cholula rather than Soconusco and
that it was related to the collapse of the Toltec Empire.[53] He supports
this proposition by referring to the accounts of López de Gómara and
Motolinía (Toribio de Benavente), which identify the cause of the migration as a drought and which maintain that the Mexicans arrived in Nicaragua by sea about a hundred years before the Spanish conquest.[54] It is
clear that these accounts are describing a migration different from the
one recorded by Torquemada, probably that of the Nahuatl.

Haberland has also favored a late arrival for the Nicarao on the basis
of archaeological evidence. He has associated the Nicarao with a ceramic
style called Managua Polychrome, which he has related to a pottery style
found in Chiapas called Nimabalari Trichrome. Since the latter is dated
A.D. 1350, the Nicarao could not have migrated from that region before
that date.[55] Despite these suggestions it is generally considered that the
Nicarao were arriving in Nicaragua about A.D. 1200.[56] Although the historical evidence is inconclusive, the presence of ceramics which exhibit
strong influences from the north provides more concrete evidence for
the arrival of the Nicarao about this time. Although the Nicarao appear
to have adopted Nicoya Polychrome pottery on their arrival in Nicaragua, they added to it northern motifs. A number of the ceramic
styles, notably Vallejo Polychrome, Mombacho Polychrome, and Castillo
Engraved, have designs in the form of Mexican gods.[57] The fact that the
Nicarao adopted Nicoya Polychrome pottery, which is generally associated with the Chorotega, also gives archaeological backing to the proposition derived from historical accounts that the Chorotega arrived in Nicaragua before the Nicarao.

From Soconusco the Nicarao continued their migration south. In
Choluteca an old man died prophesying that they would settle near a lake
in which there was an island with two mountains. They journeyed as far
as Panama and then returned north and settled at Xolotán, near Lake
Managua. Unhappy that they had not fulfilled the prophecy, they moved
to the lands of the Chorotega in sight of Ometepe Island with its two
mountains. Finally, after a war with the Chorotega, and possibly with the
Sumu, they settled on the island and on the neighboring Isthmus of
Rivas.

In the sixteenth century the Nicarao occupied the Isthmus of Rivas, and they may have had outliers to the north and south. In 1586 the Indians of El Viejo were described as *"nahuatlatos"* who spoke Naual, the same language being spoken in Chinandega and between Matiare and Managua.[58] Although, as has been indicated, it is possible that these Indian groups were descendants of early Pipil migrants, Oviedo's description of the culture of Indians living in El Viejo indicates that they were probably Nicarao.[59] Unfortunately the languages spoken by Indians living in villages in the jurisdiction of El Viejo and Chinandega are not specified in the census of 1581.[60] To the south the Nicarao appear to have occupied a wedge along the Tempisque River, between the Chorotega in the Nicoya Peninsula and the Corobici to the east.[61] It is unclear whether at the time of the Conquest the Nicarao inhabited Ometepe Island. Although they had settled there after a war with the Chorotega, in the sixteenth century the Indians living there spoke a language distinct from the language of the Indians on the isthmus, and Haberland has found no archaeological evidence to support the occupation of the island by the Nicarao on the eve of the Conquest.[62]

THE NAHUATL

At the time of the Conquest, Aztec traders had established a number of colonies in Central America, including one at the mouth of the San Juan River.[63] Torquemada recorded that there was an Indian town near the Desaguadero where the Indians spoke "a Mexican dialect not so corrupt as that of the other Pipil,"[64] which was almost certainly Nahuatl. In addition, a survey of the Desaguadero was requested in 1535 because there were reports that gold was being shipped through there to Mexico by way of Yucatán.[65]

THE SOUTH AMERICAN ZONE

The areas of eastern Honduras and Nicaragua whose unconverted Indians remained outside Spanish control were known as Taguzgalpa and Tologalpa. The boundary between the two areas was generally taken to be the río Tinto or the río Segovia, but occasionally the whole area as far south as the río San Juan was called Taguzgalpa.[66] Although there appear to have been six major Indian groups inhabiting these areas—the Sumu, the Matagalpa, the Rama, the Jicaque, the Paya, and the Lenca—there are a multitude of names for Indians in the documentary record not all of which can be assigned with any degree of certainty to any one of these major groups. For example, in 1748, Friar José Ximénez reported that in

Taguzgalpa and Tologalpa the following nations were to be found: "Lencas, Tahuas, Alhuatuynas, Xicaquez, Mexicanos, Payas, Jaras, Taupanes, Taos, Fantasmas, Gualas, Alaucas, Guanaes, Limucas, Aguagualcas, Yguyales, Cuges, Bocayes, Tomayes, Bucataguacas, Quicamas, Panamacas, Yziles, Guayaes, Mostucas, Barucas, Apazinas, Nanaycas and many others."[67] The picture is confused by the fact that a large number of these groups were often referred to by generic names such as "Xicaque," "Chontal," and "Caribe," so that it is not always clear precisely which Indian group is being referred to. The situation is most confused for the area from the Olancho Valley south to the headwaters of the río Segovia, which was inhabited by a diversity of Indian groups whose location did not remain constant over time. With these difficulties in mind an attempt will be made to identify the areas inhabited by the major Indian groups at the time of the Spanish conquest, although much of the evidence will necessarily be drawn from the documentary record of the seventeenth and eighteenth centuries.

The Sumu

The Sumu formed one of the most extensive Indian groups in Central America during the colonial period, extending south from the río Patuca in Honduras through the central highlands of Nicaragua to the río Rama. To the west they extended to Lake Nicaragua, and in the northwest they met the Matagalpa.[68] At the time of the Conquest they also inhabited the coast between Cabo de Gracias a Dios and the río Rama, but during the colonial period they retreated inland as the Zambo-Mosquito expanded.

Lehmann considered that Atlantic Nicaragua was inhabited by four linguistic groups: Miskito, Ulua, Sumo-Tauaxha, and Matagalpa.[69] The Ulua and Sumo-Tauaxha have been considered by many to be subdivisions of a single group, and the languages spoken in eastern Nicaragua are often referred to as Misumalpan—*Mis*kito-*Sum*u-Matag*alpa*—and they are generally considered to be related to Chibchan, although the relationship is not as clear for the Mosquito and the Matagalpa.[70] Johnson and Stone accept Lehmann's subdivision between the Ulua and Sumo-Tauaxha, but Conzemius has included them as two of five dialects of Sumu—Bawihka, Twahka, Panamaka, Ulwa and Kukra.[71]

Although references to the Sumu are comparatively rare in the documentary record, there are some references to the five subgroups identified by Conzemius. Most of the subgroups were recorded by Long, who in 1774 described the Indian groups living inland from the Mosquito Coast as "Pawyers, Panamakaws, Twakas, Mussues, Woolvas, Ramas, Cuckeras."[72] The most common subgroup referred to in colonial documents are the Twahka (Twaxha, Twa'ka, Taguaca), though most early references to them indicate their presence in Honduras.[73] However, all late-eighteenth- and early-nineteenth-century sources locate the Twahka south of the río Segovia, around Bocay and between the headwaters of the Wawa and Prinzapolka.[74] Although the Twahka were probably displaced there by the Zambo-Misquito, their presence in Nicaragua at the time of the Spanish conquest cannot be ruled out.

The Panamaka are mentioned briefly in the documentary record. In 1690 two missionaries reported that they had found "seven large villages of heathens called Panamacas and others called Boalies and Apaxinas which have a large number of Indians" and had settled them in the mission of San Pedro de Alcántara in the jurisdiction of Nueva Segovia.[75] In 1774, Long described the "Panamakas" as living 160 miles up the Wanks River, and on most late-eighteenth- and nineteenth-century maps the Panamaka are shown around Bocay.[76]

The Ulua (Wulwa, Olua, Ohlwa) were the most widespread of the Sumu subgroups, probably extending west into Honduras and El Salvador. Like the Twahka and Kukra, they probably lived on the Atlantic coast, but they retreated inland as the Zambo-Mosquito expanded. In the nineteenth century Wickham described the "Woolwa" as canoe men,[77] which suggests that they had been used to living on broad rivers, on lagoons, or on the coast. Their early location on the coast is suggested by a report in 1715 that "parrastras," who are considered to be Ulua, were living on the Maíz River just south of Punta Gorda.[78] By the end of the eighteenth century, however, they appear to have been living well inland. In 1757 continuous settlements of "Caribes" who spoke "Parrastra" and numbered about three thousand were living on the banks of the río Yasica, a branch of the río Tuma.[79] By the end of the eighteenth century Woolwa were to be found in the headwaters of the Escondido, Grande, and Segovia rivers.[80] The movement of the Woolwa inland can be traced by comparing contemporary maps.[81]

Farther south the Kukra also moved inland. Originally they lived at Pearl Lagoon, but by 1781 they had been reduced to about fifty and were living thirty miles up the río Escondido.[82] The only subgroup for which there is no documentary evidence from the colonial period is the Bawihka, whose dialect is closest to Mosquito. Conzemius maintains that they formerly lived on the ríos Wawa and Kukalaya but, having been expelled from that area following a war with the Twahka, settled on the río Banbana.[83]

Although some of the Sumu subgroups were identified in the colonial period, very often Indians living in eastern Nicaragua were referred to collectively as "Caribes." It is clear from documentary evidence that the Sumu and Twahka were regarded as "caribes"; in 1674, Friar Espino, while converting Indians in the Olancho Valley, noted that in the *tierra adentro* were "some Caribes called Taguacas," while in 1757 in the *partido* of Sebaco and Chontales the corregidor reported that in the Guanabana Valley there lived about five hundred "indios caribes de Sumu."[84] Nevertheless, the term "Caribe" was not restricted to the Sumu but was applied to any Indian group in southeast Honduras and eastern Nicaragua and thus included the Matagalpa and Rama.

This confused picture is not clarified by the archaeological record, since there have been few archaeological investigations in the area between the río Patuca and the río San Juan.[85] Lothrop has identified two kinds of pottery in the area east of Lake Nicaragua—Luna Ware and Zapatero Ware—both of which have been found with post-Conquest objects. Since these wares have been found in areas known to have been inhabited by the Ulua, Lothrop has attributed their manufacture to them. The greater part of Luna Ware has been found in Ulua territory, but Zapatero Ware cannot be so precisely delimited, although it is definitely associated with Luna Ware at several sites.[86] It has been suggested that Luna Ware may have had its origins in eastern Nicaragua, but Magnus maintains that there is no archaeological evidence from the Mosquito Coast to support this proposition.[87] Unfortunately no archaeological investigations have been carried out in the central highlands.

The Matagalpa

Closely allied to the Sumu-Ulua were the Matagalpa, who inhabited the region centering on the present-day town of that name in north-central Nicaragua.[88] The term was first used by Brinton in 1895 to describe a group of dialects spoken in the departments of Matagalpa, Estelí, and Nueva Segovia.[89] Both Lehmann and Brinton, however, suggest that the dialect was formerly more widespread. On the basis of geographical names and the traditions of those who inhabit the Department of Chontales, Brinton maintains that it was once spoken there. Lehmann on the basis of place-name evidence also extends the Matagalpan area to Boaco and Olama, in Chontales, where he maintains they bordered on the Ulua in Lóvago and Lovigüisca. He also suggests that it was formerly spoken in the Honduran departments of El Paraíso, Choluteca, and Tegucigalpa, where there are a number of place-names ending in *lí* (meaning "water"), which he associates with the Matagalpa: Danlí, Apalí, Ocolí, Moroselí and Combalí. Schwieriger suggests that place names ending in *-üina*, Such as Yalagüina, Palacagüina, Jiqüina and Orocüina, may also be related to the Matagalpa.[90] If these propositions are accepted, then the boundary of the Matagalpa should be placed farther north than is indicated on the accompanying map (fig. 1). The main reason for not extending the boundary so far north is that documentary evidence for the sixteenth century suggests that the area was inhabited by the Sumu-Ulua.

Unfortunately the Matagalpa are not recognized as a distinct group in the documentary record. Very often Indian groups inhabiting this region are referred to as "Chontal" or "Caribe," although these terms were also applied to other Indian groups. The term "Chontal" was derived from the Nahuatl word *chontalli,* meaning "rude, rustic person."[91] It was often used by the Spaniards to identify Indian groups that did not display a high level of civilization, and it was generally used as a term of abuse. In the sixteenth century Oviedo observed that Chondal was spoken in Nicaragua and observed that "these Chondales are very rustic people, and they live in the mountains or the foothills of them."[92] In the census taken in 1581, the following villages were included in the Province of Chontales: Olocoton, Guaxinjo, Olomega, another called Olocoton, Condega, Comoto, Teuxtepet, Boaco, Coyagalpa, Coagalpa, Xicuygalpa, Quiboga, Comana and Mayale. Two of these however, Condega and Comoto (Somoto), were identified a few years later as being inhabited by Ulua Indians.[93] Although there are no references to a language called Matagalpa in the documentary record, Lehmann maintains that the Paraka and Pantasma spoke Matagalpan.[94] In the late seventeenth and eighteenth centuries missionaries were active in converting these Indians in the vicinity of Nueva Segovia.[95]

The Rama

South of the Sumu lived the Rama. The Rama are generally considered to be a subgroup of the Voto, a member of the Chibchan family.[96] There are a number of documentary references to the Voto living in the vicinity of the San Juan River in the seventeenth century.[97] In 1620 there were said to be 1,000 Votos living between the Poco Sol and Sarapiquí rivers, southern tributaries of the San Juan River, and in 1662, 250 families of Votos were reputedly living around the Poco Sol. It is doubtful that at that time they extended north of the San Juan River, but with the increase in raids by buccaneers and the Zambo-Mosquito and the counteroffensives of the Spaniards, who all used the San Juan River as a corridor, the Votos were effectively displaced from there. In 1742, Punta Gorda was "inhabited by Englishmen mixed with Zambos; not far away was a settlement of Carib Indians of the Voto nation."[98] Three decades later Long and Kemble specifically recorded that Rama were inhabiting Punta Gorda, and Kemble also noted that they were living on the Santa Cruz River, a northern tributary of the San Juan.[99] It would appear that at that time the Rama were suffering from domination by the Zambo-Mosquito, to whom they became tributary, and were being dispersed from the area around Punta Gorda.[100] Thus, according to Roberts, writing in 1827, the Rama lived between Bluefields and the San Juan River but still had their main settlement at Punta Gorda.[101]

The maps of Tanner and Vandermaelen in the 1820s locate the Rama west of the Bluefields Lagoon and Pearl Lagoon, respectively, whereas the earlier maps of Jeffreys, Edwards, and Pinkerton place them between Punta Gorda and the Kukra River.[102] The date of their occupation of Rama Cay, in the Bluefields Lagoon, is unknown. It is possible that some Rama were taken to the area around Bluefields as slaves by the Zambo-Mosquito or the English, although it has been suggested that they arrived from Punta Gorda at the end of the eighteenth century as a result of dispersion following tribal wars. According to tribal legends recorded by missionaries in the middle of the nineteenth century, the island was given to a Rama chief by a Zambo-Mosquito king as a reward for his services during a campaign against the Tereba Indians of Costa Rica. The chief, who was called Hannibal, settled on the island and began populating it with the assistance of his three wives.[103] Although the first specific reference to Rama Indians inhabiting Rama Cay dates from 1856, Rama were working for settlers at Bluefields and Pearl Lagoon earlier in the century.[104]

There are a few references to Melchora Indians, whom Lehmann regards as Ramas.[105] On a map of Nicaragua of 1783 "caribes de Melchora" are shown north of the San Juan River and west of the Santa River.[106] Their presence in this area was confirmed in 1801 by the bishop of Nicaragua, who reported that a missionary had visited Indian villages along the eastern shore of Lake Granada and then had gone to villages "of Melchora and others between Fort San Carlos and Acoyapa."[107] In the middle of the nineteenth century Stout located the Rama between Bluefields and the Colorado River (just south of the San Juan River), and the Melchora inland from Punta Gorda, and commented that a few Melchora were also living along the San Juan.[108]

The Mosquito

There are no documentary references to the Mosquito in the early colonial period, and it would appear that they emerged from the mid-seventeenth century onward. The earliest reference to the Mosquito comes from the buccaneer Exquemelin, who in 1672 observed that they formed a small nation of 1,600 to 1,700 divided into two provinces.[109] It has been suggested, and it seems probable, that the Mosquito are a purely historic group whose origin lies in the intermixing of Sumu Indians and blacks who were shipwrecked on the Mosquito Cays in 1641.[110] In 1711 the bishop of Nicaragua described the origin of the Zambo-Mosquito as follows:

In 1641 a ship laden with Negroes was shipwrecked on the Atlantic coast, and in the part between the San Juan River, in the Province of Nicaragua, and the city of Trujillo, in the Province of Honduras . . . one-third of the Negroes were gathered together, and the rest took refuge and settled in the foothills of those mountains occupied by Carib Indians who, suspicious and fearful of those new arrivals, made war on them, and for a few years it was very bitter, and in time the Negroes defeated the Caribs, and these retired into the mountains toward the lands of Segovia and Chontales. . . . With women of the conquered, the conquerors multiplied and because these first strangers are already dead, they call their descendants Zambos because they are the sons of Negroes and Indian women. [111]

Some biological evidence supports the proposed mixed racial origin of the Mosquito. Matson and Swanson in an examination of blood groups of Mosquito and Sumu Indians from the río Segovia area found that, while all the Sumu belonged to blood group O, the distribution of blood groups among the Mosquito were 90 percent O, 8 percent A, 0.67 percent A2, and 1.33 percent B. [112] Further support for the recent origin of the Mosquito as a racially mixed group derived from Sumu Indians and blacks can also be seen in their legends and language. Heath refers to a Mosquito legend which relates that their ancestors were called Kiribi who lived in the country around Rivas, from where, after many years of fighting, they were displaced to the eastern side of Lake Nicaragua by the Nicarao, and from there they were led by a leader named Wakna to the Atlantic coast. [113] Since these events are generally thought to have affected the Sumu, the legend suggests that they were the ancestors of the Mosquito. Further association with the Sumu can been seen in a legend relating how the tribal ancestors Mai-sahana and Yapti-Misri were born from a great rock near the río Patuca and gave birth to the Mosquito, Twahka, and Ohlwa. [114] Furthermore, the Mosquito language is most like the Bawihka dialect of Sumu, and Conzemius has further suggested that, whereas the dialectical variations of the Sumu are relatively diverse so that subgroups have some difficulty in communicating, those of the Mosquito are comparatively insignificant, suggesting that the Mosquito language has a more recent origin. [115] In addition it possesses more foreign words, especially Spanish and English, and there is some evidence of African influence, although it is slight. [116]

Historical documents usually refer to the "Mosquito" or "Zambo-Mosquito," whereas social scientists generally prefer to call the group Miskito. Whatever its spelling, the origin of the name is uncertain. The most obvious suggestion is that it may have been derived from the mosquito insect, although they are not particularly prevalent on the coast. Some have suggested that the name is related to *musket,* the Mosquito being distinguished by the possession of guns which they obtained from the English. Alternatively, it may have come from either of the Spanish words *mixto* or *mestizo,* which may have been used to describe the mixed racial character of the group, or from the Mosquito word *miskaia,* meaning "fishing," an activity that would distinguish them from Indians living inland.[117] Finally, it has been suggested that it is an aboriginal name; a number of documents refer to the shipwreck taking place on the "Isla de Mosquitos," but the late date of these accounts means that the place could have been named after the Indians rather than vice versa.[118]

From a localized origin near Cabo de Gracias a Dios the Zambo-Mosquito spread along the coast, displacing and dominating Indian groups who lived there, primarily the Paya and the Sumu. As early as 1699, M. W. observed that from Cabo de Camarón to Cabo de Gracias a Dios "the Mosqueto-men inhabit the sea-shore, pretty close to the sea-side, or on the sides of some lakes or lagunes hard by."[119] From this localized origin the Zambo-Mosquito expanded rapidly to inhabit the area between the río Tinto and Punta Gorda.[120] Although several accounts extend these boundaries north and south,[121] most documentary and cartographic evidence suggests that, although the Zambo-Mosquito did carry out raids and contraband trading along the north coast of Honduras and the Matina coast of Costa Rica, they did not settle west of Trujillo or south of Punta Gorda, at least not in large numbers.[122]

Within the area delimited by the río Tinto and Punta Gorda spatial variations in the density and the racial contribution of populations were to be found. In 1757, Hodgson suggested that the average distance which the Mosquito inhabited inland was one hundred miles, but that they were established two hundred miles up the río Segovia.[123] In 1774, Long reported that the Mosquito were "most numerous near Cape Gracia a Dios, especially up the Wanks river, and about Sandy Bay, where their king resides."[124]

Although the groups resulting from the intermixing of Sumu Indians and blacks were generally referred to as Zambo-Mosquito, it is clear that there were spatial differences in their racial composition, the black influence being stronger nor.. of Cabo de Gracias a Dios and Sandy Bay and the Indian influence more dominant in the south.[125] This probably reflects the location of the shipwreck and the fact that the area to the north received larger numbers of black slaves imported by the English to work on their plantations. In 1827, Roberts divided the coast into three sections. He identified an area of mixed-racial character between the Roman River (near Cabo de Gracias a Dios) and the Patook (río Patuca), where there were "tribes of Kharibees or Caribs, Poyers, Mosquito men and some negroes." The region from Caratasca or Croata to Sandy Bay and Duckwarra (Dakura) was all "Mosquito men proper, or mixed breed of Samboes and Indians," while south from Brancman's (Bragman's Bluff) to the río Grande were "tribes of Tongulas, Towcas, Woolwas, Cookras," but there were also small colonies of "Samboes" at Pearl Cay Lagoon and Bluefields.[126] Despite these variations in the racial character of populations inhabiting the Mosquito Coast, here they are referred to collectively as Zambo-Mosquito.

THE ENVIRONMENTAL SETTING

The diversity of environments in Nicaragua paralleled the diversity of Indian cultures there, but they failed to capture the imagination of early visitors to the province. The lack of contemporary accounts has not been compensated for by recent scientific inquiries into the country's ecological history, so that any reconstruction of the natural environment on the eve of the Spanish conquest must rely heavily on inference from the nature and distribution of present-day ecosystems.[127] Nicaragua and Nicoya together can be divided into three major ecological regions: the Pacific Region, the Central Region, and the Atlantic Region. Although the correlation is by no means perfect, the Pacific Region broadly corresponds to the area inhabited by chiefdoms at the time of Conquest, while the Central and Atlantic regions were occupied by tribal groups.

The Pacific Region is characterized by its association with geologically recent volcanic activity, though within it two zones can be distinguished: the central depression and the coastal region. The central depression is formed by a structurally faulted block or graben trending northwest to southeast through Nicaragua; the Gulf of Nicoya is a product of the same fault system. The depression is associated with the large freshwater lakes of Managua and Nicaragua and with a string of about thirty volcanoes along the southern edge of the depression, some of which form islands within the lakes. The Quaternary volcanoes, which rise to 1,745 meters, form dramatic elements in the landscape, and they aroused the interest of a number of early explorers, especially the caldera of Masaya.[128] Where the depression is not composed of lakes, the land is covered with Quaternary deposits derived from the highlands to the east. Because the prevailing winds are northeasterly, these areas do not receive volcanic deposits emitted by the volcanoes, with the result that the deeply weathered tropical soils are relatively infertile. In addition, the land surrounding the mouths of the ríos Negro and Estero Real is occasionally flooded by saltwater and can support only savanna vegetation.[129]

The coastal zone of the Pacific Region consists of Cretaceous and Tertiary sediments, mainly sandstones, which have been partly covered by deposits of volcanic ash emanating from the line of volcanoes on the northeast. Within the coastal region, however, are a number of internal variations. The León-Chinandega plain, which comprises the northern part of the zone, is covered with volcanic deposits on which silty loams

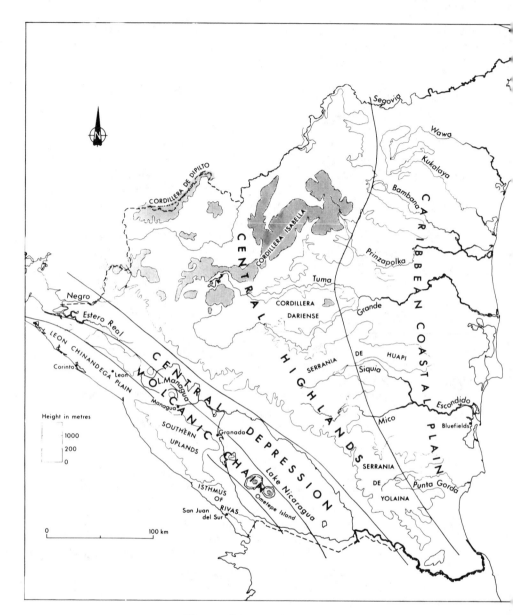

Fig. 5. Major ecological regions.

have developed to produce the most fertile soils in the country. Farther south in the southern uplands, which rise to about 1,000 meters west of Granada, the volcanic deposits are coarser, but the clay loams, ranging from dark gray-brown to light, which have developed on them are also fertile.[130]

At the time of the Conquest the area between León and Granada supported the densest Indian populations in the country. In 1540, Andagoya described it as "highly populated and very fertile with supplies of maize, beans, and many local crops and some small dogs which they also eat and many deer and fish, the land is very healthy and the Indians are very civilized in their way of life like those of Mexico."[131] South of Granada in the Isthmus of Rivas, however, volcanic deposits are few, and the Cretaceous and Tertiary sedimentary rocks produce rather infertile soils. Owing to the poor quality of the soils and the aridity of the climate in this area the region between the town of Nicaragua and the Nicoya Peninsula was uninhabited at the time of the Conquest.[132] Structurally the Nicoya Peninsula is related to Nicaragua, but it is composed of igneous and metaphoric rocks, probably of Cretaceous age, on which rather mature lateritic soils have developed.[133] Although much of the Pacific coast is low-lying and covered with mangrove swamp, there are a small number of natural harbors, such as Realejo (now Corinto) and San Juan del Sur, which became important ports during the colonial period.

Climatically the Pacific Region falls within the tierra caliente with a mean annual temperature of between 25°C and 35°C. It receives between 1,000 and 2,000 millimeters of rain a year, but there is a marked dry season between November and mid-May, while most of the rain falls in June and in September–October. The long dry season generally necessitates some form of irrigation. In pre-Columbian times Indians living in the León-Chinandega plain would have utilized rivers flowing down the slopes of the volcanoes to the northeast, while farther south wells were probably used. Despite the necessity for irrigation, the prolonged dry season would have limited the leaching of the soils, while the lack of frosts would have permitted at least two successive crops a year.[134]

Although these areas were the most densely settled in Nicaragua at the time of the Conquest, it is clear that they were more heavily forested than they are at present. In 1525 the city of León was described as situated "on the bank of the freshwater lake, with many very large gardens and trees,"[135] while on the Pacific coast Gil González de Ávila reported that there were "two beautiful ports to build ships and for this and the rest there is much wood and evergreen oaks as in Spain and many cedars, and the Indians give news of pines and I saw them and took much resin from them."[136] The forests that covered the Pacific Region were probably semievergreen forests or, in the drier areas, deciduous for-

ests.[137] Today there is little evidence of either of these forest types, for
the land has been cleared for agriculture and heavily exploited for timber.
Within the zones of semievergreen and deciduous forest there are
now areas of savanna, characterized by *jícaro* trees (*Crescentia alata*
H.B.K.), which are considered to constitute a disclimax maintained by
grazing and burning.[138]

When the forests were more extensive, game was more abundant;
the deer and peccaries that were commonly hunted in the aboriginal and
early colonial period have almost disappeared.[139] The freshwater lakes
also provided the Indians with sources of fish and turtles.[140] In 1581 the
natural resources of the region called the Chontales of León, which included the central depression, were described as follows:

> . . . the rivers are abundant in fish of different kinds. In them there are many
> caimans. There are in this land many deer, peccaries, and rabbits and arma-
> dillos and agoutis and partridges and quails, tigers and lions and jackals. The
> Indians have fisheries in the rivers and saltworks for making boiled salt on
> the coast. The birds that have been seen are herons and ducks and spar-
> row hawks and pelicans and ring doves and turtledoves and parrots and
> *catalricas*.[141]

The Central Region contains the highest land in Nicaragua, with
peaks rising to 2,000 meters. The highlands trend north to south and
consist of a number of west–east cordilleras, notably the cordilleras of
Dipilto, Isabella, and Dariense and the *serranías* of Huapí and Yolaina,
which are separated by valleys whose rivers drain to the Caribbean
coast. North of the Cordillera de Isabella granite and schists, probably of
Palaeozoic age, are to be found, whereas the rest of the Central Region
is composed of Tertiary volcanic rocks, which are mainly andesitic.
Quartz veins within the granite and schists often bear gold and silver,
which were mined in the early colonial period.[142]

In the Central Region the area north of the río Grande is more
rugged, consisting of plateau regions deeply dissected by young or re-
juvenated streams, whereas to the south, in Chontales, the mountains
are lower and constitute a gently undulating plateau with a few high
peaks and ridges. Within the Central Region variations in temperature
and rainfall are largely related to differences in relief and aspect. The
mean annual temperature is about 25°C but falls with elevation to less
than 20°C where the land enters the tierra templada. Similarly rainfall
increases with elevation, but it is also influenced by aspect; areas that
are open to the northeast trade winds receive higher levels of rainfall
than those situated in the rain shadow. The annual rainfall varies between 1,000 and 2,000 millimeters. Whereas the Pacific region is characterized by a dry season lasting for six and a half months, in the Cen-

tral Region the length of the dry season becomes shorter (about four months) from west to east, and the total amount of rainfall increases. Most of the soils in the Central Region are of only low to moderate fertility, the alluvial soils in the river valleys being the most fertile.

The Central Region was probably once covered with semievergreen forest, which gave way to seasonal evergreen forest where the dry season was short and the annual rainfall exceeded 1,800 millimeters, and to lower montane forest at about 1,200 meters.[143] Possibly the most interesting feature of the vegetation cover of the Central Region is the occurrence of pine and oak forests in Nueva Segovia. The pine forest represents the southern limit of the North American genus *Pinus,* and the species found in Nueva Segovia are *P. oocarpa* Schiede, *P. pseudostrobus* Lindl., and *P. caribaea* Mor. The pine trees, which often form pure stands, show a preference for acidic soils, but they are generally considered to be a disclimax associated with forest clearance and burning.[144] The pines themselves have been exploited for timber, and *P. oocarpa* in particular has been exploited for its resin. The pines are often found in association with oaks, particularly *Quercus peduncularis* Neé.[145]

Although the pine-oak association is clearly related to human activity, it is not a recent phenomenon. Burning and forest clearance have been occurring for several thousand years, and the pine-oak forests were well developed at the time of the Spanish conquest. In 1525 an expedition north from León found the area "highly populated, and there are large trees of yellow sandalwood and of cedars and pines and oaks and spiny oaks and cork oaks in great quantity, and from the pines they have made and make much pitch."[146] Another species which is commonly associated with the pine forest and which has been exploited for its resin is liquidambar (*Liquidambar styraciflua* L.). Wild animals in this region probably included deer, peccaries, coatimundis, sloths, monkeys, squirrels, opossums, and wildcats, many of which have been severely reduced in numbers since the pre-Columbian period.[147] Southward in present-day Chontales, much of the semievergreen forest has been replaced by savannas, which have been modified by introduced species. In the more easterly areas, where the dry season is shorter and the rain heavier, pastures are available throughout the year.[148]

The Atlantic Region is the most extensive ecological region in Nicaragua. It comprises the eastern foothills of the central highlands and an extensive coastal plain rising to between 15 and 20 meters which consists mainly of Pliocene gravels and sandy clays of marine origin.[149] The plain has been eroded to form a mesalike landscape of laterite-capped escarpments which stand above narrow, shallowly entrenched valleys. The plain is broadest in the north, where it is about 150 kilometers wide, and it narrows southward toward Bluefields, where the volcanic hills ap-

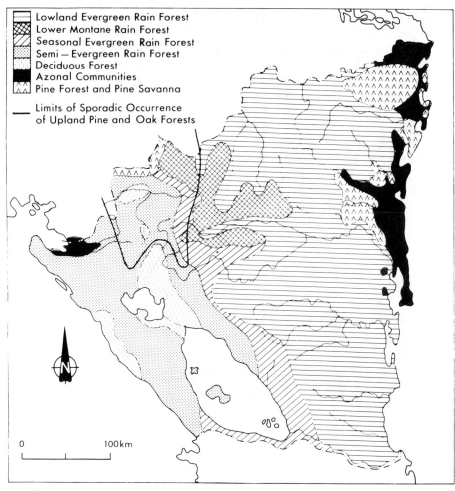

Fig. 6. Major vegetation zones (after Taylor, "Vegetation of Nicaragua," p. 33).

proach the coast. Deposits from the central highlands have formed narrow alluvial levees along the rivers, and on the coast they have created bars and spits that enclose shallow lagoons. The coastal environment possesses abundant food resources in the form of fish, manatee, and game.[150] The land offshore forms the Mosquito Bank, which is rarely more than 100 meters below sea level, and from it hundreds of coral reefs and cays rise. Here turtles, lobsters, shellfish, and fish are abundant.

Lying in the path of the northeast trade winds, this region receives the heaviest rainfall in the country, ranging from about 2,000 millimeters in the north to over 5,000 millimeters near the San Juan River, which has the highest annual rainfall in Central America. There is no marked dry season, though most of the rain falls in June to August and in the northern section of the region there is a drier period of three months from February to April. The temperatures are high with an annual mean of between 25°C and 30°C but rising to 35°C in favorable conditions. The heavy rainfall causes rapid leaching of the soils, resulting in the development of poor lateritic soils of low fertility. Where the rivers have cut into the plain, less weathered soils are to be found on the lower slopes of the valleys, while the most fertile soils are to be found on the alluvial levees. The climate and soils are not suitable for the cultivation of maize. [151]

Most of the region is covered with evergreen rain forest, but there is an extensive area of pine savanna between the río Segovia and the río Grande, [152] and there are a number of azonal communities, such as swamp forests, mangrove swamps, and beach communities along the coast. [153] The evergreen rain forest possesses a great diversity of species, and, although modified by centuries of shifting cultivation and the selective felling of trees, particularly of mahogany and cedar, it is the least modified of the forest formations in Nicaragua. [154] The variety of plant species is paralleled by the diversity of animal species that live there, including deer, tapirs, peccaries, agoutis, pacas, anteaters, sloths, monkeys, wildcats, and a great variety of birds. [155] Within the evergreen rain forest are extensive stretches of pine savanna. These are closely associated with the area of Pliocene sediments, but they are generally considered to be a fire disclimax. [156] In contrast to the evergreen rain forest, the pine savanna is poor in mammalian species. [157]

The natural environments of Nicaragua and Nicoya clearly offered a variety of possibilities and limitations for the development of Indian cultures, whose characteristics will now be examined in detail.

CHAPTER 3

The Chiefdoms

The Chorotega, Maribio, and Nicarao formed chiefdoms whose large populations were supported by various forms of intensive agricultural production. They were socially stratified and headed by hereditary chiefs or elected councils of elders; their religious practices consisted of elaborate rites and ceremonies centering around priests, temples, and idols. In general they constituted larger, more economically productive, and more complex societies than the neighboring tribes to the east.

The main sources of evidence for the Indian cultures in Nicaragua and Nicoya on the eve of the Spanish conquest are the published works of Oviedo and Andagoya, both of whom had firsthand knowledge of the region, and the secondary accounts of Martyr, López de Gómara, and Herrera. Further evidence can be derived from the early accounts of conquistadors, officials, and priests. The best sources of this kind are the accounts of the expeditions of Gil González de Ávila through the area between 1522 and 1524 the reports of the earliest governors of the province, Pedrarias Dávila and Francisco de Castañeda, and the representations of the earliest bishops, Antonio de Valdivieso and Lázaro Carrasco.[1]

The number of chiefdoms in Pacific Nicaragua and Nicoya was small, but they contained large populations. Oviedo considered that among the most powerful chiefs were Teçoatega, Nicaragua, and Nicoya.[2] Teçoatega ruled over 20,000 vassals, and in 1522 more than 9,000 subjects of Nicaragua and 6,000 subjects of Nicoya were baptized.[3] These populations were contained in hierarchies of settlements ranging from many thousands in the major administrative, market, and religious centers down to a few hundred Indians in the small communities.[4] The largest towns formed the centers of provinces: Managua, with the largest recorded population, had 40,000 inhabitants.[5] Other important towns were the residences of the caciques Teçoatega (at El Viejo), Nicaragua, Nicoya, and Mistega.[6] A number of the larger towns became centers of Spanish settlement; in 1525, Granada was established next to Jalteba, which was said to have 8,000 Indians "in its district," and León, which was said to have 15,000 *vecinos naturales* in its hinterland, was founded in the middle of the Province of Imabite.[7] Not only were the towns large, but the density of settlement in Pacific Nicaragua was high. Gil González de Ávila reported that he had passed through the province of Denochari, where he found six villages with 2,000 *vecinos* each one-half to two leagues apart.[8]

Although the towns of both the Nicarao and the Chorotega were large, those of the former exhibited greater differentiation and regularity of form, thus reflecting the more complex sociopolitical structure of the Nicarao. The palaces and houses of the Nicarao nobility were clearly distinguishable, while amongst the Chorotega there was very little differentiation between the houses of nobles and those of commoners.[9] In Nicarao towns the houses of nobles were arranged around the central square, where the cacique resided; Oviedo provides a detailed plan of the central plaza of Teçoatega (see plate).[10] The nobles who resided around the central square were the heads of provinces, and they were accompanied by a number of their subjects with whom they consulted; together they advised the cacique and formed his bodyguard.[11] The dwellings of caciques were described by Martyr as 100 paces long by 15 paces wide, with the façade open but the back wall composed of solid material. All houses were of the same construction, consisting of beams roofed with thatch, except that houses along rivers or on the edges of lakes were built on stilts.[12]

Unlike many of the other major centers in Pacific Nicaragua, Teçoatega does not appear to have possessed a temple or sacrificial mound. It is assumed that in this town the temple complex was separated from the residences of the cacique and his court, since all major centers possessed them. The temples, which were known as *orchilobos* or *teobas,* not only contained idols but also were used as armories.[13] Each major town or village also possessed a market, and in large towns separate markets were held in the suburbs.[14] There is no evidence that towns were divided into districts occupied by distinct occupational groups, except that jewelers and goldsmiths resided in the central square.[15]

Whereas Nicarao towns exhibited social and functional differentiation, Chorotegan towns were more uniform in character. Oviedo described Managua as lacking "the body of a town" and consisting of one suburb after another so that it appeared like "a rope along the lake."[16] Indian villages in Nicoya were large, but they did not reach the proportions of those found in Pacific Nicaragua. However, like villages to the north, each of the larger ones possessed a central plaza with a sacrificial mound and a temple.[17]

THE ECONOMY

In Pacific Nicaragua agriculture was the most important subsistence activity, hunting, fishing, and gathering playing secondary roles probably in that order of importance.[18] Compared with the South American zone, craft manufactures were highly developed, and markets flourished. In

Nicoya the economy appears to have been more generalized, agriculture, fishing, and collecting each making substantial contributions. At the time of the Conquest hunting appears to have played a minor role, possibly because of the overexploitation of game in previous periods.[19] The importance of agriculture in the economy is indicated by the fact that it was a predominantly male activity. This contrasts with the South American zone, where men were occupied in hunting and fishing, while the women cultivated.[20] Nobles were exempt from routine labor, and it is doubtful that Indian slaves were employed in subsistence activities; Indian slaves were few, and they were probably employed as household servants rather than as agricultural laborers.

Unfortunately there are only a few accounts of the land-tenure system at the time of the Conquest, but it would appear that land was communally owned and allocated to individuals for cultivation. Although the land could not be sold, it could be passed from father to son, or, in the absence of a son, it became the property of the deceased owner's family. If the owner left the village, the land reverted to the community for reallocation by its leaders.[21] The details of landholdings were registered in parchment books, which could be referred to in the event of a dispute.[22] No lands were owned by the temple.[23]

On these lands crops were probably grown under a semipermanent system of cultivation. Palerm has estimated that under a *barbecho* system of cultivation, which most closely approximates that practiced in the Mesoamerican zone, 2½ hectares of cultivated land are required to support a family, while two to three times as much land lies fallow.[24] In Pacific Nicaragua the rich volcanic soils would have permitted cultivation for many years before the land was abandoned to fallow. Stone axes were used to clear the land, which was then worked with digging sticks; on the island of Chira, in the Gulf of Nicoya, spades with blades made of mother-of-pearl shells were used.[25]

On the cleared plots various food crops were intercropped, the most important of which were maize, beans, manioc, and sweet potatoes. Other crops, such as cacao and cotton, required specially cleared and prepared plots. Oviedo noted that cacao groves were established on fertile soil along the banks of rivers, where they could be naturally irrigated by floodwaters. Once planted, the plots required constant attention to keep them free of weeds and browsing animals. In Nicaragua maize plots were plagued by birds, which were frightened off by boys, who shouted and threw stones at them from specially constructed cane platforms or from trees.[26] Apart from the cultivation of plots along rivers the techniques of irrigation do not appear to have been widespread. The only specific reference to irrigation is to the pot irrigation of a forty-day maize that was grown in times of shortage.[27] In addition to the cultivation of field plots permanent gardens were maintained next to dwellings, where a miscellany of fruit trees, gourds, and herb, spice, and dye plants were grown.

Maize (*Zea mays* L.) was the most important crop cultivated. It was probably introduced into southern Central America from Mexico in the Christian Era, though a South American origin cannot be ruled out.[28] Several varieties of maize—dark purple, red, white, and yellow—were known, and their productivity impressed early observers. Oviedo estimated that in Central America 1 fanega (about 1.5 bushels) of sown maize would produce 150 fanegas, which is comparable to the highest yields in Nicoya today.[29] Maize bread, known locally as *tascalpachon,* was made into tortillas as in Mexico, and drinks were made from fermented maize.[30] Beans were grown throughout the Mesoamerican zone. They probably included the common bean (*Phaseolus vulgaris* L.), the lima bean (*P. lunatus* L.), and the runner bean (*P. coccineus* L.). The jack bean (*Canavalia ensiformis* [L.] DC), a native of Central America, was probably also grown. Beans were intensively cultivated in the Province of Nagarando, where many varieties were grown, including yellow and spotted ones.[31] The squash (*Cucurbita* sp.), which is commonly associated with maize and beans in Mexico, was not native to southern Central America and does not appear to have been cultivated in Nicaragua in pre-Columbian times.[32]

At the time of the Spanish conquest the cultivation of seed crops in Pacific Nicaragua had largely supplanted that of root crops, although a few root crops, notably manioc (*Manihot esculenta* Crantz) and sweet potatoes (*Ipomoea batatas* [L.] Lam.), were still grown. The manioc root was boiled and roasted, as well as used in soups. The flour was also made into cassava bread and used in the preparation of drinks.[33] Both sweet and starchy varieties of sweet potatoes, called *camotes* in Nahua, were grown, and they could be harvested after three to six months. They were boiled, roasted, and used in stews.[34]

A variety of fruit trees were grown and they were often included as part of a girl's dowry.[35] This was probably because, as private property, they were used to indicate ownership or usufruct of land. The most important fruits cultivated were mammees (*Mammea americana* L.), *nísperos,* or sapodillas (*Manilkara bidentata* [Mill.] Fosberg), and jocotes (*Spondias purpurea* L. and *S. mombin* L.). Oviedo recorded that the Indians of Nicaragua referred to the mammee as *zapot,*[36] but it would appear that he confused the mammee with the zapote (*Calocarpum sapota* [Jacq.] Merr.), which was also grown. The latter is very similar to the mammee and often goes under the name mammee zapote.[37] The *níspero,* or sapodilla, goes under various names: it was referred to as *munonzapot* by the Chorotega, who monopolized its cultivation; it was also called chicle zapote or, by corruption, chico zapote.[38] *Spondias purpurea* L. and *S. mombin* L. were known as jocotes. It is also likely that the fruits that the Spanish called *ciruelas,* or plums, were in fact one of the species of *Spondias.*[39] Other fruits recorded in sixteenth-century accounts were papaya (*Carica papaya* L.); guava (*Psidium guajava* L.); nance (*Byrsonima crassifolia* [L.] DC); guanábana, or soursop (*Annona muricata* L.); sweetsop (*A. squamosa* L.); avocado (*Persea americana* Mill.); and pineapple (*Ananas comosus* [L.] Merr.).[40] As well as being consumed as fruits, jocotes and other plums were made into wine, while oil was extracted from the kernel of the mammee seed, and a dye was obtained from the bark of the nance tree.

Two other important plants that were grown in kitchen gardens were calabashes and peppers. Although it is possible that the bottle gourd (*Lagenaria siceraria* [Mol.] Standl) was cultivated, probably most of the fruits used as vessels came from the calabash tree (*Crescentia cujete* L.). They were particularly important in Pacific Nicaragua, where water was often in short supply and the fruits were used as water-carrying and storage vessels. Large numbers of trees were planted each year, and the fruits took forty days to mature.[41] Most gardens also contained hot and sweet peppers (*Capsicum frutescens* L. and *C. annuum* L.). The former were used to flavor food, and the leaves were added to soups and used to make sauces, while the fruits of the latter were eaten whole.[42]

A number of other crops played important roles in the Indian economy. They included cacao, cotton, tobacco, and coca. Cacao was introduced into Central America from Mexico. It was associated with the Nicarao and Nahuatl traders and was thus widely grown in Pacific Nicaragua and to a lesser extent in Nicoya.[43] Cacao trees were planted in rows placed ten to twelve feet apart and were shaded by *yaguaguit* trees (possibly *Haematoxylon campechianum* L.). The fruit was picked between February and April, and the beans were dried in the sun.[44] Cacao was eaten, drunk, and used as a medium of exchange. Cacao butter was painted on the face and taken off bit by bit with the fingers, which were then licked; it was also used as a disinfectant and as a protection against snakebites. Cacao drink was made in various ways. The Nicarao mixed about thirty ground beans with water and achiote (*Bixa orellana* L.), which gave it a red color, and then boiled and stirred it, passing it from one vessel to another to make it foam. The Chorotega made ground cacao into pellets, which were placed with a little water, heated over a low flame, and finally strained through a palm sieve.

Since cacao beans were used as a medium of exchange, only caciques could afford to drink cacao, most of which they acquired as tribute from commoners. Cacao trees were regarded as private property, and this may account for the unexpected absence of cacao from lists of items paid as tribute in Nicaragua during the colonial period. In other parts of Central America, notably El Salvador, cacao became an important item of tribute, and the difference between the two areas may reflect a difference in pre-Columbian property rights.[45]

Cotton (*Gossypium* sp.) was the most important fiber crop grown, and its cultivation probably required the establishment of special clearings. An annual variety of cotton was grown, and it was produced in such large quantities in the sixteenth century that the bishop of Nicaragua observed that the cultivation of maize and cotton was the Indians' only employment.[46] Ecological conditions in western Nicaragua were unsuitable for the cultivation of tobacco (*Nicotiana tabacum* L.), but it was grown in the east, and Indians in the west may have obtained it by trade. It was certainly smoked by Indians in Nicaragua, and Oviedo noted that the Chorotega in Nicoya smoked cigars.[47] The Nicarao also chewed coca, which they called *yaat,* to relieve pain and tiredness. It was dried, cured, sometimes mixed with ground seashells, and carried in a small bag around the neck for use in battles or on journeys.[48]

Wild animals were more abundant in the pre-Columbian period than they are at present, and on the eve of the Conquest hunting appears to have been particularly important in Pacific Nicaragua. In Nicoya it played a less significant role than it had in previous periods, possibly because of the overexploitation of game.[49] Many varieties of animals were hunted, including deer (the common deer [*Odocoileus virginiana*] and the small brocket deer [*Mazama americana*], agouti (*Dasyprocta punctata*), and peccaries (the white-lipped peccary [*Tayassu pecari*] and the collared peccary [*T. tajacu*]). Several monkey species were hunted, as were two- and three-toed sloths, opossums, rabbits, pacas, coatimundis, armadillos, raccoons, and zorillo skunks.[50] Of the animal bones encountered in archaeological sites in the Isthmus of Rivas and Nicoya, those of deer are by far the most abundant, despite the fact that the hunting of deer was a privilege reserved for nobles. Peccaries and raccoons are also represented at sites in both areas, while the remains of monkeys, agoutis and armadillos have been found in Rivas, and those of opossums and reptiles such as iguanas have been found in Nicoya.[51] Birds were also hunted, *perdices pardas* (probably tinamous) being specifically mentioned by Oviedo.[52]

The variety of animals hunted was paralleled by the diversity of techniques used to catch them. Bows and arrows, lances, spears, and snares were used to capture animals, as were various kinds of traps, including pits filled with water and nets made of henequen.[53] Poisons were not used, at least not by the Nicarao.[54] Meat was generally roasted, and the skins of deer and jaguars were worn on festive occasions. The Nicarao also used deerskins to cover books.[55]

The only domesticated animals reared in Central America were tur-
keys and mute dogs.[56] The dogs were probably used in hunting and were
also eaten.[57] In addition to ceremonial cannibalism, human flesh was
eaten by Chorotega and Nicarao chiefs. Oviedo recorded that slaves
were sold in the market, their heads cut off and their bodies cut into
pieces, stewed with salt and chili pepper, and eaten with maize.[58] These
slaves were probably war captives, because individuals who sold themselves and their children into slavery were not eaten.[59]

Fishing formed an important adjunct to the economy throughout the
area, but it was a dominant activity around the lakes in the vicinity of
León and Granada and in the Gulf of Nicoya, where shellfish were exploited. Fishing in Lake Managua was said to be better than that in Lake
Nicaragua, and in both lakes the main species caught were probably mojarras and *guapotes* (*Cichlasoma* sp.), sardines (*Characidae*), and sharks
(probably *Carcharhinus nicaraguensis*). Archaeological evidence indicates
that they also exploited freshwater turtles—the pond turtle (*Chrysemys*
sp.) and the mud turtle (*Kinosternon* sp.).[60] There is little evidence of
marine fishing off the coast of Pacific Nicaragua and Nicoya, possibly because fishing vessels were not sufficiently developed to be able to cope
with the difficult navigational conditions in those waters. Archaeological
evidence indicates that, with the exception of the exploitation of some
shellfish, fishing on the Pacific coast was undertaken in inshore waters
and estuaries.[61] In the Gulf of Nicoya the Indians collected many kinds of
shellfish, including oysters, which were not eaten but were prized for
their pearls and shells.[62] Shells were used as spades and to make jew-
elry, especially necklaces and bracelets.[63] From *Purpura* mollusks a
purple dye was extracted that was an important item of trade in pre-
Columbian times.[64]

Inasmuch as fishing occurred on the Pacific coast, canoes were
probably the most common form of vessel used. They were of a dugout
variety whose sides curved inward to afford protection against the sun
and sea spray. They were normally propelled by oars, though sails made
of cotton and rushes were also used.[65] In the Gulf of Nicoya rafts made of
four or six logs tied together and propelled by oars, were used in preference to canoes.[66] Nets and lines were made from vegetable fibers.
Notched sherds, used as gauges in the manufacture of fishing nets, and
net sinkers have been found in archaeological sites in Nicaragua and Nicoya. Neither fishhooks nor fish stupefacients appear to have been used.[67]

The collection of wild fruit and vegetable products did not play such
an important role in the economy of Indian groups in Pacific Nicaragua as
it did in the east, and it was probably undertaken in times of shortage
rather than as a regular activity.[68] In Nicoya, however, the collection of
nuts and berries appears to have played a significant role. Nutting stones

have been found in large quantities in some archaeological sites, and it seems likely that they were used to break open acorns of *Quercus oleoides* Cham. & Schl. They have not been found farther north in Nicaragua.[69] Other items collected in the pre-Columbian period included honey, beeswax, gums, resins, and balsams, the last being used for medicinal purposes. Honey and beeswax were collected from nests in trees and from under the ground.[70] Although many varieties of plants and trees were exploited for medicines, by far the most important were liquidambar (*Liquidambar styraciflua* L.) and guayacan, or lignum vitae, also called palo santo or brasil (*Guaiacum officinale* L.).[71]

Amongst the chiefdoms of the Mesoamerican zone crafts were diverse and highly developed. Although men went naked when they chose, they also wore cotton clothes consisting of tunics wrapped around with wide belts, sometimes passed between the legs to form a kind of loincloth. Women wore sleeveless blouses and shirts. Cotton blankets or shawls were also woven, and they became important items of tribute in the colonial period. For clothes and other purposes many fabrics of varying thicknesses and colors were woven.[72] Red and black dyes were obtained from *bija* (*Bixa orellana* L.) and *xagua* (Genipa americana L.) plants, respectively, and purple dye was extracted from *Purpura* mollusks in the Gulf of Nicoya.[73] Unlike the tribes of the South American zone, they did not use bark cloth for clothing, but it was used to make sandals, as was deerskin.[74]

In addition to being used for clothing, cotton was also used to make cotton canvas, which among other things was used for sails.[75] Ropes and cordage were made from cabuya, henequen, and maguey (*Agave* sp. and *Fourcroydes* sp.). Oviedo described the cabuya and henequen found in Nicaragua as the best in the Indies.[76] In Nicaragua nets were made from a fiber extracted from palm leaves, which was also used to make sails.[77] Another plant called *ozpanguazte* was used to make brooms,[78] while mats and baskets were manufactured from rushes and palm leaves. Tribute lists indicate that, in comparison with the South American zone, basketry was highly developed in Pacific Nicaragua.[79]

Many varieties of pottery bowls, pots, and pans were also made to a higher standard than that found in the South American zone. Chorotegan pottery, particularly Black Ware, was highly esteemed and in Nicoya formed an important item of trade with the highlands of Costa Rica.[80] Stone was not used for buildings but was employed in the manufacture of idols, weapons, and implements.[81] Indians in the Pacific zone also worked gold and silver, sometimes alloying the gold with silver or copper.[82] Gold was used for idols and body ornaments.[83] On an expedition through Nicoya in 1522, Gil González Dávila was given six idols of gold, and farther north he encountered the Indian leader Diriangen, whom he described as being covered with small plates of gold, and who presented him two hundred hatchets made of gold.[84] The use of gold appears to have been widespread in Nicaragua, where it was freely traded. That goldsmiths, silversmiths, and jewelers resided in the main square indicates that they were highly regarded in Nicarao society.[85]

Throughout Pacific Nicaragua and Nicoya trade was well developed. It was particularly highly developed among the Nicarao, who possessed market complexes, which were administered by two elected officials.[86] These officials were allowed in the marketplace, known as a *tianguez,* together with virgin boys, men from allied villages who spoke the same language, and slaves who were to be sold; no other men were permitted to enter the market, and trading was conducted by women.[87] Various goods were traded, including slaves, gold, and cotton cloth and blankets, as well as food.[88] Cacao beans were generally used as a medium of exchange, though cotton cloth and maize were sometimes used.[89] In Nicoya from the Middle Polychrome period onward there is evidence of trade between inland and coastal sites and in the immediate pre-Conquest period Indians living on the coast of Nicoya were trading even farther afield.[90] In 1529 the governor of Nicaragua, Francisco de Castañeda, reported that in Nicoya "the Indians of the lowlands live off trade with those in the highlands [presumably of Costa Rica] to whom they take pitchers, pots, and plates of black clay [undoubtedly Black Ware], which they make very well, and cotton blankets and beads and maize and other things which those of the highlands do not possess."[91]

THE SOCIOPOLITICAL ORGANIZATION

There is much more evidence for the social and political organization of the Nicarao than for the Chorotega, but both groups possessed social hierarchies. The class system was more highly developed among the Nicarao, whose chiefdoms were governed by a single chief; the Chorotega possessed a more democratic form of government, being ruled by elected councils.[92] Among the Nicarao were chiefs under whom were provincial leaders. These nobles were known as *calachuni* and *teite,* respectively, and they were later referred to by the Spaniards as caciques or principales. The cacique of Teçoatega had twenty-four principales resident in his court, and the cacique of Mistega had nine.[93] Among the Chorotega the old men who were elected by their communities to serve on the ruling councils were similarly regarded as caciques and principales.[94]

There appear to have been two bases to the power of Nicarao chiefs.

First, they possessed cacao groves, which produced the cacao beans that were used as money. Second, they received tribute from the commoners in the form of cacao.[95] The exact role of caciques and principales is rather difficult to define since the Spaniards assigned these titles to almost any Indian who demonstrated some authority. Nevertheless, the following contemporary observations were made. Caciques and principales were exempt from routine labor, though they did participate in hunting, but for the purpose of sport rather than subsistence.[96] Oviedo noted that in Teçoatega the heads of animals killed by the cacique were displayed to demonstrate his hunting skill. With the agreement of a council, or *monexico,* the cacique ruled in matters of war and for the general good of his subjects; the council could not meet without the cacique.[97] Wars were generally led by war leaders, but sometimes the cacique accompanied them in battle.[98] Similarly, caciques participated in religious ceremonies, though these were generally conducted by priests. It seems likely that the position of the cacique was hereditary, though there is no documentary evidence to support this assertion. On taking office, each cacique had to remain in the temple for a year, during which time he prayed and could be visited only by children who took him food. At the end of the year his nose was pierced, and a great celebration was held.[99]

Below the caciques were principales, the heads of provinces. Together with a number of their subjects they guarded the cacique and formed his court. They had the responsibility of informing the commoners of the cacique's decisions and of collecting tribute from them. For both of these purposes they employed special officials and messengers, who carried feather fans or staffs to indicate that the orders and messages they conveyed came from the cacique.[100] Caciques and other nobles were distinguished from commoners by their clothes and a distinct form of body painting.[101] Apparently they never communicated with the lower classes.[102]

As already indicated, the cacique governed with the advice of a council. Members of the council were chosen by the people to serve for periods of "four moons." Generally the oldest members of the Indian community were chosen. From among their number they elected two officials to supervise the market for periods of four months. These officials also had absolute power in the marketplace, including the punishment of offenses.[103]

Other individuals of noble rank included military and religious leaders. Military leaders among both the Nicarao and the Chorotega were chosen on the basis of their ability and could be removed from the office if they did not provide satisfactory service. They were given the title *tapaligui* by the Nicarao, and in recognition of their office their heads were shaved, a small patch of hair being left on top of the head.[104] The cacique sometimes accompanied the military leader in battle. If the latter was killed, the cacique would assume command, and another military leader would be chosen.[105] If a Nicarao military leader showed cowardice, his weapons were confiscated, and he was expelled from the army, but among the Chorotega he was often put to death.[106] The same fate befell soldiers who disobeyed the commands of military leaders.[107]

Priests resided in the temples and were supported by gifts from the people; the temple itself owned no property and did not have any form of income.[108] It is not known how priests achieved their positions or for how long they held them. According to information received by López de Gómara, priests were allowed to marry, but Herrera's source suggests the opposite.[109] The priest was the key figure in religious ceremonies, including those at which sacrifices were made, but for the judgment of religious offenses the council elected confessors.[110] They punished blasphemy and nonattendance at religious ceremonies, sentencing those they found guilty to cleaning the temple and supplying it with wood. The confessors had to be unmarried, and, unlike priests, they did not reside in the temple. They wore calabashes around their necks as signs of their official positions.

Commoners were distinguished from those of noble status in that they paid tribute and were under an obligation to fight when the occasion demanded. Most commoners participated in various economic activities including agriculture, hunting, fishing, and collecting, though it is possible that craft specialists may have been exempt from these tasks. In addition, women sold their services as prostitutes.[111]

Slaves appear to have been fairly common among the Nicarao, and they were not the exclusive property of nobles. Slaves were sold in the market for about 100 cacao beans each.[112] There were various ways in which a person might be enslaved. Those Indians who were captured in war or were found in the marketplace illegally were enslaved. These slaves, however, were often sacrificed or eaten and thus did not contribute to the formation of a distinct social class.[113] Others were enslaved in recompense for crimes they had committed, while poverty drove some families to sell their children into slavery.[114] In addition to owning slaves, each noble also possessed a number of young men who were brought up from childhood to be sacrificed, but these young men had a high social status compared with that of slaves.[115]

Among the Nicarao various people, such as confessors and those who supervised the markets, appear to have dispensed justice, but it is not clear whether there were any judges or who carried out or enforced the sentences. López de Gómara maintains that there were ministers of justice who had *moscadores* (feather fans) and staffs to indicate their official positions, but a respondent to Friar Bobadilla commissioned to investigate the customs and beliefs of Indians in Nicaragua in 1528 said that there was no judge or court of justice.[116] It was not a crime to kill a slave, but for the murder of a free person the murderer had to recompense his relatives or else become their slave. Similarly a thief had to recompense the offended party, or he was bound over with his head shaved until he had paid for his crime. A similar fate befell those who committed rape.[117]

Adultery by a man was accompanied by the loss of inheritance and exile. The same penalty applied to a man who committed bigamy, the man's inheritance being given to his first wife and the man being exiled. His first wife could then remarry as long as she had no children. A woman who committed adultery was returned to her parents and was not allowed to remarry. The severest penalty was meted out to slaves who slept with the daughters of their owners: both individuals were buried alive. Homosexuals were not tolerated and were stoned, sometimes to death.[118] A similar form of justice appears to have been administered among the Maribio, though in this group it is clear that the cacique was the judge. Murderers were publicly flogged and required to pay compensation in the form of beads, clothing, or cloth, as required by the cacique. A similar fate befell thieves and adulterers, except that an adulterer also paid compensation to the husband. Those who spoke treasonous words against the cacique had their houses burned and could not rebuild them on the same site. In addition they were required to pay a fine to the temple. Those who blasphemed against the gods were required to pay a similar fine and were flogged.[119]

Among the Nicarao monogamy generally prevailed, although caciques who could afford to support more than one wife did so; only one, however, was regarded as the legitimate wife.[120] Individuals could not marry their parents, brothers and sisters, and children, but any others from whatever class, but with the aim of keeping kin relations as close as possible.[121] Generally the boy's father asked the girl's father to allow the marriage. If the girl's father agreed, the marriage ceremony was performed, according to Oviedo by the cacique, but according to López de Gómara by a priest.[122] The custom of *jus primae noctis* was sometimes practiced whereby a girl was sent to the cacique to prove that she was a virgin and also because it was regarded as an honor.[123] The girl's father provided a dowry of fruit trees, land, and possessions, and the boy's father gave what he could. If the girl proved not to be a virgin, as had been claimed, then she was returned to her parents.[124]

Oviedo noted that among the Nicarao the women were under the control of the men whereas among the Chorotega the reverse was true.[125] Stone maintains that certain elements of the social organization of Indian groups in Pacific Nicaragua at the time of the Conquest suggest that polyandry may formerly have been the rule. For example, Nicarao women were given license once a year to sleep with whom they wished, and in independent towns it was the custom for women to choose their husbands from among young men when they gathered for feasts.[126]

There is little information about birth practices in Pacific Nicaragua. It is known, however, that head deformation was practiced in order, it was said, to make the head more attractive and a better shape for carrying loads.[127] On death the Nicarao wrapped the body in a blanket and buried it. If the individual had no heirs, his belongings were buried with him. It was believed that the body perished but the soul survived, and accordingly food was also buried, together with figurines, probably of pottery, which were broken so that the memory of the deceased would remain for twenty to thirty days.[128] When a cacique died, he was dressed in his regalia and was burned together with his symbol of office and the gold he possessed. The ashes were then placed in an urn, which was buried in front of his dwelling. There is evidence for such urn burials in the archaeological record.[129] Ritual dancing and singing accompanied the death of a cacique.[130]

Conflict between and within chiefdoms appears to have been common in Nicaragua and Nicoya, as indicated by the high social status of military leaders. The Nicarao fought both the Chorotega and the Chontal (probably the Sumu and the Matagalpa), while the Chorotega also had wars with the Guetar in Costa Rica.[131] Among the Nicarao conflict broke out over territorial claims.[132] Such disputes were obviously common since they kept records of boundaries and landholdings in parchment books for the purpose of trying to settle disagreements peacefully; such books were not kept by the Chorotega.[133] The Chorotega were considered to be more warlike than the Nicarao, and it is possible that they lacked institutional mechanisms such as this for defusing potential sources of conflict. Wars were also fought over hunting grounds and to prove which group was the more powerful; they were further stimulated by the need to obtain prisoners of war for sacrifice.[134]

The selection and role of military leaders have already been described. From accounts of attacks on the Spaniards by the Nicarao it appears that war was conducted in open battle rather than in raids. Individual soldiers could keep any booty they obtained, and prisoners were sacrificed.[135] The Nicarao used a great variety of weapons, including bows and arrows, lances, clubs, and swords and shields. The swords were made of wood with flints, and the shields of bark or light wood covered with feathers and cotton—attractive, but also light and strong.[136]

IDEOLOGY

Religion and ritual were highly developed in Pacific Nicaragua. The presence of temples and priests among the Nicarao and Chorotega has already been mentioned. The temples of both groups were considered by Oviedo to be similar, "but the language, rites, and ceremonies and customs are different." [137]

For the Nicarao the most important gods, known as *teotes,* were Tamagastad and Cipattonal. Both had human forms, but it is not clear whether they were male or female. They were considered to be the creators of all things, including human beings, the earth, the moon, and stars. [138] Other gods to whom creative powers were ascribed were Oxomogo, Calchitguegue, and Chicociagat. The power of some gods was limited to particular spheres: Quiateot was the god of rain, thunder, and lightning; Chiquinaut and Hecat were the gods of the air; Bizteot was the god of hunger; and Mixcoa, the god of trade. There were also gods of plants that were cultivated, notably maize, beans, cotton, and cacao, and of animals that were hunted: Macat was the god of deer and Toste the god of the rabbit. [139] In addition there were "angels" called *tamachas,* the most important of which were Taraacazcati and Tamacastoval. [140] Gods were represented in the form of idols made of stone, and they were petitioned for such benefits as a good harvest; a healthful climate; peace or victory in battle; freedom from plagues of insects and from floods, drought, and wild beasts. [141] To improve hunting, the heads of deer and rabbits were placed at the doors of hunters, and deer blood was dried and revered as the god of deer. [142]

Among the Nicarao gods were petitioned at ceremonies at which human sacrifices were made. Victims were sacrificed by the priest, and their blood was smeared over the idols. As mentioned earlier, the sacrificial victims included war captives, slaves, and young men reared from birth in the houses of nobles especially for the purpose. On being sacrificed, the latter were thought to go directly to heaven. [143] War captives were generally sacrificed and eaten. They were first slain and their hearts torn out. The heart was eaten by the priests and their wives and children, the hands and feet by the cacique, the intestines by the trumpeteers, and the rest by the commoners. [144] Commoners were not, however, allowed to eat the bodies of important war captives who were sacrificed. Also, women were not eaten by the priests, although they drank their blood; in fact, women were not allowed in the main temples, and female sacrifices were conducted outside; sacrifices of women did take place in lower-order temples. The heads of those who had been sacrificed were placed on trees, and the hands, feet, and entrails of slaves were buried, while the heart and the rest of the body was burned. [145]

These sacrificial ceremonies were accompanied by dancing, singing, and drinking. After the sacrifice had taken place, the priest led a procession around the town or village and back to the temple, where there were further speeches and the priest practiced self-mutilation of the tongue, ears, or genitals. The resulting blood was smeared over the relevant idol, and prayers were said.[146]

In addition to ceremonies for particular purposes, the Nicarao also held ceremonies at various times of the year in celebrations of the gods. An informant of Friar Bobadilla stated that there were 21 feast days in a year corresponding to the months, though later he noted that there were 10 *cempuales* of 20 days each, which would give a year comprised of 200 days.[147] León-Portilla suggests that the number of *cempuales* was wrongly transcribed and that it should have been 18, as in Mexico, thereby giving a year of 360 days.[148] This corresponds to the accounts of López de Gómara and Herrera, both of which state that there were 18 *cempuales* in a year.[149] On these feast days men did not sleep with their wives but became drunk.[150]

At certain ceremonies, such as that celebrating the cacao harvest, the *volador* was held. This ceremony (see plate) centered on a high pole at the top of which was a rectangular frame with an idol and from which ropes hung, twisted around the pole. Two or four men were attached to the ropes, and as they unwound rapidly, they were gradually lowered to the ground. In their hands they held bows and arrows, feather fans, and mirrors. This ceremony was also known in Mexico, and it is described in detail by Oviedo.[151] According to Brinton, the symbolism of the ceremony is that the idol at the top of the pole represented the god of fertility and the men attached to the ropes were messengers whom he sent to earth. The arrows represent lightning; the feather fans, breezes and birds; and the mirrors, water and rains. The arrival of the messengers on earth represents the ripening of the crops and the harvest.[152] A game, which was not held at ceremonies but which may have had some ritual significance, was a kind of seesaw called the *comelagatoazte* (see plate).[153] The details of rites and ceremonies, as well as notable events in the history of the chiefdoms, were recorded in deerskin books.[154]

The Nicarao possessed certain concepts and beliefs which, although recorded at an early date, appear to have been influenced by Christianity. For example, they believed that a flood had destroyed the world, which had been rebuilt by the gods, who came to earth.[155] León-Portilla maintains, however, that, while the flood story was probably introduced by the Spaniards, the idea of the destruction of the earth by a superior power was common in pre-Columbian Mesoamerica.[156] Similarly, the belief in an afterlife, with the soul, known as *yulio,* departing the body on death, may appear to have been influenced by Christianity, but such a belief was common throughout the Nahua-speaking area and appears to date back to Toltec times.[157] Those who had lived a good life, those killed in battle, and those reared from birth for sacrifice went to live with the gods; those who had lived a bad life went to a place below called Mikan-teot. There was no belief in reincarnation, except for children who died before they had been weaned.

There was also a belief in witches and sorcerers, called *texoxes,* who could transform themselves into animals, notably tigers, lions, birds, or lizards. They were in contact with the devil and could kill persons who offended them. Certain old women were supposed to have curative powers.[158]

In general terms the religions of the Nicarao and Chorotega chiefdoms were similar: they had priests, idols, and temples and practiced human sacrifice, and self-mutilation. In detail, however, there were a number of differences. Although the Chorotega may have possessed a pantheon of gods equivalent to those revered by the Nicarao, only three were recorded by Oviedo. They were Tipotani, probably the most important, and Nenbithia and Nenguitamali, a man and a woman, respectively, who were said to have created all mortal things.[159] There were also gods of water, maize, fruits, and battle.[160] The gods were often represented in the form of idols, sometimes made of gold but probably more often of clay and wood.[161] These were kept in small shrines and temples called *teyopa.*[162]

The Chorotega held three main festivals a year, at which sacrifices took place. At these ceremonies the Indians adorned themselves with paint and feathers and engaged in singing, dancing, and drinking. A sacrifice was made, the "first blood" being offered to the sun; the flesh of others who were sacrificed, which was considered to be holy, was then eaten. After the sacrifices had taken place, the women screamed and fled, being pursued by their husbands and relatives, who tried to persuade them to return by making them promises and offering them gifts. The woman who fled the farthest was the most highly esteemed.[163] On the same or the next day maize cobs were placed around the sacrificial mound, and the priests performed self-mutilation of the tongue, ears, or genitals, smearing the blood over the maize cobs, which were then distributed and eaten as holy food.[164] The Chorotega also sacrificed men and women to the volcano Masaya. Although Andagoya recorded that virgin women were sacrificed, according to Oviedo, other women, men and children were also sacrificed.[165]

CHAPTER 4

The Tribes

Although there is some archaeological evidence of the nature of Indian cultures in the South American zone at the time of the Conquest, we have virtually no documentary evidence for the sixteenth century, for the area remained largely unexplored and uncolonized. The earliest descriptions belong to missionaries who began working in the area in the early seventeenth century. In view of the inadequacy of the documentary record, critical use has been made of more recent ethnographic accounts. In general the tribes constituted smaller societies, which were essentially egalitarian and did not possess idols, temples, or an instituted priesthood. Although agriculture was practiced, other subsistence activities played more significant roles in the economy than they did in the Mesoamerican zone.

In contrast to the chiefdoms of the Mesoamerican zone, tribal settlements were small, consisting of individual houses or small clusters of dwellings. They lacked marketplaces and temple complexes, though the absence of shrines may have been more apparent than real, since the Indians were generally reluctant to reveal them to outsiders.[1] The location and the temporary or permanent nature of settlements appear to have been related to some degree to the resources exploited by the Indians. While all groups had permanent settlements, temporary ones appear to have been more common among some inland Sumu who depended heavily on wild food, particularly plantains. Their settlements lasted only as long as the sources of food, and when they were exhausted, the Indians moved on to exploit the resources of another area.[2] Archaeological evidence suggests that at the time of the Conquest other groups had permanent agricultural villages some distance inland but had temporary fishing settlements on the coast.[3] This contrasts with the settlement pattern that existed at the end of the colonial period, when permanent settlements were situated on the coast to take advantage of the employment and trading opportunities offered by the English.

Characteristically, permanent settlements were strung out along river valleys but above lands that were seasonally flooded. Among the Sumu the settlements were composed of one or more multifamily dwellings or lodges. In 1539 a member of Alonso Calero and Diego Machuca's expedition to the Mosquito Coast observed that near the río Yare (Segovia) the settlement pattern was not nucleated but that each hut stood by itself.[4] Similarly, an undated document, probably from the eighteenth century, describes the settlement pattern around Muymuy and Sebaco as follows: "They do not live in formal villages, but each family lives by itself in a very large house made of straw like a galley, and in one of these houses is collected all the lineage, and these houses are situated three to four leagues apart."[5] M. W. also observed what must have been multi-family houses among the Mosquito. In 1699 he noted that a Mosquito settlement at Sandy Bay consisted of "about 12 straggling houses, and inhabited by four hundred people in all, or thereabouts."[6] It seems that in Nicaragua these multifamily lodges were often referred to as *palenques,* for, although the term is generally used to describe pallisaded settlements, these are absent from Nicaragua.[7] There are several descriptions of multifamily houses in later ethnographic accounts.[8] In the midnineteenth century Wickham recorded that Sumu lodges normally contained four families and that each settlement consisted of two or three lodges.[9] Altogether the settlements would not have contained more than several hundred Indians, and they seldom would have reached that size.

Recent ethnographic accounts suggest that houses were either rectangular or oval. Stone was not used in construction, but the houses would have been open-sided, consisting of thatched roofs which extended almost to the ground and were supported by wooden posts. Often these houses would have been divided into compartments for individual families, and they would have possessed attics, which were used for storage and sometimes for sleeping.[10] Although hammocks were known, they were not normally used for sleeping, but were taken on journeys and were used for lazing during the day. Beds were generally made of woven palm-leaf mats and bark-cloth sheets.[11] Houses probably lasted from six to ten years; temporary shelters, which lasted only a few days, were made of wooden poles covered with plantain or *bijao* leaves.[12]

THE ECONOMY

In eastern Nicaragua, Indian groups participated in agriculture, hunting, fishing, and gathering in varying degrees. The inland Sumu and Matagalpa depended more on agriculture, though they also hunted and collected wild fruits and vegetables. The Sumu on the eastern shore of Lake Nicaragua also fished, and at the time of the Conquest they extended to the Atlantic coast, where they exploited marine resources. Recent archaeological investigations by Magnus on the Mosquito Coast suggest, however, that fishing did not play such an important role in the economy of coastal groups in the pre-Columbian times as it came to play in the colonial period; the aboriginal economy was based on agriculture, supported by riverine fishing, hunting, and gathering.[13]

In the performance of these activities there was no division of labour except that based on sex. Men generally hunted, fished, and cleared the forest for cultivation. The last activity was probably carried out on an exchange basis, male relatives and friends helping each other to clear their individual family plots.[14] Where agriculture played a more significant role in the economy, men may also have been employed in cultivation, though women generally planted, weeded, and harvested crops and gathered wild fruits and vegetables and, where possible, crabs and shell-fish. The women also made pottery and wove cotton cloth.

In pre-Columbian times crops were almost certainly grown under a system of shifting cultivation, as most crops are today. This would have involved the abandonment of plots to fallow after several years of cultivation to allow the soil to recover some of its lost fertility.[15] Nietschmann has observed that among the Mosquito at Tasbapauni plots are presently cultivated for two to three years before being abandoned for four to ten years according to their accessibility. Formerly, however, the fallowing period was between ten and fifteen years or more but had been reduced owing to land pressure created by population increase.[16] Where possible plots would have been located near the village.[17] Where the soil near the village was considered too poor for cultivation, plots might be sited some distance away, particularly on the alluvial banks of rivers. In a reconnaissance of the Mosquito Coast in 1790 the soil in the area around Cabo de Gracias a Dios was described as so poor that the Indians were forced to cultivate plots three, four, and more days' journey upriver, and around their houses they had only some fruit trees.[18] Somewhat later, in 1827, Roberts recorded that the soil in the same area was "barren whilst that inland is a much richer quality therefore the inhabitants have their provision grounds and plantain walks many miles up from the sea, with the exception of cassava which can thrive on the sandy soil near coast settlements."[19] The separation of settlements from the area that was cultivated probably occurred during the colonial period, when the arrival of European settlers on the coast forced a reorientation of the Indian economy; in the pre-Columbian period settlements were probably located away from the coast and nearer the areas under cultivation.[20] Another reason given for the distant location of cultivation plots was defense.[21]

Once the plots had been selected, the sites would have been cleared with stone axes. The actual amount of land cleared at any one time would depend on local physical conditions as well as the needs of the individual families. In his discussion of settlement patterns associated with shifting cultivation, Carneiro estimates that one acre per person is required where the land is cultivated in manioc for 2½ years and is left to fallow for 30 years.[22] Leeds considers this figure too high for an economy that is substantially dependent on wild food resources and favors an estimate of ½ acre a year.[23] This is somewhat higher that Nietschmann's estimate of 1½ acres for subsistence for a family of six or seven for the Mosquito of Tasbapauni, though this does not take into account the old plots which Nietschmann estimates provide 40 to 50 percent of the calories obtained from crops. Nor does it take into account an average of two acres per family cultivated in coconuts and rice, which were not present in pre-Columbian times, and which may have been cultivated in other subsistence crops.[24]

On many of the cleared plots many different crops were grown together in such a way that they simulated the secondary forest they replaced. In 1681, Dampier described the plots of the Mosquito as follows: "Their largest plantations have not above 20 or 30 plantain-trees, a bed of yams and potatoes, a bush of indian pepper, and a small spot of pineapples."[25] Separate plots were probably also cultivated exclusively in one crop, for plots were often referred to as *yucales, platanares, frisolares, maizales, tabacales, algodonales,* and *cacaotales,* according to which crop was being grown. Helms indicates that among the Mosquito on upper Wanks River a distinction is made between annual and perennial crops, because perennials cannot be grown in plots requiring frequent burning, which is needed for annuals.[26] It may be that the separation of plots for different crops is a response to land pressure, when the need to recultivate plots within a short time is necessary. Elsewhere plots may be abandoned though crops such as plantains may still be harvested from them.

Many varieties of crops were cultivated in the Atlantic zone. In 1672, Exquemelin observed that the food of the Mosquito consisted of "several fruits, such are called bananas, racoven, ananas, potatoes, cassava,"[27] and in 1757, Hodgson wrote that the inhabitants of the Mosquito Coast had "the greatest plenty of plantains, maize, yams, casavi (not poysonous), cocos, eddoes, and potatoes (like Jerusalem artichokes)."[28] Inland groups also grew a variety of crops. In 1783 the Indians of Matagalpa and Talamanca were said to subsist on "plaintains, yucas, camotes or potatoes, and other roots"; they also grew maize and exploited the fruit of the *pejibaye* palm.[29]

It is clear from these few descriptions that the most important crops grown by Indians in eastern Honduras and Nicaragua were root crops. Although seed crops, especially maize and beans, were grown in the pre-Columbian period, they played a far less significant role in the economy than they did in the Pacific zone. Although it is possible that root crops were domesticated in Central America, the consensus is that they were introduced from northern South America.[30] On the basis of cultural, botanical, archaeological, and linguistic evidence Chapman has suggested that sweet-manioc cultivation was introduced into Central America by a lowland Chibchan group in the third millennium B.C.[31]

Root crops have several disadvantages not shared by seed crops. First, root crops tend to be deficient in protein, fats, and oils and alone cannot provide a balanced diet; supplements are needed from other sources, notably hunting and fishing. Seed crops can supply a greater variety of nutrients, and Indians can therefore be released from their dependence on wild food resources. Second, seed crops have greater storage capabilities and can thus be used to overcome shortages.

Since seed crops possess certain advantages over root crops, it may be asked why seed crops were not adopted on a large scale in the South American zone. A number of authors have suggested that the Atlantic coast of Central America was isolated from contacts with Mesoamerica and the central Andes and that if any contacts did occur in Central America, they were effected through the Pacific zone.[32] But the fact that maize was cultivated in the South American zone and that a Mexican colony existed in the area at the time of Conquest suggests that such contacts were not altogether lacking. It seems more likely that the reason why maize was not adopted on a large scale was that the cultivation of root crops and palms supplemented by hunting, fishing, and gathering was better suited to the ecological conditions of the area and in fact provided the Indians there with a substantial and varied diet. Some parts of eastern Nicaragua appear to have been climatically unsuitable for the cultivation of seed crops, which grow better in subarid conditions. In 1627, Indians (probably Sumu) from the villages of Lóvago, Lovigüisca, and Camoapa were unable to pay tribute in maize because "the Indians have never been seen to harvest maize nor will they because it grows so badly in the area on account of the rains."[33] Not only were root-crop cultivation and exploitation of wild food resources better suited to the local ecological conditions, but there was little pressure on the Indians to change their subsistence habits. It is possible that, if the Spanish conquest had not occurred, penetration into the area by Mexican traders and colonists might ultimately have resulted in the area being incorporated into the Aztec empire, with demands for tribute and items for trade creating pressure for the adoption of new crops, including maize.[34]

The most important crops grown in the colonial period were manioc and plantains, with manioc dominant in the coastal areas and plantains more important inland.[35] There is a dispute, however, whether plantains (*Musa paradisiaca* L. var. *normalis*) were cultivated in the pre-Columbian period. They were domesticated in southeast Asia, and there is some doubt whether they reached Latin America before the Spanish conquest. Nevertheless, the diversity of varieties present and the wide distribution of the plantain in Latin America in the early sixteenth century suggest that it must have been introduced in pre-Columbian times.[36] Oviedo recorded the presence of a plant called *plátano* in the West Indies and the fringing mainland of the Caribbean, which he maintained was different from the European variety, the banana (var. *sapientum*), which was introduced to Santo Domingo from the Canary Islands in 1516.[37] When Friar Alonso Ponce visited Nicaragua in 1586, his secretary drew up a list of plants, distinguishing the indigenous ones from those introduced from Europe; among the indigenous ones he included *plátanos*.[38] It seems likely, therefore, that plantains were grown in the New World in pre-Columbian times, but if they were not, they spread very rapidly in the immediate post-Conquest period.

The inland Sumu exploited plantains as their major source of food.[39] In 1608 on a missionary expedition to the area around Muymuy, Friar Juan de Albuquerque reported that the Indians had *platanales,* "which is their food and they do not stay in one place longer than the plantains last, and when they are finished, they go to another place."[40] Plantains were probably used in the preparation of an intoxicating drink known as *mishla,* as they were in the seventeenth century. In 1672, Exquemelin described the process of making *mishla* from plantains as follows: "These they knead betwixt their hands with hot water, and afterwards put into great calabashes, which they fill up with cold water, and leave in repose for the space of eight days, during which time it ferments as well as the best sort of wine."[41]

While plantains may have been the most important staple in the inland areas, manioc (*Manihot esculenta* Crantz), though grown in those areas, assumed much greater importance on the coast. The sweet variety of manioc was cultivated, and it was probably more commonly boiled or roasted than made into bread. The first reference to manioc being grown on the Caribbean coast dates from 1539, when an account of Calero's expedition related that the land around the río Yare (Segovia) was full of "maize, yuca, and pepper."[42] The only reference to the cultivation of bitter manioc comes from M. W., who in 1699 described the method of extracting the poisonous juice from the root by grating, squeezing, and drying. He did, however, refer to the plant as "sweet cassader" and later noted that bread was made from it by the English. This suggests that the plant was probably not cultivated by the Indians in pre-Columbian times but was introduced by the English to the Mosquito Coast, probably from northern South America, where it was commonly grown.[43] In 1757, Robert Hodgson was at pains to point out that the type of cassava cultivated by the Indians there was "not poysonous."[44] The documentary evidence is backed by the absence from the archaeological record of graters or griddles associated with the baking of cassava bread.

It is unclear why the cultivation of bitter manioc should not have spread to Central America in pre-Columbian times; it has a higher starch content than sweet manioc and bread made from it can be stored for long periods. The absence of bitter manioc from Central America cannot be explained by climatic factors, though the two varieties have slightly different requirements.[45] Chapman has proposed that the cultivation of sweet manioc represents an older agricultural tradition; this is suggested by the wider distribution of sweet-manioc cultivation and its simpler form of preparation.[46] It seems likely that the more complex process of extracting the poisonous juices from bitter manioc developed later. She goes on to suggest that, while sweet manioc spread to Central America in about the third millennium B.C., from that time until the Spanish conquest the Caribbean coast of Central America remained a "cultural backwater" that was bypassed by later developments. Sauer, however, maintains that there was ample time for the diffusion of techniques of cultivation and preparation and that a more likely explanation is that the indigenous economy provided adequate supplies of food from several sources and there was no need to change to the cultivation of bitter manioc, which in other areas satisfied demands for a more substantial and reliable source of food.[47]

Other root crops grown would have included sweet potatoes, yams, and yautias. The cultivation of sweet potatoes (*Ipomoea batatas* [L.] Lam.) was noted by the earliest observers. In the documentary record they are sometimes referred to by their Nahua name camotes or are called *ages* or *batatas,* Taino names used to refer to the nonsugary and sugary races of sweet potato, respectively.[48] There is some uncertainty whether yams were cultivated in the pre-Columbian period. It is possible that the New World yam (*Dioscorea trifida* L.) was found in Central America before the Conquest, but there is no early documentary evidence for its cultivation, and the Sumu and Mosquito do not possess native names for it.[49] The yams cultivated on the Mosquito Coast during the seventeenth and eighteenth centuries were almost certainly Old World yams (*Dioscorea alata* L. and *Discorea bulbifera* L.) introduced from Africa.[50] A root crop that was almost certainly grown in the pre-Columbian period but for which there is no documentary evidence from the early colonial period is yautia (*Xanthosoma sp.*), also known as tania and malanga. It is called *duswa* by the Mosquito and *wilis* by the Sumu.[51] It is indigenous to America and is generally found in association with sweet manioc and sweet potatoes. Today it ranks second to manioc among the crops cultivated by the Mosquito.[52] A distinctive feature of agriculture on the Atlantic side of Nicaragua was the cultivation of the pejibaye palm (*Guilielma utilis* Oerst). It appears to have been domesticated in South America at an early date and was more commonly found south of Nicaragua.[53] The fruit was boiled or roasted or made into an alcoholic drink.[54]

As already indicated maize (*Zea mays* L.) was cultivated widely in eastern Nicaragua, but it appears to have been most commonly grown by the inland Sumu and Matagalpa.[55] Early visitors to the Mosquito Coast noted that maize was grown there, particularly for the preparation of drinks, but their accounts suggest that it was of secondary importance.[56] Nevertheless, archaeological investigations by Magnus on the Mosquito Coast have shown that in pre-Columbian times the Indian economy was more firmly based on agriculture than it is at present and that orientation toward the sea was the result of contact with foreigners during the colonial period. This is suggested by the discovery in archaeological sites of large numbers of metates and manos used to grind maize.[57] Nevertheless, it is difficult to estimate the importance of maize in the economy given the difficulty of finding archaeological evidence for root-crop cultivation. Maize flour was probably mixed with water to form a dough, which was then wrapped in a leaf and boiled or roasted. There is no archaeological evidence for griddles used to bake tortillas, whose method of preparation was probably introduced at a later date.[58] Much of the maize consumed by Indians in Nueva Segovia in the colonial period was eaten on the cob.[59] Given that maize was cultivated in eastern Nicaragua in pre-Columbian times, beans and chili peppers, which are commonly associated with maize cultivation, were probably grown also, though there are only a few references to them in the documentary record.[60] Today the Mosquito regard beans as a European food and eat them only occasionally, which suggests that they were probably not widely cultivated in pre-Columbian times and may have become more common through contact with the Spanish and the English.[61]

In addition to these field crops, various edible fruits and plants that provided herbs, spices, and dyes were cultivated in household gardens. Among the fruits grown were pineapples (*Ananas comosus* [L.] Merr.), papayas (*Carica papaya* L.), guavas (*Psidium guajava* L.), mammees (*Mammea americana* L.), sweetsops (*Anona squamosa* L.), soursops (*Anona muricata* L.), and sapodillas, or *nísperos* (*Manilkara achras* [Mill.]Fosberg).[62] It is worthy of note that a number of fruits currently cultivated in eastern Nicaragua were not present in the pre-Columbian period. The most notable absent fruits were the coconut (*Cocos nucifera* L.), the breadfruit (*Artocarpus communis* J. R. & G. Forst.), the mango (*Mangifera indica* L.), and all the citrus fruits (*Citrus* spp.).

Before discussing the contribution of hunting, fishing, and collecting to the economy, a few comments should be made about three other crops that were probably cultivated in the South American zone in the pre-Columbian period: cotton, tobacco, and cacao. Both wild and cultivated forms of cotton were exploited by Indians in eastern Nicaragua. Probably the most important species cultivated was *Gossypium hirsutum* L., a Mexican domesticate, and possibly the Peruvian species, *Gossypium barbadense* L.[63] Cotton was cultivated mainly by inland groups. In the sixteenth century Indians in the vicinity of Nueva Segovia wore white mantas, and in the seventeenth century some cotton cloth was worn by the Mosquito.[64] Tobacco, probably *Nicotiana tabacum* L., a South American domesticate, was used both as a stimulant and for medicinal purposes. Indians in the region of Nueva Segovia also used tobacco leaves mixed with masticated maize in water to make an alcoholic drink.[65] While cacao (*Theobroma cacao* L.) was intensively cultivated in Pacific Nicaragua, it is not clear whether the cacao used in the east came from wild or cultivated forms. Probably both were used. In 1608 the president of the Audiencia of Guatemala described the wild cacao trees around Sebaco as producing large fruits, the beans being twice the size of those found in Guatemala.[66] Nevertheless, there is a reference to *cacaotales* around Muymuy, which would seem to indicate the presence of cultivated cacao groves.[67] It is possible that Indians in the east learned the techniques of cacao cultivation from the Nicarao living on the other side of Lake Nicaragua.[68]

Hunting played an important role in the economy of tribes living in eastern Nicaragua and especially the inland Sumu and Matagalpa; on the Mosquito Coast game appears to have been more limited, and fishing would have provided a substantial proportion of the protein required.[69] The most important species hunted were deer, peccaries, and tapirs. Others mentioned in colonial documents included agoutis; pacas; coatimundis; howler, spider, and capuchin monkeys; rabbits; iguanas; hicatee turtles (land tortoises); armadillos; and crocodiles and alligators. There is archaeological evidence for the exploitation of all these species except monkeys on the Mosquito Coast.[70] The "lions and tigers" that were hunted for their skins were probably jaguars and ocelots but possibly pumas and margays.[71] Large numbers of birds were hunted, but it is difficult to identify the species from the names recorded in the early colonial period. Those most commonly mentioned were curassows, tinamous, guans, and wood pigeons, as well as various species of parrots and macaws.[72]

All groups were good hunters and hunted regularly. Hunting was a male activity, and its importance among the Mosquito can be gauged by the fact that skill in the manufacture of bows and arrows was considered a prerequisite for marriage.[73] Most animals were probably caught near cultivated plots where they came to forage; however, hunting expeditions lasting several days would have exploited more distant areas. The availability of animals varied seasonally, but the time expended in hunting would also have been affected by the demands of other subsistence activities. Among the Mosquito hunting is more important during the wet season, when turtling is not possible and animals often get trapped on islands as the waters rise.[74]

Various hunting techniques were known in eastern Nicaragua, some of which were unfamiliar to Indians living in the west. The main weapons used were bows and arrows and lances and spears. Bows and arrows were generally made from the pejibaye palm and bowstrings from silk grass (*Aechmea magdalenae* Baker) or a species of *Agave*. The tips of arrows or lances were often hardened by fire or were tipped with a hard wood such as mahogany or had points of flint, fish bones, or teeth. Small arrows, which were used to stun game, particularly birds, were sometimes tipped with blunt knobs of wood or wax. The blowgun, which was not known in the Pacific zone, was used, as were poisoned arrows. It seems likely that fire was used as a hunting device in the dry season, though there is no mention of it in the documentary record.[75]

It is doubtful that any domesticated animals were raised in the pre-Columbian period. The mute dog found in western Nicaragua was not known on the Caribbean coast,[76] and although the Muscovy duck was being raised by the Mosquito in the seventeenth century,[77] it may have been introduced to the Caribbean coast during the colonial period. Although anthropophagy was practiced by Indian groups in eastern Nicaragua, human meat did not make a significant contribution to the Indian diet; most Indians who were killed were prisoners of war.[78]

Fishing was a major economic activity among Indians living on the coast, though archaeological evidence from middens on the Mosquito shore suggests that it may not have played such an important role in the aboriginal economy but may have developed as a result of contact with Europeans.[79] Inland groups also exploited riverine resources and made occasional expeditions to the coast to catch turtles and to fish.[80]

In the latter part of the colonial period the most important animals exploited in the marine environment were turtles and manatees. Three main species of marine turtles were hunted: the green turtle (*Chelonia mydas mydas*), the hawksbill turtle (*Eretomochelys* sp.), and the loggerhead turtle (*Caretta* sp.). The first was prized for its meat, the second for its shell, and the last, which produced neither good meat nor shell, was probably exploited for its oil and eggs. The main period for turtling was during the dry season from February to April, but from then until July it was limited owing to the rough weather during the wet season and also owing to the migration of the turtles south to Tortuguero, in Costa Rica, for mating and egg laying. Turtling was resumed in August and September with the return of the turtles and the dry weather. The Indians caught turtles by turning them on their backs with a stick or harpooning or spearing them. The Mosquito were so adept at catching turtles that Hodgson observed that three men and a boy with two nets and a canoe could catch 80 to 130 turtles, each providing 150 pounds of meat.[81]

At present the green turtle accounts for about 70 percent of the meat consumed by the Mosquito at Tasbapauni, but it was probably less significant as a source of food in the precolonial period.[82] Archaeological investigations of a number of middens on the Mosquito Coast have revealed the presence of the mud or musk turtle (*Kinosternon leucostomum*), which is found in shallow, muddy waters, but the three species hunted during the colonial period are not represented.[83] The latter species are presently hunted on banks and shoals more than ten miles offshore, and it is possible that in pre-Columbian times Indians living near the coast did not possess the techniques necessary to exploit the offshore marine environment or any incentive to do so. It is also possible that the role played by turtling in the economy of coastal Indian groups increased with the arrival of Europeans, who not only created a demand for tortoise shell but indirectly encouraged Indians to locate their settlements on the coast. An important source of food for coastal Indian groups was the manatee, or sea cow (*Trichechus manatus*). It was found in the brackish river estuaries and lagoons and was generally caught with harpoons and lances.[84] One manatee was said to provide between 200 and 300 pounds of meat, and in the nineteenth century at least it was dried for storage.[85]

Many varieties of fish were caught during the pre-Columbian period. The most important species represented in middens found on the Mosquito shore were, in order of importance, sea catfish (*Ariidae*, including *Arius* sp. and *Bagre* sp.), toadfish (*Bactrachoididae, Bactrachoides* sp.), snook (*Centropomidae, Centropomus* sp.), jacks (*Carangidae, Caranx hippos*), and various members of the *Sciaenidae*, including croakers (*Micropogon* sp. and *Bairdiella* sp.), corvinas, or coppermouths (*Cynoscion* sp.), kingfish (*Mentirrhus* sp.), and sheepshead (*Arcosargus* sp.).[86] The middens also contained some bones of stingrays (*Dasyatidae*) and eagle rays (*Mylobatidae*), as well as evidence of shark species. With the exception of a number of the shark species most of these fish can be found in lagoons and estuaries at least during part of the year. Notable for their absence were the red snapper (*Lutjanus* sp.); tarpon, or *sábalo* (*Tarpon* sp.); and *carite*, or Spanish mackerel (*Scomberomorus* sp.). That all of these species are more commonly found in offshore waters adds weight to the view that most fishing occurred inshore. It is possible that the presence of a small number of bones of sharks, which are not found in lagoons or estuaries, may be from individuals that were washed ashore.

Nevertheless, it is clear from the documentary record that by the

seventeenth and eighteenth centuries Indians living on the coast were
exploiting fish from a greater variety of environments. Among those
species listed by M. W., Hodgson, and Strangeways which have not been
found in archaeological sites were snapper, tarpon, and mackerel. Other
species listed some of which were also found in the middens, were
sawfish (*Pristis* sp.); barracuda (*Sphyraena* sp.); flounders (*Bothidae*);
mullet, sometimes called *calipever* or *califavor* (*Mugil* sp.); groupers
(*Serranidae*), including jewfish (*Epinephelus* sp.); grunts (*Pomadasyidae*);
porgies (*Sparidae*); stone bass (*Diapterus* sp.); mojarras (Cichlasoma
sp.); and parrotfish (*Scaridae*).[87] Many of these fish would have entered
larger rivers and lakes, where they could have been exploited by inland
Indian groups.[88] As with turtles there were seasonal variations in the
availability and exploitation of different fish and in the contribution that
fishing made to the diet. During the wet season marine and brackish-
water fish move out from the lagoons and estuaries, and freshwater fish
take their place. Fishing is more difficult during this period owing to the
rough weather offshore and the muddying of waters in the lagoons.
Nevertheless, because of the shortage of meat from other sources at
this time, fishing is often more important then than it is during the dry
season, when conditions are more favorable.[89]

Many fairly sophisticated techniques were used to catch fish. In addition to the harpoon used to catch manatees, a throwing spear or javelin
based on the same principle was used. Spears and javelins were used
only for larger fish, smaller ones being caught with hand spears and bows
and arrows. Spear and arrow points were made of hardened wood or
teeth. Other implements used in fishing included bone and teeth hooks
and lines made of silk-grass thread. Nets were also made from the same
fibers and from the bark of the mahoe, or majagua, tree (*Hibiscus
tiliaceus* L.).[90] There are no references to the use of fish stupefacients in
colonial documents.[91] Marine fishing and most riverine fishing were
undertaken from canoes. Most observers noted that two kinds of canoes
were used. One, called a *dori*, or dory, was a keeled canoe used at sea
and in the lagoons, while the other, called a pitpan, was a flat-bottomed
canoe employed in the rivers. The latter was much smaller and lighter
than the former, which could carry up to fifty people. Canoes were made
by hollowing out single tree trunks, preferably of mahogany (*Swietenia
macrophylla* King), *cedro macho* (*Carapa guianensis* Aubl.), Santa María
(*Calophyllum brasiliense* Camb.), or silk-cotton tree (*Ceiba pentandra*
Gaertn.). In the colonial period at least, inland tribes made rough canoes
that they traded with coastal groups, who added the finishing touches.
This suggests that the inland tribes had formerly lived near the coast,
where they had developed canoe-making techniques; it is unlikely, therefore, that this trade existed in pre-Columbian times; rather it developed

during the colonial period as Indian groups moved inland and as the demands for canoes increased.[92]

In addition to turtling and fishing, Indians along the coast and estuaries collected shellfish. Unlike other fishing activities shellfish collecting was mainly a female occupation. The most important mollusks that have been found in middens were *Neocyrena* and clams (*Donax* sp.), together with a few conches (*Strombus* sp.).[93] Oysters (*Ostrea* sp.) are conspicuously absent, though they were exploited in the colonial period. Crabs were also collected from the lagoons and the seashore.[94]

The collection of wild fruits and vegetables played an integral role in the economy of Indian groups in the South American zone. Truly wild plants, feral plants, and crops from abandoned plots would have all been exploited. Collecting appears to have been particularly important among Indian groups living inland, where plant resources were probably more abundant and fishing made a smaller contribution to the economy.[95] The collection of honey and wax from bees' nests in the forests was an important economic activity. Honey was used to sweeten food before the introduction of sugarcane, and beeswax was used as a glue in making arrows and spears.[96] Salt was manufactured by mixing the ashes of burned pieces of a wild palm with water and boiling it. By this method a very white though not very strong salt was produced.[97] The Mosquito appear to have made salt by putting a piece of hot burned wood in the sea thereby causing salt crystals to condense on it.[98] Various resins, gums, and balsams were extracted for medicinal purposes. Among the species exploited were sarsaparilla (*Smilax officinalis* H.B.K.), liquidambar (*Liquidambar styraciflua* L.) and lignum vitae (*Guaiacum officinale* L.), but their frequent mention in the documentary record may reflect European interest rather than their importance in the Indian economy; all three became important items of trade in the colonial period.[99]

Compared with the crafts in the Mesoamerican zone, many crafts in eastern Nicaragua were poorly developed or unknown to the Indians. Whereas Indians in the west made extensive use of cotton, those in the east generally made their clothes, blankets, and hammocks of bark cloth. Bark cloth was made from the bark of a tree (*Castilla* sp.) closely related to the rubber tree. The bark was soaked in water and then scraped, dried, and pounded to make it soft.[100] The Indians generally went naked except for a small apron of bark cloth, though clothing was more elaborate for festive occasions, when cotton clothes were often worn. Both wild and cultivated species of cotton were probably used in the manufacture of cotton cloth, which was probably woven on a simple horizontal loom. Ropes, cords, hammocks, and bags were made from coarser fibers such as henequen and the fiber extracted from the mahoe tree (*Hibiscus tiliaceus* L.). A finer but very durable fiber, which was used for bowstrings, fishing lines, and nets, as well as for making the items already mentioned, was obtained from silk grass. [101]

Although baskets were probably made for storage and transport, basketry was not highly developed; [102] calabashes were often used for such purposes. Kitchen utensils were made of wood. Archaeological evidence indicates that pottery and stonework were well developed in the pre-Columbian period. [103] Women made pottery from clay tempered with ash, using the coil method; the wheel was unknown. The Sumu were considered to be better potters than the Mosquito, with whom they traded pottery. The loss of ceramic skills by coastal groups is likely to have been associated with cultural changes occurring in the post-Conquest period. Today the Sumu are also losing the art of pottery making. [104] Similarly, Indians in eastern Nicaragua no longer work stone, whereas archaeological evidence in the form of stone bowls and elaborate three-legged metates up to six feet long indicates that the art was once highly developed. More recently Indians have used simple, slightly hollowed-out stones as metates. [105] In contrast to the Indians in the Pacific zone, the Indians in the east possessed no knowledge of metallurgy. Gold objects found in the area were probably trade items from Pacific Nicaragua, Costa Rica, or Panama. There are no Sumu or Mosquito words for "gold" or "silver." [106]

At the time of the Conquest two forms of trade existed: intraregional trade between neighboring villages and tribes and long-distance trade with foreigners. Trade within the South American zone, which contrasted sharply with that of the west, was characterized by the lack of formal markets and mediums of exchange. The only reference to regular trading comes from M. W., who in the late seventeenth century described how at certain times of the year tribes (probably Sumu) living on the río Segovia traded with the Mosquito Indians on an island in that river, though at other times of the year they conducted raids into each other's territory. [107] The bellicose relations between tribes would have militated against the development of regular trading on a large scale. Probably all trade was conducted by barter, and it is doubtful that any mediums of exchange were used, though Conzemius maintained that the Mosquito had formerly used seashells as money. [108] Trade does not appear to have been essential for subsistence, apart perhaps from salt, and most items traded consisted of craft items and those of ornamental value. Probably the most active trade was between coastal and inland groups, who emphasized different economic activities. Conzemius noted that the Mosquito had formerly made salt and collected seashells to exchange with the Sumu for pottery, cotton goods, hammocks, bark cloth, and rough canoes.

Indians in eastern Nicaragua also traded with Mexican traders and colonists. It has already been noted that a Mexican colony probably existed at San Juan, which was used as a port from which gold was shipped north from Coclé and Veragua in Panama to Mexico by way of Chetumal Bay, in Yucatán.[109] In 1534, Francisco de Barrientos reported that he had heard from traders dealing in gold and precious stones that there was a large town called Taguzgalpa (Town of Gold) near the Desaguadero, to which Montezuma sent delegations to collect tribute in gold and other valuable items.[110] The presence of Mexican traders in the area would have afforded the Indians the opportunity to trade in items, such as gold and other metal goods and tools, which they did not possess. Gold ornaments from the Talamanca region of Costa Rica have been found in the Sumu area.[111] In exchange the Indian probably offered items similar to those traded with Europeans from the seventeenth century onward—dyes, wood, cordage and food—and feathers.

THE SOCIOPOLITICAL ORGANIZATION

The social organization of Indian groups in the South American zone was characterized by its simplicity. Descriptions from the eighteenth century of the social organization of the Mosquito suggest that there was some form of social hierarchy, but it was weak and almost certainly the result of contact with Europeans. In general there was no form of permanent leadership, although deference to age was universal, and councils of elders often acted as advisers to the community.[112] Even after the English had created the hereditary positions of king, governor, and general among the Mosquito, Hodgson observed that none of these chiefs "have much more than a negative voice and never attempt anything without a council of such old men as have influence amongst those of their countrymen who live round about them."[113] It is possible, however, that some form of emergent leadership existed. Juarros describes the activities of an old man in a community at Cabo de Gracias a Dios as follows: "This old man, even in his idolatry, had employed himself in acts of kindness; he cultivated maize to distribute among those who were in distress; he composed strifes and settled disputes among his neighbours; besides performing many other kind offices where they wanted."[114] Two other types of leadership may have existed in the form of shamans and military leaders. The shaman, who was also known as the *sukya*, was highly esteemed and acted as a healer, diviner, sorcerer, and adviser, even to the elders.[115] Because Indian groups in the South American zone lived in a state of conflict or near conflict with each other, military leaders were often required. They were generally chosen by the elders on the basis of their military ability. They were held in great esteem, but their leadership lasted only as long as the conflict, and if they did not provide good service, they were replaced.[116]

The continuous conflict within and between Indian groups may largely be explained by the lack of a true judicial authority to deal with crimes or settle disputes. Petty crimes and disputes were sometimes settled by the elders, either as individuals or in councils, but the sentences they passed were generally limited to fines.[117] Often, however, disputes between individuals and families were not settled by the leaders, and the offended parties often took justice into their own hands and settled disputes by armed conflict.[118] Chagnon has suggested that the state of chronic warfare among Yanomamö villages on the borderland between Venezuela and Brazil may be attributable to the failure of Yanomamö institutions to mediate effectively disputes arising with the villages, resulting in village fission and the establishment of mutually hostile, independent villages.[119] Conflict between groups, which may have arisen in the way that Chagnon suggests for the Yanomamö, would have been sustained by crimes and their vengeance; groups often raided each other for wives and "slaves," and it is possible that conflicts arose over access to desirable areas for cultivation and hunting.[120] Among the Guaianes and the Mosquito there were apparently many grounds for disputes, but, during the feasts which often preceded armed conflict, the women managed to hide their husbands' weapons.[121] Wars were conducted in the form of raids; there is no evidence of open battles. Before a raid a temporary war leader was chosen, and the *sukya* was consulted. Many of the ordeals at puberty and before marriage served to maintain young men in good physical condition and ready for war.[122] According to Conzemius, the Sumu organized festivals, called *asan lauwana,* at which they underwent some military training. At these sessions trials of endurance took place to train young men to tolerate pain.[123] Weapons consisted of bows and arrows, spears, and wooden clubs. They also had shields of tapir hide.[124]

A missionary of the late seventeenth or early eighteenth century summarized the sociopolitical organization of tribes living in eastern Nicaragua and Honduras as follows:

There is information that some nations in the extensive interior mountains are governed, some by leaders in the form of a republic and others by kinship and friendship, but it appears almost certain that they have not formed a republic but that they have always lived without a head or leader, natural or elected, and that at best they have been subject, not recognizing any jurisdiction, to someone who emerges in ferocity or valor or industry or goodness, so that they should have captains in war and be governed in other things which are necessary, the necessity for which having ended they remain without law, king, or court of justice.[125]

Evidence for birth, marriage, and death ceremonies and practices comes mainly from more recent ethnographic accounts. During pregnancy women lived in a separate section of the house and at the time of birth retired to a hut not far from the hamlet. A lustration ceremony was held to receive the mother and child back into the community.[126] Infanticide was practiced on deformed children.[127] Head deformation appears to have been practiced by the Sumu and the Mosquito.[128]

Although monogamy generally prevailed among Indians in the South American zone, some elders or Indians who could provide for them had more than one wife.[129] Unfortunately the only evidence for marriage rules comes from Conzemius's observations at the beginning of the twentieth century. He noted that among the Mosquito marriage between the children of two brothers or two sisters was not allowed because on the death of one partner the other generally married his or her sister- or brother-in-law, so that these cousins were in effect half brothers and sisters. However, the children of a brother and sister were not considered to be blood relatives, and marriage between cousins was permitted and indeed encouraged to strengthen family ties. Conzemius observed that among the Sumu marriage with members of other tribes was not permitted, and the offspring of such unions were killed.[130] Girls were generally betrothed at an early age, and gifts were given to the girl's father by her father-in-law. Before marriage a young man had to demonstrate his ability to provide for a wife and such skills as the manufacture of hunting and fishing equipment.[131] Sometimes a future husband took up residence in the house of his parents-in-law until the girl was old enough to return to her husband's home. Most evidence seems to suggest that on marriage a couple either resided with the husband's family or set up a separate home.[132] Pim and Seeman, however, recorded that among the Mosquito the husband and wife generally remained in the bride's home.[133] Helms has suggested that matrilocal postnuptial residence is correlated with circumstances in which men are absent from home for long periods and that it probably became more common on the Mosquito Coast after contact with Europeans, when men became involved in raids, trade, and wage labor.[134] A woman could obtain a divorce if her husband ill-treated her. In such cases she could easily remarry, but it was difficult for the husband to secure a new partner. Divorce was also possible by mutual consent, particularly in instances of illness or inability to produce children.[135]

On death bodies were wrapped in bark cloth and buried in the floors of houses, sometimes with their arms, possessions and food. The houses were then burned or abandoned. In other instances the dead were buried away from their homes, but huts were built over them. Pim and Seeman noted that Indians in the Province of Chontales placed their tombs in a circle around the village.[136] Among the Mosquito the dead were buried in canoes, which had been cut in half to form a kind of coffin, or canoes were placed over the grave. The Sumu also placed a cotton thread from the burial site to the former home or to the place where the burial feast took place. Very often the deceased's possessions, including his fruit trees and cultivation plots, were destroyed.[137] Exquemelin's account of the Mosquito contains the only reference to secondary burial. He described how a widow, after visiting her husband's grave, bringing food daily for a year, exhumed the body and washed the bones, which she then placed in a bag and carried around with her for a year. At the end of the second year she hung the bag on the doorpost and was free to remarry. A man was not obliged to perform the same ceremony for his wife.[138] As a sign of mourning women generally cut their hair and wailed, and sometimes a woman had to be restrained from committing suicide. *Mishla* feasts generally accompanied burials.[139]

Mishla feasts were held not only at burial ceremonies but also at marriages, at harvesttime, before expeditions or raids, or as a means of settling with neighbors. *Mishla* was often prepared in canoes, concocted from fruits and vegetables, notably sweet manioc, plantains, sweet potatoes, maize, pineapples, and pejibaye fruits. During the colonial period introduced fruits such as bananas, coconuts, and sugarcane were also used. The fruits were crushed and left to ferment for several days, producing an intoxicating drink. Such feasts were thus accompanied by drunken singing and dancing.[140]

THE IDEOLOGY

All observers noted the absence of idols, priests, and forms of public worship from the South American zone.[141] Some maintained that the Indians possessed no gods, while others recorded the belief in an ill-defined supernatural power. This power was said to have created the world and mankind and to be the origin of good as opposed to evil, but it was not honored by sacrifices, offerings or public worship. According to recent ethnographic accounts the power was known by different names by different Indian groups: Ma-Papak, or Ma-Papañki, by the Sumu; Matún by the Rama; and Wan-Aisa by the Mosquito.[142] Sometimes the Sumu and the Mosquito confused this god with the god of thunder. In the seventeenth century Indians living between the Guayape and Segovia rivers believed in a god, or Gualahuana (Mother of Thunder), who had created the world and brought men into being from the hairs under her arms. She was said to have had two sons, the sun and the moon. The sun had lived on the earth but had retired to heaven angry when a crab ate his arm. The moon, seeing his brother in heaven, made a fire, and the sun, seeing such a great light, went to see what it was, and the moon laid hold of him and went with him to heaven.[143] The Sumu and Mosquito also believed in a number of supernatural beings, including the sun, moon, stars, and rainbow, which were thought to have had former human existence on earth.[144] Some ancestors were also given semidivine status. According to Heath, the Mosquito revered two ancestors who were said to have given birth to the Mosquito, the Twahka and the Ohlwa (or Ulua), known as Maishana ("He Who Begot Us") and Itwana ("Our Mother"). They lived on Kounapa, a mountain between the ríos Patuca and Segovia.[145] The Indians' greatest fear appears to have been reserved for evil spirits, of which there were two: one who inhabited the earth called Wallesaw (or Woolsaw, Wlasa, Walasa, Walsa, Ulaser, Lasa or Nawal) and another who lived in the water and was known as Lerrire or Lewire.[146] There were also large numbers of bush spirits associated with plants and animals of the forest.[147] The presence and activities of these animals were regarded as omens, and many stories were told about them.[148] Charms, such as bird's claws, teeth, and seeds, were often used to bring luck in hunting and fishing, to bring courage, and to cure illnesses and relieve barrenness in women.[149]

The only religious figure among the tribes of the South American zone was the *sukya*, who acted as a healer and diviner, as well as adviser to individuals and the community. Conzemius recorded that among the Sumu and Mosquito the office of *sukya* was hereditary, although frequently he was succeeded by his nephew or son-in-law, rather than his son. Nevertheless, the person was said to have been chosen by the gods under whose influence he came. Contenders for the office made prophecies, and the person whose prophecy came true was urged to assume the office.[150] It would appear, therefore, that the hereditary character of the position was rather vaguely established and its occupancy dependent to a degree on the competence of the holder, thus suggesting that the hereditary aspect of the office was a recent development.

Religious ceremonies centered on the life cycle, and they were generally accompanied by *mishla* feasts. The nature of burials indicates that the Indians believed in an afterlife. Not only were an individual's belongings and food buried with him, but among the Mosquito a small canoe and a dead dog were also interred to assist the deceased in his passage through the underworld to paradise.[151] Among Indians living between the ríos Guayape and Segovia in the seventeenth century a man was buried with his bow and lance and a woman with her grindstone. When a person died, he went to hell, and on the fourth day an old woman called Gualavana came with another person to clean the path from hell to enable the soul to pass to heaven.[152]

Although a number of religious ceremonies were held, it appears that sacrifices did not take place. Certainly cannibalism was practiced, but it does not appear to have had any religious significance. War captives were killed and eaten, and their teeth and nails were used as ornaments. However, their deaths probably signified no more than the annihilation of the enemy and the victory of the captors.[153] Others were scalped and killed by having a pole thrust up their torso, but in these circumstances the victims were not eaten.[154] The reasons for these different practices are unknown.

CHAPTER 5

The Aboriginal Population

The controversy over estimates of the native population of the New World is even more difficult to resolve for Central America, because there the population declined very rapidly during the early colonial period, and few documents for that period have survived.[1] Estimates of the size of the Indian population on the eve of discovery range from Kroeber's calculation of 100,000 for Honduras and Nicaragua together to Dobyns's estimate of between 10.8 and 13.5 million for Central America.[2] Kroeber maintained that the estimates of early observers were exaggerated, a conclusion which he arrived at after an examination of the demographic history of Indian groups in the United States, particularly California. He assumed that the Indian population had grown at a regular rate since the time of Conquest and derived his estimates by projecting the growth rate backward from figures provided by Humboldt for the end of the eighteenth century. He therefore judged that the impact of Spanish conquest and newly introduced diseases was minimal.

Steward accepted Kroeber's conclusion that the estimates of contemporary observers were exaggerated, and, on the basis of evidence provided by contributors to the *Handbook of South American Indians,* he suggested that the population of Central America, excluding Guatemala, was 736,500. Of these 392,500 were in Honduras, Nicaragua, and El Salvador together.[3] This estimate is somewhat smaller than that of Rosenblat, who, using readily available documentary evidence, estimated that the native population of Central America was 800,000.[4] Alternative approaches have suggested that these estimates may be too low. Sapper, who had an intimate knowledge of Mexico and Central America, estimated that on the basis of the climate, resources, and available technology the native population of Central America was between 5 and 6 million.[5] More recently Dobyns has reviewed the literature available for the demographic history of the hemisphere and concluded that insufficient account has been taken of the devastating impact of disease. On this premise he suggested that Indian populations were between twenty and twenty-five times greater than they were at their nadirs, which for many Indian groups in Latin America was in the middle of the seventeenth century. He estimated that the Indian population of Central America in 1650 was 540,000, which would give figures of between 10.8 and 13.5 million Indians at the time of the Spanish conquest.[6]

In trying to estimate the aboriginal population of specific areas at the time of the Conquest, such broad estimates are clearly of limited value. For Central America, however, detailed archival research by Radell, MacLeod, and Sherman has begun to provide evidence for the size of the Indian population on the eve of Conquest, though these authors disagree over the interpretation of the documentary evidence, particularly that relating to the Indian slave trade. Radell has suggested that the population of Nicaragua was over one million at the time of Discovery, given that up to 1548 between 450,000 and 500,000 Indians were removed from the country for the slave trade; 400,000 to 600,000 probably died of disease or in war or fled the province, while 200,000 to 250,000 were probably residing in the central highlands, to be decimated during the following twenty to thirty years.[7]

Denevan adopts Radell's estimate in his calculation of the aboriginal population of Central America, which he proposes was 5.65 million in 1492.[8] Radell's estimate of the number of Indians exported for the slave trade is comparable to the 500,000 and 400,000 reported by Las Casas and Oviedo, respectively, but Sherman considers these figures too high. He suggests that a more realistic estimate of the numbers exported during the period 1524 to 1549 would be 50,000, this figure including Indian slaves exported from the whole of Central America, not just Nicaragua.[9] He estimates that the aboriginal population of Central America was about 2.25 million.[10] Although MacLeod does not provide an estimate of the Indian population of Central America, in discussing the Indian slave trade he suggests that a figure of 10,000 exported each year of the decade 1532 to 1542 would appear to be too low and 200,000 for the duration of the slave trade a conservative estimate.[11] It seems possible therefore that about half a million Indian slaves were exported from Nicaragua, though some of them would have come from elsewhere in Central America, notably Honduras.

There were few contemporary estimates of the size of the Indian population. Las Casas estimated that over 500,000 Indians had been exported from Nicaragua as slaves, another 500,000 to 600,000 had been killed in battles with the Spaniards, 20,000 to 30,000 had died of famine, and only 4,000 to 5,000 remained.[12] Although not all of these Indians would have been alive at the time of the Conquest, which had begun fourteen years earlier, the figures suggest that the aboriginal population of Nicaragua was over one million. This figure is double that estimated by Friar Motolinía in 1541. He had lived in Central America in the late 1520s, when he visited Nicaragua, and he judged that the aboriginal population had been 500,000.[13] In 1544 the *oidor* Diego de Herrera reported that there had been 600,000 Indians in the country at the time of the Conquest but that since then they had been reduced to 30,000.[14] Sherman maintains that Herrera exaggerated the figure for the aboriginal population to condemn the administration of Rodrigo de Contreras, whose residencia he conducted and for whom he had a bitter enmity.[15] But the figure for 1544 is likely to have been fairly accurate, since the *oidor* was familiar with the area at the time, and it is fairly consistent with the numbers of tributary Indians registered in the *tasaciones* made for the greater part of western Nicaragua in 1548.[16] It is important to note that none of these estimates included eastern Nicaragua, which, apart from the mining area of Nueva Segovia, remained almost entirely unexplored during the first half of the sixteenth century.

Before these estimates are judged to be exaggerated, it is worth examining additional evidence for the size of the aboriginal population. With the exception of a stretch of land between southern Nicaragua and the Nicoya Peninsula, it is clear that the Pacific lowlands at least were heavily populated. It has already been noted that in the latter area there were chiefdoms with populations running into the tens of thousands, the largest recorded settlement being that of Managua, with 40,000 Indians.[17] Evidence of the numbers of Indians baptized in the early years of the Conquest also indicates the presence of large populations. In the course of Gil González Dávila's expedition through Pacific Nicaragua and Nicoya in 1522, 32,000 Indians were baptized,[18] and in 1528 and 1529, 52,558 Indians were baptized by the Mercedarian friar Francisco de Bobadilla.[19] Of this number, 29,000 lived in the Province of Nicaragua, and more than 6,000 and 5,000, respectively, in the Provinces of Maribio and Diriá. Other conversions were effected by Francisco Fernández, who accompanied the governor of Honduras, Diego López de Salcedo, on an expedition to Nicaragua. Oviedo estimated that altogether within the first seven years of the Conquest about 100,000 Indians had been baptized.[20] Although it is impossible to obtain a figure for the total population from the numbers baptized, they do give a broad indication of its size.

In assessing the reliability of population estimates, it is worth examining whether such large populations could have been supported by the local resources, given the technology available. The following discussion represents a preliminary attempt to assess the carrying capacity of the land, and clearly more detailed research is needed before any concrete conclusions can be drawn from such evidence. In their discussion of the population of Central Mexico on the eve of Conquest, Borah and Cook estimated that 2.5 acres of land were required to support a family under intensive maize cultivation, probably either chinampas or irrigated land, 15 percent of the land being cultivated at a time. They estimated that there were 4.5 persons in a family, and this gives a population density of about 67 persons per square kilometer.[21] Chinampas were not known in Nicaragua, and techniques of irrigation were poorly developed, and it is thus unlikely that quite such high densities could have been supported.

Palerm has suggested that under a *barbecho* system of cultivation 2.5 hectares of land are required to support a family while two or three times as much land lies idle.[22] He gives no figure for the size of a family but from Borah and Cook's estimate of 4.5 persons, the population densities that could have been supported where the ratios of cultivated to uncultivated land were 1:3 and 1:2 would have been 45 and 60 persons per square kilometer, respectively. Given the fertility of the volcanic soils in Pacific Nicaragua, little land would have been left fallow so that a population density of 60 persons per square kilometer may have been possible. Farther south in Nicoya a more extensive form of cultivation appears to have been practiced, with wild resources playing a more significant role in the economy. Clark and Haswell have suggested that shifting cultivation can support 20 persons per square kilometer,[23] but given the low fertility of the mature lateritic soils in Nicoya, it is estimated that they could have supported a population density of only 15 persons per square kilometer. Although shifting cultivation was also practiced in north-central Nicaragua by the Matagalpa, there root crops predominated and consequently an even greater emphasis was placed on wild food resources as sources of protein. As such a population density of 15 persons per square kilometer seems appropriate. Farther east the Indian economy was based to a greater degree on wild food resources, and settlements were probably confined to the banks of the rivers that traversed the area. According to Clark and Haswell, those groups wholly dependent on wild food resources may achieve densities of only about 0.1 per square kilometer. However, in this area cultivation also featured in the economy, and thus a population density of 1 person per square kilometer could probably have been supported.

These estimated densities can be applied to the whole area within the different cultural and natural regions identified, but it is clear that large parts of those areas would not have been exploited at the time of the Conquest. At present about 25 percent of the land in each area in Nicaragua is cultivated, while grasslands account for 50 percent of the land in the Pacific lowlands and central highlands and 30 percent in the east; the rest is mountains, swamps, and forests.[24] Clearly this picture has changed from pre-Columbian times, the area devoted to forest having declined and that under grass having increased. If it is accepted that most of the area cultivated was worked in pre-Columbian times and that the forests were more extensive and exploited to a greater degree for subsistence, at least 50 percent of the area in each region was probably exploited, and the estimated densities can be applied to these areas. The population estimate for the Pacific lowlands, including Nicoya, assuming that only 50 percent of the land was exploited, works out at 600,000 a figure not unlike the early estimates of contemporary observers. Also,

Table 1. Estimates of Aboriginal Populations

Area	Square kilometers	Estimated population density per square kilometer	Estimated population	
			Total area	Exploited area
Pacific lowlands*	18,219	60	1,093,140	546,570
Central highlands†	23,845	15	357,675	178,838
Caribbean lowlands‡	76,295	1	76,295	38,148
Nicoya§	8,359	15	125,385	62,692
Total			1,652,495	826,248

*Present-day Departments of Chinandega, León, Managua, Masaya, Granada, Carazo, and Rivas.

†Present-day Departments of Matagalpa, Estelí, Madriz, Nueva Segovia, and half of Boaco, Chontales, and Jinotega.

‡Present-day departments of San Juan and Zelaya, and half of Boaco, Chontales, and Jinotega.

§Present-day cantons of La Cruz, Liberia, Carrillo, Santa Cruz, Nicoya, Nandayure, and the Nicoya Peninsula, and the island section of Puntarenas.

the figure for the north-central area centered on Nueva Segovia and Matagalpa is fairly similar to that proposed by Denevan, who maintains that the aboriginal population was just over half the population in the mid-1950s, which was about 350,000.[25]. With this approach the total population for Nicaragua can be estimated at 825,000, or 1.6 million if the whole area is taken into account. Of those numbers 75 percent would have been found in the Mesoamerican zone.

Part Three

CONQUEST AND SLAVERY, 1522–1550

CHAPTER 6

The Black Legend

The Conquest of Central America was a protracted affair that took a heavy toll of the native population. The region lacked the minerals and large concentrations of Indians that fired the imagination of conquistadors in Mexico and Peru, and the nature of the Indian societies themselves militated against a quick and easy conquest. In the process of conquest and colonization towns played a vital role as administrative centers within whose jurisdiction encomiendas and land grants were distributed to its citizens. With the aim of returning to Spain with an enhanced economic and social position within their short lifetimes, conquistadors and colonists looked for immediate sources of profit and advancement. Several alternatives were available. They could, and most did, aspire to become encomenderos. By obtaining an encomienda, and individual was entitled to exact tribute and labor services from the Indians encharged to him. Although only the very largest encomiendas in Nicaragua provided an income capable of supporting an "honorable" life-style,[1] the overlordship of Indians enhanced the social status of encomenderos, and in the early colonial period the possession of an encomienda provided one of the main means of access to Indian labor.

During the first half of the sixteenth century, however, the two most important sources of wealth were Indian slaves and minerals. Indian slaves were in great demand in the Caribbean islands and Panama, where the Indian population had been decimated at an early date. The demand increased further with the conquest and colonization of Peru. At the same time gold and silver commanded high prices in Europe, and handsome profits could be made by miners in Central America. Both activities were dependent, however, on supplies of Indians, which, though originally considered to be inexhaustible, soon began to decline. An alternative source of wealth that was not realized during the first half of the sixteenth century was the development of commercial agriculture. Although land grants did bestow some social status on their recipients, the development of commercial agriculture required an investment of time and money, neither of which colonists could afford. Capital was needed for the importation of crops, animals, tools, and processing equipment, as well as for the establishment of roads and ports. The realization of profits was sometimes retarded by the long maturation of crops, while transportation difficulties made the production of bulky and highly perishable crops impossible. In the early sixteenth century therefore, commercial agriculture was not regarded as a primary source of wealth; Indian slaves and minerals required less investment and brought more immediate returns.

DISCOVERY AND CONQUEST

On his fourth voyage to the New World in 1502, Columbus explored the Bay Islands (Islas de la Bahía) and the coast from Cape Honduras, which he named Punta Caxinas, south to Panama.[2] Although the Bay Islands and the northern coast of Honduras were raided for slaves, two decades passed before further exploratory expeditions to the area were mounted. In 1522 an expedition led by Gil González Dávila and Andrés Niño explored western Nicaragua as far north as the Bay of Fonseca.[3] Following the return of this expedition to Panama, the governor of Panama, Pedrarias Dávila (Pedro Arias de Ávila) on hearing news of the explored territory became eager to secure it for himself, and, while Gil González Dávila was in Santo Domingo organizing a new expedition to consolidate his position as discoverer and conqueror, Dávila dispatched Francisco Hernández de Córdoba to establish his claim to the area. In 1524, Hernández de Córdoba founded the towns of Bruselas, Granada, and León.[4] Meanwhile, several other claimants were arriving from the north. In Mexico, Cortés, hearing of the riches of Central America, dispatched one of his captains, Cristóbal de Olid, to take possession of Honduras and search for a sea link between the Atlantic and Pacific oceans. The latter arrived in 1524, but with the aim of claiming the territory for himself. Hearing of Olid's intentions, Cortés sent another captain, Francisco de las Casas, to take possession of the area in his name. Finally, in 1525, Cortés himself arrived in Honduras. Meanwhile, in 1524, Gil González Dávila had arrived from Santo Domingo in an attempt to regain possession of the territory. It was thus in Honduras and to a lesser extent in Nicaragua that rival conquistadors moving south from Mexico and Guatemala and north from Panama met and fought to gain control over the area. Thus efforts to pacify the Indians were accompanied by battles between the Spaniards themselves and even between rival elements of the same faction, very often using Indians as fighting forces.[5]

Nevertheless, the conquest of Pacific Nicaragua was relatively easy. Although first encounters between Indians and the Spaniards were not entirely amicable and the Spaniards considered it necessary to build forts in León and Granada, there was no coordinated resistance to Spanish colonization, as there was in Honduras.[6] In eastern Nicaragua, however, Indian resistance to Spanish colonization was more prolonged and in fact persisted throughout the colonial period. From the 1520s, Indians in the central highlands continually attacked the mining centers first of Santa María de Buena Esperanza and later of Nueva Segovia, and an uprising in 1544 appears to have been coordinated with revolts in Honduras.[7]

URBAN CENTERS

The difficult task of conquest was consolidated by the establishment of urban centers. Towns and cities were the primary instruments of colonization, serving as symbols of territorial possession and centers from which the surrounding countryside could be colonized and administered. The establishment of a town involved a number of processes. First, a cabildo, or town council, was selected, and then a formal plan of the town was drawn up. Towns generally followed the same plan. The central square or plaza was designated, and the land around it was divided into plots, those nearest the plaza being reserved for the church, the town hall, the official's residence, and other public buildings; the rest were allocated to citizens. At the same time the jurisdiction of the town was delineated, and within its boundaries encomiendas and lands were granted.

The Spaniards sought to establish towns in areas either where there were large numbers of Indians who could be used as sources of labor or where mineral deposits were to be found. The availability of land was not of paramount importance during the early colonial period, since conquistadors and colonists relied on the Indians for their food supplies. Many Spanish towns were founded next to well-established Indian towns; Granada was founded next to the Indian town of Jalteba, and León was sited in the middle of the populous Province of Imabite. The location of Nueva Segovia, on the other hand, was determined by the presence of minerals. Within the broad areas defined by the presence of large Indian populations or mineral resources, some consideration was given to defense, and the favored sites were those that were healthy and near good supplies of water, arable land, and pasture. During the first half of the sixteenth century towns were often abandoned or their sites changed for a number of reasons, including Indian attacks, mineral exhaustion, disease, unfavorable physical conditions, or political considerations.

The towns that emerged as major centers of population in the early colonial period were the secular and ecclesiastical administrative centers; few towns had strong economic bases. When the governorship of Nicaragua was established in 1527, León became the capital of the province. Although it was established after Granada, León was more strategically placed near the area of jurisdictional conflict and was therefore preferred.[8] At that time it possessed over 200 *vecinos,* whereas Granada had only 100.[9] By 1531 the seat of the bishop of Nicaragua had been established there, and it contained three convents, those of the Mercedarians, the Dominicans, and the Franciscans.[10] The status of León was resented by the residents of Granada, who complained that, because Granada had been founded first, it possessed more people of high social rank than did León, which they described as being dominated by lower-class Spaniards and corrupt royal officials. They thus petitioned the crown for greater independence from León in the administration of local affairs. The petition was upheld, but the additional authority given to Granada did not fundamentally alter the balance of power in the province.[11] In the 1530s the population of both towns declined as many of their citizens left in search of wealth and prestige in the newly discovered Province of Peru.[12]

Two towns in Nicaragua developed on the basis of their economic activities: Realejo and Nueva Segovia. The value of the port of Realejo was recognized in 1523 by Gil González Dávila and Andrés Niño, who named it Puerto de la Posesión. From the end of the 1520s it was a major port for the export of Indian slaves, but it was not until 1534 that it was formally established as a town by Pedro de Alvarado.[13] The town of Buena Esperanza was founded in the mining region of Nueva Segovia in 1527, but it was struck by disease, and its site was moved in 1528. This settlement fell victim to Indian attacks and was temporarily abandoned, only to be reestablished in 1531.[14] Nothing is known of the settlement after 1534, and it was probably abandoned when the town of Nueva Segovia was established sometime between 1536 and 1543.[15]

A number of other Spanish settlements were founded in eastern Nicaragua, but they were short-lived. In the 1520s, Pedrarias dispatched Benito Hurtado to establish a town between the two oceans. He apparently founded a town in the Province of Telpanega (Telpaneca), but it was abandoned in 1527 as the result of Indian attacks.[16] Finally two settlements were established on the San Juan River. In 1539 San Juan de la Cruz was established at the mouth of the San Juan by Calero and Machuca while they were on an expedition to the Desaguadero, but in 1549 it was said that it had never possessed any *vecinos* because the area lacked Indians and other necessities for a permanent settlement and that it had been established only "for effect."[17] In 1542 another town called Nueva Jaen was founded where the San Juan River enters Lake Nicaragua, but virtually nothing is known about this town.[18]

THE ENCOMIENDA

The encomienda was a grant of Indians to an individual, who in return for providing the Indians with protection and instruction in the Roman

Catholic faith could levy tribute and labor services from them. The encomienda was an attempt to reconcile the desire of the Spanish crown to
christianize the native population with the colonists' demands for labor.
It was introduced into the West Indies by Columbus and after complaints
about its operation, particularly by the Dominicans, regulations governing the encomienda were drawn up and included in the Laws of Burgos in
1512.[19] From that time until 1542, when the crown attempted to abolish
the encomienda, it was introduced throughout Spanish America.

Following the founding of a town, the Indians in its jurisdiction were
assigned in encomiendas to its *vecinos*. Before the introduction of the
New Laws conquistadors and later governors were given the right to
grant encomiendas, though titles to them had to be approved by the
crown. After the issuance of the New Laws in 1542 the Audiencia de los
Confines was given the responsibility of assigning encomiendas.[20] In
1548 a request from the governor of Nicaragua for the right to grant
encomiendas was refused by the Audiencia.[21] Initially encomiendas were
granted to those who had assisted in the Conquest according to their
merits and services. Government officials were initially allowed to hold
encomiendas, and soon many governors and their relatives and friends
held large numbers of the best encomiendas. Colonists complained that
many of those who had expended considerable effort and money in the
Conquest had been overlooked when the encomiendas were allocated. In
1536 a reminder was sent to governors to the effect that "the first conquistadors and settlers" were to be preferred as encomenderos.[22] The
first major change in the procedure for allocating encomiendas came with
the New Laws, which forbade viceroys, governors, and other government officials, monasteries, hospitals, and *cofradías* to hold encomiendas. There appears to have been little opposition to this order, but it had
little impact, mainly because royal officials had anticipated the legislation
and made over their encomiendas to their wives and children.[23]

Although encomiendas were granted following the founding of a
town, they often changed hands within a short period. In the early Conquest period Indians who had been subjugated and allocated in encomiendas often revolted, only to be pacified by a different conquistador,
who reallocated them. Even when no new campaigns were conducted, it
was common for new governors to reallocate encomiendas to their relatives and friends; in 1527 López de Salcedo reallocated the encomiendas
of León, which had originally been distributed by Pedrarias, taking for
himself the largest ones, comprising 9,000 Indians.[24]

Probably the most notable example of the appropriation of encomiendas was that by Rodrigo de Contreras, who claimed that after Pedrarias's
death the encomiendas had been badly allocated by Castañeda. He
therefore confiscated many of them, giving them to his wife, children,
servants, and "mestizos bastardos." It was estimated that he held one-

third of the encomiendas in the province and half of the best ones, which included the Provinces of Nicoya and Chira, which alone produced an annual income of 2,000 pesos.[25] Some encomiendas were also confiscated for the ill treatment or enslavement of Indians. Since many encomenderos were guilty of these offences, these charges were often used to justify suspensions of encomiendas that were politically motivated.[26] In 1533 governors were ordered not to confiscate an encomienda without hearing the encomendero's case,[27] and if the encomendero was still dissatisfied, he could always complain to the crown with varying effect; in 1532, for example, Castañeda was ordered to return some encomiendas he had seized.[28]

For these reasons the history of the encomienda during the first half of the sixteenth century was one of granting, confiscation, or voiding, and regranting, and it created an altogether unstable basis for the development of the area. A brief history of the encomienda of the village of Mistega illustrates the point well. In the space of five years Mistega was held by six encomenderos. It was given to Juan Talavera but then seized by López de Salcedo during his residence in Nicaragua, after which it was confiscated by Pedrarias, who granted it to Castañeda. Castañeda then sold it illegally, and finally it was held by Rodrigo de Contreras.[29] But the encomienda was an unstable institution not only because of confiscations and sales but also because it could be granted for only short periods. Encomiendas were initially allocated to individuals for their lifetimes only, but from an early date encomenderos petitioned the crown to permit encomiendas to be held in perpetuity, thereby allowing them to pass them on to their descendants. It was argued that "permanent" encomiendas would result in better treatment of the Indians and would encourage colonists to remain in the province.[30] The crown was reluctant to relinquish its control over the granting of encomiendas, but in 1536 it did permit the inheritance of encomiendas over two generations.[31] This concession did not satisfy encomenderos, who continued to petition the crown for encomiendas in perpetuity.[32] By that time, however, the crown had decided to abolish the encomienda.

Under the New Laws, issued in 1542, all encomiendas that fell vacant were to pass to the crown, and no new grants were to be made. There was an immediate outcry. It was argued that colonists would leave the area because they could not survive without encomiendas, mining activities would cease without the labor the Indians provided, and the Indians would be badly treated by the corregidores appointed to administer Crown encomiendas, since they were interested only in augmenting their small salaries at the expense of the Indians.[33] In 1545, as a result of protests throughout the empire, the section of the New Laws that effectively abolished the personal encomienda was revoked.[34] A few years later audiencias were given the power to allocate vacant encomiendas, with the proviso that they were to reserve the best Indian towns and ports for the crown.[35]

The number and size of encomiendas granted during the process of colonization depended on the number of soldiers who had taken part in the Conquest, most of whom aspired to become encomenderos, and on the size of the Indian population. It is ironic that the semi-nomadic tribes, which formed smaller concentrations of population, were often the most difficult to pacify and therefore required larger fighting forces. In these areas, therefore, a large number of conquistadors and soldiers had to be satisfied with only small encomiendas.

Originally the Indian population of Nicaragua, particularly in the Pacific lowlands, was large enough to provide a number of small encomiendas, but unfortunately no records exist of the original repartimientos of León and Granada made by Hernández de Córdoba in 1524.[36] The date of the repartimiento of Bruselas is unknown, but in 1529 it was reported that there were sufficient Indians in the vicinity of the town to establish thirty small encomiendas.[37] About the same time a repartimiento was made of Indians in the vicinity of Buena Esperanza, and in 1531 there were said to be seventy *vecinos* with encomiendas in the town.[38] Nothing is known of the town after 1534 or of the original repartimiento of Nueva Segovia, which was established as its successor. The general tribute assessment made in 1548 was comprehensive for Pacific Nicaragua, but it did not include encomiendas assigned in the east of the country. Of the encomiendas recorded only a small proportion possessed over two hundred Indians; those in the jurisdiction of Granada were slightly larger in size but fewer in number.[39] The small size of the encomiendas is clear when they are compared with those in Peru, where encomiendas consisting of under five thousand Indians were regarded as small.[40]

In return for being able to exact tribute and labor services from the Indians entrusted to him, an encomendero undertook to provide Christian instruction for the Indians and to maintain a horse and arms, alone or with a number of Indians, to be used in defense against rebel Indians and Spaniards, or other Europeans. He also had to maintain a fixed dwelling of stone and brick.[41] This requirement was aimed at discouraging absenteeism, which was considered to retard the development of the area and to result in the ill treatment of the Indians by irresponsible overseers. It was reinforced by a law forbidding an encomendero from absenting himself from the area for more than two years without forfeiting his encomienda.[42]

The possession of an encomienda entitled the encomendero to exact tribute and labor services from the Indians assigned to him. Until the mid-1530s the amount that encomenderos exacted was left to their discretion, but since they made excessive demands, in the early 1530s the crown assumed responsibility for the regulation of tribute and labor service and ordered official assessments, or *tasaciones,* to be drawn up. Royal officials in Central America objected to the order, arguing that the income from encomiendas would fall and as a result encomenderos would leave the area. Nevertheless, in view of the benefits that had been derived from its implementation in New Spain, the crown reaffirmed the order in 1536.[43] The following year the bishop of Nicaragua was instructed to draw up *tasaciones* for the province. By 1539, however, the assessments, for which no evidence has been found, had not been completed.[44]

When the Audiencia de los Confines was established in 1543, new *tasaciones* were ordered for the area under its jurisdiction,[45] and from that time onward the responsibility for tribute assessments lay with the audiencia. Unfortunately only fragmentary evidence of these *tasaciones* exists for Nicaragua, in the form of accounts of tribute paid by a small number of Indian villages in subsequent years.[46] The amount of tribute payable was considered to be so high that in 1548 the president of the audiencia reported that the Indians could not pay half what was due even if they were doubled in number.[47] With the *oidores* Juan Rogel and Pedro Ramírez, Alonso Lopez de Cerrato therefore set about moderating the amount of tribute to be paid. Unfortunately very few *tasaciones* exist for villages that were assessed both before Cerrato's arrival and during his

Table 2. Encomiendas in Nicaragua, 1548

	León			Granada		
Tributaries	Enco-miendas	Villages or *parciali-dades*	Total tributary population	Enco-miendas	Villages	Total tributary population
Over 200	8	23	2,026	3	8	714
100–199	9	18	1,170	14	30	1,849
50– 99	15	24	1,049	18	29	1,313
Under 50	22	25	612	8	12	218
No account	1	1	—	—	—	—
Assigned to crown		18	857		7	875
Total		109	5,714		86	4,969

Source: AGI AG 128 Libro de tasaciones 1548.

Note: Excludes Nicoya. Some of the encomiendas are larger than indicated because some encomenderos possessed villages in both jurisdictions.

term of office, but the available evidence suggests that the amount of tribute exacted was reduced by over half. For example, the numbers of fanegas of maize, beans, and cotton to be sown by the inhabitants of the village of Diriega, in the jurisdiction of Granada, were reduced from 20, 20, and 10, respectively, in 1546 to 10, 4, and 5 in 1548, while more substantial reductions were made in the number of chickens and the quantities of honey and salt payable.[48] Although these assessments did not include the service of *tamemes,* or porters, a small number of Indians were scheduled to provide personal service. Since Cerrato's assessments were made over a very short period of time, they were probably based on earlier population counts rather than on new enumerations. No *tasaciones* were made of Indian villages in eastern Nicaragua.

Even where official assessments existed, the amount of tribute and labor exacted from the Indians was excessive.[49] Although encomenderos exacted tribute in the form of foodstuffs such as maize and beans, they appear to have been more interested in using Indian labor. Perhaps the greatest burden that fell on the Indians was the provision of *tamemes,* many of whom were subsequently hired out by encomenderos.[50] Because long-distance trade had been limited in pre-Columbian times and the wheel and draft animals had been absent, few roads existed that could be used by the Spaniards. The flatness of the terrain in Pacific Nicaragua facilitated the construction of roads and the use of animal-drawn carts, but Indian carriers continued to be used.[51] From 1537 the loads Indians were required to carry were legally limited to one arroba (25 pounds), and in 1541 the employment of Indians as *tamemes* was banned. Nevertheless, the service of *tamemes* was still included in *tasaciones* drawn up in 1545, and, despite further orders forbidding the employment of Indians as porters, their employment continued illegally because of the lack of alternative means of transport.[52] As well as being employed in carrying goods to and from the mines, the Indians worked as miners. Conditions in the mines were cold and wet, and the work was described as unfit for horses.[53] As a result the death rate was high, and in 1546 the employment of Indians in mining was banned.[54] The employment of Indians in pearl fishing was also banned owing to the hazardous nature of the activity.[55]

Another task in which encomenderos employed Indians was in spinning and weaving cotton cloth. Despite orders to the contrary, women were often removed from their villages for several months at a time to work in textile workshops.[56] In 1544 the Indians of Cindega complained that their encomendero had whipped them and forced them to work till night and even on Sundays and holy days.[57] Although the textile workshops never became a really important feature in the colonial economy of Central America, the spinning and weaving of cotton issued under the *repartimiento de hilados* later became a considerable burden on Indian communities.

Particularly heavy tasks in which Indians were employed were those associated with the shipbuilding industry that was centered on Realejo. Wood for the construction of vessels was obtained from the central highlands, whence the Indians transported it on their backs to the coast. Indians were often employed in this task for three to four years at a time, and, apart from being an arduous task, it involved traveling from one climatic zone to another.[58] In 1541 the employment of Indians in this activity was banned.[59] In the same area other Indians were employed in the manufacture of pitch and tar for the shipbuilding industry.[60]

In addition to performing particular tasks, a number of Indians from each encomienda were employed by encomenderos as household servants. Originally many of these servants were Indian slaves, and they were known as *naborías,* but increasingly encomenderos employed Indians from villages that they had been granted as encomiendas. As servants these Indians were separated from their families and were subject to considerable abuse by members of the household.[61] In fact, they were treated little different from slaves to the extent that they were sometimes bought and sold, even though the practice was illegal.[62] In 1548 it was reported that in many parts of the audiencia there was not a *vecino* who did not have five or six *naborías,* and another account recorded that some households had up to twenty-five *naborías.*[63] In 1550 the crown ordered an investigation into the "condition" of *naborías.*[64]

Although various types of service were banned during the 1540s, some were included in the tribute assessments of 1548. From the 198 villages and barrios granted in encomiendas in Nicaragua, 116 Indians were allocated to work in personal service, but of those 100 gave service during the months of December to March only. The largest number provided by any one village was 8, and the average number was 1 or 2. Other kinds of services rendered included tending cattle and providing them with fodder; supplying the encomendero with fish on Fridays, Saturdays, and during Lent; clearing plots; and repairing houses. Although the commutation of tribute to personal service was forbidden in 1549 and from that date was not included in *tasaciones,* there is no doubt that it was still demanded by encomenderos.[65]

The items the Indians paid as tribute consisted of foodstuffs, vegetable products, chickens, honey, wax, salt, and various craft manufactures. The most important food crop paid as tribute was maize. There were generally two harvests of maize a year, the first being the largest but the second commanding higher prices because of its smaller size. The *tasaciones* for 1544 indicated the number of fanegas of maize that should be sown by the community and the proportion of the harvest that must be paid as tribute. The tribute assessments for 1548, however, stipulated only the amount of maize that should be sown, and it is assumed that the total product of the harvest had to be rendered as tribute. Naturally the amount of maize that was harvested from equal amounts of seed sown would have varied from year to year, but enco-menderos were forbidden to claim recompense for years of bad harvest in years of abundance.[66]

The *tasaciones* of 1548 regulated the amount of maize that was to be sown at about one fanega for every ten tributary Indians.[67] One-tenth of a fanega would have given a harvest of between five and ten fanegas, and this may be compared with about twenty fanegas required to support an Indian family for a year.[68] Beans, which were generally intercropped with maize, were also paid as tribute. It is interesting that cacao, which played such an important role in the economy of Indians in the Meso-american zone in pre-Columbian times, did not become a significant item of tribute in the colonial period; in 1548 only fourteen villages in Nica-ragua paid tribute in cacao.[69] One of the most successful sources of food, which was introduced by the Spaniards and became an important item of tribute in colonial times, was the chicken.

Other important items of tribute were fibers and goods made from them. First and foremost was cotton, which the Indians were required to cultivate and to spin and weave into mantas, or blankets. Henequen was also paid as tribute, though only by Indian tribes living on the islands in Lake Nicaragua and to the east; it was used to make ropes, cords, ham-mocks, and sandals. The extraction of this fiber was considered to be injurious to the health, since it forced the Indians to travel to a different climatic zone from the one in which they resided.[70] Comparable diffi-culties were experienced in the collection of honey and wax, which were also required as tribute. Indians employed in their collection were often absent from their villages for three months at a time, making it impos-sible for them to attend to their subsistence plots. During this time they often suffered food shortages and were forced to subsist on wild food resources, with the result that about one-third of them never returned.[71]

Finally, many manufactures were included in the *tasaciones*. Various kinds of pots and pans, jars for storage, rush mats, caps, as well as the ropes, cords, hammocks and sandals already mentioned, were all in-cluded in the *tasaciones* of 1548.[72] Although these items were of little value, they were of vital importance to Spanish colonists, since imports from Spain were inadequate and erratic.

INDIAN SLAVERY

The Indian slave trade provided colonists with probably the largest and easiest profits. The crown's attitude toward Indian slavery fluctuated throughout the first half of the sixteenth century as it tried to reconcile its humanitarian views toward the Indians with the practical needs of empire. It had been entrusted with the protection and conversion of the Indians by Pope Alexander VI in 1493, but it was being pressed by conquistadors and colonists for immediate rewards for their efforts in conquest and colonization and at the same time had to deal with the practical problem of Indians who refused to submit to Spanish authority. In general the crown upheld the freedom of the Indian as a subject of the king of Spain and permitted enslavement only as a form of punishment for rebellion or pagan practices such as cannibalism. Spaniards were also allowed to acquire Indian slaves from native owners, since it enabled them to be converted and did not result in a deterioration of their status. Indians enslaved for refusal to submit to Spanish authority were known as *esclavos de guerra,* and those acquired from native owners were called *esclavos de rescate.* The charge of cannibalism, which was used to justify the enslavement of Indians in the Caribbean, was not brought against Indians in Nicaragua, even though it could have been used against some Indian groups there. In Nicaragua the Indian slave trade became so important that its justification was unnecessary.[73]

Crown efforts to control enslaving activities in Central America were unsuccessful largely because of the scale on which enslavement took place. The sale of slaves was a profitable business and was regarded as the only means by which colonists could support themselves in the area. In 1530, however, the crown, concerned at the ill treatment of the Indians, ordered that no more slaves were to be taken in war or obtained from native owners by trade.[74] Colonists complained bitterly. They pointed to the fact that as a result of the abolition of slavery Indian resistance had increased and that Indian slaves left in the hands of native owners now ran the risk of being sacrificed. The crown relented, and *esclavos de rescate* and *esclavos de guerra* were permitted again in 1532 and 1533, respectively.[75] In 1534, however, Indians were no longer allowed to possess Indian slaves, and this effectively restricted the number of Indians that could be obtained by trade.[76] This was reinforced in 1536 by an order forbidding the acquisition of *esclavos de rescate.*[77] In the same year the export of slaves from the province was forbidden except for one or two for domestic service; this order was repeated at intervals in subsequent years.[78] Finally Indian slavery was abolished by the New Laws in 1542.

Legislation not only stipulated the circumstances in which Indians could be enslaved but specified the procedure that was to be followed. Indians had to be branded as slaves before they could be sold. Various brand marks were made on different parts of the body according to the type of slave.[79] From 1526 the branding of slaves had to be supervised by royal officials, who also collected the royal *quinto*—one-fifth of the value of the slave. The crown tried to control branding by limiting the number of branding irons and by ordering that they were to be kept in a safe with three keys in the charge of three royal officials. Theoretically the only place in Nicaragua where branding could take place was León.[80] It is clear, however, that conquistadors made counterfeit irons and sometimes openly branded slaves with irons possessing their own marks.[81] Although those who branded slaves illegally were liable for the death penalty and loss of property, these extreme punishments were seldom imposed and thus were inadequate deterrents.[82] For most Spaniards the risk involved in illegal branding was minimal, and the profits to be made were high.

Indians were enslaved in various ways. Many expeditions aimed at subjugating the Indians or colonizing or exploring new areas resulted in the enslavement of large numbers of Indians. In 1526, López de Salcedo, the governor of Honduras, led a major expedition south to Nicaragua to establish his jurisdiction over the province. He took with him more than 300 Indian slaves, including 22 caciques, to carry his personal effects and goods for sale in Nicaragua. On the way in the Olancho Valley he punished by death and mutilation 200 Indians who had taken part in a revolt. He continued south through the valley of Comayagua to León, demanding supplies and Indian slaves from villages along the way. Altogether he enslaved 2,000 Indians, only 100 of whom arrived in León, the rest having died on the journey.[83] Other, similar expeditions were led by Martín de Estete in the name of Pedrarias. On one expedition to the Province of "Chorotega" he succeeded in enslaving 4,000 Indians, and on another, which explored the territory around the Desaguadero he indiscriminately enslaved many others.[84]

In addition to these major expeditions, on which thousands of Indians were enslaved, individuals or small groups of Spaniards continually harassed Indian villages to capture Indians or obtain Indian slaves by trade. Spaniards even came down from Mexico and Guatemala for such purposes.[85] The number of Indian slaves possessed by native owners was soon exhausted, and caciques were forced to hand over free Indians.[86] Encomenderos also sold into slavery Indians from their encomiendas. Profits from the sale of slaves were greater and more immediate than any returns from Indian tribute or labor, and there was always the chance that new encomiendas would become available as colonization proceeded.[87] In desperation other Spaniards with no access to Indians conducted slave raids on Indian villages at night.[88]

Most Indians were enslaved for sale overseas; only a few were kept for personal use as household servants. Some were employed in mining until their employment in the mines was banned, but they were not used

on a large scale as agricultural laborers. The export of Indian slaves increased with demand until the 1540s, when the supply began to dwindle.
The prices of Indian slaves clearly reflected variations in demand and
supply. Sherman notes that during the early Conquest period Indian
slaves were sold for 2 or 3 pesos. Prices remained low during the 1530s
but rose to 50 or 60 pesos in the following decade. The price varied,
however, according to the sex and skills of the slave, as well as many
other external factors.[89] For example, in the 1530s the governor of Nicaragua, Francisco de Castañeda, controlled the issuance of export licenses. As such he purchased slaves cheaply, and by issuing licences
only to buyers who would accept his highly inflated prices, he forced up
the price of slaves. Thus female slaves sold for 200 pesos when they
were "worth" only 25 to 40 pesos. Despite fluctuations in the prices for
Indian slaves, it is clear that because of their greater availability in Central America they were much cheaper there than in other provinces.
While Indian slaves were selling for 2 pesos in Guatemala in the 1530s,
farther north, in Mexico, they were selling for 40 pesos.[90]

Most Indian slaves were exported to Panama, where there was an
acute shortage of labor, and to Peru.[91] Probably the first ship to sail from
Nicaragua with Indian slaves for Panama left in 1526. At first slaves were
exported by way of the island of Chira in the Gulf of Nicoya, but during
the 1530s, Realejo became the most important slave-trading port, where
the slave trade stimulated the development of the shipbuilding industry.[92]
The first mention of a slave ship leaving Realejo dates from 1529, when
charges were made for the illegal export of slaves from that port, which
must have occurred some time before.[93] This port handled all the Indian
slaves who were exported to Peru following its discovery and conquest.

To judge by the number of ships involved in the Indian slave trade, it
reached a peak in the early to mid-1530s. Bartolomé de las Casas estimated that between 1526 and 1533 five or six ships were involved in exporting slaves, and in 1529 all five ships were owned by royal officials.[94]
At that time the round trip between the island of Chira and Panama
lasted sixteen to twenty days, except during bad weather, when it took
thirty days. By 1534 the number of ships engaged in the slave trade had
risen to between fifteen and twenty caravels, which carried nothing but
Indian slaves, and in 1535 there were said to be twenty ships operating
between Nicaragua and Panama and Peru.[95] At that time it was estimated
that of a shipload of 400 Indian slaves only 50 arrived alive, and of those
who had been exported to Panama and Peru not one-twentieth were still
alive. The large load carried by the ships was also observed by Las
Casas, who recorded that "there is no ship which leaves these ports
which does not carry more than three hundred souls."[96] Using these observations on the numbers of ships engaged in the trade, the number of

trips they undertook, and their capacities, Radell has estimated that between 1527 and 1536 about 450,000 Indian slaves were exported from Nicaragua.[97]

Although the export of Indian slaves was forbidden from 1536, it is clear that it continued, but on a reduced scale, mainly because of the decline in the Indian population that supplied it. For example, in 1540 the governor of Nicaragua, Rodrigo de Contreras, was charged with having allowed the export of 2,000 Indian slaves for Peru and the Atlantic coast, probably for Panama and the Caribbean islands.[98] It seems reasonable therefore to add 50,000 for the period 1536 to 1542 to Radell's estimate of 450,000 for the period 1527 to 1536, to give a total of about 500,000 Indian slaves exported during the whole period. This figure is comparable to those given by the contemporary observers Las Casas and Oviedo. Las Casas estimated that 500,000 Indian slaves had been exported to Panama and Peru from Nicaragua, while Oviedo maintained that 400,000 had died as a result of the slave trade and the new administration.[99]

Despite the convergence of estimates, Sherman considers them to be too high. He maintains that only a few ships were involved in the early years of the trade and that the capacity of the ships was small, while in later years heavy cargo demands for space reduced that available for slaves. He suggests that 50,000 were exported from 1524 to 1549, this figure including Indian slaves exported from the whole of Central America, not just Nicaragua.[100] This figure certainly seems too low given the evidence available. Las Casas recorded that, in two years in the 1530s, 12,000 Indians had been exported to Peru and 25,000 to Panama and that up to that time 15,000 more had been shipped to Peru.[101] MacLeod also suggests that 10,000 a year for the decade 1532 to 1542 would seem to be too low and 200,000 for the duration of the Nicaraguan slave trade a conservative estimate.[102] It seems possible, therefore, that between 200,000 and 500,000 slaves were exported from Nicaragua, though some of them would have come from other parts of Central America, particularly Honduras and Guatemala.

The New Laws of 1542 aimed at abolishing Indian slavery; Indian women and children were to be set free at once, and no new slaves were to be made for whatever reason. Male slaves for whom their owners could produce a title were to remain enslaved, but all others were to be set free. The emancipation of slaves was the culmination of efforts by the Dominicans to ensure the good treatment of the Indians, and it was encouraged by practical considerations. Slavery was a wasteful institution; many Indians were killed as the result of enslaving raids, while others died on their way to markets in Central America and Peru, and those who survived often endured harsh treatment and poor living condi-

tions at their destinations. Not only was slavery wasteful in human resources, but, since Indian slaves were exempt from tribute payment, it
effectively reduced the income of the crown and the encomenderos.[103]
When the New Laws were published, the president of the audiencia pro-
tested that they would lead to economic decline: the crown would lose
the *quintos* it received from the branding of slaves and from the gold that
was mined by them, while colonists possessed no other forms of income
or wealth.[104] In 1545, Las Casas observed that the New Laws were not
being obeyed, and it was not until 1548, when Cerrato arrived as president of the audiencia, that they were effectively enforced and Indian
slaves were set free. Although the abolition of slavery also provided for
the restitution of slaves to their places of origin, very few were ever returned.[105] Sherman attributes the successful implementation of the New
Laws to the courage and integrity of Cerrato himself, but he would not
have succeeded had the circumstances in which he governed not differed
from those that had prevailed at the height of the slave trade.[106] The supply of slaves was drying up as the Indian population declined, and at the
same time the demand for slaves was decreasing; in Peru local sources of
labor were being exploited, and in Panama black slaves, mules, and
horses substituted for Indian labor. Meanwhile, local demands for labor
were increasing, and colonists had become concerned about the decline
in the Indian population.

MINING

The other major source of wealth for colonists in the early sixteenth century was mining. Gold placer deposits were found in the Segovia Mountains in 1527, and gold was soon being worked in the río San Andrés and
the río Grande.[107] The mines around the mining center of Santa María de
Buena Esperanza were sometimes known as the mines of Gracias a
Dios, and they should not be confused with the mines around the town of
that name in Honduras. Gold mines were also said to exist in the Mari-
bichicoa Valley.[108] Problems of labor shortage created by the decline in
the Indian population and by the confusion created by the reallocation of
encomiendas, as well as by Indian attacks, resulted in intermittent mining.[109] Mining activities received a slight boost in 1543, when the town of
Nueva Segovia was founded in the area, but they were still hampered by
Indian attacks and shortages of labor, the latter being exacerbated by the
ban on the employment of Indians in mining in 1546.[110]

Initially labor in the mines was provided mainly by Indians working
either in the service of encomenderos or as slaves but supplemented by
black slaves. They employed various kinds of hoes for scraping the

stream beds and excavating terraces and used wooden bowls, or bateas, sometimes paid as tribute by the Indians, for separating the gold from other substances.[111] To control the smelting of gold and ensure that the royal fifth was deducted, from 1528 refining was restricted to León.[112] Although the *quinto* was normally paid on gold, the tax was sometimes reduced, generally to one-tenth, to encourage prospecting and mining where conditions were difficult. In Nicaragua the *diezmo,* or one-tenth, appears to have been paid on gold from the beginning, and the lower tax was considered essential to attract foreign miners. The *quinto,* however, was paid on smelted silver.[113] The amounts of gold smelted were relatively small compared to the amounts in Honduras, and output appears to have declined after the mid-1530s. Up to June, 1528, 22,000 pesos of gold had been produced in Nicaragua, and in May, 1531, it was said that there were 30,000 pesos waiting to be smelted.[114] Altogether mining played a minor role in the economy and the life of the Indians, but it had the effect of extending Spanish activities into areas that otherwise would have remained outside Spanish control, at least until the next century.

AGRICULTURE

At the same time that the towns were founded, land grants were distributed to its *vecinos.* Nevertheless, during the early sixteenth century agriculture was slow to develop, and it was essentially oriented toward subsistence needs rather than export. Initially colonists were supported by imports of food from Spain or the Caribbean islands and by crops produced by Indians. Later they began to develop agriculture using Indian labor.

Initially grants of land were distributed by the conquistador, but later they were allocated by the cabildo. They were given in perpetuity to nearly all Spanish settlers according to their merits and services, and they were theoretically limited to three *caballerías* or five *peonías.*[115] These limits were often exceeded, and, despite protective legislation, the grants often resulted in the alienation of Indian lands, though they sometimes comprised savanna lands that had been underutilized by the Indians in pre-Columbian times.

Commercial crops remained insignificant in the economy during the first half of the sixteenth century. Even cacao, which had played such an important role in the economy of many Mesoamerican groups, and which was noted as one of the most important items produced in Nicaragua, does not appear to have been produced commercially in the early sixteenth century.[116] In other parts of Central America, notably Soconusco and Zapotitlán, where the cultivation of cacao was highly developed in the pre-Columbian period, commercial production continued and in fact over-shadowed developments elsewhere.[117] The fall in cacao production in Nicaragua resulted in a rapid increase in its price, from three reals a carga to between eighty and ninety reals a carga in 1549.[118] The only commercial crop the Spaniards attempted to produce in the early six-teenth century was sugarcane, but its expansion was apparently discour-aged by the imposition of the *diezmo*.[119] Other crops introduced by the Spaniards met with varying degrees of success. Wheat (*Triticum aestivum* L.) was not suited to the climatic conditions in Nicaragua, but citrus fruits—sweet orange (*Citrus sinensis* [L.] Osbeck), sour orange (*C. aurantium* L.), lime (*C. aurantifolia* [Christm.] Swingle), lemon (*C. limon* [L.] Burm.f.) and citron (*C. medica* L.)—were highly successful. Other fruits introduced during the first half of the sixteenth century were pomegranates (*Punica granatum* L.) and figs (*Ficus carica* L.), while vines were grown successfully around Granada.[120]

Horses, cattle, sheep, and pigs were introduced into Central Amer-ica by the earliest explorers and colonists. A horse was considered to be worth more than a hundred men in battle, and all *vecinos* were expected to keep horses for defensive purposes. Other livestock were regarded as essential for the maintenance of the Spaniards in the New World.[121] Most of the animals introduced were imported from the Caribbean islands.[122] Cattle in particular thrived on the formerly underutilized savannas and on the lands left deserted by declining Indian populations, though in the first half of the sixteenth century cattle and horses were also raised around León and Granada.[123] Apart from serving local needs, horses and cattle were exported to help in the conquest of Peru.[124] Probably the most important domesticated animal that was introduced by the Span-iards in terms of the diet of colonists and Indians alike was the chicken.

REGIONAL VARIATIONS IN SPANISH ACTIVITY

During the first half of the sixteenth century Spanish activities were con-centrated where there were large Indian population and minerals; at that time land was not a primary motivating force in conquest and coloniza-tion. The existence of large concentrations of Indians in Pacific Nica-ragua, which could be distributed in encomiendas or used to supply the Indian slave trade, encouraged the systematic conquest of that area at an early date. In eastern Nicaragua conquest and colonization were not undertaken with the same enthusiasm, and in fact they were prolonged throughout the colonial period. There the Indians formed smaller con-centrations of population and therefore were not as attractive as sources of slaves or tribute and labor. In addition they were more difficult to control. While the Indian population in eastern Nicaragua was too small to attract the attention of conquistadors and colonists, the presence of minerals in Nueva Segovia provided sufficient incentive for the Spanish to establish a permanent settlement there and to allocate encomiendas. The mines were not worked by local labor, however, but by black slaves or Indians imported from Pacific Nicaragua.

CHAPTER 7

Deculturation and Depopulation, 1522–1550

The first three decades of Spanish rule were disastrous for the Indians of Nicaragua and Nicoya, and undoubtedly it was the Indians in the Meso-american zone, where Spanish activities were concentrated, who suffered most. In the South American zone, with the exception of the mining area of Nueva Segovia, Indians had only temporary or indirect contacts with Spaniards, and as a result they experienced relatively minor cultural and demographic changes.

CULTURAL CHANGES IN THE MESOAMERICAN ZONE

The dramatic decline in the Indian population in the first half of the sixteenth century resulted in a reduction in the number and size of Indian settlements. Some villages were destroyed as a direct result of the Conquest, while others suffered depopulation partly as a consequence of the Indian slave trade. The large Indian populations in the Pacific lowlands attracted enslavers, and their sedentary mode of existence made it difficult for them to flee and survive on wild-food resources in the interior.[1] Although there are few references to the decline in size of particular towns and villages, a comparison of the observations of Oviedo with the list of tributary Indians drawn up in 1548 makes it clear that many suffered a severe decline.[2] Managua, which had possessed a population of over 40,000, had only 265 tributary Indians in 1548, while Jalteba had been reduced from over 8,000 inhabitants to 195 tributary Indians, and in Nicoya only 600 tributary Indians remained of more than 6,000 who had been baptized in 1522. Altogether by 1548 only 37 of 158 villages listed contained over 100 tributary Indians, and only 10 possessed more than 200.

Although there is very little evidence for changes in the form of Indian settlements during this period, the following changes are likely to have occurred. The Spanish may have taken over the palaces of nobles and public buildings for their own administrative purposes, and they would certainly have destroyed any temples and sacrificial mounds, replacing them with Christian churches. Many of the Indian markets would have continued to serve local needs; indeed, the crown encouraged their establishment as places where Indians could trade freely.[3] Since the Spaniards were eager to exploit Indian sources of labor, a number of In-

Table 3. Number and Size of Indian Villages
in Nicaragua and Nicoya, 1548

Tributary Indians	Number	Percent of total number	Tributary population	Percent of total tributary population
200 and over	10	6.3	3,074	27.1
150–199	3	1.9	658	5.8
100–149	24	15.2	2,851	25.1
50– 99	42	26.6	2,807	24.8
20– 49	56	35.4	1,687	14.9
1– 19	23	14.6	266	2.3
Total	158	100.0	11,343	100.0

Source: AGI AG 128 Libro de tasaciones 1548.

dian villages, such as Jalteba and Sutiaba, became suburbs of Spanish towns.

Following the establishment of Spanish towns, lands were allocated within their jurisdictions. Although the crown passed laws to protect Indian rights to their lands, they were largely ineffective.[4] Particularly vulnerable to encroachment were lands near towns and open stretches of land that appeared unoccupied but were exploited for wild fruits, game, wood, and water. Apart from directly usurping Indian lands, Spaniards also pressed Indians to sell their lands at low prices—"for a shirt or an arroba of wine."[5] The alienation of Indian lands was mitigated in part by the decline in the Indian population, but there was no direct correlation between losses of land and decreases in population, and undoubtedly some Indian villages were left with insufficient lands to support their populations. Even when Indians retained their lands, they were often overrun by Spanish expeditions; later straying cattle became a greater problem.[6]

The availability of labor for subsistence activities was drastically reduced by the decline in the Indian population and by Spanish demands on Indian production. To a certain extent the impact of the decline in the Indian population was moderated by the decrease in number of consumers, but in some instances the loss of a substantial proportion of the population must have weakened the community structure, thus making the cooperation needed at critical stages in the cycle of cultivation more difficult to organize. In addition Indians were often absent from their villages for extended periods while they were employed in some form of personal service. Their absences often coincided with critical periods in the agricultural calendar, such as land clearance, sowing, and harvest, even though their employment at these times was forbidden.[7] At the same time that labor inputs into Indian production decreased, the demands upon it increased. Indians were required to pay tribute in kind; for example, the amount of maize the Indians were liable to pay as tribute was equivalent to about one-quarter to one-half of their annual family needs.[8] Furthermore, some products demanded as tribute could not easily be grown or collected locally, and Indians had to spend extra time caring for crops to reach the required level of production or spend time traveling to areas where the wild products could be collected. Since tithes were payable only on crops introduced from Europe, the Indians generally remained exempt from tithe payment, though a proportion of the tribute they paid was used to support the local church and clergy.[9] The Indians were, however, required to pay for special masses and for ceremonies such as baptism and marriage. They also had to provide hospitality in the form of food and shelter for travelers, whether or not they were officials, and this placed a considerable burden on villages on major routeways.

Declining labor inputs and increased demands on Indian production had a number of effects on Indian subsistence. First, the decreased time available for subsistence activities and the reduced availability of land would have resulted in the recultivation of lands rather than the clearance of new plots, with the result that soil fertility and hence crop yields would have declined, and at a time when demands on production were increasing. The result would have been dietary deficiencies and food shortages. Second, time-consuming hunting, fishing, and gathering would have led to a decline in the importance of these activities and consequently a reduction in the importance of wild-food products in Indian diets; diets in the mines were described as inadequate, lacking the fruit and fish to which the Indians were accustomed.[10] Rather than playing an integral role in subsistence, hunting, fishing, and gathering were undertaken only in times of severe food shortage.[11] Finally, the reduction in the diversity of economic activities was paralleled by a reduction in the diversity of crops grown, low-yielding species, such as starchy varieties of the sweet potato, and those requiring high labor inputs being dropped from the assemblage of crops grown.[12] Conversely, there was an increase in the importance of maize and beans, which were adopted by the Spaniards as staples and as major items of tribute. The increased demand for maize could not always be met, however, and there were often severe shortages resulting in high prices for the crop; in one year (1528) the price of maize rose from four reals to three to four pesos a fanega.[13]

The probable loss in the variety of crops grown by the Indians was compensated for in part by the introduction of domesticated plants and animals, from both Europe and other parts of the New World from which they had not diffused in pre-Columbian times.[14] A number of the newly introduced domesticates, such as sugar and wheat, were not widely adopted by the Indians because of the difficulty of fitting them into their existing systems of cultivation, but citrus fruits were easily added to the varieties of fruit trees already cultivated. However, the introduction of livestock probably had the greatest impact on Indian agriculture. During the early colonial period the chicken became an important source of food and item of tribute; other forms of livestock were not adopted on a large scale at this time, although it was suggested that the Indians should be encouraged to acquire domesticated animals, particularly pigs and sheep.[15] There is some evidence, however, that Indians were forced to raise and tend livestock owned by encomenderos and priests.[16] The introduction of domesticated animals to Indian production was not always beneficial; very little attention was paid to the management of livestock, which were allowed to range freely and often overran Indians' plots.

Trade probably declined considerably in the early sixteenth century with the decline in the level of economic production, and hence surplus for trade, and with the disruption of long-distance trading contacts with other Indian groups. Indians would have continued to trade any surplus produce in local markets, although much of it would have been monopolized by royal officials, encomenderos, and priests.

The social organization of Indian groups in the Pacific zone was modified by population decline and by the imposition of Spanish institutions and laws. During the Conquest the social structure of the Indian groups was weakened as caciques and principales as well as commoners were enslaved and killed. Rivalries between Indian groups probably diminished as the threat of Spanish domination increased, but there is no evidence for the emergence of a military or political organization that cut across traditional loyalties; most of the armies that fought against the Spaniards do not appear to have been drawn from more than one chiefdom. Whereas in pre-Columbian times the chiefdoms of the Mesoamerican zone were characterized by a hierarchy of classes, during the colonial period the number of classes was gradually reduced. During the first half of the sixteenth century three social classes were recognized by the Spaniards: Indian leaders, or caciques; commoners; and slaves, although the last seldom formed a permanent class in the social hierarchy. Furthermore, the numbers of caciques and slaves fell relative to the number of commoners.

Throughout the New World the Spaniards sought to gain control of Indian communities through their native leaders. They found that once the Indian leaders had accepted their authority and been converted to Christianity the rest of the population would follow.[17] The Spaniards clearly preferred to communicate with one or two Indian leaders rather than with a large number of individuals. For this reason Oviedo noted that among the Chorotega, whose aboriginal form of government consisted of a council of elected elders chosen by different villages, the Spaniards insisted that the councils should be broken up and the elders made caciques of their own communities.[18] The authority of caciques was reinforced by the Spaniards, who recognized their noble rank and allowed them and their oldest sons certain privileges. These included exemption from tribute payment and routine labor and permission to wear Spanish dress, ride horses, and carry arms.[19] Initially they were also allowed to possess slaves.[20] The crown issued many decrees ordering Spanish officials not to undermine the authority of native leaders by employing them in tasks inappropriate to their status or by removing them from office and substituting their own nominees.[21] To maintain control of the Indian communities, the crown ordered that schools should be provided in Spanish towns for the instruction of the sons of Indian leaders.[22] Indian leaders thus became intermediaries between Spaniards and Indians, and, although their authority was upheld by the Spanish, the respect they commanded would have declined as they emerged as little more than instruments of Spanish control and administration.

The native councils were replaced by cabildos, which were modeled on those established in Spanish towns. They were introduced widely in Nicaragua in the 1550s. They comprised elected officials, who received salaries paid out of the tribute exacted from the community.[23] They included alcaldes and regidores, who among other things were responsible for the collection of tribute; the alcaldes could also make arrests and punish minor offenses. They were thus used to enforce Spanish laws and codes of behavior. During their period of office they were exempt from tribute payment and personal service.[24]

Most of the Indians were commoners, who were distinguished by their lack of social privileges and by their obligation to pay tribute and perform labor services. There is no evidence that specialist craftsmen were treated differently from commoners. The official status of military and religious leaders would have disappeared as their functions were taken over by the Spaniards, though it is likely that they continued to command some respect within their communities. Hence the Spaniards only recognized the noble status of caciques and their eldest sons and did not differentiate between the rest of the Indian population, with the result that a degree of social leveling occurred among those of non-noble birth.

Indian slaves formed the lowest class in Indian society until slavery was abolished in 1542. Slaves were owned by caciques, who often sold them to the Spaniards, sometimes enslaving Indians in their own communities for the purpose.[25] Gradually as large numbers of Indian slaves were sold to the Spaniards and as human sacrifices were suppressed, the size of this class within Indian communities diminished.

Other social changes occurred at the family level. Although monogamy prevailed in Nicaragua, polygamy was known, and the Spaniards sought to suppress it.[26] They also tried to discourage adultery and incest by insisting that married couples must not live with their parents or other relatives. These efforts probably achieved little success, for the Indians would not have been impressed by the example set by the Spaniards themselves. Many Spanish officials, encomenderos, and priests entered into casual relationships with Indian women, taking advantage of them when they were working in their personal service.[27] Other Spaniards were involved in hiring out Indian women as prostitutes, particularly to seamen in Realejo.[28] Although there is no evidence of marriage residence rules during the early colonial period, it seems likely that the Spaniards, following their own example, would have encouraged patrilocal residence as they did patrilineal descent.[29] Clearly, however, many families were broken up as individual members were killed during the Conquest or were enslaved and transported to other provinces.[30] In addition the prolonged absence of men and women from their villages while performing some form of labor service would have encouraged instability in marriage. These factors together would have resulted in the existence of many one-parent families and large numbers of orphans.

The Spaniards were horrified by many of the religious practices of Indians in the Mesoamerican zone and sought to abolish them and impose Christianity. Temples were destroyed or converted into churches, and idols were replaced by crucifixes and images of the Virgin Mary.[31] A contemporary observer recorded how Friar Bobadilla

destroyed many idols and oratories and burned chapels and temples of the Indians, and he placed crosses along all the roads, in the squares, and in high places where they could be clearly seen and built churches and placed in them images of Our Lady and crucifixes and holy water; and with most of the caciques he left young ladinos to instruct the Indians in the Lord's prayer and Ave Maria.[32]

Many of the Indians tried to hide their idols from the Spaniards; Castañeda noted that in the town of Imabite the Indians managed to hide two hundred idols for ten days, but when the Spaniards discovered them, they broke them into pieces.[33] Nevertheless many idols probably escaped the notice of the Spaniards and were worshiped in secret.

The Spaniards were also appalled by many of the Indian ceremonies, which often involved sacrifices and drunken dancing, and they tried to suppress them in favor of more sober, Christian ones.[34] They introduced

ceremonies related to Christian year, as well as Christian baptisms, marriages, and funerals. Mass baptisms were common in the early years
of the Conquest, but it is doubtful that many Indians were truly converted.[35] The process of conversion was continued by priests provided
by the crown or by encomenderos, but it was not easy. Some blamed the
failure of Indians to adopt Christianity on their incapacity and obstinacy,
suggesting that they should be taught not difficult concepts such as the
Trinity and the Virgin Birth but other aspects of Christianity that they
could understand more easily. Others maintained that the task of conversion was difficult because of the ill-treatment the Indians had suffered at
the hands of the Spaniards.[36] As such, with the exception of the suppression of human sacrifice, Christian instruction did not fundamentally alter
Indian religious beliefs and practices, and out of sight of the Spaniards
they continued to hold their own religious ceremonies and to respect
their own religious leaders.[37]

CULTURAL CHANGES IN THE SOUTH AMERICAN ZONE

During the first half of the sixteenth century most of the South American
zone remained remote from centers of Spanish activity, with the result
that the cultural changes experienced by the Indians there were not as
profound as those noted for the Mesoamerican zone. Two activities did,
however, bring Indians and Spaniards into contact in the east: enslaving
and mining. These primarily affected Indian groups on the margins of the
South American zone; few Spaniards penetrated as far east as the Mosquito Coast.

With the exception of the town of Nueva Segovia, the Spaniards did
not settle permanently in the South American zone, so few land grants
were issued and Indian rights to their lands probably remained more secure. However, the danger of enslaving raids forced some Indians to
abandon their lands and move into the interior, with the result that the
area the Indians could exploit for subsistence was reduced. At the same
time labor inputs into various economic activities declined. This decline
was greatest in the mining area of Nueva Segovia and in areas fringing
the South American zone that were raided for slaves. That men would
have been preferred as slaves as well as for labor in the mines may have
affected the division of labor. However, since men did not play such an
important role in agricultural production as they did the Mesoamerican
zone, the impact on agriculture of the loss of male labor would have been
less, though it would have seriously affected hunting and fishing, which
were vital in maintaining a balanced diet. Other effects of declining labor
resources on economic production would have been similar to those already noted for the Mesoamerican zone.

Probably few changes occurred in the assemblage of crops and animals raised by Indians in the South American zone even though members of expeditions through the area carried plants and animals with them both for their maintenance and for colonization. Contreras maintained that he had supplied Calero and Machuca's expedition to the Desaguadero in 1539 with various plants including pineapples, bananas, oranges, lemons, figs, radishes, onions, cabbages, beans, and garlic.[38] However, the short-lived presence of such expeditions in the area would not have allowed time for the adoption of new crops.

There is very little evidence for changes in the social and political organization of Indian groups in the South American zone during the first half of the sixteenth century, but it seems likely that, because contacts with the Spaniards were not very intense, the changes were minor. The most sustained contact between Spaniards and Indians occurred in the mining areas. There some Indians were employed, but more banded together to attack Spanish settlements.[39] Conflict with the Spaniards appears to have resulted in a decline in intertribal rivalries, and it may also have resulted in the strengthening of the status of military leaders. The absence of men engaged in these activities was probably not long enough to influence the division of labor or marriage residence rules.

The lack of sustained contact would not have permitted the imposition of Christianity resulting in the removal of shamans in favor of Catholic priests or the suppression of polygamy in favor of Christian marriage. Although Indians may have been baptized and idols and shrines destroyed when Spanish exploratory expeditions penetrated the area, Indian beliefs and religious practices were not altered to any great degree.

DEMOGRAPHIC CHANGES

It is clear that the Indian population suffered a dramatic decline during the early sixteenth century, but there are very few contemporary estimates of the numbers involved. In 1544 the *oidor* Diego de Herrera estimated that the Indian population of Nicaragua had ben reduced to 30,000, though this figure probably did not take into account Indians living in the eastern region of the country, which, except for the mining area around Nueva Segovia, had not yet been brought under Spanish control.[40] This figure is comparable to the number of tributary Indians recorded in the *tasaciones* of 1548 by President Cerrato and the *oidores* Rogel and Ramírez.[41] Unfortunately the *tasaciones* cover only the Pacific lowlands and Nicoya. They give details of the population and the amount of tribute to be paid by 198 villages and barrios. There were 5,714 Indians in the jurisdiction of León, 4,969 in the jurisdiction of Granada, and 660 in Nicoya, a total of 11,343. These figures refer to tributary Indians, and it is assumed that they were married male Indians, since at that time single men were not liable for tribute payment.[42]

Unfortunately there is no contemporary evidence for family sizes that could be used to estimate the total Indian population from these figures. However, in the tributary lists drawn up in 1581, which will be discussed later,[43] the average ratio of married male Indians to the total population was 1:4.1. It seems reasonable, therefore, to multiply the population figures for 1548 by a factor of four, which gives estimates of 42,732 for the total Indian population of Nicaragua and 2,640 for Nicoya.[44] These figures exclude Indians who worked in Spanish households and were classified as *naborías*. Given that most households probably possessed between 2 and 5 *naborías*[45] and that at that time there were about 350 *vecinos* in León, Granada, and Realejo together, it seems likely that there were about 1,000 *naborías* in the whole country.[46] Thus by 1548 the Indian population of the Mesoamerican zone had fallen to 46,372 from an estimated aboriginal population of 609,262, a decline of 92.4 percent.

Although there are no accounts of the Indian population in the South American zone during this period, it seems probable that the population suffered a substantial reduction, owing mainly to disease but also to enslaving raids and the disruptive effect of Spanish colonization in the vicinity of Nueva Segovia.[47] A reduction in the Indian population of about one-half to one-third seems possible, but it would have been concentrated on the western fringes of the area, where contact with the Spaniards was most intense. If yellow fever and malaria were present on the Caribbean coast at this time, the decline may have been greater.

The causes of this dramatic decline in the Indian population were numerous and complex to a degree that most contemporary observers failed to recognize. They generally blamed the decline on one major factor: the Indian slave trade. As early as 1535, Francisco Sánchez, a royal official, claimed that one-third of the Indian population of Nicaragua had been lost as a result of the slave trade.[48] Estimates of the numbers of Indians involved in the slave trade have already been discussed, and it seems likely that over 200,000 were exported from Nicaragua. It is worthy of note, however, that the spatial impact of the slave trade was not uniform. For the most part Indians in the eastern part of the country were protected by their remoteness from the centers of enslaving activities, while those living near Realejo and León and around the Gulf of Nicoya, near the ports of export, suffered the most.[49]

Undoubtedly another major factor in the decline of the Indian population was disease, though estimating its precise impact is difficult. First, there is the difficulty of identifying diseases from sixteenth-century descriptions of the symptoms; many illnesses have similar symptoms. It is important that the diseases are correctly identified since the mortality rates associated with different diseases vary considerably. Even after the disease has been identified, it is extremely difficult to assess its precise impact, since diseases do not act uniformly, rather their spread is affected by such environmental factors as population density, the degree of interpersonal contact, sanitation, dietary habits, and immunity, as well as the presence of vectors for carrying the disease.[50] In the absence of such detailed information in the documentary record, the fractional estimates of the impact diseases made by contemporary observers, which note a reduction of one-third or one-half of the population, must be relied on. It is likely, however, that reductions of such large proportions did not apply to extensive areas, such as the whole country, but were local maxima.

Throughout the colonial period epidemic diseases attracted the greatest attention from contemporary observers, but it is important to note that dysentery, typhoid, hookworm, and other helminthic diseases took their toll and increased the susceptibility of the Indians to more deadly diseases. The first recorded epidemic disease in Middle America was smallpox, which was introduced into Mexico in 1520.[51] Between 1520 and 1521, Guatemala was ravaged by a disease that was either smallpox or influenza.[52] The only possible reference to the disease spreading south at this time comes from an account written in 1527, which noted that it was necessary to introduce slaves to "Panama City, Nata, and the port of Honduras" because smallpox had killed off the Indians there.[53] It seems likely that this disease spread south from Honduras to Panama through Nicaragua. In 1529 it was reported that the mines of San Andrés and Gracias a Dios had been depopulated as a result of "figo y enfermedades," which had killed many Indians and some Spaniards.[54] MacLeod suggests that the disease was pneumonic plague.[55] This outbreak appears to have been distinct from a major epidemic that occurred two years later.

In 1531 Indians around León were said to be dying of "stomach pains and fevers" and "pains in the stomach and sides" as a result of disease known as "landres."[56] The term "landres" was used in Europe to describe the buboes associated with bubonic plague, but Ashburn maintains that the disease did not reach America.[57] MacLeod suggests that the descriptions of the disease fit pneumonic plague.[58]

The difference between the two types of plague is significant because pneumonic plague has a much higher mortality rate. Bubonic plague is contracted through the bite of a flea that has obtained the disease from an infected rat. The presence of the disease is therefore dependent on a reservoir of infected rats, and it tends to spread slowly and sporadically. Pneumonic plague, however, can be spread from person to person through the inhalation of droplets expelled into the air by coughing and sneezing of an infected person, and its spread is therefore more rapid. The origin of pneumonic plague is uncertain, but it has been suggested that it develops when a person suffering from a respiratory infection contracts bubonic plague. Plague flourishes between 10°C and 30°C, with pneumonic plague found at the lower end of the temperature range and bubonic plague at the higher end of the range, although not over 30°C or in dry conditions. Pneumonic plague thus tends to be a winter disease, and when the climate becomes warmer and drier, it changes to bubonic plague.[59] Given these climatic conditions, it seems likely that the epidemic of 1531 was bubonic plague rather than pneumonic plague. This is supported by Castañeda's observation that two-thirds of the Indians had buboes. These are generally associated with bubonic plague rather than with pneumonic plague, which is so virulent that buboes do not have time to develop before the infected person dies. Furthermore, it was noted that those who were most affected were those who were living in the houses of Spaniards, where European rats—the black rat (*Rattus rattus*) and the brown rat (*R. norvegicus*), which carry the disease—would have been most common.[60]

This epidemic was followed two years later by an outbreak of measles. Herrera describes the epidemic as follows:

At this time there was such a great epidemic of measles in the Province of Honduras spreading from house to house and village to village, that many people died; and although the disease also affected the Spaniards, . . . none of them died. . . . This same disease of measles and dysentery passed to Nicaragua, where also many Indians died. . . . and two years ago there was a general epidemic of pains in the side and stomach which also carried away many Indians.[61]

It was estimated that in Nicaragua the disease killed 6,000 Indians, which was said to be one-third of the population.[62] Over a decade later, in 1545, an epidemic of either pneumonic plague or typhus also afflicted Mexico and Guatemala, but it does not appear to have spread farther south.[63]

There is considerable controversy over the origins of the tropical diseases yellow fever and malaria and whether either was present in Central America in the sixteenth century. Yellow fever is generally considered to be an introduction from the Old World. The first agreed epidemic of yellow fever occurred in Yucatán in 1648. Ashburn effectively argues that the skin coloration recorded in the sixteenth century was the result of starvation rather than yellow fever.[64] Recent zoological and historical research suggests that sylvan yellow fever may have been present in Latin America in pre-Columbian times.[65] If this was the case, then outbreaks of the disease in the tropical coastal lowlands of Central America in the sixteenth century cannot be ruled out. Nevertheless, it was only later that these coasts, and particularly Panama, earned the reputation of being unhealthy.[66] Similar comments can be made with respect to malaria. It now seems certain that malaria was introduced from the Old World. This is based on the fact that Indian populations in Latin America do not produce polymorphisms resistant to malaria, whereas those in Africa do, and the fact that in Latin America malarial parasites are relatively unspecialized and have a restricted number of hosts, thus suggesting that malaria is a relative newcomer to the New World.[67]

Another cause of the decline in the Indian population was conflict with the Spaniards. Conquest and enslavement went hand in hand, and it is difficult to estimate the numbers that were killed in battle as opposed to those who were enslaved. Las Casas maintained that, by 1542, 500,000 to 600,000 Indians had been killed in encounters with the Spaniards in Nicaragua.[68] This figure seems to be a considerable overestimate, given the estimated size of the aboriginal population and the relative ease with which the Spaniards succeeded in pacifying the country.

As long as the Indian population could be seen to provide an inexhaustible supply of labor, little attention was paid to its preservation, with the result that Indians were subject to ill-treatment and forced to work long hours under poor conditions on inadequate diets and under threat of punishment for shortcomings. Many of the tasks in which Indians were employed were strenuous and directly contributed to illness and death; these included working as porters, miners, lumberjacks, and shipbuilders. For example, in 1533 one miner lost two hundred Indians in one *demora* (work period) as a result of ill-treatment and poor working conditions.[69] Other Indians who fell ill in the mines tried to find their way home, but they often died before reaching their villages. It was said that it was possible to tell the routes from León and Granada to the mines by the skeletons of Indians along the roadside. Because these activities contributed significantly to the high death toll, the employment of Indians in them was later banned or permitted only under certain circumstances. Even if the Indians did not die as a direct result of their employment in such tasks, the exhausting work, long traveling distances, and poor diets they had to suffer often increased their susceptibility to illness and disease. The incidence of ill-treatment and overwork was greatest where Spanish demands for labor were the highest. In 1547 the bishop of Nicaragua reported that around Realejo, León, and Granada the population of Indian villages had declined to between twelve and fifteen Indians each whereas "in other villages which are not located near the Spanish they are increasing."[70] Ill-treatment and overwork made a greater contribution to the decline in the Indian population in the Mesoamerican zone, because Spanish activities were concentrated there. Although the mines were in the South American zone, they were worked by black slaves or Indians imported from the Mesoamerican zone, rather than by local Indians, who were difficult to pacify.[71]

Although very few contemporary observers attributed the decline in the Indian population to changes in economy, social and political organizations, and ideology of Indian groups brought about by Spanish conquest, it is clear that their effects were considerable. Disruption of the Indian economy led indirectly to food shortages and famines and hence to a decline in the Indian population. Many Indians, fearing attack and enslavement by the Spaniards, abandoned their lands and fled to the hills, where they tried unsuccessfully to survive on wild fruits, vegetables, fish, and game.[72] Meanwhile, those who remained suffered food shortages as their lands were alienated and their labor diverted into other economic activities. A major famine ocurred in Nicaragua in 1528, when it was estimated that two-thirds of the population died. Andrés de Cerezeda reported that the famine was caused by a drought, whereas other observers noted that it was due to the inability of the Indians to cultivate their lands.[73] Herrera recorded that one famine, probably that of 1528, had resulted in a "very high mortality, so that many Indian villages were devastated, and in parts it was not possible to walk in the streets because of the smell of the dead."[74] This was probably also the same famine referred to by Sebastian Rodríguez and Las Casas, both of whom claimed that 20,000 to 30,000 people had died of hunger and that food had been so scarce that there had been an increase in cannibalism.[75] Even if overwork was not responsible for the famine in 1528, it was probably an important contributory factor, and legislation was soon passed prohibiting the employment of Indians at sowing and harvest times. Nevertheless, food shortages continued throughout the period.

There is some evidence to suggest that the breakdown of social organization of Indian communities and the psychological impact of the Conquest resulted in a lowering of the birth rate. While disease and famines probably took their heaviest toll on the youngest and oldest segments of the population, enslavement, ill-treatment, and overwork had greater effects on able-bodied males and in some cases may have resulted in an imbalance in the sex ratio. It is uncertain whether this imbalance directly affected the birth rate. Nevertheless, it seems likely that the endless, tiring work that the Indians were forced to do would have dampened their desires to procreate, particularly since additional children would have placed increased burdens on already inadequate sources of food. Furthermore, Indians did not wish to bear children who would be born into slavery. Hence they practiced birth control by abstaining from sexual intercourse, inducing miscarriages, and practicing infanticide.[76] There are harrowing tales of children being buried alive or killed to feed adult male members of the family.

Although racial intermixing occurred during the early sixteenth century, it did not make as significant a contribution to the decline in the Indian population then as it did in succeeding centuries. The degree of mixing was dependent on the intensity of contact between the races and was stimulated by the predominance of men among the European and black segments of the population. The lack of European women in Latin America in the decades following the Conquest resulted in the emergence of mestizos. Although mixed marriages were legal from 1501, they were not encouraged by the crown. As a result most interracial relationships were of a casual nature, and most of the resulting offspring illegitimate. However, some mestizos were brought up as whites, for there were numerous complaints that "bastard mestizos" had been granted privileges, especially encomiendas, while other worthy colonists had been overlooked.[77] Nevertheless, most of the mestizos were probably brought up as Indians by their Indian mothers. In addition there were large numbers of mestizo orphans. The governor of Nicaragua, Francisco de Castañeda, was said to have cared for fifteen or sixteen mestizo orphans in his own home,[78] and in 1554 the number of mestizo orphans was large enough to prompt the suggestion that special orphanages should be founded for them.[79]

Blacks made an early appearance in Central America. They were imported primarily to perform tasks that were considered too arduous for Indians, though they were also employed as overseers and domestic servants. Although there were a few shipments of black slaves from Africa during this period, most of the blacks were probably introduced from Spain under individual licenses. The numbers introduced under these licenses generally did not exceed five, although in 1527 the city of Granada petitioned the crown to allow colonists to introduce twelve black slaves each.[80] Unfortunately there are no accounts of the numbers of black slaves in Nicaragua at this time.

During the sixteenth century most non-Indians resided in the towns, and it was there that racial mixing occurred most readily. Although the crown discouraged the permanent residence of Indians in Spanish towns by legislation, contact between the races occurred while they were employed there either as *naborías* or in the personal service of encomenderos. Since there is only fragmentary evidence for the numbers of persons of mixed races in Nicaragua during the first half of the sixteenth century, it is difficult to estimate the loss of Indian population that might be attributable to racial mixing, but the qualitative evidence suggests that compared with the other factors described, it was relatively insignificant.

Thus although it is difficult to estimate the precise impact of different factors in the decline of the Indian population and therefore to be certain about their relative importance, the general impression is that the Indian slave trade and disease were of equal importance, perhaps accounting for one-third each of the total decline. The remaining one-third can be attributed to the ill-treatment and overwork of the Indians and to the disruption of Indian communities brought about by Spanish conquest and colonization.

Part Four

COLONIAL CONSOLIDATION AND INDIAN
DECULTURATION, 1550–1720

CHAPTER 8

Centers of European Activity: Towns, Estates, and the English

From the midsixteenth century the nature and distribution of Spanish activities in Nicaragua changed, as did the institutions the Spaniards used to control and exploit the Indians. Once the Indian slave trade and mining had ceased and the decline in the Indian population had reduced the income available from encomiendas, many colonists deserted the province. Those who remained moved to their estates and turned to the development of agriculture. The towns were essentially sustained by their administrative functions and by trade and shipbuilding, which were based on the province's favorable location. While changes in the nature and distribution of Spanish activities made different demands on Indian lands and labor, the encomienda and other official and nonofficial exactions continued to make demands on Indian production. At the same time the arena of Spanish activities expanded eastward as missions were established on the frontier and more Indian villages were brought under Spanish administration. The political control of eastern Nicaragua became more urgent from the midseventeenth century, when the security of the province was threatened by the settlement of the English on the Mosquito Coast.

URBAN CENTERS

In the early sixteenth century towns and cities were essentially administrative centers; very few possessed well-developed economic bases. Their existence and persistence had depended to a large extent on the presence of large Indian populations, which not only provided the day-to-day necessities of domestic service and food, as well as a small income for the encomenderos to whom they paid tribute, but also formed the basis of the Indian slave trade that sustained the coastal ports. The decline in the Indian population thus threatened the existence of many towns.

In most towns and cities their administrative functions helped stem their decline. There were always a number of posts to which *vecinos* could aspire, even if the most important officials were brought in from outside the province and generally from Spain, and the existence of these posts had a multiplier effect on employment opportunities within

127

the city as a whole. León was economically inferior to the second city, Granada, but its administrative functions helped it retain its status as capital city even though it lost many of its citizens when its site was moved in 1610. Given the importance of the administrative functions of towns and cities and the fact that there appears to have been a relationship between the number and type of officials appointed and the decline in the Indian population, it is desirable to discuss their distribution in slightly more detail. León remained the major administrative center in Nicaragua during the late sixteenth and seventeenth centuries, with the governor of the province and treasury officials residing there; the latter had deputies in the towns of Realejo and Granada. In addition each town possessed a cabildo consisting of two alcaldes (magistrates), an alguacil (constable), an *escribano* (notary) and a number of regidores (councilors), the number depending on the size of the town; in Nicaragua in the midseventeenth century the number varied between two and six.[1]

With the exception of alcaldes, who had civil and criminal powers as courts of first instance within the towns' jurisdictions, and treasury officials, who collected tribute from *lavoríos,* contact between most of the royal and local officials and the Indians was probably small. The most important officials as far as the Indians were concerned were the corregidores and the alcaldes mayores. In Nicaragua the number of *corregimientos* varied over time, but the most important four were Monimbo-Masaya, Caçaloaque-Posoltega (later called Sutiaba), Realejo, and Sebaco.[2] Nicoya was subject at times to the rule of the corregidores and at others to alcaldes mayores. Corregidores and alcaldes mayores were probably the worst oppressors of the Indians. They were originally charged with the collection of tribute from crown villages, but later their powers were widened to include the distribution of labor under the repartimiento. They were also given civil and criminal jurisdiction in cases between Indians and Spaniards and those between Indians.[3]

Corregidores and alcaldes mayores were generally appointed for three or five years.[4] The posts were poorly paid, particularly those of corregidores, who received annual salaries of only 150 to 200 pesos. However, the lack of remuneration for these posts and the short term for which they could be held were compensated for by the illegal profits they could yield. Corregidores and alcaldes mayores exercised almost exclusive control over contacts between Spaniards and Indians, and hence they were in a unique position to exploit both parties. They accepted bribes from *vecinos* for access to Indian labor under the repartimiento and for support in court cases. From the Indians they exacted goods and services with little or no payment, and they forced them to buy items of little value at highly inflated prices. Similar forms of bribes and exactions were made by other poorly paid officials, notably *jueces de milpas,* during the exercise of their short terms of office.[5] Given the considerable profits that could be made from various offices and the lack of other opportunities for creating wealth, it is not surprising that, despite the very low salaries paid to officials, there were far more potential officeholders than there were posts available.[6]

Although most of the contacts between the aforementioned officials and Indians occurred in the rural areas, rather than in the towns, the nearer villages were to the residences of officials, the greater the likelihood and degree of exploitation they suffered. Certainly contemporary observers noted the greater decline in the Indian population in areas where corregidores and *jueces de milpas* had been appointed.[7]

In addition to secular officials, the capital city, León, attracted a large number of clergy, both secular and regular. The cathedral was located there, but after the change in the city's site in 1610 and owing to the greater commercial importance of Granada, the bishop requested the transfer of the seat of the bishopric to Granada.[8] Despite a long correspondence between the bishop and the crown, nothing appears to have been done, and the idea was probably put to rest by pirate attacks on Granada in the latter part of the century. These two cities remained the main centers of ecclesiastical activity in Nicaragua, both possessing Franciscan and Mercedarian convents, as well as hospitals of San Juan de Dios.[9]

Despite the extensive secular and ecclesiastical administrative bureaucracies, there were clearly insufficient posts available for all would-be office holders, and other sources of income had to be found. From the beginning of the sixteenth century trade provided a substantial source of income for a small number of individuals and perhaps more than any other factor accounts for the fluctuations in the fortunes and hence size of towns in Nicaragua. Those towns and ports through which trade passed were generally wealthy and had large populations. The most notable were Realejo and Granada. León, on the other hand, according to Dampier, was "a place of no great trade, and therefore not rich in money. Their wealth lies in their pastures, and cattle, and plantations of sugar."[10]

During the first half of the sixteenth century the ports of Puerto de Caballos and Trujillo, on the northern coast of Honduras, flourished as ports of call for the Spanish fleets. Toward the end of the century, however, the fleets stopped there less regularly, exports fell, and the presence of foreign corsairs in Honduran waters increased. As the fortunes of the northern Honduran ports declined, those on the Pacific coast flourished. In 1648, Thomas Gage described Granada as possessing more inhabitants than León, "among whom there are some few merchants of very great wealth, and many of inferior degree very well to pass, who trade with Cartagena, Guatemala, San Salvador and Comayagua and some by the South Sea to Peru and Panama."[11] Chinese goods that had been imported through Acapulco were among the items that passed illegally through Granada and Realejo to Peru.[12] The importance of Realejo was heightened by its shipbuilding activities and by its role as the port of export for pine pitch to Peru.[13] Although the images of both Realejo and Granada were tarnished by the attacks of pirates and corsairs in the 1670s and 1680s, trade recovered quickly afterward, though much of it became contraband.

From the end of the sixteenth century towns and cities began to lose their residents to the rural areas. The causes of this movement are discussed as part of the development of landed estates, but it is interesting to note that for León and Granada a number of noneconomic factors accelerated the process. In León the major period of desertion accompanied its movement to the present-day site in 1610. Many *vecinos* failed to erect houses at the new site, and by the middle of the seventeenth century about three-quarters of its *vecinos* were living on their estates.[14] At that time most of Granada's *vecinos* were living in the town, but the situation changed following pirate attacks. Thus, in 1679, Granada possessed about 200 *vecinos,* but only about 30 were living in the city, while the rest had retreated inland and were living on haciendas or in Indian villages around Masaya, Managua, Nueva Segovia, and the Valley of Nicaragua.[15] Hence in 1711 the bishop of Nicaragua reported that the province's *vecinos* were living "like blind gentiles because, attracted by the abundance and freedom of the countryside, they have gone to live there, leaving almost deserted the towns and villages living on farms, ranches, and in miserable huts, without remembering that they are Christians."[16]

Table 4. Number of Spanish *Vecinos* in Nicaragua, 1571–1723

Towns	1571–74[a]	1570s[b]	1570s[c]	1594[d]	ca. 1620[e]	1646[f]	1683[g]	1723[h]
León	150	62 (37)	60	120	80	50	282[i]	
Granada	200	65 (35)	60	100+	250+	100	200[i]	25–30
Realejo	30	50 (—)	25	30	100	46	77	
Nueva Segovia	40	26 (20)	24	15		50	187	100
Total	420	203 (92)	169	265	430	246	746	

[a] *CDI,* 15: 409–572 no author, n.d.; López de Velasco, *Geografía,* 317–27.
[b] AGI IG 1528 no author, n.d., but written while Villalobos was president of the Audiencia, 1573–78. Encomenderos in brackets.
[c] AGI AG 167 no author, n.d., probably the early 1570s.
[d] Serrano y Sanz, *Relaciones Históricas,* 417–71 Juan de Pineda 1594.
[e] Vázquez de Espinosa, *Compendium,* 235–63.
[f] Díaz de la Calle, *Noticias Sacras,* 125–32.
[g] AGI CO 815 Razón de las ciudades . . . 1683, AG 29 Navia Bolaños 28.7.1685.
[h] AGI Mapas y Planos (AG) 18 Mapa de la Provincia de Honduras . . . Onofre Núñez.
[i] Spaniards and mestizos.

At the same time that Spaniards and people of mixed race were moving to the countryside, Indians were being attracted to the towns. Some Indians settled in the Indian barrios of the major towns; if the towns did not possess distinct Indian barrios, they resided in the homes of their employers. It was not until the seventeenth century that attempts were made to segregate the races by establishing distinct barrios for Indians on the one hand and for mestizos, mulattoes, and blacks on the other. These attempts at racial segregation were never very successful, however, because the races were brought into frequent contact at their places of work. As such the towns emerged as racial and cultural melting pots.

AGRICULTURAL ESTATES

Once the wealth generated by the Indian slave trade, mining and Indian tribute had been exhausted, alternative sources of income had to be found. The acquisition of lands and the development of commercial agriculture appeared to be the main alternative available, and in the 1550s bishop Carrasco concluded that the only way to prevent the mass exodus of Spaniards from Nicaragua to Peru was to import six thousand black slaves for the production of cacao, silk, and cochineal.[17]

There is no doubt that from the second half of the sixteenth century *vecinos* of towns and cities in Nicaragua began taking up residence on their estates and turning their attention to the development of agriculture. MacLeod views the movement of Spaniards to the countryside as a response to the high cost of living in the towns and the lack of opportunities for wealth creation there. He sees the Spaniards as retreating into a semisubsistence form of existence in the rural areas, where they raised a few cattle and grew some maize and sometimes cultivated a small amount of indigo for sale.[18] His argument is similar to that proposed by Chevalier and supported by Wolf for the emergence of the landed estate in Mexico.[19] They see the economic depression in Mexico, particularly in the mining industry, and the decline in commerce with Spain as a result of the recession there, as causing a retreat into self-sufficiency. While Borah acknowledges that Mexico experienced an economic depression during the seventeenth century, he sees the hacienda as emerging in response to increased demands for food at a time when its availability decreased as the Indian population declined. Thus high prices for food stimulated the development of haciendas.[20]

The evidence from Nicaragua is far from clear. While it seems likely that the movement to the countryside was a response to the lack of economic opportunities in the towns—although this may be disputed with respect to Granada and Realejo, where trade maintained a number of

wealthy merchants—not all of those who moved to the countryside retreated into a subsistence form of existence. Cattle raising sustained
some wealthy ranchers, and indigo production was clearly geared to an
external market and was sufficiently profitable to enable the producers
to incorporate fines as part of their running costs. On the other hand,
many hacendados barely scraped a living; in 1691 the *vecinos* of Nicaragua were described as poor, the richest possessing a cattle ranch and
few horses, and many estates were mortgaged or burdened with an-
nuities assigned to the church. [21]

The stimulus for agricultural production came from the external demand for hides and indigo, though there was some difficulty in finding
outlets for the latter toward the end of the seventeenth century. In addition beef began to play a more important role in the local diet, though it is
uncertain whether the development of livestock production was stimulated by rising prices for foodstuffs, particularly maize. As Figure 7 indicates, there was no consistent upward trend in the price of maize at the
end of the sixteenth century; rather, the price fluctuated from year to
year, between the first harvest and the second, and from region to region. In León the average price of maize for the first harvest was between 3 and 4 reals a fanega and between 4 and 5 reals a fanega in Granada, and it was slightly higher in both areas for the second harvest. [22] By
the 1620s, however, it was selling at between 6 and 8 reals. [23]

Although the establishment of estates and the movement of *vecinos*
to the countryside may have been stimulated by the lack of alternative
sources of wealth in the towns, with the exception of trade the enterprises that were established supplied both internal and external markets, and they were not operated purely to supply the subsistence needs
of estates. Part of the confusion in the debate over self-sufficiency and
market orientation arises from the different levels at which they are discussed. Clearly provinces and regions became more self-sufficient in agricultural production in terms of providing for their own needs and in
terms of the percentage of produce going to the internal rather than external market, but few estates operated as self-contained economic units
with no market orientation.

A prerequisite for the development of agriculture was acquisition of
lands. Although land grants had been given to early settlers, most of
them were near the towns of which they were *vecinos* and it was not until
the second half of the sixteenth century that the colonized area expanded, with grants of land being made in remoter parts of the country, particularly to the east and south. Acquisition of lands by Spaniards
often conflicted with Indian claims to lands, and it had other, less direct
disruptive effects on the Indian economy. The degree of conflict between
Spaniards and Indians over the possession and use of land was mitigated

by two factors: first, the decline in the Indian population meant that the Indians no longer required such extensive areas of land for exploitation, even though their needs would not have declined in parallel with the population; second, most of the grasslands had been unutilized or underutilized by the Indians in pre-Columbian times, and the acquisition of these areas by the Spanish thus caused minimal disruption, though the livestock they introduced to them became a menace to Indian agriculture.

Although the crown recognized the rights of Indians to lands they held at the time of the Spanish conquest, by the middle of the sixteenth century they were already being alienated. In 1549 the crown decreed that all lands taken from Indians should be returned[24] and in 1550 ordered that Indians were to be paid adequate sums for land they rented.[25] There were several ways in which Spaniards might acquire Indian lands. First, they could illegally usurp it. This was probably the most common means of acquiring land in the period of confusion immediately following the Conquest, but later it was probably easier to secure it through legal channels, which though theoretically biased in favor of Indian possession, in practice favored non-Indian petitioners.

The second means of acquiring land was through purchase followed by a request for a formal title. Spaniards might purchase land from individual Indians or from caciques acting on behalf of the community. Indians were often forced to sell their lands to meet tribute demands, and in such circumstances encomenderos were in an advantageous position to acquire land. Many land sales were in fact illegal, since individual Indians usually possessed only the usufruct of the land, which was legally the property of the community. Since most Indian lands were communally owned, the pressure to sell was probably greatest on Indian leaders and members of the cabildo, who controlled its allocation.

Even though the sale of communal lands was illegal,[26] there is no doubt that leaders were bribed to sell land either for private gain or to meet tribute demands and other financial obligations of the community. These demands were particularly difficult to meet in times of crisis, such as during an epidemic or famine. Land sales to non-Indians increased during the sixteenth century as the population declined and communal lands fell out of cultivation, thus making more land available, at the same time that Indian communities were finding it increasingly difficult to meet their obligations with a decreased population. The sale of land provided an easy and immediate means of acquiring cash which could be used to purchase food or discharge obligations.

The crown sought to control the sale of Indian lands in the 1530s by ordering that all transactions were to take place before a Spanish judge, and later in 1571 by requiring that all Indian lands should be sold by auction over thirty days to allow higher bids to be made and to prevent

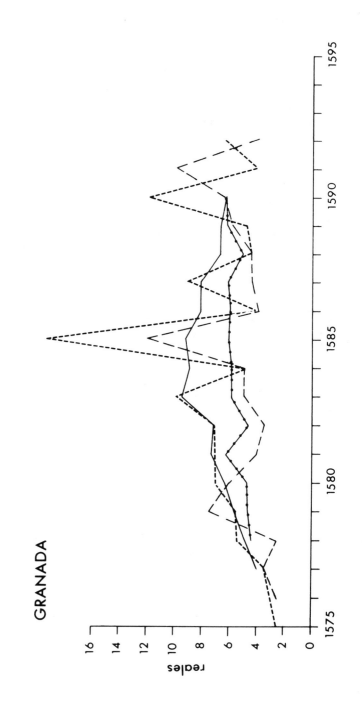

GRANADA

reales

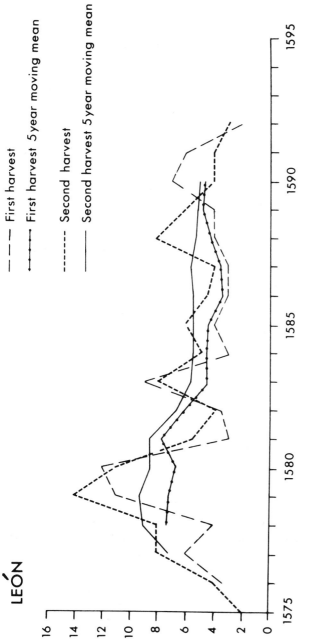

Fig. 7. Prices of royal-tribute maize, 1575–92 (AGI CO 984 and 985).

would-be purchasers from coercing Indians into selling their lands at low prices.[27] The deeds of sale of a piece of land formed the basis on which Spaniards could then petition for title to the land. Despite the previous decrees and the decree that land titles would not be given for lands that had been taken from Indians against their will,[28] there is no doubt that bribery and coercion were rife, and this was one of the means by which Spaniards secured formal titles to Indian lands.

The third means by which Spaniards might acquire lands was through declaring an area unoccupied and requesting a grant. The main stipulation was that the grant should not conflict with the claims or rights of other parties, including Indians.[29] Before the grant was made, the area had to be surveyed, the boundaries marked, and an inquiry held at which Indian communities and neighboring landlords could object. Although Indian communities often objected, sometimes their silence at the inquiry was bought.

In 1591 a decisive piece of legislation was introduced. It consisted of two cedulas. The first cedula ordered that all land that had been illegally occupied by Spaniards was to be returned to the crown. This by itself would have dealt a blow to the illegal occupation of Indian land. The second cedula declared that anyone who possessed land without a legal title could obtain one by paying a fee, or *composición*.[30] At that time considerations of defense were uppermost in the crown's mind, and this was seen as one way of raising revenue. The effect was to legitimize the illegal occupation of Indian lands.[31] The law was to apply not only to lands that had been illegally possessed but also to those that were to be occupied in the future. A common means of obtaining land grants, therefore, particularly from the seventeenth century onward, was to declare a tract of land unoccupied or uncultivated, that is, to make a *denuncia,* and then pay the corresponding *composición*. The land was supposed to be held for ten years without prejudice to a third party before a title could be obtained by payment.[32]

The major problem with the new laws was that many of the lands regarded by the Spaniards as unoccupied in fact played an important role in the Indian economy; these lands might comprise those lying fallow as part of the shifting cultivation cycle, or they could constitute valuable hunting, fishing, and collecting grounds, as well as essential sources of fuel, house-building materials, and sometimes water. In fact, the Spaniards regarded all lands beyond the 600-vara limit and the ejido as fit for occupation even though they fell within the *términos* of the village. One way around the problem was for the Indian community itself to make a *denuncia* and pay the corresponding *composición*. Legally Indian communities were to be favored over private individuals in this respect, but the stronger financial position of most Spanish purchasers would have

Table 5. Land Grants on Which *Media Anatas* Were Paid, 1713–1733

| Jurisdiction | No. | Total *caballerías* | |
		Total area	Average size
León	52	335.0	6.4
Realejo	2	10.0	5.0
Granada	44	622.0	14.1
Nicaragua	29	231.5	8.0
Nicoya	9	49.5	5.5
Nueva Segovia	19	109.0	5.7
Chontales	20	302.5	15.1
Sebaco	4	41.0	10.3
Total	179	1,700.5	9.5

Source: AGI AG 252. Where possible the location of the grant rather than the residence of the person to whom the grant was made has been used. In some instances where the location of the grant is uncertain, the residence of the recipient has been used. The boundaries of the jurisdictions are similarly unclear, particularly with respect to the division between Granada and Chontales. In the calculation of the total area fractions of smaller than one-half *caballería* were ignored.

enabled them to pay higher *composiciones,* which would have ensured the success of their claims.

Evidence for the size and location of land grants, as well as the cost of lands in Nicaragua, is extremely fragmentary. Although a small number of titles to lands granted between 1694 and 1720 are to be found in the Archivo General de Centro América in *legajos* A1.24 1569–1583, it is difficult to obtain a general view of their character and distribution over time. The only comprehensive evidence that exists is for 1713 to 1733, and it comes from the lists of *media anatas* paid on lands when titles were granted.[33] During this period 179 grants were made. Most (78 percent) of the grants were of 10 *caballerías* and under, and nearly half (49 percent) were of 5 *caballerías* and under. The largest grant was of 193 *caballerías,* which was given to a *vecino* of Granada, but in this instance the owner had possessed the land for a long time without a title. Slightly larger grants were made in Chontales and Sebaco, and slightly smaller ones in the hinterlands of León and Nueva Segovia, which had been colonized at an early date. The high average figure for land grants in the jurisdiction of Granada is influenced by the one very large grant of 193 *caballerías.* If this figure is excluded, then the average falls to 10 *caballerías,* making it fairly comparable to that found in the jurisdiction of Nicaragua; both areas were developed for livestock raising from the end of the seventeenth century.

Within the separate jurisdictions there were considerable variations in the size of land grants. The size does not appear to have varied between Spaniards and Indians, though there were far fewer grants to Indians. Some of the largest grants were given to the church or its members; in 1714 the Mercedarian Convent in Nicaragua received a grant of 28 *caballerías* in Chontales, and in 1729 a parish priest secured a grant of 41 *caballerías* in the same region.

The extension of the colonized area in Nicaragua occurred in two directions: first, eastward to the lush grasslands of Chontales; second, south to the Isthmus of Rivas and Nicoya. During the seventeenth century cattle from the Pacific coastal plain were pastured on the grasslands of Chontales during the dry season, but toward the end of the century ranchers, mainly from Granada, began requesting formal land grants in the area, many of which were fairly extensive.[34] The movement south to the Isthmus of Rivas began at an earlier date, when *vecinos* of Granada established cacao plantations and livestock ranches in the area. It continued south through the century, arriving in Nicoya at the beginning of the eighteenth century.[35] In Nicaragua land shortages do not appear to have been a major problem, though of course there were conflicts, particularly between Spaniards and Indians, over the ownership of desirable stretches of land. A more significant problem was the shortage of labor.

From 1549, Indians were no longer required to perform labor services for their encomenderos, and the repartimiento was introduced with the aim of ensuring a supply of labor for all approved tasks, which included most agricultural activities; work in sugar mills and indigo works was banned. Unfortunately there were never enough Indians to supply all the demands made upon them, and for most estate owners the introduction of black slaves on a large scale was not an economical proposition. Although colonists complained bitterly about the lack of black slaves to perform agricultural tasks, there were few requests for imports except in the sixteenth century, when they were establishing commercial enterprises. Their complaints were largely used to justify forms of Indian labor that were unacceptable to the crown.

Since the repartimiento failed to supply estate owners with the agricultural labor they required, employers soon resorted to encouraging or coercing Indians to work for them as private employees. By the end of the seventeenth century wage labor had emerged as the dominant labor system in agriculture.[36] In addition, estate owners employed a small number of free blacks and people of mixed race. These workers commanded higher wages, and their footloose existence made them an unreliable source of labor. By the end of the seventeenth century most estates probably possessed a few black slaves, who were employed mainly as household servants; a few free blacks and persons of mixed race, who undertook supervisory activities; and a larger number of Indian workers, mostly free laborers, who were either resident on the estate or worked as day laborers.

The production of crops for export had been undertaken only halfheartedly in the early sixteenth century. Spanish interest had focused on the Indian slave trade and mining, both of which promised quicker and more substantial profits. At that time agricultural production centered on livestock raising. This was encouraged by the presence of extensive and largely unutilized grasslands, by the existence of internal markets in the mining areas and ports for animals and animal products, and by the demand for animals during the conquest and colonization of Peru. Nevertheless, production remained at a low level, and few ranchers made great fortunes from the activity.

During the second half of the sixteenth century the search began for products that might be produced commercially. It was inevitable that cacao, which had been one of the most important crops in pre-Columbian times, should be the first to be considered, even though there were important cacao-producing areas farther north, in Soconusco and Zapotitlán, and there was only a small market for chocolate in Mexico and Europe.[37] Bishop Carrasco observed that sixty leagues of land along the Pacific coast of Nicaragua constituted more extensive and better cacao land than that in Guatemala.[38] However, a major problem with the development of cacao production in Nicaragua was that it required high labor inputs. Although cacao is not normally labor-intensive, the local cacao trees were not very hardy and needed constant care and attention. Furthermore, the cacao groves established on the Pacific coastal plain required irrigation during the dry season.[39] As the Indian population declined, the cacao groves could not be maintained, and fewer Indians were left to revive production. As early as the midsixteenth century it was estimated that to reestablish the cultivation of cacao and other crops in Nicaragua would require six thousand black slaves.[40] Its cultivation was also constrained by the capital required to establish cacao groves, because the slow maturation of the crop meant that profits could be realized only after seven to eight years. For these reasons cacao never became a major export crop, though it was produced on a small scale.[41]

In the major cacao-producing areas of Soconusco and Zapotitlán cacao cultivation remained in Indian hands, and the Spaniards obtained the crop from them in the form of tribute or by trade.[42] In Nicaragua cacao production passed into the hands of the Spaniards, who employed Indians to cultivate it.[43] The control of cacao production by the Spaniards may have been encouraged by the inadequacy of Indian production largely brought about by the decline in the Indian population. The Spaniards generally acquired already established groves from Indians by purchase, by illegal occupation, or in payment of tribute or other debts.[44] Initially cacao production was concentrated around Granada, but later cacao groves were established farther south on the Isthmus of Rivas and in the Valley of Nicaragua, mostly by *vecinos* from Granada. Vázquez de Espinosa maintained that the best cacao was produced on the slopes of the Mombacho Volcano.[45] Despite efforts to expand the production of cacao, it never became an important item of export, and it even failed to meet local needs. In 1626, in an effort to protect cacao production in Central America, a ban was placed on the import of cheap cacao from Guayaquil. While other provinces were glad of the protection the ban provided, Nicaragua complained that it suffered from shortages of cacao and that the export of indigo, pitch, and tobacco depended on the importation of cacao from Peru.[46] Later the demand for cacao in Nicaragua was met by imports from the Matina coast of Costa Rica and by contraband trade through the Mosquito Coast.[47] As well as being used to make drinking chocolate, cacao beans continued to be used as a medium of exchange throughout the seventeenth century.[48]

Two products associated with cacao production in pre-Columbian times were vanilla (*Vanilla planifolia* Andr.) and achiote (*Bixa orellana* L.), which were used for flavoring and coloring chocolate, respectively. Although vanilla could probably have been developed as an export crop, particularly on the Pacific coastal plain,[49] as an epiphyte it is difficult to produce commercially, and in Central America its production appears to have been dominated by Oaxaca.[50] However, at the beginning of the eighteenth century the very high prices for vanilla in Europe appear to have stimulated the governor of Nicaragua to order Indians in the village of Nicaragua and on Ometepe island to produce vanilla and achiote.[51]

Although indigo dye was used by the Indians in Nicaragua in pre-Columbian times, it was not until the last quarter of the sixteenth century that it emerged as an item of commercial value to supplant cacao. In 1558 samples of the plant, including details of its cultivation, were requested by the crown in the hope that it could be developed as a source of blue dye, for which there was a demand in Spain.[52] The commercial production of indigo in Central America appears to have begun in Nicaragua in the early 1570s, when small amounts were exported to New Spain to be used for dyeing cloth; at that time indigo dye was worth 1 peso (of 12 reals) a fanega in Nicaragua, while in New Spain it was worth about three times as much (7 to 8 tostones).[53] By 1577, 100 quintals (2,500 pounds), were being exported from Nicaragua, and two years later, in anticipation of increased indigo production there, the president of the audiencia requested the importation of 400 to 500 black slaves, arguing that taxes on indigo dye over two years would more than pay for them.[54] In 1583 the governor declared indigo Nicaragua's major product.[55] The Pacific coastal plain was the most important area of production, though cultivation occurred around Managua, and there is even evidence for its production in Nueva Segovia.[56] While indigo production began in Nicaragua, more important areas of cultivation emerged farther north in San Salvador and to a lesser extent in southeast Guatemala and southern Honduras.

The species of indigo plant originally grown was probably *Indigofera suffruticosa* Mill., the more common Southeast Asian *Indigofera tinctoria* L. being introduced at a later date. The plant was known in Central America by its Nahuatl name *xiquilite*, while the dye it produced was known as *añil* or *tinta añil*. In the early stages of the development of indigo production the indigo processing works, known as *obrajes*, depended on the collection of leaves from wild indigo plants, but with the realization that indigo could become an important commercial crop, lands were purchased and dedicated to its cultivation. Although cultivated indigo thus became the major source of supply for the *obrajes*, as late as the eighteenth century Indians were still being sent into the mountains to collect wild indigo.[57]

The cultivation of indigo plants and their processing to form blocks of dye are described in detail in contemporary accounts.[58] The cultivation of indigo began with the burning of the land, over which the seeds were then broadcast and trampled into the soil by cattle or horses. Sowing normally took place at the beginning of the rainy season, in April or May, to take advantage of the rains. After an initial period of weeding, the weeds were kept down by grazing livestock, which do not eat indigo plants. The leaves of the plant were not normally picked in their first year of growth but were harvested in the July of the following year. The plants could last for up to ten years, but the quality of dye they produced declined after three years. From this short description of its cultivation, it is clear that indigo possessed two advantages over other crops, particularly cacao. First, it could be easily combined with livestock raising, which had already demonstrated its success in many areas where indigo cultivation was introduced. Second, it required only a small investment of capital and a small seasonal supply of labor.

The process of making indigo dye began with the collection of the leaves, which were then placed in vats, known as *pilas* or *canoas*, and steeped in water for about twenty-four hours or until the water turned blue. At this stage the water was drained into another vat, the rotting leaves being left behind. The water was then beaten with wooden poles or sticks; initially the beating was done by Indians, who stood in the water; later the beaters were driven by water- or horsepower. After several hours of beating, the dye was left to settle before it was scooped out and placed in linen cloths to strain out the water. Finally the dye was dried in the sun, after which it was divided into blocks for sale. Tasks of different degrees of skill were involved in the processing of indigo; relatively unskilled Indians, and to a lesser extent persons of mixed race, were employed on a seasonal basis to bring the leaves to the processing works in carts or on horseback, but the timing of the different processes involved in making the dye was a skilled job in which free laborers, either blacks or persons of mixed race, were generally employed. Particularly important was the task of judging the point at which the beating of the liquid should stop and the dye allowed to settle; over- or underbeating could adversely affect the quality of the dye.

Although indigo production possessed many advantages over other economic activities, it had one disadvantage, which was noted from the beginning: the unhealthy character of the method of processing.[59] The draining of the first vats, the removal of the rotting leaves, and the beating of the water in the second vats very often forced workers to stand for several hours in warm water that gave off vapors and caused colds and other respiratory infections. In addition, the rotting leaves attracted insects, which spread disease and helped to earn the *obrajes* the reputation of being unhealthy places of work.[60] Even though the construction of self-draining vats and the use of water- and horsepower helped improve conditions in the processing plants, their reputation remained with them. The early recognition of the unhealthiness of indigo processing resulted in a ban on the employment of repartimiento labor in *obrajes*.[61] Until 1601, Indians could work there voluntarily, but after that date the employment of Indians in *obrajes* was banned completely.[62] At first *obrajeros* tried to seek alternative sources of labor. In the 1580s there were many petitions to the crown requesting the introduction of black slaves or the removal of the 1581 ban on the grounds that it had resulted in the "ruin and total destruction" of the province.[63] An advantage of importing black slaves was that indigo production only required labor for several months a year, and the rest of the time they could be employed in other activities, such as, it was suggested, shipbuilding.[64] Black slaves were not sought after by many producers, however. Slaves were an expensive proposition, particularly for owners who could not usefully employ them in complementary economic activities. Most indigo planters preferred to use Indian labor illegally and employ free laborers as they could. Although following the ban on the employment of Indians in *obrajes* in 1601 alcaldes were charged with undertaking annual tours of inspection of indigo works and taking proceedings against those who were suspected of having used Indian labor, the threat of being fined did not deter employers. Many claimed that they had not used Indians to work inside the *obrajes* but only to bring in plants from the fields; others tried to shift the blame onto their overseers. Generally, however, indigo producers accepted the fines that were imposed on them; they were not very high, and they could often be reduced by bribing the inspector. The fines were incorporated in the running costs of the enterprise and represented a smaller outlay than the importation of black slaves would have required. Thus with high profits to be made in indigo production, fines failed to check the illegal employment of Indians in *obrajes,* about which higher officials, ecclesiastics, and Indians themselves continued to complain.[65]

The production of indigo expanded at the end of the sixteenth and beginning of the seventeenth centuries, but during the remainder of the latter century it seems to have stagnated owing mainly to difficulties of access to markets in Europe. Initially indigo from Central America was transported to ports on the northern Honduran coast or to Portobello and Cartagena by way of Granada and the Desaguadero. However, with the penetration of pirates and corsairs into the area and the breakdown of the Spanish commercial system, which resulted in fewer vessels with smaller cargoes sailing to Latin America, priority was given to the ports through which silver was shipped to Spain, notably Veracruz and Portobello; thereafter trade with Central America became irregular and hence unreliable. Given the unreliability of trade on the northern coast of Honduras, indigo producers in Central America began to ship their produce through Granada, which became the major port of export for indigo.[66] The route from Granada by way of the Desaguadero was not ideal, however, since only small vessels could be used, and, more important, it was vulnerable to pirate attacks, which were at their peak between 1660 and 1685. Despite the difficulties of finding markets for indigo, its production continued throughout the century, and gradually new outlets were found in the form of foreign traders whose presence increased in Caribbean waters.[67]

Another dyestuff that became a minor export was cochineal. Cochineal is produced from the dead bodies of insects that are cultivated on the tuna or nopal cactus, which itself might be wild or cultivated. The techniques of cochineal production appear to have been developed by the Indians of Mixteca and Oaxaca in pre-Columbian times, and those areas remained the most important centers of production during the colonial period.[68] Spaniards showed a reluctance to become involved in the techniques of production, which consisted of raising and drying the insects at the rate of about 70,000 insects per pound of dye; they preferred to allow the Indians to produce the cochineal and then obtain it from them by trade.[69] It seems likely that the techniques of cochineal production were known to Indians in Nicaragua in pre-Columbian times, but if they were not, they were introduced soon after the Conquest. Cochineal was being produced in Nicaragua in 1586, very good cochineal powder being made in Managua.[70] In 1595 the crown ordered the authorities in Central

America to encourage the planting of tuna cactuses for the production of cochineal, and small quantities were produced for export throughout the seventeenth century.[71] Despite further efforts to promote the production of cochineal in 1709, it never became more than a minor product.[72]

Although physical conditions in Nicaragua were suitable for the cultivation of sugar, sugar production never provided for more than a small proportion of domestic needs. There were two main reasons for this. First, sugar was a bulky product, and the costs of transport rose rapidly with distance from markets. Thus sugar produced in Central America could not compete in European markets with that produced in the nearer Caribbean islands. Second, even if the profits from sugar production had been high, the establishment of a sugar mill required a high investment of capital, and few residents in Nicaragua possessed the necessary financial resources. Some sugar was produced in the jurisdiction of León, particularly near Chichigalpa, and small quantities were grown in Nueva Segovia.[73] In 1684 sugar production in Nicaragua was summarized by its governor as follows: "There are no more enterprises and products than some livestock and in the same haciendas some 4 or 5 residents sow a little sugar cane without the form of a mill in which some harvest 20 or 30 arrobas [500–750 pounds] all so little that it does not supply the province for a quarter of the year."[74] The demand for sugar was met by imports from Peru.[75]

A crop that was produced for export but to which there are few references during the period under study was tobacco (*Nicotiana tabacum* L.). This crop was mainly grown in eastern Nicaragua, where it was suited to the cooler and wetter climatic conditions.[76] It was exported to Spain by way of Portobello and Cartagena and exchanged for cacao coming from Peru.[77]

When the Spaniards turned their attention to agriculture, their intention was to produce for external markets, mainly Spain, and to rely on Indian agriculture for their own subsistence needs. This clear-cut distinction in the orientation of Spanish and Indian production was never realized; as already indicated, commercial crops had difficulty reaching external markets, and production tended to languish and shift to those crops for which there was an internal market. These included subsistence crops, particularly maize and beans, which were not being supplied in sufficient quantities by the Indians. Although the Spaniards had a preference for wheat flour, wheat could not be grown easily in Nicaragua and had to be imported, mainly from Costa Rica. Consequently it was always more expensive than maize. In 1649 in Nicaragua wheat cost one real a pound, whereas one real could buy fourteen to eighteen pounds of maize; most Spaniards became resigned to eating maize tortillas.[78]

During the late sixteenth and seventeenth centuries livestock production expanded to become one of the most important agricultural activities in Nicaragua. The early importance of livestock raising is indicated by the fact that in 1586 there were said to be three kinds of people in Granada; encomenderos, merchants and traders, and cattle ranchers.[79] Cattle were raised mainly for their hides and tallow, which were exported to Spain,[80] but they also provided meat for the internal market in Nicaragua and neighboring provinces. Cattle raising expanded rapidly during the sixteenth century, and by 1608 there were said to be 80 *hatos* (ranches) around Granada, many of which contained 2,500 to 3,000 cattle.[81]

Despite the expansion in cattle raising, by the end of the century shortages of meat were common in the major cities of Central America and especially in Santiago de Guatemala. Blame for this state of affairs was placed on a variety of factors: the concentration of production on hides for export, the indiscriminate slaughter of animals in the countryside, lack of animal care, the unorganized system of marketing, and finally the rise in the consumption of meat by Indians. In an attempt to overcome shortages of meat, ordinances were introduced restricting the slaughter of animals to Spanish towns, where the pricing and marketing of the meat was organized and monopolized by a *veedor*, whose post was auctioned.[82]

It is clear that the meat shortages mainly affected Santiago de Guatemala, and citizens of Nicaragua objected to the new ordinances since there were no shortages of meat there. In Nicaragua meat was cheap: a cow could be bought for three to four pesos, and one real could buy 16 to 50 pounds of meat.[83] But even if there were no shortages of meat in Nicaragua, some of the criticisms of the lack of animal husbandry were justified. Cattle were often hunted down like wild animals, stripped of their hides and tallow, and a daily ration of meat taken; the rest was left to rot. Peons were sometimes employed to round up cattle and provide rudimentary care for sick animals,[84] but little attention was given to the improvement of pastures. Instead, a form of transhumance was practiced, cattle in the jurisdiction of Granada being moved in the dry season to the lush grasslands around Lake Granada and to the more inaccessible Chontales.[85] Furthermore, there were many cattle rustlers and hunters of feral cattle, particularly in the east.[86]

Next in importance to cattle were mules and horses.[87] They were used in small numbers in sugar milling and in the collection of indigo, but most important was their use for transport. From the end of the sixteenth century the mule-raising industry developed to supply the mule trains that plied the route from San Salvador, San Miguel, and Choluteca through Nicaragua and south to Costa Rica and Panama. It also supplied the mule trains that traveled across the Isthmus of Panama, and merchants from Costa Rica, Panama, and Colombia went to Nicaragua to buy mules.[88]

MINING

Mineral production declined so markedly in Nicaragua in the late sixteenth century that in 1583 the governor of Nicaragua, Hernando Casco, claimed that neither gold nor silver was mined in the country.[89] This was a slight exaggeration, for some miners were still panning gold in Nueva Segovia, where silver deposits were also found in the 1570s. Nevertheless, because of shortages of labor, production remained at a very low level.[90] In 1573 only 865 pesos of gold or silver were smelted, though production appears to have risen to 4,033 pesos of silver bars, or *planchas,* in 1597.[91] Virtually nothing is heard of the mining industry in Nicaragua until the end of the seventeenth century, when gold mines were rediscovered in Nueva Segovia in 1699.[92]

SHIPBUILDING AND THE PINE-PITCH INDUSTRY

Shipbuilding in Nicaragua was concentrated on the Pacific coast, mainly at Realejo, but also at Cosiguina and San Juan del Sur.[93] The dockyards stood on deep-water harbours, and in the hinterlands were good supplies of materials for the construction of vessels—good hardwoods that were resistant to burrowing insects and worms, pitch for caulking, various forms of canvas cloth for sails, and many types of cables and cords, all manufactured by the Indians. Many royal vessels were constructed in Realejo, including two galleons for the Manila fleet, while smaller ships were built for the coast traffic between Mexico and Panama.[94] Initially Indians were employed both in cutting wood and in constructing the vessels, but the employment of Indians in the former activity was banned in 1579 because it took a heavy toll of the Indian population.[95] Although henceforth Indians were largely replaced with free labor or black slave labor, a century later corregidores were still coercing Indians to work in shipbuilding.[96] Although ships were built at Realejo throughout the seventeenth century, the industry declined slightly toward the end of the century in the face of competition from the shipyards at Guayaquil and in the Philippines, and when the Pacific trade declined as ships were harassed by pirates.[97]

The extensive stands of pine trees that the Spaniards encountered in Nueva Segovia became an important source of pitch, which was used for caulking ships and lining wine barrels.[98] Although some of the pitch was consumed in the local shipyards, probably most was transported to Peru by way of Realejo, where it was exchanged for Peruvian cacao and wine. Small amounts were shipped north to Acapulco by way of Realejo and Amapala and south through Granada to Panama.[99] Although the techniques of production were rather primitive, the pitch being extracted in crude ovens, the profits from its manufacture were high. Vázquez de Espinosa noted that, while a quintal of pitch was worth 20 reals in Realejo, in Callao it fetched 96 reals, which, discounting the cost of transport, enabled merchants to make a profit of about 30 reals on every quintal. The pine-pitch trade was said to have made many men rich.[100] By 1647 the production of pitch in Nueva Segovia had reached 22,000 to 23,000 quintals a year and had become so profitable that a suggestion was made, though not followed, that the crown should take over the industry, making contracts with individuals for its production in return for a percentage of the profits.[101] The employment of forced labor in the manufacture and transport of pitch was banned in 1564, and the order was repeated in 1649.[102] By that time, however, most of the labor was undertaken by free workers, including Indians. An attempt to limit their employment in the industry to six months a year, to allow them to attend to their plots, provoked the response that in Nueva Segovia the transport of tar and pitch was the Indians' main source of income.[103] Although pitch was produced throughout the century, production declined slightly with the decline of the shipbuilding industry and trade with Peru, and possibly with the exhaustion of some of the pine forests.

ENGLISH ACTIVITIES ON THE MOSQUITO COAST

For both ideological and practical reasons Spain sought to prohibit "foreigners" from settling and trading in the New World.[104] Nevertheless, owing to the lack of skilled personnel in the peninsula, the crown was obliged to grant special licences to foreign merchants, sailors, and miners to sail to and settle in the New World. Thus from the earliest years of colonial rule in Central America a small number of foreigners, mainly seamen and miners, were present in the area. Most of them were Roman Catholics, mostly Portuguese and Italians; the English, French, and Dutch were officially excluded because they were Protestants and political rivals, but they arrived in Central America as raiders and smugglers. It was this last group of foreigners that had the greatest impact on Indian life in Nicaragua.

From the middle of the sixteenth century foreign corsairs led by the French and later the English attacked Spanish vessels and ports. Trujillo and Puerto de Caballos were particularly vulnerable to attack since there the Spanish fleets took on board goods produced in Central America and supplied it with European manufactures. Despite efforts to protect vessels and ports from attack by changing the routes of ships, providing coastguards, and fortifying the established ports, these raids became a fact of life during the late sixteenth century.[105]

Several factors contributed to a lull in the activities of corsairs at the beginning of the seventeenth century. Spanish trade was concentrated on the newly constructed and more easily defended port of Santo Tomás de Castilla, in the Bay of Amatique, while the attention of Europeans was focused on the colonization of North America, the Guianas, and the unoccupied islands in the Caribbean. In addition the stimulus for attacking Spanish settlements and trade routes was reduced by European peace treaties.[106] Conversely, the outbreak of war between England and Spain in 1625 encouraged the revival of piratical activities and renewed efforts at establishing settlements within Spanish territory as a means of weakening its power. While attacks by corsairs continued on the northern coast of Honduras, several English settlements were established by the Providence Company.[107]

The English first settled in Providencia in 1629, and within five years they had occupied the islands of Tortuga and Roatán and had established settlements in Belize and at Cabo de Gracias a Dios and Bluefields. Within a short time the Spaniards managed to drive the English from their establishments on the islands—from Tortuga in 1635, from Providencia in 1641, and from Roatán in 1642—but those on the Mosquito Coast and in Belize remained. In 1655 these setbacks for the English were in part compensated for by the seizure of Jamaica, which became a vital base from which attacks and colonizing expeditions could be mounted.

The most outrageous attacks were perpetrated on the major cities of Nicaragua. Granada suffered the most, being easily accessible from the Caribbean coast by way of the San Juan River and also offering most in terms of booty. Many of the goods exported from Central America no longer went through the northern Honduran ports but passed south to Granada and through the Desaguadero to the Caribbean coast to meet the fleets in Portobello and Cartagena before sailing to Spain. The first attacks took place in 1665 and 1666, and despite the completion of Fort San Carlos in 1667 another attack occurred in 1670.[108] The Spaniards replied by building the massive Fort Inmaculada Concepción on the San Juan River. Although the heavily defended fort effectively blocked the easy passage of corsairs up the San Juan River, it was not difficult for them to cross the narrow isthmus farther south and approach the city from the Pacific side. This they did in 1685. Eight months later the cities of León and Realejo were sacked, the former having scarcely recovered from an earlier attack in 1681.[109]

CHAPTER 9

Institutions and Mechanisms of Control and Exploitation: Encomiendas and Missions

During the first half of the sixteenth century Indians in the Mesoamerican zone were brought under Spanish control and allocated in encomiendas, but those in the South American zone had only irregular contacts with the Spaniards. From the mid-sixteenth century onward, however, the boundary of the Spanish-controlled area was gradually extended eastward; more Indian communities were brought under Spanish administration and granted in encomiendas, while missions were established on the frontier. Nevertheless, for most of the colonial period many Indians in the eastern Nicaragua remained outside Spanish control, and from the middle of the seventeenth century onward the greatest influence on their way of life was the presence of the English on the Mosquito Coast.

THE ENCOMIENDA

In the early sixteenth century the encomienda was the most influential institution on Indian life, but from that time onward its importance declined. Even though the crown failed to abolish the encomienda in 1542, throughout the colonial period it sought to limit the power of encomenderos by taking over the administration of encomiendas, controlling the amount of tribute that encomenderos could exact, and abolishing their privileged access to Indian labor. Encomiendas also declined in importance because the amount of tribute and labor they could yield fell with the dwindling Indian population. Moreover, from the Indians' point of view tribute became a less significant burden than many other demands that were made upon them, and the repartimiento and free labor assumed greater importance in terms of the numbers of Indians they involved and their impact on native communities. Despite the decline in the importance of the encomienda, it persisted into the eighteenth century long after it had been abolished in other parts of the empire. It seems likely that its survival in Nicaragua, as in Chile and in Paraguay, was due to the economic backwardness of the area.

Part of Cerrato's task as president of the audiencia from 1548 was to revise the allocation of the encomiendas and to redistribute those that had fallen vacant since the passing of the New Laws in 1542.[1] In the revision of the allocation a number of smaller encomiendas were confiscated from encomenderos for levying too much tribute, for ill-treating Indians, and for exporting them from the province.[2] In the redistribution conquistadors and first settlers and their wives and children were to be preferred, and in 1549, Cerrato reported that he had given seven encomiendas to "poor conquistadors."[3] There were, however, numerous complaints from colonists that in the reallocation Cerrato had favored his relatives and friends: for example, Nindirí, one of the largest encomiendas in Nicaragua, which Las Casas estimated yielded an annual income of 6,500 pesos, was given to his brother Dr. Cerrato. This encomienda was substantial by the standards of Nicaragua, and early conquistadors and settlers, who did not possess encomiendas, justifiably complained bitterly. However, the attacks on Cerrato were probably more vicious than the offenses warranted and reflected the colonists' general dissatisfaction with his reforms, which included the emancipation of Indian slaves and the moderation of tribute. Nepotism was after all a fact of life in Central America. Notwithstanding the hyperbole of the accusations, it is true to say that Cerrato did little to modify the prevailing allocation of encomiendas, and in particular he failed to break up the larger encomiendas to provide for a greater number of deserving people, as colonists had hoped.[4]

Initially encomiendas were granted for two years, but in New Spain the crown permitted extensions for three lives in 1555 and four lives in 1607.[5] It is uncertain, however, whether encomiendas were ever granted for three or four lives in Central America. In 1637 the crown ordered that encomiendas were to be granted for two lives only, and confirmations of titles to encomiendas in Nicaragua recorded between 1615 and 1675 indicate that they were granted for only that period.[6] Encomiendas were not to be given to those living outside the jurisdiction of the audiencia, nor were they to be held in two provinces.[7] While the former order was seldom contravened, many were held in two provinces. The list of encomiendas in the audiencia in 1662 indicates that 35 percent of those who held encomiendas in Nicaragua also possessed villages in other provinces, particularly Chiapas; Guatemala, especially Chiquimula; San Miguel; and San Salvador. These encomiendas generally yielded higher annual incomes averaging about 840 pesos, while those composed solely of villages in Nicaragua averaged only 350 pesos.[8] Even within Nicaragua villages comprising one encomienda might be many miles apart, thus making the obligations of the encomendero difficult to meet.

The number, size, and value of encomiendas declined steadily through the colonial period. From 95 in 1548 the number had fallen to 66 in 1581 and 52 in 1662.[9] The decline must have been even more marked in areas where encomiendas had been granted at an early date, since the figures for 1581 and 1662 include villages, mainly in eastern Nicaragua, that were incorporated from the second half of the sixteenth century onward as a result of missionary and colonizing expeditions. The number of encomiendas declined with the Indian population and as they were amalgamated to form encomiendas of sufficient size to justify the provision of a parish priest.[10] Compared with the amalgamation in other areas within the audiencia, however, the degree of amalgamation in Nicaragua was small because, despite population decline, many villages remained large enough to form separate encomiendas. In fact, some villages could provide for several encomenderos; in 1662, Managua was divided between nine encomenderos.[11] Most encomiendas in Nicaragua were, however, composed of one or two villages, or *parcialidades*. One reason for the decline in the number of encomiendas was that villages were not always reallocated when they reverted to the crown. Nevertheless, during the late sixteenth and seventeenth centuries the percentage of Indian villages and *parcialidades* paying tribute to the crown did not change significantly.[12] The income from vacant *encomiendas* was used for defensive purposes; for wine and oil for churches, convents, and monasteries; and for pensions and *ayudas de costa*.[13] By the beginning of the eighteenth century about 20 percent of the total income from Indian tribute, including that received by individuals, was spent on defense within the audiencia. It was used to fortify San Felipe del Golfo and San Juan on the Desaguadero, to protect the port of Trujillo, and to support the Armada de Barlovento.[14] To compensate for the loss of personal encomiendas, the crown granted fixed sums in the form of pensions and *ayudas de costa* to deserving colonists, their wives, and their children, and in this way it was able to provide a small income for a larger number of people. The number of encomiendas, pensions, and *ayudas de costa* assigned was restricted after 1687, when a moratorium was placed on new allocations until enough income had been obtained from vacant encomiendas to provide for the needs of defense. By 1703 the amount collected was insufficient.[15] In 1701 the crown ordered that all encomiendas held in absentia were to revert to the crown on the death of the owner, and finally in 1718 the encomienda as a grant to a private individual was abolished. The crown argued that the conditions under which encomiendas had been granted at the time of the Conquest no longer prevailed; there were no soldiers to be remunerated for their services, and it was no longer necessary to make special provision for the instruction of Indians.[16] Although personal encomiendas were abolished, the provision of pensions continued.

Gradually during the colonial period, therefore, the number of personal encomiendas declined. In 1581 88.5 percent of the villages and *parcialidades* in Nicaragua were held by private individuals, but by 1704

Table 6. Assignment of Indian Villages and
"Value" of Indian Tribute, 1704

Assigned to	Villages or parcialidades		Value in terms of the servicio del tostón *		
	No.	Percent	Tostón	Real	Percent
Private individuals	22.2	19.3	1,775	2	32.3
Crown	20.0	17.4	1,041	0	18.9
Defense	18.1	15.7	1,103	1	20.0
Wine and oil	1.2	1.1	76	2	1.4
Vacant	53.5	46.5	1,506	3	27.4
Total	115.0	100.0	5,503	0	100.0

Source: AGCA A3.16 146 989 tasaciones 1704.
*As a capitation tax the *servicio del tostón* can be used as a rough guide to the size of encomiendas but not to their total value, because there were spatial variations in the amount of tribute paid by the Indians.

the figure had fallen to 19.3 percent, though the latter accounted for 32.3 percent of the total income from Indian tribute.[17] In 1662 only eight of the thirty-three encomiendas that were composed solely of Indian villages in Nicaragua were worth more than five hundred pesos, the limit placed on the value of encomiendas in 1687.[18] The income from encomiendas in Nicaragua had never been great, and it declined with the Indian population. Their value was also reduced by tighter official control over the amount of tribute that could be levied and because tribute income was subject to the tithe.[19] During the seventeenth century the crown imposed further levies on encomenderos to increase revenue. From 1631 recipients of encomiendas had to pay the *media anata* before receiving confirmation of their titles, and in 1636 those wishing to extend the possession of an encomienda for a second or third life had to pay the total income for the first two or three years after receiving the concession.[20] Other levies were also made for defensive purposes. In 1684 a 5 percent tax was imposed on all encomenderos to pay for the fortification of the San Juan river, and between 1687 and 1694 encomenderos were required to pay the *media anata* each year to help pay the costs of defense.[21] It was levied again for two years from 1703. The encomienda had become a less attractive proposition.

When official tribute assessments were introduced from the 1530s, the task of assessment was encharged to *oidores* of the audiencia. An *oidor* was expected to visit Indian villages, count the number of tributary Indians, assess the quality of the land, and note the crops grown by the community.[22] If it was impossible for an *oidor* to visit villages in his juris-diction because of their distant location and the cost of visiting them, as was common in Nicaragua, the responsibility for the count lay with gov-ernors, alcaldes mayores, and corregidores within their respective juris-dictions, while the assessment remained with the *oidor*.[23] Counts were supposed to be made every three years and whenever an encomienda was reassigned. In 1591 an annual capitation tax of four reals known as the *servicio del tostón* was introduced to help pay the costs of defense, and after that date counts were to be made every year.[24] The *tasación* had to be approved by the cacique and a copy of it kept in the Indian village, while other copies were to be lodged with the encomendero and the audiencia.[25] A recount or reassessment could be requested at any time by any one of the three parties involved,[26] but the process was long, and the petitioner had to pay the costs. It seems likely that the abuses involved in tribute assessments documented by Zorita for New Spain were also common in Nicaragua.[27] In the former area encomenderos found it relatively easy to secure the appointment of sympathetic officials to undertake the enumeration and to bribe caciques to give their ap-proval to the *tasación*. The latter abuse was so common that in 1552 the crown specifically forbade agreements between encomenderos and In-dian caciques.[28] Indians, on the other hand, soon became tired of wasting their time and money entering into lawsuits that they never won.

During the sixteenth century *visitas* were conducted by *oidores* at extended intervals, but during the seventeenth century they were rare, and counts were generally undertaken by local officials and parish priests. The first official assessments were made in the 1530s, but the *tasaciones* made by Cerrato and the *oidores* Rogel and Ramírez in 1548 represent the first attempt to cover the whole audiencia. Although some reassessments were made in Nicaragua in the second half of the six-teenth century, very little evidence of them remains. Following the order in 1549 prohibiting personal service and requiring tribute to be moder-ated, in 1555 the alcalde mayor of Nicaragua, *licenciado* Juan Cavallón, reported that he had visited the province twice, on both occasions mod-erating the amount of tribute paid by the Indians and punishing excessive exactions.[29] Apparently the next *visita* by an *oidor* did not take place until the early 1560s when Dr. Manuel Barros was commissioned by the au-diencia to undertake *visitas* of Villa de la Trinidad, San Salvador, San Mi-guel, Honduras, and Nicaragua. The degree of tribute moderation he effected was considerable.[30]

In 1571 the governor of Nicaragua, Alonso de Casaos, assessed the amount of tribute to be paid by Indians in the Province of Chontales, in the eastern part of the jurisdiction of Granada, and with the exception of this area, most of Nicaragua was visited and reassessed by the *oidor li-*

cenciado Diego García de Palacio in 1578–79.[31] He also drew up instructions for the conduct of *visitas,* indicating the manner in which Indians should live, how they should be treated by the Spaniards, and the punishments that were to be imposed for infringements.[32] During the *visita* over thirty charges were made for excessive exaction of tribute and services, for ill-treatment of Indians, and for seizure of and encroachment on Indian lands. Most of the charges were against encomenderos, but there were a few against caciques.[33] In 1581 the governor, Don Artieda de Cherino, conducted a similar survey employing *jueces de comisión* and parish priests. Ten *jueces* were appointed, most of them local *vecinos,* and they were instructed to enumerate the entire population, indicate whether single people paid tribute, and note the person responsible for the last *tasación.* Most of the *tasaciones* recorded were those made by *licenciado* García de Palacio, and apparently they were the first assessments to be made on a per capita basis. He identified three categories of Indians who paid different amounts of tribute: married Indians; widowers and single men; and widows and single women. The only other *visita* of Nicaragua known to have taken place in the sixteenth century was in 1587.[34] Little is known of this *visita* either in terms of the *tasaciones* made or whether it extended farther than the jurisdiction of León.

Tribute reassessments during the seventeenth century were made irregularly. In 1609, Alonso Criado de Castilla, president of the audiencia, ordered a review of tribute payments to ascertain whether they were excessive and to inquire whether the Indians should be allowed to pay tribute in money.[35] Probably in response to this order a *visita* of Nicaragua was undertaken in 1612 by the *oidor,* Dr. Sánchez de Araque, who apparently ensured that Indians paid tribute on a per capita rather than communal basis.[36] There does not appear to have been another *visita* until 1663. Little is known of this *visita,* which was conducted by the *fiscal* of the audiencia, Don Pedro Frasso, though the numbers of tributary Indians counted were probably those included in a report from the governor of Nicaragua, Pablo de Loyola, in 1674.[37]

Although there were few general assessments in the early seventeenth century, some villages were reassessed when they were reassigned in encomiendas, while other villages were reassessed on request, and separate districts were enumerated at irregular intervals. These enumerations, which often involved bribery and corruption, were conducted by local officials together with parish priests.[38] In 1682 the long time lapse since the last general assessment prompted the crown to order the enumeration of tributary Indians in Honduras, Nicaragua, Sonsonate, and San Salvador.[39] Unfortunately the account of this enumeration omits large sections of the Province of León and the whole of Nueva Segovia, but figures for these regions are included in a later report written by the *oidor,* Antonio Navia Bolaños, in 1685.[40] This count probably formed the basis of many *tasaciones* made in 1686, though the numbers of Indians registered in the enumeration and *tasaciones* do not correspond in detail.[41]

A large number of villages particularly in the jurisdiction of León, Sebaco, and Nicoya appear to have been reassessed in 1694 or 1696, but villages in other jurisdictions were assessed individually and at irregular intervals.[42] Apparently there was another general reassessment in 1701, but no evidence of the enumeration has been found.[43] Nor is there any evidence of a count being made in 1708, when Ayón maintains that a major reassessment occurred.[44] There is evidence, however, in the form of both *padrones* and *tasaciones* for individual villages, particularly in the eastern part of the country and in the jurisdiction of León, between 1717 and 1719.[45] In conclusion it can be said that throughout the seventeenth century and the beginning of the eighteenth century counts and *tasaciones* were made irregularly and covered only limited areas. The extended time intervals between assessments meant that Indians had to pay according to counts that were out of date and often included dead or absent Indians. The result was that Indian communities began to fall into debts they were never able to repay.[46]

Early lists of tributary Indians refer only to *"indios tributarios,"* and it is assumed that they were male married Indians. This assumption is based on the fact that in 1578 the crown found it necessary to order single people to pay tribute, because Indians were postponing marriage often indefinitely in order not to pay tribute.[47] As a result, lists of tributary Indians drawn up by the governor in 1581 included married Indians, widowers, and single men.[48] Nevertheless single men became tributary only from age twenty-five and women only when they married, with the result that men and women still postponed marriage.[49] Later the age at which single people became liable to pay tribute was reduced to seventeen and fifteen for men and women, respectively.[50] In 1587 married male Indians paid from age sixteen and females from age thirteen, but the ages were raised to seventeen and fifteen respectively, in 1612, and dropped again to sixteen and fourteen in 1663.[51] Thus it is clear that in Nicaragua Indians paid tribute at earlier ages than eighteen as specified by the crown. Single people paid only half the amount of tribute paid by married Indians or less. Other groups who paid half tribute were married Indians whose spouses were non-Indians, Indians who were either exempt from tribute payment or paid tribute in other villages, or Indians who were absent or classified as *naborías.* Male tributary Indians continued to pay tribute up to the age of fifty-five, and females up to fifty. In other parts of the empire women did not pay tribute, but in the audiencia of Guatemala it seems to have become "the custom" for them to pay.

Women married to men who were exempt from tribute payment were exempt for the duration of their husband's lives, but when they died, they were liable to pay tribute as widows.[52]

Indians who were automatically exempt from tribute payment included caciques and their oldest sons, as well as those who had an official status.[53] In the sixteenth century Indians were theoretically exempt if they owned property comprising over one thousand *"pies de cacao"* and fifty cattle, or were craftsmen, in which case they were regarded as *lavorios* and paid tribute in money.[54] It is unclear whether these criteria were ever used to claim exemption; while individuals may have claimed exemption as craftsmen, very few would have owned enough property to substantiate such claims. Indians who had been recently converted were also exempt, except that they were required to pay the *servicio del tostón,* which was introduced in 1591. The period for which they were exempt was originally ten years, but by 1686 it had been extended to twenty years.[55]

Other forms of exemption had to be obtained from the audiencia.[56] Individuals could petition for tribute exemption on grounds of disablement or racial or social status. A child with a non-Indian parent often claimed exemption as a non-Indian or sought to be classified as a *lavorio* and therefore pay less tribute. The rule that was followed was that a child assumed the same status as its mother, but the racial status of individuals became increasingly difficult to establish as racial intermarriage increased, and baptismal records were not always available. There were other, less formal ways in which Indians could avoid tribute payment. Although Indians were liable to pay tribute in their place of birth even though they resided elsewhere, Indian officials charged with the collection of the tribute often found it difficult to find absent Indians, particularly in the towns. This situation led to conflict between the absentees and their home villages, because the burdens of tribute payment, the repartimiento, and officeholding became heavier on those that remained. Nevertheless disputes between the two parties were generally concluded by the crown reaffirming the right of an Indian to reside where he wished as long as he paid tribute in the village of his birth.[57]

Another way in which Indians could escape tribute payment was by avoiding being placed on a tributary list. Opportunities for this kind of evasion increased as marriages between individuals from different villages became more common. Although a wife generally took up residence in her husband's village, their children were supposed to be included in the tributary list of the mother's village, but often they were not.[58] Similarly, when such lists were drawn up, individuals could claim, without justification, that they paid tribute elsewhere. That such forms of evasion were common is clear from comparisons of *padrones* drawn up at the same time for nearby villages, for the birthplaces of individuals often do not correspond; that is, individuals claiming to pay tribute in villages other than those in which they resided do not appear in the tributary lists for those villages.

Whole villages could also claim exemption for periods of years in the event of disasters, such as epidemics, famines, earthquakes, and pirate attacks, or if the church required rebuilding. Such claims had to be supported by a Spanish official and the local parish priest.[59] Some observers complained about the ease with which Indians obtained relief from tribute payment, but it is clear that often exemption was not granted, and villages were allowed only to defer payment.[60]

Several changes in the nature of tribute payment were introduced during the late sixteenth and seventeenth centuries. From 1549 tribute could no longer be commuted to personal service.[61] As will be shown, personal service did continue illegally, but from that date onward it was not included in the schedule of items that each village had to provide. There was a gradual reduction in the number of items demanded in line with an order in 1552 stating that Indians should pay tribute in two or three items that were produced in the local area.[62]

Most tribute was paid in agricultural produce, such as maize, some beans, cotton cloth and chickens; many of the items previously paid as tribute, such as rush mats, sandals, pots, pans, and jars, were omitted. The simplification of tribute made its collection easier, but it meant that little account was taken of the nature of local production. Thus in 1627 villages near Sebaco found it impossible to pay their tribute in maize and cotton since neither crop grew well in the humid climate.[63] Most villages in Nicaragua paid tribute in maize and cotton, but the other items they paid varied: Indians in the jurisdiction of León and the village of Nicaragua contributed salt, which they obtained from seawater; those in the jurisdiction of Granada collected cabuya or henequen; and Posoltega, Nandaime, and villages in Nueva Segovia paid tribute in honey.[64] Honey and wax, which had featured strongly in early tribute assessments, were gradually dropped in most areas because collecting them from the mountains forced the Indians to spend several months traveling.[65]

Maize as a vital foodstuff remained an essential item of tribute payment throughout the colonial period. As soon as the amount of maize demanded as tribute was reduced or commuted to a money payment, colonists complained of food shortages. At first the assessments regulated that 1 fanega should be sown by ten to twelve Indians, but in the early 1560s Dr. Barros reduced the amount to 1 fanega per twenty-four to twenty-five Indians.[66] In 1581 each Indian was required to sow 1 almud of maize, divided between two sowings.[67] This levy appears to have persisted until at least 1610,[68] and it seems likely that the changeover to levies in the form of harvested maize occurred as a result of the 1612 *visita*. In Nicaragua a levy of 1 almud of sown maize was replaced by 1½ fanegas of harvested maize.[69] Although this probably represented a reduction in the amount of maize paid as tribute in most years, the responsibility for production fell on the Indians, and when yields were low or the harvest failed, they were forced to buy maize elsewhere at highly inflated prices to meet their tribute demands.

By the end of the seventeenth century the amount of annual tribute paid by a married couple was 1½ fanegas of maize, 6 yards of cotton cloth, 1 chicken, and either one-half almud of salt or 6 pounds of cabuya or henequen or 1 *quartillo* of honey. Most also paid one-half almud of beans. Male half tributaries paid the same minus the cotton cloth, and women half tributaries paid only 4 yards of cotton cloth and sometimes 1 chicken.[70] In addition, from 1591 tributary Indians were required to pay the *servicio del tostón*.[71]

According to a royal cedula of 1551, Indians were not obliged to take their tribute to the residence of their encomendero or to the nearest town where a royal official resided.[72] Initially encomenderos or their overseers or servants collected the tribute from the Indian villages, while the corregidor was responsible for its collection from those villages that paid tribute to the crown. Because of abuses perpetrated by the overseers and servants of encomenderos, in 1553 they were forbidden to collect tribute, and in 1605 the same order was applied to encomenderos themselves. From that time on tribute from all Indian villages was collected by royal officials, and encomenderos had to collect the amount they were due from the *real caja*.[73] However, royal officials were no less guilty of the charges made against the earlier tribute collectors, and the abuses continued. The actual responsibility for the collection of tribute from individuals lay with Indian leaders, who if they could not meet the necessary demands were liable to fines or imprisonment. This became an increasing possibility as *tasaciones* failed to keep pace with demographic changes, as Indian absenteeism increased, and as heavy exactions by royal officials rendered the communities less able to meet tribute demands. In 1695 the cabildo of Granada complained that, for the above reasons, the jails were often full of caciques and tribute collectors who had been unable to collect the amount specified.[74]

Once collected, tribute items were sold in the marketplace, and the revenue entered the royal coffers. The value of items auctioned varied considerably from year to year; between 1572 and 1594 the price of maize in León and Granada varied from 1 to 23 reals a fanega, depending on the state of the harvest and the region in which it was grown.[75] Because of the variable price of items auctioned, the income from tribute is an extremely unreliable guide to the size of the Indian population and to its change over time. It was a common practice for individuals, particularly royal officials with preferential access to tribute items, to purchase them at low prices and by monopolizing production create shortages that enabled them to resell them at inflated prices. Profits of over 100 percent were common and were particularly high when harvests were poor.[76]

By now it will be clear that there were many abuses of the tributary system. Little notice was taken of the *tasaciones,* and collectors often levied as much tribute as they could, visiting Indian villages at harvesttime and taking what they wanted.[77] Although the practice was illegal, they forced Indians to pay for absent or dead Indians,[78] and when they failed to meet the demands, Indian leaders were either fined or imprisoned. Individual Indians who defaulted were often required to compensate for their failure to pay tribute in kind by paying in cash or labor. The prices of items that should have been paid were generally set above their true value, and since Indians found it equally difficult to pay in cash, because the wages they earned were paid in kind, they were often taken from their villages to work as servants.[79]

Before passing on to discuss the labor demands made upon tributary Indians, it is worth noting that *lavoríos,* Indians who were privately employed, paid tribute in cash rather than kind.[80] The amount payable appears to have been two pesos for a married couple and one peso for a single person. This was less than that paid by tributary Indians, who as such tried to get themselves designated *lavoríos.* The *lavoríos* were free to reside where they wished, but they were required to pay tribute in the towns where they were registered.

Throughout the colonial period Indians remained the most important source of labor in Central America, though the form of their employment changed. Until 1549 encomenderos could legally exact labor services from Indians in their charge which meant that they had almost exclusive access to sources of labor. From that time onward, however, the inclusion of personal service in tribute assessments and the commutation of tribute to personal service was strictly forbidden. The order was repeated in the ordinances of 1601 and 1609.[81] Nevertheless, during the late sixteenth and early seventeenth centuries at least, there were complaints from Indians and Spaniards too numerous to mention that encomenderos still employed Indians in their personal service often without payment, treating them like "slaves." Gradually, however, the control that encomenderos exercised over Indian labor was eroded as new labor systems emerged.

The crown intended that the abolition of personal service should open the way to a free labor market, but it feared that, if Indians were given the freedom to work, they would refuse, and so in 1549 it introduced a new labor system, which in Central America was later known as the repartimiento. Indians were to offer themselves for work at approved tasks for stipulated periods for fixed wages. It was envisaged that the provision of adequate wages would be sufficient to attract Indian labor, so that coercion would be unnecessary, but since wages were poor and the tasks at which Indians were employed were demanding in time and energy, few worked voluntarily.

Each Indian village, whether it paid tribute to the crown or to an encomendero, was required to make available for work a quota of its tributary population. Applications for the hire of Indian labor had to be made to the audiencia, and the actual allocation of Indians was undertaken by the *juez repartidor,* who in the seventeenth century received from the employer one-half real for each Indian hired.[82] The Indians then worked for the stipulated period, at the end of which they received their pay and returned to their communities. Their places were immediately filled by a new group of Indians who had been collected and allocated in the same way. Since the hiring of Indian labor was open to all employers, the introduction of the repartimiento satisfied requests from non-encomenderos for access to sources of Indian labor, but since demands for labor increased, the amount available to any one employer was restricted. Despite some minor changes in the administration and operation of the repartimiento in the ordinances of 1601 and 1609, it continued to function in almost the same form throughout the period.[83]

In 1555 the repartimiento in the audiencia of Guatemala required each Indian village to provide 2 percent of its tributary Indians for *"servicio ordinario"*—that is, repairing houses and supplying households with food, water, and firewood. Indians could not be employed more than half a day's journey from their homes or for more than one week at a time. Given the distance from which Indians could be drawn, this proportion proved inadequate to meet demands, and it was later increased. Indians were to be provided with food and paid three reals a week, or their value in cacao, and extra for any time spent traveling.[84] By the seventeenth century requests for Indian servants normally amounted to one female and one male Indian per household, and the quota of tributary Indians required to provide *servicio ordinario* had been increased to 10 percent. In addition, Indian villages had to provide 5 percent of their tributary populations for *"servicio extraordinario,"* which included a variety of approved tasks.[85] From the beginning repartimiento labor could not be employed in mining or transporting goods, though Indians could undertake these tasks voluntarily, and in 1581 the employment of forced labor in indigo manufacture was also banned, though it continued illegally.[86]

During the third quarter of the sixteenth century Indians were employed in shipbuilding at Realejo, but it is not clear whether they were employed under the repartimiento. In 1578 the villages of Chinandega, El Viejo, Posoltega, Quesalquaque, Telica, Sutiaba, and Granada provided 372 Indians for the task, about one-fourth of whom were women employed to provide food for male workers. Those employed in cutting wood were paid two reals a week, and those working on the construction of ships three reals. The Indians were employed for one month at a time and sometimes for longer periods, which clearly exceeded that allowed under the repartimiento. Also, although a fixed proportion (20 percent) of the tributary population of each village was assigned, it is not clear whether they were employed on a rotational basis.[87] Whatever labor system was in operation, in 1579 the employment of Indians in this heavy work was banned, and the crown ordered that they should be replaced with black slaves.[88]

During the seventeenth century the collection of honey, wax, salt, and sarsaparilla and the manufacture of pitch were added to the list of prohibited tasks.[89] The most important tasks in which repartimiento labor was employed into the eighteenth century were agriculture, mining, and defense, though the Indians also repaired houses, built roads, and were employed in similar public works.

Unfortunately there is very little evidence of the importance of the repartimiento as a source of agricultural labor, though it is clear that such labor was used for this purpose.[90] One informative account lists the numbers of Indians allocated for various tasks from the villages of Sutiaba, Quesalquaque, Posoltega, and Telica in the *corregimiento* of Sutiaba in 1705. Of 216 Indians allocated, 94 were assigned to 14 *vecinos* mostly for employment on their estates. They were called *"peones de continuo,"* and it is assumed that they were permanent employees, and they may even have resided there. The rest were divided between the *vecinos* of León on the basis of one or two per *vecino*, generally one *leñatero* and one *molendera*.[91]

Although the employment of repartimiento labor in mining was banned in the sixteenth century, because of its importance to the Central American economy it was permitted again in 1645.[92] Mining was a relatively unimportant economic activity in Nicaragua, however, and it made few demands on repartimiento labor, except at the end of the seventeenth century, when attempts were made to expand production in Nueva Segovia. At that time the crown agreed to the provision of eighty male Indians and ten female cooks to be drawn from the villages of Telpaneca, Yalagüina, Palacagüina, Somoto, Totogalpa, Sebaco, and Jinotega.[93]

Servicio extraordinario was also used for defensive purposes. Indians were employed as guards and to repair the damage to houses and lands inflicted by hostile Indian and pirate attacks. These demands were greatest in the late seventeenth century, when the English and Zambo-

Mosquito threatened the security of the Caribbean coast, and the major towns in Nicaragua were attacked by pirates. Levies on Indian villages for defensive purposes were particularly onerous since they were more demanding in the numbers of Indians required and in the duration for which they were employed. As a result Indian villages were often able to claim exemption from providing *servicio ordinario* or from tribute payment on the grounds that they were employed in defensive duties.[94] The problem of providing sufficient Indians for defense was a major one in Nueva Segovia, where villages were small; in 1663 it was possible to collect only twelve Indians from seventeen villages since only one Indian out of thirty tributary Indians was required to serve.[95]

Although the quotas required for *servicio ordinario* and *servicio extraordinario* were fixed at 10 and 5 percent, respectively, the percentages were often exceeded.[96] Furthermore, individual Indians were sometimes required to do more than their fair share of service as other Indians left their communities in search of wage labor. Although these Indians were theoretically liable to the repartimiento, their employers were often able to bribe officials to release them from this duty, with the result that the burden of supplying a fixed number of workers fell on those who remained and with increasing frequency.[97] Sometimes caciques were forced to hire Indians themselves to fulfill the quota.[98]

Not only did the number of turns of employment increase over time, but so did their duration. In the sixteenth century Indians were employed under the repartimiento for between one week and one month, but during the seventeenth century there were increasing numbers of complaints that employers had retained Indians in their employment for extended periods of over a year,[99] often ignoring the fact that the repartimiento was supposed to be suspended for the months of April, May, September, and October, when the Indians were to be free to work their own lands.[100] Thus the repartimiento gradually converted the Indians into wage laborers.

The recompense Indians received for working under the repartimiento was always low; private employment always offered better wages. At the end of the seventeenth century Indians working under the repartimiento were paid less than half the wages paid to private employees.[101] In the sixteenth century Indians working under the repartimiento were paid about 2 or 3 reals a week, and although wages rose to 1 or 1½ reals a day in the second half of the seventeenth century, they remained low.[102] Workers were supposed to be paid in money, but more often they were paid in cacao or goods, and sometimes not at all.[103]

There is some evidence that as early as the late sixteenth century employers began turning away from the repartimiento as a source of Indian labor.[104] The repartimiento was unable to meet the demands made on it, and its rotational character brought other disadvantages: an employer could not build up a skilled and permanent labor force, and he was forced to pay employees for the unproductive time they spent traveling to and from their place of work. Although it was more expensive to hire voluntary workers, these disadvantages of the repartimiento were overcome as long as the workers remained in their employ. The wages paid to voluntary workers were often double those paid for similar work under the repartimiento, and employers often offered other incentives, such as agreeing to discharge the Indians' tribute debts or arranging for their exemption from work under the repartimiento.[105] But this free-labor system was not always as free as it appeared. Sometimes employers made advances to workers with the express purpose of binding them to their places of work through debts. The debts incurred were inherited by the deceased's family, so that widows were often forced to work for their husbands' former employers to pay them off. Such advances to Indians were forbidden in the sixteenth century, but they continued to the extent that in the late seventeenth century the authorities found it necessary to try to limit advances to the equivalent of four months' wages.[106]

Most Indians who offered themselves for private employment probably started as day laborers, but over time many settled on estates. The persistent absence of Indians from their communities led to conflicts between their employers and village leaders, as well as with those who relied on the repartimiento as their basic source of labor. Indian communities complained that, owing to the absence of Indians who were privately employed, they were unable to produce sufficient food or meet their tribute and repartimiento obligations.[107] In 1671 an order was issued requiring all Indians who were resident on estates to return to their villages. Naturally their employers complained. They argued that the Indians were well treated on estates and received good wages with which they could pay tribute; they were instructed in the Catholic faith and became civilized ladinos to the extent that they did not wish to return to their "uncivilized" villages. The employers went on to argue that agriculture was dependent on free labor and that if the Indians returned to their villages production would cease, and the fall in income would seriously affect the work of the church and the defense of the area, resulting in the eventual loss of the American colonies.[108] Although the order was not revoked, by 1709 at least the restitution of Indians to their villages had not been effected.

It is difficult to estimate the proportion of Indians who were privately employed during the seventeenth century. Initially Indians who were servants and permanent residents in Spanish households were known as *naborías*. From the late sixteenth century onward, however, the terms *naborías* and *lavoríos* were applied to household servants and those privately employed, not only Indians but also mulattoes and blacks. The number of *lavoríos* was always small; in 1685 in the jurisdictions of León and Granada only 9.3 and 4.5 percent, respectively of the tributary population were classified as *lavoríos*.[109] These figures probably considerably underestimate the numbers of Indians who were privately employed, and it seems likely that most continued to pay tribute in their villages of origin and were not reclassified as *lavoríos*.

In addition to supplying tribute and labor, Indians were subjected to many other exactions that were often more oppressive. These exactions were usually made by royal officials, particularly corregidores, alcaldes mayores and *jueces de milpas,* but also by governors, the clergy, and travelers. Corregidores and alcaldes mayores were probably the worst oppressors of the Indians. With the exception of parish priests, they came into the most sustained contact with the Indians and were thus in the best position to exploit them. Corregidores and alcaldes mayores compensated for the short duration of their posts and the lack of remuneration they provided by exploiting the Indians. In 1582 the governor of Nicaragua argued that the salaries of royal officials should be increased to conserve the Indian population.[110]

There were several ways in which corregidores and alcaldes mayores made profits at the expense of the Indians. One of the principal means was by trade, though it was illegal.[111] They forced Indians to sell them such items as cotton, indigo, salt, cacao, and tobacco at below market prices and then resold them at substantially increased prices. They also forced Indians to buy items of low value, such as "soap, candles and combs," at high prices, sometimes offering them advances that were repayable at harvesttime. This *repartimiento de generos* became a considerable burden on Indian communities, and it continued throughout the colonial period despite royal prohibitions.[112] The result was that many Indians fell into the debt of corregidores and alcaldes mayores. In 1706 eighty Indians were endebted to the corregidor of Sutiaba for sums up to sixty pesos.[113] Officials also required Indians to sow milpas, tend their horses and cattle, weave cotton, and provide a multitude of other services for which they were paid poorly if at all. The distribution of cotton for spinning and weaving was known as the *repartimiento de hilados,* and it became a very heavy burden on female Indians. Women were often taken from their communities to work in textile workshops, where they were required to produce fixed amounts of spun or woven cotton often from inadequate amounts of raw fiber.[114]

Jueces de milpas were appointed to ensure that the Indians planted maize so that they would not suffer food shortages. These officials were badly paid from the *cajas de comunidad,* but their positions enabled them to supplement their income by levying goods and services from the Indians, as well as by trading.[115] The *jueces de milpas* were so notorious in their exploitation of the Indians that in 1585 the crown forbade their appointment.[116] Nevertheless, in the Audiencia of Guatemala *jueces de milpas* continued to be appointed, and it was not until 1619, when the order was repeated,[117] that the crown brought charges against two presidents of the audiencia, Alonso Criado de Castilla and Conde de la Gómera, for having allowed the appointment of *jueces de milpas*. At the same time an investigation into the conduct of all those who had been appointed since 1585 was ordered.[118] It would appear that in the whole audiencia more than eighty *jueces de milpas* had been appointed for different periods of time; in Nicaragua the longest appointment was for five years, while most held office for only two years. It is known that at least twelve were appointed in Nicaragua, but the figure may be higher because the document containing the information has been badly burned. The salaries were generally five hundred *tostones* a year, though only three hundred *tostones* in Nueva Segovia. The illegal activities they indulged in were broadly similar to those of corregidores and alcaldes mayores, on top of which they failed to conduct their duties conscientiously. Their examinations of the milpas were often cursory, and they meted out punishments by flogging at will. On one occasion the Indians of Masaya were in the hills sowing maize, and because they refused to sow a milpa for the *juez,* he had two hundred of them whipped, including the alcaldes and the regidores. Officials of the audiencia repeatedly petitioned the crown to permit the appointment of *jueces,* but the crown did not relent and in fact reaffirmed the order forbidding their appointment in 1630, 1632, 1640, 1644, and 1669.[119] Even so it is clear that such officials were appointed; in Nicaragua in 1651 a residencia was held on a *juez de milpas* of Monimbó, while in 1672 there were three *jueces de milpas* in the province.[120] When *jueces* were not appointed, however, their duties were carried out by the equally exploitative corregidores.[121]

Parish priests were allowed to receive a certain amount of free goods and services. Although the crown tried to limit the amount they could receive, they often exacted more. Despite repeated prohibitions, many levied taxes called *derramas,* which were purportedly for the support of local bishops when they were conducting *visitas,* and, like alcaldes mayores and corregidores they forced Indians to cultivate milpas, tend their cattle, and spin and weave cotton with little or no payment.[122] For church festivals and other services such as baptisms, marriages, and burials, they often demanded wine and food.[123]

Indians were also obliged to provide gifts for official visitors and food and lodging for travelers. Although the crown tried to limit the number of visits undertaken by royal officials—governors, alcaldes mayores and corregidores being limited to one visit in their terms of office—many officials had different forms of jurisdiction within the same area, with the result that visits were frequent. The problem was aggravated by the fact that many officials took with them large numbers of assistants and servants, though again the crown attempted to limit their number.[124] The burden that travelers placed on Indian communities was heaviest on those on major routeways, to the extent that the villages of Nagarote, Matiare, and Pueblo Nuevo, which were on the *camino real*, were exempt from providing labor under the repartimiento because of the heavy demands they made.[125]

THE MISSIONS

Representatives of missionary orders accompanied early colonizing expeditions in Central America, but it was not until the second half of the sixteenth century that they arrived in substantial numbers to undertake the conversion of those Indians who still remained outside Spanish control. The most important mendicant orders that worked in Nicaragua were the Franciscans and the Mercedarians. It was envisaged that the missionary orders would undertake the preliminary conversion and "civilization" of Indians on the frontier, but because of the shortage of secular clergy in Nicaragua, some were also employed as parish priests. Most, however, worked in remote areas where the Indians lived a nomadic existence or were scattered in small settlements over wide areas. The missionaries tried instructing the Indians in their native villages, but since they could not control and discipline them, they decided to establish missions or *reducciones*. Theoretically after ten years the missions were to be handed over to the secular authorities, and the Indians were to become full-fledged members of society, with the obligations of paying tribute and providing labor services. The missionaries were then to move on, "pushing back the frontier" by establishing new missions in even more remote areas.

The earliest convents established in Nicaragua belonged to the Mercedarians. One was established in León in 1537, and by the end of the century two more had been established in Granada and Sebaco. The Franciscans arrived in 1574 and by 1579 had founded a convent at León.[126] Both missionary orders at times possessed daughter convents and hospices, which were used as bases from which they embarked on the conversion of the Indians in the eastern part of the country; they were not occupied continuously, however, owing to Indian attacks and the shortage of missionaries.

Missionary efforts in Nicaragua were initiated in 1606 by Mercedarians based at Sebaco. Friar Juan de Albuquerque made three entradas in the mountains of Tabavaca, and by 1608 he had gathered together by persuasion more than two hundred Indians, who were settled near Muymuy. [127] The work of Friar Albuquerque was consolidated by the establishment of the missions of Santa Cruz and San Juan on the Muymuy River in the Indians' home area. Nevertheless, in 1623 the Indians revolted and fled to the mountains. Three years later Friar García de Loaysa again tried to draw the Indians from the hills by offering them gifts, but this time he resolved to establish them away from their home territory to discourage them from fleeing. He therefore settled them at Metapa, and in 1627 the settlement had a population of eighty-five. [128] Meanwhile, in the mountains of Cacaobaca, Friar Juan Godoy de Santa Cruz converted an unspecified number of Indians and settled them away from the mountains at San Ramón Nonnato, near Matagalpa. Later in the century, in 1697, Friar Diego Alarcón converted fifty-five Indians around Muymuy. Some of the Indians subsequently fled, and to prevent the rest from fleeing, the missionaries moved them to Posoltega. [129]

Farther south, near Boaco, at the beginning of the century a number of Indians came down from the mountains and voluntarily settled at Camoapa, Lóvago, Lovigüisca, and Carra, The last-named village appears to have been amalgamated with Lovigüisca in about 1614, and, although the other three villages have persisted to the present day, during the seventeenth century their populations fluctuated considerably. [130] Unlike the Indians in the missions, these Indians were administered by the secular clergy, and in 1663 they were made tributary to the crown.

Although the Franciscans had convents in Nicaragua and also administered some of the tributary Indian villages there, they were not active in converting Indians until the last quarter of the seventeenth century. At the request of Indians from Tologalpa, Franciscans began work in the area known as Paraka and Pantasma. In 1674, Friar Pedro Lagares entered the Valley of Culcalí and finally established two villages, San José de Paraka and San Francisco Nanaica, which by 1678 together held more than two hundred Indians. [131] The missions continued in existence until 1691, when the missionary who administered them died and was not replaced. In 1693 an account of the Franciscan missions founded since 1681 included two missions, Limpia Concepción de Paraka and Nuestra Senora de la Asumpción de Pantasma. [132] It is unclear whether these were new missions or whether their names had been changed. Missionary work in the area was not resumed in earnest until 1721, although there is some evidence that Franciscans were still working in the vicinity of Nueva Segovia in the early eighteenth century. [133]

In the seventeenth century missionary efforts in Nicaragua met with little success. This was due partly to the lack of financial and military support provided by the crown but also to the methods the missionaries employed and the nature of the Indian societies they encountered. One problem they faced was the diversity of languages spoken by the Indians.[134] Although the missionaries were criticized for not speaking Indian languages, the task of learning all of them would have been impossible. Instead the missionaries adopted the strategy of capturing and converting a small number of Indians, who then acted as interpreters. As far as possible, the missionaries tried to convert the Indians by persuasion and with gifts of trinkets, such as "belts, beads, and knives," which in the early years of contact were highly appreciated; by the eighteenth century, however, the Indians were not as easily won over by such gifts, many of which they could obtain from the Zambo-Mosquito and the English.[135] They also feared the diseases the missionaries introduced.[136] If persuasion failed, soldiers were often employed to bring the Indians into the missions by force. There was considerable controversy over the employment of force in converting the Indians; some argued that the task was impossible without it, while others regarded persuasion as the only way of effecting lasting conversions, otherwise no sooner would the Indians be settled in a mission than they would flee.[137] But it was not only resentment of the force that had been employed to bring the Indians into the missions that encouraged them to escape. The Indians were generally unfamiliar with a sedentary way of life, and they were said to yearn to return to the forests. Also, the Indians gathered together in one mission village were often drawn from several, sometimes hostile, communities, and they possessed few common interests to encourage them to remain in the mission. The missionaries responded to the problem of fugitivism in two ways: first, by using soldiers to prevent the Indians fleeing, and second, by establishing the missions away from the Indians' home area.[138] The latter strategy was employed at the beginning of the seventeenth century, when Indians from the Muymuy region were moved to Metapa and Matagalpa, and their settlements in the hills were destroyed.[139] An alternative strategy was to settle Indians in small numbers in already established Indian villages, such as occurred at the end of the century, when Indians from Muymuy were settled at Posoltega.[140] Both strategies proved unsuccessful, however, for the Indians still fled and those who remained became depressed and ill.

REGIONAL VARIATIONS IN EUROPEAN ACTIVITY

Indians living in the Mesoamerican and South American zones had different colonial experiences. The former region came under Spanish control at an early date, and the encomienda was introduced to control and exploit the Indians. Indians were liable to pay tribute and were required to provide labor under the repartimiento. From the late sixteenth century onward they began to work as free laborers. At the same time the development of agriculture made demands on Indian lands. The impact of these institutions and activities varied and was positively correlated with the distribution of the non-Indian population. Demands for Indian labor were highest in the towns of León and Granada, on rural estates, and in the shipbuilding industry at Realejo, while demands on Indian production were closely correlated with the distribution of Spanish officials and the clergy, most of whom resided in the towns. During this period some Indians living in the South American zone were assigned in encomiendas and required to provide labor under the repartimiento, and thus similar kinds of demands were made on Indian labor and production, with similar variations occurring in response to the distribution of non-Indian activities. In these areas the level of Spanish activity was lower—mining had more or less ceased, and the agricultural colonization of the area was just beginning—but their impact was probably equally profound because the tribal communities that they affected were less able to withstand the extralocal demands made upon them.

Throughout this period most of the South American zone remained outside Spanish control, though intermittent missionary activity profoundly affected those Indians who were living in the frontier region. Between the latter area and the Mosquito Coast a large number of Indians remained outside Spanish control, though they had intermittent contacts with them and with the English and the Zambo-Mosquito who resided on the coast. On the Mosquito Coast itself the dominant cultural influence came from the English, whose presence indirectly resulted in major changes in the racial and cultural character of its inhabitants.

CHAPTER 10

Cultural Change in the Mesoamerican Zone, 1550–1720

A number of institutions that had been introduced in the first half of the sixteenth century continued to exist throughout this period, although their character changed. As a consequence their impact on Indian cultures was broadly similar, but there were some differences of detail. Although the Indian slave trade had been abolished and legislation had been introduced restricting the excessive exploitation of the Indians, new forms of exaction emerged to take their place that were often more subtle but had equally penetrating effects on the Indian way of life. Official and formal contacts between non-Indians and Indians directly affected the Indians, but developments in the Nicaraguan economy and society also had profound repercussions. Probably the most important was the expansion of agriculture, which made demands on Indian lands, attracted Indian labor, and indirectly led to the breakup of Indian communities.

The decline in the number and size of Indian settlements in the Mesoamerican zone during the first half of the sixteenth century tailed off subsequently. In Pacific Nicaragua, unlike other parts of the audiencia, there was little amalgamation of Indian villages because most of the villages were large enough to permit their effective administration; many villages were in fact composed of a number of *parcialidades,* or suburbs, each of adequate size to be assigned as a separate encomienda. For example, in the late seventeenth century Managua and Jalteba each had seven suburbs, and Sutiaba eleven; thus some villages had several hundred tributary Indians and well over a thousand Indians altogether.[1]

Just as there was little change in the number of Indian villages during this period, the average number of tributary Indians (married males) in each village or suburb did not differ significantly. Whereas in 1581 the average number was 38.8, in 1685–86 it was 34.9.[2] If the average number of tributary Indians per village only is calculated for the latter date, then the figure rises to 117.6. This figure is not significantly different from that calculated from an incomplete list of villages and their number of tributary Indians drawn up in 1663: twenty-seven villages were recorded as possessing 3,499 tributary Indians, giving an average of 129.6 per village.[3] Unfortunately there are no comprehensive lists of villages in Nicaragua during the first half of the seventeenth century, and thus it is difficult to determine the extent of the likely decline between the two

Table 7. Numbers and Sizes of Indian Villages in Nicaragua,
1581 to 1676–86

Number	León		Granada		East	
	1581*	1685[†]	1581	1685	1581	1685
Number of villages or suburbs	44.0	47.0[‡]	40.0	44.0	24.0	25.0
Number of villages	—	7.0[‡]	—	20.0	—	22.0
Number of married men	1,486.0	1,378.0[‡]	1,777.0	1,796.0	559.0	1,426.0
Average number of married men per village or suburb	33.7	29.3	44.4	40.8	23.3	57.0
Average number of married men per village	—	196.9	—	89.8	—	64.8

*AGI AG 966 census 1581.

[†]AGGA A3.16 147 999 tasaciones 1676–86. Most of the figures are for 1685 or 1686, a few villages in the east were counted between 1676 and 1683.

[‡]Folios 1–9 are missing from the document and probably referred to villages in the jurisdiction of León. These figures should therefore be slightly larger.

dates. The only area in the Mesoamerican zone that appears to have suffered from an irreparable decline in the number and size of its villages was Nicoya. Although there is no account of the number of villages existing in Nicoya in the late sixteenth century, the area was said to possess 3,500 Indians in 1569.[4] In 1684 there were only seven villages containing 442 tributary Indians, and ten years later they had been reduced to only 288, most of whom lived in the village of Nicoya, a large number having been captured or killed during pirate attacks.[5] In 1711 the bishop of Nicaragua reported that only one village still existed in the peninsula, that of Nicoya itself, which possessed over 100 souls.[6]

Although there appears to have been little change in the number and size of Indian villages during the late sixteenth and seventeenth centuries, it is clear that Indians were abandoning their villages in search of employment or to escape tribute payment, the repartimiento, or pirate attacks.[7] The degree to which Indians began to desert their villages is difficult to estimate, since Indians were enumerated in their places of birth rather than their current places of employment or residence. Thus demographic evidence suggests that the settlement pattern was more nucleated than it was in reality. The fact that in the 1670s the authorities found it necessary to order Indians to return to their villages indicates the extent to which Indians had deserted their communities. Similarly, the establishment of separate barrios in the major Spanish towns and of new villages nearby reflects the degree of rural-urban migration; León had two settlements next to the town, as well as the village of Metapa some distance away, which in 1683 together possessed 172 *lavoríos*.[8] Two other villages of *lavoríos* were established in 1653, one at Pueblo Nuevo de San Nicolás, between Sutiaba and Nagarote, consisting of Indians mainly from Managua and Jalteba, and the other at Santísima Trinidad, near Nueva Segovia.[9]

At the same time that Indians were moving to Spanish centers of employment, non-Indians were migrating from the towns to rural estates and, though they were forbidden to do so by law, to Indian villages.[10] The drift of non-Indians to the countryside, including Indian villages, was motivated by economic considerations, but it was given added stimulus by pirate attacks. Before the prohibition on Spaniards living in Indian villages in 1603, there were numerous complaints about their presence there,[11] and despite the introduction of legislation it would appear that non-Indians, and particularly mulattoes and mestizos, did take up residence in Indian villages to the extent that most villages possessed at least one or two persons of either race. In the midseventeenth century an attempt was made to segregate the races by establishing the mulattoes, mestizos and blacks in separate settlements near the four Spanish towns. The experiment was unsuccessful, however, since the settlements became little more than bases from which these races attacked and robbed Indian villages.[12] In 1679 a suggestion was made, though not taken up, that all mulattoes and blacks should form two large settlements at Granada and San Juan, where they could assist in the defense of the province.[13]

THE ECONOMY

The process of change in the Indian economy that began in the early sixteenth century continued along the same lines through the late sixteenth and seventeenth centuries, though with increasing momentum; in the second half of the sixteenth century the alienation of Indian lands began in earnest, and although the decline in the Indian population occurred at a slower rate, official and unofficial demands on Indian labor and production increased. The loss of lands for cultivation and for the exploitation of wild-food resources, together with the decline in labor inputs resulted in a decrease in production for subsistence needs, forcing Indians to desert their lands and become dependent on wage labor. Not all branches of the

Indian economy declined equally, however; the production of crops and goods demanded by the Spaniards as tribute and for other purposes probably increased, while those of little interest to colonists and with low-yielding qualities would have been cultivated or produced less frequently.

In general, crop yields probably declined as falling labor inputs allowed less attention to be paid to weeding and cultivation. Similarly, the time-consuming nature of hunting and collecting may have forced a decline in the importance of these activities, though fishing may have increased with the introduction of the Roman Catholic requirement of eating fish on Fridays and selected holy days. In general the contribution of wild-food sources probably declined, but wild fruits, roots, fish, and shellfish continued to be eaten in times of shortage.[14] Not all changes in the Indian economy were negative: domesticated animals introduced from Europe, particularly chickens and cattle, were readily adopted by the Indians and constituted valuable protein additions to their diet. Also, some of the crafts practiced by the Indians were stimulated by Spanish demands for goods, but since most Indians produced barely enough for their own subsistence, they had few items to trade.

Although an attempt has been made to establish the nature of the pre-Columbian landholding system, the picture is far from clear, and little evidence is available for the nature and distribution of landholdings during the first half of the sixteenth century. This situation reflects not only the lack of evidence available but also the Spanish preoccupation with Indian tribute and labor, rather than land, as sources of wealth. It was not until the second half of the century, as the income from Indian sources declined with the population and as markets for agricultural produce became clearly established, that the Spaniards turned their attention to land. Once the potential value of land had been realized, the alienation of Indian lands began in earnest.

The crown was eager for Indian villages to possess adequate lands to raise crops and animals for their own subsistence and for tribute purposes and tried to protect their rights to the land.[15] Indian communities were also eager to protect their lands, not only to safeguard their livelihood but also to discourage individuals from deserting their villages, since the tribute and repartimiento obligations of absentees fell on those that remained.[16] The crown and Indian leaders were thus united in the aim of preserving the Indian population in distinct villages, and the provision of adequate lands was seen as one way of encouraging it.

Most Indian lands were communally owned, and they consisted of *ejidos* or *pastos,* which were communal pastures, and *sementeras* or *labranzas,* which were cultivated lands. In addition most Indian communities originally possessed considerable stretches of *monte,* which were used for grazing and exploited for fuel, building materials, and wild-food resources. These lands constituted the *terminos,* or jurisdiction, of the village. It is not known to what extent the limits of landholdings coincided with those that had existed in pre-Columbian times, but the *terminos* appear to have been well defined, for land titles granted to Spaniards often specified that the land fell within the jurisdiction of a particular Indian village. Since the rights of Indians to lands they had held at the time of the Conquest were recognized in law, Indian communities did not usually seek formal titles to their lands. This became a serious problem later, when their rights were disputed by potential purchasers; the Indians could only weakly claim that they had possessed the land since "time immemorial."

Initially the size of Indian landholdings was not specified, but Indians were regarded as proprietors of the land that they had held at the time of the Conquest. With the rapid alienation of Indian lands, however, it became clear that some form of protective legislation was required that stipulated the minimum amount of land an Indian community should hold. According to Gibson, in 1567 it was specified that each Indian village was to hold land within a 500-vara (one-fourth mile) radius; this was increased to 600 varas in 1687.[17] It seems likely that, as in the Valley of Mexico, the 500 varas were measured from the outermost houses of the settlement; therefore houses were purposely located some distance from the center to obtain the maximum extension of land possible. At the same time the crown tried to protect Indian holdings from being overrun by straying livestock. In 1550 a general order was issued prohibiting the establishment of cattle ranches near Indian villages, and in 1618 another decree specified that such ranches had to be 1½ leagues (about 3.9 miles) from already established Indian settlements and 3 leagues from those that were to be established in the future.[18]

The other form of landholding whose minimum dimensions were specified was the ejido. This generally comprised communal pastureland, though increasingly the term was used to refer to all communal lands, including those under cultivation.[19] In 1573 it was stipulated that each Indian village should have one square league of land for its ejido (approximately 4,338 acres).[20] It is interesting that this specification took no account of the size of an Indian village and was therefore adequate for smaller Indian villages but only just sufficient for those in Pacific Nicaragua, where from the end of the seventeenth century onward some villages possessed several thousand Indians. In 1705 the Indians of Sutiaba complained that Indians were leaving the village because their lands had been encroached on by citizens of the city of León, leaving them with only one-half league of ejido, insufficient for a population that in 1694 consisted of 1,491 tributary Indians.[21] In fact, in both instances in which legal minimums were set to protect Indian lands from encroachment, potential landowners viewed them as maximums, and any lands over and above these limits, even though they might be possessed legally by Indian communities, were regarded as fit for alienation.

Apart from communal pastures, Indian villages also held within their jurisdictions other lands that were used for cultivation. Some of these lands were worked communally, but it appears that most were allocated to individuals by the cabildo. During the sixteenth century at least crops produced for tribute payment were raised on communally worked plots, the actual size of the plots, which were specified in the *tasaciones,* varying with the number of tributary Indians. In 1587 the villages of San Pedro Sutiaba and Tusta were required to plant two communal milpas. The milpa of maize was to be 400 by 400 varas, and the field of cotton, from which blankets were to be made as items of tribute, was to be 60 by 60 varas. The produce from the two milpas was divided between the encomendero, who received two-thirds, and the community, whose portion entered the *caja de comunidad.* [22]

It is not clear whether during the seventeenth century, following the introduction of per capita tribute payments, items grown for tribute payment were cultivated communally or whether individuals grew them on their own plots. What is clear is that the crown was eager that Indian communities should have an income that could provide security in the event of a disaster, such as an epidemic or a harvest failure, and for meeting extraordinary demands, such as those made by royal officials on *visitas.* For these purposes, in 1577 the crown ordered that a *sementera* or *milpa de comunidad* should be established in each Indian village. [23] Each Indian was required to cultivate ten *brazas* of land, or one hundred Indians were required to sow one *fanega de sembradura.* [24] From 1683, Indian communities were also required to maintain a community ranch. [25] The produce from all community lands was sold, and the income entered the *caja de comunidad.* Despite repeated orders that each Indian village should establish a *caja de comunidad,* it appears that those villages that were small or too poor did not do so. [26] The *cajas* were administered by the cacique, the parish priest, and the corregidor, each of whom possessed a key to the chest. Although it was intended that the income should be used for community purposes, the funds were often used by these officials as their own private capital. As early as the 1580s the cacique of Juigalpa was charged with having taken 41 tostones from the *caja de comunidad,* which the village had agreed to spend on ornaments for the church. He was removed from office and ordered to repay the amount he had taken. [27]

Most of the cultivated lands owned by the community were worked individually as in pre-Columbian times. The land was allotted to the heads of families, and *visitas* of five Indian *pueblos* in Pacific Nicaragua between 1663 and 1676 indicate that on average each milpa supported 6.3 persons.[28] Unfortunately there is no evidence for the size of the milpas, and it seems likely that many of them were little more than garden plots. The land could be inherited by male descendants. If there were no heirs or the holder moved to another village, then the land reverted to the community for reallocation by the cabildo. With the rapid decline in the Indian population during the sixteenth century this must have been a common occurrence.

In addition to lands that were owned by the community by right, there were other lands, generally in the vicinity of the village, which had been purchased either by the community or by individual Indians. Although, as has been indicated, Indians were in theory the proprietors of the land they held at the time of the Spanish conquest, as pressure on Indian lands increased and as the memories of the definite limits of landholdings at the time of the Conquest began to fade, Indian lands came under greater threat. The means by which the Spaniards acquired Indian lands has already been described; one way in which Indian villages could forestall disputes was to petition for formal grants in the same way as non-Indians.[29] Although Indian communities were free to buy lands, the *cajas de comunidad* had limited funds, and the opportunity for individual Indians to buy land was restricted by their low income and consequent lack of savings.[30] Although the evidence is scant, it appears that most Indians who purchased land were caciques and principales.

Other lands worked by the community were those belonging to *cofradías,* or religious brotherhoods. In 1655 it was said that each convent and Indian parish in Nicaragua had two *cofradías* and that each *cofradía* possessed a cattle ranch.[31] If land was not owned by the *cofradía,* cattle were grazed on ejido lands. It is not clear how the *cofradías* acquired their lands. Originally they may have formed part of the communal lands, whose product was designated for the celebration of particular saints. Likewise it is possible that individuals may have designated the lands they had been allocated for the same purpose, receiving certain privileges in return. In addition *cofradías* purchased land from the funds they accumulated from members' dues. Work on the land was undertaken by members of the brotherhood, and it appears that such work exempted individuals from other community obligations, such as the repartimiento, leaving the burden of the latter to fall on nonmembers. This problem, together with official complaints that the income derived from the land was spent on drunken fiestas in celebration of various saints at which the Indians reverted to their pagan practices, encouraged the crown to try to limit the establishment of *cofradías.*[32] Although from 1637 *cofradías* could not be established without permission, they continued to be founded, and in 1663 the audiencia reported that they had been established in such large numbers that in villages where there were no more than one hundred Indians there were ten to twelve *cofradías*.

Apart from the loss of land, perhaps the most important change that affected Indian agriculture was the decline in labor inputs. During the second half of the sixteenth century and the first half of the seventeenth century the Indian population continued to decline, and, although some legislation, such as the abolition of personal service, was designed to relieve the burden of work falling on those that remained, other forms of exploitation soon emerged to take their place. Although the payment of tribute remained a constant drain on Indian resources, more complaints were made about the repartimiento and about the services and forced sales demanded by local priests, official visitors, and other Spanish officials.[33]

Communal labor would have been discouraged by the extended absences of individuals and by the introduction of per capita tribute payments. Irrigation systems fell into disrepair, to the extent that in 1663 the audiencia found it necessary to order Indian villages to continue the irrigation of lands for maize cultivation.[34] The decline in labor inputs must have also led to a gradual fall in production and to a reduction in the number of species and varieties of crops grown, though these losses were compensated for in part by the introduction of new plants and animals from Europe and later from other parts of the world. Nevertheless, maize remained by far the most important crop grown, its status being reinforced by its adoption as a staple by the Spaniards. In the seventeenth century Vázquez de Espinosa estimated that in Nicaragua (El Viejo) 2 *celemines* would provide tortillas for several days.[35] Given an estimate of about 6 *celemines* a week for a family, the total yearly requirement would have been 26 fanegas a year. This corresponds to Borah and Cook's estimate of 25 fanegas a year for a family of 4.5 persons in Mexico, and both are somewhat higher than Gibson's estimate of about 20 fanegas per family in the Valley of Mexico.[36] Given an average yield of about 1:100 in Nicaragua,[37] to reach 26 fanegas it would be necessary to sow 0.26 fanegas. At the official conversion rate of one *fanega de sembradura* for 8.8 acres,[38] it would have been necessary to cultivate about 2.3 acres a year. It has been suggested that under a semipermanent system of cultivation families in Pacific Nicaragua probably cultivated about 6 acres[39] and that the cultivation of maize probably accounted for about one-third of agricultural production, though this does not include any maize that might have been sown for tribute purposes. Each family was required to provide 1 or 1.5 fanegas of maize as tribute; there was no Indian village in Nicaragua that did not pay part of its tribute in maize.

Despite these general estimates of production, it is clear that there were considerable variations in yields according to local edaphic and climatic conditions. The volcanic soils of Pacific Nicaragua probably generated higher returns than soils elsewhere, while farther south in Nicoya the mature lateritic soils produced low yields. Apart from normal regional variations in climate that affected production, sometimes a flood or a drought might destroy the harvest. Other reasons given for shortages in production were that the Indians had had insufficient time to cultivate their lands, that their plots had been overrun by straying animals, and that the Indians were naturally lazy. The authorities considered it necessary to force Indians to plant maize by insisting that they pay it as tribute and by appointing *jueces de milpas*.[40] In 1566 the governor of Nicaragua complained that since the amount of maize paid as tribute had been reduced from 1 almud to 0.5 almud of sown maize per tributary, its price had risen to 9 tostones (36 reals),[41] whereas the normal price was between 2 and 4 reals. A similar rise in price was noted following the abolition of *jueces de milpas* in the early seventeenth century.[42] Sometimes the price of maize was also inflated by the export of large quantities of the crop to Panama and Nombre de Dios, though occasionally the authorities issued orders prohibiting its export.[43] All these factors were reflected in considerable fluctuations in the price of maize.[44]

Other subsistence crops that had been widely cultivated in the pre-Columbian period and continued to be grown in the colonial period included various varieties of beans, sweet and chili peppers, plantains, and sweet potatoes. Beans were an important item of tribute, though they were not levied as universally as maize, and occasionally chili peppers were also paid as tribute.[45] Against these native staples crops introduced from Europe made little headway. In addition Indians continued to cultivate a small number of fruit trees in yards or gardens. Native fruits remained by far the most important, and they could be bought for six or eight cacao beans, a small fraction of a real.[46]

Cacao had played an important role in the economy of the Nicarao, but it declined markedly in importance during the colonial period. Cacao groves were difficult to maintain with a reduced labor force, and many passed into Spanish hands.[47] A *visita* of the *partido* of Monimbo in 1651 revealed that only a few cacao trees remained in Diriomo and Diriá, because most of them had been destroyed by drought and had not been replaced.[48] The decline in Indian cacao production was reflected in its decline as an item of tribute. In 1548, 14 of the 158 tributary villages in Nicaragua paid in cacao, but by the end of the seventeenth century no village in the province was paying in cacao.[49]

Cotton remained one of the most important crops grown by the Indians in Nicaragua, especially on the Pacific coast, where it was suited to the warm, dry climate; Vázquez de Espinosa maintained that the area produced the best cotton in the Indies.[50] Next to maize and chickens it was the most important item paid as tribute in terms of both the number of villages which paid in cotton cloth and the total value of tribute they paid. Each tributary Indian generally had to provide one piece of cloth three varas or three *piernas* (approximately three yards) long, the price of which varied between sixteen and twenty reals a *pierna*.[51] Indian women were also forced to spin and weave cotton under the *repartimiento de hilados*.[52]

During the second half of the sixteenth century sources of animal protein increased as the Indians became familiar with European domesticates and began raising them. Chickens, which had been adopted most readily in the first half of the sixteenth century, continued to be an important source of food and item of tribute. All Indian households were required to raise chickens, and when *visitas* were conducted, those that did not possess them were fined.[53] Initially the Indians had been frightened of the larger domesticated animals, but as they became more familiar with them, they began raising them. Colonists hoping to monopolize production initially objected to the raising of livestock by Indians, but in 1551 the crown ordered that Indians were to be free to raise livestock as they wished.[54] By the beginning of the seventeenth century it was said that the Indians had become so accustomed to eating meat that if it was not available they would die of hunger.[55] Although most of the meat that was consumed was probably fresh, some was also dried for storage. By the end of the seventeenth century livestock had been so widely adopted by the Indians that ordinances required that each Indian village was to possess an *estancia de ganado* as well as a *milpa de comunidad*.[56] By the beginning of the eighteenth century probably most Indian villages possessed several hundred head of cattle, most of which were probably communally owned and grazed on village ejidos; other large herds were owned by *cofradías*.[57]

While the large-scale production of horses and mules generally remained in Spanish hands, some were raised by Indians for transport and for certain types of repartimiento labor, such as the collection of indigo leaves.[58] Although Indians, with the exception of caciques, were forbidden to ride horses, they did raise them in small numbers.[59] However, horses were particularly vulnerable to confiscation for failure to meet tribute demands and other debts.[60] In addition to raising their own mules and horses, Indians were also obliged to tend those owned by local Spanish officials and clergy.[61] Although the smaller domesticated animals—sheep, pigs, and goats—might have provided the Indians with additional sources of food, there is no evidence that they were raised in large numbers in Nicaragua.

The decline in the availability of labor probably led to a decline in the time-consuming activities of collecting and hunting. The main exceptions to this rule were the collection of honey and beeswax, both of which were demanded as items of tribute despite efforts to prohibit their exaction. Other wild-vegetable products that attracted Spanish interest were medicinal plants, such as sarsaparilla, which became an important item of export, and resins, gums, and balsams, the most important of which was liquidambar.[62]

There is little evidence for change in the nature and role of hunting in the economy. Probably the most important animals hunted continued to be deer, peccaries, pacas, and birds.[63] There were no recorded innovations in the techniques used to capture animals; certainly the Indians would have found it difficult to acquire firearms, which by law they were prohibited from using.[64] In contrast to hunting, fishing seems to have remained an important activity, and it may well have been stimulated by the introduction of fish eating on Fridays and holy days. The most important fishing areas were the Pacific coast and Lakes Managua and Nicaragua. The most important fish caught were mojarras and sabalos, the former selling at eighteen to twenty for a real.[65] The production of *hilo morado* (purple dye) from *Purpura* mollusks continued in Nicoya throughout the colonial period,[66] while salt was extracted from seawater and paid as tribute by Indians living in villages near the Pacific coast of Nicaragua.[67]

Many activities were undertaken by the Indians either as part of their repartimiento obligations or under coercion from Spanish officials and priests. These activities have been described in detail elsewhere and included cutting wood, making pitch for shipbuilding, manufacturing canvas sails and cordage, and weaving cotton cloth. In addition many household items and articles of clothing were demanded as tribute and traded in local markets. Early tribute demands included household furniture and utensils: rush and palm mats, wooden chairs, and cooking and storage vessels. Also demanded were cotton cloth and leather and rope shoes and sandals. A craft that probably developed significantly in the colonial period was leatherworking. Although deer hides had been used for many purposes in the pre-Columbian period, leather in the form of cattle hides became more generally available during the colonial period, and it was commonly used for footwear and riding equipment.[68] Other Indian craftsmen who Herrera noted were present in Nicaragua included silversmiths, musicians, wax-workers, tailors, and blacksmiths.[69]

Whereas in pre-Columbian times a proportion of extracommunal trade consisted of luxury items and slaves, during the colonial period most trade was in agricultural produce and craft products. By law Indians were free to market their produce where they wished, and they were not required to pay the *alcabala* on goods they sold.[70] As has been shown, however, Indians were often coerced into selling their goods at low prices to Spanish officials, encomenderos, and priests.[71] Other non-

Indian merchants and traders had shops or stalls in Indian villages. Initially most traders were peripatetic because they could stay in Indian villages for only three days, but from 1632 at least non-Indians were permitted to establish retail outlets in the villages on payment of an annual tax.[72] In all their dealings with Spanish officials and traders Indians complained about the prices they were charged and the currency frauds that were committed. Cacao beans were used as a medium of exchange even in Spanish towns to the eighteenth century, though by that time metal coins were becoming more common. Since silver coins were often debased with lead, the Indians generally preferred to trade in cacao.[73]

THE SOCIOPOLITICAL ORGANIZATION

Modifications to the social and political organization of Indian communities that had been introduced in the first half of the sixteenth century were subsequently consolidated. The legal status of caciques was more clearly specified, and many secular and ecclesiastical posts to which Indians were either elected or appointed were created in Indian villages. While these posts maintained a hierarchical element in the social organization of Indian communities, in general the Indians experienced social leveling.

The social status of individuals was determined by the status of their pre-Columbian ancestors and by the political role they played in the colonial period. At the top of the social ladder were caciques, whose superior social position was reinforced by legal privileges.[74] However, compared to their rights in pre-Columbian times, the privileges of caciques were now restricted; they were no longer permitted to own Indian slaves or levy tribute and services from their subjects.[75] Furthermore, their legal privileges were often ignored; there were frequent complaints that Spanish officials forced them to perform tasks that were humiliating and caused them to lose respect in their communities.[76] The position of cacique was supposed to be hereditary passing through the male line, but the authorities sometimes interfered with the succession of officeholders. Probably from the sixteenth century onward, governors began to appoint *indios gobernadores,* particularly when there was a problem over the succession created by the absence of a male heir or an heir who was too young to assume office. They were also appointed to take over the duties of corregidores when the corregimientos of Monimbó and Sutiaba were abolished in 1673.[77] While the title *indio gobernador* could be given to a cacique, it is clear that the faculty of Spanish officials to make such appointments opened the way for the imposition of Indian leaders or even non-Indians on Indian communities in full denial of the hereditary claims of caciques.[78]

Despite the gradual erosion of their powers and status, caciques still held a privileged position in Indian society. Their status was reinforced by their relative wealth, which had its origins in the pre-Columbian period; it is significant that most of the Indians who purchased land in the colonial period were caciques and principales. Although the income of caciques was reduced by the loss of tribute, it was compensated for in part by the access to community funds that their official positions provided. The authorities tried to control the use of community funds and the sale of Indian lands by caciques by ordering that all transactions were to be made before Spanish officials.[79] Occasionally charges were brought against caciques for malpractice, but the order was largely ineffective.[80] Caciques also supplemented their incomes with bribes from non-Indians for the rent or purchase of lands and for the use of Indian labor, as well as from Indians hoping to gain exemption from the repartimiento.

Despite the reduction in the powers and status of caciques, the fact that other Indians tried to establish themselves as caciques indicates that their position was still regarded as superior; the main advantages the position bestowed were exemption from tribute payment and labor services. Gibson notes that Indians in the Valley of Mexico often achieved some social status by enterprise or sponsorship by a local encomendero or priest, which over time was recognized by the award of the title of principal. In the absence of a legitimate heir to the position of cacique, the principal might then assume office, or in some cases be appointed as an *indio gobernador* in defiance of the claims of other caciques and principales.[81] This may have been a common occurrence in Nicaragua, where Indian communities were much smaller than those in the Valley of Mexico and where noble families did not emerge as strong social units to oppose such maneuvers. There must have been many occasions, when the succession was interrupted or in doubt, that provided opportunities for official intervention.

Beneath the caciques and *indios gobernadores* in the social structure were the elected Indian officials, the alcaldes and regidores, who formed the cabildo modeled on those established in Spanish towns. Indian cabildos were widely introduced in Nicaragua in the early 1550s, and they were considered essential for the "civilization" of the Indians and to establish law and order.[82] The number of alcaldes and regidores elected in any one village was established by law; villages of fewer than eighty houses were to have only one alcalde and one regidor, and those of more than eighty houses were to have two alcaldes and between two and four regidores, depending on the size of the village.[83] Elections to the cabildo were to be made annually, and Indians were not to serve for consecutive periods. Spanish officials were to ensure that people of bad character were not elected and were to encourage the election of those who spoke Spanish. Although all adult male Indians were eligible for election, the posts probably circulated among relatively small groups of Indians who held office for a number of consecutive years. Offices had to be confirmed by the Spanish authorities, and for this purpose Indians often had to travel miles to Spanish towns to receive the vara—the insignia of office. With the cacique the cabildo controlled all political affairs in the community. The tasks performed by alcaldes and regidores were very similar, though the former acted as judges in local courts and were accorded greater respect; in the absence of a Spanish alcalde mayor or corregidor they could even arrest non-Indians for committing offences in Indian communities.[84] The most important duties undertaken by these Indian officials were the collection of tribute and the selection of Indians to serve under the repartimiento. Other duties included the regulation of land sales and rents, the prevention and punishment of minor crimes, the maintenance of public buildings and roads, the supervision of markets, the provision of adequate water supplies, and the organization of public ceremonies. They also represented the community in its contacts with the Spanish administration in such matters as excessive tribute exactions or land encroachment.

The offices of alcalde and regidor brought with them exemption from tribute payment and labor services. They also enabled individuals to improve their financial positions through manipulating the tribute system and receiving bribes in the same way as caciques. Despite the advantages these positions bestowed, Indians were generally reluctant to stand for election. On the whole the social, political, and financial advantages the offices offered were outweighed by the burden of work they imposed; the failure of alcaldes and regidores to submit the required amount of tribute or quota of Indians to work under the repartimiento could result in their being fined, having their goods confiscated, or being imprisoned.[85] Furthermore, since Indian cabildos enforced Spanish laws, and organized the collection of tribute and labor under the repartimiento, the Indians tended to view them as institutions for their exploitation rather than as platforms for the expression of their political views. To most Indians officeholding was yet another burden that had to be borne, and the Indians preferred to abandon their villages rather than assume office.[86]

Other members of Indian cabildos included alguaciles, who were local constables; *escribanos,* who looked after the community records; and *alfereces,* or standard-bearers. Some alguaciles had special responsibilities for the collection of tribute and for supervising the local hostelry; they were known as *alguaciles de mandón* and *alguaciles de mesón,* respectively. Officials of lesser importance who were not members of the cabildo were mayordomos, who were appointed to look after the community and *cofradía* lands, and *cantores, sacristanes,* and *fiscales,* who were attached to the local church and were appointed by the clergy. *Cantores* and *sacristanes* assisted at services and looked after the ornaments and church buildings, while *fiscales* summoned people to mass. All these officials were exempt from tribute payment and the repartimiento. Church musicians were probably also exempt.[87]

Although the Spaniards recognized only the higher social status of caciques, their oldest sons, and Indian officials, within the largest class of commoners there were probably considerable variations in the socioeconomic status of individuals. These variations are not, however, clearly revealed in the documentary record until the eighteenth century,[88] and they fade into insignificance when compared with the differences between Indians and other races.

At the family level of social organization the Spaniards tried to impose monogamy and Christian standards of morality in family life. Bigamy was made illegal and adultery punished, but the Inquisition was never introduced to investigate, try, and punish Indian offenses.[89] Legally Indians were free to choose their own marriage partners.[90] Although in theory this meant that they could choose non-Indian spouses, such unions were indirectly discouraged by other legislation that promoted the residential segregation of the races.[91] Most Indians married spouses from their own villages, and the number who married non-Indians was very small at least among those who lived in Indian communities; in Indian villages in Pacific Nicaragua in the late seventeenth century only 0.9 percent of married couples included one partner of a non-Indian race, and this compared with 0.5 percent in the South American zone.[92] There was undoubtedly more contact between the races than these figures suggest, but many of the relationships between Indians and non-Indians were casual and were formed in the towns and on haciendas for which detailed evidence is not available.

Marriage records are not available in parish registers until the end of the eighteenth century; thus the few comments here are based on censuses drawn up at single points in time generally for the purpose of tribute assessment. Of particular interest are accounts of the number of Indians marrying out of their villages, since they may indicate the stability or breakdown of communities. The most comprehensive evidence for Indian marriage patterns can be gleaned from the tribute assessments drawn up for the whole of Nicaragua between 1676 and 1686. From this document it is possible to ascertain the number of Indians married to partners from their own villages or barrios and whether those partners were tributary Indians, *lavoríos,* or people of a non-Indian race. A summary of the marriage patterns is included in Table 8.

As presented the evidence suggests that outmarriage was more common in Pacific Nicaragua (66.6 percent of couples consisting of one partner from another village or barrio) than it was in the east (49.2 percent). In fact the opposite is likely to have been the case. In Pacific Nicaragua villages were much larger and consisted of several barrios. Indians were therefore considered to be marrying outside the community if they married a person from another barrio in the same village. Unfortunately it is not possible to tell from this document whether Indians were marrying partners from another village or from another barrio of the same village, but it is likely that if marriages outside villages could be calculated the percentage of Indians classified as marrying out would be far smaller and probably smaller than in the east. In the east villages were generally smaller and were not subdivided into separate barrios, and outmarriage

Table 8. Character of Indian Marriages in Nicaragua, 1676–86

Number	León*	Granada†	Nueva Segovia‡	Sebaco§
No. and percent of married couples both from the same village	551 (23.9%)	660 (23.2%)	659 (48.1%)	219 (46.9%)
No. and percent of couples man from village marrying woman from another village	711 (30.9%)	1,023 (36.0%)	305 (22.3%)	187 (27.5%)
No. and percent of couples woman from village marrying man from another village	770 (33.4%)	902 (31.7%)	317 (23.1%)	200 (29.4%)
No. and percent of men married to *lavorías*	68 (2.9%)	67 (2.4%)	9 (0.6%)	12 (1.7%)
No. and percent of women married to *lavoríos*	104 (4.5%)	89 (3.1%)	25 (1.8%)	34 (5.0%)
No. and percent married to people of non-Indian race	23 (1.0%)	22 (0.7%)	5 (0.3%)	5 (0.7%)

Source: AGCA A3.16 147 999 tasaciones 1676–86.
*The Jurisdiction of León contains 7 villages and a total of 46 barrios. The *tasaciones* for this jurisdiction are incomplete; the first 9 folios are missing from the document. Dates of *tasaciones* 1686.
†Jurisdiction of Granada contains 20 villages and 44 barrios. Dates of *tasaciones* 1685 to 1686.
‡Jurisdiction of Nueva Segovia contains 14 villages. Dates of *tasaciones* 1676 to 1685.
§Jurisdiction of Sebaco contains 11 villages. Dates of *tasaciones* 1685.

Table 8. *Continued*

Number	Mesoamerican zone	South American zone
No. and percent of married couples from same village	1,211 (23.3%)	878 (42.8%)
No. and percent of couples outmarrying	3,466 (66.6%)	1,009 (49.2%)
No. and percent marrying *lavoríos*	328 (6.3%)	80 (3.9%)
No. and percent marrying those of non-Indian race	45 (0.9%)	10 (0.5%)
No. and percent of other marriages	154 (2.9%)	73 (3.6%)
Total	5,204 (100%)	2,050 (100%)

did mean marriage to a person from another village.[93] The evidence as presented is therefore inconclusive, but two points should be made. First, the closer proximity of villages in Pacific Nicaragua would have encouraged intermarriage between Indians from different villages. Second, even if a large proportion of the Indians were marrying partners from different barrios rather than different villages, it means that the social distinctiveness of separate barrios was breaking down. Less comprehensive data for four villages in the jurisdiction of León and four villages in the jurisdiction of Nueva Segovia for the period 1685 to 1718 show that in both regions outmarriage was increasing.[94]

All the available evidence indicates that most Indians married. In the jurisdiction of Granada in 1581, 95.9 percent of the adult population was or had been married,[95] and the corresponding figure for the east was 96.3 percent. In 1676–86 the marriage rate in the jurisdiction of Granada had fallen to 82.7 percent, but in the east it remained high at 93.4 percent.[96] Although the latter figures are likely to be underestimates, since the counts did not include Indians who were exempt from tribute payment, notably caciques and Indian officials, who would probably have been married, it is tempting to suggest that the lower marriage rate in the seventeenth century, and particularly in the Mesoamerican zone, was related to the greater participation of the Indian population in the regional economy through the repartimiento and wage labor, which resulted in the prolonged absence of Indians from their communities.

Unfortunately there is little evidence for family sizes during the period under study. Most population counts were undertaken for the purpose of tribute assessment, and as such they do not include the number of children. Even where the numbers of children and tributary Indians are included, many of those who might have been defined as children on the basis of age would have been included in the latter category on the basis of their marital status. This is a greater problem with sixteenth-century evidence; later tributary Indians were defined on the basis of age. Even where detailed censuses give the ages of individuals, it is still impossible to estimate family size since the relationship between the individuals is not specified. Once an individual married, he was generally listed as heading a separate household; thus a couple might have had a family of six children, but if, say, three of them were married, they would have been registered as three separate family units, and their parents would have been listed as a family with three children. It is therefore impossible to calculate completed family size. The best that can be achieved is to calculate, where possible, the ratio of adults (generally those over age eighteen) to children, to gain a general impression of family size and whether it was increasing or decreasing.

The census of Nicaragua of 1581, excluding the towns of Posoltega and Chichigalpa, for which figures for the numbers of children are not available, shows that the number of children per adult was 0.82 for both zones, though there were considerable variations between villages. It is interesting to note that Sebaco, which had been brought under Spanish administration most recently, had a higher ratio of 1.40.[97] On the whole the figures tend to suggest that the population was failing to maintain itself. Unfortunately there is no comprehensive census from the seventeenth century that includes the number of children in each village with which these figures can be compared, but information is available for a small number of villages in both zones between 1717 and 1719. Evidence from two villages in the Mesoamerican zone suggests that there was a decline in the adult-child ratio between the two dates to about 0.48, and the four villages in the South American zone show an even more dramatic decline, to an average of 0.29 children per adult.[98] Although family size probably fell during the seventeenth century, these particularly low ratios also reflect the impact of an epidemic in 1717.[99]

The Spaniards sought to encourage the establishment of nuclear family households, primarily to achieve Christian standards of morality; the cohabitation of married families and the existence of extended families were considered undesirable because they encouraged incest and adultery. Newly married couples were therefore required to build separate houses, and Spanish officials undertook tours of inspection to ensure that each nuclear family had its own house. Although failure to comply with this rule was punished by a fine and flogging,[100] the inspector's accounts and censuses reveal that many houses were occupied by more than two adults; it was particularly common for households to accommodate single or widowed relations. The *padrones* for Diriamba and Posoltega in 1663 and for Posoteguilla in 1676 reveal that households contained on average 3.9, 2.8, and 2.8 adults, respectively.[101]

A short comment must be made about orphans. Although the number of children described as orphans can be used as a guide to the high mortality rate and collapse of family structure, they are not consistently recorded in censuses. It is clear, however, that in the sixteenth century a large number of children were orphans; in 1581, 1 in 16 children in Managua (85 of 1,369 children) were orphans.[102] Later censuses do not always record the numbers of orphans, but they appear to have declined. The question of the upbringing of orphans was debated in the sixteenth century. Many orphans were adopted by Spaniards with the aim of rearing them to be household servants; it was said that each household possessed three or four orphans. This was considered to be undesirable by the Spanish authorities who argued that the orphans

never return to their homes, and the men become wayward and vagrants, and the women marry Negroes and Mulattoes, and, although some of them return and marry in their native villages, they do not settle there because of the great poverty that exists among the Indians and the different food they eat, and they do not know how to wait on their husbands, and for this reason their is little love between the said Indians.[103]

From the above observation it is clear that the authorities were concerned about the loss of the Indians' racial and cultural identity, probably because it signified a loss of tribute income. As a result the adoption of Indian orphans by Spaniards was forbidden in 1571, and the responsibility for rearing them was placed on their nearest relatives.[104] It may be that the Christian practice of specifying godparents at the time of baptism eventually overcame the problem, though it is equally clear that Spaniards continued to adopt Indian orphans for use as servants and that priests were probably the worst offenders in this respect.

The social organization of Indians who were designated as *lavoríos* is difficult to determine because of the lack of documentary evidence. The origins of *lavoríos* are diverse. Initially they consisted of a large number of single persons—widows, unmarried men and women, and orphans. Most lived in the towns or on Spanish estates, where they were often persuaded or forced to stay by the employers for whom they had worked under the repartimiento. Although these Indians often lived in distinct urban barrios, in the course of their employment they came into contact with non-Indians. As such the racial distinctiveness of urban barrios probably declined, a process that Lutz has documented for Santiago de Guatemala.[105] Similarly, those who resided on the estates gradually lost their racial and cultural identities to an extent that in the late seventeenth century efforts to make them return to their villages were disastrous because, having become ladinos, they could not accustom themselves to the "poverty" and "uncivilized life" of their villages.[106]

IDEOLOGY

Although the task of converting the Indians to the Roman Catholic faith had been charged to the Spanish crown by Pope Alexander VI in 1493, it did not begin in earnest until political stability had been achieved, which in Central America was in the middle of the sixteenth century.

It was envisaged that members of the secular clergy, the parish priests, should be responsible for the instruction of Indians in villages that had been granted as encomiendas, their salaries being paid out of the tribute they paid to their encomenderos or the crown. The relatively small size and poverty of Indian communities in Nicaragua, compared with others in the New World, meant that they could provide only low salaries for parish priests, and consequently they failed to attract good-quality candidates. As a result there were always shortages of secular clergy and constant complaints that those who were appointed were creoles of little ability and experience who did not understand the local Indian languages and were more interested in supplementing their incomes by trading with the Indians than in converting them. Because of the difficulties of recruiting parish priests, therefore, the missionary orders were permitted to minister to Indians who lived in tributary villages, though it was the crown's intention that they should be employed primarily in the preliminary conversion of Indians who remained outside Spanish control. The activities of the mendicant orders were supervised, however, by the local bishop, whose permission they required to work in his jurisdiction. The missionary orders seem to have achieved greater success in converting the Indians; most of them came from Spain, whereas the difficulty of obtaining secular clergy meant that most of them were creoles who had received little formal training because of the lack of seminaries and colleges in the area.[107]

For the purposes of religious administration Indian villages were grouped into *partidos,* which were assigned either to a parish priest or to a missionary. It was the crown's intention that the Indians should be instructed in the faith independently of other races, but owing to the lack of clergy a parish priest might find himself responsible for the whole population, irrespective of race, distributed in towns, villages, and estates over a vast area. Although there was some reorganization of *partidos* as a result of demographic changes and the opening up of new areas of economic activity, the numbers of *partidos* and the proportion of posts held by the regular clergy remained fairly constant. In 1591 there were fifteen *partidos* in Nicaragua, nine of which were administered by Mercedarians.[108] Although the Mercedarians tried to acquire jurisdiction over more Indian villages, they gained control of only the small *doctrina* of Somoto and Condega.[109] In 1663 the Mercedarians were working in the *partidos* of El Viejo, Chinandega, Jinotepe, Nicaragua, Isla Ometepe, Nandaime, and Nicoya, while the Franciscans worked in Posoltega and Sebaco.[110] In this way the missionary orders played a significant role in instructing Indians who were already under Spanish administration.

The duties of priests were manifold. They provided the Indians with regular Christian instruction either in their native languages or in *mexicana,* which was used as a lingua franca at least in the Pacific region.[111] At the same time they suppressed and punished idolatry, witchcraft, concubinage, drunkenness, and truancy. In this task the clergy were aided by secular officials, in particular alcaldes mayores, corregidores, and *tenientes de gobernadores.*[112] Punishments generally consisted of imprisonment and flogging and were sometimes extremely severe. In 1712 three Indians accused of witchcraft were so severely punished that they died.[113]

Indians not only were required to accept the Catholic faith but also were forced to support the church financially by paying fees for services, contributing alms for charitable purposes, and providing goods and services for the support of the local church and clergy. Although the clergy were not allowed to exact fees for masses or baptisms, they could charge for marriages and burials.[114] From the seventeenth century at least the maximum charges for these services were laid down in *aranceles,* but they were not always adhered to. Since priests were not allowed to charge for performing the Sacraments, they often asked Indians to contribute a *limosna,* or donation, to the church. Although such donations were meant to be voluntary, they soon became another compulsory levy on the Indians. In addition, for special religious festivals Indians were often required to provide "bottles of wine, calves, chickens, and candle wax,"[115] though most of the money for such activities came from the *cajas de comunidad* and the *cofradías.* The priests also made many illegal demands for goods and services, which have already been described.[116]

The *cofradías,* or religious brotherhoods, also made demands on their members. Members of *cofradías* paid dues that were used for saying special masses and for celebrating saints' days, particularly the saint after whom the *cofradía* was named. The dues they paid were often substantial and sometimes exceeded the amount of tribute paid by the Indians.[117] Since *cofradías* were normally organized by the different races, they emerged as institutions that supported the Indians' corporate identity.[118] Thus, although *cofradías* made demands on the Indians, they were readily adopted by them. It is significant that *cofradías* did not emerge until the seventeenth century, and then very rapidly, probably in response to the breakup of Indian communities. Later *cofradías* became important landowners, and the income they derived from their agricultural activities gave them a measure of economic independence. Gibson has suggested that *cofradías* were also encouraged by parish priests as alternative sources of income for the church at a time when the amount of tribute, and hence the money that entered the *caja de comunidad* for the support of the local church, was falling.[119] Thus even though the membership of *cofradías* imposed certain financial burdens on its members, Indian communities and the church alike benefited from their establishment.

Although the imposition of Christianity affected the daily life of the Indians, it is difficult to assess the degree to which they accepted Christian beliefs. The outward symbols of religious adherence changed: temples and idols were destroyed and replaced with churches and convents containing Christian images. However, Indian communities may have managed to conceal some idols and worship them in secret. Similarly, pagan rites and ceremonies, including sacrifices, were forbidden and replaced with Christian services related to the life cycle and the Christian calendar. Nevertheless, it was a common complaint that at supposedly Christian festivals Indians engaged in drinking and dancing, which, in the eyes of the complainants, encouraged immoral and irreverent behavior and caused the Indians to revert to their former beliefs and practices.[120] Thus, although Christian symbols of religious adherence dominated aboriginal ones, Indian beliefs probably remained in essence aboriginal with aspects of Christianity grafted onto them. Hence they probably added the Virgin Mary and Jesus Christ to the host of gods they already worshiped, ignoring the concept of monotheism that Christianity demanded.

CHAPTER 11

Cultural Change in the South American Zone, 1550–1720

The cultural changes experienced by Indians living in the South American zone varied according to the nature and intensity of contact they had with different non-Indian groups. During the period under study the area was colonized from two directions: from the already settled Pacific lowlands and from the Caribbean coast. Colonization from the west came in two streams, one secular and the other ecclesiastical. From the time of the Conquest the eastern frontier of settlement was gradually pushed farther east until about the third quarter of the sixteenth century, when it came to a halt largely because the mining industry, which had initially encouraged the settlement of the area, had declined. No other economic incentives existed in the area to stimulate the pushing back of the frontier, and from the end of the sixteenth century it was the missionary orders that carried the limits of colonization farther east. Missionary activity was intermittent, however, and although some of the more successful missions were later taken over by the secular authorities, many were short-lived. On the Caribbean coast contact with non-Indians intensified from the middle of the seventeenth century as the English settled on the shore.

Indians living in tributary villages and on the Caribbean coast maintained regular contact with other races, but Indians who were brought under the control of the missionary orders experienced the most profound cultural changes because the missionaries attempted to restructure their culture completely. Indians who remained outside the control or influence of Spaniards, missionaries, and other Europeans experienced only minor cultural changes brought about by intermittent contact with them and with other Indians under their control.

Because of the remoteness of eastern Nicaragua and the difficulties of accessibility within the region, the documentary evidence for the area is very fragmentary. Missionary accounts, which might be expected to provide more detailed information, are also incomplete because the missions were short-lived. Evidence for the Indian population living outside Spanish control is, for obvious reasons, even more inadequate. Nevertheless, an attempt will be made to describe the cultural changes experienced by Indian groups living in the South American zone, though the inadequacy of the evidence should always be borne in mind.

TRIBUTARY INDIAN VILLAGES

During the middle of the sixteenth century Spanish colonization was consolidated on the western fringes of the South American zone. A fairly large number of small villages were made tributary to individuals or the crown, and Spanish forms of secular and ecclesiastical administration were introduced as in the Mesoamerican zone. The process of cultural change experienced by these communities was thus broadly similar to that described for the Pacific region, although there were a number of differences stemming from the lower intensity of contact and from differences in the Indian cultures and the environments in which they lived.

Superficially villages in eastern Nicaragua do not appear to have declined in number during the late sixteenth and early seventeenth centuries. In 1581, twenty-four Indian villages paid tribute, though none of the villages appeared in the 1548 *tasaciones,* and in 1676–85 twenty-five villages were paying tribute.[1] There is no suggestion of a decline in the interim period; in 1663 there were twenty-two tributary villages in the vicinity of Nueva Segovia and Sebaco.[2] Nevertheless, it is clear from a cursory examination of the names of the villages that there was considerable instability in the settlement pattern; about half of the villages recorded in 1581 were not present in 1685, and vice versa. Compared with the villages in the Pacific region, Indian villages in the east were smaller, though they grew during the seventeenth century; the average number of married men per village rose from 23.3 in 1581 to 57 in 1685.[3] Although there was no forced amalgamation of villages such as occurred in other parts of Central America, we have some evidence of voluntary consolidation resulting from population decline: in 1703 four villages in the jurisdiction of Nueva Segovia—Ula, Siguateca, Cacalguaste, and Telpanequilla—were amalgamated to form San Miguel del Jícaro.[4]

The settlement pattern was unstable because of enemy attacks and migration. From the 1660s hostile Indians led attacks in the valleys of Jalapa and Mozonte, in Nueva Segovia,[5] and from the beginning of the eighteenth century the Zambo-Mosquito carried out raids on frontier towns, even though their main efforts were concentrated on the Matina coast of Costa Rica, where they obtained cacao and Indian slaves.[6] These attacks and the Indians' desire to escape tribute payment, the repartimiento, and ill-treatment, drove them to desert the hills. These movements were more common in the South American zone, where the Indians were more familiar with a seminomadic form of existence. Other Indians deserted to Spanish towns and estates.[7] By 1653 at least enough *lavoríos* were working in Nueva Segovia to justify the establishment of a separate Indian barrio in the town, and an order issued in 1679 for the return of Indians employed by *vecinos* in Nueva Segovia appears to have had little effect.[8]

The major changes in the Indian economy were associated with the increasing importance of agriculture, which was encouraged by the sedentary life the Spaniards imposed, the nature of tribute demands, and the introduction of livestock. Whereas in the pre-Columbian period the Indians had practiced shifting cultivation based on an assemblage of crops in which root crops figured significantly, in the colonial period cultivation became more permanent, seed crops assuming greater importance and livestock largely supplanting wild animals and fish as sources of animal protein. As a consequence, settlements and landholdings became more permanent, although some shifts occurred in response to enemy attacks. Nevertheless, since the Indians were unfamiliar with the concept of landownership as opposed to land use, and since there was less pressure on land in eastern Nicaragua, they did not seek formal titles to their lands. This became a serious problem in the eighteenth century, when their lands came under pressure from ranchers in the west.

Changes in the nature of landholding were paralleled by changes in the allocation of labor among the various economic activities. The major change was that time had to be set aside to meet Spanish demands for tribute and labor; previously Indian communities had not produced surpluses or provided labor to meet extracommunal demands. Furthermore, the burden of tribute payment was sometimes greater in the east than in the west because the products demanded were often unsuited to the physical conditions of the region. In common with the Mesoamerican zone, the burdens of the repartimiento and other demands for labor services by Spanish officials and priests reduced the time available for subsistence activities. In addition to carrying out the tasks in which Indians were commonly employed in the west,[9] Indians in the east were also engaged in establishing tobacco plantations and transporting tar and pitch to the Pacific coast.[10] Although Indians complained about the burdens these demands imposed, they were probably not as great as those experienced in the west, since the area was remote and there were fewer Spanish officials, priests, colonists, and travelers to make exactions. In 1649 the absence of a corregidor in Nueva Segovia was given as the reason for the rise in population there, since not only were the Indians free from exploitation by a corregidor but Indians from other regions with corregidores fled there to escape their demands.[11] On the other hand, the remoteness of the eastern areas from official surveillance may have encouraged greater exploitation of the Indians, albeit by a smaller number of people, who imposed burdens on communities that were excessive given their small size and the Indians' lack of familiarity with providing goods and services to meet extracommunal demands.

Although the assemblage of crops cultivated by the Indians in this zone did not alter significantly, the emphasis of production did change. The tribute items the Spaniards in Nicaragua usually demanded were maize, beans, and cotton. Although these items were produced in small quantities in eastern Nicaragua in pre-Columbian times, Indian subsistence depended to a greater degree on the cultivation of root crops. The need to pay tribute in the crops specified led to an increase in their cultivation, though some were not naturally suited to the climate of the region.[12] During the period under study the main subsistence crops cultivated were maize and plantains; a survey of the village of Boaco in 1701 showed that the inhabitants possessed 106 milpas of maize, 12 plots of plantains, and one cattle ranch.[13] Other food crops cultivated included beans and sweet potatoes, and it is assumed that the Indians continued to cultivate indigenous fruit trees; there is no evidence that Indians adopted European fruits, such as citrus fruits. Other crops commonly grown in this area were tobacco and sugar.[14]

Domesticated animals, particularly cattle, spread rapidly in eastern Nicaragua, where they could graze on the extensive year-round pastures. Cattle were introduced at an early date, and it was probably not long before the Indians began to raise them.[15] From about the midseventeenth century they also raised mules, which were used in the tar-and-pitch industry.[16] Meanwhile, chickens remained one of the most important sources of food; they were also required as tribute and by Spanish officials and clergy as part of their weekly rations.

The exploitation of wild-food resources probably continued throughout the period, though at a reduced level of intensity owing to the decline in available labor and alternative sources of protein in the form of domesticated animals. Hunting and collecting remained more important than fishing, particularly in times of shortage, and honey and wax were paid as tribute.[17] Craft activities probably did not vary significantly from those of the pre-Columbian period. Spanish demands for cotton cloth and their insistence on more "decent" forms of clothing than the bark cloth the Indians normally wore, probably encouraged its wider use.

In the pre-Columbian period the Indians produced few food surpluses or craft items for exchange, and any trade that occurred was by barter. During the colonial period trade probably expanded, and it is possible that formal markets and mediums of exchange were introduced. However, most goods were probably bought and sold under coercion from Spanish officials and colonists rather than being traded freely in the open market.[18] In eastern Nicaragua the Spaniards were particularly interested in obtaining tar, pitch, and mules; in 1695 the governor of Nicaragua had a special agent in Nueva Segovia who undertook purchases of these items.[19]

Although the social and political institutions the Spaniards imposed on the Indians in eastern Nicaragua were the same as those introduced in the Mesoamerican zone, their effects were different. Whereas in the Mesoamerican zone the political organization of the chiefdoms was changed and the Indians experienced a degree of social leveling, in the South American zone the tribal groups, which had been essentially egalitarian, underwent social differentiation and witnessed the introduction of a form of political organization, albeit a weak one. As such there was a convergence in the political and social structure of the Indian communities in the two zones. Social differentiation in the South American zone occurred through the creation of permanent leaders and town councils. Whereas in pre-Columbian times Indian leaders had been elected on a temporary basis, now the position of the cacique was made permanent and hereditary, and caciques and cabildo officials were differentiated from the common people by being granted certain privileges.[20]

At the family level of organization the Spaniards sought to impose monogamy and Christian standards of morality in marriage. They tried to suppress polygamy and the cohabitation of families in multifamily households. Polygamy was easier to control because it was not widespread and because parish priests could effectively prevent such marriages. The multifamily occupancy of houses was more difficult to counter. A *visita* of the village of Jinotega in 1663 showed an average of 3.3 adults per household.[21] Although the average fell to just over 2 in the early eighteenth century, it seems likely that the decrease was due to the general decline in the Indian population rather than to the success of Spanish officials in enforcing nuclear-family residence.[22]

Although the marriage rate was higher in eastern Nicaragua, outmarriage was more common there. The figures for the pattern of outmarriages at the end of the seventeenth century suggest that outmarriages were common in the west, accounting for 66.6 percent of all marriages as opposed to 49.2 percent in the east, but the figure for the Mesoamerican zone is inflated by the number of Indians who married partners from their own villages but from different barrios of those villages. If, as has already been suggested, the number of Indians marrying out of their villages as opposed to their barrios is calculated, the percentage is less than that calculated for the South American zone.[23] One reason for the higher percentage of outmarriages in the east was the smaller size of the villages, which restricted the choice of marriage partners. It is also clear, however, that the population was more mobile, with individuals moving around the countryside in search of employment. Most villages experienced the loss of a number of tributary Indians, and sometimes they accounted for a substantial percentage of the total population: in 1718 no less than 25 percent of the total adult population of Teustepet (221) was registered as absent. Although the destinations of about half of those absent are unknown, of the remainder one-third were living on haciendas, one-third had migrated to the west (to Masaya, Diriá, and Granada), and the others were living in other Indian villages.[24]

Although the marriage rate in the east was high, and there were fewer single people, which might suggest a higher degree of social stability, villages were clearly losing their population through migration, and the small number of children suggests that Indian communities were beginning to break down. Whereas in 1581 the average number of children per adult was 0.66 for the four villages Teustepet, Boaco, Jinotega, and Linagüina, between 1717 and 1718 the figure was 0.29.[25] Although it is clear that the area was suffering from epidemics at this time, the absence of able-bodied adults probably contributed to the low birthrate.

The religious affairs of Indians residing in tributary Indian villages in the east fell under the jurisdiction of the secular clergy, and thus the comments about the organization of the church and its nature and impact on the economic, social, and political life of the Indians apply equally to the South American zone. However, the adoption of Christianity by Indians living in this zone was even more superficial than it was in the west. Here the task of conversion was made more difficult by the dispersed settlement pattern, the greater diversity of Indian languages, and the greater difficulty of persuading clergy to work in these remote and unattractive areas. Therefore, Indian villages were visited irregularly by priests who had little training and knowledge of Indian languages and were more interested in trading with the Indians than converting them.[26]

THE MISSIONS

During the late sixteenth and seventeenth centuries, among all the Indians who lived in the South American zone, those who were brought under the control of the missionary orders experienced the most radical cultural changes, even though they were moderated to some extent by the short life of the missions.[27]

Before the missions were established, the Indians in the area had a seminomadic existence, subsisting on the products of cultivation, hunting, fishing, and gathering.[28] One of the primary aims of the missionary orders was to "civilize" the Indians, and this meant congregating them in permanent nucleated settlements, or *reducciones,* where they could be instructed in techniques of cultivation, livestock raising, and craft manufacture. Mission villages were established as miniature versions of Spanish towns, with houses erected around a central plaza on which the church and administrative buildings were built. According to an order of 1713, all *reducciones* were also to have adequate "water, lands, and *montes,*" as well as "an ejido consisting of one league of land, for the grazing of livestock."[29]

At first the Indians were fed on provisions, mainly maize and meat, imported by the missionaries, but at the same time they were given plots of land, tools, and animals—notably chickens, cattle, and some horses—with which to establish a permanent form of agriculture. Since it was intended that the missions would eventually be secularized, it seems likely that a landholding system similar to that found in the tributary Indian villages was introduced in the missions. Hence the community probably owned the land, but plots were allocated to individuals for cultivation. Unfortunately we have no information about the organization of labor in the missions, but the burden of work imposed on the Indians was probably not very great, for the missions aimed only at self-sufficiency, and the Indians were not subject to tribute payment and the repartimiento. Nevertheless, it is clear that the Indians resented working in the missions and preferred their seminomadic existence in the forests.

There is little evidence about the character of mission agriculture, but what we have suggests that maize was the dominant crop regardless of the area in which the mission was situated. For Indian groups living in areas that were not naturally suited for the crop, this would have been an innovation. In many settlements the missionaries had to teach the Indians how to cultivate the newly introduced crops and sometimes even the basic techniques of cultivation. The missionaries also distributed livestock to the Indians, not only for their subsistence but also to encourage them to remain in the missions. The raising of domesticated animals supplanted hunting and fishing as sources of animal protein. Although the earlier activities may have continued on a small scale, they were not encouraged or even permitted by the missionaries because of the opportunities they afforded for desertion. Thus, although the diet of the Indians in this area may have been adequate in terms of the amount of protein and calories consumed, its variety was probably reduced. Again, since the missions aimed only at self-sufficiency and agricultural production remained at a low level, trade did not expand as it did in the tributary Indian villages. Furthermore, the missionaries discouraged all contacts with persons outside the missions, because they were thought to have a corrupting influence.

Like the tributary Indians in eastern Nicaragua, the Indians who came under the control of the missionary orders experienced changes in their social organization at both community and family levels. The changes were of a different character, however, and they were largely destructive. During the process of missionization Indian communities were often broken up, and the Indians who were established in one mission were often drawn from several, often mutually hostile, communities. They possessed few common interests and dissension among them was often aggravated by contacts with outside groups. The task of integrating the Indians into communities and imposing discipline was therefore a formidable one. Unfortunately, the missionaries chose to supervise closely all aspects of Indian life, thus divesting the Indians of the faculty to regulate their own lives and establish some form of community organization that might have encouraged them to remain in the missions. Hence the missions suffered continual desertions, and any Indians that remained when the missionaries died or left rapidly dispersed to resume their former way of life in the forests.

Within the missions Indian cabildos were established by the missionaries to enable them to impose discipline and to provide the Indians with the political experience they would require when the missions were secularized. The introduction of Indian cabildos established a social hierarchy among Indians whose social organization had formerly been egalitarian. Meanwhile, more sweeping changes took place in their family life. Some family units were destroyed during the process of missionization, particularly when force was employed. It is clear that the missionaries had greater success in gathering children, women, and old people into the missions. This imbalance in the age and sex structure did not change over time owing to the greater ability of able-bodied males to flee. Also the missionaries' efforts to suppress polygamy did little more than arouse resentment, and as soon as the missionaries left, the Indians reverted to their own marriage customs and rites.[30]

The organizational structure of the Franciscan and Mercedarian orders and their aims, activities, and means of converting the Indians have already been described, and the comments made here will be confined to their impact on the Indians' religious beliefs and practices. When the missionaries arrived, the absence of idols, temples, priests, and sacrificial ceremonies gladdened their hearts and suggested that the task of converting the Indians would be relatively easy.[31] Their initial optimism was soon dispelled, however, as the absence of native leaders made quick and easy conversions impossible and the Indians proved reluctant to move into the missions. The force that was often employed created resentment and discouraged the Indians from adopting Christian beliefs, on top of which the diversity of languages spoken by the Indians made their instruction difficult. In addition, many of the concepts the missionaries introduced were less familiar to Indians in the South American zone than they were in the west, where, although the content of the native religion differed from Christianity, the Indians were familiar with formal ceremonies, permanent religious buildings, and instituted priesthoods. The lack of true conversion is demonstrated by the desire of the Indians to revert to their former way of life and by the constant supervision required to keep them in the missions. Thus, despite the apparent lack of religious beliefs in the east, the missionaries found the task of converting the Indians there more difficult.

INDIAN GROUPS OUTSIDE SPANISH CONTROL

There are few accounts of the cultural changes experienced by Indian groups outside Spanish control, but it is clear that some changes occurred as a result of the activities of missionaries and the settlement of the English on the Mosquito Coast. The area outside Spanish control remained heavily populated even though some Indians were collected into the missions or enslaved by the Zambo-Mosquito. Rumors persisted about villages with populations of 3,000 and 6,000 Indians in the mountains of Chontales, but most accounts record large numbers of small settlements; in 1699, eighteen settlements of Guaianes were enumerated in the headwaters of the río Segovia.[32] The settlements were composed of a number of extended-family or multifamily houses; the latter were more common among the Sumu, though individual families were scattered throughout the countryside.[33] In addition, there were temporary or semipermanent settlements belonging to Indians who still depended largely on wild-food resources but were sedentary for a few months of the year when they cultivated plantains or maize.[34] In the colonial period settlements may have been established away from the rivers to escape missionary expeditions and the enslaving raids of the Zambo-Mosquito.

The constant conflict between Indians and those seeking to incorporate them into missions or capture them for sale as slaves may have brought about slight changes in their social organization. Although the presence of common aggressors may have reduced intertribal warfare, war leaders probably became more common features of Indian society, even though their positions remained temporary.[35] The raids also broke up families as women and children in particular were removed to the missions or enslaved. It is not known whether these changes affected marriage residence rules. Both monogamy and polygamy prevailed, and multifamily households were common.[36]

THE MOSQUITO COAST

Although in the late sixteenth and early seventeenth centuries buccaneers camped temporarily on the Mosquito Coast while they provisioned themselves before attacking the north coast of Honduras, cultural changes experienced by Indians living on the coast did not begin in earnest until the English settled there permanently in the 1630s and a large number of black slaves were shipwrecked there in 1641. There is some doubt about the origin of the shipwrecked vessel, but Holm has suggested that the slaves may have been fleeing from Providencia, which was recaptured by the Spaniards in that year.[37] Documentary evidence about the location of the shipwreck is also vague, though two documents mention that it occurred on the "Isla de Mosquitos."[38] In the conflicts that soon arose between the newly arrived black slaves and the Indians, the blacks were the victors and took the Indian women for wives. It was from these unions that the so-called Zambo-Mosquito emerged.[39] The black contribution to this racial mixture was maintained by the English, who imported black slaves from the Caribbean islands, especially Jamaica, to work on their plantations. Other blacks arrived as runaway slaves from the interior areas of Honduras and Nicaragua, notably from the mining areas of Teguicigalpa and Comayagua, and also from plantations on the Caribbean coast and the islands. Although the racial changes on the Mosquito Coast were profound, the cultural changes that accompanied them occurred more slowly and were not fully apparent until the eighteenth century.

The arrival of the English and the emergence of the Zambo-Mosquito brought changes in the settlement pattern on the Mosquito Coast. Whereas in pre-Columbian times the Indians had had temporary fishing settlements on the coast and permanent agricultural villages some distance inland, during the second half of the seventeenth century the Zambo-Mosquito established permanent settlements on the coast, particularly at Cabo de Gracias a Dios, Sandy Bay, and Bluefields.[40] These settlements were established so that the inhabitants could take advantage of employment and trading opportunities offered by the English. There is no evidence of changes in the forms of houses or settlements; the Mosquito apparently lived in multifamily houses.[41]

The primary aim of the English who settled on the Mosquito Coast was trade; they had no intention of directly altering the Indian economy. That they came as traders rather than colonists, at least in the early years of the settlement of the coast, meant that only small stretches of land were alienated, and these were mainly areas that had not been cultivated by Indians. A small number of Indians were employed by the English as sailors on vessels that traded between the coast and the Caribbean islands, particularly Jamaica,[42] but work on the plantations was undertaken by imported black slaves. Nevertheless, the presence of foreigners diverted Indian labor away from subsistence activities and to the acquisition of trade items.

The Indian economy was based on the cultivation of crops, heavily supplemented by fishing, and, farther inland, by hunting. Root crops were the most important crops grown, while maize was grown in small quantities for beverages rather than bread.[43] In 1714 it was reported that the Mosquito lived on "fish, wild game, plantains, and roots of plants and different vegetables, and from maize they make their drinks."[44] During the seventeenth century bitter manioc was introduced to the area, and the coconut palm became well established on the Caribbean coast.[45] There is no evidence that the blacks who settled on the coast introduced any African domesticates, unless the yams recorded by Dampier were an African variety. Indeed, Raveneau de Lussan noted that around Cabo de Gracias a Dios the Indians taught the shipwrecked blacks how to plant maize, bananas, and manioc and also how to make a drink called hoon from an indigenous palm tree, probably the pejibaye palm.[46]

Although the Europeans introduced domesticated animals, particularly cattle and horses, to the Mosquito Coast, it is doubtful that the Indians adopted them to any great extent; wild animals were abundant, and firearms made hunting more efficient. Thus in 1707 the economy of the Mosquito was described as follows: "The maize they sow they use in chichas, and they subsist on plantains and other edible roots, and there is no domesticated meat, only wild meat, which they usually eat, fish, some chickens, and beans."[47] Firearms were greatly sought after by the Indians, to the extent that men were said to offer their wives to the English in exchange for muskets.[48] The acquisition of firearms would certainly have aided in the hunting of rapidly moving animals, especially birds, and enabled the Indians to conduct more effective enslaving raids. In 1721 the governor of Costa Rica reported that the Mosquito used firearms "like fish in the sea and birds in the air," such that they could compete with the Spaniards in war.[49]

Most of the characteristics of trade between the Europeans and Zambo-Mosquito have already been described, and it is clear that this trade dominated over that among the Zambo-Mosquito themselves. Generally speaking, European manufactures, especially guns, were exchanged for turtle shells, cacao, and Indian slaves, though other wild products, such as honey, wax, and sarsaparilla, were also traded.[50] No mediums of exchange appear to have been used; nor were formal markets established.

Only slight changes occurred in the social organization of Indian groups living on the Mosquito Coast during the late seventeenth and early eighteenth centuries. While marriage-residence rules may have begun to change to accommodate the prolonged absence of men from their households, polygamy appears to have continued, and the rudimentary political organization that the English introduced did little to modify the essentially egalitarian character of the society.

From the observations of early visitors to the Mosquito Coast it would appear that the newcomers adopted the customs of the Indians. The Mosquito were polygamous, marrying as many wives as they could support; on the Isla de Mosquitos each man was said to have six or seven wives.[51] Trial marriages occurred, formal marriage taking place after children had been born. There was no concept of adultery.[52] The documentary evidence is unclear about the marriage-residence rules in effect at this time. Dampier provides the only comment on the matter, recording that upon marriage a couple built a separate house, but this clearly did not occur in all instances, as the existence of multifamily houses indicates.[53] Helms has suggested that there was a tendency to matrilocality stimulated by changes in the Indian economy during the seventeenth century.[54] Although in pre-Columbian times men would have been absent from their homes on hunting and fishing expeditions and in times of war, their absences became more frequent and prolonged with the arrival of the English in the area. Not only were the Mosquito drawn into working as sailors and obtaining items for trade, but the acquisition of firearms enabled them to carry out more effective raids, which became more frequent. When men are absent from their communities for long periods, it is advantageous in terms of cultural continuity for the men to move to their wives' villages or homes on marriage so that a stable consanguineal core of women remains to stabilize the community. Should patrilocality prevail in communities where men are absent from their homes for extended periods, the deserted wives tend to drift back to their parents' home with the result that the composition of the community tends to be unstable. Helms suggests fairly convincingly that in former times individual families had foraged together for part of the year but that when more distant expeditions were mounted the men probably left their families at home, thereby initiating matrilocality, which later became institutionalized. She concludes that, although the case for the development of matrilocality during the colonial period cannot be proved, it would be wrong to assume that it originated in the pre-Columbian period.

There is very little evidence for precise family sizes in the seventeenth century, but it is clear that they were large. One observation noted that each family was composed of 10 or 12 people, but it is not clear whether they were large nuclear families or extended families.[55] The rapid increase of Zambo-Mosquito from their origin in the 1640s to a population of 5,000 to 6,000 in 1711 suggests a high fertility rate,[56] which would have been encouraged by polygamy and the acquisition of wives and children from other Indian groups.[57]

In the pre-Columbian period Indians living on the Mosquito Coast were essentially egalitarian, temporary leaders being chosen to lead expeditions against hostile neighbors; at other times they had no form of government.[58] According to Conzemius (quoting Exquemelin), after contact the Mosquito selected leaders in times of war, but the preferred leaders were those who had sailed with the buccaneers.[59] This reflects the friendship that had developed between the Mosquito and the English and the prestige the latter were accorded because of their ability to supply them with the firearms that were essential for their domination of the coast.

In addition to the temporary war leaders the English created a number of official positions to substantiate their claims to the coast. They attempted to found the Kingdom of Mosquitia with a king at its head. The date of the origin of the kingship is uncertain; it had certainly been established by 1687, when the chief at Cabo de Gracias a Dios was crowned King Jeremy I.[60] From that time onward the king was chosen by the governor of Jamaica, theoretically from a list of candidates. The king was then crowned and received a scepter as his symbol of office. The governor of Jamaica later found it desirable to extend the support of the Zambo-Mosquito by creating a number of other offices along the coast: a general was installed at Black River, a governor at Tuapí Lagoon, and an admiral at Pearl Lagoon. Nevertheless, it was the king who commanded the greatest respect. He resided in a thatched palace at Sandy Bay during the turtle season and in another palace on the río Segovia for the rest of the year. The king was generally a zambo or mulatto, at least from the early eighteenth century, whereas farther south the governor at Tuapí Lagoon was generally a Mosquito, with more Indian than black blood.[61] During the eighteenth century these officials were supported by tribute levied from defeated tribes, but it is not clear when these exactions began; they may have begun as compensations for goods acquired during raids, which the English were eager to discourage for political reasons.[62] The items paid as "tribute" included turtle shell, canoes, hammocks, and cotton lines. The Mosquito appear to have respected the appointed officials as intermediaries with the English, but they did not recognize their power within their own communities; the social organization remained, at least during the seventeenth century, essentially egalitarian but with temporary war leaders and the *sukyas* (shamans) commanding some authority.[63]

Through the acquisition of firearms the Zambo-Mosquito were able to dominate their Indian neighbors, carrying out raids and seizing Indian slaves. These raids were an extension of the intertribal conflicts that had occurred in the pre-Columbian period, but they were intensified by the Zambo-Mosquito, who, having acquired firearms, were able to carry out raids with impunity. The Zambo-Mosquito regarded inland Indian groups as fit for enslavement and referred to them as Alboawinneys, meaning "slave meat" in Miskito (*alba* = slave; *wina* = meat).[64] Most enslaved men would have been sold to Europeans, while the women would have been kept as wives and the children brought up as their own.[65] Thus Indian slaves did not form a distinct social class but were either exported or rapidly absorbed into Mosquito society.

There is no evidence that Europeans living on the Mosquito Coast attempted to convert the Indians to Christianity; certainly the descriptions of their religion by early travelers and settlers do not suggest any Christian influence.[66]

PLATES

Plate 1. *Map of Nicaragua by Sebastián de Aranzibia y Sasi, 1716 (AGI Mapas y Planos [Guatemala], no. 17; courtesy Archivo General de Indias, Seville).*

Rio de le san tarrua

Jslas mosquitos

Jsla depulas

Rio de maiaga

Puntagorda

piedrasaas

Rio de san Juan

LESTE

Rio de Steuro

Rio Colorado

Chontales

Castillo

Granada

Pueuelo de san Juan

Plate 2. *Benzoni in conversation with an Indian cacique in Nicaragua (Theodore de Bry,* Americae Pars Quinta, *1595, plate 20; courtesy British Library).*

Plate 3. *Nicoya Polychrome wares (courtesy British Museum).*

Plate 4. *Luna Ware vessels from Nicaragua (above, courtesy British Museum; below, courtesy Peabody Museum, Harvard University, photograph by Hillel Burger, photo no. N27605, cat. no. 78-42-20/16985).*

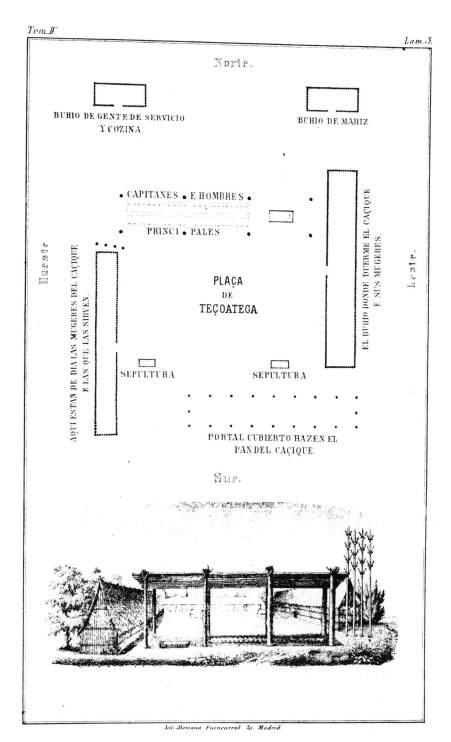

Plate 5. *Plan of the Indian town El Viejo (from Oviedo,* Historia general, lám. *3).*

Plate 6. *Method of making maize tortillas in Central America (after Benzoni; courtesy British Library).*

Plate 7. *Cacao trees and methods of drying cacao and fire making (after Benzoni; courtesy British Library).*

Plate 8. *Stone metate from Nicoya (courtesy Marjorie de Oduber and the Detroit Institute of Arts; photograph by Dirk Bakker).*

Plate 9. *Black Ware and other vessels from Nicaragua (courtesy British Museum).*

Plate 10. *Burial urn from Nicaragua (courtesy British Museum).*

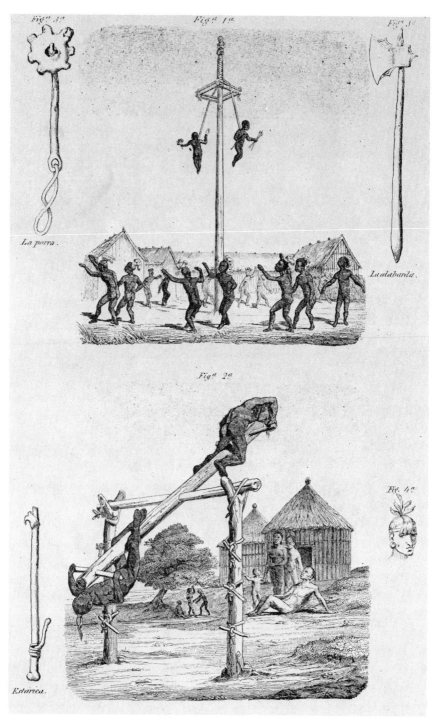

Plates 11 and 12. *Top: the* volador; *below: the* comelagatoazte *(Oviedo,* Historia general, lám. *5, figs. 1, 2).*

Plate 13. *Ceremonial dance in Nicaragua (Theodore de Bry,* Americae Pars Quinta, *1595, plate 21; courtesy British Library).*

Plate 14. *Stone statues, here and on facing page, from Isla Zapatera (Bovallius,* Nicaraguan Antiquities, *plates 9, 12; courtesy British Library).*

Plate 15. *Stone statues from Isla Zapatera (above) and Pensacola (facing page)
(Squier,* Nicaragua, *pp. 451, 483).*

Plate 16. *Modern-day settlement of Kukra Indians near Bluefields.*

Plate 17. *Stone tripod bowl from the Mosquito Coast (courtesy British Museum).*

Plate 18. Stone statues from Chontales (Richardson, "Non-Maya Monumental Sculpture," p. 411).

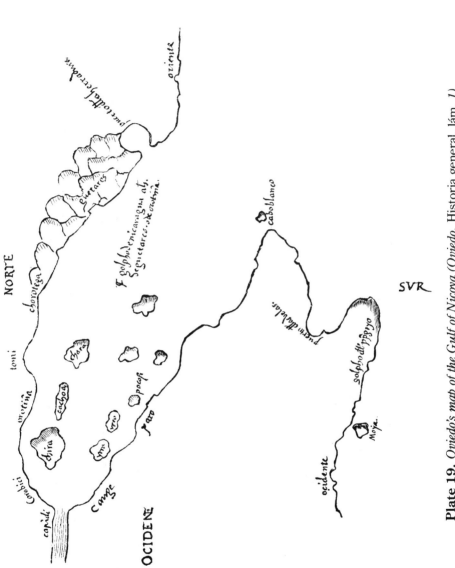

Plate 19. *Oviedo's map of the Gulf of Nicoya (Oviedo, Historia general, lám. 1).*

Plate 20. *Franciscan church with the Chapel of María Auxiliadora, Granada.*

Plate 21. *Nineteenth-century engraving of indigo works (Squier, "Nicaragua," p. 746; courtesy University of London Library).*

Plate 22. *Map of the mouth of the San Juan River by Martín de Andújar, 1673 (AGI Mapas y Planos [Guatemala], no. 5; courtesy Archivo General de Indias).*

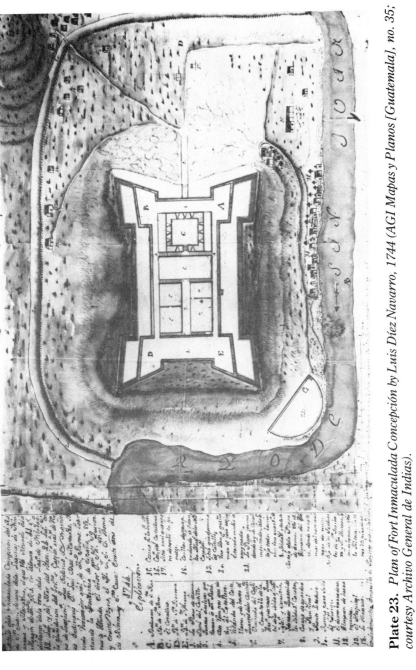

Plate 23. *Plan of Fort Inmaculada Concepción by Luis Díez Navarro, 1744 (AGI Mapas y Planos [Guatemala], no. 35; courtesy Archivo General de Indias).*

Plate 24. *Parish church of Sutiaba.*

Plate 25. *Church of San Blas, Nicoya.*

The Turning Tide: Demographic Change, 1550–1720

Estimates of the Indian population during the late sixteenth, seventeenth, and early eighteenth centuries are mainly based on or can be derived from lists of Indians drawn up for the purposes of tribute assessment. A major disadvantage of using such lists, other than the problems of inaccuracies and the possibilities of exaggeration or depression of numbers, is that they give only the numbers of tributary Indians, excluding those exempt by virtue of age, status, or physical disability. It is therefore difficult to estimate the total population from these counts. The only enumeration that includes children and covers the whole country was made in 1581; all other comprehensive counts include only the numbers of tributary Indians, though there are a few *padrones* for individual Indian villages from the end of the seventeenth century. Most general estimates of the Indian population by Spanish officials appear to have been based on lists of tributary Indians.

The most comprehensive account of the Indian population in Nicaragua was drawn up in 1581, but before a discussion of this account it is worthwhile to examine a few general estimates of the size of the Indian population made by contemporary observers. In 1553 the Dominican friar Tomás de la Torre reported that in the whole of the Province of Nicaragua there were not 7,000 *hombres*.[1] This friar had recently visited Nicaragua, and his estimate is likely to be fairly accurate. Probably in the 1550s, Juan de Estrada, a *vecino* of Guadalajara, suggested that there were 3,000 Indians in Nicaragua, but he admitted that it would be necessary to look at the *libro de tasaciones* to ascertain the precise number.[2] Some years later the dean of the Cathedral of León, Pedro del Pozo, reported that there were 6,750 *vecinos naturales* in Nicaragua and Nicoya, 6,050 of these forming separate Indian parishes, and 700 being administered by the parish priests of Granada and Nueva Segovia.[3] Although the document is undated, the same bundle contains several letters from the dean written in the early 1570s. The letter in question, however, was written a year after Indian sacristans and church musicians, who had formerly been exempt from tribute payment, were placed on the tribute rolls, and MacLeod suggests that this probably occurred in the early 1560s.[4] Finally, in 1578, the bishop of Nicaragua reported that forty years before there had been 300,000 Indians in Nicaragua, but that at that time, according to the *padrones* of priests and vicars, there were

Table 9. Contemporary Population Counts and Estimates to 1685

Year	Count or Estimate	Source and Comment
1548	10,683 *tributarios*	Excludes Nicoya with 660. Does not cover the jurisdictions of Sebaco and Nueva Segovia. Tributarios are married males. AGI AG 128 Libro de tasaciones.
1553	7,000 *hombres*	Fr. Tomás de la Torre. AGI AG 8 22.5.1553.
1550s	3,000 Indians	Juan de Estrada. AGI IG 857, no date.
ca. 1570	6,750 *vecinos naturales*	Dean of the Cathedral of León, Pedro del Pozo. AGI AG 167, no date.
1571–74	10,580 *tributarios*	López de Velasco. Clearly based on 1548 tributary lists with some errors in transcription. In the text he rounds the figures upward to give a total of 12,000 to 12,500 Indians. López de Velasco, *Geografía*, 318–26.
1578	8,000 Indians	Bishop of Nicaragua reported that forty years before there had been 300,000 Indians but that they had since been reduced to 8,000. AGI AG 162 12.1.1578.
1581	8,333 *tributarios* 3,822 married males 15,694 total Indians	The most comprehensive count for the sixteenth century, since it includes eastern Nicaragua. AGI AG 966 census.
1607	6,000 Indians	Governor of Nicaragua. Figure probably refers to tributary Indians. AGI AG 40 29.6.1607.
1612	28,490 *personas*	*Visita* by *oidor* Sánchez Araque counted this number. May include other races as well as Indians. AGI AG 13 26.1.1613; AGCA A1.23 1514 fols. 232–35 cedula 24.1.1613.
1649	5,000 Indians	Population declining because of *molestias* of the corregidores. AGCA A1.23 1517 fols. 207–208 cedula 12.12.1649; AGI AG 25 1672.

Table 9. *Continued*

Year	Count or Estimate	Source and Comment
1652	4,000 *tributarios*	Of these only 600 were tributary to the crown. AGI CO 986 Oficiales reales.
1663	5,078 *tributarios*	Pedro Frasso's *visita*. AGI AG 21 25.11.1663.
	5,100 *tributarios*	Same *visita* but figures rounded and some omitted. AGI AG 40 Certificación sacada de los libros reales 2.1.1674.
1674	4,540 *tributarios*	Compares the figures with those for 1663. AGI AG 40 Certificación sacada de los libros reales 2.1.1674.
1676–86	11,675 *tributarios* 2,089 *casados enteros* 4,600 married males	Taken from the Libro de tasaciones. Telica and Matiare missing from the jurisdiction of León. AGCA A3.16 147 999 tasaciones.
1685	10,918 *tributarios* 3,368 *casados enteros*	Comprehensive count. In addition there were 363 newly converted Indians. AGI AG 29 Navia Bolaños 28.7.1685.

only 8,000.[5] This information also appears in a letter from Juan Moreno de Toledo to the crown in the same year, but the letter says that the 8,000 figure was according to *"los padrones antiguos,"*[6] and it may therefore have been twelve years old for an *oidor* had not visited the province since that time.[7] It seems probable, therefore, that the figure refers to the mid-1560s, but it is not clear whether it refers to the total Indian population or just the tributary Indians.

Although it is clear that some reassessments of the amount of tribute paid by the Indians in Nicaragua were made in the second half of the sixteenth century,[8] very little evidence of the accompanying enumerations remains. The list of tributary Indians published by López de Velasco in 1571–74 appears to be fairly comprehensive, but, like the *tasaciones* of 1548, it includes only Indian villages in the jurisdictions of León and Granada, omitting those in the eastern part of the country. A careful examination of his account reveals that in fact it was based on the *tasaciones* of 1548 with some minor errors in transcription so that his figures total

Table 10. Indian Population in Nicaragua, 1581

Jurisdiction	Number of villages or barrios	Number of tributary Indians	Number of married males	Number of children	Number of reservados	Total	Ratio of tributary to non-tributary Indians	Ratio of married males to total
León								
Sutiaba	12	1,040	481	865	68	1,973	1:1.9	1:4.1
El Viejo and Chinandega	21	1,367	617	1,039	55	2,461	1:1.8	1:4.0
Posoltega and Chichigalpa	11	776	388	791		1,567	1:2.0	1:4.0
Total	44	3,183	1,486	2,818		6,001	1:1.9	1:4.0
Granada								
Diriá	9	1,008	476	823	6	1,837	1:1.8	1:3.9
Managua	12	1,199	564	1,369	45	2,613	1:2.2	1:4.6
Nandaime and Jinotepe	19	1,679	737	1,220	6	2,905	1:1.7	1:3.9
Total	40	3,886	1,777	3,412	57	7,355	1:1.9	1:4.1
East								
Chontales—León	6	263	125	167		430	1:1.6	1:3.4
Chontales—Granada	8	412	197	312	1	725	1:1.8	1:3.7
Sebaco	3	161	71	238	8	407	1:2.5	1:5.7
Nueva Segovia	7	428	166	333	15	776	1:1.8	1:4.7
Total	24	1,264	559	1,050	24	2,338	1:1.9	1:4.2
Grand total	108	8,333	3,822	7,361		15,694	1:1.9	1:4.1

Source: AGI AG 966 census 1581.

10,580 for Nicaragua and Nicoya rather than 11,343.[9] In the text López de Velasco rounds the figure up to give a general estimate of 12,000 to 12,500 tributary Indians. With the exception of the Chontales of Granada, most of Nicaragua was visited by *jueces de comisión,* and new *tasaciones* were drawn up by the *oidor* García de Palacio in 1578–79.[10] The *jueces* were instructed to count the entire population, including women, children, and old people. The accuracy of the counts appears to have varied particularly with respect to the nontributary population—for example, children appear to have been inconsistently enumerated in the east. The number of male married Indians was 3,822, while the total tributary population, which included able-bodied females, was 8,333 and the total population 15,694. The detailed figures indicate that the ratio of male married Indians to the total Indian population was 1:4.1, but this is likely to be an underestimate owing to the underenumeration of children. The range for the individual villages was 1:3.44 to 1:4.77.

To the figures for tributary Indians should be added those of *lavoríos.* Unfortunately there are no accounts of the population of *lavoríos* for the late sixteenth century, but a conservative estimate of their numbers, including women and children, would be about 500, 400 of whom would have been in the Mesoamerican zone.

The estimated total Indian population for the Mesoamerican zone, excluding Nicoya, for which data are not available for 1581, declined from 43,732 in 1548 to 13,756 in 1581, a decline of 68.5 percent at the rate of 3.7 percent a year.[11] Although the dean's account written in the 1570s recorded that there were 6,750 *vecinos naturales* in Nicaragua and Nicoya and gave a regional breakdown of the figures, in the absence of a precise date for the account it is impossible to calculate yearly rates of decline between the three dates, although they clearly indicate that in the last quarter of the sixteenth century the Indian population was still declining at a rapid rate. Similarly, it is impossible to calculate the rate of decline in the South American zone during the second half of the sixteenth century because the Indians there were not enumerated until at least the 1570s.

Unfortunately there are no counts comparable to that made in 1581 for the seventeenth century. Most accounts of the Indian population refer to *indios tributarios* and since they do not specify the categories of tributary Indians that were included, it is difficult to compare them. In the sixteenth century tributary lists generally included *casados,* and the term was often used synonymously with *tributario* or *vecino natural.* At that time *casados* accounted for about 90 percent of the total male tributary population. In the seventeenth century however, *casados* were divided into subcategories according to the origins, racial character, and social status of their wives. The category of tributary Indians most com-

Table 11. Decline in the Tributary Indian Population (Married Males)
in the Sixteenth Century

Jurisdiction	1548	ca. 1570s	1581	1548– ca. 1570s, %	ca. 1570s– 1581, %
León	5,714	2,400	1,486	−58.0	−38.1
Granada	4,969	3,000	1,777	−39.6	−40.8
Nicoya	660	450	NA	−31.8	
East	NA	900	559		−37.9

Sources: AGI AG 128 Libro de tasaciones 1548, AG 167 no author, no date (ca. 1570s), AG 966 census 1581.

monly recorded was that of *casados enteros,* tributary Indians whose wives also paid tribute and came from the same village. This category accounted for about 40 percent of the total male tributary population. Comparisons of the numbers of *casados* and *casados enteros* at different times during the sixteenth and seventeenth centuries can therefore be misleading when used to indicate demographic trends.

Several reports from the first half of the seventeenth century give general estimates of the number of Indians. In 1607 the governor of Nicaragua reported that there were 6,000 "*indios*" in the country, while by 1649 there were only 5,000 "*indios.*"[12] A document written three years later noted that there were 4,000 tributary Indians in the province,[13] and thus by comparison it seems likely that the two earlier accounts also referred to tributary Indians. A *visita* of Nicaragua undertaken by the *oidor* Sánchez Araque in 1612 revealed that there were 28,490 *personas,*[14] but unfortunately there are no further details of this *visita.* It is assumed that the figure included people of all ages and races. This is suggested by the large size of the figure compared to that of 15,694 for the total Indian population in 1581, especially considering that other evidence indicates that the Indian population was continuing to decline. For example, the tributary populations of villages and barrios (twenty-six in number) in the provinces of El Viejo, Chinandega, and Chichigalpa in the jurisdiction of León declined by 22.6 percent, or 0.6 percent a year, between 1581 and 1621. There were, however, enormous variations in the degree of change, ranging from the complete disappearance of three villages to four villages that registered increases.[15]

Two accounts of the Indian population in the mid-seventeenth century give estimates on a regional basis. The numbers of *indios tributarios* in 1663 were extracted retrospectively from treasury accounts in 1674. The figures were then slightly modified by being rounded up or down and compared with the number existing at that time.[16] A comparison of the figures for 1663 and 1674 indicates that between the two dates the population had declined, and this was confirmed in a letter from the *contador* of Nicaragua in 1676, who attributed the decline since 1663 to enemy invasions and disease.[17] The percentage decline calculated from the original and more accurate figures recorded in 1663 was just over 10 percent. If these figures are compared with the total number of tributary Indians registered in 1581, the percentage decline between the two dates (1581 and 1663) is quite dramatic—over 50 percent for the Mesoamerican zone. Meanwhile the tributary population of the South American zone increased owing to the incorporation of new Indian villages under Spanish administration at the beginning of the century, mainly as a result of missionary activity. A major problem in the interpretation of all these figures emerges when they are compared with two sets of figures for the total number of tributary Indians in the 1680s. One account was drawn up by the *oidor* Antonio Navia Bolaños in 1685, and the other can be obtained by summing the number of tributary Indians obtained from the *tasaciones* made between 1676 and 1686.[18] Most of the latter *tasaciones* were in fact made in 1685 and 1686; only villages in the jurisdiction of Nueva Segovia were assessed at different dates between 1676 and 1686. The figures given by Bolaños were probably drawn from earlier tribute assessments, and they indicate the presence of a smaller number of tributary Indians than that recorded in the *tasaciones* for 1676–1686. The figures for the total tributary population from the two accounts are fairly comparable—10,918 in 1685 and 11,675 in 1676–86—but the categories of tributary Indians identified in the accounts are different.[19] However, when the total figures are compared with those for 1663 and 1674, which were 5,078 and 4,540, respectively, they suggest that the Indian population was experiencing a dramatic increase—on the basis of the figures for 1674 and 1685 an increase of 140 percent. Such an increase is extremely unlikely, and it must reflect a difference in the categories of Indians recorded as tributaries at the two dates. It is possible that the figures for 1663 and 1674 referred to married male tributary Indians only, and in comparing them with the different categories recorded in the *tasaciones* of 1676 to 1686, they are most comparable to those of married male tributary Indians. If, however, the figures for 1663 and 1674 are compared with the male married tributary Indians only for 1581, then the decrease already noted and supported by qualitative evidence is converted into an increase. It is difficult, therefore, to ascertain the categories of Indians included in the figures for 1663 and 1674 and thus to draw any conclusions about demographic trends during the late sixteenth and seventeenth centuries. In comparing the figures for the total tributary population in 1581 and 1676 to

1686, there appears to have been a slight increase, but the evidence already described suggests that the increase was just beginning and that up to about 1675 the population had been declining.

Unfortunately there are no comprehensive accounts of the Indian population at the very end of the seventeenth and early eighteenth cen-

Table 12. Tributary Indians in Nicaragua, 1663 and 1674

				1663a–74	
Jurisdiction	1663a	1663b	1674	% decline	Rate of decline ω
León					
Quesalquaque and Sutiaba	1,045	1,100	950		
Nagarote and Matiare	66	—	—		
El Viejo	450	430	380		
Total	1,561	1,530	1,330	14.80	1.45
Granada					
Jalteba and Monimbó	1,938	1,900	1,750		
Total	1,938	1,900	1,750	9.70	0.93
Nueva Segovia	1,127	1,150	1,000		
Sebaco	512	520	460		
Total	1,639	1,670	1,460	10.92	1.05
Grand Total	5,078	5,100	4,540	10.95	1.02

Sources: 1663a AGI AG 21 Frasso 25.11.1663, 1663b and 1674 AGI AG 40 Certificación sacada de los libros reales 2.1.1674.

Table 13. Tributary Indians in Nicaragua 1581–1663

Jurisdiction	1581	1663a	% change	Rate of change ω
León	3,183	1,561	−50.96	−0.89
Granada	3,886	1,938	−50.13	−0.86
East	1,264	1,639	+29.67	+0.32
Total	8,333	5,078	−39.06	−0.61

Sources: AGI AG 966 census 1581, AG 21 Frasso 25.11.1663.

turies. There are, however, a few *tasaciones* for individual villages in the 1690s and between 1717 and 1718.[20] A comparison of these confirms that, with the exception of one village, which was suffering from an epidemic in 1718, the decline in the Indian population had been halted and was being converted into an increase. The increase was most marked in the Mesoamerican zone.

Both accounts of the Indian population in the third quarter of the seventeenth century include tributary Indians only, ignoring those who were exempt, were *lavoríos,* or were living in missions or in areas outside Spanish control. There is little evidence for the ratio of tributary to nontributary Indians living in Indian villages. There are only a few *padrones* for villages between 1663 and 1719, and of the five available the range in the ratio is from 1:2.0 to 1:2.9.[21] For the South American zone *padrones* are available only for the beginning of the eighteenth century, when for five villages between 1717 and 1718 the ratio was not dissimilar, ranging from 1:2.0 and 1:3.0.[22] It is reasonable therefore to double or triple the total number of tributary Indians to obtain a figure for the total population. On the basis of the far more detailed figures drawn from the *tasaciones* in 1676–86, the total Indian population living in tributary villages in Nicaragua can be estimated at between 23,350 and 35,025.

The numbers of *lavoríos* are inconsistently recorded during the seventeenth century despite the fact that they were required to pay tribute. In 1685 there were 231 *lavoríos* in the jurisdiction of León and 188 in the jurisdiction of Granada, but none were recorded for the east of the country, even though it is known that a separate barrio for *lavoríos* had been

Table 14. Tributary Indians in Nicaragua, 1685 and 1676–86

| | 1685* | | 1676–86* | | | |
| | | | | Tributaries | | |
Jurisdictions	*Casados enteros*	Total tribu- taries	*Casados enteros*	Married male	All male	Total
León	1,648	3,580	551	1,378	1,770	3,538
Granada	832	3,918	660	1,796	2,370	4,760
Nueva Segovia	679	1,059	659	996	1,141	2,339
Sebaco	209	2,361	219	430	504	1,038
Total	3,368	10,918	2,089	4,600	5,785	11,675

Sources: AGI AG 29 Navia Bolaños 28.7.1685; AGCA A3.16 147 999 tasaciones 1676–86.
*Both sets of figures exclude *lavoríos* and *reservados*. In addition the figure for Sebaco for 1685 excludes the villages of Lóvago, Lovigüisca, and Camoapa, which contained 253 newly converted Indians.

Table 15. Estimated Indian Population in Nicaragua and Nicoya at the End of the Seventeenth Century

Indian population	Mesoamerican zone	South American zone
Tributary population (multiplication factor 2.5)		
Nicaragua	20,745	8,443
Nicoya	718	
Lavoríos	800	200
Missions		200
Outside Spanish control		30,000
Total	22,263	38,843

established in Nueva Segovia in the middle of the century.[23] To judge from the qualitative accounts of Indians leaving their villages in search of employment on estates or in the towns, the number of Indians who were registered as *lavoríos* underestimated the number of Indians who were privately employed and no longer resided in their communities. It may be that, in changing their place of residence and employment, tributary Indians were able to escape registration as either *tributarios* or *lavoríos*. Although there is no evidence for the ratio of tributary *lavoríos* to the total *lavorío* population, it is not unreasonable to suggest that the tributary figure should be doubled to obtain the total population. This may be an overestimate, however, since under conditions of private employment and urban living children would have constituted a more apparent burden, and hence family sizes may have been smaller.

The Indian population contained within the missions is more difficult to estimate because missions were constantly being founded and abandoned. Missionary activity was concentrated in the first part of the seventeenth century, when missionary expeditions resulted in the establishment of a number of Indian villages some of which became tributary to individuals or the crown. The only attempt at further conversions was at the end of the seventeenth century, when in 1678 it was reported that two missions had been founded containing a total of 200 "almas de confesión" and many children, who together comprised 40 families.[24]

The numbers of Indians who resided in areas outside Spanish control is extremely difficult to estimate. From the end of the sixteenth century we have comments on the numbers residing on the Caribbean coast, but few comments on the area between the coast and the frontier of Spanish settlement, though it is clear from later accounts that the area contained substantial Indian populations.[25] One account in 1681 recorded that on the banks of the río Bocay alone there were 6,000 Indians, without counting others living in surrounding valleys.[26] This area formed only a small part of the total area outside Spanish control, and thus it may be suggested that, taking account of observations made in the eighteenth century, the Indian population of this area was about 30,000. There is more evidence for the number of inhabitants on the Mosquito Coast. In 1672, Exquemelin described the Mosquito as a nation of 1,600 to 1,700,[27] but by 1707 there were said to be 1,000 men under the protection of the English and about 2,000 to 3,000 women and children.[28] In 1711 the bishop of Nicaragua estimated that between 5,000 and 6,000 Indians were living on the coast.[29]

Taking into account all the Indians not designated as tributary Indians, but excluding the Zambo-Mosquito, the total Indian population in the last quarter of the seventeenth century was about 61,106. The figures for *lavoríos* are likely to be underestimates, and the number of them included for the South American zone is a pure guess. The inclusion of the figure of 30,000 for the area between the Mosquito Coast and the frontier of Spanish settlement is also an intelligent guess. The major problem in comparing demographic trends in the two zones is that much of the east of the country was not brought under Spanish control until the end of the sixteenth century, so that the tributary population appears to be increasing, whereas in fact it is being recorded for the first time. In addition it is virtually impossible to obtain accurate figures for the whole of the South American zone. Nevertheless two comparisons are worth making: first, between the tributary population of the Mesoamerican zone in the middle of the sixteenth century and the last quarter of the seventeenth century and, second, between estimates of the Indian population in both zones at the time of Conquest and in the last quarter of the seventeenth century. According to the lists of tributary Indians drawn up in 1548 and 1676–86, the Indian population of the Mesoamerican zone, excluding *lavoríos,* declined from 45,372 (multiplication factor of 4) to 21,463 (multiplication factor 2.5).[30] This was a decline of 52.7 percent or 0.55 percent a year, but it masks the considerable temporal variations that have been noted. From a comparison of the figures for the aboriginal population with those for the end of the seventeenth century it would appear that the total Indian population in the Mesoamerican zone (including *lavoríos*) suffered a greater decline than that of the population in the east: 96.6 percent compared to 82.1 percent, respectively.

The major factors responsible for the decline in the Indian population changed in the late sixteenth and seventeenth centuries. Whereas conquest and to a greater extent the Indian slave trade had taken a heavy toll on the Indian population in the first half of the sixteenth century, by 1550 political stability had been achieved, and the slave trade had ceased.

Also, although there were many instances of overwork and excessive demands for goods and services, the New Laws went some way toward improving the treatment of the Indians to the extent that the proportion of the decline that can be attributed to these causes decreased. The most significant factors during this period were disease, the disruption of Indian economies and societies, and racial intermixing, the last assuming greater importance as time progressed.

Once political stability had been achieved, casualties resulting from conflict between Indians and non-Indians accounted for an insignificant proportion of the decline in the Indian population, though three areas of conflict remained. First, Indians were killed during missionary expeditions. Second, from the last quarter of the seventeenth century the Zambo-Mosquito conducted raids inland from the Mosquito Coast as far west as Lake Granada. Finally, pirate attacks on Spanish towns in the seventeenth century resulted in some Indian casualties.

The burden of work that fell on the Indians in providing tribute and meeting the repartimiento quota and other demands for goods and services was considerable. Although each exaction may have been small, together they combined to keep the Indians in continual labor, leaving them little time to attend to their subsistence needs. In addition some of the tasks in which Indians were employed were injurious to health and directly contributed to the death rate. It was estimated that before the prohibition on the employment of Indians in shipbuilding at Realejo in 1579, 500 Indians died,[31] while many others died in the unhealthy indigo factories. Although the crown attempted to prohibit the employment of Indians in tasks regarded as strenuous and unhealthy, their employment often continued illegally. Even when the tasks in which Indians were employed were not particularly arduous, there were instances of ill-treatment. This was particularly true among Indians who worked under the repartimiento, for employers had little incentive to preserve the labor supply, which was available for only limited periods.

There is no doubt that in many instances the illegal exactions mainly by corregidores, alcaldes mayores, *jueces de milpas,* and priests in the form of goods and labor services far exceeded the legal demands of tribute and the repartimiento.[32] In 1649 the reason given for the decline in the Indian population of León and Granada was the presence of corregidores and *jueces de milpas* which had encouraged the Indians to migrate to Nueva Segovia.[33] Later when corregidores were appointed in Nueva Segovia and Sebaco the bishop of Nicaragua noted that

there have been two epidemics in two years but they have not caused the ruin that this tyranny [of the *corregidor*] has introduced in this province with his treatment of these poor Indians and illegal trade in cloth, pitch and indigo taking from the poor Indians publicly their mules, cattle, wax, honey and horses, which are the products of the province, without leaving them the means by which they can survive.[34]

The heavy demands made on the Indians encouraged them to flee to the uncolonized interior or to desert their villages for the towns and rural estates, where they were often able to escape enumeration. For these reasons part of the loss in the Indian population was more apparent than real.

During the late sixteenth and seventeenth centuries disease continued to take its toll on the Indian population. Its demographic effects were not as devastating in the Mesoamerican zone, because there the Indians had built up some immunity to such diseases as smallpox and measles. In the remoter eastern parts of the country, however, where Indians were brought under Spanish control by missionaries for the first time, the impact of disease was devastating. Although it is difficult to be precise about the impact of particular diseases, the epidemiography of Nicaragua suggests that it did not suffer as badly as Guatemala. Pneumonic plague and typhus were among the most important diseases that ravaged highland Guatemala at regular intervals during the late sixteenth and seventeenth centuries,[35] but these diseases prefer cooler climates,[36] and they were therefore less common in the warmer climate of Nicaragua. On the other hand, it is assumed that the tropical diseases yellow fever and malaria were introduced sometime during the seventeenth century, but, because of the lack of documentary evidence for the Caribbean coast, no precise dates can be given for their introduction or any assessment made of their impact, though it must have been considerable.

During the sixteenth century the highlands of Guatemala were afflicted with plague, smallpox, and a number of other diseases generally referred to in the documentary record as *"pestes,"*[37] but the only reference to disease in Nicaragua at this time is to an outbreak of *"romadizo"* (catarrh or hay fever) in 1578. This disease affected Spaniards as well as Indians but caused only a few deaths.[38] Given these descriptions of the disease and the fact that pneumonic plague was present in Guatemala at that time, it is possible that *"romadizo"* was in fact a mild form of the disease that failed to become more virulent owing to the unfavorable climatic conditions. Farther south in Nicoya in 1573 there was an unidentified epidemic which claimed 300 people in twenty days.[39] Since no comparable disease was recorded farther north at this time, it is possible that it was introduced from the south.

In the early seventeenth century Guatemala was ravaged by smallpox, followed by typhus and pneumonic plague. The pneumonic plague epidemic was vividly described by the president of the audiencia, Alonso

Criado de Castilla, who recorded that it did not affect Spaniards but was worst among hispanicized Indians and those who lived in the coldest regions.[40] This disease does not appear to have spread farther south, but in 1617 smallpox, typhus, and measles were reported as having killed many Indians in Honduras.[41] It seems likely that some of these diseases would also have affected Nicaragua. Reports of diseases during the rest of the century are so vague that it is impossible to identify them, let alone assess their impact. It would appear that during the 1670s parts of Nicaragua and Nicoya were afflicted by *"enfermedades y pestes."*[42] In the 1690s measles and smallpox were introduced to Honduras and Nicaragua by missionaries; they probably carried it from Guatemala, where epidemics occurred between 1693 and 1694. The impact of disease in the missions was so devastating that it discouraged other Indians from settling in them and encouraged those that remained to flee.[43] Eastern Nicaragua also suffered from a *"peste"* in the second decade of the eighteenth century.[44]

During the late sixteenth century and throughout the seventeenth century it is clear that pressure on Indian lands and labor put strains on Indian economies that were expressed in food shortages and famines. In 1672 the *vecinos* of Granada complained that there were food shortages every year,[45] and in addition there were a number of severe famines in Nicaragua in 1586 and 1610.[46] The famines not only resulted directly in an increase in the mortality rate but also increased the susceptibility of Indians to diseases that often followed in their wake. Although drought and the excessive export of maize contributed to food shortages, it is clear that many resulted from excessive labor demands which rendered the Indians unable either to sow or to harvest crops.[47] For example, in 1629 the priests of the villages of El Viejo and Chinandega reported that because the Indians had been employed on the repartimiento they had been unable to grow maize, so that there was not a fanega to be found between the villages, and, since they could not afford to buy it elsewhere at highly inflated prices, they were dying of hunger.[48] The impact of crop shortages was mitigated to a certain extent, however, by the raising of domesticated animals, particularly chickens and cattle.

Although it might be supposed that the degree of economic disruption caused by demands for land, labor, and goods was not as great in Indian communities on the western fringe of the South American zone owing to its remoteness and lack of attractive resources, it should be remembered that Indians in this area had subsisted on the products of shifting cultivation supplemented by hunting and gathering to varying degrees; they did not produce agricultural surpluses or provide labor for extracommunal purposes, so that even though the demands made on them by outsiders were probably smaller than those in the Mesoamerican zone, they probably represented a greater burden. As a result the Indians suffered food shortages, fell behind in their tribute payments, and were forced either to offer themselves for private employment to meet these demands or else to try to survive on wild food resources.[49] Meanwhile, the economy of Indians brought into the missions was largely destroyed. During the short life of the missions the Indians were largely supported by imported provisions, and they lived a precarious existence often resorting to wild food resources for survival. This was particularly true in the early years following the establishment of the missions.[50] Later, as agriculture developed, the missions became economically more stable, largely as a result of the development of livestock raising. On the Caribbean coast there is no evidence for food shortages and famines during this period. This may be attributed in part to the relative lack of disruption of the Indian economy at this time, the ability of Indians to take advantage of firearms which made hunting more efficient, and the variety of wild resources available for exploitation with little effort.

It is difficult to estimate the contribution that social disorganization made to the decline in the Indian population, though it is clear that it must have contributed significantly to the fall in the fertility rate, particularly in the east. This fall would have occurred through the breakdown of Indian communities, brought about by the prolonged absences of individuals working under the repartimiento or as free laborers and by an increase in the number of outmarriages. Similarly, Indian populations in the missions failed to sustain themselves, and on the Caribbean coast racial mixing among Indians, blacks, and the English resulted in an increase in the numbers of Zambo-Mosquito at the expense of the Indian population.

During the colonial period racial mixing accounted for an increasing proportion of the decline in the Indian population, despite the fact that the crown tried to minimize interracial contact by passing laws prohibiting non-Indians, with the exception of a small number of authorized secular and ecclesiastical officials, from residing in Indian villages and barrios. The laws achieved a degree of success, and they were reinforced in Nicaragua in the midseventeenth century by the residential segregation of mestizos, mulattoes, and blacks in four new villages near the towns of León, Granada, Realejo and Nueva Segovia.[51] With the places of residence of Indians and non-Indians fairly well regulated, the main opportunities for interracial contact were in the towns, on the estates, and in the mining areas, where Indians were employed either under the repartimiento or as private workers. Since employment under the repartimiento was normally temporary, the intensity of contact with other groups was probably less than in regions where Indians were employed

Table 16. Distribution of Non-Indians, 1683

Jurisdiction	Span-iards	Mestizos	Mulat-toes	Blacks	Zambos	Slaves
León		220		150		—
Metapa		62		74		—
Realejo	77	19	87	16	—	—
Granada		200	160	—	—	—
Nicaragua			172		—	25
Nueva Segovia	187	61	133	20	—	—
Nicoya (village)	1	—	6	2	—	—
Nicoya (haciendas)	3	17	12	2	—	—

Sources: AGI CO 815 Razón de las ciudades . . . 1683 and AG 29 Navia Bolaños 28.7.1685.

on a permanent basis and often resided in their places of employment. It is clear therefore that, as more and more Indians turned to private employment, the likelihood of the loss of Indian population through racial intermixing increased.

Clearly the degree of interracial mixing depended on the distribution of non-Indian groups. A large proportion was to be found in the urban areas. By law Spaniards were required to live in towns, and a substantial number of blacks who were imported as slaves during the early colonial period were also to be found in the towns, where they were employed as domestic servants.[52] Although some black slaves were also employed as field hands, they were extremely expensive, and for agricultural labor Indians were generally preferred.[53] The propensity of Indians to marry blacks or mulattoes they met in the towns or on estates during the course of their employment under the repartimiento[54] led to a ban on assigning female workers to places of work where there were slaves.[55] During the seventeenth century most of the free blacks and mulattoes resided in the towns, where they formed the basis of the urban militia. In 1662, the mestizos, mulattoes, and blacks in the militia numbered 176 in León, 113 in Granada, and 100 in Realejo.[56] Blacks and mulattoes were also commonly employed as overseers of estates and later as supervisors of mule trains to Costa Rica and Panama.[57]

With the exception of Spanish *vecinos,* the population of non-Indians is haphazardly recorded in the documentary record. Even where their numbers are recorded, it is not clear whether the figures refer to the town only or to the whole area under its jurisdiction. The numbers of non-Indians recorded for Nicaragua in 1683 are indicated in table 16. The most interesting feature is the predominance of mulattoes among the mixed races, although the number of mestizos may be small because many of them were classified as Spaniards, particularly those in outlying areas where the white population was small.

As indicated in the discussion of social organization, the numbers of Indians who married people of non-Indian races and continued to reside in Indian villages was small, but it seems likely that most interracial marriages and unions occurred in other areas that were not well documented, notably in the towns and on estates. For this reason it is extremely difficult to be precise about the contribution that interracial mixing made to the decline in the Indian population.

Part Five

COLONIAL REORGANIZATION AND INDIAN
ACCULTURATION, 1720–1821

CHAPTER 13

Administrative Reforms and Territorial Incorporation

During the eighteenth century Nicaragua was subject to the same administrative and economic reforms aimed at revitalizing the empire as other parts of the New World, but in Nicaragua they never achieved the desired effects. Undoubtedly one reason for lack of response to the reforms was the preoccupation of the government with matters of defense that acted as a constant drain on sources of capital and labor.

By the beginning of the eighteenth century the English had a number of footholds along the Caribbean coast from Belize down to Costa Rica. From these settlements, which were concentrated between the Black River and Bluefields, the English carried out extensive contraband trading, which Floyd estimates was worth about 300,000 pesos in 1745.[1] By the second quarter of the eighteenth century the crown recognized that an offensive was needed to root the English out of the Mosquito Coast. This was to be undertaken by two means: first, by strengthening coastal fortifications, and, second, by increased missionary activity on the frontier to extend the area of Spanish control. The failure of the latter strategy will be described fully elsewhere, but it is worthy of note that, in common with other areas in Latin America, the missionaries were being used essentially for a military purpose.

The choice of a well-defended site from which an offensive could be mounted was a difficult one. Although the Spaniards had control of Fort Inmaculada, on the San Juan River, it was difficult to defend, and it was an unsuitable site from which to launch an offensive. Trujillo was also considered unsuitable because it was difficult to fortify and because it was too close to the English settlements at the Black River and on the Bay Islands, the English having seized the latter in 1742. It was recommended, therefore, that the basis of the military offensive should be a new fort that would be established at Omoa, in Honduras. Although the establishment of Fort Omoa was recommended in 1744, work did not commence until 1752, and it was not completed until 1775. In the meantime, in recognition of the importance of defense, the administration of military affairs in Nicaragua was entrusted to a *comandante general de armas*. However, when the intendancy system was introduced into Central America in 1786, the intendant of Nicaragua resumed control over matters of defense.[2] The intendant was charged with among other duties, establishing regular forces and organizing the militia, as well as ensuring supplies for the fort. During the middle of the eighteenth century preparations were made for a coastal offensive, which was to involve both land forces from the mainland and naval forces prepared in the Caribbean. During the offensive between 1779 and 1783 the Spaniards established themselves at Trujillo whence they managed to retake Roatán and move to the Black River. Farther south they managed to hold on to Fort Inmaculada. Further Anglo-Spanish hostilities were forestalled by the Treaty of Versailles in 1783 and the associated Mosquito Convention of 1786, which required the English to evacuate the Mosquito Coast. Following the evacuation of the coast, the Spaniards attempted to keep control over the evacuated area by establishing garrisons and colonies of immigrants from Spain and the Canaries. They recruited 1,298 colonists in Spain and the Canaries (992 and 306, respectively), but not all arrived: 22 died, 54 deserted before leaving Spain, and 290 died en route. Those that survived went mainly to Trujillo; a few went to the Black River and Cabo de Gracias a Dios, but none went to Bluefields.[3] Unaccustomed to agricultural labor in the tropics, the colonists lived a precarious existence, and the settlements consisted largely of soldiers supported by government rations; in 1791 there were 135 soldiers and only 3 colonists at Cabo de Gracias a Dios.[4] The threat of English attack finally resulted in the abandonment of Roatán and the colony at Cabo de Gracias a Dios in 1795, while an attack by the Zambo-Mosquito in 1800 drove the Spaniards from the Black River, after which Trujillo once again became the frontier town.[5]

Parallel with changes taking place in the organization of military affairs, at the end of the eighteenth century Nicaragua was subject to the same administrative reforms as other parts of the empire. Throughout the colonial period the economic backwardness of Nicaragua and the low salaries paid to officials meant that the province failed to attract good-quality administrators; in 1737 the salary of the governor of Nicaragua was 1,378 pesos, and the corregidores and alcaldes mayores received between 250 and 275 pesos each. These officials compensated for their low salaries by illegal trade and bribes, which could bring in an additional 4,000 to 5,000 pesos a year.[6]

The inefficiency of administration and the fact that a considerable proportion of what should have been government revenue was not entering the royal coffers, not only in Nicaragua but in most other parts of the empire, resulted in administrative reforms in the 1780s. The intendancy system was first introduced to the Viceroyalty of La Plata in 1782 and was applied to New Spain in 1786.[7] The intendancy system drastically reduced the number of administrators with governors, alcaldes mayores and corregidores being replaced by intendants, who carried out their combined political, judicial, and military functions; they also had jurisdiction over financial affairs. In New Spain about 200 governors, alcaldes mayores and corregidores were replaced by 12 intendants.[8] Appointed by the king, the intendants were answerable to him alone. The intendencias were subdivided into *partidos,* which were administered by *subdelegados,* who were appointed by the intendant and approved by the viceroy.

When the intendancy system was introduced into New Spain in 1786, the Gobierno of León became a separate intendancy.[9] Although it was divided into *partidos,* the creation of the intendancy and the concentration of power in the hands of one individual, to the extent that the intendant of León had jurisdiction over the former Gobierno of León and two *corregimientos,* as well as Nicoya and Costa Rica, created resentment in peripheral areas where the administration had been conducted with a degree of autonomy. These seeds of political conflict grew in the Wars of Independence.

With the aim of increasing royal revenue, intendants were to be particularly concerned with the promotion of agriculture, industry, and commerce and with the improvement of financial administration. Although the administrative reforms appear to have had a considerable impact in increasing royal revenue from other parts of the empire, in Nicaragua it appears to have declined. Whereas the average annual royal income for the period 1790–1804 was 32,463 pesos, between 1805 and 1819 it declined to 18,736 pesos, a decline of 43 percent.[10] During the whole period from 1790 to 1819, however, over half the revenue from the intendancy came from the interior areas, which suggests that the reforms may have had some effect in increasing royal revenue from those areas. It is clear, however, that no administrative reforms could overcome the more fundamental problems of shortages of capital and labor, which were rendered more serious by the demands of the defense. To understand the lack of economic revival in Nicaragua at the end of the eighteenth century, it is necessary to look more closely at the evolution of different economic activities throughout the century.

URBAN CENTERS

To a large extent the fortunes of cities reflected the prosperity of their hinterlands, but they were also affected by changes in administration and the needs of defense. During the eighteenth century two major changes took place in Nicaragua's urban hierarchy: the town of Nicaragua rose in importance, and Realejo declined. These changes shifted the balance of population and wealth against the jurisdiction of León in favor of that of Granada. This heightened the rivalry that already existed between the

Table 17. *Diezmos* in Pesos for Selected Years, 1731–1775

Year	León*	Granada†	Nueva Segovia
1731	1,640	2,867	500
1735	1,559	3,000	500
1740	2,425	4,725	1,150
1745	3,500	4,262	1,299
—			
1760	5,663	16,062	988
1765	4,709	12,459	2,499
1770	5,679	14,686	1,095
1775	8,403	18,667	2,529

Sources: AGI AG 950 1731–45, AG 909 1760–75.
*León includes Realejo.
†Granada includes Nicaragua, Sebaco, and Nicoya.

two regions, which was further encouraged by the establishment of León as the center of the intendencia.

From a population of 2,958 in 1717 the town of Nicaragua grew to 4,534 in 1752 and to 11,908 in 1778.[11] The town's growth was based on cacao production and its citizens' ownership of cattle ranches in Sebaco and, more commonly, in Nicoya. The town managed to attract a good number of wealthy Spaniards of distinction, and by 1778 14 percent of its population could be described as Spanish.[12] The formal title of "villa" was given to Nicaragua in 1720 with the proviso that confirmation was to be sought within five years. At that time its elevation to the status of villa was opposed by Granada, which presumably did not want to lose administrative control over the wealthiest part of the region under its jurisdiction. The town did not request a formal title again until 1778, and it was granted in 1783.[13] The growth in the importance of Nicaragua is clearly reflected in the increase in *diezmos* for Granada up to that time. Meanwhile, the town of Realejo went into decline. It had never really recovered after the pirate invasion of 1685, which had occurred against a background of economic stagnation brought about by the decline of the shipbuilding industry and trade with Peru. Its most distinguished citizens, including the corregidor, abandoned Realejo in favor of the neighboring Indian village of El Viejo.[14] The Franciscan and Mercedarian convents and best houses were allowed to fall into disrepair, and it became "un compendio de miserias y respiradero de pobreza."[15] By the middle of the century its population consisted of only a few black and mulatto carpenters and porters.[16]

The populations of León and Granàda remained fairly evenly balanced throughout the eighteenth century, although, as would be expected,

León, as capital of the province, had a greater proportion of whites and mestizos than Granada (in 1778, 22.3 percent as opposed to 21.5 percent). However, royal revenue from the jurisdiction of Granada, which included the villa of Nicaragua, was considerably higher than that of León, and after the establishment of the intendancy only a small part of the income of the province came from the jurisdiction of León. Resentment of the dominance of León by citizens of Granada led to a four-month rebellion in 1811, which ended with forces from León besieging the town and the imprisonment of some of the city's leading families.[17] Granada's defeat dealt a blow to its status; in 1825, Thompson said that the town had only 1,000 houses, which was only half those it had possessed a century before.[18]

Meanwhile, on the frontier the town of Nueva Segovia just managed to survive. Although the town was continually being replenished with militia, the permanent population appears to have declined as a result of attacks by the Zambo-Mosquito.[19] By 1752 many of its citizens had moved to Estelí, while others were reported as living in surrounding villages, and only a few people "of all colors" were living in the town.[20] Its population of 375 at that date had risen to only 604 by 1778.

Although the towns and cities remained identifiable entities in the settlement pattern, it was no longer possible to equate the settlements of non-Indians with the towns and Indians with the rural areas. The seventeenth century had witnessed the movement of landowners to their rural estates, but during the eighteenth century more comments were made about ladinos settling in Indian villages or on Indian lands. An account of the distribution of Spaniards and ladinos in Nicaragua in 1804 indicates that most (58 percent) were living in Indian villages, 24 percent in rural valleys and haciendas, and only 18 percent were living in towns and *reducciones*.[12]

Table 18. Urban Population of Nicaragua in the Eighteenth Century

Jurisdiction	1752 *almas*	1778 total	Span-iards	Mes-tizos	Ladinos	Indians
León	5,439	7,571	1,061	626	5,740	144
Realejo	320					
Granada	5,058	8,233	863	910	4,765	1,659
Nicaragua	4,534	11,908	1,637	554	7,152	2,664
Nueva Segovia	375	604	151		453	

Sources: AGI AG 950 Bishop Morel 8.9.1752 ("almas de confesión y comunión"); Juarros, *Compendium,* 63–67 (except Nicaragua AGI AG 535 on the erection of the Villa of Rivas 5.11.1778).

AGRICULTURE

Agriculture remained the dominant economic activity in Nicaragua during this period, as shipbuilding declined and mining experienced only a very minor revival. A few commercial crops were exported to Spain, the main ones being indigo and cacao, but agriculture appears to have developed as much in response to demands for meat and other provisions within the audiencia. Livestock raising was particularly well suited to the grasslands of Nicaragua, and it had the advantage that it required lower labor inputs than many other crops. There were basically two kinds of holdings. First, there were large estates, where there was a tendency to cultivate one commercial crop but where small quantities of provisions, such as maize, beans and sugar, were also grown. These estates probably provided most of the commercial crops, particularly cacao, indigo, and tobacco, which were exported to Spain, and also most of the livestock that were destined for the Guatemalan market. The smaller holdings generally raised a few cattle and produced a variety of crops which were used for domestic consumption. In contrast to the haciendas they generally grew a greater variety of crops, including fruit trees. Provisions generally included maize, beans, plantains, rice, and sugar; fruits included bananas, limes, pawpaws, mammees, avocadoes, and pineapples.[22]

Whereas the seventeenth century had witnessed a decline in the population, the eighteenth century experienced an increase. This naturally led to greater demands for land and to increasing conflict between potential and actual users. The emerging mixed races entered into the conflict that already existed between Spaniards and Indians. The mixed races originally formed a landless group, and they earned their livings by working as overseers of estates or artisans or tradesmen in the towns. However, over time some accumulated small amounts of capital with which they were able to purchase or rent lands, very often from Indian communities; those less fortunate became squatters on the margins of the already settled area.

During the eighteenth century colonization proceeded eastward and southward, where land was cheaper; in 1743 land in Nueva Segovia and the valley of Nicaragua was valued at 6 pesos a *caballería,* whereas in León it cost 10 to 12 pesos.[23] Colonization is perhaps the wrong word, since during the seventeenth century livestock from haciendas in the jurisdiction of León and Granada had been pastured on these lands during the dry season. During the eighteenth century, however, under pressure from the authorities, ranchers in León and Granada began obtaining formal titles to lands in those areas, particularly in Chontales.[24] Although some small grants were made to persons of mixed race who had previously lived by hunting down feral cattle,[25] many large grants went to *vecinos* of León and Granada. In 1787 it was noted that one *vecino* of León possessed five haciendas in Chontales, one of which, called Jaen, contained over 1,000 *caballerías* (111,000 acres) of land and 30,000 head of cattle.[26] The expansion east as far as the Mosquito Coast was effectively discouraged by the presence of the hostile Zambo-Mosquito. To the south lands in Nicoya were purchased with profits from cacao production in the valley of Nicaragua. Observers claimed that the whole of Nicoya was owned by *vecinos* from Nicaragua, but this was an exaggeration, for although they did possess the largest herds, in fact they owned less than one-fourth of the *hatos* (ranches) and haciendas.[27]

Agricultural development during the eighteenth century suffered considerably from shortages of labor and capital, and control of markets for particular products by merchants and the city council of Santiago de Guatemala, and later Guatemala City, created additional difficulties for landowners in Nicaragua.

Where possible, landowners attempted to secure labor under the repartimiento, but, given the small number of Indians available and the great demand for them, only the most important landowners succeeded in obtaining them; others were forced to employ free labor. Although the wages paid to free workers were higher than those paid to Indians working under the repartimiento, they failed to attract sufficient labor, and hacendados were forced to fall back on less demanding forms of agriculture, such as livestock raising, rather than produce more labor-intensive crops for which the land was equally suited.

Despite various efforts to promote the cultivation of new commercial crops, indigo and cacao remained dominant, although sugar and tobacco acquired some local importance. To encourage the cultivation of crops for export to Spain, sales taxes (*alcabala*) and export-import taxes (*almojarifazgo*) were often removed.[28] In 1803 commercial crop production was also promoted by the abolition of sales taxes and tithes on new plantings of indigo, cacao, sugar, cotton, and coffee for ten years to run from the day of the first harvest; taxes on the import of tools and machinery for the processing of sugar and coffee had been removed in 1792.[29] In addition new plants were introduced to Central Amerca, mainly from Asia. In 1801 more productive varieties of sugarcane—the Otaheite and Bourbon varieties—were introduced through Trujillo, and about the same time the breadfruit (*Artocarpus communis* J. R. and G. Forst), mango (*Mangifera indica* L.), cinnamon (*Cinnamomum zeylanicum* Breyn), and black pepper (*Piper nigrum* L.) were also introduced.[30] However, the newly introduced crops made only slow progress against those that were well established.

Indigo remained one of the most important commercial crops grown in Nicaragua, although its cultivation was localized, and its production only accounted for a small proportion of that produced within the audiencia—most of it was produced in El Salvador and to a lesser extent in Honduras and Guatemala. However, good-quality indigo was produced in Nicaragua, and the main areas of production were around León, particularly to the north, on the León-Chinandega plain, and in the valley of Nicaragua.[31]

The two main factors limiting the production of indigo were labor and capital, although physical problems such as drought and locusts also caused difficulties in some years. The problems of securing labor arose from the small population and from the official ban on the employment of Indians in indigo *obrajes* which remained in force throughout the period. Nevertheless, some Indian labor was employed illegally; employers claimed that the Indians wanted to work because they earned high wages with which they could provide for themselves and their families, as well as pay their tribute.[32] The annual tours of inspection occurred at irregular intervals, and the fines that were imposed did not deter employers from using Indian labor. However, most of those who worked in the *obrajes* were mulattoes, ladinos and some black slaves. The difficulties of securing labor often forced indigo producers to abandon cultivation of the crop and rely on the collection of wild indigo.

Throughout the eighteenth century indigo producers had to struggle against merchants for control over production.[33] Until 1782 indigo production depended on loans from merchants, which were repayable in indigo generally at a price unfavorable to the grower. Smith suggests that the difference amounted to about 1 real a pound less than the official price paid at the annual fair in Apastepeque.[34] To oppose the domination of production by merchants, the indigo growers formed an organization called the Sociedad de Cosecheros de Añil and obtained a loan of 100,000 pesos from the crown. From this capital fund loans were made to growers at a 4 percent rate of interest, and the fund was supplemented by a tax of 4 pesos on each *zurrón* (214 pounds) that was levied when the indigo was sold by the grower.[35] Even those who did not receive loans from the society were required to pay the tax. Initially, the headquarters of the society was in San Vicente, but in 1786 it was moved to San Salvador. The number of growers who received loans increased steadily into the nineteenth century; in 1820 the amount been borrowed was 496,628 pesos and the interest outstanding was 169,624 pesos.[36] However, the number of borrowers from Nicaragua was very small. Between 1782 and the beginning of 1793 the society loaned 282,935 pesos, but only 15,000 (5.3 percent) went into eight growers in Nicaragua. The small number of recipients in Nicaragua was accorded some attention at a conference of indigo producers and traders held in 1794. It was suggested that, since the area was good for indigo production, 60,000 pesos should be set aside for loans to growers in Nicaragua.[37] This suggestion does not appear to have been taken up, however, and the proportion they received remained small. By 1801 the total figure loaned had risen to 435,204 pesos, and the proportion going to growers in Nicaragua had risen to 39,000 pesos (9 percent).[38]

The other means by which merchants sought to benefit from indigo production was through fixing the price of indigo. Before the establishment of the Society of Indigo Growers prices had been set by the major producers and merchants at the fair in Apastepeque. When the society was established, it took over responsibility for setting prices under government supervision at the fair, which was moved to San Vicente. It is uncertain to what extent these prices were adhered to; probably merchants and growers continued to make private arrangements for the purchase and sale of indigo. In 1792 the fair was abolished, and the free trade of indigo was authorized. Previously indigo had to be sent to San Vicente for registering before being shipped to Spain, but the abolition of the fair also resulted in the abolition of this requirement.[39]

Apart from the conflicts between merchants and growers, and the fact that the industry was largely controlled by interests outside the province, indigo production was also hampered by the taxes levied on indigo and its export. Apart from the 4-peso tax on each *zurrón*, which was reduced to a 2 percent ad valorem tax in 1817,[40] it was subject to the tithe and *alcabala*, and further high costs were involved in warehousing and transport. Salvatierra has estimated that in Guatemala taxes on indigo amounted to 12 percent of its value, and by the time it had reached Spain 20 percent had been added to the value of the dye.[41] This was an undesirable situation, for it was facing competition in European markets from indigo produced in the Dutch and English colonies in Asia.[42] To overcome this problem and to encourage the production of high-quality indigo—*flor* and *sobresaliente*—the tithe and *alcabala* were reduced to the level payable on poorer quality indigos—*corte*. Also in recognition of the potential of Nicaragua to produce indigo of high quality, the crown abolished the payment of these taxes on new plantings for ten years beginning with the first harvest.[43]

The general trend of indigo production in the audiencia during the latter part of the colonial period was a gradual expansion to the end of the eighteenth century, after which it declined. Its expansion was stimulated according to the growers by the availability of credit, and according to the merchants by the freeing of trade. However, the expansion could not be maintained in the face of competition from other indigo-producing areas of the world and because of irregularities in trade during the pre-Independence period.[44] Although Nicaraguan production accounted for only a small proportion of the total produced in the audiencia, the same changes in the level of production can be discerned. While about 40,000 pounds were being produced in Nicaragua in the late 1790s, just over 14,000 pounds were being produced by 1810, and this represented only 2.5 percent of the total production of the audiencia.[45] Nevertheless, taxes on indigo amounted to about 160,000 pesos at the end of the eighteenth century.[46]

The main areas of cacao production in Central America in the eighteenth century were Soconusco; Matina, on the Caribbean coast of Costa Rica; and the valley of Nicaragua.[47] The last area dominated production in Nicaragua, although some was grown around Granada; in 1752, 310 of the 353 cacao haciendas enumerated by Bishop Morel were in the valley of Nicaragua, which in 1757 were said to produce over 5,000 fanegas of cacao a year.[48] In 1769 these cacao haciendas were described as "one of the riches of the province," and at the turn of the century they were yielding about 220,000 pesos a year.[49] Even though the price of cacao fell at the beginning of the nineteenth century, there were still 700 haciendas in the valley of Nicaragua in 1817.[50] Most of the cacao produced in Nicaragua was probably exported to neighboring provinces, notably San Salvador and San Miguel, though small amounts were shipped to Spain.[51] At the beginning of the nineteenth century cacao production suffered a decline owing to plagues of locusts, competition from cheap cacao from Guayaquil, and high export duties. The price fell from between 30 and 50 pesos a *fardo* towards the end of the century to 10 pesos in 1815, but it recovered somewhat two years later when it rose again to 25 pesos. At that time there was a good market for cacao in Mexico, where it sold for 65 to 80 pesos, so that, discounting the costs of transport by way of Realejo and Acapulco and the duties payable on exports, which amounted to 20 pesos, there was still nearly 30 percent profit to be made.[52]

Although sugar did not develop into a major export crop, its cultivation expanded considerably during the eighteenth century. Many estates grew sugarcane on a small scale, but some concentrated on the production of sugar. The crop was cultivated throughout Nicaragua, but it was particularly important around León, where it was grown on irrigated lands.[53] It was said that its expansion in eastern Nicaragua was inhibited by the lack of capital. Some good-quality sugar was produced in Nicaragua, some of which was exported to Spain, but in 1800 it accounted for only about 1 percent of the exports of the province.[54] At the end of the colonial period there were a number of attempts to encourage the cultivation of sugar,[55] but there is no evidence that its production and export expanded, and this would have been unlikely given the high transport costs of shipping such a bulky product.

It is worth noting that the production of tobacco could have been increased considerably in Nicaragua, notably in Nueva Segovia, but its cultivation was banned because of the dangers of contraband trade. From the mideighteenth century the crown established a royal monopoly over the manufacture and sale of tobacco. The royal monopoly was introduced into Central America in 1766, and warehouses and factories were established in the region.[56] About that time the ban on the cultivation of tobacco in Nicaragua was introduced to minimize losses of revenue through contraband trade. The ban was finally lifted in 1792 owing to the poor quality of the tobacco produced in Costa Rica, to which its cultivation had been restricted in 1787.[59] However, by 1817 the cultivation of tobacco had still not been reestablished in Nueva Segovia.[58]

During the eighteenth century several major changes occurred in the spatial distribution of livestock raising. On the Pacific lowlands livestock raising was carried on in association with indigo production, but the difficulties of pasturing during the dry season resulted in the grazing of animals in the east, and gradually this seasonal movement was transformed into a more permanent one with animals being raised there. At the same time there was an expansion of livestock raising in Nicoya.

By far the most important animals raised were cattle, followed by mules and horses. There are no general estimates of the total number of livestock in Nicaragua, but some of the ranches were very extensive—in 1757, *vecinos* of Granada were said to have 100,000 cattle in Chontales.[59] Ranches on the Pacific coastal plain were smaller; in 1740 a *visita* of the *corregimiento* for Realejo listed 17 large estates and 27 small ones with only 3,038 cattle altogether.[60] Although there were clearly more cattle in the east, the number sold at the annual fair appears to have been smaller than that from the two Pacific jurisdictions of León and Granada because the seller's residence was registered as the origin of cattle, and many cattle raised in Chontales were listed as having come from Granada. However, the smaller number from the east may also reflect the slightly lower levels of production there; a substantial proportion of the cattle found in Chontales were in fact feral cattle that were hunted down, killed, and consumed there, rather than raised for export.[61]

Contemporary observers noted that four problems beset livestock production: the laziness of the inhabitants, a disease known as "*morrina*" (murrain), the killing off of female cattle, and thefts.[62] In an effort to increase cattle production an order was passed that no female cattle were to be killed. The effect of this ban was to create larger herds, which resulted in reduced animal care and larger numbers of feral cattle. These cattle were particularly vulnerable to theft, either by people of mixed race who led a nomadic existence, stealing cattle and living off wild fruits and vegetables, or by the Zambo-Mosquito, who raided ranches on the eastern borders of Chontales.[63] Except in Chontales, an

Table 19. Origins of Cattle Destined for the Annual Cattle Fair,
1791–1801

Origin	1791	1793	1796	1797	1799	1801
León	5,983	6,842	5,191	4,094	5,095	2,068
Granada	5,911	2,063	5,082	982	1,519	—
Nueva Segovia	1,666	1,729	4,275	857	1,766	1,353
Sebaco (Chontales)	—	548	231	560	1,005	—
Total	13,560	11,182	14,779	6,493	9,385	3,421
Total for audiencia	23,468	22,914	25,259	10,159	16,448	4,750
Nicaraguan percent of total	58.8	48.8	58.5	61.7	57.1	72.0

Sources: 1791 AGCA A3.3 38 743; 1793 AGCA A3.3 39 768; 1796 AGCA A3.3 2446 35830; 1797 AGCA A3.3 35 805; 1799 AGCA A3.3 2368 34956; 1801 AGCA A3.3 2446 35841. Fairs of 1791, 1799, and 1801 were in Chalchuapa. Fairs of 1793, 1796, and 1797 were in Jalpatagua.

additional problem was the shortage of pasture in the dry season. In Nueva Segovia cattle were driven to higher and moister altitudes or to the lowland marshy areas along the coast or lakes, and around León and Granada they were moved to the Bay of Fonseca and the shores of Lake Nicaragua, respectively.[64]

In addition to these problems, livestock production was hampered by the domination of interests in Guatemala City, which suffered from shortages of meat. It appears that up to 1781 an annual fair was held in January at Las Lagunas, to which producers in Nicaragua sent cattle.[65] *Vecinos* and merchants in Guatemala complained that on the way to the fair many cattle were sold in San Salvador and San Vicente, where *vecinos* burned the pastures so that the cattle weakened and had to be sold.[66] At that time Nicaragua also exported some hides and tallow to Costa Rica and Panama, as did Nicoya, which also exported mules.[67] This free trade in livestock was abolished in 1781, when because of shortages of meat in Guatemala City the sale of cattle outside the fair was forbidden on pain of confiscation.[68] This ban on the export of cattle except for sale at the annual fair was particularly detrimental to producers in the more distant regions of Granada and Nicoya for a variety of reasons. First, the long journey from Nicaragua to the fair held at either Jalpatagua or Chalchuapa caused the cattle to lose weight, with the result that they could command only low prices compared to those they could have fetched in their regions of origin. One rancher in Granada maintained that the local prices for cattle were 10 to 12 pesos for good-quality animals, 7 to 8 pesos for medium-quality, and 5 to 6 pesos for others, whereas the respective prices in Guatemala were only 6 to 7 pesos, 4 to 5 pesos, and 28 reals.[69] One reason given for the low prices in Guatemala was that purchasers were aware that sellers had no option but to sell their cattle there; the long journey home would have resulted in the loss of nearly all the weakened cattle. Officials in Guatemala maintained that the prices for cattle in Guatemala were not low, that in 1791 they had been sold at an average price of 6 to 9 pesos, and that if prices were set in León, they would be fixed by interested parties, since the producers were the same people who held official positions, whereas in Guatemala the prices were set by impartial administrators.[70]

Producers complained not only about the low prices the were paid for cattle but also about the losses they incurred on the way to the fair. These were brought about by the weakening of the cattle, as a result of the long journey and the shortage of pasture, and the fact that, to arrive at the fair on time, cattle had to leave Nicaragua at the end of the rainy season before their hooves had hardened for the journey. There were also problems of disease, such as that which afflicted herds in San Salvador in 1795, resulting in the loss of over 7,000 cattle.[71] Other cattle were killed in stampedes or escaped, or else the mules that escorted the herds died and the cattle had to be killed and sold.[72] Others were killed by drovers for food. Altogether about 25 percent of the cattle destined for the fair never arrived.[73] The most vociferous complaints came from producers in Nicoya, who were farthest from the fair. They argued that other nearby provinces such as Chiquimula and Honduras could easily supply Guatemala City.[74] Officials in Guatemala were unimpressed and said that if necessary cattle from Nicoya could recuperate on the pastures around León.[75] Producers also complained that the rule was unfair to other provinces such as San Miguel, San Vicente, Sonsonate, and San Salvador, which also suffered shortages of meat, and they felt that if there was to be a fair it should be held somewhere between the places of production and sale, so that the costs could be borne more equally by sellers and purchasers; it was suggested that the fair should be held in the "llanos de la Asumpción."[76] The fair remained in Jalpatagua until 1791, when an order was issued for its transferral to Chalchuapa, making the journey from Nicaragua four days shorter.[77] Despite this order the fair was still held in Jalpatagua until 1797, after which it was transferred to Chalchuapa. Another problem with the organization of the fair was that cattle had to be registered at the Garita del Platanar on a particular day, and if the traders arrived early they had to wait there and incur losses in their herds, whereas if they arrived late, they had to pay a fine. Producers petitioned for a more flexible timetable, but like their other requests it was ignored.[78]

The reason officials in Guatemala refused to pay attention to the complaints of producers outside the province was that they believed that the failure of the fair was caused by drovers who sold cattle illegally on the journey.[79] Weak or dead cattle could be sold on the way, and drovers took advantage of this loophole. Officials in Guatemala tried to make the fair more successful by issuing orders prohibiting the sale of cattle outside the fair, but finally in 1800, in recognition of the falling numbers arriving there, the free sale of cattle was permitted.[80]

MINING

Mining activities in Nicaragua continued intermittently at a low level during the eighteenth century. Silver was discovered in Nueva Segovia in 1735, and in the 1740s gold was being worked near Villanueva.[81] There were difficulties in securing labor for the mines because the corregidor of Sutiaba and Posoltega refused to allow Indians to work under the repartimiento because of the ill-treatment they received. Later in the 1770s gold was discovered at El Peñon, and production was high enough to warrant the appointment of an administrator in 1780.[82] The post was abolished four years later, however, probably because the output from the mines could not justify the salary of 800 pesos. The few figures available for mineral production, which are taken from *quinto* receipts, indicate that production was low; although figures are available for only a few years, the peak year of production was 1772, when 110 marks of silver were produced.[83] In 1814 rich silver deposits were discovered in Nueva Segovia at Macuelizo and Marimacho, but there were considerable problems in securing labor.[84] Small quantities of pearls were produced in Nicoya throughout the colonial period, but they made an insignificant contribution to royal revenue.[85]

OTHER ECONOMIC ACTIVITIES

There were a number of nonagricultural activities that used Indian labor. These mainly comprised the collection of wild vegetable products. Sarsaparilla and a variety of balsams, gums, and resins were of particular interest to the Spaniards. Sarsaparilla was also shipped to Europe by the English, who employed blacks and Zambo-Mosquito in its collection.[86] Dyewoods and woods for construction, notably cedar and mahogany, were also exported, mainly to Peru, and in 1800 these exports were worth about 8,000 pesos a year. Although wood accounted for only 4.5 percent of the .total exports of the province by value, it was third in its list of exports.[87] Some of the wood was consumed locally by the ship-building industry at Realejo and to a lesser extent by small yards established on Lake Granada.[88] During the eighteenth century, however, the shipbuilding industry declined despite the availability of good flexible wood and the durability of vessels constructed at Realejo.[89] In 1742 the port still launched a vessel of about 300 tons every year for use in trade with Peru, but by the beginning of the nineteenth century vessels of only 70 and 80 tons were being built, partly because the port was silting up.[90] Several reasons were given for the decline in the shipbuilding industry: the lack of skilled labor, the decline in trade with Peru, and the incompetent handling of merchandise in the port and its maladministration, which discouraged foreign merchants from operating there.[91] In fact, Realejo never really recovered after the pirate attacks of the seventeenth century, when a large proportion of its population moved to El Viejo; in its state of decline the shipbuilding industry was unable to take advantage of the liberalization of trade from 1774.[92]

With the decline in the shipbuilding industry and trade with Peru the production of several other products associated with it also declined. These included the manufacture of cordage and sailcloth, which generally employed Indian labor under coercion from local officials. The decline in the production of these items was blamed, however, on the lack of care the Indians had given to the cultivation of the fiber-producing plants.[93] The production of tar and pitch also declined in importance, although by the beginning of the nineteenth century its export, mainly to Peru, was still worth 10,000 pesos, and it was second in Nicaragua's list of exports.[94] Its production was erratic, however, for it was produced only when ships arrived from Peru to purchase it.[95]

ENGLISH COLONIES ON THE MOSQUITO COAST

During the first half of the eighteenth century the English consolidated their position on the Mosquito Coast by making it a protectorate. In 1739, in return for English protection, the inhabitants of the coast surrendered their territorial rights.[96] Despite the consolidation of the English position on the coast, the number of non-Indian inhabitants does not appear to have increased substantially. The earliest settlements of non-Indians were at the río Tinto or Black River (in Honduras), Cabo de Gracias a Dios, Bluefields, and Punta Gorda, though small numbers of Europeans were scattered all along the coast.[97] When the protectorate was established, the headquarters of the superintendent were established at the mouth of the Black River, and it was the northern part of Mosquito coast which attracted most non-Indian settlement. In 1757 about three

Table 20. Inhabitants of the Mosquito Coast, 1757

Location	Whites	Mulat- toes and Mestizos	Negro slaves	Indian slaves	Total
Cabo de Gracias a Dios	6	—	28	—	34
Sandy Bay	5	7	3	8	23
Bragman's Bluff	11	6	8	20	45
Pearl Key Lagoon	2	2	3	11	18
Corn Islands	3	23	10	30	66
Bluefields	2	2	10	3	17
Punta Gorda	4	10	12	16	42
Brewer's Lagoon*	3	16	19		38
Plantain River*	2	14	10		26
Black River (eastern lagoon)*	1	5	1	6	13
Black River*	31	17	254		302
Mistire Creek*	9	51	127		187
Cape River*	25	17	201		243
Not fixed	50	—		20	70
Total	154	170	800		1,124

Source: PRO CO 123/1 fols. 55–79 Hodgson 1757.
*In Honduras.

fourths of the 1,124 inhabitants of the coast lived in the Honduran sector.[98] During the next 30 years about 200 to 300 whites were living on the coast with 900 to 1,000 slaves.[99] The main interests of the English were trading in dyewood, mahogany, sarsaparilla, and turtleshell. In 1769, 800,000 feet of mahogany, 200,000 pounds of sarsaparilla, and 10,000 pounds of turtleshell where exported to England, and in 1783 the export of these items was said to be worth £30,000.[100] The dyewood was exported to England, Holland, and North America for use in the textile industries.[101] Although much of the wood was obtained by trade, the English also established wood-cutting enterprises in which they employed both black slaves and the Zambo-Mosquito. A few families established sugar plantations at Cabo de Gracias a Dios and farther north in Honduras, while some possessed cacao plantations up the río Segovia, and others raised livestock.[102]

The activities of the English on the Mosquito Coast were brought to an abrupt halt in 1786, when under the Mosquito Convention the English agreed to evacuate the coast. In 1787, 517 freemen and 903 slaves left for Jamaica and Belize, but 202 remained, 46 of whom were slaves who had deserted during the evacuation.[103] From that time until 1800 the Spaniards tried unsuccessfully to gain control of the Mosquito Coast by establishing colonists at the Black River, Cabo de Gracias a Dios, and Bluefields. Meanwhile, the English established in Jamaica and Belize maintained contraband trading contacts with the Zambo-Mosquito on the Coast.[104]

CHAPTER 14

Instruments of Indian Integration

During the eighteenth and early nineteenth centuries there was no change in the eastern boundary of the area under Spanish administration, despite the fact that military and missionary activities attempted to establish greater control over the eastern part of the country. Although the encomienda was abolished in 1721, the Indians continued to pay tribute and provide labor under the repartimiento into the nineteenth century, although by that time free labor had become the dominant labor system. Meanwhile, in eastern Nicaragua missionary activities were encouraged by the crown to counteract the foreign threat on the Mosquito Coast, but most of the missions they established were short-lived.

THE ENCOMIENDA, THE REPARTIMIENTO AND FREE LABOR

The encomienda persisted longer in Central America than in many other parts of Latin America, and in the early nineteenth century Indian tribute constituted the most important source of royal income from the area. This reflected not only the survival of fairly large Indian populations but also the small income the crown derived from other sources, notably from *alcabalas* and *quintos*.[1]

In the first quarter of the eighteenth century the crown decided to take over the administration of encomiendas as they fell vacant. In 1701 an order was issued that encomiendas of absent encomenderos were to revert to the crown, and in 1718 the encomienda was abolished. It was not until 1721, however, that the order was put into effect in the Audiencia of Guatemala.[2] There was little opposition to the order, for by that time the encomienda had become a less attractive proposition. The crown's justification for the abolition of the encomienda was that conditions had changed since the Conquest period; there were no conquistadors to be remunerated for their services, and the custodial duties of *encomenderos* had been taken over by Spanish officials. Nevertheless, the crown did undertake to provide pensions for deserving subjects. The abolition of encomiendas marked the end of the crown's efforts to gain control over the administration of the Indians; it also increased royal revenue. Although at that time there were problems with tribute debts, the step was well timed for the crown to take advantage of the increase in Indian population that was just beginning. Although encomiendas were abolished in Nicaragua in 1721, the Indians continued to pay tribute until the end of the colonial period, except for a brief period between 1811 and 1816 when payments were suspended.[3] Nevertheless, there were many changes in the way Indians were counted and assessed and in the amount of tribute they paid.

At the beginning of the eighteenth century governors, alcaldes mayores, and corregidores were responsible for drawing up lists of tributary Indians in each village, and on the basis of these counts the amount payable by the village was assessed by an *oidor*. At that time counts were made at irregular intervals, and there were many complaints from Indian villages that their *tasaciones* were out of date and they were forced to pay for Indians who were either dead or absent. Although pressure was brought on Indian officials to pay the assessed tribute in full, most Indian villages fell into arrears. In 1734 the *contador* of Nicaragua reported that, with the exception of the villages of Sutiaba, Jalteba, and Jinotepe, the Indians had not been counted for 17 years, and that in Nueva Segovia tribute lists were 20 years out of date.[4] Villages in the jurisdiction of Matagalpa and some in the jurisdiction of León were in fact counted within the next two years,[5] but in 1740 the governor complained that most of the villages had not been counted for more than 30 years mainly because of the inadequate salaries and expenses paid to enumerators.[6] The last *tasaciones* for villages in the jurisdiction of Granada in the book of *tasaciones* drawn up in 1753 were 45 years old.[7]

The exemption of women from tribute payment in 1754, confirmed by the Audiencia of Guatemala in 1756, necessitated the drawing up of new *tasaciones*.[8] There were few adjustments in these *tasaciones* during the early 1760s, with the exception of the jurisdiction of Sutiaba and Matagalpa.[9] The reason given was that the number of tributaries had increased and that the governor was therefore levying increased amounts of tribute but rendering to the exchequer only the amount of tribute required by the last assessment. Since he was making a profit, he was not inclined to undertake a new count.[10] From the 1760s special commissioners (*apoderados fiscales*) were appointed to enumerate the Indians. Although this change may have been stimulated by the recommendation that the enumerators should not be the same persons as those who collected the tribute, since this encouraged various forms of fraud,[11] probably the main reason for introducing the new procedure was the increasing difficulty of counting the number of Indians belonging to each village. Head counts undertaken in Indian villages were clearly inadequate because substantial proportions of those born there resided elsewhere. To obtain a complete count of the Indians belonging to each village, therefore, enumerators had to refer to the parish registers of baptisms, marriages, and deaths. Although it is clear that parish records were inadequately kept and that Indians could still escape the notice of the authorities, the new system did produce more accurate and comprehensive counts.

The main disadvantages of the new system were that it was time-consuming and expensive; a count of the tributaries in Nicaragua in the 1770s took from July, 1775 to March, 1777.[12] This meant that enumerations could not be undertaken by governors and other high-ranking officials, otherwise they would have been unable to attend to other administrative matters. The appointment of special commissioners, however, brought another disadvantage, that of cost. The *apoderados fiscales* were to receive the salary of three pesos a day, which was assessed on the basis of thirty-five *tributarios* counted and six leagues traveled per day, plus nine days for preparing the *tasaciones*. Half of the costs were to be borne by the exchequer and the rest by the Indians at the rate of one real for each *casado entero* and half a real for each *medio*. Three or four *apoderados fiscales* were appointed for Nicaragua. The costs of the counts proved to be high, and officials of the Audiencia maintained that they did not do the job properly. As a result they petitioned the crown to permit governors, corregidores and alcaldes mayores to undertake enumerations as they had in the past. The crown rejected the proposal, arguing that the new procedure was preferable since it had resulted in a rise in the number of tributary Indians registered.[13] However, in order to mitigate the costs, counts were to be undertaken every five years rather than every three years, which had theoretically been the norm previously.[14] By the beginning of the nineteenth century the cost of enumerating Indians in the whole of the Audiencia of Guatemala amounted to 30,000 pesos, which was equivalent to about one-seventh the annual income from tribute.[15] To dispense with the costs of drawing up tributary lists, the enumerations were finally entrusted to parish priests, and in 1805 instructions were drawn up for their guidance.[16]

Villages could obtain exemption from tribute payments at times of crisis, and individuals could claim exemption on the basis of their official position, disablement, or racial status. As racial mixing increased during the eighteenth century, the number of petitions for tribute exemption on racial grounds rose. The rule that was followed was that a child was classified as being of the same race as his or her mother, with the exception of the offspring of a Spanish father and an Indian mother who were legally married, in which case he or she was classified as a mestizo; illegitimate mestizos were classed as Indians and liable to pay tribute.[17] To obtain exemption from tribute as a non-Indian, a petitioner generally had to provide marriage and birth certificates. Needless to say, in many cases, if not most, petitioners were unable to produce these, and a review of the outcomes of claims indicates that without them exemption was seldom granted.[18] In the late eighteenth century, when regular militia were established in Nicaragua, Indians who enlisted could also claim exemption under the *fuero militar*.[19] Although these legal channels existed, undoubtedly more Indians became exempt by deserting their communities and taking up residence on estates or in the towns, where they could often escape enumeration.

The threefold classification of tributary Indians, outlined of the previous period, lasted until the middle of the eighteenth century, when the crown exempted women from tribute payment. Although the cedula providing for the exemption of women was issued on September 13, 1754, the audiencia questioned its introduction on the grounds that it conflicted with an earlier cedula issued in 1702, which stated that women should pay tribute. Nevertheless, the crown reaffirmed the order on December 11, 1756, and it was implemented in the following year.[20] One issue that emerged as a result of the exemption of women from tribute payment was the payment of the *servicio del tostón*. Formerly married Indians had paid four reals a year, whereas single men had paid only two reals, and it was suggested that the two contributions should be made equal. Theoretically the contribution of married male Indians should have been reduced to two reals, but since this would have resulted in a loss of revenue, in 1759 it was decided to regulate it at four reals.[21] A few years later other adjustments were made to equalize the amount of tribute paid by married and single Indians.[22] The existence of a single category of tributary Indians must have made tribute assessments much easier.

Indians in Nicaragua continued to pay tribute in kind throughout the eighteenth century. The most important items levied were maize, cotton cloth, beans, and chickens, although in western Nicaragua salt and cabuya were exacted, and in the east, honey. After the exemption of women from tribute payment cotton cloth ceased to be paid as tribute. Although the Indians would have preferred to pay their tribute in money, collectors pressed them to pay in goods since it afforded them opportunities to make illegal profits; they argued that the Indians did not possess sufficient money to pay in cash.[23]

Although the amount of tribute payable was specified on a per capita basis and its value was regulated, nevertheless there were variations in the amount paid by Indians in different regions, even though the amount paid in Nicaragua was generally considered to be low compared to amounts paid in other parts of the empire. Indians paid the equivalent of between 12 and 24 reals, while in the east a number of villages paid 11 reals, Muymuy paid 4, and Lóvago, Lovigüisca, and Camoapa paid only 2. The small amount of tribute paid by the latter villages was a reward

for having been peacefully converted.[24] It is worth noting that these figures represent the value of tribute paid in kind according to official
prices, which were always regulated below those of the market. Thus in
1779 the Indians of Masaya complained that, although the value of the
tribute was regulated between 14 to 18 reals, in fact it was worth 4 to 5
pesos.[25] In 1787 the audiencia requested information from governors
within its jurisdiction about the introduction of a uniform tax of 3 pesos a
year. The governor of Nicaragua replied that Indians in his province
could easily pay 3 pesos, since they earned about 16 to 20 reals a month
and spent much of it on fiestas.[26] Nevertheless, the audiencia finally decided that each tributary Indian should pay 2 pesos, and it attempted to
introduce this uniform tax from the mid-1790s.[27] However, by 1811 few
changes had been made in Nicaragua, where the Indians were still paying
varied amounts between 2 and 23¼ reals.[28]

Although governors, corregidores, and alcaldes mayores were ultimately responsible for the delivery of the money derived from the sale of
tribute into the royal coffers, the actual collection of the tribute items
was undertaken by the local Indian officials. During the early eighteenth
century these officials exprienced extreme difficulty in collecting tribute
since many Indians had died in epidemics and the places of residence of
absent Indians were often unknown.[29] Even if the residences of Indians
were known, employers sometimes concealed their presence or pre-
vented collectors from exacting tribute from them by "dismissing them
with sticks and with ignomony."[30] Because the *tasaciones* were not re-
adjusted and the collection of tribute was difficult, tribute arrears began
to mount to very substantial sums.[31] Between 1725 and 1738 the tribute
arrears of five villages in Nueva Segovia amounted to no less than 20,101
pesos.[32] Unable to deliver the stipulated amount of tribute, Indian officials were often imprisoned or fined or had their goods confiscated.[33]

The problem of tribute arrears prompted the suggestion, which was
taken up by the crown in 1737, that governors, corregidores, and alcaldes mayores should provide security for tribute payment on taking
office.[34] Normally the official collector would obtain security through
bondsmen, and if the amount of tribute was inadequate, the official and
the bondsmen were held liable from their own funds.[35] In 1739 it proved
impossible to find people who would act as bondsmen. The reason given
was that the people were too poor, but it is equally likely that they realized the difficulties that tribute collection posed.[36] It is not clear whether
this practice operated throughout the rest of the century or whether it
was discontinued as impracticable.

Like full tributary Indians, *lavoríos* continued to pay tribute until the
end of the colonial period, women being exempt from the middle of the
eighteenth century. Although the century witnessed more frequent

changes in the residence and place of employment of Indians, the number of Indians who were reclassified as *lavoríos* did not increase substantially. There appear to have been some regional variations in the classification of *lavoríos*. In parts of Nicaragua, notably the east, Indians born outside the villages in which they resided who claimed to be *lavoríos* were generally classified as such,[37] but in the jurisdiction of León only those Indians residing in specially designated barrios were regarded as *lavoríos*. In the latter circumstance it was argued that the Indians had been classified as *lavoríos* and paid a reduced amount of tribute on the basis of the services they provided for the adjacent towns and that, if they moved away and no longer performed them, then they could no longer claim to be *lavoríos*.[38] They were sometimes likened to *yanaconas* in Peru. Although *lavoríos* paid a reduced amount of tribute, they were generally considered to be better off than other Indians since they could earn wages in the town. Thus it was suggested that they should be liable to pay the same amount of tribute as full tributary Indians.[39] In Nicaragua they generally paid eight reals, although from 1752 *lavoríos* in the jurisdiction of El Viejo paid ten reals.[40]

During the eighteenth century demands on Indian labor were considerable, and they took a variety of forms. The repartimiento remained an important source of labor in agriculture until it was abolished in 1812,[41] although it is difficult to assess its precise importance relative to free labor because of the lack of documentary evidence. Other forms of forced labor, such as the *repartimiento de hilados* (see below), became common, and they attracted the most frequent complaints from Indians.

In the eighteenth century the repartimiento for agriculture and other approved tasks was regulated at one quarter of the adult male population aged between eighteen and fifty-five (later fifty). Although Indians generally worked on a rotational basis, instructions for the repartimiento of Sutiaba stipulated that the most destitute should be chosen and not those who possessed "a cart, oxen, or plot or garden of maize sufficient to support their families and pay their tribute."[42] Many Indians were assigned to work in *obrajes* and sugar mills, even though the prohibitions against their employment in these enterprises continued.[43] During the eighteenth century wages did not rise; Indians were generally paid one real a day if they were assigned to work in agricultural tasks, although more skilled workers, such as bricklayers, received one and a half reals.[44]

The continuing importance of the repartimiento in Nicaragua into the nineteenth century compared to other parts of Latin America, notably Mexico, where it ceased to be significant from the seventeenth century, can probably be explained by the shortage of labor and the unprofitability of economic enterprises in Nicaragua. In Mexico the decline in the Indian population encouraged the change from the repartimiento to free labor at the beginning of the seventeenth century, but only because profits from economic activities were high enough to enable employers to pay the higher wages necessary to attract free labor. In Nicaragua many enterprises were insufficiently profitable to enable employers to pay the high wages commanded by free laborers, which in eastern Nicaragua were three times higher than those paid to repartimiento workers.[45] As such the change from the repartimiento to a predominantly free labor system took place more gradually. Thus the repartimiento continued into the nineteenth century, but because it was unable to meet all the demands made on it, most employers were forced to rely on free labor and to minimize costs by falling back on less labor-intensive forms of production.

Although personal service was generally abolished in 1549, important government officials and members of the clergy could to employ a small number of Indians to provide household services.[46] In some instances the amount of service required by an official was considerable, and it could place a heavy burden on the labor resources of a village. In 1785 the governor of Nicaragua employed thirty-one Indians from the village of Masaya: six servants, eight nightwatchmen, two stable hands, one shepherd, four collectors of fodder, one cook, one worker to carry milk from Masaya, two millers, one baker, and five fishermen. According to the current rates of pay, this labor force would have cost over 2,000 pesos in salaries, not counting 800 pesos' worth of goods the Indians were required to provide.[47] In many instances, however, Indians providing such services and goods were not paid in full; sometimes they were paid a small fraction and then often in goods or cacao. Although the numbers of Indians who were employed by parish priests were generally fewer than those who worked for government officials, a priest typically had the services of a cook, a servant, a stable hand, and a collector of wood and fodder, as well as the help of a *mayordomo portero* and a *fiscal* to assist in the running of parish affairs.[48] Villages near episcopal centers were also required to provide services for the bishop's palace and convents.[49] These kinds of services were finally abolished with the repartimiento in 1812.[50]

The payment of tribute and the provision of Indians to work under the repartimiento and provide services for officials were not the only levies made on Indian communities. During the colonial period a number of unauthorized exactions emerged which often placed even greater burdens on them. Probably the most important exaction was the *repartimiento de hilados,* whereby Indians were forced to spin and weave cloth at very low rates of pay. Indians were also subject to the *repartimiento de generos,* by which they were forced to buy poor-quality goods at exorbitant prices and sell items that they produced at low prices. These last two practices were illegal, as was the coercion of Indians to work in particular tasks against their will and for low pay. The most important officials involved in these activities were the corregidores, although other government officials and even parish priests also participated.[51] Most of the activities were widespread, although the *repartimiento de hilados* was most common in the cotton-producing area surrounding León, and to a lesser extent around Granada. Officials also required Indians to dye cotton using the *tinta de caracol* (see below), but this practice was limited to Nicoya, where the dye-producing mollusks were to be found.

The *repartimiento de hilados* began in the seventeenth century, but it seems to have reached its peak in the first half of the eighteenth century. At three month intervals corregidores distributed raw cotton to female Indians for spinning. From each 4 pounds of raw cotton the Indians were expected to spin 1 pound of thread, for which they were normally paid 4 reals, though the price paid varied between 2 and 6 reals according to the quality of the thread produced.[52] The corregidores sold the thread for between 7 and 12 reals, again depending on its quality. In 1768 the corregidor of Sutiaba was employing no less than 1,010 female Indians as both spinners and weavers, and a few years later the village was said to be producing produced 6,000 pounds of thread a year, giving the corregidor an annual income of 5,000 pesos.[53]

Other officials established mills for weaving the thread. Such a mill existed in Sutiaba, where three skilled weavers each supervised 20 to 25 Indian workers, who worked for two hours each morning and afternoon. Each worker was required to produce about 9 yards of cloth in three months, for which she was paid 2 pesos, about half its market value.[54] In 1789, following complaints from the Indians that they were locked in the mills and unable to visit their families, a royal provision ordered that Indians should not be coerced into leaving their villages to work in the mills or be forcibly retained there.[55]

A form of *repartimiento de hilados* was practiced in Nicoya under which Indians were required to dye cotton thread with purple dye obtained from *Purpura* mollusks. The mollusks were collected from the seashore, and the dye was applied directly to the thread. When the dye had been exhausted, the mollusks were replaced, and the dyers moved on to exploit those of another bay, returning to the same bay a month later. In the mideighteenth century the corregidor distributed between 1 and 2 pounds of thread a month to about 15 to 20 Indians, who in theory received 3 pesos for each pound of dyed thread they produced; in practice they were often paid less and in kind.[56] Sometimes this work imposed a considerable burden. In 1781 the Indians complained that the corregidor had forced them to leave their homes to work in dyeing, giving them each up to 8 pounds every two weeks and paying them only 2 reals a pound for the dyed thread they produced. Since two weeks were insufficient to ensure the rich dyeing of the thread, the dyed cloth they produced was of poor color, and the Indians were punished by being pilloried or flogged.[57]

In addition to being forced to work in spinning, weaving, and dyeing cotton, there were other tasks over and above those undertaken under the heading of personal service, which corregidores in particular required Indians in their charge to perform. They included such work as building houses, clearing milpas, transporting goods, and lumbering.[58]

Officials continued to trade in Indian villages, making illegal exactions and committing frauds.[59] In the eighteenth century they were particularly interested in acquiring cabuya, which was used among other things, for cordage. Officials obtained it by advancing the Indians cacao; in 1725, Indian villages in the jurisdiction of Granada were advanced between 10 and 20 pesos of cacao, for which they had to provide 1 arroba of cabuya for each peso each week. The quality of the cacao they were given was generally poor, and it was regulated at 60 beans a real, whereas the current rate of exchange was 70 good-quality beans for ½ real. The heavy demands for cabuya soon exhausted local supplies, and Indians were forced to travel up to 30 leagues to Sutiaba to buy it at the rate of 140 beans a real or else go to the valley of Nicaragua, where they bought it for 8 silver reals an arroba.[60] Similarly, in the villages of Quesalquaque, Posoltega, and Posolteguilla the corregidor was demanding 1 arroba and 3 pounds of cabuya for each peso of cacao that was worth 4 reals in silver.[61]

THE MISSIONS

Missionary activity in Nicaragua was more intense during the eighteenth century because the threat to imperial security posed by the attacks of the Zambo-Mosquito and by the settlement of the English on the Mosquito Coast persuaded the crown to provide the missionaries with greater financial and military support.[62] Despite the increased level of missionary activity, it is difficult to obtain a clear picture of the number and size of missions that were founded, because of their lack of stability and the incompleteness of the documentary record. Furthermore, it is difficult to distinguish missionary activities from those of the secular authorities who attempted to pacify hostile Indians and counteract the foreign threat.

From the end of the seventeenth century until 1721, when the Franciscans resumed their work in Nueva Segovia, there appears to have been little or no missionary activity in Nicaragua. In 1721 Friar Juan Baptista de Alfara and Friar Miguel de Aguirre entered Nueva Segovia, where they found that the former mission settlement at Paraka contained only fifty Indians. To this settlement they managed to gather another twelve Indians, but the mission was soon attacked by hostile Indians, and its site was moved. Following another attack in 1724 the site was moved again to an unspecified place fifty leagues from where the Indians had originally been settled and from which they subsequently fled.[63]

During the eighteenth century Indians in eastern Nicaragua gradually moved inland to escape the attacks of the Zambo-Mosquito. Some of these Indians remained hostile to Spanish rule, and it was difficult to distinguish between them and the Zambo-Mosquito. Others moved inland and voluntarily settled on the fringes of the colonized area, where they presented work for the missionary orders. In 1730 it was reported that Indians fleeing from the Zambo-Mosquito had settled at a place called Yasica, near Matagalpa, where a mission called Nuestra Señora de los Dolores del Manchen was founded. At the same time it was suggested that another mission should be established at San Roque, near Muymuy, where a distinct group of Indians had settled.[64]

Although there were continuous attacks on Indian villages along the frontier, it was the attack on Jinotega in 1743 by the Zambo-Mosquito, Carib, and English that persuaded the crown to support the work of Recollect missionaries in the area. The Recollect Order had been established by the Franciscans in 1682. Their primary duty was the conversion of heathen Indians in frontier regions. Beginning in 1744 Friar Antonio de Aguila and Friar Antonio Cáceres undertook to convert Indians in the areas around Matagalpa and Boaco. One document mentions that they founded five missions, but it does not give their names, whereas another records that only four missions were founded, at San Ramón (near Matagalpa), Aguarcha, Olama, and Boaco Viejo.[65] There is some discrepancy in the names of the missions recorded in other accounts, but it would appear that the initial population of the four or five missions originally founded was about 700.[66] As a result of Indian attacks, amalgamations and fugitivism, only two missions remained in 1751, with 244 Indians;[67] one of those was San Ramón, which had about 100 Indians in 1752.[68]

Despite their initial success the missionaries became disheartened, because no sooner had they established the missions than the Indians fled. Part of the problem was that at the same time punitive raids were being conducted on the Carib by the secular authorities using soldiers and Indian militiamen drawn from frontier villages. In 1749 an expedition managed to capture about 100 Carib who were thought to have been responsible for the recent raids on Indian villages, including Muymuy,

Camoapa, and Lóvago. These Carib were transported to Granada, whence they fled back to the mountains and took vengeance by attacking the village of Boaco, killing the missionary and capturing 70 to 80 Indians.[69] Although the missionaries were provided with a guard of 16 soldiers in 1752, they were reluctant to continue working in the area, since they could see no means of converting the Indians while they were in league with the Zambo-Mosquito. They suspended their activities there in 1756.[70]

Meanwhile Franciscan Observants continued to work in Nueva Segovia and Chontales. In 1748 the Franciscans had renewed their work in Jalapa and Jícaro, where Friar Nicolás Guerra and Friar Joseph de Aguilar encountered a few Indians who had been converted on a previous expedition.[71] The missionaries had great difficulty maintaining the Indians in the missions. In 1768, Friar Sebastián de Orozco reported that he had settled 50 Indians at a place called Cacalguaste, near Jalapa, but 8 had died and the rest had fled because, he maintained, he did not have enough gifts to encourage them to remain in the mission. He also settled 23 Indians at Jalapa, but many of them died of measles.[72] Because of the slow progress of the missions the bishop finally ordered the missionaries to withdraw.[73]

The evidence for the establishment of missions in Chontales is rather vague. It seems that a mission called Nuestra Señora de Guadalupe was established by Recollects at Lovigüisca probably in the 1740s, but during the twenty years of its existence the missionaries managed to convert only 100 Indians.[74] Another attempt was made to settle Indians near Lóvago by Don José Lozado y Zomoca sometime during the second half of the century.[75] In addition, in 1768, 47 Carib led by Yarrince voluntarily settled at Apompua, near Juigalpa.[76] Apparently no mission was founded there, but Captain Don Antonio Vargas, on whose hacienda they settled, arranged to supply them with food, clothes, and other items.[77]

Following the English evacuation of Mosquito Coast in 1787, the urgent need of the Spaniards to control these frontier regions receded, and missionary activity lapsed. There were clearly many "heathen" Indians in these areas, but they were considered difficult to convert, and, in the absence of a strong political motive, it was not considered to be worth the crown's money or the time and effort of the missionaries. Nevertheless, in 1801 the bishop of Nicaragua suggested that three new missions should be established: one near the site where Yarrince had settled at Olama Real, to which it was thought that Indians living between the Olama and Tomotoya rivers could be gathered; another for Indians who lived at Melchora and between the Mico and Carca rivers; and the third at Tortuga for the Indians that were already established there, for those from El Tular, and for any Guatuso Indians that might be converted.[78]

Missionaries began working in the area again in 1806, and by 1811 they had founded two missions, at Yasica and Guadalupe.[79] Although four missionaries were still working there in 1813, to combat fugitivism they decided to transport the Indians to Chichigalpa.[80] There they formed the settlement of Nuevo Guadalupe, together with Indians from the island of Solentiname, who in 1770 had come down from the mountains requesting Christian instruction.[81] Despite the problem of disease in the initial stages of its foundation, by 1815 Nuevo Guadalupe had a population of 121, and it was suggested that 500 more Indians from Matagalpa should be captured and transferred there.[82] It is not known whether the suggestion was taken up.

REGIONAL VARIATIONS IN CULTURAL INFLUENCES

Although the Nicaraguan economy remained fairly stagnant during the eighteenth and early nineteenth centuries, the distribution of economic activities expanded with the increase in the non-Indian population. Agricultural enterprises, particularly livestock raising, were established in eastern Nicaragua and to the south in the isthmus of Rivas and Nicoya, thereby creating demands on Indian lands and labor on a wider scale. Despite this expansion in the distribution of the non-Indian population, most non-Indians, and particularly the royal officials, remained concentrated in the Pacific region, where heavy demands on Indian labor and production continued and probably increased with the development of the *repartimiento de hilados*. The expansion of the non-Indian population into the countryside and the integration of the Indians into the Nicaraguan economy as free laborers brought the races into closer and more sustained contact, resulting in Indian acculturation and racial mixing.

In the east the activities of the Spaniards and the English converged. Military and missionary operations extended the sphere of Spanish influence eastwards, while the English allied with the Zambo-Mosquito extended their domination of the interior tribal areas westward from the Mosquito Coast. Thus Indians who had formerly lived outside the influence of both parties were gradually brought into contact with them. Although the English evacuated the Mosquito Coast in 1787, their influence remained through the trading contacts they maintained with the Zambo-Mosquito.

CHAPTER 15

Cultural Change in the Mesoamerican Zone, 1720–1821

With the extension of agricultural activities this period witnessed the increasing alienation of Indians lands and the incorporation of Indians into the national economy as wage laborers. Although tribute and the repartimiento continued to be levied throughout the eighteenth century, and other exactions made heavy demands on Indian production and labor, it was the gradual incorporation of the Indians into the Nicaraguan economy and the disintegration of Indian communities which accompanied it that brought about the greatest changes in the Indian way of life.

The Indian settlement pattern reflected many of the changes that were occuring in Nicaragua's economic and social structure. Although the population figures for individual villages give the impression that they were fairly stable entities whose populations were increasing, in reality they had a high population turnover, for as Indians abandoned their communities, their places were being filled by non-Indians. Accounts of Indian villages in western Nicaragua at the beginning of the nineteenth century show that desertion was common; nearly 10 percent of the tributary population was absent from Realejo, Chinandega, and Chichigalpa.[1] Many Indians were attracted to the nearby towns, but others moved to developing rural areas. The development of the Rivas Valley and the establishment of the Villa de Nicaragua in particular appear to have attracted Indians from many jurisdictions so that, it was said, they could escape tribute payment and other exactions.[2] In 1717 there were 935 Indians in the Rivas Valley and the suburbs of the Villa de Nicaragua; by 1778 their numbers had risen to 2,664.[3] Although by law Indians were free to reside where they wished,[4] various measures were taken to encourage them to return to their villages. These included burning their homes and fining estate owners who retained Indians in their employment.[5] Apart from these piecemeal efforts to encourage Indians to return to their communities, which were largely ineffective, in Nicaragua there was no program for the establishment of distinct Indian and non-Indian settlements during the eighteenth century as there was in other parts of Central America.

Meanwhile, Indian villages were becoming more ladino in character, although the pattern of change was uneven.[6] For example, in the jurisdiction of León in 1776, the villages of Sutiaba, Telica, and Quesalquaque were overwhelmingly Indian, altogether possessing 6,764 Indians and only 318 ladinos, but the population of the other six villages was 54.5 percent ladino.[7] By the turn of the century the settlements in the Meso-american zone that could still be described as Indian were El Viejo, Sutiaba, and Masaya, whereas León, Granada, and Nicaragua were dominated by ladinos, and there were more or less equal numbers of In-dians and ladinos in Managua.[8]

The dispersion of Indians from their communities and the movement of non-Indians into the countryside meant that at the beginning of the nineteenth century a very different settlement pattern existed from that which had been envisaged at the beginning of the colonial period. In Nicaragua more than 20 percent of the Spaniards and ladinos were living on haciendas or small holdings, but what is more interesting is that nearly 60 percent resided in Indian villages.[9] The rest were living in the towns or other non-Indian settlements.

Although the settlement pattern changed substantially during the eighteenth and early nineteenth centuries, the number and size of settle-ments did not. According to Bishop Morel's *visita* in 1752 the average size of settlements in the east was about 500 inhabitants, compared to 1,000 in the west, where the largest settlements were to be found in the vicinity of Granada.[10] However, his figures include persons of all races "de confesión y comunión," and probably much of the difference between the two zones can be attributed to the presence of larger numbers of non-Indians in the Mesoamerican zone.

There are few accounts of the form of Indian villages during the eigh-teenth and nineteenth centuries, but Bishop Morel's *visita* does provide some details on the physical character of the settlements. The larger Indian villages had a regular form near the center of the settlement, which was marked by the presence of a plaza, a cathedral or church, a town hall, a prison, and shops. Away from the center, however, the plan

Table 21. Settlement Pattern in Nicaragua, 1752

Jurisdiction	Number of settle-ments	Number of persons*	Average size of settle-ments	Number of houses		Average household size
				Stone	Straw	
León	17	18,669	1,098	347	3,162	5.3
Granada	17	28,249	1,662	712	4,376	5.6
Nueva Segovia	13	6,992	538	12	653	10.5
Sebaco	11	6,027	548	4	681	8.8

Source: AGI AG 950 Bishop Morel 8.9.1752.
*Generally persons "de confesión y comunión."

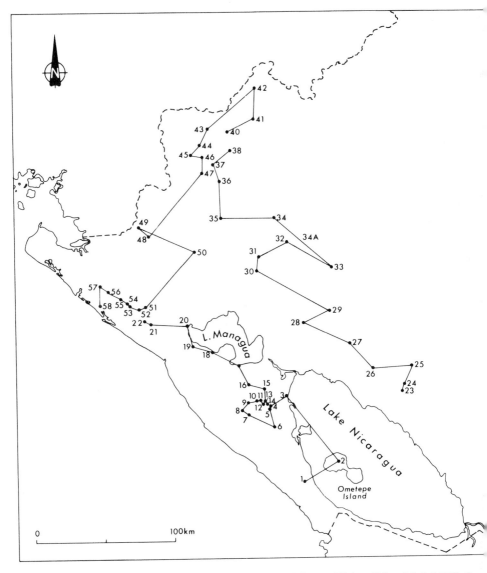

Fig. 8. Route of Bishop Morel's *visita* (AGI AG 950 Bishop Morel 8.9.1752).*

1. Nicaragua (villa and pueblo)	7. Jinotepe	14. San Juan Namotiba
2. Isla de Ometepe	8. Diriamba	15. Masaya
3. Granada and Jalteba	9. Masatepe	16. Nindirí
4. Diriá	10. Jalata	17. Managua
5. Diriomo	11. Nandasmo	18. Matiare
6. Nandaime	12. Niquinohomo	19. Nagarote
	13. Santa Catalina Namotiba	20. Pueblo Nuevo, or

often became irregular, individual families establishing houses where they wished and houses being separated by garden plots and orchards.[11] Smaller villages had a more irregular form, houses being clustered around a center marked by a church, a village hall, and a prison. Most houses were built of thatch; the church and the priest's house very often were the only stone buildings; in the larger settlements the number of stone buildings increased. A *visita* of the Indian villages of El Viejo, Chinandega, and Chichigalpa in 1740 showed that a few families owned several houses, which they rented out.[12] Although there is little evidence for household size, that which exists suggests that households were generally smaller in the Mesoamerican zone than they were in the east. Not only that, but Indian households were smaller than those of other racial groups. Evidence from the *visita* of the *partido* of Realejo in 1740 reveals that Indian households averaged about 3.7 persons, whereas those of Spaniards and mixed races contained 4.6 and 5.2 persons, respectively.[13]

THE ECONOMY

The eighteenth century witnessed the increasing control of Indian lands and labor by non-Indians. While Indian lands were often inadequate and subject to alienation by non-Indians during the seventeenth century, the situation deteriorated during the eighteenth century, when the population as a whole increased, thereby creating greater demands for land. At the same time official and nonofficial demands on Indian labor continued. With inadequate lands and a lack of labor time to cultivate them, many individuals abandoned their villages in search of wage labor. This process was further encouraged by the development of exactions such as the *repartimiento de hilados,* which added to the burdens that Indian production had to bear. Production was often geared to satisfy official and non-

---

Momotombo	34. Jinotega	46. Yalagüina
21. Sutiaba	34A. San Ramón	47. Pueblo Nuevo
22. León	35. Estelí	48. Villa Nueva
23. Acoyapa	36. Condega	49. Somotillo
24. Lovigüisca	37. Palacagüina	50. El Sauce
25. Lóvago	38. Litelpaneca	51. Telica
26. Juigalpa	39. Comalteca	52. Quesalquaque
27. Comalapa	40. Nueva Segovia	53. Posolteguilla
28. Teustepe	(Ciudad Antigua)	54. Posoltega
29. Boaco	41. Jícaro	55. Chichigalpa
30. Metapa (Ciudad Darío)	42. Jalapa	56. Chinandega
31. Sebaco	43. Mozonte	57. El Viejo
32. Matagalpa	44. Totogalpa	58. Realejo
33. Muymuy	45. Tepesomoto	

official demands, rather than to meet Indian subsistence needs, and the only real bonus for the Indians during the eighteenth century, in terms of their diet and income, was the expansion of livestock raising.

The eighteenth century witnessed increasing conflict between Indians and non-Indians over the use of land as the population of both groups increased; while the mixed races emerged as a landless group reduced to renting or squatting on lands, the Indians were anxious to prevent the further alienation of their lands, which were now required to support their expanding populations. During this time of rapid economic and social change, the *cajas de comunidad* and *cofradías* grew in importance to provide a form of economic and social security.

The loss of Indian lands by sale or illegal occupation that began in the late sixteenth century was a serious problem when the population was decreasing but became more acute at the beginning of the eighteenth century when the population increased and many Indian villages found themselves with inadequate lands to support their populations. Although some villages managed to extend their lands by purchase, many others lost land to non-Indians. Indians constantly complained that *vecinos* had either cultivated plots on their lands or, more commonly, grazed their livestock there, resulting in damage to crops and the intermixing of herds.[14] Particularly vulnerable to encroachment were Indian lands in the vicinity of major towns. One *vecino* from León, who held land contiguous to the ejidos of Sutiaba, moved the boundary markers and tried to charge the Indians rent for use of their land.[15] Preventing the illegal occupation of Indian lands was made difficult by two factors: first, the land often appeared unoccupied since it consisted of untended stretches of grassland, scrub, or woodland; and, second, few villages possessed formal titles to their lands. Nevertheless, for administrative reasons the crown was eager for the Indians to remain in their villages, and one way it could encourage this was by assuring them rights to their lands. A cedula issued in 1754 ordered that *jueces subdeledados* in charge of the allocation of land grants should assure Indian rights to their lands, including "community lands and those granted to villages for *pastos* and ejidos," even if they did not posses formal titles to them. They were also to provide them with additional lands if these should not be sufficient.[16] Nevertheless, it became clear that the only really effective way for the Indians to protect their lands was through the acquisition of formal titles.

The standard measure for an ejido was one square league, or about 3,885 acres, equivalent to 37 *caballerías*.[17] Ejidos included communal pastures and milpas, monte, and lands alloted to individual families for cultivation. The latter were distributed by the Indian cabildo. There were instances of favoritism and petty jealousies affecting the allocation and revocation of lands, a problem that was made more acute by the frequent changes of officeholders. An account drawn up by don Antonio Larrazábal on the state of agriculture in the Audiencia of Guatemala in 1810 noted with respect to ejidos that

their apportionment depends on the whim of their own officials, who arbitrarily give out lands at their fancy, take them away and give them out again, when and as they wish, leaving them without the opportunity most of the time to sow for themselves or others, and the worst is that with this mismanagement and arbitrariness the Indian will never be secure in the labor of his land to be a useful farmer, even if only of maize and vegetables.[18]

The account went on to recommend that Indians should be given plots of land that were inalienable and could be inherited, since, it was argued, this would provide them with an incentive to increase production. This recommendation appears to have produced some effect a few years later. A decree issued in 1812 and repeated in 1820 ordered that all married Indians and those over age twenty-five should be given lands as near as possible to Indian villages, but not those which belonged to individuals or Indian commuities, except where the lands owned by the latter were extensive compared to the size of the population, in which case up to 50 percent could be used for the purpose.[19] The decree clearly reflected the dilemma which the authorities faced; while they clearly wished to develop agriculture, they also wanted to preserve the community lands of Indian villages to keep the Indians there. Unfortunately, there is no evidence of the extent to which Indians received private holdings following the issue of the decreee.

Apart from lands allotted to individual families for cultivation, Indians were also required to sow a *milpa de comunidad* or cultivate 10 *brazas* of land each to provide for emergencies. The relationship between the *milpa de comunidad* and the 10 *brazas* of land cultivated is far from clear. While the product from both these lands went into the *caja de comunidad*, it is not known whether they were alternatives or whether the *milpa de comunidad* was worked communally and the 10 *brazas* individually. In addition to cultivated lands, many Indian communities also possessed livestock, particularly cattle, which were raised on communal lands, and the profits of which entered the *caja de comunidad*. However, some communities could cultivate only enough for their own subsistence, and others were too small even to cultivate a *milpa de comunidad*.[20] In some instances contributions to the *caja de comunidad* were commuted to money payments. This occurred where Indians were privately employed or spent extended periods away from home working under the repartimiento and were thus unable to cultivate lands for this purpose. During the late eighteenth century the community contribution appears to have been regulated at between one and a half and two reals per person.[21] Its collection was suspended with the suspension of tribute payments between 1811 and 1815. The contributions made by individuals and the income from the working of community lands formed only part of the total income of the *cajas de comunidad;* the rest came from the rent and sale of lands, from the hire of animals and canoes for transport, and from other commercial activities.

The *cajas de comunidad* were originally administered by Indian officials, but during the colonial period the secular authorities gained greater control over community funds by insisting that one of the keys to the chest should be held by a corregidor and by establishing central depositories for the funds.[22] A central depository, or *arca,* was supposed to be established in each *cabecera* to contain the community funds from all nearby villages, but the extent to which community funds were transferred to provincial centers in Nicaragua is unknown. Nevertheless, even though community funds increased over time, the amount of money that remained under the control of Indian officials in their communities decreased as more and more was lent out to borrowers; in 1819 only 19.6 percent of the total community funds remained at their disposal, while 53.1 percent was on loan and 27.3 percent formed part of a consolidated fund established in Guatemala in 1815.[23]

Community funds were supposed to be used to support the elderly, sick, widows, and orphans; to maintain the church; and to establish schools.[24] They also contributed to the salaries of intendants and were used to pay tribute arrears and provide security in times of crisis. For other than routine purposes Indian communities had to petition the audiencia to use their own funds. In many instances permission was denied, either because the audiencia did not accept the case for expenditure or because the existing funds were inadequate for the purpose. In 1791 a request to the audiencia from Indians of El Viejo to use 300 pesos to construct two canoes to transport goods to the port was opposed by the governor of Nicaragua on the grounds that the community as a whole did not wish to use its money in this way and that the principales only wanted to spent it on drunken fiestas. Nevertheless, the audiencia upheld the village's request.[25] The actual amount of community funds possessed by villages varied with the size of their populations and the type and level of agricultural production. In general terms they were larger in Pacific Nicaragua, for although Indian communities there owned 80 percent of the total community assets, they comprised only 60 percent of the Indian population.[26]

While access to community funds by Indian communities themselves became more difficult, other groups found it relatively easy to use their funds. Indian officials, secular authorities, especially *gobernadores, tenientes,* corregidores and parish priests with privileged access to community funds often used them for their own purposes, either by taking money direct from the *cajas* or by selling agricultural produce belonging to the community.[27] The greater part of community funds was, however, used for loans to individuals. Requests for loans had to be made to the audiencia. Loans generally exceeded 1,000 pesos, and they were made over 3 to 4 years at 5 percent interest, although one large loan of 4,000 pesos made to the cabildo of León was repayable over 10 years.[28] It is uncertain how much of the money was ever paid back; if the example of *cofradía* funds is anything to go by, then probably some money was lost through bankruptcy,[29] though the dramatic increase in community funds toward the end of the eighteenth century suggests that some profits were being made. Owing to the great demand for loans, in 1791 the amount granted to any one individual was limited to 1,000 pesos, repayable over two years. At the same time Indian villages received some protection by being allowed to retain a minimum of one-quarter of their funds to meet emergencies.[30]

Toward the end of the eighteenth century community funds were being used not only by private individuals but also by the authorities to promote the economic development of the province. In 1793 the governor of Nicaragua obtained a loan of 1,500 pesos at 5 percent interest to encourage agricultural development by making small loans, which were repayable in produce, notably maize.[31] This was extended in 1815, when the audiencia authorized the granting of loans at 8 percent interest from community funds to promote agricultural production, and three years later it authorized the use of community funds for the development of cochineal production.[32] Thus the situation had been reached where community funds were no longer being used to support Indian communities but were being employed to promote the general economic development of the province; Indian communities were thus subsidizing the non-Indian sector, while Indians who required loans were having to pay interest on them, even though they themselves had provided the capital.

Cofradías, or religious brotherhoods, became important institutions in the economic, social, and religious life of Indian villages during the eighteenth century. Despite the financial burdens that membership of *cofradías* imposed, they provided the Indians with a form of corporate identity at a time when outside influences were undermining their communities and, as their wealth increased, gave them security and a small degree of economic independence. Even though the crown tried to limit the founding of *cofradías,* they continued to be established until the end of the colonial period. Although separate *cofradías* were established for whites, ladinos, and Indians, most documents fail to indicate the racial identity of their members; consequently the following observations are drawn from accounts of *cofradías* as a whole, and they may not accurately reflect the characteristics Indian *cofradías*. It seems likely that *cofradías,* in terms of their assets, were most important among whites and ladinos, in the first case because of their greater financial resources and in the second because ladino settlements did not have alternative sources of income in the form of community lands that could provide security in the event of disasters; in the case of Indian communities *cajas de comunidad* generally covered such emergencies.

Although the origins of *cajas de comunidad* and *cofradías* were different, in their economic organization they were very similar—so much so that there was often confusion about which lands and animals were owned by the community and which by *cofradías. Cofradías* were originally founded to celebrate various saints and hold special services, but they soon developed economic interests. Many *cofradías* owned land, while others possessed livestock, which they grazed on ejidos. Most of the cattle were probably consumed locally, although some found their way to the cattle fair at Japaltagua in Guatemala.[33] In addition some subsistence crops, particularly maize and plantains, were also grown on *cofradía* lands.[34] The lands owned by *cofradías* were not always worked by their members but were rented out to tenants. In addition the capital owned by *cofradías* was lent at 5 percent interest. From these sources and membership dues the *cofradías* received their income.

There is little information on the income of *cofradías* in Nicaragua with the exception of Nicoya, where individual *cofradías* branded over 1,000 cattle a year, but there is no doubt that they were wealthier than the *cofradías* described by Gibson in the Valley of Mexico, where, he suggests, in a good year a *cofradía* would probably make only 10 to 20 pesos profit.[35] The *cofradías* were administered by Indian mayordomos, who appear to have been unsalaried and were appointed by the corregidor.[36] They kept the acounts and supervised the sale and purchase of lands and agricultural produce. The keys to the chests in which the funds of the *cofradías* were kept were held by the alcaldes and parish priests, again a parallel with the *cajas de comunidad* and indicating their close integration into the organization of Indian communities. Although the administration of the *cofradías* was supposedly in the hands of Indian mayordomos, it is clear that in many instances the *cofradías'* assets were disposed of by parish priests.[37]

Apart from community lands, which were worked either communally or individually, a small number of Indians owned lands they had purchased. However, fewer Indians were able to buy land in the eighteenth century, when the increased demand for land caused prices to rise. The few grants to individuals averaged three to five *caballerías,* while most grants to Indians went to Indian communities and *cofradías.*[38]

Although the Indian population increased during the eighteenth century, the sources of labor that could be employed in subsistence activities did not expand at a parallel rate, because Indians were increasingly turning to wage labor and those who remained were called on to meet their communities' obligations under the repartimiento in full. As a result there were constant complaints from Indians that because they were working on the *repartimiento* they were unable to provide for their own subsistence needs.[39] However, the greater concentration of population and economic activities in the Pacific zone meant that Indians there were able to return to their villages more easily and frequently than were Indians in other parts of the province, where they often resided far from their places of employment. But even if the Indians were not drawn off to work away from their places of residence, they were often not available for agricultural labor since they were burdened by many demands for personal service. The Indians complained that they suffered food shortages to the extent that they had to sell their personal belongings to buy food.[40]

The most important influences on agricultural production emanated from these increased pressures on Indian lands and labor; there appear to have been a few changes in the nature of production, including the types of crops and animals raised and the techniques employed. Probably most Indian families cultivated a small milpa of maize and beans, and many may have possessed a *platanar* from which they obtained plantains. In addition they probably had a kitchen garden, where they raised spices, such as peppers and garlic, a few vegetables, and fruit trees. Small patches of sugarcane and cotton may also have been cultivated.

Owing to tradition and because it remained the major item paid as tribute by the Indians, maize continued to be the most important crop raised. Maize generally grew well in Nicaragua, while Nicoya produced little else in the way of crops. The only area where its cultivation proved difficult was in Nueva Segovia, which was sometimes hit by drought and where the soils were poor and acidic.[41] Although maize yields were high, there were nevertheless difficulties, in addition to those of increasing shortages of land and labour already discussed, which intervened to cause shortages of the crop. Some of the difficulties were more widespread than others, and some affected other crops as well as maize. First, maize was often attacked by plagues of locusts. This appears to have been a fairly common problem that also affected other cereal crops and cotton.[42] As a result Indians were encouraged to grow root crops, such as "yuca, ñame, camote, y papas" which were not affected by locusts and could grow on any soil.[43] The second threat to standing crops was straying cattle. In addition there were normal seasonal and regional variations in yields of maize, which led to fluctuations in its price. In Nicaragua the price of maize was generally 4 reals a fanega for the first harvest and double that for the second, but in times of shortage the price reached 2 to 3 pesos.[44] There were also some regional variations in prices; in Nicaragua in 1803 maize was cheapest in Telica, El Viejo, and Chinandega, where it sold for 10 reals a fanega, followed by Masaya and Granada, where it sold for 12 reals, and it was most expensive in León, where it cost 2 pesos.[45]

Although maize remained the Indian staple, it appears that other crops, particularly root crops and fruit trees, which were less affected by problems of weather, locusts, and straying animals, assumed more important roles in the Indian diet. Plantains in particular are noted much more frequently in the documentary record for the eighteenth century, even in the Pacific lowlands, where there were probably fewer difficulties with food supplies.[46] In many instances, however plantains were not cultivated but were harvested from wild sources. Cultivated tree crops also provided food, although individual families probably never possessed more than a few trees. The most important fruit trees cultivated remained the native ones, such as papayas, annonas, jocotes, mammees, sapotes, nisperos (sapodilla), avocado pears, and pineapples, although a few introduced species such as citrus fruits and bananas, were probably adopted widely. At the beginning of the nineteenth century, if not earlier, a number of trees of Asian origin were introduced to Central America through Trujillo. They included the now familiar mango (*Mangifera indica* L.), cinnamon (*Cinnamomum zeylanicum* Breyn.) and the breadfruit (*Artocarpus communis* J. R. and G. Forst).[47] Meanwhile, the cultivation of cacao by Indians declined as its production passed into Spanish hands. Nevertheless, Indians continued to consume chocolate; in the province of Realejo in the eighteenth century each household was said to possess a stone for grinding cacao.[48]

By the eighteenth century livestock raising had achieved a prominent position in the Indian economy. Most families raised chickens and possessed horses, mules, and oxen for use in agriculture and for transport. An account of the villages of El Viejo, Chinandega, and Chichigalpa in 1740 indicates that, of 424 families, 152 owned horses (276 horses, 36 percent), and 62 owned yokes of oxen (82 yokes, 15 percent).[49] Most livestock, including cattle, which were generally communally owned, were raised on ejidos or *cofradía* lands.

Although herds of cattle, horses, and mules were sometimes extensive, a number of problems occurred in raising them. As with the production of maize, the raising of livestock was at the mercy of the weather. The droughts that afflicted maize production also resulted in dry pastures and loss of animals, so that in times of shortage one form of production could not always substitute for another.[50] Also, there appears to have been little in the way of livestock husbandry. The lands on which livestock were grazed were sometimes distant from villages, and the heavy demands on Indian labor meant that little care could be taken of herds.[51] Animals were thus subject to attacks by coyotes, and they often died of diseases such as murrain. Cattle on ranches situated near indigo works, which attracted insects, were said to be particularly vulnerable to disease.[52] Older animals were probably consumed in the village, while horses and mules were used for transport or hired out. Other animals were branded and sold locally, the profit entering the *caja de comunidad* or the funds of the *cofradía*. Although most animals raised by commercial producers were sold at the annual cattle fair at Jalpatagua, few animals from Indian villages appear to have been sent there, although they may have ended up at the fair after being sold to middlemen. Many cattle and other livestock never benefited the community, however, because they were appropriated by Indian leaders, Spanish officials, and parish priests.[53]

The exploitation of wild food resources declined considerably during the eighteenth century, although perhaps not as dramatically as the lack of documentary evidence might suggest. Hunting and gathering declined as the areas that could be exploited were reduced along with the labor time to conduct them. The need for the dietary supplements that these activities provided also declined as the availability of meat increased. Hunting and collecting thus became activities which were undertaken in times of shortage or where plants and animals were very readily available or were regarded as having commercial value. Fishing remained an important subsistence activity along the coasts and around the lakes, where mojarras, *guapotes,* and sardines were caught.[54] However, the activities which attracted most attention from observers were pearl fishing and the collection of mother-of-pearl and *Purpura* mollusks in Nicoya.[55]

Apart from meeting their own subsistence needs and the numerous demands for goods and services, Indians also manufactured items of everyday use both for themselves and for sale. The production of leather goods, made of cattle hides, and also from deerskins, became more important during the eighteenth century as cattle raising increased. Production was greatest in the livestock-raising areas, where many products associated with horse riding and ranching, such as bridles, halters, reins, whips, saddles, leather seats, and saddlebags, were manufactured.[56] The increased availability of leather resulted in a decline in the importance of various kinds of cords and ropes, although the reason given for the decline in the industry was the lack of care the Indians had given to the fiber-producing plants. For domestic purposes Indians continued to make earthenware pots and bowls, and they used reeds, rushes, and palms to manufacture hats, mats, baskets, and chairs and other items of furniture.[57]

During the eighteenth century the monopolization of trade by secular officials continued. Although officials were prohibited from trading with Indians, they did so through the purchase of tribute items and through the repartimiento of cotton, cabuya, and other goods. In addition they coerced Indians into selling them other items at very low prices, which they resold at profits of 200 to 400 percent.[58] Officials also sold manufactures from neighboring provinces and from Europe, although their control of this trade appears to have been less than complete, since they had to compete with other merchants and traders. There were 30 to 35 commercial houses in Guatemala, which together received about 1,000 pesos worth of goods from Cádiz every year. These goods were then distributed to merchants and traders for sale through shops in the major towns. Few imported manufactures were freely purchased by Indians; most were bought under pressure from officials. Often the Indians did not want the goods, nor could they afford them.[59] Most European manufactures were extremely expensive; the wholesale price of European cloth was 60 percent higher in Nicaragua than in Cádiz, and the retail price was 90 percent higher.[60] The most that Indians could have afforded would have been cloth made in Guatemala and El Salvador, which they could wear on festive occasions. Complaints about the control of trade by officials and the high prices they charged for goods appears to have been greatest in the jurisdictions of corregidores.[61]

After satisfying their own subsistence needs and all external demands, few Indians had any goods to sell or money with which to purchase others. A few may have sold livestock, but mostly traded only small quantities of food they had processed, such as cheese or sweets, and a few craft items, such as hats, baskets, pots, and leather articles.[62] Since the Indians possessed few items for sale and trade was monopolized by officials, it is uncertain whether regular markets were held. Even in the eighteenth century coins were not widely used as a medium of exchange partly owing to their shortage. Indians very often paid for goods they purchased with other products, including crops and cattle. In Nicaragua cacao was used as a medium of exchange up to about the middle of the eighteenth century, the wages of workers being paid half in money and half in cacao.[63]

THE SOCIOPOLITICAL ORGANIZATION

By the end of the colonial period the power of caciques and other nobles within their communities had been almost completely eroded; the only privileges that caciques and their eldest sons still enjoyed were exemption from tribute payment and the repartimiento. The decreased authority and status of caciques was not replaced by that of elected leaders, since the power and privileges of the latter appear to have diminished as their responsibilities increased. Most Indian villages elected one or two alcaldes and several regidores according to the size of village. In 1752, Indian communities in Nicaragua elected one or two alcaldes and one to eight regidores.[64] These officials were supposed to be freely elected, but since those elected had to be confirmed in office by the Spanish authorities, opportunities existed for outside intervention. Such cases of intervention were not common, however, although in 1770 the governor tried to force his own candidate for alcalde on the village of Jalteba.[65]

Although the offices of alcalde and regidor brought with them exemption from tribute payment and the repartimiento, they were insufficient rewards for the multitude of duties the offices brought, which during the eighteenth century became even more onerous. The collection of tribute and provision of labor under the repartimiento became more difficult as Indians began deserting their villages in search of employment elsewhere. Alcaldes were thus forced to travel around the countryside, sometimes with the help of *alguaciles de mandón,* searching for absent Indians. At such times any shortfalls in tribute or the provision of labor faced them with fines, confiscation of goods, or imprisonment.[66] Although these duties imposed considerable burdens on elected officials, they did provide them with opportunities to make some profits at the expense of both the Indians and the Spanish authorities.[67]

At the family level there appears to have been very little change to social organization. Most of the documentary evidence for marriage patterns and family size is for the Indian villages, while there is little information for rural estates and the towns where changes were taking place. Nevertheless, it is clear that marriage patterns were becoming more complex as the Indian population became more mobile.

Unfortunately, few marriage records exist for Nicaragua during the eighteenth century, and from 1754, when women were exempted from tribute payment, the information available from tributary lists declines. Very often women are not included at all in *padrones* or, if they are, their origin, race, or legal status is not recorded. For this reason most of the following comments are drawn from *padrones* and *tasaciones* for the first half of the eighteenth century.

Changes in the pattern of marriages in Pacific Nicaragua are difficult to analyze because of differences in the way the information was recorded. Whereas in the seventeenth century accounts specified whether Indians married within or outside their barrios rather than their villages, in the eighteenth century they often recorded both or only marriages between Indians from different villages. Nevertheless, it appears that there was a slight increase in out-marriage during the eighteenth century. In the jurisdiction of León the proportion of men marrying spouses from other barrios rose from 60 percent to 64.1 percent between 1676–86 and 1759, though in 1759, 87 percent married women from their own villages.[68] The evidence for the jurisdiction of Granada is less complete, but in the villages of Nindirí, Masaya, and Managua the proportion of men with spouses from their own villages was smaller and fell from 42.2 percent in 1686 to 39.4 percent in 1759.[69]

The available evidence suggests that most people married, although the marriage rate appears to have fallen slightly during the eighteenth century. Figures for a number of villages in the jurisdiction of León and Granada in 1759 indicate that males who were or had been married accounted for 77.5 percent and 71.5 percent of the male tributary population, respectively.[70] Unfortunately, there is no evidence for marriage rates among females, but they were probably as low; in western Nicaragua one reason given for the failure of women to marry was that they were forcibly retained in the *casa de maestres*, where they were employed in spinning and weaving cotton and were unable to meet potential husbands.[71] Officials were concerned about the falling marriage rate because it suggested a fall in the birthrate and a loss of tribute income, and also because it implied immoral conduct. However, the increase in the Indian population indicates that the falling marriage rate did not affect the birthrate; indeed, there were complaints that many people had children without being married. Although the falling marriage rate may have represented a retarded rejection of Christian ideals, more likely it reflected the increasing mobility of the population encouraged by wage labor. The latter is certainly suggested by the fact that the marriage rates were lowest in areas of high employment opportunities.

Indians were legally free to marry persons of their choice, but the authorities encouraged marriages between Indians to safeguard the crown's tribute income.[72] This was reinforced by a decree in 1798 that Indians wishing to marry had to obtain permission from their parents or the parish priest.[73] During the eighteenth century the numbers of Indians resident in Indian villages who married non-Indians remained small, though the evidence is available only for males. In the middle of the eighteenth century interracial marriages constituted only 0.3 percent of all Indian marriages, but the *padrones* for El Viejo, Chinandega, and Chichigalpa in 1817 indicate that by the beginning of the nineteenth century that figure had risen considerably, to 23.1, 17.1 and 10.7 percent, respectively. At that time all the non-Indian marriage partners were mulattoes.[74]

The evidence for family size during the eighteenth century is very fragmentary. Many of the data problems outlined in the discussion of family size in the seventeenth century remain and are exacerbated by the fact that tributary lists did not register children born to women who came from another village, so that many couples appear childless. The best evidence is for the corregimiento of Realejo in 1740. This *visita* provides information on household size and the number of children per couple, although as usual married children are regarded as forming a separate household which makes it impossible to calculate the average completed family size. The *visita* reveals that the average Indian household contained about three persons and that the adult-child ratio was 1:0.74.[75] Unfortunately there is no evidence for family size for the end of the eighteenth century with which these figures can be compared. The greater mobility of the Indian population in the eighteenth century was reflected in the higher percentage of orphans. Whereas previously only 1 to 2 percent of children were classified as orphans, in the eighteenth century this figure sometimes passed 10 percent for individual villages.[76] The evidence is not comprehensive enough to indicate any regional variations in the incidence of orphanage, and it would appear that variations were more related to the size of Indian villages, the smallest villages possessing the largest number of orphans.

There is very little evidence for the social organization of *lavoríos*. While some *lavoríos* would have become residents of distinct Indian barrios within the major towns, most were scattered through the countryside, living either on estates or in Indian villages. The difficulty of enumerating such a dispersed population means that few figures are available, and where they are available, they are for tributary *lavoríos* only. As a consequence there are few guides to changes in their marriage patterns or family sizes. The only evidence available is for 1741 for several villages in the jurisdiction of Nueva Segovia, where the marriage rate was much lower than that among tributary Indians, as was the ratio of adults to children.[77] It seems likely that these characteristics were also common among *lavoríos* in the Mesoamerican zone.

THE IDEOLOGY

Although Indian conversion proceeded, it was beset by a number of problems, among which was the shortage of clergy. The poverty of the province resulted in its failure to attract good-quality clerics in large numbers, and this was evident in the employment of regular clergy to administer Indians in already well-established communities. The Mercedarians had charge of two fairly large villages in the Mesoamerican zone—Posoltega and Chichigalpa—while the Franciscans were employed in Chinandega, El Viejo, Jinotepe, Nandaime, Nicaragua, and the island of Ometepe.[78] The inability of the province to attract good-quality clerics was reflected in the fact that less than one-third of the Franciscans who worked in the area were from Europe,[79] and, since the proportion of those coming from Spain was generally higher for the regular clergy, most of those employed as parish priests would have been creoles. These priests were poorly trained, and they were often eager to compensate for their small salaries by making exactions from the Indians. There were many complaints that parish priests charged too much, often in goods, for church services, that they made *repartimientos de generos,* that they exacted too much in the form of personal service, that they used community and *cofradía* funds for their own purposes, and that they led immoral lives. The shortcomings of the clergy retarded the conversion of the Indians. Even in Sutiaba, a large Indian village next to the capital, León, the conversion of the Indians had not been very successful, for a *visita* of that village by the bishop in 1746 revealed intolerable "vices, superstitions, and idolatry."[80]

Although the acceptance of Christan beliefs on anything other than a superficial level appears to have proceeded very slowly, the number, size and wealth of *cofradías* grew rapidly. Their growth should be viewed not as reflecting a new enthusiasm for Christianity but as providing Indian communities with a sense of identity and independence in a way that was acceptable to the Spanish authorities and at a time when other influences worked to undermine them.

CHAPTER 16

Cultural Change in the South American Zone, 1720–1821

Although the Indians in eastern Nicaragua could still be divided into four groups according to the cultural changes they experienced, during the eighteenth century they became less distinct as contacts between them increased and their activities became more interdependent. The missionaries, who had been important agents of cultural change in the seventeenth century, played a minor role relative to the English and the Zambo-Mosquito, who became dominant influences on the life of the Indians; their influence even extended to the Spanish settled area, where they had trading contacts.

TRIBUTARY INDIAN VILLAGES

During the eighteenth century Indian groups living in tributary villages in the east experienced a greater variety of cultural changes than those in the Mesoamerican zone. These changes were largely brought about by the effective colonization of the area for the first time by non-Indians and through contact with the Zambo-Mosquito. The colonization of the area resulted in increased demands for land and labor, while contacts with the Zambo-Mosquito took the form of trade or raids. These influences severely affected the economic and social organization of Indian communities and accelerated the process of cultural change.

Many of the changes were reflected in the fluctuations in the number, size, and location of Indian villages; settlements were constantly being attacked and destroyed by the Zambo-Mosquito, following which they were often relocated away from the frontier. By 1768, Jinotega, Boaco, Camoapa, Lóvago, and Lovigüisca had all been attacked, and Muymuy had been attacked three times.[1] Nevertheless, the average number of tributary Indians in sixteen Indian villages in eastern Nicaragua rose from 180 to 1777 to 265 in 1806.[2] Although the populations of Indian villages apparently increased, many tributary Indians no longer resided there but lived on haciendas or plots in the countryside, or else they had migrated to the towns. From the beginning of the eighteenth century Indian desertion was common in eastern Nicaragua. In 1726 villages in the jurisdiction of Sebaco and Chontales were said to possess 2,000 Indians, 1,500 of whom were living in the countryside.[3] Similarly, in the neighboring jurisdiction of Nueva Segovia, *tasaciones* drawn up in 1741 indicate that 546 Indians were missing, and an examination of the detailed *padrones* for five villages reveals that on average 17 percent of the adults were absent, although the proportions for individual villages ranged from 11 to 47.2 percent, the smaller villages registering the most absentees.[4] An account of the residences of absentees from the village of Yalagüina two years earlier recorded that 45 were living in the households or haciendas of local *vecinos,* while another 31 were living in other jurisdictions of the province, El Salvador, Choluteca, and the mining districts of Honduras.[5]

As Indians were abandoning their villages, so ladinos were moving into them, though the pattern of immigration was uneven. Villages in Nueva Segovia attracted a small number of ladinos, but they remained essentially "Indian" in character, whereas those in the jurisdiction of Sebaco became progressively ladino so that by the end of the eighteenth century they contained more or less equal number of Indians and ladinos.[6]

Most of the villages in eastern Nicaragua consisted of an unorganized cluster of houses many of which were unoccupied for a large part of the week or year. Many of the "residents" in fact lived in ranchos, *chacras,* or *bohíos* scattered throughout the countryside. Others did not maintain houses in the village but stayed with relatives or friends or camped under the trees when they came to hear mass.[7] This dispersed settlement pattern served the needs of defense; large nucleated settlements, it was said, attracted raids, and fewer people were able to survive.[8] Although dwellings were dispersed, household sizes were large. The evidence from Bishop Morel's *visita* suggests that the average household size in eastern Nicaragua was about 9.6 persons, although the figure refers to all racial groups.[9] Nevertheless it is nearly twice that of households found in the Pacific zone, and it suggests that extended family residence was the norm.

On the western fringes of the South American zone Indian economic activities were subject to changes similar to those outlined for the Mesoamerican zone. The main differences were of degree rather than substance. During the eighteenth century the demand for land in eastern Nicaragua increased. Owing to the relative lack of land pressure at an early date, few Indian villages had sought legal titles to their lands; in 1740 the corregidor of Sebaco reported that because of the general availability of land, ejidos had never been designated, and it was impossible for Indian villages to safeguard their rights to the land.[10] Hence, as land pressure increased, Indian lands were alienated more frequently and more widely. The establishment of haciendas and ranches also created new demands for labor, reducing that available for subsistence production. These changes undermined the structure of Indian communities to the extent that each individual or family eked out a living as best it could either by farming its own plot, which might be in the hills, or by leaving the village in search of wage labor. In times of shortage the Indians resorted to eating "palmitos, piñuelas, guanacastes, frutas silvestres y otras yerbas."[11] Although community funds and *cofradías* were also established in eastern Nicaragua, they were not as wealthy as those in the Mesoamerican zone. In 1801 there were 17 *cajas de comunidad* in the jurisdictions of Nueva Segovia and Sebaco, and their assets together amounted to 11,136 pesos 5½ reals. This accounted for only 20.1 percent of the total assets of *cajas de comunidad* in Nicaragua, whereas the Indians there accounted for about 40 percent of the total Indian population of the province.[12] However, some of the *cofradías* in eastern Nicaragua probably became quite wealthy from their livestock-raising activities.

There appear to have been few changes in the nature of agricultural production; the only significant developments were in livestock raising.[13] Cattle were raised in large numbers; the village of Lovigüisca even sent herds to the annual fair in Jalpatagua.[14] In addition some villages on the frontier developed a contraband trade in cattle either with inland Indian groups who sold them to the Zambo-Mosquito or with the Zambo-Mosquito themselves.[15] However, legal forms of trade appear to have been controlled by royal officials. In 1788 the Indians of Matagalpa complained that the corregidor had monopolized the trade in meat and other provisions, clothes, riding equipment, salt, and soap, storing the goods in the *casa real*.[16]

The major changes in the social organization of tributary Indian villages in eastern Nicaragua took place at the family level, and they were related to the increasing mobility of the Indian population. First, although most people married, the marriage rate appears to have been falling. A *visita* of the corregimiento of Sebaco in 1726 revealed that about 500 men and women were unmarried and that women often practiced infanticide so as not to be punished for bearing illegitimate children.[17] While the marriage rates was probably falling, there was a slight decrease in the proportion of intravillage marriages. The *padrones* for Nueva Segovia for 1741 and for Sebaco in 1755 indicate that, compared to 1676–86, the percentage of out-marriages remained about the same in Nueva Segovia (44.5 percent compared to 45.4 percent respectively), but in Sebaco it increased from 56.9 percent to 64.4 percent.[18] This suggests that the population was becoming more mobile, although a detailed examination of the out-marriages indicates that most marriages still took place within the region, with very few Indians migrating to the Pacific zone. The correlation between the size of villages and the percentage of out-marriages appears to have been weaker than in previous periods;

thus it seems likely that, whereas previously out-marriages had been stimulated by the lack of potential marriage partners within villages, later it was motivated by other factors, notably economic ones.

The outward orientation of Indian communities was also reflected in the increased number of mixed marriages, which were also encouraged by the influx of *libres,* many of whom arrived in the middle of the century to form the militia for defense against the Zambo-Mosquito. In 1741 Indian villages in Nueva Segovia contained only one or two Indians who had non-Indian spouses, but the *padrones* for seven villages in Sebaco and Chontales in 1755 indicate that about 14 percent of married Indians were married to *libres.*[19] There were, however, considerable local variations, the highest incidences of interracial marriage being in Juigalpa and Boaco, where 83 percent and 37 percent of couples, respectively, comprised one person of non-Indian race.

There is only fragmentary evidence for family sizes, and there are problems in its interpretation which have been outlined in the discussion of the social organization of Indians in the Mesoamerican zone. In 1741 five villages in Nueva Segovia had a low average ratio of adults to children of 1:0.62, the range for the individual villages being 0.39 to 0.75.[20] A fairly substantial proportion of the children (on average 7 percent) were classified as orphans, and this probably reflected the increasing mobility of the population.

The only evidence for the social organization of *lavoríos* is for several villages in the jurisdiction of Nueva Segovia in 1741. This evidence suggests that the marriage rate was lower among *lavoríos*: only 45.3 percent of adults were married compared to 86.6 percent of tributary Indians in the same area. Of the married couples 59.7 percent of *lavoríos* were married to tributary Indians, and the rest were married to other *lavoríos.* Over 75 percent of the single persons appear to have been women, but since many of these women in fact possessed several children, it may be that they were married to non-Indians or to absentees, neither of whom were included in the *padrones.* In this case the marriage rate would have been somewhat higher than the 45.3 percent already indicated, although a lower marriage rate for *lavoríos* would be expected owing to their greater mobility. The same *padrones* indicate that the ratio of adults to children was higher than that of tributary Indians—1:1.06 compared to 1:0.62, although this would be lower if, as seems likely, many of the single women were in fact married.[21] Nevertheless, it would be consistent with the view that couples of higher social status generally have more children.

There appears to have been little change in the ideology of Indians living in tributary villages in the east. Their effective conversion continued to be hampered by the dispersed settlement pattern; in Nueva

Segovia in 1752 it was said that the parishoners were so scattered that they heard mass very rarely, not even once a year.[22] Despite requests for the reorganization of parishes and for more clergy for these areas, no changes appear to have been made.

THE MISSIONS

The level of missionary activity in eastern Honduras and Nicaragua fluctuated considerably during the eighteenth century as the threat of attack by foreigners or the Zambo-Mosquito grew and subsided; at times when these threats were greatest, the crown gave greater support to missionary activities. In the eighteenth century the work of the missionaries was severely hampered by the increased reluctance of Indians to settle in the missions, by the attacks of the Zambo-Mosquito, and by trading contacts the Indians maintained with groups outside. As a result the missions were highly unstable; few survived more than a few years, and those that did often changed sites. As a result their impact on the economic and social life of the Indians was often superficial.

The missions were generally established on open sites where the Indians could cultivate their plots and raise livestock; in areas where land was restricted the Indians had to locate their plots in the hills, and this was considered undesirable since it afforded them opportunities to flee. Nevertheless, even where land was freely available, the Indians still returned to the hills to hunt, collect wild fruits, and tend their plots. The mission lands comprised communal milpas and pastureland, as well as plots that were allotted to individual families for cultivation. Livestock, especially cattle, were vital to the existence of the missions. They were an essential source of food, particularly in the initial stages of the missions' foundation, and they were distributed to Indians to encourage them to remain in the missions. Following the experience of previous decades, plans to renew missionary activity in Nicaragua at the beginning of the nineteenth century suggested that each Indian should be given a cow and a mare and that the Indians should be provided with pigs and chickens, as well as tools with which to cultivate plantains, maize, beans, wheat and cotton, and, where possible, sugar and cacao.[23] Evidence for some of these types of agricultural activities can be found in the inventory of the mission of San Ramón. In 1767 the mission possessed ten yoke of oxen, a field of plantains and 190 *surcos* of sugarcane, which they processed themselves.[24] In addition the mission possessed two *cofradías* each with a *hato,* one of 300 cattle and the other of 125, as well as a small number of mules and mares. Although most mission produce was probably consumed in the mission itself, small quantities may have been sold in the surrounding area. There is little evidence of food shortages in the missions, and their failure to survive was usually attributable to other factors, such as attack by the Zambo-Mosquito or desertion, rather than inadequacies in the subsistence base.

The political organization the missionaries imposed in the missions did little to integrate its members, who had often been drawn from distant communities and among whom women and children, for whom it was less easy to escape, predominated. This imbalance in the age and sex composition was not rectified over time because able-bodied men fled more frequently. Unfortunately there is no evidence for the size of families in the missions during the eighteenth century. Although the missionaries would have insisted on monogamy and tried to encourage nuclear family residence in conformity with Christian ideals, they did not achieve much success. Thus in 1773 it was suggested that missionaries should be accompanied by women on their expeditions to demonstrate that a man could be satisfied with one woman.[25]

The small number of missionaries involved and the short life of the missions limited the effectiveness of Indian conversion. Furthermore, the resentment aroused by the missionaries in their surprise attacks and the force they employed in bringing the Indians into the missions discouraged the adoption of Christian beliefs. The Indians probably practiced Christianity only under duress, and once the missionaries had departed, they returned to their former religious practices. It is doubtful that at any stage there were real changes in Indian beliefs. Even during the existence of the missions the missionaries constantly faced the problem of Indians being lured back to the forests by "spirits."

INDIAN GROUPS OUTSIDE SPANISH CONTROL

Indian groups that had lived outside Spanish control during the seventeenth century came into more intense contact with the English, Zambo-Mosquito and ladinos during the eighteenth century. This contact appears to have had significant effects on the distribution of Indian settlements and their economic activities; there appear to have been less significant changes in the social organization and ideology of these groups. Although this may partly reflect the inadequacy of the documentary record, it also underlines the economic nature of contact.

The response of unconverted Indians to contact with outside groups varied. Those Indians who lived closest to the Zambo-Mosquito entered into alliance with them, helping them in their raids on frontier towns and villages and entering into trading relations with them. Other Indian groups nearer the Spanish settled area were fearful of the raids of the

Zambo-Mosquito and their Indian allies, and they began moving inland in small numbers, voluntarily settling on estates and in tributary Indian villages on the frontier.[26] Thus in 1759 it was possible to distinguish two groups of Indians: *caribes alzados,* who were allied with the Zambo-Mosquito, and *caribes manzos,* who lived on the edge of the Spanish settled area.[27]

As a result of contact with outside groups and their confinement inland, the economy of these Indian groups changed. While cultivation and hunting were still practiced, fishing probably declined in importance, and, to provide goods demanded by traders, collecting probably increased. Root crops, notably plantains, cassava, sweet potatoes, and the fruit of the pejibaye palm, remained the most important crops cultivated and collected. Plantains appear to have been particularly abundant; *platanares* extended for leagues along riverbanks. Some maize was grown, but it was not made into bread but rather was eaten on the cob or made into a paste or beverage.[28] In some areas cultivation provided food for only part of the year; collecting and hunting supplied it other times. Numerous animals were hunted, mainly with lances and bows and arrows, sometimes with poisoned tips. The animals hunted included peccaries, pacas, coatimundis, agoutis, armadillos, iguanas, rabbits, tapirs, and deer. The Sumu traded peccaries and iguanas with groups living on the coast.[29]

Trade had an important influence on economic activities. Formerly the Zambo-Mosquito had conducted enslaving raids on Indians in this zone, but, encouraged by the English, who wanted to establish more peaceful contraband trading, they turned the relationship from one of enslaving and exacting "protection money" to one of trading and exacting tribute. During the 1720s the Zambo-Mosquito defeated the Paya in Honduras and from that time on exacted tribute in the form of cattle from the Paya and Twahka (Sumu), while from the Rama they demanded "tortoise shell, canoes, hammocks, and cotton lines."[30] The cattle paid as tribute were not raised by the Indians themselves but were acquired from ladinos by trade, through raids on nearby estates or by hunting feral cattle. The main items sought by the English, who often employed the Zambo-Mosquito as intermediaries, were dyewoods and medicinal products such as sarsaparilla, balsams, gums, and resins. In return the Indians received European manufactures, mostly tools, firearms, and trinkets.

Despite increased contacts with outside groups, the social and political organization of the Indians in this zone did not change significantly. They remained essentially egalitarian, "without god, nor law, nor king," and continued to appoint temporary leaders only as community requirements demanded.[31] It seems likely that with increased contact with outside groups, either through raids or later through trade, there would have been an increased demand for leaders who could act as military leaders or community spokesmen. Nevertheless, there is no evidence that these positions became permanent. Similarly, there is no evidence that a lower social status was accorded to certain groups within the community, such as slaves. Slaves were either sacrificed or sold to the Zambo-Mosquito.[32]

Although the missionaries were outspoken in their criticism of polygamous practices among the inland Indian groups,[33] they were generally considered to be monogamous, and only the elders had several wives.[34] Marriages generally occurred at a young age and took place within the third degree of collateralty.[35] One account suggests that a form of trial marriage existed, the bridegroom residing in the father-in-law's house until his fiancée was ready to be taken to his own lodge.[36] Although the place of residence of the newly married couple is not specified, the latter observation suggests that it was with the bridegroom's family, or else the couple established a separate home. This contrasts with marriage residence rules among the Zambo-Mosquito, which were matrilocal. It is tempting to suggest that patrilocal residence was the aboriginal form of marriage residence, which had been preserved to a greater degree among the inland groups; in the case of the Zambo-Mosquito contact resulted in the prolonged absence of men from their villages, and this probably encouraged the development of matrilocality.

Unfortunately there is very little evidence for changes in the religious beliefs and practices of the inland groups during this period, but later ethnographic accounts, such as those of Wickham, Heath, and Conzemius, suggest that they were probably minimal.[37]

THE MOSQUITO COAST

The area inhabited by the Zambo-Mosquito expanded with the population, and by the middle of the eighteenth century they were dispersed in more than twenty settlements or rancherias from the río Tinto in Honduras south to Punta Gorda.[38] Many of these settlements, particularly those in Honduras and northern Nicaragua, were some distance inland due to the poor quality of the soil on the coast; in some areas the soil was too sandy, and in others it was covered with mangrove swamp. Farther south, near Bluefields, the soil was said to be more fertile.[39] Other settlements were established in the foothills of the mountains, though sited on riverbanks for easy communication with the coast by canoe.[40] A settlement generally consisted of a small cluster of dwellings that together housed 50 to 150 people; the largest settlements were at río Tinto, Cabo de Gracias a Dios, Sandy Bay, Pearl Lagoon, and Bluefields.[41] The only fortified settlement was that of the Mosquito king at Cabo de Gracias a Dios, which was surrounded by a wall and a moat.[42] The settlements appear to have been racially mixed, with a few whites and their slaves living in the same settlements as Indians. There is no evidence on the size of households.

During the eighteenth century the economy of the inhabitants of the coast was profoundly altered by the presence of the English. Although the English did purchase some Indian lands,[43] on which they established sugar and cacao plantations, they often raised livestock on the open savanna lands that had been underutilized by the Indians. More profound changes in the economy were brought about indirectly by the diversion of Indian labor into activities encouraged by the English. Males were drawn away from subsistence activities either into paid employment as lumberjacks, collectors of sarsaparilla, or turtle fishers or into trading activities. As a result agriculture became a predominantly female activity.[44]

Even though settlements were often situated near the coast to take advantage of employment and trading opportunities, cultivation generally took place several miles inland, where the soils were more fertile. Even there crops took about a year to mature, and the roots they produced were small. The crops most commonly grown were plantains, manioc, sweet potatoes, and yams. There were considerable problems with food shortages, which were overcome in part by the exploitation of wild food resources.[45] Although the Indians possessed many ingenious methods of capturing animals and fish, undoubtedly the guns and fishing equipment they obtained from the English made such activities more efficient. Canoes were generally made by inland groups, who traded them in a half-finished state with Indians living on the coast. Archaeological evidence indicates that these developments in fishing equipment and marine transport enabled the Indians to expand their fishing activities to offshore waters.[46] Because hunting on the coast was generally poor, the Zambo-Mosquito conducted inland expeditions or obtained game by trade with inland groups. Although the English kept cattle and horses, and there were said to be large numbers of pigs and poultry on the coast, there is no evidence that the Indians raised them themselves.[47] They obtained cattle as tribute from inland groups, by raids on frontier estates, and through contraband trade with the Spaniards. They did not consume the cattle, however, but traded them with the English.

The acquisition of items for trade with English consumed much of the Zambo-Mosquito' time. The most sought after items were sarsaparilla, wood (particularly mahogany and dyewoods), and turtleshell, and in the early part of the century Indian slaves were also traded. In return the Zambo-Mosquito received guns and gunpowder, various tools, fishing equipment, and European cloth.[48]

During the eighteenth century the social organization of the Indians living on the Mosquito Coast changed so much that in 1809 Henderson was able to remark that "neither the Poyers nor the Towkcas possess anything like the civilization of the Mosquito people."[49] The alliance between the English and the Zambo-Mosquito resulted in the imposition of leaders on what had formerly been an egalitarian society. The most important officials were the king, who resided at Sandy Bay, and the governor, who lived at Tuapí Lagoon. Originally the position of king was not hereditary, and when the king died, candidates for the post, who were generally principales, went to Jamaica, where the English selected one for office for life.[50] When the English evacuated the coast, however, it appears that the most important positions at least became hereditary. In 1809, Henderson observed that "the government of the Mosquito Indians is hereditary; and a very exact and perfect idea of the British law of succession is entertained by them."[51] There was some rivalry between the king and governor, and also between less important leaders among the Mosquito branch of the Zambo-Mosquito. Although the governor had jurisdiction over the area from Tuapí Lagoon to Bluefields, he was generally regarded as second in rank to the king at Sandy Bay.[52] Thus goods for distribution to the Zambo-Mosquito were generally given to the king, and the Mosquito often complained that they were not receiving their fair share. However, the brief friendships they developed with the Spaniards assured them no better deal, and for the most part they remained allied with the English.[53]

Even though all the Zambo-Mosquito were under the authority of the king, they were divided into *parcialidades* and battalions of about 100 to 150 Indians, which were under the command of captains.[54] It is uncertain how these captains were selected, but they were probably those who had demonstrated greatest dexterity in raiding and warfare. The king, the governor, and many lesser captains were clearly able to muster large fighting forces, and the former were respected as key men in relations with the English, from whom they received British army uniforms and other insignia, which they continued to wear long after the English had evacuated the coast.[55] At first the power of officials was not very great; Hodgson observed that they undertook no action without consulting the elders and that their directions were followed rather than their orders obeyed.[56] By the end of the century, however, their power was considerable. In 1793 it was said that the king was respected and feared, and Henderson observed that

"legislative and judicial power resides exclusively in the will of him who governs. The king, or chief is completely despotic. Whenever he dispatches a messenger, his commands are always accompanied by his cane; this establishes credibility of the bearer and a sudden compliance with the purport of his errand. In this way decrees are enforced, the punishment due to offence remitted or the severest sentence annexed to it carried into instant execution.[57]

Although the power of these high officials increased, they did not exercise power in domestic disputes; those were resolved by village elders.

While political leaders were imposed on an essentially egalitarian society, there were other ways in which the society may have become differentiated. First, some of the Indians captured as slaves, normally for sale to the English, may have been retained by the Zambo-Mosquito. Roberts noted that "these Indians [Zambo-Mosquito] used to make frequent incursions on the neighboring Cookras, Woolwas and Toacas bordering on the Spanish territory for the purpose of seizing and selling them for slaves to the settlers and chief men of different parts of the Mosquito Shore."[58] Whether the chief men were Zambo-Mosquito and what they may have done with the slaves is unknown; they may easily have been resold to the English rather than kept as slaves. Second, by the end of the eighteenth century the Zambo-Mosquito were collecting tribute from all their neighboring Indian groups. The payment of tribute, however, was a formal means of trading rather than a reflection of class divisions, for these Indian groups remained outside Zambo-Mosquito society and were not incorporated into it as a distinct class.

Other changes in the social organization of the Zambo-Mosquito occurred at the family level. First, the division of labor changed, women assuming responsibility for cultivation and all other forms of routine domestic work, while men assisted in land clearance and spent much of their time acquiring items for trade with the English, by whom many of them were employed.[59] As has already been suggested, this may have favored an increase in matrilocal residence, which was better adapted to the prolonged absence of men, particularly given their diverse racial and cultural backgrounds. Polygamy appears to have been common among the Zambo-Mosquito. Many men had two to six wives, while one king possessed twenty-two.[60] Marriage generally took place at an early age, about ten years old, whilst betrothal often occured at birth.[61] Despite the existence of polygamy, adultery was punishable. The offending man had to pay the offended husband an ox, and, if he was unable to pay, the fine was paid by the village headman, and the offender had to cancel the debt by serving a period of servitude.[62]

Despite the greater contact between the inhabitants of the Mosquito Coast and outsiders, there are relatively few accounts of their religious beliefs. Those that exist record that the Indians possessed no religion or modes of public worship, nor did they posses "a priest, physician or lawyer."[63] However, they did believe in evil spirits and had a "Sokee, or Conjurer." Hodgson noted that they had contact with "an evil spirit Woollesaw who if he is too much neglected does mischief but never any good, and they hold that their creator does not concern himself with them except that he places them after death in countries good for hunting in proportion to their merits."[64] There is no evidence that the English, with whom they had sustained contact, were accompanied by priests or that they attempted to convert the Indians to Christianity.

CHAPTER 17

Demographic Recovery

Although the information relating to the Indian population in the eighteenth and early nineteenth centuries is generaly more abundant, it is often lacking in detail and coverage. Moreover, the figures available are often difficult to interpret and analyze. Perhaps surprisingly, the data on the tributary population are more useful for ascertaining demographic trends than the secular and episcopal censuses that were taken from the last quarter of the eighteenth century onward.

Excluding the *visita* made by Bishop Augustín Morel de Santa Cruz in 1752, which does not give a separate account of the Indian population, the first comprehensive counts of both tributary and nontributary Indians are those of 1777. There are, however a few *padrones* for different regions before that date which may give some insights into demographic trends. These include four *padrones* for villages in the jurisdiction of León made in 1735; a *visita* of all villages in the *partido* of Realejo in 1740; and *padrones* for villages in Nueva Segovia in 1741, and Sebaco and Chontales in 1755.

For the villages in the jurisdiction of León in 1735 only summary accounts of the number of tributary Indians are available. These indicate that the tributary population had increased by an average of 24.3 percent since 1676–86, although there were considerable spatial variations between the villages.[1] Further evidence for demographic trends in the jurisdiction of León is available for the *partido* of Realejo, where a *visita* was made in 1740.[2] At that time a small number of Indians (10) were living in the Spanish settlements at Realejo and El Viejo, but most resided in the Indian villages of Chinandega, Chichigalpa, and El Viejo. Indians were specified in the *visita* as adults or children, and it is assumed that the distinguishing age was eighteen. The total number of adults for the three villages was 757. This figure is a slight decrease compared with 786 for 1686, and, taking into account that not all adults recorded in 1740 would have been tributary Indians, the decrease must have been much greater. The fact that the Indian population was declining is also suggested by the small sizes of families and the low ratios of children to adults in all three villages. The decline in the *partido* of Realejo was probably a local phenomenon, however, for it goes against the trend already noted for the jurisdiction, and it was probably partly due to racial intermixing, since there were large numbers of non-Indians living nearby.

The picture in the east is not much clearer. Five *padrones* of Indian villages in Nueva Segovia together show an increase of 22.5 percent from 1676–86 to 1741, but again the pattern is uneven.[3] It would seem that the larger villages registered the larger increases while the smaller ones declined or showed only small increases. The small number of children enumerated suggests that the population was increasing only slowly. The rate of population growth for the five villages (using 1681 as a midpoint for 1676–86) was only 0.34 percent a year. The only other account of the Indian population in the east at this time is contained in a *visita* of the *partido* of Sebaco and Chontales in 1740. Unfortunately, the figures for individual villages included in this account are not comparable, some being given in numbers of Indians and others in numbers of families. Indian villages in Sebaco (consisting of Sebaco, Matagalpa, Jinotega, and Muymuy) possessed 3,410 Indians "de ambos sexos," while the seven villages of Chontales had 1,160 families.[4] *Padrones* of the latter villages for 1755 indicate that there the rate of increase from 1685 was higher (1.19 percent a year) than in Nueva Segovia but that the pattern of increase was similar with the largest villages increasing the most and small settlements actually losing population.[5]

Before passing on to discuss the more comprehensive lists that are available for the latter part of the eighteenth century, I should comment on two episcopal *visitas* undertaken in 1746 and 1752. The former appears to have been less extensive, covering only the jurisdiction of León. The accounts of some villages list the number of Indians (Sutiaba was said to have about 1,000 Indians), but most give only the number of families. Furthermore, there is no distinction between the races, and those living on haciendas are not included.[6] The most detailed *visita* conducted in Nicaragua during the eighteenth century was the one undertaken by Bishop Augstín Morel de Santa Cruz in 1752.[7] The bishop gives a detailed account of all parishes in terms of the form of their settlements, the number of public buildings and houses present, and the type of agriculture practiced. The population is recorded in terms of "personas de confesión y comunión" or in some cases "todas edades." From these figures it is extremely difficult to estimate the total population, and, since they are not broken down by race, it is impossible to obtain a figure for the Indian population. However, they do show that 78 percent of the population lived in the Mesoamerican zone and that there families were slightly larger.

New *tasaciones* were drawn up for Nicaragua following the exemption of women from tribute payment in 1754. Unfortunately, the tributary lists that were drawn up in 1759 cover only the Mesoamerican zone.[8] Two lists were made in 1759, one at the beginning of the year and the other at the end. The lists are not comprehensive for both dates, but where figures are available for the same area for both dates, the later list indicates a population increase over the earlier one. The list compiled at the beginning of the year was probably based on existing *tasaciones* drawn up on the basis of counts made perhaps several years earlier, while it is assumed that the later list was based on new *padrones* drawn up in response to the order exempting women from tribute payment. It seems likely, therefore, that the figures from the earlier *tasaciones* underestimate the actual number of tributary Indians at that time. Despite this disadvantage, the earlier *tasaciones* are more complete for León than are the later ones. The *tasaciones* for Granada were made at the beginning of the year, but they were probably based on *tasaciones* made in 1754. The *tasaciones* for both jurisdictions indicate a considerable increase of 63.8 percent in the number of male tributaries since 1676–86, the increase being much more marked in the jurisdiction of Granada, where it was 99.1 percent, compared to 15.3 percent in León.

In 1765 the crown ordered the audiencia to introduce the new system for enumerating tributary Indians involving the appointment of special commissioners.[9] Enumerators were instructed to include the names of male Indians and their status as caciques, widowers, single men, persons exempt from tribute (*reservados*), male married Indians (*enteros*), half-tributary Indians (*medios*), persons about to pay tribute (*próximos*), or children. An account was also to be made of *lavoríos*. The new enu-

Table 22. Population of Nicaragua in 1752

Jurisdiction or zone*	Number of persons	Families	Family size	Number of settlements	Average size of settlements
León (nos. 18–22, 30, 48–58)	18,669	4,053	4.6	17	1,098
Granada (nos. 1–19)	28,249	5,187	5.5	17	1,662
Nueva Segovia (nos. 35–47)	6,992	1,648	4.2	13	538
Sebaco (nos. 23–29, 31–34)	6,027	1,574	3.8	11	548
Mesoamerican zone	46,918	9,241	5.1	34	1,380
South American zone	13,019	3,222	4.0	24	542
Total	59,937	12,463		58	

Source: AGI AG 950 Bishop Morel 8.9.1752.
*This table excludes the mission of·San Ramón in Sebaco, which had 100 Indians. Numbers refer to those in fig. 8, showing the route taken by Bishop Morel.

merations, which covered all settlements, not just Indian villages, were made in 1767, the *tasaciones* being drawn up in 1768 and 1769. Unfortunately, only the summary figures for these *tasaciones* are available, and the boundaries of the jurisdictions to which they refer are unclear. Nevertheless, they do show an increase over the previous *tasaciones,* which were said to have been made for the following jurisdictions at the following dates: Sutiaba, 1763 and 1764; Realejo, 1757; Granada, 1728 and 1754; Segovia, 1713, 1738, 1750, and 1754; and Matagalpa, 1761.[10] Another comprehensive count of Indians in Nicaragua and Nicoya was undertaken between July, 1775, and March, 1777.[11] The resulting figures were probably used in reply to the order of 1776 for a census of all

Table 23. Tributary Indians in Nicaragua, 1768–69

Jurisdiction	Previous *tasaciones* (various dates)	*Tasaciones* of 1768–69
Sutiaba	1,447	1,457
Realejo	335	458 (110)
León and Segovia	656	1,134
Granada	2,146	4,115
Sebaco and Matagalpa	1,640 (550)	2,457
Total	6,224	9,621
Nicoya	55	94

Source: AGI AG 560 15.1.1771. It is apparent from another list that these figures included *lavoríos.* Those that are known are given in parentheses (AGCA A3.16 151 1054 tasaciones 1770).

Table 24. Tributary Indians in Nicaragua, 1777

Jurisdiction	Number of villages	Number of tributaries	Number of *lavoríos*
Nicaragua	28	1,968	943
Sutiaba	5	1,466	—
Realejo	3	396	129
Matagalpa	12	1,375	599
Total	48	6,205	1,671
Nicoya	1	88	—

Source: AGI AG 560 1777.

Spanish overseas territories.[12] The numbers of Indians resulting from this survey are available only in summary form, and again the actual jurisdictions to which the figures refer are uncertain. If this count is complete, then it registers a decline in the tributary population, although if the *lavoríos* are included, it shows little change. The figure for Nicaragua, which presumably included the jurisdictions of Granada and Nueva Segovia because of the large number of villages counted, appears to be very low compared to previous and later counts. What appears to have happened is that an error was made in transcription. It is known from another document that the *tasación* for Nueva Segovia in 1776 was for 502 *tributarios*.[13] If this figure is subtracted from that given for Nicaragua, the result is 1,466, exactly the same figure as that given for Sutiaba. This suggests that the figure for Sutiaba has been included twice, whereas that of Granada has been omitted. This very muddled picture is not made much clearer by the fact that in a later *matrícula,* made in 1793, based on counts taken between 1788 and 1792, where the figures are compared with the last count, which it says was made in 1777, the figures correspond to figures from various dates. Those for Granada are identical to those given for 1759,[14] and the figure for Nueva Segovia does not correspond to that of 502 already noted for that date. In fact, only the figures for Sutiaba and Realejo appear to be those recorded for 1777.[15] Similarly, it is not certain that the figures given for 1788–92 and 1795–98 in the same document actually refer to those dates; most of the figures for villages in the jurisdiction of Matagalpa and

Table 25. Tributary Indians in Nicaragua, 1759 to 1817

Jurisdiction	1676–86*	1759	"1777"	1788–92	1795–98	1806	1811	1816–17
León	1,770	2,041	1,900	1,376	1,684	1,556	1,317	1,185
Granada	2,370	4,719	4,719	4,576	4,753	4,632	4,523	4,223[†]
Nueva Segovia	1,141		680	715	913	817	815	740
Sebaco	504		2,499	2,445	2,444[‡]	3,430[§]		2,790
Total	5,785		9,586	9,112	9,794	10,435		8,938
Nicoya	135		88	113	94	102	78	

Sources: 1676–86: AGCA A3.16 147 999; 1759: AGCA A3.16 149 1027, 1029, A3.16 503 3899, 3891; "1777", 1788–92, 1795–98: AGI AG 560 1777; AGCA A3.16 153 1101, A3.16 246 4912 (see text comments on "1777"); 1806: *BAGG* 3:217–20 8.7.1806; 1811: AGCA A3.16 153 1103; 1816–17: AGCA A3.16 152 1073–97, A3.16 153 1104–11.

*Male tributary Indians.

[†]Jalteba and Isla Ometepe are missing; they probably possessed about 400 Indians.

[‡]Many villages with populations the same as those registered in "1777."

[§]Probably includes the mission of San Ramón.

Sebaco are identical to those for 1777. Further lists of *tributarios* are available for 1806, 1811, 1816–17 in various states of completeness. These problems being kept in mind, if the figures for 1777 are compared to those of 1788–92, they show a slight decline, which is likely to have been due to disease. There appears to have been a slight increase in the tributary population in the late 1790s, but in the nineteenth century all areas registered declines.

There are no detailed and comprehensive records of the total population of Nicaragua at the end of the eighteenth century, but a few summary lists exist, although not all differentiate the races. Two lists of those who could purchase indulgences exist for 1776, and they vary only slightly in the figures they provide, the list to be found in the *Archivo General de Centro América* being more detailed. [16] Many persons, particularly Indians, could not afford to purchase indulgences and were therefore excluded from the lists; a comment on one of the lists suggested that only about half of the population was able to purchase them. [17] Thus, although the numbers purchasing indulgences are distinguished by race, the Indian population is clearly underrepresented and probably not consistently underrepresented to gain any true guide to its total size. These figures cannot be compared in detail with the census of 1776 that was ordered for all Spanish overseas territories, because the latter has not

Table 26. Purchasers of *Bulas* de Santa Cruzada, 1776

Jurisdiction or zone	Spaniards	Ladinos*	Indians	Total	Percent Spanish	Percent ladino*	Percent Indian
León	1,365	9,870	2,080	13,315	10.3	74.1	15.6
Sutiaba	—	651	7,406	8,057	—	8.1	91.9
Realejo	59	2,344	1,695	4,098	1.4	57.2	41.4
Granada	447	8,615	8,880	17,942	2.5	48.0	49.5
Nicaragua	656	5,532	1,487	7,675	8.5	72.1	19.4
Nueva Segovia	380	3,564	1,897	5,841	6.5	61.0	32.5
Sebaco and Matagalpa	236	2,007	6,344	8,587	2.7	23.4	73.9
Mesoamerican zone	2,527	27,012	21,548	51,087	4.9	52.9	42.2
South American zone	616	5,571	8,241	14,428	4.3	38.6	57.1
Total	3,143	32,583	29,789	65,515	4.8	49.7	45.5

Source: AGCA A3.29 1749 28130 Extracto del numero de personas . . . capaces de tomar bulas de Santa Cruzada.

*Includes mestizos, mulattoes, and blacks.

survived for Nicaragua. The census was certainly taken, since summary figures for the total undifferentiated population have survived in transcripts in the Gaçeta de Guatemala and in Juarros's *Compendium*.[18] The total population according to this census was 103,943 with an additional 2,983 in Nicoya, of which 83,988 (80.8 percent) of the total were living in the Mesoamerican zone. There are several references to other censuses being taken at the turn of the century, but the censuses themselves have not been found. In 1802 the Gaçeta de Guatemala recorded that an episcopal census had been initiated in 1796 and that so far 112,559 *almas* had been counted in 51 villages.[19] Eight years later an episcopal survey was said to have enumerated 131,932 people, but it is not known whether the figure refers to the same census.[20] Another document which lists the number of settlements and population by parishes could equally well correspond to the same episcopal census, but unfortunately it has no author or date. It records that there were 158,903 *almas* in Nicaragua and 3,998 in Nicoya.[21] Finally, another general account of the population about 1800 gives a similar total figure of 151,000 for Nicaragua plus 8,000 for Nicoya.[22] One census which exists for the early nineteenth century was taken in 1813; it recorded a population of 149,751, although Squier maintained that it was highly inaccurate since it was undertaken by untrained enumerators.[23] He also noted that Miguel González Sarabia published an account of the population in 1823 under the title *Bosquejo político estadístico*, in which he estimated that Indians and ladinos ac-

Table 27. Total Population of Nicaragua and Nicoya in the Last Quarter of the Eighteenth Century

Jurisdiction	Bulas		Census, 1776c	No date *	No date[+]
	1776a	1776b			
León	51,604	25,470	83,988	45,662	52,000
Granada		25,617		81,625	67,000
Nueva Segovia	6,204	5,841	19,955	31,616	10,000
Sebaco		8,587			22,000
Total	57,808	65,515	103,943	158,903	151,000
Nicoya	1,828	1,893	2,983	3,998	8,000
Total	59,636	78,408	106,926	162,901	159,000

Sources: 1776a: AGI AG 562 Estado de las bulas de Santa Cruzada 23.7.1779; 1776b: AGCA A 3.29 1749 28130 Extracto del numero de personas . . . capaces de tomar bulas de Santa Cruzada 6.6.1778; 1776c: Juarros, *Compendium*, 497; AGI AG 656 vol. 6 N256 26.4.1802.
  *No date: AGCA A1.11 76 620, no author, no date.
  [+]No date: *BAGG* 7:157–75 ca. 1800.

counted for two-fifths of the population each, the remaining one-fifth being creole.[24]

In the absence of figures for the total Indian population at the end of the eighteenth century, it can be estimated by using the tributary population and a multiplication factor derived from a few surviving *padrones* for that period. For 1777 the tributary population and the total Indian population of the jurisdictions of León and El Viejo are known, but in the latter case the total population corresponds very closely to the tributary population and is therefore likely to have been inaccurate. For the jurisdiction of León the ratio of tributary to nontributary Indians was 1:5.1, although the range for the villages listed was between 1:4.1 and 1:5.5.[25] Later the ratios for the villages of El Viejo, Chinandega, and Chichigalpa for 1798 and 1816–17 were 1:3.9 and 1:4.5, respectively.[26] The only ratios that can be calculated for the South American zone are for three villages in Nueva Segovia in 1796, and their average is 1:3.6, with a range between 1:3.1 and 1:5.[27] It is suggested, therefore, that the tributary figures for the Mesoamerican zone should be multiplied by 4 and 4.5, and those for the South American zone by 3.5 and 4. This is done only in the absence of further evidence, and the drawbacks of so doing are fully recognized. The tributary figures for 1806 are used as being the most comprehensive, and they give a total population of between 24,752 and 27,846 for the Mesoamerican zone and between 14,865 and 16,988 for the South American zone.

To these figures should be added those for Nicoya. The tributary population of Nicoya appears to have fluctuated slightly around 100; the largest number recorded was 113 in 1788–92, and the smallest was 62 in 1760.[28] The total population of the area increased substantially, but the increase was due to an influx of non-Indians. The proportion of the population that was Indian declined through the century; Thiel reported that in 1700 the population of Nicoya taken from parish registers was 1,499, 647 (43.2 percent) of whom were Indians, whereas in 1801 there were 662 Indians (19.6 percent) in a total population of 3,420.[29] Given that the tributary population at the latter date was about 120, the ratio of tributary Indians to nontributary Indians was low, about 1:5.

Lavoríos continued to be recorded intermittently throughout the eighteenth century. Those residing in separate barios or villages in the jurisdiction of León were counted most regularly, whereas in the jurisdiction of Granada and in the east, where *lavoríos* were not as clearly residentially segregated, they were included in the *padrones* of Indian villages and not recorded separately. Accounts of *lavoríos* in the 1720s and 1730s indicate that most of them resided in the Mesoamerican zone and particularly in the jurisdiction of León but that they formed only a small proportion of the total tributary population.[30] By the 1770s, however, their numbers had increased substantially. The most detailed evidence available is included in a document giving an account of the tributary population in 1793, although some of the figures clearly refer to 1777 or earlier.[31] Unfortunately, the number of *lavoríos* in Granada or Nueva Segovia are not included, although it is known that they did comprise a small proportion of the population in those regions. In the jurisdiction of León there were 708 *lavoríos* compared with 1,990 *tributarios,* and for Sebaco the same figures were 677 and 2,484 respectively. *Lavoríos* therefore accounted for 26.2 percent and 22.2 percent, respectively, of the total tributary population. This was a considerable increase on the figures for the 1720s and 1730s, especially when it is considered that the earlier figures included female *lavoríos* who were exempted from tribute payment in 1754. By 1811 the number of *lavoríos* in the jurisdiction of León had risen to 783, although it fell again to 616 in 1816–17.[32] At the latter date 807 *lavoríos* were to be found in Sebaco, but the *tasaciones* for *lavoríos* are incomplete, since a number of villages that had formerly possessed fairly substantial numbers of *lavoríos* are not included. None of the later accounts contain any references to *lavoríos* in the jurisdictions of Granada and Nueva Segovia, although they are known to have existed. It is possible that *lavoríos* in those areas were subsumed under the general heading of tributary Indians, so to avoid possible double counting, no estimate of their numbers will be added to the figures for the jurisdictions of León and Sebaco. Thus, in the absence of further information, it is suggested that at the turn of the century there were about 1,500 tributary *lavoríos* (750 in León and 750 in Sebaco). Figures for the number of tributary *lavoríos* and the total population of *lavoríos* for El Viejo and Chinandega in 1816–17 suggest that the ratio may have been about 1:5.[33] Hence it can be estimated that the total population of *lavoríos* for Nicaragua was about 7,500.

The difficulties that beset missionary efforts in Nicaragua meant that the missions were short-lived and never housed large numbers of Indians; in fact, for a large part of the eighteenth and nineteenth centuries missionary efforts were suspended in the area. Thus any Indians living in the missions can be calculated as part of the number that were living outside Spanish control. Population estimates for Indians living in this zone are the most difficult to calculate. It is clear that the area was densely populated; it was said to have more Indians "than the hairs on a deer,"[34] and another account reported that the Carib were "very many" and proceeded to list the number of tribes they comprised: "aguilas, muimuyes, tomayes, musutepes, tunlas, taguacas, guylubaganas, yuscos, panamagas, yalasanes, bocaes."[35] The latter account, by a missionary who obviously knew the area well, also noted that there were 100,000 Indians in the area between the Spanish settled zone and the

Table 28. Estimates of the Population of Zambo–Mosquito

Year		Estimate and Source
1730	12–14,000	*personas* (AGCA A1.17 210 5018 Corregidor of Sebaco and Chontales 8.7.1743)
1731	7,000	*personas bien armados* (*CDHCR* 9:187–205 Informe of the Zambo–Mosquito 16.2.1731)
1737	2,000	*armados* (AGI AG 302 Rivera 10.5.1737; AGCA A1.17 335 7088 Rivera 23.11.1742)
1743	10,000	*hombres de armas* (AGI AG 303 Averiguación en razón de la fortificación 26.2.1743)
1757	Under 8,000	1,500 of whom were able to bear arms (PRO CO 123/1 fols. 55–79 Hodgson 1757)
1759	3,000	*bien armados y diestros en el fusil* (AGI AG 449 and AGCA A1.12 117 2473 Yarrince 18.9.1759 [at Black river only])
1761	3,521	*indios* (MNM B ª-XI-C ª-B-n º-1, Hodgson and Hodgson 1782)
1773	7,000–10,000	"fighting men" (Edwards, "British Settlements," 210 10.11.1773)
1774	6,000–7,000	"fighting men; so that the whole number possibly amounts to 20,000–30,000" (Long, *History of Jamaica* 1:316)
1776	5,000	*indios* offered to the English to help in the American Civil War (AGI AG 665 and *CDHCN*: 198–205 Diario de Antonio de Gastelu 11.7.1776)
1778	Under 30,000	(Anon, *Present State*, 48)
1780s	1,500	"sencible [*sic*] men" and four or five times that number of women and children (BM Add. 12,431 f.202 Request for information from Captain Kimberley, n.d.)
1784	10,000	"warriors" (PRO CO 123/3 fols. 1–6 White 16.1.1784)
1804	1,500–2,000	"capable of using arms" (Henderson, *British Settlement*, 190)

Zambo-Mosquito on the coast. Unfortunately, the northern and southern limits of the area to which he referred are not specified, but the size of the estimate suggests that it may have included Honduras, Nicaragua, and Costa Rica. Nevertheless, the size of the Indian population in Nicaragua should not be underestimated; an account in 1757 noted that Carib occupied fifty leagues along the banks of the río Yasica and that they numbered "3,000 hombres", while farther south 500 "indios caribes de

Sumu" were living in the Guanabana valley.[36] By the 1920s only 3,000 to 3,500 Sumu Indians were left.[37] Given that at the same time the Jicaque Indians in Honduras numbered only between 1,200 and 1,500, whereas at the end of the eighteenth century it was estimated that there had been 12,280,[38] it is not unreasonable to suggest that the Sumu experienced a similar rate of decline during that period. Thus the population at the beginning of the nineteenth century can be estimated at about 27,300 to 31,850, to which should be added 500 Rama Indians living between Bluefields and the San Juan River.[39]

Although as indicated in the previous chapter there were spatial variations in the racial character of the Zambo-Mosquito, the coast they inhabited from Trujillo, in northern Honduras, to Punta Gorda was regarded as a common cultural area. Therefore, most population estimates cover the whole area, and it is impossible to indicate the proportions to be found in Honduras and Nicaragua. Nevertheless, the figures as a whole illustrate the expansion of the Zambo-Mosquito from a localized origin near Cabo de Gracias a Dios in the midseventeenth century. Despite discrepancies in the accounts, by the beginning of the nineteenth century the Zambo-Mosquito probably numbered between 15,000 and 30,000. Being a mixed racial group, however, they are not included in the estimate for the Indian population at that time.

Thus by the end of the eighteenth century the total Indian population in the Mesoamerican zone of Nicaragua was 31,596. This represents an increase of 46.7 percent over the population calculated at the end of the seventeenth century. The rate of increase was low, however, averaging only 0.32 percent a year, and it appears to have slowed down toward the

Table 29. Estimated Indian Population in Nicaragua and Nicoya at the Beginning of the Nineteenth Century

Population	Mesoamerican zone	South American zone
Tributary Indians		
Nicaragua	27,846 (Multiplication factor: 4.5)	16,988 (Multiplication factor: 4)
Nicoya	650 (Multiplication factor: 5)	
Lavoríos	3,750	3,750
Outside Spanish control		30,075
Total	32,246	50,813

beginning of the nineteenth century, when it was converted to a decrease.[40] Meanwhile, the population of Nicoya declined by about 10 percent during the century. The Indian population in the South American zone increased less dramatically, by 30.8 percent but it constituted about 60 percent of the total Indian population of the province.

CAUSES OF DEMOGRAPHIC CHANGE

During the eighteenth century the Indian population began to increase, but a number of factors reduced the level of recovery. Whereas during earlier periods the major causes of decline had been disease, ill-treatment, overwork, and the economic and social disruption caused by conquest and colonization, during the eighteenth century losses in the Indian population can be attributed more to continued disruption caused by the expansion of the non-Indian population into Indian villages and the continued demands for tribute and labor, as well as to racial intermixing. Diseases also took their toll.

Although considerable demands were made on Indian labor and production, the demographic effects of those demands were indirect. While there are a number of instances of Indians employed under the repartimiento being ill-treated, overworked, and ill-fed to the extent that some died, cruelty appears to have been more localized than at previous times. Other Indians died as a result of being forced to work in unhealthy occupations and in areas to which they were not acclimatized. There is insufficient evidence to indicate that free laborers were treated better than Indians who worked under the repartimiento, but to attract and maintain them in their employment, employers would have found it necessary to offer them better wages and working conditions. Nevertheless, many employers failed to attract free workers and this suggests that conditions were not greatly improved; often it was the desire to escape the burdens of tribute payment and the repartimiento or to earn wages to subsist, particularly where access to land was limited, that drove Indians to become wage laborers. Push factors seem to have been more significant than pull factors in encouraging migration.[41]

Extracommunal demands on Indian labor, lands, and production continued throughout the eighteenth century, reducing the ability of the Indian population to maintain itself. The employment of labor under the repartimiento reduced the labor available for subsistence activities. Complaints about the disastrous effects of the repartimiento on Indian agriculture are numerous in the documentary record. The repartimiento was not, however, the only institution that placed a burden on Indian sources of labor; labor was needed to produce items for tribute payment, to spin and weave cotton under the *repartimiento de hilados,* and to provide the numerous services and goods required by secular and ecclesiastical officials. However, it was the increased alienation of Indian lands that had the greatest impact on Indian communities in the eighteenth century. This occurred as a result of the expansion of the non-Indian population and particularly the landless mixed races, who because of the lack of alternative employment opportunities often purchased, rented, or usurped Indian lands. The loss of land came at a time when the Indian population was beginning to increase and create greater demands for food. These demands for Indian labor and lands contributed to food shortages, which were common throughout the eighteenth century. Although many of the shortages and famines were initiated by droughts and plagues of locusts, their impact would have been moderated if the general level of production had been higher and the economy more diversified. The funds of *cajas de comunidad* and *cofradías* provided some relief in times of shortage, but the assistance they could give was limited since their funds were largely controlled by non-Indian officials. Nevertheless, by the eighteenth century many possessed more reliable sources of food in the form of livestock.

As demands for labor and goods increased, and as less or no land was available for production, increasingly Indians were forced to seek employment as wage laborers. By this means they could be assured of a regular income and often food, clothing, and accommodation. In addition they might escape the surveillance of officials who were charged with the collection of tribute and with the organization of labor under the repartimiento. In their places of employment Indians came into more sustained contact with other races, and this encouraged intermarriage. In addition it made the enumeration of the Indian population more difficult, so that although population loss through racial mixing was high, it was probably not as high as censuses might suggest; many individual Indians would have escaped the notice of enumerators in their new places of residence, or else they would have been reclassified as ladinos.

Although the aim of the missionaries in eastern Nicaragua was to create self-sufficient communities based on agriculture, the short life of the missions meant that that goal was not achieved to any great degree. Had it been achieved, it would have resulted in a radical transformation of the Indian economy. As it was, although a number of livestock were introduced, the Indians remained very much dependent on the plots they cultivated in the hills and the wild food products they obtained from the forest. The impact of missionary activity on the economy of Indian groups that remained outside the missions is difficult to assess. Probably greater effects were brought about by the contacts they had with ladinos and with the Zambo-Mosquito, who created demands for a variety of wild products and thereby diverted Indian labor into those activities and away from subsistence. Any fall in food production was not compensated for by trade, which returned to the Indians only cheap manufactures, tools, and trinkets. The evidence is too scant to indicate whether food shortages occurred in these areas, and they cannot be inferred from demographic changes, which are also inadequately recorded.

On the Mosquito Coast several economic changes occurred which had different effects. Agriculture had always been difficult on the coast, and much of the food consumed by Indians was obtained from wild food resources. With the expansion of the population and its increased contact with Europeans several changes occurred: agriculture became more inadequate to meet the demands made on it, and labor was withdrawn from fishing into the collection of wild animal and vegetable products demanded by the Europeans, but this loss of food production was probably compensated for in part by the introduction of livestock. That the balance was on the negative side, however, can be seen by the references to food shortages on the coast.

Although several changes occurred in the social organization of different Indian groups, it is difficult to assess their demographic impact. As far as it is possible to judge, the fertility rate among most groups, with perhaps the exception of those who were collected into the missions, increased. At the same time social relationships appear to have become more fluid, the marriage rate falling and partners being chosen from a greater variety of social, racial, and geographical backgrounds. This was encouraged by the repartimiento, which removed men from their villages for extended periods, and, more important, by the emergence of wage labor, which attracted Indians to the towns and local estates. Probably the only group among whom the fertility rate fell were those who were collected into the missions. Villages and missions on the frontier of the Spanish colonized area also lost population as a result of raids by the Zambo-Mosquito. These raids were at a peak during the first half of the eighteenth century, but they declined later as the English persuaded their allies to turn to contraband trading, rather than slaving, as a source of income.[42] Some of the most devastating attacks occurred in eastern Nicaragua in 1749, when several villages were attacked and about 70 to 80 Indians from Boaco alone were captured; one report estimated that during the series of attacks, which affected five villages, about 500 Indians were captured.[43] To these well-documented raids should be added numerous minor attacks all along the frontier. The Indians captured were either absorbed into Zambo-Mosquito society, particularly the women as wives, or they were sold to the English and shipped to Jamaica.

Some of the epidemics that occurred in Guatemala during the eighteenth and early nineteenth centuries[44] appear to have spread farther south to Honduras and Nicaragua. The most notable exceptions appear to have been the typhus epidemics, whose spread in Nicaragua would have been discouraged by the warm climate. While the documentary record is incomplete for Nicaragua, it should contain some reference to at least one of the five typhus epidemics in Guatemala, if they spread farther south. In general there seem to have been relatively few epidemics, although this may reflect the inadequacy of the documentary record. The most notable epidemics were those in 1725–28, 1741–45, 1748–51, 1780–82, and 1816, and they were all either smallpox or measles. Many documents simply speak of *"pestes," "epidemias,"* and *"enfermedades,"* which might refer to a number of diseases. Also, the evidence is too fragmentary to obtain a clear picture of the areas that were affected, and whether there was any regional or urban-rural variations in mortality rates.

The first epidemic recorded in this period occurred between 1725 and 1728. It was identified in Honduras as measles,[45] and although it is not mentioned by name in Nicaragua,[46] it is assumed that it was the same disease that was also afflicting Guatemala at the time.[47] Observers recorded that as result of the epidemic one-half of the tributary Indians in Boaco and two-thirds of those in Teustepet had died since the last *tasación,* which was probably in 1718.[48]

A number of documents from the 1730s refer to the inability of Indians to pay tribute owing to the decline in the population as a result of *"epidemias," "pestes,"* or *"enfermedades."* There is no mention of a specific disease, and it is possible that the complaints were a retarded response to the measles epidemic just described. Alternatively, it is possible that the smallpox epidemic in Guatemala in 1733[49] did spread farther south. In that year the villages of Matagalpa, Jinotega, and Sebaco were reported as being unable to harvest their maize because of *"enfermedades."*[50]

Between 1741 and 1745 a "terrible *peste*" ravaged Nicaragua and Nicoya, arriving from Honduras, but the characteristics of the disease are not specified.[51] An outbreak of *tabardillo,* or typhus, occurred in Guatemala in 1741, and it may be that the disease did advance farther south, although, as already suggested, the climate of Nicaragua would not have favored its spread.

Between 1750 and 1751 smallpox appears to have ravaged the missions in eastern Nicaragua, where the Indians had little immunity to the disease; there is no evidence that it reached epidemic proportions in other parts of the country. The disease claimed 112 neophytes in the Matagalpan missions.[52] By then Nueva Segovia had been struck by smallpox, measles, German measles (*alfombrilla*), and *males de mollera,*

Table 30. Epidemics in Nicaragua and Nicoya During the Eighteenth and Early Nineteenth Centuries

Year	Disease	Source
1717	*"Epidemia"*	Nicaragua (Sebaco). Date probably earlier. Documents refer to the epidemic which the Indians had been suffering. It may have been the same as the 1714 epidemic in Honduras. AGCA A1.23 1582 10226 cedula 11.5.1717.
1725–28	Measles	Nicaragua (General) AGI AG 251 Betancurt 29.5.1727; (León-Sutiaba) AGCA A1.23 1586 fol. 434 cedula 9.12.1728; (Granada) AGCA A1.23 1526 fol. 255 cedula 29.5.1727; (Sebaco) AGCA A1.23 1586 fol. 83 and fol. 239 cedulas 30.1.1728.
1732–34	*"Epidemias y enfermedades"* *"Enfermedades"*	Nicaragua (General) AGI AG 230 Contador de cuentas reales 27.9.1734. Nicaragua (Sebaco and Matagalpa) AGCA A1.23 1589 fol. 169 cedula 23.5.1733.
1741–45	*"Peste"*	Nicaragua (Pueblo of Nicaragua) AGCA A3.16 148 1017 Pueblo of Nicaragua 1732; Nicoya AGCA A3.16 83 1190 Cura of Nicoya 13.2.1745 (Costa Rica).
1750–51	Smallpox	Nicaragua (Matagalpa) AGCA A3.16 503 3900 22.9.1751; ANCR CC5290 Bishop of Nicaragua 3.7.1815; Nicaragua (Nueva Segovia) AGCA A3.16 501 3869 Rector of Nueva Segovia 12.12.1749, 30.9.1751.
1753	Smallpox	Nicaragua (Nueva Segovia) AGCA A3.12 186 Villages of Nueva Segovia 1753.
1769?	Measles	Nicaragua (Missions of Jalapa and Jícaro) AGCA A1.23 117 2474 Autos relativos a las misiones de Paraka y Pantasma 1769.
1780–82	*"Peste de viruelas"* [smallpox]	Major epidemic. Nicaragua (General) AGCA A3.16 503 3901 and 1092 Estado . . . de los indios tributarios que han fallecidos 11.10.1782, 31.1.1783.
1801	*"La tos epidémica"*	Nicaragua (León) AGCA A1.26 199 1639 Fiscal 7.9.1801.
1809	Yellow fever	Honduras (Trujillo) AGCA A1.46 107 1315 20.9.1809.
1816	Smallpox	Nicaragua (Matagalpa) AGCA A3.16 152 10713 Matrículas for Matagalpa 25.12.1816.

which, translated as "headaches," may refer to meningitis.[53] Smallpox struck the area again in 1753, and shortly afterward the missions of Jalapa and Jícaro were devastated by measles.[54]

Probably the major epidemic of the century was a smallpox outbreak which occurred between 1780 and 1782. This epidemic affected all parts of Nicaragua, and it was so devastating that accounts were drawn up of the numbers that had died. A total of 682 tributary Indians, or 9 percent of the total tributary population, died in the epidemic;[55] its impact is likely to have been even greater among children. Even so, in León at least, the decline in the tributary population was not regarded as sufficient to justify a reduction or postponement of tribute payments. This major epidemic was probably followed shortly afterward by an outbreak of measles, which was present in Guatemala and Honduras in the late 1780s.[56] Finally, in 1816 there was another localized epidemic of smallpox in Matagalpa.[57]

Two diseases are worth mentioning because of their more unusual occurrence. First, there was a report in 1801 that children in León had contracted *"la tos epidémica"* from which many in Quetzaltenango, Totonicapán, and Chimaltenango had died in the same year.[58] This disease was probably either whooping cough or diphtheria. Second, there was an outbreak of yellow fever in Trujillo in 1809 which was described as follows: "This colony [Trujillo] is infested with the disease they call *vomito prieto* [black vomit], it is so malignant that is scarcely gives those who are suffering from it time to receive the sacraments because then they lose their minds and begin to emit blood through the mouth and from these symptoms death follows."[59] Although this outbreak of yellow fever is unlikely to have spread inland owing to the cooler climate there, it may well have spread east and south along the Mosquito Coast.

The loss of Indian population that can be attributed to racial intermixing increased in Nicaragua during the eighteenth century as the size of the non-Indian population increased. Although eighteenth-century documents generally distinguish between the numbers of Spaniards and the numbers of mixed race, they make less distinction between the mixed races, who were collectively called ladinos. Most of the ladinos were mestizos and mulattoes in the ratio of about 1:3, but small numbers of zambos and blacks were also included in this category.

In Nicaragua the number of non-Indians increased from about 1,663 adult males in 1683 to 35,726 adults (3,143 Spaniards and 32,583 ladinos) in 1778.[60] The latter figure is an imperfect guide to the total non-Indian population, since it includes only those who could purchase indulgences, thereby excluding those who were too poor. Nevertheless, it is a more reliable guide to the non-Indian population than to the Indian population, which was largely exempt for the same reason. It is impossible to say to what extent the apparently large increase in the non-

Indian population at the end of the century was due to natural increase, for clearly their numbers were boosted by Indians being reclassified as ladinos. Nevertheless, it is clear that the non-Indian population was increasing dramatically, with racial mixing eroding the Indian population at a faster and faster rate as the number of people of mixed race increased.

The proportion of Spaniards in the total population was generally small—about 5 percent—although the proportion was slightly higher in the major cities. Spaniards were the most important landowners and merchants and they generally held the most important secular and ecclesiastical offices, while mestizos had to be satisfied with minor posts. Most of the mulattoes worked as artisans and routine laborers, although some were employed as overseers, and others may have managed to acquire small holdings.[61] In Nicaragua mulattoes were often referred to as *pardos,* and in 1810 there were said to be three kinds of *pardos:* artisans, such as painters, sculptors, silversmiths, carpenters, weavers, tailors, shoemakers, and blacksmiths; agriculturalists and muleteers; and those who did not work but lived by rustling and stealing produce from estates.[62] Many of the latter group lived in the frontier regions, where they conducted a lucrative contraband trade with the Mosquito Coast.[63] Also stationed there were mulattoes, who formed the ranks of the militia.[64]

By the end of the nineteenth century less than 20 percent of all Spaniards and ladinos were living in the towns; the rest resided in the rural areas. However, their migration to the countryside occurred unevenly, and some jurisdictions became almost entirely ladino in character, while others remained Indian. In 1800 the only *partidos* described as Indian were El Viejo, Sutiaba, Matagalpa, and Masaya,[65] but they remained Indian not only because they attracted fewer non-Indians but also because they had always been large Indian settlements. Although most accounts give the racial character of the population by *partidos,* it is clear that the generalizations they provide gloss over a very complex racial pattern, for within *partidos* villages ranged from being almost pure Indian to being predominantly ladino.[66]

In the absence of detailed marriage records, the loss of the Indian population through racial intermixing is difficult to gauge. Indians might be encouraged to marry non-Indians in the hope that their children might be relieved of their tributary status. However, with the exception of legitimate children of Spaniards and Indians, who were probably few and who were classified as mestizos, all other children followed the status of their mother. Hence the children of Indian women married to people of other races would have remained tributary Indians, particularly if they remained in their communities, where their genealogical history was known. However, in the anonymous environment of the towns, where individual histories were unknown and where it was expected that most

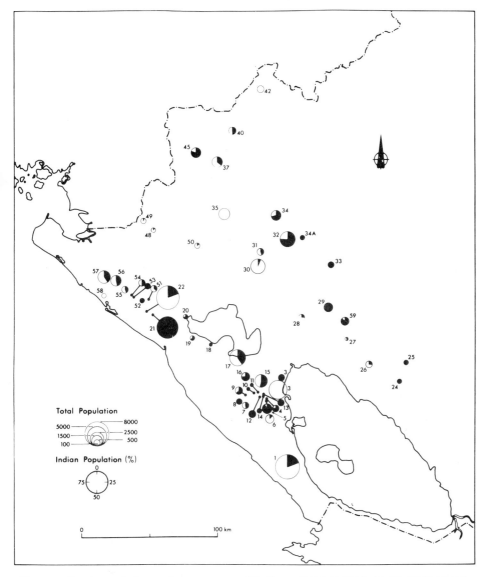

Fig. 9. Total population and percentage of Indians, 1776 (AGCA A3.29 1749 28130 Extracto del numero de personas . . . capaces de tomar Bulas de Santa Cruzada 6.6.1778). Numbers refer to settlements indicated in Fig. 8, page 286.

of the population would be ladino, it seems likely that the offspring of mixed marriages would have stood a better chance of achieving ladino status, particularly if they had dark skins. The evidence suggests that, while there were a number of mixed marriages in the Indian villages, probably most occurred in ladino-dominated environments. This was not true in eastern Nicaragua, where the militia was stationed and where the smaller size of the villages limited the availability of Indian marriage partners; it appears that many Indians in the east, having met non-Indians, deserted their communities to try to escape tribute payment.

Racial intermixing appears to have occurred quite freely on the Mosquito Coast, and by the middle of the century it may have begun to affect inland groups. Besides the Zambo-Mosquito, by the middle of the eighteenth century there were about 200 whites, 200 people of mixed race, and just under 1,000 slaves on the coast. Although there may have been some discrimination at the individual level, there appears to have been no legal or social restriction on contact between the races. As such the numbers identified as being of mixed race, most of whom were mestizos, is surprisingly small.[67] It may be that many children born of English men and Indian women were not defined as mestizos but were absorbed into Zambo-Mosquito society along with the offspring of Indian men who had captured Spanish women for wives.[68] The few mulattoes present on the coast probably originally came from the settled parts of Honduras and Nicaragua. The mixed racial character of the Zambo-Mosquito was maintained through contacts with the mixed races and blacks, and racial mixing was regarded as beneficial: Henderson considered the Zambo-Mosquito "more active, industrious and enterprising than the aboriginal."[69]

Part Six

CONCLUSION

CHAPTER 18

Indian Survival in Colonial Nicaragua

At the time of the Spanish conquest Nicaragua was inhabited by Indian groups representative of two cultural types: chiefdoms and tribes. These two cultural types had different histories, and they inhabited relatively distinct areas, which have been termed "zones of tradition." The zone of Mesoamerican tradition comprised the Pacific lowlands, where socially stratified chiefdoms formed dense populations supported by intensive forms of agricultural production; the zone of South American tradition encompassed eastern Nicaragua, which was inhabited by essentially egalitarian tribes who subsisted on a combination of shifting cultivation, hunting, fishing, and gathering. Historical, ecological, ethnological, and archaeological evidence suggests that at the time of the Spanish conquest the Indian population of the province was about 800,000, and probably another 60,000 were living in Nicoya. Conservative estimates of the carrying capacity of the land have been adopted and it is possible that the estimate of over one million for the aboriginal population suggested by Radell and accepted by Denevan is more realistic.[1] The estimate of 800,000 is fairly consistent with estimates of contemporary observers of the Conquest period, when it is remembered that their assessments referred only to the Pacific lowlands, which at that time contained just over 70 percent of the total population.

From the time of discovery the Mesoamerican zone attracted a disproportionate number of Spanish colonists. In the first half of the sixteenth century they were attracted there by the large Indian populations that could be distributed in encomiendas or used to supply the Indian slave trade. The smaller concentrations of Indians in the South American zone were less attractive as sources of tribute, labor, or slaves. These Indians had not paid tribute in pre-Columbian times, nor had they provided labor for extracommunal purposes, and to exact them would have required the creation of a special organizational structure. Since these Indians produced only small surpluses, if any, and could provide only small sources of labor, the undertaking was not considered worthwhile. Only in the vicinity of the mines in Nueva Segovia was it considered desirable to control the Indian population and exploit its sources of labor through the introduction of the encomienda. However, the encomiendas granted there were few and small, and the labor the Indians provided, which proved difficult to control, was inadequate to meet the demands of miners. Thus the miners were forced to import Indians from the Pacific

Table 31. Estimated Indian Population Change in Nicaragua and Nicoya During the Colonial Period

	Population estimates				Percent of change			
Region	Aboriginal population	About 1550	End of 17th century	Beginning of 19th century	Aboriginal to 1550	1550 to end of 17th century	End of 17th to beginning of 19th century	Aboriginal to beginning of 19th century
Mesoamerican zone	546,570	43,732	21,545	31,596	−92.0	−50.7	+46.7	−94.2
Nicoya	62,692	2,640	718	650	−95.8	−72.8	−9.5	−99.0
South American zone	216,986	144,657	38,843	50,813	−33.3	−73.1	+30.8	−76.6
Area under Spanish control*	178,838		8,843	20,738		−95.1[†]	+134.5	−88.4
Area outside Spanish control*	38,148		30,000	30,075		−21.4[†]	+0.3	−21.2
Total	826,248	191,029	61,106	83,059	−76.9	−68.0	+35.9	−89.9

* Areas under and outside Spanish control at the end of the seventeenth century. The aboriginal population is calculated from these areas and the estimated aboriginal population density (see chap. 5).

[†] Decline from the time of the Conquest to the end of the seventeenth century.

lowlands and, when possible, black slaves. For the same reasons Indians in the South American zone were also less desirable as slaves. Although slavery could be justified more easily in eastern Nicaragua, where the Indians offered greater resistance to Spanish rule, their smaller numbers and their more nomadic mode of existence meant that their enslavement involved greater efforts and fewer rewards than those in the Mesoamerican zone. Although the level of Spanish activity in the South American zone was clearly lower than that in the west, colonization in the vicinity of Nueva Segovia and slaving raids took their toll on the Indian population, which also suffered from the impact of newly introduced diseases. It is possible that the Indian population in this zone was reduced by about one-third during the first half of the sixteenth century.

It was in the Mesoamerican zone, therefore, that Spanish activities were concentrated. The large concentrations of Indians in the Pacific lowlands constituted the major attraction for Spaniards. It was in this area, therefore, that towns were founded and encomiendas granted within their jurisdictions. In these areas contact between Spaniards and Indians was greatest, with the result that here the Indians suffered most from overwork and ill-treatment and their communities experienced the most profound economic and social changes. Spanish demands for tribute and labor put strains on the Indian economy, leading to food shortages and famines and increasing the susceptibility of the Indians to deadly Old World diseases. Population losses in their turn led to social disorganization, which together with the psychological impact of conquest and colonization contributed to a lowering of the fertility rate. The larger concentrations of Indians in the Mesoamerican zone also made the area the most attractive for slaving activities. The Indian slave trade in Nicaragua was in many ways unique in the history of the early colonial period in Latin America. It was unique in its scale and the fact that it involved Indians from highly developed aboriginal societies; in other areas, such as the Caribbean, northern Mexico, Argentina, and southern Chile, slavery was used to control the exploit bands or tribal groups. In Nicaragua the Indian slave trade was encouraged by the lack of local enterprises in which they could be employed and by the discovery of Peru a decade before the introduction of the New Laws.

As a result of conquest and colonization the Indian population in Pacific Nicaragua was reduced from about 600,000 at the time of discovery to about 45,000 in 1550. This amounts to a reduction of about 92.5 percent and a depopulation ratio of 13.3:1. As would be expected, this ratio is higher than that recorded for central Mexico and the central Andean area, but it is also higher than the depopulation ratios that can be calculated for other chiefdoms, such as the Chibcha.[2] Undoubtedly the major reason for the exceptionally high level of decline in Nicaragua was the Indian slave trade.

Although many factors worked against Indian survival in Pacific Nicaragua during the first half of the sixteenth century, other factors reduced the level of decline. First, the highly structured character of the chiefdoms enabled the Spaniards to achieve political control relatively easily through a small number of native leaders, so that the number of Indian casualties during conquest was minimized. Second, the introduction of the encomienda caused less disruption to the economic and social organization of Indian communities than it did among the tribal groups, since, although demands for tribute and labor increased under Spanish rule, such forms of exaction had existed in pre-Columbian times.

During the second half of the sixteenth century and the seventeenth century the Indian population continued to decline, reaching its nadir at the end of the period, when only about 60,000 Indians were left in the province. During this period the Indian population in the South American zone experienced the greater decline. There the Indian population fell by over 70 percent while in the Mesoamerican zone it was halved. The greater decline in the South American zone during this period, compared to that of the first half of the sixteenth century, can be accounted for by the greater intensity of contacts between the Indians and other races, resulting in the widespread introduction of Old World diseases and the beginnings of profound cultural change.

During the second half of the sixteenth century and the seventeenth century the Mesoamerican zone continued to be the focus of Spanish activities, although Spanish colonization extended into the South American zone, where some Indian villages were granted in encomiendas and other Indians were settled in missions. Meanwhile, the presence of the English and blacks on the Mosquito Coast from the midseventeenth century onward indirectly resulted in changes in the Indian cultures there. For reasons which have already been described, the introduction of encomiendas was more disruptive to the economic and social life of the Indians living in the South American zone than it was to those in the west, while missionary activity destroyed the Indian cultures it affected, precipitating considerable population losses. Within the South American zones all these changes were concentrated in the areas which were brought under Spanish administration, where the Indian population declined by about 95 percent; in the areas outside Spanish control the decline would have been much smaller—possibly about 20 percent.

In the Mesoamerican zone the Indian population continued to decline through the late sixteenth and seventeenth centuries, though at a reduced rate. However, the relative importance of different factors responsible for the decline changed. The Indian slave trade had been abolished, and the treatment of the Indians gradually improved with legislation. Apart from epidemic diseases, which continued to take their toll, the main sources of cultural and demographic change during this period were

Spanish demands on Indian communities and their response to them. Demands for tribute and for labor under the repartimiento were a constant drain on Indian production and labor, but probably more oppressive were the unofficial exactions made by Spanish officials, encomenderos, and priests. These forms of direct exploitation were coupled with demands for lands and labor created by the establishment of estates and the development of commercial agriculture. Indian labor was also in demand in the towns and in the shipbuilding industry. Reductions in Indian lands and in labor time to work them undermined production at a time when external demands upon it were increasing. As a result Indians were forced to abandon their villages and seek employment as wage laborers to provide for their own subsistence and to escape tribute payment and other exactions. Through sustained contact with non-Indians in the towns and on estates Indians experienced acculturation, and racial intermixing increased.

By the end of the seventeenth century the Indian population of the province, excluding Nicoya, had reached its nadir, having declined by 92.1 percent from the time of the Spanish conquest. The depopulation ratio for the province was 12.6:1, but that figure masks a marked difference between the two zones. The level of decline was much higher in the Mesoamerican zone, whose depopulation ratio of 25.4:1 is comparable with Dobyns's depopulation ratios of 20:1 and 25:1 for the American continent.[3] The lower ratio of 5.6:1 for the South American zone may be attributed to the lower intensity of contact up to the end of the seventeenth century.

During the eighteenth century the Indian population in both zones increased, reaching a peak in the first decade of the nineteenth century, after which it began to decline again. The increase was most marked in the Mesoamerican zone, which registered nearly a 50 percent increase in its Indian population. This increase may be related to the absence of the most destructive forces that had been present in the early colonial period, the improvement in sources of food, and the effective establishment of a new social and political order. However, conditions were still bad enough in some areas to drive Indians to desert their villages and seek employment elsewhere. The movement of non-Indians to the countryside put additional pressure on Indian lands, labor, and production, forcing Indians to abandon their communities and seek employment as wage laborers. These processes brought Indians and non-Indians into more frequent and intense contact, causing them to lose their cultural and racial identities. Thus, although the Indian population increased during the eighteenth century, the rate of increase was slow, and finally racial intermixing outstripped the rate of natural increase, converting the increase into a decline.

During the eighteenth century the Indian population in areas that had been outside Spanish control during the previous century declined by about 10 percent as contacts increased with Spanish colonists, soldiers, and missionaries, on the one hand, and with the Zambo-Mosquito, on the other. A proportion of the decline experienced in these areas contributed to the increase in the Indian population under Spanish control and to the growth of the Zambo-Mosquito population on the Mosquito Coast. Thus the more marked increase in the Indian population under Spanish administration in the South American zone (134.5 percent) compared to the increase in the Mesoamerican zone was due in part to the extension of the frontier of settlement; it was also due to smaller losses in Indian population through intermixing, which resulted from the presence of smaller numbers of non-Indians in the area—in 1776 only 17.3 percent of the total Spanish and ladino population lived in the South American zone.

During the colonial period the Indian population of Nicaragua and Nicoya was reduced by 90 percent, although a more marked decrease in the sixteenth and early seventeenth centuries was mitigated by an increase in the eighteenth century. The decline was most marked in the Mesoamerican zone, particularly Nicoya, which did not experience a demographic recovery in the eighteenth century. The smaller decline in the South American zone may appear to be contrary to what was predicted at the beginning of this study; it was suggested that the chiefdoms of the Pacific lowlands would have a greater chance of surviving contact with the Spaniards than would the tribal groups to the east. A number of factors were responsible for the unpredicted conclusions of this study. The smaller decline in the South American zone may largely be explained by the fact that by the end of the colonial period a large proportion (about 60 percent) of its Indian population had not been brought under Spanish control and therefore experienced intense contact with non-Indians. Nevertheless, if only those Indians who were brought under Spanish control are considered, the decline is still greater than that estimated for the Mesoamerican zone (excluding Nicoya), being 88.4 percent as opposed to 94.2 percent. While it is possible that the difference of 5.8 percent could be a function of errors in estimation, it can probably be accounted for by the other major factor deemed to be significant in the survival of Indian populations: the nearness of Indian groups to the socioeconomic centers of the province and the empire.

Although the nature of Indian cultures at the time of Spanish conquest influenced their level of survival in a positive way—for example, the existence of a hierarchical social and political structure in the chiefdoms enabled the Spaniards to achieve political control with little bloodshed—it had one major negative effect. The dense Indian populations associated with the more highly developed chiefdoms provided the only source of profit in the province in the early colonial period. The Indians

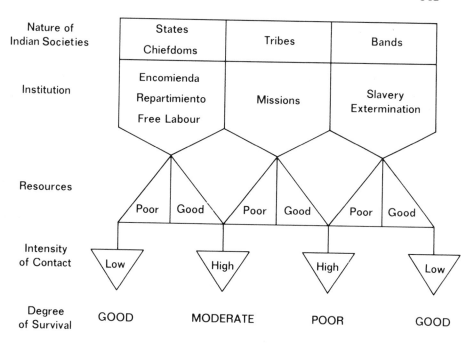

Fig. 10. Degree of Indian survival in colonial Spanish America.

were used to supply the Indian slave trade, and those that were left in the second half of the sixteenth century formed the basic source of labor for the development of commercial agriculture. The existence of sources of Indian labor and the rich volcanic soils in the Mesoamerican zone combined to make this area the continued focus of Spanish activities, the four major towns and cities being established there. In 1776, 80.4 percent of the Spanish population lived in the Mesoamerican zone, together with 82.9 percent of the ladino population.[4] It was in this zone, therefore, that contact between Indians and non-Indians was most intense and demands on Indian lands, labor, and production were greatest; in the South American zone, where Indian groups formed smaller concentrations of population and where land was not sought after on a large scale until the eighteenth century, the Indians were able to survive to a greater degree. However, comparing the Mesoamerican zone with the parts of the South American zone that were brought under Spanish control, the difference in the degree of survival is small and can almost certainly be explained by the devastating impact of the Indian slave trade. Indeed, in the absence of the slave trade the level of Indian survival in the Mesoamerican zone at the end of the colonial period would undoubtedly have been greater.

Thus it would appear that in Nicaragua the cultural advantages that chiefdoms possessed over tribes with respect to the survival in the face of contact were outweighed by the greater demands made upon them. Therefore the degrees of Indian survival in both zones may be described as "moderate" (See fig. 10), although, as this book has attempted to show, the processes that contributed to these levels of survival were quite different.

Glossary

Alcabala. Sales tax.

Alcalde. Magistrate.

Alcalde mayor. Spanish official with political and judicial authority over a district.

Alférez. Standard-bearer

Alguacil. Constable, police officer.

Alguacil de mandón. Constable charged with locating Indians with the purpose of collecting tribute from them.

Alguacil de mesón. Constable charged with supervising inns.

Almas de confesión y comunión. People who had been confirmed, generally those over the age of seven or eight.

Almojarifazgo. Import and export duty.

Almud. Measure of capacity equivalent to one-twelfth fanega, or one *celemín.*

Añil. Indigo.

Apoderado fiscal. Spanish official appointed for specific purpose; special commissioner.

Arancel. List of fixed prices or fees.

Arca. Treasury chest.

Arroba. Weight equivalent to about 25 pounds.

Armada de barlovento. Armed ships charged with the protection of Spanish fleets in Caribbean waters.

Audiencia. High judicial court and governing body of a region, and, by extension, the area under its jurisdiction.

Ayuda de costa. Grant toward expenses or a pension.

Barbecho. System of cultivation by which land is left fallow for short periods.

Barrio. District or suburb of town.

Batea. Wooden pan for washing alluvial gold.

Bohío. Hut made of wood and straw.

Braza. Linear measure equivalent to 2 varas.

Caballería. Area measurement; in the region discussed in this book about 111 acres.

Cabecera. Main village of a district, generally with several other villages under its jurisdiction.

Cabildo. Municipal council.

Cacique. Indian leader or chief.

Caja. Strongbox or chest.

Caja de comunidad. Community chest.

Camino real. Royal road.

Canoa. Vat for making indigo dye.

Cantor. Singer.

Carga. Load and weight measure of about 200 pounds.

Casa real. Governor's or official's residence.

Casado/a. Married person.

Casado entero. Male Indian married to female Indian from the same village or barrio.

Cédula. Decree.

Celemín. Measure of capacity equivalent to an almud or one-twelfth fanega.

Chacra. Small holding or farm.

Chinampas. Artificially created islands in shallow freshwater lakes.

Cofradía. Religious brotherhood.

Comandante general de armas. Spanish official in charge of military affairs.

Composición. Payment of a fee to regularize illegal or irregular occupation of land.

Contador. Treasurer.

Corregidor. Royal official with administrative and judicial authority.

Corte. Type of indigo of poor quality.

Demora. Period during which mines were worked.

Denuncia. Accusation; claim to unoccupied land.

Derrama. Tax levied for the support of a bishop while he was conducting a *visita.*

Diezmo. One-tenth, or tithe.

Doctrina. Indian parish under the care of the regular clergy.

Ejido. Communal lands.

Encomendero/a. Holder of an encomienda.

Encomienda. Grant of Indians given to an eminent colonist as a personal reward for merits or services, to whom the Indians were required to pay tribute in the form of goods, money and, until 1549, labor services.

Enfermedades. Illnesses, diseases.

Entrada. Expedition, military or religious, into unexplored or unconquered territory.

Epidemia. Epidemic; disease.

Esclavos de guerra. Indian slaves taken in war or rebellion.

Esclavos de rescate. Indian slaves obtained by trade.

Escribano. Notary.

Estancia. Ranch for livestock; generally 6¾ *caballerías* for a *ganado mayor* and half that for *ganado menor.*

Fanega. Measure of capacity, about 1½ bushels.

Fanega de sembradura. Amount of land that could be sown with one fanega of seed; a *fanega de sembradura* of maize was 8.8 acres.

Fardo. Measure of about 100 pounds.

Fiscal. Attorney general.

Flor. Type of indigo of good quality.

Fuero. Privilege; the *fuero eclesiástico* and the *fuero militar* bestowed certain privileges on clerics and soldiers, respectively, including exemption from tithe payment and trial in civil courts.

Ganado mayor. Cattle, horses, and mules.
Ganado menor. Pigs, sheep, and goats.
Gobierno. Area under the jurisdiction of a governor.

Hacendado/a. Owner of a hacienda.
Hato. Cattle ranch.
Hilo morado. Cotton thread dyed with purple shellfish dye.

Indio gobernador. Indian leader appointed during the colonial period.
Intendencia. Jurisdiction of an *intendente.*
Intendente. Royal official with extensive powers, appointed from the third quarter of the eighteenth century.

Juez de comisión. Judge or inspector appointed for specific purpose.
Juez de milpas. Inspector encharged with ensuring that Indians grew maize.
Juez repartidor. Spanish official in charge of the allocation of Indians under the repartimiento.

Labranza. Cultivated plot of land.
Ladino. A non-Indian. Generally a person of mixed race, including an Indian who had experienced a degree of cultural and racial change.
Lavorío. Originally an Indian who worked as a household servant. Later an Indian living in a non-Indian settlement, who was not included in an encomienda and paid a distinct form of tribute.
Legajo. Bundle; in this book, bundle of documents.
Leñatero. Supplier of firewood.
Libre. Freeman or free woman.
Libro de tasaciónes. Book in which *tasaciones* of Indian villages were recorded.
Limosna. Alms, charity.

Mano. Pestle for grinding maize.
Manta. Blanket or shawl.
Matrícula. Register of inhabitants of an Indian village drawn up for the purpose of assessing tribute payment.
Mayordomo. Overseer or manager.
Media anata. Payment equivalent to half a year's income. Often paid on the acquisition of encomiendas or land grants, and on receipt of public office.
Medio/a. Indian paying half tribute, normally a widower, widow, or a single person, or one married to an Indian from another village. Also, a measure of capacity equivalent to one-half *celemín* or almud.
Mestizo. Offspring of an Indian and a European.
Metate. Mortar for grinding maize.

Milpa. Plot cultivated in maize, often with beans.
Milpa de comunidad. Plot of maize cultivated communally.
Mita. See *repartimiento.*
Molendera. Miller of maize, who generally baked bread.
Monte. Uncultivated land or scrub, often used as a source of fuel and timber.

Naboría. See *lavorío. Naboría* was the more commonly used term in the first
  half of the sixteenth century.

Obraje. Workshop; here a workshop in which indigo dye or textiles were
  made.
Obrajero. Owner of an *obraje.*
Oidor. Spanish official; judge and member of the audiencia.

Padrón. Detailed list of inhabitants of a settlement, Indian or Spanish.
Palenque. Multifamily house, possibly a fortified settlement.
Parcialidad. Suburb of a town or village or kinship group within an Indian
  community.
Pardo. Dark-skinned person; generally used to refer to a mulatto in the eigh-
  teenth century.
Partido. Subordinate administrative unit.
Pasto. Pasture.
Peonía. Area measurement; 5 *peonías* were originally equivalent to 1 caba-
  llería.
Peso. Monetary unit equal to 8 reals.
Peste. Disease, generally used to refer to smallpox.
Pierna. Linear measurement equivalent to about 33 inches.
Pila. Vat for making indigo dye.
Plancha. Bar of silver.
Platanar. Plot of wild or cultivated plantains.
Principal. Indian leader, generally with less authority than that of a cacique.
Próximo. Indian about to reach tributary status, generally an Indian between
  the ages of fifteen and seventeen.

Quartillo. One-quarter of a *celemín* or almud.
Quintal. Measurement of weight, about 25 pounds.
Quinto. Tax of one-fifth the value of an item; paid on Indian slaves, silver, etc.

Ranchería. Small rural settlement.
Rancho. Ranch.
Real. Monetary unit comprised of 34 maravedis. Eight reals constituted 1
  peso.
Real caja. Royal treasury.
Reducción. Settlement formed of nonconverted Indians or by the amalgama-
  tion of several Indian settlements.
Regidor. Councilor attached to a cabildo.
Repartimiento. Draft labor system whereby each Indian village provided a

quota of its tributary Indians to work in approved tasks for specified periods.

Repartimiento de generos. Forced distribution and sale of goods among Indians generally by royal officials and clergy.

Repartimiento de hilados. Forced distribution of cotton to Indians for spinning and weaving.

Reservado/a. Indian exempt from tribute payment by virtue of age, status, or physical incapacity.

Residencia. Judicial review of a Spanish official's conduct at the end of his term of office.

Sarampión. Measles.

Sementera. Sowing. There were two sowings a year, the *primera sementera* and the *segunda sementera.*

Servicio del tostón. Capitation tax of four reals on each tributary Indian, introduced in 1591 to help pay for costs of defense.

Sobresaliente. Type of indigo of good quality.

Subdelegado. Royal official in charge of a *partido* and under the authority of an *intendente.*

Surco. Row of sugarcane plants.

Tameme. Indian carrier or porter.

Tasación. Official tribute assessment.

Teniente. Governor's lieutenant.

Terminos. Limits of jurisdiction.

Tierra caliente. Area with hot climate.

Tierra templada. Area with temperate climate.

Tinta de caracol. Shellfish dye.

Tortilla. Thin, round, flat cakes of maize bread.

Tostón. Four reals, or one-half peso.

Vara. Linear measure of about 33 inches; staff of office.

Vecino. Householder in Spanish town.

Vecino natural. Indian householder in Indian village.

Veedor. Inspector.

Viruelas. Smallpox.

Visita. Tour of inspection of an area.

Zambo. Offspring of an Indian and a black.

Zurrón. Sack of indigo weighing 214 pounds.

Abbreviations Used in Notes and Bibliography

UNPUBLISHED SOURCES

AGCA	Archivo General de Centro América, Guatemala City
AGI	Archivo General de Indias
	AG Audiencia de Guatemala
	CO Contaduría
	EG Escribanía de Camara
	IG Indiferente General
	JU Justicia
	MP Mapas y Planos
	PAT Patronato
AHNM	Archivo Histórico Nacional, Madrid
ANCR	Archivo Nacional, Costa Rica
	CC Complementario Colonial
ANH	Archivo Nacional de Historia, Honduras
BM	British Museum, London
	Add. Additional Manuscripts
BNM	Biblioteca Nacional, Madrid
BPR	Biblioteca del Palacio Real, Madrid
	MA Miscelánea de Ayala
MNM	Museo Naval, Madrid
PRO	Public Record Office, London
	CO Colonial Office
RAHM	Real Academia de la Historia, Madrid
	CM Colección Muñoz
SHM	Servicio Histórico Militar, Madrid

PUBLISHED SOURCES

AEA   *Anuario de Estudios Americanos.*
ASGH   *Anales de la Sociedad de Geografía e Historia* (Guatemala).
BAGG   *Boletín del Archivo General del Gobierno,* Guatemala City.
CDHCN   *Colección de documentos referentes a la historia colonial de Nicaragua.* Recuerdo del Centenario de Independencia Nacional, 1821–1921. Managua: Tip. y Enc. Nacionales, 1921.
CDHCR   *Colección de documentos para la historia de Costa Rica.* Compiled by L. Fernández. 10 vols. Paris: Imp. Dupont, 1883–1901.
CDI   *Colección de documentos inéditos relativos al descubrimiento, conquista y organización de las antiguas posesiones españolas de América y Oceanía.* 42 vols. Madrid, 1864–84.
CDIU   *Colección de documentos inéditos relativos al descubrimeinto, con-*

        quista y organización de las antiguas posesiones españolas de Ultra-
        mar. 25 vols. Madrid, 1885–1932.
CS   *Colección Somoza: Documentos para la historia de Nicaragua.* Edited
        by A. Vega Bolaños. 17 vols. Madrid, 1954–57.
HAHR *Hispanic American Historical Review.*
HMAI *Handbook of Middle American Indians.* 17 vols. to date. (Austin:
        University of Texas, 1964–).
HSAI   *Handbook of South American Indians.* 6 vols. Smithsonian Institu-
        tion, Bureau of American Ethnology Bulletin 143. Washington D.C.,
        1946–50.
JLAS   *Journal of Latin American Studies.*
LARR *Latin American Research Review.*
RABNH *Revista del Archivo y Biblioteca Nacionales* (Honduras).

Notes

CHAPTER 1

1. Dobyns, "Estimating Aboriginal American Population," 415. Depopulation ratios are an unsatisfactory means of estimating the aboriginal population, since they cannot be calculated where the population becomes extinct.

2. Smith, "Depopulation of the Central Andes," 459.

3. Cook, *Demographic Collapse,* 94.

4. Cook and Borah, *Essays,* 1:82.

5. Dobyns, "Estimating Aboriginal American Population," 429; Denevan, *Llanos de Mojos,* 120; Denevan, ed., *Native Population,* 212.

6. For example, the rates of decline for different Indian groups in Colombia vary considerably. For the Chibcha areas the following depopulation ratios have been calculated: Tunja (1537–1755), 9.3:1 (Friede, "Tunja," 13); and the Sabana de Bogotá (1537–1778), 5.2:1 (Villamarin and Villamarin, *Indian Labor,* 83–84). Meanwhile, the tribal Indians of Pamplona were reduced by 10:1 during the colonial period (Colmenares, *Encomienda y población,* 47) and the Andakí and Quimbaya had become almost extinct by the seventeenth century (Friede, *Los Andakí,* 188–89; Friede, *Los Quimbayas,* 253).

7. Borah maintains that the Indian population of New Spain began to increase in the last decades of the seventeenth century (Borah, *Century of Depression,* 42), whereas Miranda believes that the increase started earlier, in the 1620s and 1630s, and that the bishoprics of Mexico, Puebla, and Michoacán registered average increases of 20 percent during the second half of the seventeenth century (Miranda, "Población indígena," 184–85). Dobyns ("Estimating Aboriginal American Population," 413) places the nadir for the Indian population of Mexico at 1650, while studies of smaller areas such as central Mexico by Gibson (*Aztecs,* 140–41) and Mixteca Alta, Nueva Galicia, and adjacent areas in New Spain by Cook and Borah (Cook and Borah, *Mixteca Alta,* 38, 57; Cook and Borah, *Essays,* 1:355) also suggest that the increase had begun by midcentury.

8. Veblen, "Native Population Decline," 497–99; Lovell, "Cuchumatán Highlands," 240. An exception is Lutz's study of the Quinizalapa valley, near Antigua, in Guatemala, which suggests that the population began to increase in the 1620s and 1630s (Lutz, "Quinizalapa Valley," 187).

9. Cook, "Población indígena," 96.

10. For a more detailed account of regional variations in depopulation and recovery see Newson, "Indian Population Patterns."

11. Caso, "Definición del indio," 239–47; Kubler, *Indian Caste,* 36–38; Borah, "Race and Class," 331–42; Pitt-Rivers, "Race, Colour and Class," 549–53.

12. Borah, "Race and Class," 338.

13. Tannenbaum, "Acculturation Studies," 205.

14. Wagley, "Cultural Influences on a Population," 95–104.

15. Steward and Faron, *Native Peoples,* 429–30.

16. Cook, "Demographic Consequences," 108–109; Vellard, "Causas bio-lógicas," 77–93; Cook and Borah, *Indian Population;* Dobyns, "Andean Epidemic History," 493–515; Borah, "America as Model," 379–87; Dobyns, "Estimating Aboriginal American Population," 410–11; Crosby, "Conquistador y Pestilencia," 321–37; Jacobs, "Tip of the Iceberg," 123–32; Sánchez-Albornoz, *Population of Latin America,* 60; Crosby, "Virgin Soil Epidemics," 289–99; Denevan, ed., *Native Population,* 4–6; Dobyns, *Native American Historical Demography,* 22–25.

17. Dobyns, "Estimating Aboriginal American Population," 410–11; Jacobs, "Tip of the Iceberg," 126; Crosby, "Virgin Soil Epidemics," 293–99; Dobyns, *Native Historical Demography,* 25–34; McNeill, *Plagues and Peoples,* 204–205.

18. Borah and Cook, *Aboriginal Population,* 89; Thompson, "Maya Central Area," 24–26; Crosby, *Columbian Exchange,* 38.

19. Ashburn, *Ranks of Death,* 130–34; Vivó Escoto, "Climate of Mexico and Central America," 213–14; Dunn, "Antiquity of Malaria," 385–93; Sauer, *Early Spanish Main,* 279; Thompson, "Maya Central Area," 54–55; Duffy, *Epidemics,* 140; Wood, "Late Introduction of Malaria," 93–104; McNeill, *Plagues and Peoples,* 213.

20. Denevan, ed., *Native Population,* 5; Brown, "Yellow Fever," 390; Bustamante, "Fiebre amarilla," 28.

21. These may have included typhoid, paratyphoid, bacilliary, and amoebic dysentery, hookworm, and other helminthic infections most of which are waterborne and are more prevalent in the humid tropics (Sangster, "Diarrhoeal Diseases," 145–74).

22. Smallpox: Dixon, *Smallpox,* 7–8; Crosby, "Conquistador y Pestilencia," 333; plague: Manson-Bahr, *Manson's Tropical Diseases,* 256–57, 418, 451; Shrewsbury, *Bubonic Plague,* 1–6; MacLeod, *Spanish Central America,* 8–9; typhus: Ashburn, *Ranks of Death,* 81, 95–96.

23. Black, "Infectious Diseases," 515–18; Shea, "Defense of Small Population Estimates," 159–61.

24. Shea, "Defense of Small Population Estimates," 160–61. The differential impact of disease is clearly demonstrated in Swann, "Demographic Impact of Disease and Famine," 97–109; Malvido, "Efectos de las epidemias," 1: 179–97.

25. Zavala, *New Viewpoints,* 68; Service, "Indian-European Relations," 413–14; Harris, *Patterns of Race,* 3–13; Villamarin and Villamarin, *Indian Labor,* 24–30.

26. Tannenbaum, "Acculturation Studies," 204; Steward, *Theory of Culture Change,* 43–63; Service, "Indian-European Relations," 416; Mason, *Patterns of Dominance,* 112–113.

27. For examples see Steward, *Theory of Culture Change,* 43–63; Gibson, *Aztecs,* 220–21, 403.

28. Sahlins and Service, *Evolution and Culture,* 37–38; Ginsberg, *Essays in Sociology,* 104; Segraves, "Ecological Generalization," 538–40.

29. Benedict, "Two Patterns," 207–12.

30. Jiménez Moreno, "Mestizaje y la transaculturación," 81–83; Gibson, *Aztecs,* 144; Cámara Barbachano, "Mestizaje en Mexico," 34; Phelan, *Kingdom of Quito,* 49; Moreno Navarro, *Cuadros de mestizaje,* 84.

31. Kubler, *Indian Caste,* 65; Miranda, "Población indígena," 187; Jaramillo Uribe, "Población indígena," 282–83; González and Mellafe, "Función de la fa-

milia," 68; Israel, *Race, Class and Politics*, 33; Newson, "The Law of Cultural Dominance," 81–82; Grieshaber, "Hacienda-Indian Community Relations," 107–108. For an attempt at identifying economic centers, intermediate zones, and peripheries, see Slicher Van Bath, "Economic Diversification in Spanish America," 53–95; Newson, "Indian Population Patterns," 62–65.

32. MacLeod, *Spanish Central America.*

CHAPTER 2

1. Cooper, "Areal and Temporal Aspects of South American Culture," 1–38.
2. Steward, ed., *Marginal Tribes*, 4.
3. Steward, ed., *Circum-Caribbean Tribes*, 6–9.
4. Ibid., 11–15; Steward, ed., *Comparative Ethnology*, 769–71; Steward and Faron, *Native Peoples*, 284, 453.
5. Steward, ed., *Marginal Tribes*, 12.
6. Chapman, "Tropical Forest Tribes," 158–60.
7. Ibid., 161–67. She accepts the northern origin proposed for the Jicaque by the linguistics Greenberg and Swadesh and suggests that they probably migrated from the north as hunters and gatherers at about the same time or somewhat later and became assimilated to the Chibchan tropical forest culture. Other linguists are more hesitant to identify an origin for the Jicaque given the unreliability of the linguistic evidence (Kaufman, "Mesoamerican Indian Languages," 960).
8. Steward and Faron, *Native Peoples*, 13.
9. Kirchhoff, "Mesoamérica," 92–107.
10. Stone, "Eastern Frontier," 118–21.
11. Baudez, *Central America*, 227 n. 2.
12. Oviedo and Andagoya accompanied Pedrarias Dávila to the New World in 1514, and in official capacities they were involved in the early conquest and administration of southern Central America, including Nicaragua. Their first-hand experience of the region at that early date and their access to documentary sources now lost, mean that their works constitute valuable sources of evidence for the nature of Indian cultures at the time of Spanish conquest. The Franciscan friar Torquemada spent most of his life in Mexico and his *Monarquía indiana,* for which he used native Indian sources, constitutes an invaluable source for ethnohistorians of that country. Apparently the friar also visited Guatemala and Honduras, but probably not Nicaragua, and as a source for those areas his works are more limited. Nevertheless, he is a useful secondary source of information on the early migrations of Mesoamerican peoples to Nicaragua and Nicoya. Two travellers through Nicaragua in the sixteenth century were the Italian Girolamo Benzoni and the Franciscan friar Alonso Ponce. Benzoni traveled through Nicaragua in the 1540s, but his *Historia del Nuevo Mundo* contains only a few ethnographic details. The same it not true of the account of Friar Ponce's journey. He visited Franciscan convents between Guadalajara and Nicaragua between 1584 and 1589, and the long account of this journey, in fact written by his secretary Ciudad Real, includes many observations on the Indian communities he visited, including the nature of their settlements and livelihood, as well as the languages that were spoken. However, since the account was written over sixty years

after Spanish conquest, some care is needed in interpreting the evidence it provides, particularly the linguistic evidence (Oviedo y Valdés, *Historia general;* Andagoya, *Narrative of Pascual de Andagoya*). A copy of Andagoya's manuscript is housed in the Real Academia de la Historia in Madrid (RAHM Colección Muñoz A/71 fols. 27–68); Torquemada, *Monarquía indiana;* Benzoni, *Historia del Nuevo Mundo;* Ponce, *Relación breve.*

13. This was particularly true of Martyr, who held the position at the beginning of the sixteenth century. Written at a later date, Herrera's *Historia general* draws on earlier works, notably those of Oviedo, López de Velasco, and López de Gómara. López de Gómara was secretary-chaplain to Cortés until his death in 1547, and as such he utilized information supplied to him by the conquistador and by his captain, Andrés de Tapia. His *Historia general* is best on the conquest of Mexico; his account of Nicaragua is largely drawn from Oviedo (Martyr D'Anghera, *Orbe novo;* López de Velasco, *Geografía;* Herrera y Tordesillas, *Historia general;* López de Gómara, *Hispania Victrix*).

14. Oviedo, *Historia general,* 4 lib. 42 cap. 1:363. "Nicaragua" was undoubtedly Nahuat, while Orotiña belonged to the Oto-Manguean stock and was spoken by Chorotega Indians in Nicoya. Chondal was a collective name for the languages spoken in eastern Nicaragua.

15. López de Gómara, *Hispania Victrix,* 283.

16. *CDI,* 6:5–40 García de Palacio 8.3.1576. Pipil corrupta probably referred to the Nahuat dialect spoken by the Nicarao. Potón may have been spoken by the Lenca, who may have been living in Nueva Segovia on the border with Honduras (Stone, "Synthesis," 213).

17. Mason, "Native Languages," 58–59; Johnson, "Central American Cultures," 63.

18. Torquemada, *Monarquía indiana,* 1 lib. 3 cap. 40:331–33.

19. Although Stone suggests that they displaced the Corobici, they are not specifically mentioned by Torquemada (Stone, *Pre-Columbian Man,* 133; Torquemada, *Monarquía indiana,* 1 lib. 3 cap. 40:331–33).

20. Stone suggests that, while oppression by the Olmec may have led to the departure of Manguean speakers south from Soconusco (Chiapas), where they became known as Chiapaneca, the hostile environment created by Maya groups may have been responsible for their migration south to El Salvador, Honduras, Nicaragua, and Nicoya. Unfortunately, she gives no precise date for the migration, although she suggests that they originally left Cholula owing to the conquest of the area by the Olmec about A.D. 800. This suggests that she is following Torquemada's description of the migrations of the Chorotega and Nicarao. She arrives at the same date for the start of the migration but assumes that it referred to their departure from Cholula rather than Soconusco. See Stone, *Pre-Columbian Man,* 133.

21. Chapman, "Tropical Forest Tribes," 12; Healy, "Chorotega y Nicarao," 259.

22. Lothrop, *Pottery of Costa Rica,* 390–91; Strong, "Archaeology of Costa Rica," 141; Healy, "Chorotega y Nicarao," 258–60; Healy, *Archaeology of the Rivas Region,* 336, 345. For archaeological investigations in Nicoya see Hartman, *Archaeological Reconnaissance;* Lothrop, *Pottery of Costa Rica;* Coe, "Costa Rican Archaeology," 170–83; Coe, "Archaeological Investigations in Coastal Guanacaste," 358–65; Baudez and Coe, "Archaeological Sequences,"

366–73; Baudez, *Recherches archéologiques;* Lange, "Sapoa River Valley." For a summary of this work to 1966 see Lothrop, "Archaeology of Lower Central America," 184–91.

23. Lehmann, *Zentral-Amerika,* 789–94; Mason, "Native Languages," 80; Stone, "Synthesis," 210; Kaufman, "Mesoamerican Indian Languages," 959.

24. Johnson, "Linguistic Map," 63–64; Chapman, *Los Nicarao,* 79; Kaufman, "Mesoamerican Indian Languages," 959.

25. AGI PAT 26–5 and *CS,* 1:457–70 Cerezeda, Governor of Honduras, 20.1.1529, JU 1030–32 and *CS,* 2:95–100 Diligencias seguidas en León . . . 2.9.1529, PAT 26–5 and *CS,* 2:283–87 Pedrarias Dávila 25.11.1529; Oviedo, *Historia general,* 4 lib. 39 cap. 3:347.

26. Ponce, *Relación breve,* 337–38; Lehmann, *Zentral-Amerika,* 647; Stone, "Grupos Mexicanos," 44.

27. *CS,* 1:434–8 cedula 2.10.1528; AGI JU 1030 and *CS,* 2:219–77 Informaciones de Francisco de Castañeda 1529, JU 1030 and *CS,* 2:189–92 Acuerdo para que se manda entregar a Martín Estete el hierro . . . 1.10.1529, AG 9 and *CS,* 3:68–78 Castañeda 30.5.1531; *CDHCR,* 6:199–211 Rodríguez 9.7.1545; Ponce, *Relación breve,* 356–60.

28. Oviedo, *Historia general,* 4 lib. 42 cap. 5:391.

29. Lothrop, *Pottery of Costa Rica,* 9; Stone, "Synthesis," 214.

30. Squier, "Archaeology and Ethnology of Nicaragua," 95–97.

31. Levy, *Notas geográficas,* 7 based on Alcedo.

32. Oviedo, *Historia general,* 3 lib. 29 cap. 21:300.

33. Brinton, *American Race,* 159–60; Lothrop, *Pottery of Costa Rica,* 11; Johnson, "Central American Cultures," 64; Stone, *Pre-Columbian Man,* 134.

34. Mason, "Native Languages," 61–62; Chapman, *Los Nicarao,* 17; Stone, "Synthesis," 210; Kaufman, "Mesoamerican Indian Languages," 960.

35. Ponce, *Relación breve,* 354–56.

36. AGI AG 966 census 1581. The census of this province was drawn up by Duarte de Salazar on commission from Governor Artieda Cherinos.

37. AGI AG 966 census 1581; Ponce, *Relación breve,* 356; Stone, "Synthesis," 213, 228.

38. For a discussion of the Nahua language and its dialects see Lehmann, *Zentral-Amerika,* 978–80; Rivet, Stresser-Péan, and Loukotka, "Langues du Méxique," 1057–60; Wolf, *Shaking Earth,* 37–42.

39. Chapman, "Tropical Forest Tribes," 13. There appear to be differences of opinion about the number of Nahuat-Pipil migrations to Central America and the times at which they occurred. Stone suggests that there were three migrations. The first migration to Guatemala and El Salvador occurred between A.D. 300 and 600. Some scholars maintain that this migration did not extend farther east to Honduras, but Stone suggests that the presence of artifacts at Travesía and Playa de los Muertos in the Sula plain indicates more than just a mere influence from the central Mexican plateau and may be due to the presence of Nahuat-Pipil in the area or else to the diffusion of traits from Copán, which shows evidence of Nahuat culture at this time. The second migration, she suggests, occurred between A.D. 700 and 900 and entered Honduras by a northern route through Tabasco, the Petén, and the Golfo Dulce. Finally, a third migration following the same route took place about A.D. 1000 (Stone, "Nahuat Traits," 532–33; Stone, *Pre-Columbian Man,* 112–15, 136, 142–51). Thompson agrees

that the first migration of the Nahuat-Pipil occurred in the Early Classic, A.D. 300–600 (Willey, *Introduction to American Archaeology,* 539–40, comment by Thompson).

40. Vázquez, *Crónica,* 81.

41. Ibid., 1:31: ". . . es lo mismo que el mexicano en sus voces, aunque basto y serrano."

42. Wolf, *Shaking Earth,* 41; Kaufman, "Mesoamerican Indian Languages," 962.

43. Roys, *Indian Background,* 118.

44. Lothrop, "South America as Seen from Middle America," 427; Stone, *Central and Southern Honduras,* 127.

45. Ponce, *Relación breve,* 352.

46. Oviedo, *Historia general,* 4 lib. 42 cap. 11:413–14.

47. Ponce, *Relación breve,* 343, 354, 359, 379.

48. Oviedo, *Historia general,* 4 lib. 42 caps. 2–3:366–84. Friar Bobadilla's interviews were conducted in 1528, not 1538. The published version wrongly transcribed the date. Oviedo stated elsewhere that Friar Bobadilla, having concluded his investigation, gave a sermon in the Nicarao town of Totoaca on October 2, 1528 (Oviedo, *Historia general,* 4 lib. 42 cap. 3:381). Also, Pedrarias Dávila died in 1531 and thus could not have commissioned Friar Bobadilla to conduct the inquiry in 1538. Furthermore, Friar Bobadilla was in Peru in 1538 (León-Portilla, *Religión,* 19).

49. Torquemada, *Monarquía indiana,* 1 lib. 3 cap. 40:331–33.

50. Lehmann, *Zentral-Amerika,* 994–95.

51. Torquemada, *Monarquía indiana,* 1 lib. 3 cap. 40:332.

52. Thompson, *Archaeological Reconnaissance,* 11; Jiménez Moreno, *Síntesis de la historia pre-tolteca,* 2:1077; Chapman, *Los Nicarao,* 74–75.

53. Lothrop, *Pottery of Costa Rica,* 8; León-Portilla, *Religión,* 32–33.

54. López de Gómara, *Hispania Victrix,* 284; Motolinía, *Memoriales,* 197.

55. Haberland, "Evidence for the Nicarao and Pipil Migrations," 556–59.

56. Chapman, "Tropical Forest Tribes," 13; Coe, "Costa Rican Archaeology," 180; Stone, *Pre-Columbian Man,* 171–72; Healy, "Chorotega y Nicarao," 260–61; Healy, *Archaeology of the Rivas Region,* 339.

57. Lothrop, *Pottery of Costa Rica,* 398; Strong, "Archaeology of Costa Rica," 141; León-Portilla, *Religión,* 30–32; Healy, "Chorotega y Nicarao," 261; Healy, *Archaeology of the Rivas Region,* 339.

58. Ponce, *Relación breve,* 352, 354, 359.

59. Oviedo, *Historia general,* 4 lib. 42 cap. 11:413–14.

60. AGI AG 966 census 1581.

61. Oviedo, *Historia general,* 4 lib. 42 cap. 12:426–27.

62. Ponce, *Relación breve,* 369; Haberland, "Nicarao and Pipil Migrations," 552. In Ponce's account it states, ". . . en la isla de la laguna se hable otra lengua particular."

63. Chapman, "Port of Trade Enclaves," 114–53.

64. Torquemada, *Monarquía Indiana,* 1 lib. 3 cap. 40:333; Brasseur de Bourbourg, *Histoire de Nations Civilisées,* 2:109.

65. AGI AG 52 and CS, 3:406–12 Sánchez 2.8.1535; Lothrop, *Pottery of Costa Rica,* 10.

66. AGI AG 371 Fr. Ximénez 9.9.1748; Vallejo, *Historia documentada,* 30–31; Vázquez, *Crónica,* 4:78–79.

67. AGI AG 371 Fr. Ximénez 9.9.1748.

68. Chapman, "Tropical Forest Tribes," 58–59; Stone, "Synthesis," map opposite p. 216.

69. Lehmann, *Zentral-Amerika,* 461–62.

70. Mason, "Native Languages," 76.

71. Conzemius, "Miskito and Sumu Languages," 59–66; Johnson, "Linguistic Map"; Stone, "Synthesis."

72. Long, *History of Jamaica,* 1:320.

73. AGI AG 183 Frs. Ovalle and Guevara 4.3.1681; AGCA A3.2 1075 19750 Doctrinas 1761; Vázquez, *Crónica,* 4:123–24.

74. Roberts, *Narrative of Voyages,* 127; Tanner, "Map of North America"; Vandermaelen, "Partie du Guatemala."

75. AGCA A3.1 800 14832 fol. 33 Frs. Santa Cruz and Mosquera 28.11.1690, Al. 12 77 626 Fr. José María Magdalena 15.1.1693.

76. Long, *History of Jamaica,* 1:320, 322, 323; Thompson, "Map 13"; Pinkerton, "Spanish Dominions"; Strangeways, "Map of Mosquitia"; Tanner, "Map of North America"; Vandermaelen, "Partie du Guatemala."

77. Wickham, *Journey Among the Woolwa,* 160.

78. AGI AG 302 Lic. Santaella Melgarejo 3.4.1715; Brinton, *American Race,* 163.

79. AGI AG 449 Corregidor of Sebaco and Chontales 20.11.1757.

80. AGCA A1.17 4501 38303 Porta Costas 1.8.1790; Roberts, *Narrative of Voyages,* 103, 116–18; Stout, *Nicaragua,* map; Anon., "Report on the Mosquito Country," 422; Brinton, *American Race,* 163.

81. Jeffreys, "Bay of Honduras"; Edwards, "New Map of the West Indies"; Thompson, "Map 13"; Pinkerton, "Spanish Dominions"; Strangeways, "Map of Mosquitia"; Vandermaelen, "Partie du Guatemala"; Squier, *Notes on Central America,* map.

82. Anon., "Mosquito Country," 422; Roberts, *Narrative of Voyages,* 112, 116–18.

83. Conzemius, "Miskito and Sumu Languages," 65; Conzemius, *Ethnographical Survey,* 15.

84. *BAGG* 5:283–308 Fr. Espino 16.9.1674; AGI AG 449 Corregidor of Sebaco and Chontales 20.11.1757.

85. Exceptions are Magnus, "Prehistory of the Miskito Coast"; Magnus, "Prehistoric Cultural Relationships," 568–78; Magnus, "Costa Atlántica," 67–74; Magnus, "Prehistoric and Modern Subsistence Patterns," 61–80.

86. Lothrop, *Pottery of Costa Rica,* 386–87, 392.

87. Magnus, "Prehistory of the Miskito Coast," 15, 43, 220–21; Magnus, "Prehistoric Cultural Relationships," 570.

88. Lehmann, *Zentral-Amerika,* 479.

89. Brinton, "Matagalpan Linguistic Stock," 403.

90. Lehmann, *Zentral-Amerika,* 480.

91. Ibid.; Herrera, *Historia general,* dec. 4 lib. 8 cap. 3:107–108; Alcedo, *Diccionario,* 1:553; Brinton, "Matagalpan Linguistic Stock," 403; Vázquez de Espinosa, *Compendium,* 261.

92. Oviedo, *Historia general,* 4 lib. 42 cap. 1:363.

93. AGI AG 966 census 1581; Ponce, *Relación breve,* 341–42.

94. Lehmann, *Zentral-Amerika,* 480–81.

95. *BAGG* 5:283–308 Fr. Ovalle 11.9.1675; AGCA A3.1 800 14832 fol. 33

Frs. Santa Cruz and Mosquera 28.11.1690, A1.12 77 626 Fr. José María Magdalena 15.1.1693, A1.3 382 2466 22.8.1722, A1.12 134 1504 13.12.1722, A3.2 1075 19570 Doctrinas 1761, A1.12 117 2473 Autos relativos a la solicitud del indio carive . . . 1768.

96. Lehmann, *Zentral-Amerika*, 417–20, Mason, "Native Languages," 76, 86; Johnson, "Central American Cultures," 55, 65; Stone, "Synthesis," 212.

97. Peralta, *Río de San Juan*, 16–19; Lehmann, *Zentral-Amerika*, 416–17; Conzemius, "Rama Indianer," 298–99; Holm, "Creole English," 363–64.

98. AGI AG 303 Rivera 23.11.1742; Peralta, *Costa Rica y Costa de Mosquitos*, 125.

99. Long, *History of Jamaica*, 1: 320; Anon., "Mosquito Country," 421–22.

100. Long, *History of Jamaica*, 1: 320, 322; Anon., "Mosquito Country," 421; Roberts, *Narrative of Voyages*, 100.

101. Roberts, *Narrative of Voyages*, 98, 170.

102. Edwards, "A New Map"; Pinkerton, "Spanish Dominions"; Tanner, "Map of North America"; Vandermaelen, "Partie du Guatemala."

103. Conzemius, "Rama-Indianer," 305.

104. Roberts, *Narrative of Voyages*, 111; Holm, "Creole English," 367.

105. Lehmann, *Zentral-Amerika*, 419–20.

106. MNM Bª-XII-Cª-C-n° 2 1783.

107. *BAGG* 7: 119–45 Bishop of Nicaragua 23.9.1801.

108. Stout, *Nicaragua*, 113 and map.

109. Esquemeling, *Buccaneers*, 234. See also Raveneau de Lussan, *Voyage into the South Seas*, 15.

110. Conzemius, *Ethnographical Survey*, 17; Chapman, "Tropical Forest Tribes," 55–57; Helms, *Asang*, 16–19. One eighteenth-century account gives the date of the shipwreck as 1652 (AGI AG 302 Lic. Santaella Melgarejo 3.4.1715).

111. AGI AG 229 Bishop of Nicaragua 30.11.1711.

112. Matson and Swanson, "Hereditary Blood Antigens," 545–57.

113. Heath, "Miskuto Grammar," 49; Lehmann, *Zentral-Amerika*, 462–63. Heath refers to the invaders as Nahautl, but they were clearly the Nicarao.

114. Heath, "Miskuto Grammar," 48; Conzemius, *Ethnographical Survey*, 16–17.

115. Conzemius, "Miskito and Sumu Languages," 59–60, 64, 67; Conzemius, *Ethnographical Survey*, 12–14; Chapman, "Tropical Forest Tribes," 56; Helms, *Asang*, 19.

116. Helms, *Asang*, 19. For a recent detailed analysis of African influences on the Mosquito language see Holm, "Creole English," 314–23.

117. For a full discussion of the derivation of the name Mosquito see Heath, "Miskuto Grammar," 51; Helms, *Asang*, 15–16; Holm, "Creole English," 306–309.

118. *CDHCN*, 12–63 Fiscal 5.6.1713; AGCA A1.17 335 7088 Rivera 23.11.1742.

119. M. W., "Mosqueto Indian," 300.

120. AGI AG 299 Bishop of Nicaragua 30.11.1711; *CDHCN*, 12–63 Fiscal 5.6.1713, AG 449 Díaz Navarro 30.11.1758 written in 1743–44 and accompanying map AGI MP 49 1758; PRO CO 123/1 fols. 55–79 Hodgson 1757; MNM Bª-XI-Cª-B-n°-1 1782; *BAGG* 7: 157–75 President Domas y Valle 5.3.1800.

121. AGCA A1.17 335 7088 Rivera 23.11.1742; AHNM Estado 4227

Fuertes 24.6.1784; Long, *History of Jamaica*, 1: 314; Henderson, *British Settlement*, 177–78.

122. Gámez, *Costa de Mosquitos*, 90, describes their raids on the Matina coast.

123. PRO CO 123/1 fols. 55–79 Hodgson 1757.

124. Long, *History of Jamaica*, 1: 323.

125. For example, PRO CO 123/1 fols. 55–79 Hodgson 1757; Floyd, *Anglo-Spanish Struggle*, 63–64.

126. Roberts, *Narrative of Voyages*, 146–47. The "Kharibees or Caribs" probably refers to the Black Caribs who were transferred to Trujillo from the Bay Islands by the Spaniards at the end of the eighteenth century.

127. The most accessible accounts of present-day ecosystems are geology: Hershey, "Geological Reconnaisance," 493–516; Schuchert, *Historical Geology;* Roberts and Irving, *Mineral Deposits;* West, "Surface Configuration," 33–83; climate: Vivó Escoto, "Climate of Mexico and Central America"; Portig, "Central American Rainfall," 68–90; soils: Pendleton, "Soil Conditions," 403–407; Stevens, "Soils of Middle America," 265–315; vegetation: Lauer, "Klimatische und Planzengeographie," 344–54; Taylor, "Vegetation of Nicaragua," 27–54; general: Wagner, *Nicoya*, 195–200; Denevan, *Upland Pine Forests;* West and Augelli, *Middle America;* Incer, *Nueva geografía.*

128. For example, Oviedo, *Historia general*, 4 lib. 42 caps. 6–10: 398–413.

129. Taylor, "Vegetation of Nicaragua," 43.

130. Pendleton, "Soil Conditions," 406.

131. RAHM CM A/71 29 no. 306 fols. 27–68 Andagoya 1540.

132. *CS,* 1: 446–48 Relación de tierras, costas y puertos . . . Pedrarias Dávila 1529.

133. Stevens, "Soils of Middle America," 309.

134. Vivó Escoto, "Climate of Mexico and Middle America," 214–15.

135. *CS,* 1: 128–33 Pedrarias Dávila April, 1525.

136. AGI PAT 26–17 and *CS,* 1: 89–107 Gil González de Avila 6.3.1524.

137. For descriptions of the species composition of these formations see Denevan, *Upland Pine Forests,* 272–73; Taylor, "Vegetation of Nicaragua," 37–38; Wagner, "Natural Vegetation," 246–47.

138. Taylor, "Vegetation of Nicaragua," 49.

139. Incer, *Nueva geografía,* 159; Healy, *Archaeology of the Rivas Region,* 288–90.

140. Healy, *Archaeology of the Rivas Region,* 287–91.

141. AGI AG 966 census 1581. It is not known what *catalricas* were.

142. Denevan, *Upland Pine Forests,* 260.

143. Ibid., 273.

144. Cook, *Vegetation Affected by Agriculture,* 19–22; Denevan, *Upland Pine Forests,* 300; Taylor, "Vegetation of Nicaragua," 44–48.

145. Denevan, *Upland Pine Forests,* 274; Taylor, "Vegetation of Nicaragua," 47.

146. *CS,* 1: 128–33 Pedrarias Dávila April, 1525. For an early description of the extraction of pine resin see Oviedo, *Historia general,* 1 lib. 6 cap. 16: 177.

147. Incer, *Nueva geografía,* 159.

148. Taylor, "Vegetation of Nicaragua," 49–50; Radell, "Historical Geography," 151–54.

149. West, "Surface Configuration," 81.

150. Nietschmann, *Between Land and Water,* 91.

151. Pendleton, "Soil Conditions," 404–405; Stevens, "Soils of Middle America," 310.

152. Harshberger, *Phytogeographic Survey,* 665; Parsons, "Miskito Pine Savannas," 36–63.

153. Taylor, "Vegetation of Nicaragua," 40–44.

154. For the species composition of the evergreen rain forest see ibid., 35–36.

155. Incer, *Nueva geografía,* 148–52; Nietschmann, *Between Land and Water,* 83.

156. Parsons, "Miskito Pine Savannas," 45–47; Taylor, "Vegetation of Nicaragua," 48–49.

157. Nietschmann, *Between Land and Water,* 85–88.

CHAPTER 3

1. For comments on published sources see chapter 2, nn. 12, 13.

2. Oviedo, *Historia general,* 3 lib. 29 cap. 21:292, 4, lib. 42 cap. 1:365.

3. AGI PAT 26–17 and *CS,* 1:89–107 Gil González de Ávila 6.3.1524; Oviedo, *Historia general,* 4 lib. 42 cap. 11:413.

4. Torquemada, *Monarquía indiana,* 1 lib. 3 cap. 38:329; López de Gómara, *Hispania Victrix,* 282.

5. Oviedo, *Historia general,* 4 lib. 42 cap. 5:391.

6. Ibid. cap. 1:365. The Spaniards adopted the term *cacique* from the Arawak whom they encountered in the Caribbean, and they applied it to anyone who demonstrated authority.

7. *CS,* 1:128–33 and RAHM CM A/77 fols. 140–49 Pedrarias Dávila April, 1525.

8. AGI PAT 26–17 and *CS,* 1:89–107 Gil González de Avila 6.3.1524.

9. Herrera, *Historia general,* 6 dec. 3 lib. 4 cap. 7:393; López de Gómara, *Hispania Victrix,* 282.

10. Herrera, *Historia general,* 6 dec. 3 lib. 4 cap. 7:393; Martyr, *Orbe novo,* 2 dec. 6 lib. 5:227; Oviedo, *Historia general,* 4 lib. 42 cap. 13:427–29.

11. Oviedo, *Historia general,* 4 lib. 42 cap. 1:365, cap. 3:377.

12. Martyr, *Orbe novo,* 2 dec. 6 lib. 5:227; López de Gómara, *Hispania Victrix,* 283.

13. Martyr, *Orbe novo,* 2 dec. 6 caps. 5–6:227–28; Oviedo *Historia general,* 4 lib. 42 cap. 1:364, cap. 2:372. According to Lothrop the term *orchilobos* comes from the Mexican name Huitzilopochtii (Lothrop, *Pottery of Costa Rica,* 1:65). Teoba was probably Oviedo's corruption of the Mexican term *teopan,* meaning 'place of the gods.'

14. RAHM CM A/71 29 no. 306 fols. 27–68 Andagoya 1540; Martyr, *Orbe novo,* 2 dec. 6 lib. 6:228; Oviedo, *Historia general,* 4 lib. 42 cap. 1:364, cap. 3:379.

15. López de Gómara, *Hispania Victrix,* 283.

16. Oviedo, *Historia general,* 4 lib. 42 cap. 5:391.

17. AGI PAT 20–1–3 and *CS,* 1:84–89 Relación del viaje que hizo Gil González de Ávila, n.d. [1522?], PAT 26–17 and *CS,* 1:89–107 Gil González de

Ávila 6.3.1524; Oviedo, *Historia general,* 3 lib. 29 cap. 21:300, 4 lib. 42 cap. 11:417–18.

18. On the basis of data obtained from the sites of San Francisco, between Lake Managua and Lake Nicaragua, and Santa Isabel, about 4 kilometers north of Puerto San Jorge on the west shore of Lake Nicaragua, Wyckoff has suggested that there was an increase in hunting in the Late Polychrome period and a decline in the exploitation of shellfish. Lange suggests, however, that faunal collection methods at both sites may not have been adequate to determine ecological trends (Lange, "Coastal Settlement," 112). Healy maintains that there was a decline in hunting in the Late Polychrome period, possibly owing to the introduction of hunting regulations which restricted exploitation (Healy, *Archaeology of the Rivas Region,* 288–90).

19. Wagner, *Nicoya,* 214–15; Lange, "Northwestern Costa Rica," 48–53; Lange, "Coastal Settlement," 110–13.

20. Martyr, *Orbe novo,* 2 dec. 6 cap. 5:225; Oviedo, *Historia general,* 4 lib. 42 cap. 1:366.

21. López de Gómara, *Hispania Victrix,* 283; Oviedo, *Historia general,* cap. 3:376, 380.

22. Oviedo, *Historia general,* 4 lib. 42 cap. 1:364.

23. Ibid., cap. 3:381.

24. Palerm, "Agricultural Systems," 38.

25. Oviedo, *Historia general,* 3 lib. 29 cap. 21:299. They were also used as oars.

26. Ibid., 1 lib. 7 cap. 1:227–28; Benzoni, *Historia del Nuevo Mundo,* 167.

27. Oviedo, *Historia general,* 1 lib. 7 cap. 1:227, lib. 8 cap. 30:269, 4 lib. 42 cap. 12:423–24.

28. For evidence of the early cultivation of maize in lower Central America see Bartlett, Barghoorn, and Berger, "Fossil Maize," 389–90; Linares, Sheets, and Rosenthal, "Prehistoric Agriculture," 137–45; Snarskis, "Stratigraphic Excavations," 342–53.

29. Oviedo, *Historia general,* 1 lib. 7 cap. 1:229. Present-day yields in Nicoya are between 1:60 and 1:120 (Wagner, *Nicoya,* 217), and the soil there is generally not as fertile as that in Pacific Nicaragua. In the nineteenth century Levy estimated that one *medio* of maize planted in good soil produced 5 to 8 fanegas for the first harvest and 3 to 4 fanegas for the second harvest (Levy, *Notas geográficas,* 459). This gives yields of 1:120–192 and 1:72–96, respectively.

30. Oviedo, *Historia general,* 1 lib. 7 cap. 1:229.

31. Ibid., cap. 18:243–44.

32. Stanislawski, *Transformation of Nicaragua,* 29.

33. Oviedo, *Historia general,* 1 lib. 7 cap. 2:231, 233.

34. Ibid., cap. 4:234.

35. Ibid., 4 lib. 42 cap. 3:375.

36. Ibid., 1 lib. 8 cap. 21:260.

37. Sauer, "Cultivated Plants," 351; Sauer, *Agricultural Origins,* 532.

38. Ponce, *Relación breve,* 351; Oviedo, *Historia general,* 4 lib. 42 cap. 1:385; Sauer, "Cultivated Plants," 532.

39. Sauer, "Cultivated Plants," 530.

40. For accounts of fruit trees see AGI PAT 180–27 and CS, 1:479–508

Castañeda 30.3.1529; Herrera, *Historia general,* 9 dec. 4 lib. 8 cap. 7:127–82; Ponce, *Relación breve,* 351; López de Gómara, *Hispania Victrix,* 282; Vázquez de Espinosa, *Compendium,* 250; Oviedo, *Historia general,* 1 lib. 7 cap. 14: 239–43, lib. 8 caps. 17–22:257–62, cap. 33:273–74, lib. 9 cap. 20:294–95, cap. 23:297, 4 lib. 42 cap. 1:385, cap. 12:423, cap. 13:429.

41. Herrera, *Historia general,* 6 dec. 3 lib. 4 cap. 7:392; López de Gómara, *Hispania Victrix,* 282; Oviedo, *Historia general,* 1 lib. 7 cap. 8:236, lib. 8 cap. 4:251–52, 4 lib. 42 cap. 13:429.

42. Oviedo, *Historia general,* 1 lib. 7 cap. 7:235–36.

43. Ibid., 4 lib. 42 cap. 4:385. *Chocolate* is a Nahuatl word, whereas *cacao* is a Nahua word borrowed from Mixe-Zoque (Campbell and Kaufman, "Linguistic Look at the Olmecs," 84).

44. For a full discussion of cacao cultivation and its socioeconomic significance see Oviedo, *Historia general,* 1 lib. 8 cap. 30:267–71; Millon, "Trade, Tree Cultivation, and the Development of Private Property," 698–712; Thompson, "Notes on the Use of Cacao," 102–106; Benzoni, *Historia del Nuevo Mundo,* 168.

45. AGI AG 162 and *CS,* 11:468–76 Fr. Valdivieso, Bishop of Nicaragua, 15.7.1545 records ". . . aquella provincia no diezman los vecinos del cacao siendo heredamiento." See also Bergmann "Distribution of Cacao," 89–96.

46. *CDI,* 5:522–29 Lic. Carrasco, Bishop elect of Nicaragua, n.d.

47. Oviedo, *Historia general,* 4 lib. 42 cap. 11:416; Benzoni, *Historia del Nuevo Mundo,* 98.

48. Oviedo, *Historia general,* 1 lib. 6 cap. 30:179–80.

49. Lange, "Coastal Settlement," 112–13; Healy, *Archaeology of the Rivas Region,* 288–90.

50. References to animals and birds include Torquemada, *Monarquía indiana,* 1 cap. 29:331; Alcedo, *Diccionario,* 3:322; Oviedo, *Historia general,* 2 lib. 12 caps. 10, 11, 16, 19–21, 23–24:39–49, 3 lib. 29 cap. 21:297–99, 4 lib. 42 cap. 1:364, cap. 3:380.

51. Coe, "Archaeological Investigations in Coastal Guanacaste," 360; Lange, "Coastal Settlement," 113; Healy, *Archaeology of the Rivas Region,* 288–90.

52. Oviedo, *Historia general,* 4 lib. 42 cap. 12:423. For a list of birds that could be hunted for food around Realejo in the eighteenth century see MNM MS 570 fols. 263–79, n.d.

53. RAHM CM A/71 29 no. 306 fols. 27–68 Andagoya 1540; Oviedo, *Historia general,* 2 lib. 10 cap. 10:40, cap. 19:45, 4 lib. 42 cap. 3:380.

54. Oviedo, *Historia general,* 4 lib. 42 cap. 1:365.

55. Ibid., 364.

56. RAHM CM A/71 29 no. 306 fols. 27–68 Andagoya 1540; Oviedo, *Historia general,* 2 lib. 12 cap. 18:45, 4 lib. 42 cap. 3:375, cap. 12:426; Benzoni, *Historia del Nuevo Mundo,* 168.

57. Sauer doubts that dogs were used in hunting, believing that they were kept as pets or for food (Sauer, *Early Spanish Main,* 59).

58. Oviedo, *Historia general,* 4 lib. 42 cap. 1:364, cap. 2:373, cap. 3:377.

59. Herrera, *Historia general,* 6 dec. 3 lib. 4 cap. 7:394; López de Gómara, *Hispania Victrix,* 284.

60. AGI AG 940 Memorial of the life of Don Hurtado y Plaza 15.11.1783;

Ponce, *Relación breve*, 358, 364; Cobo, *Obras*, 2 lib. 7 cap. 38:302; Healy, *Archaeology of the Rivas Region*, 287, 290. For a list of the types of fish caught off the Pacific coast at Realejo, see MNM MS 570 fols. 263–79, n.d.

61. Coe, "Archaeological Investigations in Coastal Guanacaste," 360; Lange, "Northwestern Costa Rica," 51–53. *Spondylus* and *Purpura* mollusks are generally found in deep water, and Healy suggests that a special procurement industry developed on the coast (Healy, *Archaeology of the Rivas Region*, 291).

62. AGI AG 181 Fr. Andrés, Bishop of Nicaragua 15.7.1683; Alcedo, *Diccionario*, 3:370; Juarros, *Statistical and Commercial History*, 72; Oviedo, *Historia general*, 2 lib. 19 cap. 9:204–205, 3 lib. 29 cap. 21:299.

63. Oviedo, *Historia general*, 3 lib. 29 cap. 21:299.

64. Ibid., 4 lib. 42 cap. 12:424; Gerhard, "Shellfish Dye," 179; Lange, "Northwestern Costa Rica," 235–36. Lange suggests that the dye may have been extracted from *Murex* mollusks rather than *Purpura* mollusks.

65. Ponce, *Relación breve*, 375–76.

66. Oviedo, *Historia general*, 3 lib. 29 cap. 21:299.

67. Lange, "Sapoa River Valley," 301; Lange, "Northwestern Costa Rica," 51–53; Healy, *Archaeology of the Rivas Region*, 290.

68. AGI AG 965 Lic. Alvarez de Ortega, Archdean of León, n.d.

69. Lange, "Sapoa River Valley," 261–63; Lange, "Northwestern Costa Rica," 53.

70. RAHM CM A/105 4840 fols. 137–40 Castañeda, Governor of Nicaragua 30.3.1529; AGI AG 162 and *CS* 11:468–76 Fr. Valdivieso, Bishop of Nicaragua 15.7.1545, AG 50 and RAHM CM A/114 4851 Factor y Veedor Arteaga 15.5.1555, AG 168 30.1.1560; Benzoni, *Historia del Nuevo Mundo*, 167.

71. Herrera, *Historia general*, 9 dec. 4 lib. 8 cap. 7:128; Alcedo, *Diccionario*, 3:321; Oviedo, *Historia general*, 2 lib. 10 caps. 2–3:9–13, 4 lib. 42 cap. 12:423, 425.

72. Ponce, *Relación breve*, 352; López de Gómara, *Hispania Victrix*, 281; Oviedo, *Historia general*, 4 lib. 42 cap. 1:364, 366, cap. 12:424.

73. Oviedo, *Historia general*, 1 lib. 8 caps. 5 and 6:252–54, 4 lib. 42 cap. 12:424.

74. RAHM CM A/71 29 no. 306 fols. 27–68 Andagoya 1540; López de Gómara, *Hispania Victrix*, 281; Oviedo, *Historia general*, 4 lib. 42 cap. 1:366.

75. RAHM CM A/71 29 no. 306 fols. 27–68 Andagoya 1540; Ponce, *Relación breve*, 375–76.

76. Oviedo, *Historia general*, 4 lib. 42 cap. 12:425.

77. Ibid.; Ponce, *Relación breve*, 375–76.

78. Oviedo, *Historia general*, 4 lib. 42 cap. 12:425.

79. López de Velasco, *Geografía*, 329.

80. Oviedo, *Historia general*, 3 lib. 28 cap. 21:298, 4 lib. 42 cap. 12:424; Levy, *Notas geográficas*, 9.

81. Martyr, *Orbe novo*, 2 dec. 6 lib. 5–6:227–29; Levy, *Notas geográficas*, 9.

82. Herrera, *Historia general*, 9 dec. 4 lib. 8 cap. 7:126; Alcedo, *Diccionario*, 3:322; Levy, *Notas geográficas*, 9; Oviedo, *Historia general*, 1 lib. 6 cap. 8:165.

83. Martyr, *Orbe novo*, 2 dec. 6 lib. 6:228.

84. AGI PAT 26–17 and *CS*, 1:89–107 Gil González de Ávila 6.3.1524;

Herrera, *Historia general,* 6 dec. 3 lib. 4 caps. 5–6:381–90; Oviedo, *Historia general,* 3 lib. 29 cap. 21:291, 293.

85. Herrera, *Historia general,* 6 dec. 3 lib. 4 cap. 7:393; Martyr, *Orbe novo,* 2 dec. 6 lib. 6:228; López de Gómara, *Hispania Victrix,* 283.

86. Oviedo, *Historia general,* 4 lib. 42 cap. 12:423.

87. Ibid., 4 lib. 42 cap. 1:364, cap. 3:379, cap. 12:423.

88. Ibid., 4 lib. 42 cap. 3:379, cap. 11:420.

89. RAHM CM A/71 29 no. 306 fols. 27–68 Andagoya 1540.

90. Lange, "Coastal Settlement," 110; Healy, *Archaeology of the Rivas Region,* 291.

91. AGI PAT 180–27, RAHM CM A/105 fols. 137–40 and *CS,* 1:479–508 Castañeda 30.3.1529.

92. Herrera, *Historia general,* 9 dec. 3 lib. 4 cap. 7:393; Torquemada, *Monarquía indiana,* 2 lib. 11 cap. 21:346; López de Gómara, *Hispania Victrix,* 283; Oviedo, *Historia general,* 4 lib. 42 cap. 1:364, cap. 12:427. The first two authors distinguish between the two types of government, while the latter two identify them with the Nicarao and the Chorotega.

93. Oviedo, *Historia general,* 1 lib. 8 cap. 30:268, 4 lib. 42 cap. 3:377, cap. 13:428. *Teite* is a corruption of the Nahuatl *teuctli,* meaning "lord" (León-Portilla, *Religión,* 95).

94. López de Gómara, *Hispania Victrix,* 283; Oviedo, *Historia general,* 4 lib. 42 cap. 1:364, cap. 12:427.

95. Oviedo, *Historia general,* 1 lib. 8 cap. 30:267–68, 4 lib. 42 cap. 13:428.

96. Martyr, *Orbe novo,* 2 dec. 6 cap. 5:225; Oviedo, *Historia general,* 4 lib. 42 cap. 13:429.

97. Herrera, *Historia general,* 6 dec. 3 lib. 4 cap. 7:394; López de Gómara, *Hispania Victrix,* 283; Oviedo, *Historia general,* 4 lib. 42 cap. 2:377, cap. 3:379.

98. Oviedo, *Historia general,* 3 lib. 29 cap. 21:295. Another reference to the role of caciques in war by Oviedo denies that they participated (ibid., 4 lib. 42 cap. 3:379).

99. Ibid., 4 lib. 42 cap. 2:372–73.

100. Ibid., cap. 1:365.

101. Ibid.

102. Ibid., cap. 3:377.

103. Ibid., cap. 12:423.

104. Ibid., cap. 1:364–65. Tapaligui corresponds to the Nahuatl *tlapaliuhqui,* meaning "strong and courageous one" (León-Portilla, *Religión,* 100).

105. Oviedo, *Historia general,* 3 lib. 29, cap. 21:295, 4 lib. 42 cap. 3:379.

106. Herrera, *Historia general,* 6 dec. 3 lib. 4 cap. 7:394–95; López de Gómara, *Hispania Victrix,* 283; Oviedo, *Historia general,* 4 lib. 42 cap. 1:364.

107. Oviedo, *Historia general,* 4 lib. 42 cap. 3:379.

108. Ibid., cap. 2:373–74, cap. 3:381.

109. Herrera, *Historia general,* 6 dec. 3 lib. 4 cap. 7:396; López de Gómara, *Hispania Victrix,* 284.

110. Herrera, *Historia general,* 6 dec. 3 lib. 4 cap. 7:396; Martyr, *Orbe novo,* 2 dec. 6 caps. 6–7:228–33; López de Gómara, *Hispania Victrix,* 284; Oviedo, *Historia general,* 4 lib. 42 cap. 1:364, cap. 3:380–81; León-Portilla

(*Religión*, 107) says that the role of confessors was more highly developed there than in central Mexico and suggests that it may have been due to Maya influence.

111. Oviedo, *Historia general*, 1 lib. 8 cap. 30:268, 4 lib. 42 cap. 1:364, cap. 3:377, cap. 12:421.

112. Oviedo, *Historia general*, 1 lib. 8 cap. 30:268. Thompson thinks that this price is an error. For a general description of slavery in pre-Columbian times see Sherman, *Forced Native Labor*, 15–19.

113. Martyr, *Orbe novo*, 2 dec. 6 cap. 6:229; Oviedo, *Historia general*, 4 lib. 42 cap. 1:364, cap. 2:373, cap. 3:379.

114. Herrera, *Historia general*, 6 dec. 3 lib. 4 cap. 7:396; Oviedo, *Historia general*, 4 lib. 42 cap. 3:376–77, cap. 11:420.

115. Martyr, *Orbe novo*, 2 dec. 6 cap. 6:229.

116. López de Gómara, *Hispania Victrix*, 283; Oviedo, *Historia general*, 4 lib. 42 cap. 3:376.

117. López de Gómara, *Hispania Victrix*, 283; Oviedo, *Historia general*, 4 lib. 42 cap. 3:377–78.

118. Herrera, *Historia general*, 6 dec. 3 lib. 4 cap. 7:394; López de Gómara, *Hispania Victrix*, 283; Oviedo, *Historia general*, 4 lib. 42 cap. 3:376–78.

119. AGI AG 966 census 1581.

120. López de Gómara, *Hispania Victrix*, 283; Oviedo, *Historia general* 4 lib. 42 cap. 1:365.

121. Oviedo, *Historia general*, 4 lib. 42 cap. 3:377.

122. López de Gómara, *Hispania Victrix*, 283; Oviedo, *Historia general*, 4 lib. 42 cap. 3:376.

123. RAHM CM A/71 29 no. 306 fols. 27–68 Andagoya 1540.

124. Oviedo, *Historia general*, 4 lib. 42 cap. 3:376.

125. Ibid., cap. 4:385.

126. López de Gómara, *Hispania Victrix*, 283; Oviedo, *Historia general*, 4 lib. 42 cap. 12:421; Stone, "Synthesis," 225.

127. Oviedo, *Historia general*, 4 lib. 42 cap. 3:380; León-Portilla, *Religión*, 107–108.

128. Oviedo, *Historia general*, 4 lib. 42 cap. 2:374–75.

129. Ibid. For archaeological evidence of urn burials see Lothrop, *Pottery of Costa Rica*, 1:96–97; Healy, *Archaeology of the Rivas Region*, 218–19.

130. Oviedo, *Historia general*, 4 lib. 42 cap. 11:415.

131. Ibid., 1 lib. 8 cap. 21:261, 4 lib. 42 cap. 3:378; Thiel, "Población de la República de Costa Rica," 84.

132. Oviedo, *Historia general*, 4 lib. 42 cap. 1:364.

133. López de Gómara, *Hispania Victrix*, 283; Oviedo, *Historia general*, 4 lib. 42 cap. 3:347.

134. Herrera, *Historia general*, 6 dec. 3 lib. 4 cap. 7:394; López de Gómara, *Hispania Victrix*, 283; Oviedo, *Historia general*, 4 lib. 42 cap. 3:379.

135. Herrera, *Historia general*, 6 dec. 3 lib. 4 cap. 7:395; Oviedo, *Historia general*, 4 lib. 42 cap. 3:379.

136. AGI PAT 26–17 and *CS*, 1:89–107 Gil González de Ávila 6.3.1524; Martyr, *Orbe novo*, 2 dec. 6 cap. 5:227; Oviedo, *Historia general*, 4 lib. 42 cap. 3:378.

137. Oviedo, *Historia general*, 4 lib. 42 cap. 1:364.

138. Ibid., cap. 2:367–75. Many of these gods have Mexican affiliations (Lothrop, *Pottery of Costa Rica*, 1:65–70; León-Portilla, *Religión*, 63–72).

139. Oviedo, *Historia general*, 4 lib. 42 cap. 1:364–65, cap. 3:378, 380, cap. 11:413.

140. Ibid., cap. 11:421.

141. Martyr, *Orbe novo*, 2 dec. 6 cap. 7:231.

142. Oviedo, *Historia general*, 4 lib. 42 cap. 3:380.

143. Martyr, *Orbe novo*, 2 dec. 6 cap. 6:229.

144. Oviedo, *Historia general*, 4 lib. 42 cap. 2:372–73; Herrera, *Historia general*, 6 dec. 3 lib. 4 cap. 7:396; Martyr, *Orbe novo*, 2 dec. 6 cap. 6:229, López de Gómara, *Hispania Victrix*, 284.

145. Hererra, *Historia general*, 6 dec. 3 lib. 4 cap. 7:396–97; Martyr, *Orbe novo*, 2 dec. 6 cap. 7:229–30; López de Gómara, *Hispania Victrix*, 284.

146. Martyr, *Orbe novo*, 2 dec. 6 cap. 7:231–32.

147. Oviedo, *Historia general*, 4 lib. 42 caps. 2–3:373, 378.

148. León-Portilla, *Religión*, 87. The names of the twenty days correspond to those of the Nahua calendar.

149. Herrera, *Historia general*, 6 dec. 3 lib. 4 cap. 7:396–97; López de Gómara, *Hispania Victrix*, 284.

150. Oviedo, *Historia general*, 4 lib. 42 cap. 3:378.

151. Ibid.; León-Portilla, *Religión*, 56–57, 78–79.

152. Lothrop, *Pottery of Costa Rica*, 1:76.

153. Oviedo, *Historia general*, 4 lib. 42 cap. 11:430.

154. López de Gómara, *Hispania Victrix*, 284.

155. Oviedo, *Historia general*, 4 lib. 42 cap. 2:367–71.

156. León-Portilla, *Religión*, 72–73.

157. Martyr, *Orbe novo*, 2 dec. 6 cap. 6:229; Oviedo, *Historia general*, 4 lib. 42 cap. 2:368–75; León-Portilla, *Religión*, 82–84. *Yulio* may be the equivalent of the Nahuatl *yollotl*, meaning "heart" (León-Portilla, *Filosofía náhuatl*, 345.

158. Herrera, *Historia general*, 6 dec. 3 lib. 4 cap. 7:395; López de Gómara, *Hispania Victrix*, 283; Oviedo, *Historia general*, 4 lib. 42 cap. 1:365, cap. 11:420–21, cap. 12:426.

159. Oviedo, *Historia general*, 4 lib. 42 cap. 11:421.

160. Ibid., cap. 11:419.

161. AGI PAT 26–17 and *CS*, 1–89–107 Gil González de Ávila 6.3.1524; Herrera, *Historia general*, 6 dec. 3 lib. 4 caps. 5–6:381–90; López de Gómara, *Hispania Victrix*, 281; Oviedo, *Historia general*, 3 lib. 29 cap. 21:291, 300.

162. Oviedo, *Historia general*, 3 lib. 20 cap. 21:300. Although Oviedo specifically states that the Chorotega called their temples *teyopas*, he was probably mistaken, since the term *teyopa* is likely to have been derived from the Mexican *teopan* (See n. 13).

163. Ibid., 4 lib. 42 cap. 11:417–18. Stone ("Synthesis," 230) notes that this game is played annually by the Guatuso and that it may have been derived from the Corobici.

164. Oviedo, *Historia general*, 4 lib. 42 cap. 11:418.

165. RAHM CM A/71 29 no. 306 fols. 27–68 Andagoya 1540; Oviedo, *Historia general*, 4 lib. 42 cap. 5:397.

CHAPTER 4

1. Chapman, "Tropical Forest Tribes," 94.

2. AGI AG 233 Fr. Pedro de la Concepción 13.1.1699, AG 371 Fr. Ximénez 9.9.1748; Vázquez, *Crónica,* 4:113–43.

3. Magnus, "Prehistoric and Modern Subsistence Patterns," 72–97; Helms, "Coastal Adaptations," 130.

4. Peralta, *Costa Rica,* 728–40, ref. to p. 734, n.d.

5. AGCA A1.12 78 646, n.d.

6. M. W., "Mosqueto Indian," 301.

7. For example, *CDHCN,* 12–83 Aranzibia, Governor of Nicaragua, 14.1.1715; *BAGG* 7:157–75 President Domas y Valle 5.3.1800, *BAGG* 7: 119–45 Instancia presentada por el Fiscal . . . 23.9.1801; Termer, "Habitación rural," 398–99.

8. Young, *Residence on the Mosquito Shore,* 98; Wickham, *Journey Among the Woolwa,* 162–63; Wickham, "Notes on the Soumoo," 199; Conzemius, *Ethnographical Survey,* 31–32.

9. Wickham, *Journey Among the Woolwa,* 162–63.

10. M. W., "Mosqueto Indian," 301, 307; Strangeways, *Sketch of the Mosquito Shore,* 334; Young, *Residence of the Mosquito Shore,* 98; Cotheal, "Grammatical Sketch," 238; Wickham, "Notes on a Journey," 59; Wickham, *Journey Among the Woolwa,* 162–63; Wickham, "Notes on the Soumoo," 199; Bell, *Tangweera,* 84.

11. Strangeways, *Sketch of the Mosquito Shore,* 335; Young, *Residence on the Mosquito Shore,* 14; Pim and Seeman, *Dottings on the Roadside,* 415; *Límites,* 172 (1882); Conzemius, *Ethnographical Survey,* 32; Raveneau de Lussan, *Voyage into the South Seas,* 287.

12. AGI AG 174 Mercedarian friars 15.8.1608, AG 371 Fr. Ximénez 9.9.1748; Vázquez, *Crónica,* 4:113–14; Conzemius, *Ethnographical Survey,* 30.

13. For descriptions of the economies of different Indian groups see AGI AG 371 Fr. Ximénez 9.9.1748; Vázquez, *Crónica,* 4:114 (Sumu or Matagalpa); AGI AG 174 Mercedarian friars 15.8.1608 (Sumu); AGI AG 940 Memorial of the life of Don Hurtado y Plaza 1783 (Matagalpa). For archaeological evidence of the economy of Indian groups inhabiting the Mosquito Coast see Magnus, "Prehistoric and Modern Subsistence Patterns." For descriptions of the Mosquito economy see *CDHCN,* 12–63 Fiscal to Bishop of Nicaragua 5.6.1713; PRO CO 123/1 fols. 55–79 Hodgson 1757; M. W., "Mosqueto Indian," 300–301, 307–12; Esquemeling, *Buccaneers,* 235; Raveneau de Lussan, *Voyage into the South Seas,* 285–87; Dampier, *New Voyage,* 16–17.

14. This is the case among the Mosquito of Asang and Tasbapauni today (Helms, *Asang,* 129; Nietschmann, *Between Land and Water,* 133).

15. For a general description of the cycle of shifting cultivation see Palerm, "Agricultural Systems," 29–34.

16. Nietschmann, *Between Land and Water,* 149.

17. Ibid., 84, 132, 145. He notes that among the Mosquito of Tasbapauni the maximum distance that plots are located for attendance by people traveling on foot is 6 miles and by canoe 10 to 15 miles if no overnight stop is to be involved. They do, however, possess plots 20 to 30 miles away.

18. *BAGG* 6:274–86 Porta Costas 1.8.1790.

19. Roberts, *Narrative of Voyages*, 115, 150.

20. Magnus, "Prehistoric and Modern Subsistence Patterns."

21. For example, PRO CO 123/1 fols. 55–79 Hodgson 1757.

22. Carneiro, "Slash and Burn Agriculture," 231–33.

33. Leeds, "Yaruro Incipient Tropical Forest Horticulture," 20.

24. Nietschmann, *Between Land and Water*, 134, 148.

25. Dampier, *New Voyage*, 16.

26. Helms, *Asang*, 125.

27. Esquemeling, *Buccaneers*, 235. Conzemius (*Ethnographical Survey*, 62) suggests that racoven were bananas; *ananas* was the Spanish name for pineapples.

28. PRO CO 123/1 fols. 55–79 Hodgson 1757.

29. AGI AG 940 Memorial of the life of Don Hurtado y Plaza 15.11.1783.

30. Sauer, *Agricultural Origins*, 40–48; Harris, "Agricultural Systems," 3–15; Lathrap, *Upper Amazon*, 47–60; Helms, *Asang*, 24–27.

31. Chapman, "Tropical Forest Tribes," 165.

32. Ibid., 165–66; Magnus, "Prehistory of the Miskito Coast," 216–18; Helms, *Middle America*, 117–18.

33. AGCA A1.12 77 623 13.4.1627.

34. Helms, *Middle America*, 119.

35. Roberts, *Narrative of Voyages*, 115; Heath, "Miskuto Grammar," 50; Conzemius, *Ethnographical Survey*, 61–62.

36. Sauer, "Cultivated Plants," 527; Smole, "*Musa* Cultivation," 47–50.

37. Oviedo, *Historia general*, 1 lib. 8 cap. 1:247–48.

38. Ponce, *Relación breve*, 351.

39. To the extent that Conzemius noted that the Rama call plantains *sumu* (Conzemius, "Rama-Indianer," 311).

40. AGI AG 174 Mercedarian friars 15.8.1608.

41. Esquemeling, *Buccaneers*, 235. For other accounts of *mishla* preparation see Raveneau de Lussan, *Voyage into the South Seas*, 285; M. W., "Mosqueto Indian," 307.

42. *CS*, 6:75–88, and Peralta, *Costa Rica*, 728–400, on the expedition of Calero and Machuca, n.d. (the expedition took place in 1539).

43. M. W., "Mosqueto Indian," 310.

44. PRO CO 123/1 fols. 55–79 Hodgson 1757.

45. Sauer, "Cultivated Plants," 508. The sweet variety is more tolerant of severe dry periods and lower temperatures than is the bitter variety.

46. Chapman, "Tropical Forest Tribes," 162–66. Purseglove (*Tropical Crops*, 173) is of the same opinion.

47. Sauer, "Cultivated Plants," 507–508.

48. AGI AG 966 census 19.12.1581; Martyr, *Orbe novo*, 1 dec. 3 lib. 4:318; Patiño, *Plantas cultivadas*, 2:62.

49. Sauer, "Cultivated Plants," 511; Conzemius, *Ethnographical Survey*, 62–63. They do, however, refer to a semiwild variety of yam as *usi*.

50. PRO CO 123/1 fols. 55–79 Hodgson 1757.

51. Conzemius, *Ethnographical Survey*, 62.

52. Helms, *Asang*, 142; Nietschmann, *Between Land and Water*, 149.

53. Sauer, "Cultivated Plants," 525.

54. AGI AG 940 Memorial of the life of Don Hurtado y Plaza 15.11.1783; M. W., "Mosqueto Indian," 310; Raveneau de Lussan, *Voyage to the South Seas,* 285.

55. Evidence for maize grown by the Sumu, see *CS,* 6:75–88, and Peralta, *Costa Rica,* 728–40, on the expedition of Calero and Machuca 1539; AGCA A1.12 77 635 1731; maize grown by the Sumu and Matagalpa, AGI AG 223 Fr. Pedro de la Concepción 13.1.1699, AGCA A3.16 501 3870 Pueblo of Santiago de Boaco 1.5.1750; Vázquez, *Crónica* 4:114; maize grown by the Matagalpa, *CDHCN,* 131–34 Villa of Nueva Segovia 20.10.1664; *BAGG* 5:214–36 Informe relativo a que 47 indios caribes de la provincia de Matagalpa . . . 14.11.1768.

56. *CDHCN,* 12–63 Fiscal in Madrid 5.6.1713; PRO CO 123/1 fols. 55–79 Hodgson 1757; M. W., "Mosqueto Indian," 308, 310; Raveneau de Lussan, *Voyage to the South Seas,* 285. Exquemelin and Dampier do not mention the cultivation of maize.

57. Magnus, "Prehistoric and Modern Subsistence Patterns." For additional archaeological evidence of mortars and grindstones see Stone, *Central and Southern Honduras,* 79–81. Among the Sumu or Matagalpa, women were buried with their grindstones (AGI AG 223 Fr. Pedro de la Concepción 13.1.1699).

58. Stone, "Synthesis," 219.

59. AGI AG 371 Fr. Ximénez 9.9.1748; Vázquez, *Crónica,* 4:114.

60. AGCA A1.12 77 635 1731; Dampier, *New Voyage,* 16.

61. Helms, *Asang,* 128; Nietschmann, *Between Land and Water,* 105.

62. *CS,* 6:75–88 and Peralta, *Costa Rica,* 728–40 on the expedition of Calero and Machuca 1539; M. W., "Mosqueto Indian," 308, 310; Esquemeling, *Buccaneers,* 114; Dampier, *New Voyage,* 16. Pineapples were also grown in Nueva Segovia (AGI AG 966 census 19.12.1581).

63. Sauer, "Cultivated Plants," 533–35; Mangelsdorf, MacNeish, and Willey, "Origins of Agriculture," 439–40.

64. AGI AG 966 census 19.12.1581; M. W., "Mosqueto Indian," 307–308; Esquemeling, *Buccaneers,* 235. The Mosquito also made cotton bedclothes.

65. AGI AG 371 Fr. Ximénez 9.9.1748; Vázquez, *Crónica,* 4:114. It was probably smoked and used to drive out evil spirits, as noted in more recent ethnographic accounts (Wickham, "Notes on the Soumoo," 206; Conzemius, *Ethnographical Survey,* 91).

66. AGI AG 12 Criado de Castilla 30.11.1608.

67. AGCA A1.12 77 635 1731.

68. Chapman, "Tropical Forest Tribes," 100.

69. Roberts, *Narrative of Voyages,* 150. For more recent accounts of hunting among Indian groups see Henderson, *British Settlement,* 180; Young, *Residence on the Mosquito Shore,* 102–105; Fröebel, *Seven Years' Travel,* 132; Pim and Seeman, *Dottings on the Roadside,* 418; Squier, *Adventures,* 128–29; Wickham, "Notes on the Soumoo," 203; Bell, *Tangweera,* 159, 232; Conzemius, "Rama-Indianer," 314; Conzemius, *Ethnographical Survey,* 73–81; Helms, *Asang,* 115–17; Nietschmann, "Hunting and Fishing Focus," 50–54; Nietschmann, *Between Land and Water,* 152–80.

70. Magnus, "Prehistoric and Modern Subsistence Patterns."

71. AGI AG 966 census 19.12.1581, AG 223 Fr. Pedro de la Concepción 13.1.1699; M. W., "Mosqueto Indian," 310–11; PRO CO 123/1 fols. 55–79 Hodgson 1757; AGI AG 940 Memorial of the life of Don Hurtado y Plaza 15.11.1783; Dampier, *New Voyage*, 16, 36; Anon., "Mosquito Country," 421 (1781).

72. AGI AG 966 census 19.12.1581, AG 223 Fr. Pedro de la Concepción 13.1.1699; M. W., "Mosqueto Country," 421 (1781); Dampier, *New Voyage*, 36.

73. Esquemeling, *Buccaneers*, 237.

74. Young, *Residence on the Mosquito Shore*, 104; Bell, *Tangweera*, 246; Nietschmann, *Between Land and Water*, 162.

75. AGI AG 299 Bishop of Nicaragua 30.11.1711, AG 371 Fr. Ximénez 9.9.1748; BNM 18740[44] Diario del viaje . . . 18.3.1781; AGI AG 940 Memorial of the life of Don Hurtado y Plaza 15.11.1783. For more recent accounts of hunting equipment see references in n. 69.

76. Conzemius, *Ethnographical Survey*, 60.

77. M. W., "Mosqueto Indian," 311.

78. AGI AG 371 Fr. Ximénez 9.9.1748; M. W., "Mosqueto Indian," 305; Esquemeling, *Buccaneers*, 114; Vázquez, *Crónica*, 4:123–24.

79. Magnus, "Prehistoric and Modern Subsistence Patterns," 78–79. For recent accounts of fishing see Strangeways, *Sketch of the Mosquito Shore*, 30, 36–42, 50, 83, 85–86; Roberts, *Narrative of Voyages*, 93–94, 97, 100, 119–20, 156; Young, *Residence on the Mosquito Shore*, 11, 17, 21–22, 46–47, 59, 87; Anon., *Bericht über das Mosquitoland*, 129–30; Fröebel, *Seven Years' Travel*, 132; Pim and Seeman, *Dottings on the Roadside*, 402–404; Wickham, *Journey Among the Woolwa*, 179; Squier, *Adventures*, 58, 100–19, 131–37, 185, 244; Wickham, "Notes on the Soumoo," 202, 206; Conzemius, "Rama-Indianer," 312–14; Conzemius, *Ethnographical Survey*, 40, 65–72; Craig, *Fishing in British Honduras;* Helms, *Asang*, 117–18; Nietschmann, *Between Land and Water*, 152–80.

80. AGI AG 449 Díaz Navarro 1743–44; M. W., "Mosqueto Indian," 301; Anon., "Mosquito Country," 420 (1781).

81. Oviedo, *Historia general*, 2 lib. 13 cap. 8:63; M. W., "Mosqueto Indian," 312; PRO CO 123/1 fols. 55–79 Hodgson 1757; Long, *History of Jamaica*, 1:326; BAGG 7:157–75 President Domas y Valle 5.3.1800; Strangeways, *Sketch of the Mosquito Shore*, 217–20; Anon., "Mosquito Country," 420 (1781); Esquemeling, *Buccaneers*, 235; Dampier, *New Voyage*, 34–36; Nietschmann, *Between Land and Water*, 93–95, 123–26. For a recent account of the characteristics and development of the turtle-fishing industry on the Mosquito coast see Parsons, *Green Turtle*, 30–34.

82. Nietschmann, *Between Land and Water*, 165.

83. Magnus, "Prehistoric and Modern Subsistence Patterns," 67–76.

84. Oviedo, *Historia general*, 2 lib. 13 cap. 9:64; M. W., "Mosqueto Indian," 312; PRO CO 123/1 fols. 55–79 Hodgson 1757; Strangeways, *Sketch of the Mosquito Shore*, 337; Esquemeling, *Buccaneers*, 234; Dampier, *New Voyage*, 32, 34–6. Dampier in particular gives a very detailed account of the techniques used in catching manatee.

85. Roberts, *Narrative of Voyages*, 97; Squier, *Adventures*, 137.

86. Magnus, "Prehistoric and Modern Subsistence Patterns," 70–73.

87. M. W., "Mosqueto Indian," 312; PRO CO 123/1 fols. 55–79 Hodgson 1757; Strangeways, *Sketch of the Mosquito Shore,* 208–17.

88. For accounts of present-day fishing in the Atlantic waters of Nicaragua and neighboring areas see Collier, "American Mediterranean," 122–42; Hubbs and Roden, "Oceanography," 143–86; Stuart, "Fauna of Middle America," 332–35; Craig, *Fishing in British Honduras;* Incer, *Nueva geografía,* 177–80.

89. Nietschmann, *Between Land and Water,* 118–22, 160.

90. *CS,* 6:75–88, and Peralta, *Costa Rica,* 728–40, on the expedition of Calero and Machuca 1539; *BAGG* 5:214–36 Informe relativo a que 47 indios caribes de la provincia de Matagalpa . . . 1768; M. W., "Mosqueto Indian," 301; PRO CO 123/1 fols. 55–79 Hodgson 1757; Strangeways, *Sketch of the Mosquito Shore,* 335; Dampier, *New Voyage,* 15–17, 32–37.

91. But they were used by Indians just to the north in Honduras (Squier, *Adventures,* 301–302; Conzemius, "Rama-Indianer," 290; Conzemius, *Ethnographical Survey,* 70; Von Hagen, "The Jicaque," 52–53.

92. AGI AG 299 Bishop of Nicaragua 30.11.1711; M. W., "Mosqueto Indian," 307; PRO CO 123/1 fols. 55–79 Hodgson 1757; AGCA A1.17 4501 38303 and *BAGG* 6:274–86 Porta Costas 1.8.1790; Strangeways, *Sketch of the Mosquito Shore,* 70–71, 90–92; Dampier, *New Voyage,* 17, 32–35.

93. Magnus, "Prehistoric and Modern Subsistence Patterns," 68–76.

94. PRO CO 123/1 fols. 55–79 Hodgson 1757; AGCA A1.17 4501 38303 and *BAGG* 6:274–86 Porta Costas 1.8.1790; Edwards, "British Settlements," 208 (1773); Anon., "Mosquito Country," 421–22 (1781); Esquemeling, *Buccaneers,* 235.

95. For the role of collecting in the economy of the Sumu and Matagalpa see AGI AG 223 Fr. Pedro de la Concepción 13.1.1699, AG 371 Fr. Ximénez 9.9.1748; Vázquez, *Crónica,* 4:114; and, for the Mosquito, AGCA A1.17 4501 38303 and *BAGG* 6:274–86 Porta Costas 1.8.1790. For wild fruits most commonly exploited by the Mosquito today see Conzemius, *Ethnographical Survey,* 90–91; Nietschmann, *Between Land and Water,* 251–52.

96. AGI AG 966 census 19.12.1581; Vázquez de Espinosa, *Compendium,* 244, 246; M. W., "Mosqueto Indian," 300, 308; Conzemius, *Ethnographical Survey,* 58.

97. AGI AG 371 Fr. Ximénez 9.9.1748.

98. M. W., "Mosqueto Indian," 302.

99. AGCA A1.17 4501 38303 and *BAGG* 6:274–86 Porta Costas 1.8.1790; M. W., "Mosqueto Indian," 300; PRO CO 123/1 fols. 55–79 Hodgson 1757.

100. AGI AG 223 Fr. Pedro de la Concepción 13.1.1699, AG 371 Fr. Ximénez 9.9.1748; M. W., "Mosqueto Indian," 307; Esquemeling, *Buccaneers,* 234.

101. PRO CO 123/1 fols. 55–79 Hodgson 1757; Dampier, *New Voyage,* 35; Patiño, *Plantas cultivadas,* 3:26.

102. Conzemius, *Ethnographical Survey,* 52; Chapman, "Tropical Forest Tribes," 112. It is considered to be more highly developed among the Mosquito than among the Sumu or the Rama (Harrower, "Rama, Mosquito, and Sumu," 46).

103. PRO CO 123/1 fols. 55–79 Hodgson 1757; Strangeways, *Sketch of the Mosquito Shore,* 335; Conzemius, *Ethnographical Survey,* 40, 42–44, 48–50.

104. Wickham, "Notes on the Soumoo," 207; Harrower, "Rama, Mosquito, and Sumu," 47; Conzemius, *Ethnographical Survey,* 40, 48; Palmer, *Through Unknown Nicaragua,* 45.

105. Conzemius, *Ethnographical Survey,* 42–44; Kirchhoff, "Caribbean Lowland Tribes," 223–24.

106. Wickham, "Notes on the Soumoo," 207; Conzemius, *Ethnographical Survey,* 41–42.

107. M. W., "Mosqueto Indian," 304.

108. Conzemius, *Ethnographical Survey,* 40.

109. Chapman, "Tropical Forest Tribes," 117.

110. AGI AG 49 Barrientos 25.7.1534; Vásquez de Espinosa, 247.

111. Conzemius, *Ethnographical Survey,* 41.

112. Sloane, *Voyage to the Islands,* lxxvii; Juarros, *Statistical and Commercial History,* 363; Levy, *Notas geográficas,* 295; Squier, *Adventures,* 202; Wickham, "Notes on the Soumoo," 201; Esquemeling, *Buccaneers,* 234; Dampier, *New Voyage,* 17.

113. PRO CO 123/1 fols. 55–79 Hodgson 1757.

114. Juarros, *Statistical and Commercial History,* 363.

115. Henderson, *British Settlement,* 186–87; Strangeways, *Sketch of the Mosquito Shore,* 331; Roberts, *Narrative of Voyages,* 267; Squier, *Adventures,* 231, 251–55; Bell, *Tangweera,* 97; Conzemius, *Ethnographical Survey,* 101, 123, 139–42; Landero "Taoajkas," 46–8; Dampier, *New Voyage,* 16.

116. AGI AG 12 and *CDHCN,* 92–122 President Criado de Castilla 30.11.1608; M. W., "Mosqueto Indian," 301, 307; Conzemius, *Ethnographical Survey,* 81.

117. Levy, *Notas geográficas,* 295.

118. Wickham, *Journey Among the Woolwa,* 162; Levy, *Notas geográficas,* 295; Conzemius, *Ethnographical Survey,* 102–103; Dampier, *New Voyage,* 17.

119. Chagnon, "Yanomamö Social Organization," 112.

120. M. W., "Mosqueto Indian," 302, 304; Long, *History of Jamaica,* 1:323, 326–27; Levy, *Notas geográficas,* 295; Conzemius, *Ethnographical Survey,* 81–87.

121. AGI AG 223 and 297 Fr. Pedro de la Concepción 13.1.1699; Dampier, *New Voyage,* 17.

122. Collinson, "Indians of the Mosquito Territory," 153; Wickham, "Notes on the Soumoo," 201; Conzemius, *Ethnographical Survey,* 146.

123. Conzemius, *Ethnographical Survey,* 81–82.

124. AGI AG 940 Memorial of the life of Don Hurtado y Plaza 15.11.1783; Esquemeling, *Buccaneers,* 235; Conzemius, *Ethnographical Survey,* 81; Dampier, *New Voyage,* 17.

125. AGI AG 371 Fr. Ximénez 9.9.1748.

126. Henderson, *British Settlement,* 188; Young, *Residence on the Mosquito Shore,* 75, 98; Pim and Seeman, *Dottings on the Roadside,* 302; Conzemius, *Ethnographical Survey,* 150–51; Landero, "Taoajkas," 46. Conzemius observed traces of the couvade among the Sumu and the Mosquito.

127. Young, *Residence on the Mosquito Shore,* 75; Squier, *Adventures,* 243.

128. M. W., "Mosqueto Indian," 304; Wickham, "Notes on a Journey," 58–59; Wickham, *Journey Among the Woolwa,* 161; Wickham, "Notes on the Soumoo," 200–201; Conzemius, *Ethnographical Survey,* 146.

129. AGCA A1.12 5802 48962 Mercedarian friars 1610; *CDHCN*, 12–63 Aranzibia, Governor of Nicaragua 14.1.1715; AGI AG 371 Fr. Ximénez 9.9.1748; Strangeways, *Sketch of the Mosquito Shore*, 187–88; Fröebel, *Seven Years' Travel*, 137; Wickham, "Notes on the Soumoo," 205; Squier, *Adventures*, 202.

130. Conzemius, *Ethnographical Survey*, 146–47.

131. M. W., "Mosqueto Indian," 309; Esquemeling, *Buccaneers*, 236–37; Conzemius, *Ethnographical Survey*, 145.

132. M. W., "Mosqueto Indian," 309; Young, *Residence on the Mosquito Shore*, 98; Squier, *Adventures*, 203, 297; Bell, *Tangweera*, 88; Esquemeling, *Buccaneers*, 236–37; Dampier, *New Voyage*, 16.

133. Pim and Seeman, *Dottings on the Roadside*, 307.

134. Helms, "Matrilocality," 197–212; Helms, *Asang*, 24–27; Helms and Loveland, eds., *Frontier Adaptations*, 14.

135. Bell, *Tangweera*, 86–87; Conzemius, *Ethnographical Survey*, 150.

136. Pim and Seeman, *Dottings on the Roadside*, 126.

137. M. W., "Mosqueto Indian," 309; Young, *Residence on the Mosquito Shore*, 30; Fröbel, *Seven Years' Travel*, 137; Pim and Seeman, *Dottings on the Roadside*, 307–308; Squier, *Adventures*, 68; Wickham, "Notes on a Journey," 68; Wickham, "Notes on the Soumoo," 207; Bell, *Tangweera*, 89; Conzemius, *Ethnographical Survey*, 155–56.

138. Esquemeling, *Buccaneers*, 237.

139. M. W., "Mosqueto Indian," 309; Fröebel, *Seven Years' Travel*, 137; Pim and Seeman, *Dottings on the Roadside*, 308; Wickham, "Notes on the Soumoo," 207; Bell, *Tangweera*, 95; Conzemius, *Ethnographical Survey*, 153–55.

140. M. W., "Mosqueto Indian," 308; Roberts, *Narrative of Voyages*, 128–30; Young, *Residence on the Mosquito Shore*, 30–31; Pim and Seeman, *Dottings on the Roadside*, 306, 405; Wickham, "Notes on a Journey," 60; Wickham, *Journey Among the Woolwa*, 189; Wickham, "Notes on the Soumoo," 201–203; Squier, *Adventures*, 203–11; Bell, *Tangweera*, 89–96; Esquemeling, *Buccaneers*, 235–36; Conzemius, *Ethnographical Survey*, 99; Dampier, *New Voyage*, 17. Squier in particular gives a long description of a marriage ceremony at which *mishla* was consumed.

141. AGCA A1.12 5802 48962 Mercedarian friars 1610, A1.12 78 646, n.d.; Serrano y Sanz, *Relaciones históricas*, 285–328 Varias noticias del Río de San Juan 1791–1804; M. W., "Mosqueto Indian," 309; Henderson, *British Settlement*, 186; Strangeways, *Sketch of the Mosquito Shore*, 331; Levy, *Notas geográficas*, 296; Wickham, "Notes on the Soumoo," 207; Esquemeling, *Buccaneers*, 235.

142. Conzemius, "Rama-Indianer," 325; Conzemius, *Ethnographical Survey*, 126; Chapman, "Tropical Forest Tribes," 140.

143. AGI AG 223 and 297 Fr. Pedro de la Concepción 13.1.1699. Elements of this account appear in a legend recorded by Grossman at the beginning of this century (Conzemius, *Ethnographical Survey*, 127, 130).

144. Conzemius, *Ethnographical Survey*, 126.

145. Heath, "Miskuto Grammar," 48.

146. Henderson, *British Settlement of Honduras*, 186; Strangeways, *Sketch of the Mosquito Shore*, 331; Roberts, *Narrative of Voyages*, 267; Cotheal, "Grammatical Sketch," 238; Levy, *Notas geográficas*, 296; Squier, *Adventures*, 243;

Límites, 177, 182; Conzemius, "Rama-Indianer," 325; Conzemius, *Ethnographical Survey,* 127–28; Landero, "Taoajkas," 47; Dampier, *New Voyage,* 16.

147. Conzemius, "Rama-Indianer," 326; Conzemius, *Ethnographical Survey,* 128.

148. Pim and Seeman, *Dottings on the Roadside,* 401; Conzemius, *Ethnographical Survey,* 132–34, 165–70. Stories told by the Rama today surrounding the tapir and manatee have been related by Loveland (Loveland, "Tapirs and Manatees," 67–83).

149. Wickham, "Notes on the Soumoo," 207; Conzemius, *Ethnographical Survey,* 128, 132–35.

150. Conzemius, *Ethnographical Survey,* 140–42.

151. AGI AG 223 and 297 Fr. Pedro de la Concepción 13.1.1699; M. W., "Mosqueto Indian," 309; Stout, *Nicaragua,* 184; Conzemius, "Rama-Indianer," 323; Conzemius, *Ethnographical Survey,* 155.

152. AGI AG 223 and 297 Fr. Pedro de la Concepción 13.1.1699.

153. W. M., "Mosqueto Indian," 305; Esquemeling, *Buccaneers,* 114; Conzemius, *Ethnographical Survey,* 85, 89; Chapman, "Tropical Forest Tribes," 145.

154. Cockburn, *Journey Overland,* 237.

CHAPTER 5

1. An earlier version of this chapter has been published as "Depopulation of Nicaragua," 254–59.

2. Kroeber, *Cultural and Natural Areas,* 166; Dobyns, "Estimating Aboriginal American Population," 415.

3. Steward, ed., *Comparative Ethnology,* 664.

4. Rosenblat, *Población indígena,* 1:102.

5. Sapper, "Die Zahl und die Volksdichte," 100.

6. Dobyns, "Estimating Aboriginal American Population," 415.

7. Radell, "Indian Slave Trade," 67, 75.

8. Denevan, ed., *Native Population,* 291. His estimates for the Central American countries are: Guatemala, 2,000,000; Honduras and Belize, 750,000; El Salvador, 500,000; Nicaragua, 1,000,000; Costa Rica, 400,000; and Panama, 1,000,000.

9. For a full discussion of the volume of the Indian slave trade see Sherman, *Forced Native Labor,* 74–82. See also chap. 6.

10. Sherman, *Forced Native Labor,* 4–5.

11. MacLeod, *Spanish Central America,* 52.

12. Las Casas, *Breve relación,* 43–45.

13. Motolinía, *Memoriales,* 197.

14. AGI AG 9, *CDI,* 24:397–420 and RAHM CM A/110 4845 fols. 224–26 Herrera 24.12.1544.

15. Sherman, *Forced Native Labor,* 78.

16. See chap. 6.

17. See chap. 3.

18. AGI PAT 20-1-3 and *CS,* 1:84–89 Relación del viaje . . . , n.d. [1522?], PAT 26-17 and *CS,* 1:26–107 Gil González Dávila 6.3.1524; *CS,* 1:107–109 and BNM 13,020 fols. 209–10v. Gil González Dávila 8.3.1524. Figures for the

numbers of Indians baptized who were vassals of different caciques were as follows: Chorotega, 487; Nicoya, 6,063; Papagayo, 137; Isla de Chira, 713; Sabdni, not given; Nicaragua, 9,018; Chomi, not given—Indians fled; Corevisi, 210; Denochari Province, 12,608; Pocosi, not given; Diria, 150; Paro, 1,016; Nampiapi, 6; Canjen, 1,118; Orosi, 134. When Castañeda visited Nicoya in 1529, he found that Nicoya had 2,000 able-bodied males as subjects; Chira, 400; Corobeci, 200; Orotiña, 200; and Cangen, 200 (AGI PAT 180–27 and *CS*, 1:479–508 Castañeda 30.3.1529).

19. Oviedo, *Historia general*, 4 lib. 42 cap. 3:382–83.

20. Ibid., 4 lib. 42 cap. 2:366–67, cap. 4:385.

21. Borah and Cook, *Aboriginal Population*, 91.

22. Palerm, "Agricultural Systems," 38.

23. Clark and Haswell, *Economics of Subsistence Agriculture*, 37.

24. Incer, *Nueva geografía*, 419. The distribution of land uses in 1963 was as follows:

Type of land	Pacific region, percent	Central region, percent	Caribbean region, percent
Cultivated lands	24.8	22.6	21.0
Grasslands	49.0	49.5	28.8
Mountains, forests, swamps, and other	26.2	27.9	50.2

25. Denevan, *Upland Pine Forests*, 283.

CHAPTER 6

1. According to Rodríguez Becerra (*Encomienda y conquista*, 112–13), an income of 500 pesos a year was sufficient to maintain a house, and a man could live "honorably" on 1,000 pesos. Very few encomiendas in Nicaragua provided an income of over 500 pesos.

2. Morison, *Admiral of the Ocean Sea*, 596; Colón, *Vida del Almirante*, 271–79; Sauer, *Early Spanish Main*, 121–25.

3. AGI PAT 20–1–13 and *CS*, 1:84–89 Relación del viaje . . ., n.d. [1522?], PAT 26–17 and *CS*, 1:89–107 Gil González Dávila 6.3.1524.

4. *CS*, 1:128–33 Pedrarias Dávila April, 1525.

5. For a full discussion of the rivalries between conquistadors see Bancroft, *Native Races*, 2:144–65; Alvarez Rubiano, *Pedrarias Dávila*, 319–77; Molina Argüello, *Gobernador de Nicaragua*, 25–37; Chamberlain, *Conquest and Colonization of Honduras*, 9–18.

6. AGI PAT 26–17 and *CS*, 1:89–107 Gil González Dávila 6.3.1524; Oviedo, *Historia general*, 3 lib. 29 cap. 21:294.

7. For examples of Indian attacks on the mining area of Neuva Segovia see AGI PAT 26–5 and *CS*, 1:457–70 Cerezeda 20.1.1529, PAT 180–27 and *CS*, 1:479–508 Castañeda 30.3.1529, PAT 26–5 and *CS*, 2:283–87 Pedrarias Dávila 25.11.1529, PAT 26–5 and *CS*, 2:401–403 Pedrarias Dávila 1.3.1530, IG 1081 and *CS*, 3:258–72 Cabildo of León 1532, AG 9 and *CS*, 3:272–78

Castañeda 1.5.1533, AG 9 and *CS,* 11:454–68 Herrera 10.7.1545, AG 9 and *CS,* 12:449–60 Oidors of the Audiencia 30.12.1545; RAHM CM A/111 4846 fols. 145v.–6 García 8.2.1546.

    8. Radell, "Historical Geography," 63.

    9. Oviedo, *Historia general,* 4 lib. 42 cap. 1:363.

    10. AGI PAT 26–5 and *CS,* 1:448–57 Pedrarias Dávila 15.1.1529, PAT 26–5 and *CS,* 1:457–70 Cerezeda 20.1.1529, AG 9 and *CS,* 3:68–78 Castañeda 30.5.1531; *CS,* 3:330–34 Bula pontífica 3.11.1534.

    11. AGI JU 297 and *CS,* 9:1–558 Juicio de residencia . . . Contreras 28.6.1544 (petition 20.4.1537).

    12. AGI AG 110 and *CS,* 3:113–16 Alvarez Osorio 30.11.1531, AG 9 and *CS,* 3:272–78 Castañeda 1.5.1533, JU 293 and *CS,* 4:1–760 Juicio de residencia de Castañeda 23.1.1536, AG 41 Cabildo of Santiago de Guatemala 30.4.1549, AG 162 Lic. Carrasco, n.d.; *CDI,* 5:522–29 Lic. Carrasco, n.d.

    13. López de Gómara, *Hispania Victrix,* 280–81; Fuentes y Guzmán, *Recordación Florida* 3:293, 295 (map); Juarros, *Statistical and Commercial History,* 70; Radell and Parsons, "Realejo," 298–301.

    14. *CDHCR,* 6:5–48 Interrogatorios presentados por Pedrarias Dávilla 1527; AGI PAT 180–22 and *CS,* 1:373–431 Información recibida en León 13.7.1528, PAT 26–5 and *CS,* 1:448–57 Pedrarias Dávila 15.1.1529, JU 1030–2 and *CS,* 2:26–28 Acuerdo . . . 25.5.1529, PAT 26–5 and *CS,* 2:283–87 Pedrarias Dávila 25.11.1529, AG 42 and *CS,* 3:85–97 Testimonio . . . 1531; Oviedo, *Historia general,* 4 lib. 42 cap. 11:424.

    15. Peralta, *Costa Rica,* 816; Lozoya, *Vida del Segoviano,* 65–66; AGI JU 298 and *CS,* 10:1–168 Juicio de residencia . . . de Pedro de los Ríos 28.6.1544, AG 162 and *CS,* 11:468–76 Fr. Valdivieso 15.7.1545, AG 9 and *CS,* 12:449–60 Oidors of the Audiencia 30.12.1545. The site was at the junction of the río Segovia and the río Jícaro, where the ruins of Ciudad Vieja exist today (Denevan, *Upland Pine Forests,* 289–90).

    16. *CDHCR,* 6:5–48 Interrogatorios presentados por Pedrarias Dávila 1527; *CS,* 1:277–80 Alvitez 20.11.1527; RAHM CM A/105 4840 Información . . . 13.7.1528; Oviedo, *Historia general,* 4 lib. 42 cap. 11:424.

    17. AGI AG 52 and *CS,* 6:74–75 Calero, n.d., JU 1037 and *CS,* 15:108–229 Juicio promovido por Contreras 18.11.1549; Peralta, *Costa Rica,* 728–40; Oviedo, *Historia general,* 4 lib. 42 cap. 4:386.

    18. It was apparently founded on the site of the former Fort San Carlos. Peralta suggests that it was founded in 1542, but Juarros maintains that it was founded by Gabriel de Rojas under orders from López de Salcedo, in which case it must have been founded before 1530, when López de Salcedo died. It is possible that Juarros mistook Nueva Jaen for Buena Esperanza, which was reestablished by Gabriel de Rojas in 1529 but under orders from Pedrarias (Juarros, *Statistical and Commercial History,* 335; López de Velasco, *Geografía,* 326; Peralta, *Costa Rica,* 397, 816).

    19. For the Spanish background to the encomienda see Chamberlain, *Castilian Backgrounds;* and Hanke, *Spanish Struggle for Justice,* 19–20, 23–25, 86–87.

    20. AGCA A1.23 1511 fol. 56 cedula 30.6.1547, fol. 76 cedula 18.8.1548; AGI AG 9 Audiencia 23.9.1547.

    21. AGCA A1.23 1511 fol. 77 cedula 1.9.1548.

22. AGCA A1.23 4575 fol. 37v. cedula 9.9.1536.

23. AGCA A1.24 2195 15749 fol. 288 cedula 22.10.1541, A1.23 1511 fol. 17 cedula 7.9.1543; AGI PAT 21–1–4 and *CS*, 11:285–305 Información a solicitud de Herrera 16.8.1544, AG 162 and *CS*, 11:355–58 Fr. Valdivieso 15.11.1544, AG 402–2 cedula 9.7.1546.

24. AGI PAT 26–5 and *CS*, 1:448–57 Pedrarias Dávila 15.1.1529, AG 49 and *CS*, 2:404–40 Cerezeda 31.3.1530.

25. The total income from encomiendas was estimated at between 8,000 and 9,000 pesos, which was considered enough to support 15 to 20 conquistadors. For information on the encomiendas held by Contreras, see AGI AG 40 and *CS*, 3:444–46 Contreras 6.7.1536, AG 43 and *CS*, 5:200–207 Governor of Nicaragua 25.1.1537, IG 1206 and *CS*, 6:103–16 Capítulo de cargos . . . contra Contreras 1.7.1540, AG 52 and *CS*, 7:349–75 Quejas . . . contra Contreras, n.d., AG 43 and *CS*, 11:146–53 Cabildo of León 24.6.1544, JU 297 and *CS*, 9:1–558 Juicio de residencia . . . de Contreras 28.6.1544, AG 162 and *CS*, 11:355–58 Fr. Valdivieso 15.11.1544, AG 44 and *CS*, 11:362–76 Cuidad de Granada 28.11.1544, AG 9 and *CDI*, 24:397–420 Herrera 24.12.1544; RAHM CM A/112 4849 fols. 60–61v. Ciudad de León 10.2.1548.

26. For examples of the confiscation of encomiendas for the ill-treatment of Indians, see AGI AG 401–2 and *CS*, 3:31 cedula 4.4.1631; *CS*, 15:31–40 Cerrato 8.4.1549; AGI AG 393–3 cedula 11.9.1550.

27. AGI AG 422–16 and *CS*, 3:304–305 cedula 25.10.1533.

28. *CS*, 3:133–35 cedula 31.1.1532, *CS*, 3:157–58 cedula 20.2.1532.

29. AGI JU 1030 and *CS*, 2:91–93 Repartimiento 26.8.1529, JU 1030 and *CS*, 2:102–16 Información . . . 6.9.1529, JU 293 and *CS*, 4:1–760 Juicio de residencia de Castañeda 23.1.1536, AG 43 and *CS*, 11:146–53 Cabildo of León 24.6.1544.

30. AGI AG 965 and *CS*, 1:248–53 Cabildo of Granada 10.7.1527, PAT 180–27 and *CS*, 1:479–508 Castañeda 30.3.1529.

31. AGCA A1.23 4575 fol. 29 cedula 23.2.1536; AGI AG 401–3 and *CS*, 6:64–68 Carta acordada . . . 18.10.1539.

32. AGI AG 43 and *CS*, 5:494–96 Carta de . . . León 8.4.1538, AG 43 and *CS*, 6:88–90 Cabildo of León 25.3.1540; CDI 7:555–73 Exposición . . . de la ciudad de Granada 24.11.1544.

33. AGI AG 162 and *CS*, 11:355–58 Fr. Valdivieso 15.11.1544, AG 9 and *CS*, 12:449–60 Oidors of the Audiencia 30.12.1545.

34. AGCA A1.23 1511 fol. 35 cedulas 20.10.1545, 26.3.1546.

35. AGCA A1.23 1511 fol. 56 cedulas 30.6.1547, fol. 65 23.4.1548; AGI AG 402–3 cedula 7.7.1550.

36. *CS*, 1:128–33 Pedrarias Dávila April, 1525.

37. AGI PAT 180–27 and *CS*, 1:479–508 Castañeda 30.3.1529.

38. AGI AG 43 and *CS*, 3:85–97 Testimonio . . . 1531.

39. AGI AG 128 Libro de tasaciones 1548.

40. Keith, *Conquest and Agrarian Change*, 33–36.

41. AGCA A1.23 4575 fol. 42v. cedula 20.12.1538.

42. AGCA A1.24 2195 fol. 302 cedula 1.7.1535. Several cedulas gave permission to encomenderos to absent themselves for two years: AGI AG 401–3 cedulas 18.7.1539, 22.8.1539, 18.10.1539.

43. AGCA A1.23 4575 fol. 28v. 23.3.1536 (cedula 28.3.1536); Fuentes y

Guzmán, *Recordación Florida*, 2:256–58. It would appear that tasaciones were made for parts of Guatemala, San Miguel, San Salvador, and Chiapas by the *visitador* Lic. Maldonado and the bishop of Guatemala, Francisco Marroquín (AGI AG 156 Bishop Marroquín 20.1.1539; Rodríguez Becerra, *Encomienda y conquista*, 117).

44. AGI AG 401–3 and *CS*, 5:342–45 cedula 30.12.1537, AG 401–3 and *CS*, 6:64–68 Carta acordada 18.10.1539, AG 9 and *CS*, 11:454–68 Herrera 10.7.1545; Fuentes y Guzmán, *Recordación Florida*, 2:348–55. Herrera mentions that *tasaciones* were drawn up by the bishop of Nicaragua, but he does not give the date.

45. AGCA A1.23 1551 fol. 25 cedula 23.10.1543.

46. AGI CO 984 Cargo de tributos 1544–47 provides some evidence of tribute payments for Posoltega, Diría, Diriega, and Nindirí. It is possible that these payments may have been made according to the aforementioned bishop's tasaciones.

47. AGI AG 9 and *CS*, 14:344–50 Cerrato 28.9.1548.

48. AGI CO 984 Cargo de tributos and AG 128 Libro de tasaciones 1548.

49. AGI AG 401–3 and *CS*, 5:342–45 cedula 30.12.1537, AG 401–3 and *CS*, 6:64–68 Carta acordada and *CS*, 6:64–68 18.10.1539.

50. AGI CO 984 Cargo de tributos 1547. The employment of *tamemes* is discussed at length by Sherman (*Forced Native Labor*, 111–18).

51. AGI JU 301 and *CS*, 15:232–489 Juicio contra Diego Herrera, June, 1548.

52. AGI AG 43 and *CS*, 5:200–307 Governor of Nicaragua 25.6.1537; RAHM CM A/108 4843 Contreras 25.7.1537; AGI AG JU 279 Ordenanzas de Contreras 1537; AGCA A1.23 4575 fol. 50 cedulas 28.1.1541, 31.5.1541; AGI AG 9 and *CS*, 12:429–40 Herrera 24.12.1545; AGCA A1.23 1511 fol. 40 cedula 5.7.1546; AGI AG 402–2 cedula 9.7.1546; *CDI* 24:447–63 Maldonado 20.9.1547; AGI AG 9 Ramírez 25.5.1549; AGCA A1.23 1511 fols. 113, 116 cedulas 1.6.1549.

53. AGI AG 9 and *CS*, 3:272–78 Castañeda 1.5.1533.

54. AGI JU 393 and *CS*, 4:1–760 Juicio de residencia . . . contra Castañeda 23.1.1536; AGCA A1.23 1511 fol. 40 cedula 5.7.1546 and repeated in 1549 (AGCA A1.23 1511 fol. 93 cedula 22.2.1549).

55. AGCA A1.23 1511 fol. 13 cedula 28.8.1543.

56. AGI AG 43 and *CS*, 5:200–307 Governor of Nicaragua 25.6.1537, JU 279 Ordenanzas de Contreras 1537, AG 401–3 and *CS* 7:118–20 cedula 31.5.1541; Pardo *Efemérides*, 74; Sherman, *Forced Native Labor*, 92 cedula 13.2.1531. A similar order was issued in 1549 (AGCA A1.23 4575 fol. 108v. cedula 9.9.1549).

57. AGI JU 297 and *CS*, 9:1–558 Juicio de residencia . . . de Contreras 28.6.1544.

58. AGI AG 401–3 and *CS*, 7:118–20 cedula 31.5.1541, JU 297 and *CS*, 9:1–558 Juicio de residencia . . . de Contreras 28.6.1544, AG 9 and *CDI*, 24:397–420 Herrera 24.12.1544; AGCA A1.23 1511 fol. 137 and *CS*, 17:2–3 cedula 11.3.1550.

59. AGI AG 401–3 and *CS*, 7:118–20 cedula 31.5.1541.

60. AGI AG 965 Archdean of León, n.d.

61. AGI AG 401–3 and *CS*, 8:201–203 cedula 7.10.1543, AG 401–3 and *CS*, 17:2–3 cedula 11.3.1550.

62. AGCA A1.23 4575 fol. 49v. cedula 28.11.1540.

63. AGCA A1.23 1511 fol. 91 cedula 15.12.1548; AGI AG 965 Archdean of León, n.d.

64. AGCA A1.23 4575 fol. 107 cedula 7.6.1550.

65. AGI AG 128 Libro de tasaciones 1548; AGCA A1.23 4575 fol. 94 cedula 22.2.1549.

66. AGCA A1.23 1511 fol. 121 cedula 7.8.1549.

67. AGI AG 128 Libro de tasaciones 1548.

68. Borah and Cook (*Aboriginal Population*, 90–91) have estimated that 25 fanegas were required to support a family for a year in central Mexico at the time of the Conquest, whilst Gibson (*Aztecs*, 311) has suggested that between 10 and 20 fanegas were required to support a family during the colonial period in the same area.

69. AGI AG 128 Libro de tasaciones 1548.

70. AGI AG 301 and *CS*, 15:232–489 Juicio contra Herrera, June, 1548.

71. AGI AG 401–3 and *CS*, 7:118–20 cedula 31.5.1541, AG 965 Archdean of León, n.d.

72. AGI AG 128 Libro de tasaciones 1548.

73. There are several very detailed accounts of slaving activities in Central America: Saco, *Historia de la esclavitud;* Sherman, "Indian Slavery"; and Sherman, *Forced Native Labor.*

74. AGCA A1.24 2197 15752 fol. 17v. cedula 2.8.1530; AGI IG 422-15 and *CS*, 3:4–5 cedula 25.1.1531; Puga, *Provisiones*, 65v., 66; Zavala, *Instituciones coloniales*, 13–14.

75. AGCA A1.24 2197 15752 fol. 4 cedula 30.6.1532, fol. 5v. and AGI AG 393-1 cedula 19.3.1530; Zavala, *Instituciones coloniales*, 14–20; Sherman, *Forced Native Labor*, 35–36.

76. *CDIU*, 10:192–203 cedula 20.2.1534.

77. AGI AG 401-2 and *CS*, 3:442–43 cedula 26.5.1536, AG 401–2 and *CS*, 3:458–60 cedula 9.9.1536.

78. AGI AG 401–2 and *CS*, 3:442–43 cedula 26.5.1536; AGCA A1.24 2195 15749 fol. 218v. cedula 29.1.1538; AGI AG 402–2 and *CS*, 14:339–40 cedula 1.9.1548.

79. For a full discussion of the branding of slaves see Sherman, *Forced Native Labor*, 64–67.

80. AGI PAT 26–5 and *CS*, 2:196–215 Castañeda 5.10.1529; Sherman, *Forced Native Labor*, 67.

81. For example, when the regidor of Trujillo, Vasco de Herrera, went on an expedition to Nicaragua, he took with him the royal branding iron and made two counterfeit irons (AGI AG 49 and *CS*, 2:404–40 Cerezeda 31.3.1530).

82. The death penalty was removed in 1528, but the loss of property, which remained in force, should have acted as a strong deterrent (Sherman, *Forced Native Labor*, 384 n. 1).

83. *CS*, 1:293–99 Castillo, n.d.; AGI PAT 20-4 and *CS*, 1:473–78 Testimonio de información por López de Salcedo 28.2.1529, AG 44 Cabildo of Trujillo 20.3.1530; RAHM CM A/106 4841 Castillo 1531; Herrera, *Historia general*, 8

dec. 4 lib. 1 cap. 7:46–47; Sherman, *Forced Native Labor*, 44–48. The details of the treatment meted out to the Indians make horrific reading: Indians were often killed by being roasted alive or being torn to pieces by dogs; others were punished by having their limbs cut off. Those enslaved were placed in neck chains and if they flagged on the journey, they were decapitated.

84. AGI JU 1030 and *CS*, 2:219–77 Informaciones de Castañeda 1529; AGI PAT 26-5 and *CS*, 2:196–215 Castañeda 5.10.1529, AG 9 and *CS*, 3: 68–78 Castañeda 30.5.1531; *CDHCR*, 6:199–211 Rodríguez 9.7.1545.

85. AGI AG 965 Archdean of León, n.d.

86. AGI AG 401-3 and *CS*, 7:118–20 cedula 31.5.1531.

87. *CDHCR*, 6:199–211 Rodríguez 9.7.1545; Sherman, "Indian Slavery," 56–57.

88. AGI AG 52 and *CS*, 7:349–75 Quejas de vecinos de León y Granada 1542; Sherman, *Forced Native Labor*, 54.

89. Sherman, *Forced Native Labor*, 68–70.

90. Saco, *Historia de la escalvitud*, 2:180–81.

91. For the slave trade with Panama see AGI AG 965 and *CS*, 1:248–53 Cabildo of Granada 10.7.1527; *CS*, 1:293–99 Castillo, n.d.; AGI PAT 26-5 and *CS*, 1:448–57 Pedrarias Dávila 15.1.1529, JU 1030 and *CS*, 2:16–25 Fiscal Villalobos 8.4.1529, JU 1030 and *CS*, 2:28–71 Juicio contra Ruiz 3.7.1529, PAT 26-5 and *CS*, 2:196–215 Castañeda 5.10.1529, JU 1030 and *CS*, 2:219–77 Información de Castañeda 1529; RAHM CM A/106 4841 Castañeda 1.5.1533; Borah, *Early Colonial Trade*, 4. For the slave trade with Peru see AGI AG 52 and *CS*, 3:406–12 Sánchez 2.8.1535, JU 293 and *CS*, 4:1–760 Juicio de residencia . . . de Castañeda 23.1.1536; *CDI*, 7:555–73 Ciudad de Granada 24.11.1544; AGI AG 9, *CS*, 14:344–50 and RAHM CM A/112 4849 Cerrato 28.9.1548, AGI AG 401-3 and *CS*, 15:72–74 cedula 1.6.1549.

92. AGI PAT 180–27 and *CS*, 1:479–508 Castañeda 30.3.1529, JU 1030-2 and *CS*, 2:16–25 Fiscal Villalobos 8.4.1529, PAT 26-5 and *CS*, 2:196–215 Castañeda 5.10.1529; Radell and Parsons, "Realejo," 300–301.

93. In 1529, Bartolomé Ruiz was charged with having exported 80 to 90 Indians from "el puerto del río de la posesión" without a license (AGI JU 1032-2 and *CS*, 2:28–71 Juicio contra Ruiz 3.7.1529).

94. Las Casas, *Breve relación*, 45; AGI PAT 180-27 and *CS*, 1:479–508 Castañeda 30.3.1529.

95. AGI AG 52, RAHM CM A/107 4842, and *CS*, 3:406–12 Sánchez 2.8.1535; Herrera, *Historia general*, 11 dec. 5 lib. 7 cap. 2:102. Borah (*Early Colonial Trade*, 132) is doubtful that all of them were caravels; they may have been brigantines.

96. Las Casas, *Obras escogidas*, 5:59–68 15.10.1535; Zavala, *Instituciones coloniales*, 22–23.

97. Radell, "Historical Georgaphy," 72–77; Radell, "Indian Slave Trade," 71–75. Radell places the peak years of the slave trade between 1533 and 1536, during which time, he assumes there were an average of 17 ships on the Panama run doing 12 trips a year and another 2 to 3 ships traveling to Peru once or twice a year. The average capacity of the ships he estimates at 350 slaves.

98. AGI IG 1206 and *CS*, 6:103–16 Capítulo de cargos . . . contra Contreras 1.7.1540.

99. Las Casas, *Breve relación,* 45; Oviedo, *Historia general,* 4 lib. 42 cap. 4:385.

100. Sherman, *Forced Native Labor,* 74–82.

101. Las Casas, *Obras escogidas,* 5:59–68 15.10.1535; Zavala, *Instituciones coloniales,* 22–23.

102. MacLeod, *Spanish Central America,* 52.

103. Simpson, *Administration of New Spain,* 3–4; MacLeod, *Spanish Central America,* 52–56.

104. AGI AG 9, *CDI,* 24:421–22 and *CDHCN,* 30–41 Audiencia 30.12.1545.

105. Despite the numerous orders that Indian slaves were to be returned to their places of origin (for example, AGI IG 423-20 and *CS,* 7:464–66 cedula 1543, IG 423-20 and *CS,* 7:535 cedula 28.9.1543; AGCA A1.23 1511 fol. 72 cedula 25.6.1548), very few were ever returned. A list of 821 slaves freed in Panama in 1550 included only 158 from Nicaragua, 18 from Guatemala, 5 from Honduras, 2 from Veragua, and 2 from Realejo. The largest number came from Cubagua (272). The Nicaraguan Indians were supposed to be settled at Cerro de Cabra (Simpson, *Administration of New Spain,* 17–18).

106. AGI AG 9 and *CS,* 14:344–50 Cerrato 28.9.1548, JU 301 and 302 1553. The enforcement of the New Laws in the Audiencia of Guatemala by Cerrato has been studied in detail by a number of scholars: Bataillon, "Las Casas et le Licencié Cerrato," 79–87; Sherman, "Indian Slavery"; Sherman, "Cerrato Reforms," 25–50; Sherman, *Forced Native Labor,* 129–88; MacLeod, *Spanish Central America,* 108–19.

107. AGI PAT 170-30 and *CS,* 1:246–58 Castillo 1.7.1527, PAT 26-5 and *CS,* 1:225–28 Castillo 26.5.1527.

108. Oviedo, *Historia general,* 4 lib. 42 cap. 11:425.

109. AGI PAT 180-22 and *CS,* 1:374–431 Información recibida en León 13.7.1528, PAT 26-5 and *CS,* 1:448–57 Pedrarias Dávila 15.1.1529, PAT 26-5 and *CS,* 1:457-70 Cerezeda 20.1.1529, PAT 180-27 and *CS,* 1:479–508 Castañeda 30.3.1529, JU 1030 and *CS,* 2:26–28 Acuerdo . . . 25.5.1529, PAT 26-5 and *CS,* 2:283–87 Pedrarias Dávila 25.11.1529, PAT 26-5 and *CS,* 2:401–403 Pedrarias Dávila 1.3.1530, IG 1081 and *CS,* 3:258–72 Cabildo of León 1532/3, AG 9 and *CS,* 3:272–78 Castañeda 1.5.1533, JU 293 and *CS,* 4:1–760 Juicio de residencia . . . Castañeda 23.1.1536.

110. AGI JU 298 and *CS,* 10:1–168 Juicio de residencia . . . Pedro de los Ríos 28.6.1544, AG 9 and *CS,* 11:454–68 Herrera 10.7.1545, AG 162 and *CS,* 11:468–76 Fr. Valdivieso 15.7.1545, AG 9 and *CS,* 12:449–60 Oidors of the Audiencia 30.12.1545, AG 402-2, AGCA A1.23 1511 fol. 40 and *CS,* 13:486–87 cedula 5.7.1546, AG 401-3 and *CS,* 15:6–7 cedula 22.2.1549, AG 9 and *CS,* 15:31–40 Cerrato 8.4.1549.

111. AGI AG 128 Libro de tasaciones 1548. The equipment used in mining was probably similar to that described by West for Honduras (West, "Mining Economy," 767–77).

112. *CS,* 1:303–305 cedula 7.2.1528, *CS,* 1:439 cedula 2.10.1558.

113. AGI AG 402-1 and *CS,* 2:440–41 cedula 5.4.1530, AG 401-3 and *CS,* 5:224–25 cedula 5.9.1537; Salvatierra, *Historia de Centro América,* 1:282.

114. AGI PAT 26-5 and *CS,* 1:457–70 Cerezeda 20.1.1529, AG 9 and *CS,* 3:68–78 Castañeda 30.5.1531.

115. Ots Capdequí, *España en América,* 7–28. The dimensions of *caballerías* and *peonías* appear to have varied during the early colonial period. In the West Indies they were measured in terms of the number of *montones* that could be constructed, and a *caballería* was twice the size of a *peonía.* However, measurements specified in the Ordinances of 1573 indicated that *caballerías* were to be five times the size of *peonías.* A *peonía* consisted of a house plot of 50 × 100 feet; 100 fanegas of land for wheat and barley; 10 fanegas for maize; 2 *huebras* of land for a garden and 8 for trees; and pastureland for 10 pigs, 20 cows, 5 horses, 100 sheep, and 20 goats. A *caballería* was to consist of a house plot of 100 × 200 feet, and the rest was to be equivalent to 5 *peonías.* It is doubtful that such precise dimensions were adhered to in the early colonial period, but unfortunately there is no evidence available. In the middle of the eighteenth century a *caballería* in Central America was equivalent to 111 acres, while an estancia for ganado mayor was 6¾ *caballerías* and an estancia for *ganado menor* was half that (AGI AG 264 Ventas y composiciones de tierras 1749–51).

116. RAHM CM A/111 4846 Fr. Valdivieso 15.7.1545.

117. MacLeod, *Spanish Central America,* 68–95.

118. AGI AG 9 and *CS,* 15:31–40 Cerrato 8.4.1549.

119. It had been anticipated that sugar produced in Nicaragua could be exported to Peru, Panama and even Spain (*CDHCR,* 6:199–211 Rodríguez 9.7.1545).

120. AGI JU 297 and *CS,* 9:1–558 Juicio de residencia de Contreras 28.6.1544, JU 287 and *CS,* 13:1–304 Juicio promovido por Contreras 31.7.1548.

121. AGI AG 39 Las cosas que se han remediado . . . , n.d.; García Peláez, *Memorias,* 1:173; Newson, *Aboriginal and Spanish Colonial Trinidad,* 88. Cortés introduced livestock to Honduras from Mexico in 1525 and from Spain in 1529.

122. AGI AG 44 Cabildo of Trujillo 20.3.1530.

123. AGI JU 297 and *CS,* 9:1–558 Juicio de residencia . . . Contreras 28.6.1544, AG 965 Archdean of León, n.d.; Radell, "Historical Geography," 149.

124. AGI JU 293 and *CS,* 4:1–760 Juicio de residencia . . . de Castañeda 23.1.1536.

CHAPTER 7

1. RAHM CM A/105 4840 fols. 138–40 Castañeda 30.3.1529; AGI AG 49, *CS,* 2:404–40 and RAHM CM A/105 4840 fols. 277–80 Cerezeda 31.3.1530; Saco, *Historia de la esclavitud,* 2:172.

2. RAHM CM A/77 fols. 140–9 and *CS,* 1:128–33 Pedrarias Dávila, April 1525; AGI AG 128 Libro de tasaciones 1548; Oviedo, *Historia general,* 4 lib. 42 cap. 5:391.

3. AGI AG 402-3 and *CS,* 15:106–108 cedula 9.10.1549.

4. AGCA A1.23 4575 fol. 103v. cedula 29.5.1549, fol. 110v. cedula 9.10.1549.

5. AGCA A1.23 4575 fol. 110v. cedula 9.10.1549.

6. AGI AG 965 Archdean of León, n.d.; *CDHCR,* 6:199–211 Rodríguez 9.7.1545.

7. AGI JU 279 Ordenanzas de Contreras 1537; RAHM CM A/108 4843 Contreras 25.7.1537; AGI PAT 26-5 and *CS*, 1:448–57 Pedrarias Dávila 15.1.1529, JU 1030 and *CS*, 2:26–28 Acuerdo . . . 25.5.1529, JU 297 and *CS*, 3:454–55 Ordenanzas que hizo Contreras 3.9.1536, AG 401-3 and *CS*, 7: 118–20 cedula 31.5.1541.

8. *CDHCR*, 6:199–211 Rodríguez 9.7.1545. For estimates of the proportion of production paid as tribute see the earlier discussion in chap. 6.

9. Haring, *Spanish Empire*, 266.

10. AGI AG 9 and *CS*, 3:272–78 Castañeda 1.5.1533.

11. AGI AG 43 and *CS*, 5:200–307 Governor of Nicaragua 25.6.1537, AG 965 Archdean of León, n.d.

12. For losses in varieties of crops cultivated in Middle America, see Sauer, *Early Spanish Main*, 54.

13. AGI PAT 180-22 and *CS*, 1:374–431 Información recibida en León 13.7.1528, AG 39 Las cosas que se han remediado . . ., n.d., AG 965 Archdean of León, n.d.

14. See chap. 6.

15. AGI AG 402-3 and *CS*, 15:106–108 cedula 9.10.1549.

16. AGI AG 402-3 and *CS*, 15:104 cedula 9.10.1549.

17. Fuentes y Guzmán, *Recordación Florida*, 2:157–58.

18. Oviedo, *Historia general*, 4 lib. 42 cap. 1:364.

19. AGI JU and *CS*, 2:91–93 Repartimiento . . . 26.6.1529, JU 297 and *CS*, 9:1–558 Juicio de residencia de Contreras 28.6.1544, AG 965 Archdean of León, no date; *Recopilación* 2 lib. 6 tít. 5 ley 18:230 17.7.1572; Gibson, "Transformation of the Indian Community," 587; Gibson, *Aztecs*, 150.

20. AGCA A1.23 4575 fol. 22 cedula 20.2.1534.

21. AGI JU 297 and *CS*, 9:1–558 Juicio de residencia de Contreras 28.6.1544; AGCA A1.23 1511 fol. 59 cedula 26.8.1547; AGI AG 402-3 and *CS*, 15:106–108 cedula 9.10.1549; AGI AG 965 Archdean of León, n.d.

22. AGI AG 9 Herrera 24.9.1545, AG 402-2 and *CS*, 13:490–91 cedula 10.9.1546.

23. AGI AG 128 Libro de tasaciones 1548, AG 402-3 and *CS*, 15:106–108 cedulas 9.10.1549.

24. Haring, *Spanish Empire*, 162; Gibson, *Aztecs*, 148–49.

25. AGCA A1.23 4575 fol. 22 cedula 20.2.1534, A1.24 2195 fol. 188 cedula 30.1.1538; AGI JU 297 and *CS*, 9:1–558 Juicio de residencia de Contreras 28.6.1544 (cedula 31.1.1539).

26. *CDI*, 24:513–57 Lic. López 9.6.1550.

27. AGI AG 401-3 and *CS*, 7:118–20 cedula 31.1.1541, AG 402-2 and *CS*, 17:2–3 cedula 11.3.1550.

28. AGI IG 1206 and *CS*, 6:103–16 Capítulos de cargos . . . 1.7.1540; *CDHCR*, 6:199–211 Rodríguez 9.7.1545; AGI AG 162 and *CS*, 14:229–305 Bishop of Nicaragua 1547.

29. Gibson, "Transformation of the Indian Community," 587.

30. AGI AG 975 Archdean of León, n.d.

31. AGI PAT 26-17 and *CS*, 1:89–107 Gil González Dávila 6.3.1524; *CS*, 1:128–33 Pedrarias Dávila, April, 1525; Brasseur de Bourbourg, *Histoire de nations civilisées*, 4:615; López de Gómara, *Hispania Victrix*, 281; Oviedo, *Historia general*, 3 lib. 29 cap. 21:292, 4 lib. 42 cap. 4:381–83; Fuentes y Guzmán, *Recordación Florida*, 2:157–58.

32. Oviedo, *Historia general,* 4 lib. 42 cap. 4: 383.

33. AGI AG 9 and *CS,* 3: 68–78 Castañeda 30.5.1531.

34. Ibid.

35. AGI PAT 20-3-1 and *CS,* 1: 84–89 Relación del viaje . . ., n.d. [1522?]; PAT 26-17 and *CS,* 1: 89–107 Gil González Dávila 6.3.1524; López de Gómara, *Hispania Victrix,* 281–82; Oviedo, *Historia general,* 4 lib. 42 cap. 2: 266, cap. 3: 381–83.

36. *CDHCR,* 6: 199–211 Rodríguez 9.7.1545.

37. Oviedo, *Historia general,* 4 lib. 42 cap. 4: 385.

38. AGI JU 387 and *CS,* 13: 1–304 Juicio promovido por Contreras 31.7.1548.

39. AGI PAT 26-5 and *CS,* 2: 283–87 Pedrarias Dávila 25.11.1529, PAT 26-5 and *CS,* 2: 401–403 Pedrarias Dávila 1.3.1530.

40. AGI AG 9, *CDI,* 24: 397–420, RAHM CM A/110 4845 fols. 224–26 Herrera 24.12.1544.

41. AGI AG 128 Libro de tasaciones 1548 for the jurisdiction of León November 24 to 29 and for the jurisdiction of Granada December 1 to 8, 1548.

42. *Recopilación,* 2 lib. 6 tít. 5 ley 7: 226–27 5.7.1578.

43. See chap. 12.

44. A multiplication factor of 4 may be conservative for 1548 since after that date the number of adult males is likely to have increased relative to other sections of the Indian population owing to the cessation of the slave trade. A multiplication factor of 4.5 or 5 might be preferable. Barón Castro (*Población de El Salvador,* 200) believes that the figures for tributary Indians in the 1548 tasaciones referred to able-bodied adults, which he claims constituted 46 percent of the total Indian population. Since single persons were not liable for tribute until later in the century, this would appear to be an error of judgment. The ratio of tributary to nontributary Indians in Mexico in 1548 was 1: 3.3 (Borah and Cook, *Population of Central Mexico,* 102).

45. See chap. 6.

46. Oviedo recorded that León had over 200 *vecinos* and Granada about 100 (Oviedo, *Historia general,* 4 lib. 422 cap. 1: 363), whereas López de Velasco noted that León had 150 *vecinos,* Granada 200, and Realejo 30 (López de Velasco, *Geografía,* 317–27). The latter figures also appear in *CDI,* 15: 409–572 no author, n.d.

47. AGI JU 293 and *CS,* 4: 1–760 Juicio de residencia de Castañeda 23.1.1536.

48. AGI AG 52 and *CS,* 3: 406–12 Sánchez 2.8.1535.

49. *CDHCR,* 6: 199–211 Rodríguez 9.7.1545.

50. Shea, "Defense of Small Population Estimates," 159–60.

51. Crosby, *Columbian Exchange,* 47.

52. McBryde, "Influenza in America," 296–302; Thompson, "Maya Central Area," 24; Crosby, *Columbian Exchange,* 49, 58; Veblen, "Native Population Decline," 490–91.

53. *CDHCR,* 4: 7–11 Instrucciones a los procuradores de la ciudad de Granada 10.7.1527; Crosby, *Columbian Exchange,* 51.

54. AGI PAT 26-5 and *CS,* 1: 448–57 Pedrarias Dávila 15.1.1529.

55. MacLeod, *Spanish Central America,* 98.

56. AGI AG 9, *CDI,* 24: 178–92 and *CS,* 3: 68–78 Castañeda 30.5.1531, AG 110 and *CS,* 3: 113–6 Alvarez Osorio 30.11.1531.

57. Ashburn, *Ranks of Death,* 200, 217, 227–28.

58. MacLeod, *Spanish Central America,* 98.

59. Pollitzer, *Plague,* 418, 483, 510–13, 535–38; Shrewsbury, *Bubonic Plague,* 1–6; MacLeod, *Spanish Central America,* 8–9; McNeill, *Plagues and Peoples,* 124.

60. AGI AG 9, *CDI,* 24:178–92 and *CS,* 3:68–78 Castañeda 30.5.1531.

61. Herrera, *Historia general,* 10 dec. 5 lib. 1 cap. 10:72. Ashburn translates *cámaras de sangre* as "dysentery" (Ashburn, *Ranks of Death,* 91).

62. RAHM CM A/106 4841 fols. 334–35 Pedro de los Ríos 28.4.1533; AGI AG 9 and *CS,* 3:272–78 Castañeda 1.5.1533.

63. AGI AG 9 and *CDI* 24:442–47 Audiencia 31.12.1545; Zinsser, *Rats, Lice, and History,* 194–95; Thompson, "Maya Central Area," 24; MacLeod, *Spanish Central America,* 98; McNeill, *Plagues and Peoples,* 209.

64. Ashburn, *Ranks of Death,* 130–34; Duffy, *Epidemics,* 140; Thompson, "Maya Central Area," 24; McNeill, *Plagues and Peoples,* 213.

65. Denevan, *Native Population,* 5.

66. Sauer, *Early Spanish Main,* 279.

67. Dunn, "Antiquity of Malaria," 385–93; Wood, "Late Introduction of Malaria," 93–104.

68. Las Casas, *Breve relación,* 45.

69. AGI AG 9, *CS,* 3:272–78 and RAHM CM A/106 4841 Castañeda 1.5.1533. The document does not specify the length of the demora, but it would have been less than a year.

70. RAHM CM A/111 4846 fols. 230–31v. Fr. Valdivieso 1547; AGI AG 162 and *CS,* 14:229–305 Bishop of Nicaragua 1547.

71. AGI AG 9 and *CS,* 3:272-8 Castañeda 1.5.1533. Indians from the jurisdictions of León and Granada were employed in the mines of Nueva Segovia. See chap. 6.

72. RAHM CM A/105 4840 fols. 138–40 Castañeda 30.3.1529.

73. AGI PAT 180-22 and *CS* 1:374–431 Información recibida en León 13.7.1528, PAT 26-5 and *CS,* 1:448–57 Pedrarias Dávila 15.1.1529, PAT 26-5 and *CS,* 1:457–70 Cerezeda 20.1.1529, AG 110 and *CS* 3:113–16 Alvarez Osorio 30.11.1531.

74. Herrera, *Historia general,* 10 dec. 5 lib. 1 cap. 10:72.

75. *CDHCR,* 6:119–211 Rodríguez 9.7.1545; Las Casas, *Relación breve,* 43.

76. AGI JU 293 and *CS,* 7:151–224 Petición sobre la conducta de Castañeda 16.11.1541; *CDHCR,* 6:199–211 Rodríguez 9.7.1545; Herrera, *Historia general,* 8 dec. 4 lib. 3 cap. 2:149; Saco, *Historia de la esclavitud,* 2:168; García Peláez, *Memorias,* 1:96.

77. AGI IG 1206 and *CS,* 6:103–16 Capítulos de cargos . . . 1.7.1540, JU 297 and *CS,* 9:1–558 Juicio de residencia de Contreras 28.6.1544, PAT 21-1-4 and *CS,* 11:285–305 Información a solicitud de Herrera 16.8.1544; AG 162 and *CS,* 11:468–78 Fr. Valdivieso 15.7.1545; *CDI,* 24:397–420 and RAHM CM A/110 4845 fols. 224–26 Herrera 24.12.1544.

78. AGI JU 293 and *CS,* 4:1–760 Juicio de residencia de Contreras 23.1.1536.

79. AGI AG 9 and *CDI,* 25:37–49 Audiencia 6.9.1554.

80. *CDHCR,* 4:7–11 Instrucciones a los procuradores de la ciudad de Granada 10.7.1527. For examples of the small numbers bought from Spain, see AGI

AG 402-2 and *CS,* 3: 171 cedula 29.11.1532, IG 1206 and *CS,* 6: 118–28 Relación de las bienes de Juan Tellez 8.7.1540.

CHAPTER 8

1. Díaz de la Calle, *Noticias sacras y reales,* 130–32. León, Granada, and Nueva Segovia had six, and Realejo three.
2. Gerhard "Colonial New Spain," 133–36.
3. Molina Argüello, "Communidades y territorialidad," 451. Molina Argüello maintains that the jurisdiction of corregidores was not extended to non-crown villages until after 1570. An interesting case is the corregimiento of Realejo, which when it was established in 1600 had no Indians in its jurisdiction; later it included the Indian village of El Viejo (Molina Arguello, "Gobernaciones," 126).
4. *Recopilación,* 2 lib. 5 tít. 3 ley 10: 118 15.7.1584 but generally appointed for five years (Molina Argüello, "Gobernaciones," 126).
5. See chap. 9.
6. AGI AG 27 Audiencia 11.5.1681.
7. See chap. 12.
8. AGI AG 162 Bishop of Nicaragua 14.7.1647, 20.7.1647, 20.8.1651, AG 167 King to Dean of León, n.d.; AGCA A1.23 1516 fol. 162 cedula 20.8.1648, 1518 fol. 56 cedula 12.6.1652.
9. AGI AG 29 Navia Bolaños 12.11.1684, 28.7.1685; Díaz de la Calle, *Noticias sacras y reales,* 130–31; Vázquez de Espinosa, *Compendium,* 248–57.
10. Dampier, *New Voyage,* 154.
11. Gage, *English-American,* 342.
12. García Peláez, *Memorías* 2: 37; Borah, *Early Colonial Trade,* 117–27; MacLeod *Spanish Central America,* 165–66.
13. Vázquez de Espinosa, *Compendium,* 249.
14. AGI AG 162 Bishop of Nicaragua 20.7.1647, 20.8.1651.
15. AGI AG 162 Bishop of Nicaragua 12.4.1679.
16. AGI AG 362 and BNM 20,0545 Visita of the Bishop of Nicaragua 1.11.1711.
17. RAHM CM A/115 4852 fol. 73–76v. Bishop Carrasco, n.d. but probably ca. 1557; AGI AG 162 and *CDI,* 5: 522–29 Bishop Carrasco, n.d.
18. MacLeod, *Spanish Central America,* 217–21.
19. Chevalier, *Land and Society,* 48, 66, 180; Wolf, *Shaking Earth,* 202, 204.
20. Borah, *Century of Depression,* 32–33. Frank also believes that the growth of haciendas was stimulated by the high prices for agricultural produce (Frank, *Mexican Agriculture,* 56).
21. AGI AG 40 Enríquez 18.1.1691, AG 44 Cabildo of Granada 2.7.1695.
22. AGI CO 984 and 985 Cargo de tributos 1572–94 (the accounts are incomplete for 1572–74 and 1592–94).
23. AGI IG 1528 Mercado 23.1.1620; Vázquez de Espinosa, *Compendium,* 252.
24. AGCA A1.23 4575 fols. 103, 110v. cedulas 29.4.1549, 9.10.1549; A1.23 1513 fol. 51 cedula 18.11.1576.
25. AGCA A1.23 4575 fol. 122 cedula 4.8.1550.

26. AGCA A1.38 4778 41245 Ordenanzas 23.10.1683.

27. Gibson, *Aztecs,* 281; *Recopilación,* 2 lib. 6 tít. 1 ley 27: 195–96 24.5. 1571, 23.7.1571, 6.5.1572, 18.5.1572.

28. *Recopilación,* 2 lib. 4 tít. 12 ley 17: 43–44 30.6.1646.

29. Ibid., 2 lib. 4 tít. 12 ley 7: 41 6.4.1588 and ley 9: 41 11.9.1594.

30. AGCA A1.15 6943 fol. 37, A1.23 1513 fol. 722 and A1.23 4610 fol. 293 cedulas 1.11.1591.

31. Ots Capdequí, *España en América,* 30; Martínez Peláez, *Patria del criollo,* 149–53.

32. *Recopilación,* 2 lib. 4 tít. 12 ley 19: 44 30.6.1646.

33. AGI AG 252 *Media anatas* on lands 1713–33.

34. Ibid.; Radell, "Historical Geography," 150–55.

35. AGI AG 252 *Media anatas* on lands 1713–33; ANCR CC 260 Title to land in Nicoya given to a *vecino* of Nicaragua 30.10.1692; Salvatierra, *Historia de Centro América,* 1: 302; Radell, "Historical Geography," 162–63; Meléndez, *Costa Rica,* 167.

36. AGI AG 44 Cabildo of Granada 2.7.1695.

37. MacLeod, *Spanish Central America,* 68–79.

38. RAHM CM A/115 4852 fols. 73–76v. Bishop Carrasco, n.d. but probably ca. 1557; AGI AG 162 and CDI, 5: 522–29 Bishop Carrasco, n.d.

39. MacLeod, *Spanish Central America,* 72.

40. RAHM CM A/115 4852 fols. 73–76v. Bishop Carrasco, n.d., but probably ca. 1557; AGI AG 162 and CDI 5: 522–29 Bishop Carrasco, n.d.

41. Radell, "Historical Geography," 165.

42. MacLeod, *Spanish Central America,* 73.

43. AGI AG 181 Bishop of Nicaragua 15.7.1683.

44. AGI AG 131 Franciscans 1640; AGCA A1.23 1517 fols. 99 cedula 7.5. 1646; AGI AG 181 Bishop of Nicaragua 15.7.1683; AGCA A3.16 496 3807 Pueblo of Masaya 1709.

45. Ponce, *Relación breve,* 248, 252; López de Velasco, *Geografía,* 317, 321; AGI AG 43 Recaudos de la provincia de Nicaragua 1627–28; RPM 2537 fol. 286v. Descripción general de todos los dominios, n.d.; Vázquez de Espinosa, *Compendium,* 261; AGCA A1.12 32 293 Guardián of the convent of Granada 16.5.1709; Ayón, *Historia de Nicaragua* 2: 13; Salvatierra, *Historia de Centro América,* 1: 302; Radell, "Historical Geography," 164–65.

46. AGI AG 43 Recaudos de la provincia de Nicaragua 1627–28, 21.2.1631 auto 6.10.1626; MacLeod, *Spanish Central America,* 244–49.

47. Floyd, *Anglo-Spanish Struggle,* 40–70; MacLeod, *Spanish Central America,* 340.

48. AGI AG 167 Ciudad de Granada 15.12.1649.

49. AGI AG 25 Vecino of Granada 14.3.1671. Vázquez de Espinosa (*Compendium,* 253) noted that it was collected in Chichigalpa.

50. See Bruman, "Culture History of Mexican Vanilla," 360–76.

51. AGCA A3.16 496 3807 Governor of Nicaragua 6.4.1709.

52. AGCA A1.23 1511 fol. 237 cedula 14.6.1588.

53. AGI AG 10 Venegas de los Ríos, n.d., AG 10 Venegas de los Ríos 6.9.1575.

54. AGI AG 55 Alvarez de Toledo 8.1.1578, AG 10 President of the Audiencia 20.3.1579.

55. AGI AG 40 Casco 17.3.1583.

56. *CDHCN,* 131–34 Town of Nueva Segovia 24.10.1664; AGI AG 44 Vecino of Nueva Segovia 1674; Vázquez de Espinosa, *Compendium,* 252, 260.

57. AGI AG 257 Corregimeinto of Sutiaba 15.2.1705.

58. AGI AG 13 Relación de la siembra y calidad de xiquilite . . ., n.d.; AGCA A1.23 1514 fol. cedula 1.11.1610; Vázquez de Espinosa, *Compendium,* 236; Rubio Sánchez, "El Añil," 317–18; Smith, "Indigo Production," 181–84.

59. AGI AG 162 Bishop of Nicaragua 2.4.1578, AG 10 Audiencia 4.4.1580.

60. Smith, "Indigo Production," 185–86.

61. AGCA A1.23 1513 fol. 594 cedula 15.5.1581.

62. AGCA A1.23 4576 fol. 46 cedula 24.11.1601 and repeated in 1601 and 1627 (AGCA A1.23 4577 fol. 45 cedula 8.10.1631).

63. AGI AG 43 Cabildo of León 10.12.1582. Other requests: AGI AG 40 Artieda 18.3.1582, AG 40 Casco 17.2.1583, AG 43 Cabildo of León 22.1.1586.

64. AGI AG 56 Crown to Audiencia 15.3.1582.

65. AGI AG 40 Lara de Cordova 8.4.1603, AG 40 Audiencia 10.3.1607, AG 40 real provisión 12.2.1609; AGCA A1.53 459 3002 Cura of Masaya 1631 and A3.12 491 3726 Morillo, vecino of Granada 1631.

66. AGI AG 43 Procurador of Granada 18.6.1646, AG 162 Bishop of Nicaragua 20.7.1647; Vázquez de Espinosa, *Compendium,* 249; Gage, *English-American,* 343; MacLeod, *Spanish Central America,* 200–201.

67. BPR 2537 fol. 286v. Descripción General . . ., n.d.; AGI AG 40 Rodríguez Bravo 14.5.1688. The critical role that the availability of markets played in indigo production is described by MacLeod, *Spanish Central America,* 195–203.

68. Lee, "Cochineal Production," 449–73; MacLeod, *Spanish Central America,* 174.

69. Vázquez de Espinosa, *Compendium,* 260.

70. Ponce, *Relación breve,* 351, 360.

71. AGCA A1.23 4588 fol. 252–53 cedula 13.15.1595; AGI AG 40 Ciudad de Granada 14.5.1688; Vázquez de Espinosa, *Compendium,* 249, 260. For exports of cochineal from Central America see Chaunu, *Séville et l'Atlantique,* 6:980–81.

72. AGCA A3.16 496 3807 Governor of Nicaragua 6.4.1709.

73. AGI AG 40 Cabildo of León 7.9.1635, AG 167 Ciudad de Granada 15.12.1649, AG 21 Frasso 26.11.1663; *CDHCN,* 131–34 Town of Nueva Segovia 24.10.1664. Vázquez de Espinosa, Compendium, 248, 261; Dampier, *New Voyage,* 153–54, 157.

74. AGI AG 40 Governor of Nicaragua 10.3.1684.

75. Vázquez de Espinosa, *Compendium,* 251.

76. AGI AG 44 Vecino of Nueva Segovia 1674; *CDHCN,* 131–34 Town of Nueva Segovia 24.10.1664; Vázquez de Espinosa, *Compendium,* 249, 261.

77. AGI AG 43 Recaudos de la provincia de Nicaragua 1627–28, AG 40 Cabildo of Leon 7.9.1635; Vázquez de Espinosa, *Compendium,* 249.

78. AGCA A3.12 491 3725 Mexía, vecino of Granada 12.3.1609; AGI AG 167 Ciudad de Granada 15.12.1649; Ponce, *Relación breve,* 351; López de Velasco, *Geografía,* 317, 327–28; Vázquez de Espinosa, *Compendium,* 248.

79. Ponce, *Relación breve,* 363. For later comments on cattle raising, see AGI AG 40 Rodríguez Bravo 14.5.1688; AG 240 Governor of Costa Rica

15.11.1719; Ponce, *Relación breve,* 351; López de Velasco, *Geografía,* 317, 327; Vázquez de Espinosa, *Compendium,* 248, 253; Herrera, *Historia general,* 9 dec. 4 lib. 8 cap. 7:127–28.

80. AGCA A1.38 258 1955 Ordinances for the reform of estancias de ganado 1608; BPR 2537 fol. 286v, 387v, Descripción General . . ., n.d.; Gage, *English-American,* 342–43; Vázquez de Espinosa, *Compendium,* 249.

81. AGCA A1.38 258 1955 Ordinances for the reform of estancias de ganado 1608.

82. Ibid.; MacLeod, *Spanish Central America,* 211.

83. AGCA A1.38 258 1955 Ordinances for the reform of estancias de ganado 1608; AGI AG 1528 Mercado 23.1.1620; AG 167 Ciudad de Granada 15.12.1649; Gage, *English-American,* 340; Vázquez de Espinosa, *Compendium,* 252.

84. AGCA A3.12 491 3732 Cabildo of Granada 4.5.1709.

85. Radell, "Historical Geography," 152–55.

86. AGI AG 63 Villavicencio, vecino of Jerez de la Frontera 1615; Radell, "Historical Geography," 154–55.

87. AGI AG 167 Ciudad de Granada 15.12.1649, AG 362 Bishop of Nicaragua 20.6.1708; Alcedo, *Diccionario,* 3:321; Ponce, *Relación breve,* 351; López de Velasco, *Geografía,* 317.

88. AGI AG 40 Cabildo of León 7.9.1735; BNM 3178 Frutas mas principales que hay . . ., n.d.; AGI AG 167 Ciudad de Granada 15.12.1649; AGCA A3.16 76 1066–67 Pasaje de mulas 1683–88, 74 1058–60 Pasaje de mulas 1710–19 (Costa Rica); Herrera, *Historia general,* 9 dec. 4 lib. 8 cap. 7:126; Gage, *English-American,* 342–43; Vázquez de Espinosa, *Compendium,* 253.

89. AGI AG 40 Casco 17.2.1583.

90. AGI AG 162 and *CDI,* 5:522–29 Bishop Carrasco, n.d.; AG 386-2 King to Audiencia 23.5.1574; AGCA A1.23 1514 fol. 61 cedula 20.10.1604.

91. AGI PAT 182-1-43 Relación de las rentas, n.d., AG 11 Cuenta de Nicaragua 9.7.1597.

92. AGCA A3.9 481 3643 and 3644 Aguilar, miner of Nueva Segovia 13.6.1699, 7.4.1713.

93. AGI AG 10 Venegas de los Ríos, n.d.; AGI AG 14 On the ports of Nicaragua 1629; BNM 2468 fol. 100 Descripciones geográficas 24.6.1632; AGI IG 1528 Mercado 23.1.1620; BPR 2537 fol. 380v. Descripción general, n.d.; Serrano y Sanz, *Relaciones históricas,* 468 Pineda (1594); Vázquez de Espinosa, *Compendium,* 250–51; Borah, *Early Colonial Trade,* 5; Radell and Parsons, "Realejo," 301–302.

94. AGI AG 10 Lic. Palacio 20.11.1578, AG 50 Oficiales reales 26.3.1579, Alvarez de Toledo 24.5.1580, Alvarez de Toledo 15.9.1580.

95. AGI AG 40 Artieda 12.11.1579, AG 55 Arias Riquel 4.3.1580; ANCR CC 5142 Fr. Ortiz 6.2.1583; AGCA A1.23 1513 fol. 565 cedula 6.9.1679.

96. AGI AG 162 Bishop of Nicaragua 6.4.1679.

97. AGI AG 247 Treasurer of Nicaragua 2.8.1712; Radell, "Historical Geography," 113–19; Radell and Parsons, "Realejo," 305–306; MacLeod, *Spanish Central America,* 276.

98. AGI AG 44 Montoso Castillo 3.8.1590; BNM 3178 Frutas mas principales que hay . . ., n.d.; BNM 3047 fols. 128–35v. no author, n.d.; *CDHCN,*

131–34 Town of Nueva Segovia 24.10.1644; AGI AG 40 Ciudad de Granada 14.5.1688, AG 44 Vecino of Nueva Segovia 1674, AG 362 Bishop of Nicaragua 18.6.1702, AG 247 Treasurer of Nicaragua 2.8.1712; Vázquez de Espinosa, *Compendium*, 250–51.

99. BNM 3064 Descripción de Panama 1607; AGI AG 43 Recaudos de la provincia de Nicaragua 1627–28; BNM 2468 fol. 100 Descripciones geográficas . . . 24.6.1632; AGI AG 40 Cabildo de León 7.9.1635; BPR 2537 fol. 387v. Descripción general, n.d.; AGI AG 21 Frasso 26.11.1663; Dampier, *New Voyage*, 137; Vázquez de Espinosa, *Compendium*, 249, 250–51.

100. Vazquez de Espinosa, *Compendium*, 251. See also AGI IG 1528 Mercado 23.1.1620, AG 14 On the ports of Nicaragua 1629.

101. AGI AG 162 Bishop of Nicaragua 14.7.1647; MacLeod, *Spanish Central America*, 277–78.

102. AGI AG 401-4 cedula 3.3.1564; AGCA A1.24 1560 10204 fol. 152 cedula 5.5.1649.

103. AGCA A3.12 491 3727 Vecinos of Nueva Segovia 2.11.1669.

104. Moreno, "Extranjeros y el ejercicio de comercio," 441–54; Konetske, "Legislación sobre inmigración," 269–99.

105. Floyd, *Anglo-Spanish Struggle*, 12–16, MacLeod, *Spanish Central America*, 156. There are numerous references to the presence of foreigners in the sixteenth century: AGI AG 52 Vecino of Trujillo 1558, AG 9 Audiencia 22.8.1559, AG 394-4 King to Audiencia 5.5.1561, AG 386-2 King to Audiencia 26.5.1573, AG 39 Cap. López 20.5 1575, AG 39 Relación de las cartas, 1575, AG 55 Cap. López 1577, AG 43 Cabildo of Comayagua 7.4.1578, AG 10 Audiencia 17.3.1578; AGCA A1.23 1513 fol. 561 cedula 22.5.1579, AGI AG 10 Ciudad de Trujillo 16.5.1583, AG 49 Romero 26.2.1595, AG 39 Cap. Carrança 17.8.1595, AG 10 no author 21.9.1595, AG 1 Consejo de Indias 7.3.1596, AG 10 Audiencia 4.4.1596, AG 386-2 King to Audiencia 28.11.1596, AG 164 Bishop of Honduras 12.10.1598, AG 39 Alvarado 20.5.1603.

106. Floyd, *Anglo-Spanish Struggle*, 15–17.

107. AGI AG 44 Cabildo of Trujillo 6.2.1643, AG 16 Dávila y Lugo 4.10. 1643; BNM 3047 fols. 128–35 no author, n.d.; AGCA A1.23 1520 10075 fol. 137 Merits of Escoto 11.12.1674. The activities of the Providence Company are described fully in Newton, *Colonizing Activities*, and summarized in Parsons, *Green Turtle*, 5–13.

108. AGI AG 40 Governor of Nicaragua 18.6.1670, Cabildo eclesiástico of León 24.1.1671, AG 162 Bishop of Nicaragua 23.12.1673, 12.4.1679; AGCA A3.16 1.9.1689; Haring, *Buccaneers in the West Indies*, 137–39, 162; Newton, *Colonizing Activities*, 272; Cruikshank, *Life of Sir Henry Morgan*, 57–59, 153–54; Trigueros, "Defensas estratégicas," 432–59; Floyd, *Anglo-Spanish Struggle*, 29–33. The attack of 1665 included the notorious Henry Morgan.

109. The buccaneer-historians Raveneau de Lussan and Dampier were involved in these attacks (Raveneau de Lussan, *Voyage into the South Seas*, 129–31, 134; Dampier, *New Voyage*, 152–57). For comments on the impact of these attacks see AGCA A3.16 495 3782 Fiscal 14.10.1686, A3.16 147 999 1686; AGI AG 255 Indians of Sutiaba 1690, AG 44 Cabildo of Granada 1695; Trigueros, "Defensas estratégicas," 459–60; Floyd, *Anglo-Spanish Struggle*, 36–38.

CHAPTER 9

1. AGI AG 402-2 cedula 18.8.1548.

2. For example, AGI JU 287 and *CS,* 14:124–249 Juicio promovido . . . 22.8.1548, AG 9, *CDI,* 24:494–501 and *CS,* 15:491–512 cedula 26.1. 1550, AG 393-3 cedula 11.9.1550.

3. AGI AG 402-2 cedula 1.9.1548, AG 9 and *CS,* 15:31–40 Cerrato 8.4.1549.

4. AGI AG 386-1 cedula 11.7.1552; Bataillon, "Las Casas et le Licencié Cerrato," 82–84; Sherman, "Cerrato Reforms," 39–40, *Forced Native Labor,* 168–72; MacLeod, *Spanish Central America,* 112–16.

5. *Recopilación,* 2 lib. 6 tít. 11 ley 14:282–83 3.6.1555, ley 16:283 9.6.1569; Haring, *Spanish Empire,* 54.

6. AGCA A1.23 4579 fol. 137v. cedula 25.11.1637; AGI AG 418 Confirmation of titles to encomiendas 1615–75. See also a list of encomiendas drawn up in 1662 (AGI CO 983A Relación de todas la rentas 29.12.1662).

7. *Recopilación,* 2 lib. 6 tít. 9 ley 24:269 24.11.1527; AGCA A1.23 4576 fol. 176v. cedula 1.5.1608.

8. AGI CO 983A Relación de todas las rentas 29.12.1662.

9. AGI AG 128 Libro de tasaciones 1548, AG 966 census 1581, CO 983A Relación de todas las rentas 29.12.1662.

10. *Recopilación* 2 lib. 6 tít. 10 leyes 21–24:255–56 10.10.1618.

11. AGI CO 983A Relación de todas las rentas 29.12.1662.

12. AGCA A1.23 1512 fol. 283 cedula 1.10.1560. In 1581 11.5 percent of Indian villages or *parcialidades* paid tribute to the crown, while in 1652 it was said that only 600 out of 4,000 tributary Indians in Nicaragua (15 percent) were under crown administration (AGI CO 986 Oficiales reales 10.11.1652).

13. From 1627 all encomiendas had to remain vacant for a year before being reassigned (AGCA A1.23 1518 fol. 78 cedula 10.4.1627).

14. The use of income from vacant encomiendas for defense appears to have begun in Central America in 1572, when 1,000 pesos were assigned for the defense of the port of Trujillo (AGCA A1.23 1512 fol. 425 cedula 1.12.1572).

15. The order was issued on 26.2.1687. By 1703, 7,000 pesos had been collected from vacant encomiendas, but another 9,000 pesos were still required (AGI AG 246 cedula 28.4.1703, AG 256 Memorial 1703).

16. AGI AG 246 Oficiales reales 15.11.1703 (cedula 9.6.1701), AG 259 cedulas 23.1.1718 and 27.9.1721.

17. AGI AG 966 census 1581; AGCA A3.16 146 989 tasaciones 1704. See table 6.

18. AGI CO 938A Relación de todas las rentas 29.12.1662, AG 258 cedula 31.1.1687. The value and number of provincial encomiendas in 1662 was: over 500 pesos, 8; 200–499 pesos, 7; 100–199 pesos, 17; under 100 pesos, 1.

19. See discussion of tribute in chap. 6. For the payment of tithes on tribute see AGCA A1.23 4576 fol. 67v. cedulas 13.2.1595, 16.1.1621.

20. AGCA A3.16 2566 37647 fol. 33 cedula 1.2.1636. There was an order for the payment of the *media anata* in 1648 (AGCA A1.23 1517 fol. 141 cedula 1.2.1648), but Haring maintains that it was introduced in 1631 (Haring, *Spanish Empire,* 273).

21. AGCA A1.23 256 fol. 244 cedula 19.12.1684, A1.23 2025 14035 fol. 31v. cedula 28.4.1694; Haring, *Spanish Empire,* 67.

22. *Recopilación,* 2 lib. 6 tít. 5 ley 27:233 11.7.1552.

23. AGI AG 9 Audiencia 30.6.1560; AGCA A1.23 1517 fol. 203 cedulas 2.10.1624, 30.9.1639, 12.12.1649; *Recopilación* 2 lib. 6 tít. 5 leyes 55 and 56:239 23.12.1595, 13.6.1623, 9.10.1623, 2.10.1624. In 1582 it was estimated that in Nicaragua a *visita* by an *oidor* cost 3,000 pesos (AGI AG 40 Artieda 18.3.1582), while in 1573 the crown's annual income from encomiendas in Nicaragua was only 3,528 pesos.

24. AGCA A1.23 1512 fol. 375 cedula 1.7.1567, A1.23 4581 fol. 28v. cedula 1.6.1577, A1.23 1515 fol. 52 cedula 12.12.1619.

25. AGCA A1.23 1511 fol. 253 cedula 22.6.1559; Puga, *Provisiones* fols. 127–28, 152–53 8.6.1551.

26. AGCA A1.23 4577 fol. 13v. cedula 12.12.1619.

27. Zorita, *Lords of New Spain,* 219–29.

28. Puga, *Provisiones,* fol. 139v. 18.12.1552; Miranda, *Tributo indígena,* 115.

29. AGI AG 52 Lic. Cavallón 27.2.1555; Bancroft, *Native Races,* 2:359.

30. AGI JU 323 Commission given 12.3.1562, AG 50 Arteaga 1.5.1563, Venegas de los Ríos 13.11.1566. Details of the *visita* of Granada by Dr. Barros are contained in JU 328 fols. 281–304 1563.

31. AGCA A1.23 1513 fol. 506 cedula 15.10.1576; AGI AG 966 census 1581, CO 984 tasaciones 1579, AG 966 census 1581.

32. AGI AG 966 census 1581. His instructions for the conduct of *visitas* are contained in AGI AG 128, n.d., and in Paso y Troncoso, ed., *Epistolario,* 15:104–25.

33. For charges and sentences see AGI AG 966 1578, JU 330 1578–80. There are 5 in the former *legajo* and 31 in the latter.

34. AGCA A3.16 494 3763 26.1.1605.

35. AGCA A1.23 1514 fol. 131 cedula 26.5.1609.

36. AGI AG 13 Sánchez Araque 13.1.1613.

37. AGI AG 40 Certificación sacada de los libros reales . . . 2.1.1674. The figures included with the account of the *visita* written in 1663 were probably taken from earlier tasaciones (AGI AG 133 Fiscal 6.5.1633).

38. AGI AG 29 Audiencia 14.5.1681 (cedula 21.6.1680).

39. AGCA A1.23 1522 fol. 42 cedula 12.8.1682.

40. AGI CO 815 Razón de las ciudades 1683, AG 29 Navia Bolaños 28.7.1685.

41. For the 1686 *tasaciones* see AGCA A3.16 147 999. These indicate the presence of a slightly higher tributary population than that indicated by Navia Bolaños in 1685.

42. *Tasaciones* for various dates between 1676 and 1696 can be found in AGCA A3.16 147 999.

43. AGCA A1.23 1583 fol. 131 cedula 5.5.1719.

44. Ayón, *Historia de Nicaragua,* 2:232.

45. For example, AGCA A3.16 497 3817 1717 (Jinotega), 3818 1718 (Teustepet), 3821 1718 (Boaco), 3822 1719 (Quesalquaque), 3823 1719 (Teustepet), 3824 1719 (Quesalquaque), 3826 1719 (Posolteguilla); for the towns of Chichigalpa, El Viejo, and Chinandega see A3.16 1605 26438 1718.

46. AGI AG 247 Oficiales reales 15.2.1709.

47. *Recopilación,* 2 lib. 6 tít. 5 ley 7:226–27 5.7 1578.

48. Despite orders to the contrary, AGCA A1.23 1513 fol. 591 cedula 17.4.1581.

49. AGCA A3.16 494 3763 26.1.1605, A3.16 511 5315 Padrón of Litelpaneca 17.4.1581.

50. AGCA A1.38 4778 41245 Ordenanzas 21.10.1683.

51. AGCA A3.16 494 3763 tasación of Sutiaba 17.12.1587; AGI AG 133 Fiscal 6.5.1663.

52. AGCA A1.23 1512 fol. 407 cedula 18.5.1572.

53. AGCA A1.23 1512 fol. 407 18.5.1572; *Recopilación,* 2 lib. 6 tít. 5 ley 18:230 17.7.1572. In fact, between 1572 and 1576 Indian officials in Nicaragua paid half tribute, which was regulated at 7 tostones (AGI CO 984).

54. AGCA A3.16 494 3763 26.1.1605; *Recopilación,* 2 lib. 6 tít. 5 ley 11:227, n.d.; AGCA A1.23 4585 fol. 240 cedula 14.5.1686.

55. AGCA A1.23 1524 fol. 3 cedula 21.3.1702.

56. AGCA A1.23 1561 fol. 23 cedula 16.2.1655.

57. AGCA A1.23 1559 fol. 212 cedula 2.5.1642, A1.23 1561 fol. 102 cedula 27.4.1655, A1.23 1567 fol. 167 cedula 3.3.1683, A1.23 1583 fol. 62 cedula 18.5.1719.

58. Generally the children of a married couple were to be included in the tributary list of the father's village, while children of single women were to be included in that of the mother's village (*Recopilación,* 2 lib. 6 tít. 1 ley 10 10.10.1618), but *padrones* for Nicaragua do not include children when the mother is from another village, thus suggesting that children were registered in the mother's village regardless of her marital status.

59. AGI AG 133 Fiscal 6.5.1633.

60. AGCA A1.23 1524 fol. 189 cedula 2.8.1704.

61. AGI AG 402-3 and *CS,* 15:3–6 cedula 22.2.1549; AGCA A1.23 4575 fol. 94 cedula 22.2.1549; Zavala, *Instituciones coloniales,* 70.

62. *Recopilación,* 2 lib. 6 tít. 5 ley 22:231–32 18.12.1552.

63. AGCA A1.12 77 623 Villages of Camoapa, Lóvago, and Lovigüisca 31.1.1614, 13.4.1627.

64. AGI AG 40 Lara de Cordova 27.7.1604; AGCA A3.16 147 999 tasaciones 1676–96.

65. See chap. 10; AGI AG 965 Archdean of León, n.d.; AG 50 Venegas de los Rios 13.11.1566.

66. AGI AG 128 Libro de tasaciones 1548, AG 50 Venegas de los Ríos 13.11.1566; Radell, "Historical Geography," 87.

67. AGI AG 966 census 1581.

68. AGI AG 50 Oficiales reales 3.8.1604; AGCA A3.16 494 3764 tasaciones 1605–10.

69. In 1614 married male Indians in Sebaco paid 1½ fanegas of maize.

70. AGCA A3.16 147 999 tasaciones 1676–96.

71. AGCA A1.23 1513 fol. 719 cedula 1.11.1591; *Recopilación,* 2 lib. 6 tít. 5 ley 16:228.

72. *Recopilación,* 2 lib. 6 tít. 5 ley 44:237. On his *visita* Lic. Palacio brought a number óf charges against encomenderos for having forced Indians to carry their tribute to the nearest town without payment (AGI JU 330 1578–80).

73. AGCA A1.24 2195 fols. 99 and 345 cedulas 17.3.1553, A1.23 1514 fol. 77 cedula 22.12.1605, A1.23 1516 fol. 12v. cedula 12.12.1619, A1.23 4596 fol. 32 cédula 28.3.1620.

74. AGI AG 44 Cabildo of Granada 2.7.1695.

75. For the prices of maize in León and Granada, 1572–94, see AGI CO 984 and 985 Cargo de tributos, and fig. 7.

76. AGI AG 43 Ramírez, procurador of León 1631[?]; AGCA A1.23 1526 fol. 141 cedula 11.11.1719; Salvatierra, *Historia de Centro América,* 2:153.

77. AGI AG 401-4 cedula 18.3.1564, JU 330 Sentences of Lic. Palacio 1580; ANCR Guatemala 19 Case against Enciso 1606; AGI AG 240 Aranzibia 16.3.1718.

78. AGI AG 965 Archdean of León, n.d.; AGCA A3.16 491 3726 Pueblo of Boaco 31.1.1631, A3.16 495 3781 Contador of Nicaragua 29.11.1676.

79. AGI AG 131 1640; AGCA A3.16 491 3729 Indians of Condega and Telpaneca 8.5.1696, A3.16 491 3732 Cabildo of Granada 4.5.1709, A3.16 491 3734 1711.

80. *Recopilación,* 2 lib. 6 tít. 5 leyes 9–10:227 15.2.1575 and 4.7.1593; AGI CO 986 Cargo de tributos 1625; AGCA A3.16 146 990 Cuaderno . . . de lavoríos 1.1.1707.

81. *Recopilación,* 2 lib. 6 tít. 5 ley 24:232 22.2.1549; AGCA A1.23 4576 39529 Ordenanzas for the repartimiento 24.11.1601, 26.5.1609.

82. García Peláez, *Memorias,* 1:226. Martínez Peláez (*Patria del criollo,* 471–73) and Sherman (*Forced Native Labor,* 191–207) describe the operation of the repartimiento in the Audiencia of Guatemala.

83. AGCA A1.23 4576 39529 Ordenanzas for the repartimiento 24.11. 1601, 26.5.1609.

84. AGI AG 9 Ramírez and Quesada 25.5.1555.

85. AGCA A3.16 491 3728 24.11.1695; AGI AG 44 Cabildo of Granada 1695. At that time Indian villages in the jurisdiction of Granada supplied 300 Indians for *servicio ordinario* and 150 for *servicio extraordinario.* The administration of the *servicio ordinario* was apparently undertaken by corregidores and alcaldes mayores, while *servicio extraordinario* was in the hands of the governor. In 1621 Indians in the corregimiento of El Viejo complained that the corregidor had exceeded his authority in ordering them to work on tasks which fell into the category of *servicio extraordinario* (AGCA A1.30 210 1713 Residencia on the corregidor of Realejo 1621).

86. AGCA A1.23 1512 fol. 478 cedula 27.4.1575 See also chap. 8.

87. AGI AG 968A Memorial de los indios alquilones . . . 1,578. For other descriptions of the heavy work involved in shipbuilding, see AGCA A1.23 1511 fol. 137 cedula 11.5.1550; AGI AG 50 Venegas de los Ríos 15.6.1564 and AG 55 Arias Riquel 4.3.1580.

88. AGCA A1.23 1513 fol. 565 cedula 6.9.1579.

89. AGCA A1.23 1516 fol. 179 cedula 15.4.1640, A1.23 1560 fol. 152 cedula 5.5.1649.

90. For example, AGCA A3.1 520 4101 Morales, vecino of León 28.4. 1634.

91. AGI AG 257 Indians of the corregimiento of Sutiaba 1705.

92. AGI AG 968B Oficiales reales of Guatemala 13.10.1646 (cedula 30.12. 1645).

93. AGCA A3.9 155 3005 Miners of Nueva Segovia 26.4.1699.

94. For example, following pirate attacks on Granada (AGCA A3.16 495 3782 Pueblos of Jinotepet and Diriamba 14.10.1686; AGI AG 225 Indians of Sutiaba 1690).

95. AGI AG 44 Autos . . . la ciudad de Nueva Segovia 1663.

96. In 1631 the encomendero of Boaco complained that more Indians had been assigned to work under the repartimiento then were permitted according to the *tasación* (AGCA A3.12 491 3726 Morillo, vecino of Granada 31.1.1631).

97. AGCA A1.23 1515 fol. 81 cedula 24.6.1607, A3.16 496 3807 Pueblo of Masaya 1709.

98. AGCA A1.23 1514 fol. 132 cedula 26.5.1609.

99. AGCA A3.12 491 3731 Vecinos of Granada 18.5.1709.

100. AGI AG 40 Governor Cordova y Guzmán 29.6.1607; AGCA A1.23 4576 39529 fol. 7 Ordenanzas for the repartimiento 26.5.1609; AGI AG 133 Ordenanzas 6.5.1663.

101. AGCA A3.12 491 3729 Indians of Condega and Telpaneca 8.5.1696.

102. AGI AG 9 Ramírez and Quesada 25.5.1555, JU 328 fols. 281–304 Ordenanzas of Dr. Barros for Granada 1563, AG 968A Memorial de los indios alquilones 1578, AG 133 Ordenanzas 6.5.1633; AGCA A1.38 4778 41245 Ordenanzas 21.10.1683; AGI AG 44 Cabildo of Granada 2.7.1695. Vázquez de Espinosa recorded that one real would buy two *celemines* of maize, which would make tortillas for several days (*Compendium*, 252).

103. AGI JU 328 fols. 281–304 Ordenanzas of Dr. Barros for Granada 1563; AGCA A3.12 491 3729 Indians of Condega and Telpaneca 8.5.1696, A3.12 491 3734 1711 cedula 12.9.1709.

104. In 1586 a *vecino* of Nueva Segovia complained that Indians from his encomienda were living on estates, where their presence was concealed by the owners, and that it was impossible to make them return to their villages (AGCA A3.16 520 4110 Sigueyra, vecino of Nueva Segovia 18.3.1586).

105. Ibid.; AGCA A1.23 1515 fol. 81 cedula 24.6.1607, A3.12 491 3729 Indians of Condega and Telpaneca 8.5.1696.

106. Pardo, *Efemérides*, 20 2.6.1584; AGCA A1.23 4579 fol. 42 cedula 8.10.1631, A1.38 4778 41245 Ordenanzas 21.10.1683.

107. AGCA A3.16 491 3729 Indians of Condega and Telpaneca 8.5.1696, A3.16 496 3807 Pueblo of Masaya 1709.

108. AGCA A1.12 77 630 Cabildo of Granada 29.7.1689, A3.12 491 3730 Pueblo of Managua 17.5.1709, A3.12 491 3731 18.5.1709, A3.12 491 3732 Cabildo of Granada 12.9.1709.

109. AGI CO 815 Razón de las ciudades 1683.

110. AGI AG 40 Artieda 18.3.1582, AG 40 Casco 12.4.1584.

111. *Recopilación* 2 lib. 5 tít. 2 ley 47:237 10.7.1530; AGCA A1.24 4575 fol. 468v. cedula 21.2.1604.

112. There are numerous examples of corregidores and alcaldes mayores coercing Indians to trade with them, for example: AGI AG 11 Fiscal 17.4.1702, AG 40 Lara de Cordova 8.4.1603, AG 40 Cordova y Guzmán 29.6.1607; AGCA A1.30 210 1714 Charges against the corregidor of Chontales 1623; AGI AG 43 Procurador of Nicaragua 4.11.1631; AGCA A1.30 211 1720 Charges against the corregidor of Realejo 1634; AGI AG 131 1640; AG 20 Oidor of the Audiencia 30.8.1659; AGCA A3.12 491 3733 cedula 3.9.1673; AGI AG 162 Bishop of Nica-

ragua 6.4.1679, AG 43 Instrucción de la ciudad de León, n.d. Trade occurred despite orders to the contrary (AGCA A1.23 1517 fol. 99 cedula 15.4.1640, A1.23 1520 fol. 242 cedula 11.8.1676, A1.23 4592 fol. 22 cedula 2.8.1679).

113. AGI AG 257 Memorial of debts to corregidor 11.3.1706; AGCA A1.30 213 1726 Charges against corregidor Solorzano 1718. At the rate of pay of 3 reals a day, 60 pesos represented the equivalent to about 4½ months' work. Debts of 5 pesos or less were more common and represented less than 2 weeks' work.

114. AGCA A1.30 210 1714 and 1715 Charges against the corredigor of Chontales 1623, A1.30 211 1718 Charges against the corregidor of Realejo 1626; AGI AG 43 Procurador of Nicaragua 4.11.1631; AGCA A1.30 211 1720 Charges against the corregidor of Realejo 1634; AGI AG 156 Bishop of Guatemala 3.7.1637, AG 25 Testimonio . . . 1672.

115. AGI AG 40 Casco 12.4.1584.

116. AGCA A1.23 1513 fol. 646 cedula 8.6.1585; Pardo, *Efemérides,* 20 8.6.1585. However, in 1587 they were still being appointed. Fuentes y Guzmán (*Recordación Florida,* 3:307) maintains that the officials were first introduced into Guatemala in 1539.

117. AGCA A1.23 1515 fol. 231 cedula 12.12.1619.

118. The investigation of the conduct of *jueces de milpas* in the Audiencia of Guatemala makes fascinating reading, it is contained in four *legajos*—AGI AG 971A, 971B, 972A and 972B—all of which have been badly burned and are difficult to handle and read.

119. AGCA A1.23 1515 fol. 231 and 4576 fol. 38v. cedula 28.5.1630, A1.24 2197 f.13 cedula 4.9.1640, A1.23 4582 f.113 cedula 14.11.1699; García Peláez, *Memorias,* 1:235–37. Part of the reason why the audiencia permitted their appointment was to appease would-be officeholders; the crown, however, tried to limit such appointments for financial reasons and to protect the Indians from exploitation (MacLeod, *Spanish Central America,* 317–18).

120. AGCA A1.30 252 1910 Residencia on Don Cristóbal Torres 1651; AGI AG 25 Testimonio . . . 1672.

121. AGCA A1.23 1515 fol. 231 cedula 12.12.1619, A1.23 1524 fol. 164 cédula 2.8.1704.

122. For *derramas* see AGCA A1.23 1513 fol. 619 cedula 3.11.1582, A1.23 4577 39530 cedula 12.12.1619, A1.23 1521 fol. 235 cedula 19.6.1680 cedula confirming prohibition 21.5.1678, A1.38 4778 41245 Ordenanzas 21.10.1683. For priests exacting goods and labor see AGI AG 50 Venegas de los Ríos 15.6.1564, 13.11.1566; AGCA A1.23 1514 fol. 219 cedula 21.5.1611, A1.73 476 3149 Pueblo of Chinandega 1613; AGI AG 40 Memorial on the instruction of Indians 1631, 17.5.1631, AG 167 Oidor 23.8.1678; AGCA A1.23 1526 f.96 cedula 7.2.1718.

123. AGI AG 40 Memorial on the instruction of Indians 1631.

124. AGCA A1.23 4579 39532 fol. 86 cedula 17.8.1636 and *Recopilación* 2 lib. 5 tít. 2 ley 21:120. For the burden imposed by *visitas* see AGI AG 162 Bishop Carrasco, n.d., AG 40 Casco 17.2.1583, AG 40 Lara de Cordova 8.4. 1603.

125. AGI AG 131 1640; AGCA A1.23 1517 fol. 99 cedula 7.5.1646, A3.12 491 3731 Vecinos of Granada 12.9.1709.

126. AGI AG 10 Audiencia 22.10.1577, AG 50 Oficiales reales 15.7.1597;

Juarros, *Statistical and Commercial History,* 64; Nolasco Pérez, *Mercedarias,* 115–17, 122–23.

127. AGCA A1.12 5802 48962 Fr. Albuquerque 1608; AGI AG 174 Fr. de Rivera 15.8.1608; *CDHCN,* 92–122 Criado de Castilla 30.11.1608; Nolasco Pérez, *Mercedarias,* 123–27.

128. AGI AG 15 Fr. de las Casas, n.d.; Nolasco Pérez, *Mercedarias,* 130.

129. AGI AG 297 Fr. Alarcón 18.2.1699.

130. AGCA A1.12 78 646 n.d., A1.12 77 623 Pueblos of the corregimiento of Sebaco 31.1.1614, 1627; AGI AG 133 Frasso 1.1.1663.

131. *BAGG,* 5:283–308 Fr. Espino 17.9.1674; AGI AG 183 Fr. Guevara 22.3.1681, Frs. Ovalle and Guevara 4.3.1681; AGCA A1.24 1566 10210 fol. 72 real provisión 5.5.1681; AGI AG 371 Fr. Ximénez 9.9.1748; Bancroft, *Native Races,* 2:448; Ayón, *Historia de Nicaragua,* 2:138–40; Vázquez, *Crónica,* 4:202–207.

132. AGCA A1.12 77 626 Fr. Magdalena 15.1.1693; Vázquez, *Crónica,* 4:212.

133. AGCA A1.12 77 629 Fr. Santa Cruz 17.7.1711; ANCR CC 3728 Bishop of Nicaragua 1.11.1711.

134. AGI AG 223 Fr. Concepción 13.1.1699, AG 371 Fr. Ximénez 9.9.1748.

135. AGI AG 10 Lic. Palacio 2.6.1578, AG 15 Fr. de las Casas, n.d.; ANCR CC 3728 Bishop of Nicaragua 1.11.1711.

136. AGI AG 297 Fr. Concepción 13.1.1699.

137. AGI AG 223 Various documents dated 1699; AGCA A1.12 77 629 Fr. Santa Cruz 17.7.1711.

138. AGI AG 39 Alvarado 15.5.1600.

139. AGI AG 15 Fr. de las Casas, n.d.

140. AGI AG 297 Fr. Alarcón 18.2.1699.

CHAPTER 10

1. AGCA A3.16 147 999 tasaciones 1676–96.

2. AGI AG 966 census 1581; AGCA A3.16 147 999 tasaciones 1676–96.

3. AGI AG 21 Frasso 25 and 26.11.1663. The figure for 1663 is higher because it probably included other categories of tributary Indians.

4. Cabrera, *Guanacaste,* 228; Thiel, "Población de la República de Costa Rica," 88.

5. AGCA A3.16 147 999 tasaciones 1676–96; Thiel, "Población de la República de Costa Rica," 92.

6. ANCR CC 3728 Bishop of Nicaragua 1.11.1711.

7. See chap. 9 and AGI AG 43 Procurador of Nicaragua 4.11.1631, AG 43 Arbieto 13.12.1653; AGCA A3.16 495 3782 Pueblos of Jinotepet and Diriamba 14.10.1686.

8. AGI AG 40 Governor of Nicaragua 1.12.1670, CO 815 Razón de las ciudades 1683.

9. AGI AG 43 8.1.1653; AGCA A3.1 520 4102 Justicias of Pueblo de la Trinidad 10.1.1673.

10. AGCA A1.23 4578 fol. 31v. cedula 11.1.1569, A1.23 1513 fol. 557 cedula 25.11.1578, A1.23 1514 fol. 37 cedula 26.5.1603; *Recopilación,* 2 lib. 6

tít. 3 ley 21:212 2.5.1563 etc.; MacLeod, *Spanish Central America,* 220–24.

11. For example, AGI AG 50 Moreno, Treasurer of Nicaragua 15.9.1580.

12. AGI AG 43 Arbieto 19.7.1653; AGCA A1.23 1518 fol. 211 cedula 17.3.1657.

13. AGI AG 162 Bishop of Nicaragua 12.4.1679.

14. See chap. 12 and AGI AG 50 Venegas de los Ríos 15.6.1564; AGCA A1.38 258 1955 Ordinances for the reform of estancias de ganado 1608.

15. *Recopilación,* 2 lib. 4 tít. 12 leyes 7 and 9:209 6.4.1588, 11.6.1594.

16. AGI AG 257 Corregimiento of Sutiaba 15.2.1705. This situation was common throughout the audiencia (AGCA A1.23 1516 fols. 12–14 cedula 9.8. 1631; Martínez Peláez, *Patria del criollo,* 156–58).

17. Gibson, *Aztecs,* 281, 285, 293.

18. *Recopilación,* 2 lib. 4 tít. 12 ley 12:42 24.3.1550 and 2.5.1550, lib. 6 tít. 3 ley 20:211–11 10.10.1618.

19. AGCA A1.23 2347 17672 fol. 6v. cedula 26.4.1549.

20. *Recopilación,* 2 lib. 6 tít. 3 ley 8:209 1.12.1573, 10.10.1618.

21. AGCA A3.16 495 3798 tasaciones 1694; AGI AG 257 Corregimiento of Sutiaba 15.2.1705.

22. AGCA A13.6 494 3763 Tasación of Sutiaba 17.12.1587.

23. AGCA A1.23 1513 fol. 525 cedula 8.5.1577, A1.23 1524 10079 fol. 164 cedula 2.8.1704.

24. AGCA A1.38 4778 41245 Ordenanzas 21.10.1683, A1.23 1523 fol. 185 cedula 27.11.1697, A1.38 4778 41248 Instrucción . . . 20.2.1709. The cultivation of 10 brazas was introduced into the Viceroyalty of Peru in 1582, after it had been in operation in New Spain (*Recopilación,* 2 lib. 6 tít. 4 ley 31:222 4.6.1582; García Peláez, *Memorias,* 1:223), and it is possible that it was introduced at the same time as the sementeras and *milpas de comunidad* and may very well have been the same thing.

25. AGCA A1.38 4778 4125 Ordenanzas 21.10.1683.

26. AGCA A1.23 1523 fols. 184–85 cedulas 26.3.1689, 27.11.1697.

27. AGI JU 330 Sentences of Palacio 1580.

28. AGCA A3.16 495 3773 Padrón of Diriamba 11.3.1663. A3.16 146 984 Padrón of Nicoya 26.3.1675, A3.16 495 3778 Padrones of Posoltega, Guacama, and Miagalpa 18.1.1676.

29. See chap. 8.

30. Of 179 land grants made in Nicaragua between 1713 and 1733, only 10 were made to individual Indians (AGI AG 252 Media anatas paid on lands 1713–33).

31. AGI AG 40 Arbieto 12.10.1655.

32. AGI AG 133 20.4.1663, Fiscal 6.5.1663.

33. See chap. 9. There were many complaints from Indians that owing to the demands of the repartimiento and other labor services they were unable to sow or harvest their milpas. For example, AGCA A1.12 32 268 Priests of El Viejo 9.8.1629, A1.23 1517 10072 fol. 3 cedula 25.5.1641, A1.23 1519 fol. 213 cedula 10.3.1660. For complaints against secular and ecclesiastical officials for employing them to sow milpas or spin and weave cotton so that they could not attend to their subsitence needs, see: AGI AG 50 Venegas de los Ríos 15.6.1564, AG 40 Memorial 1632; AGCA A1.30 211 1720 Charges against the

corregidor of Realejo 1634, A1.23 1516 fol. 179 cedula 15.4.1560, A1.23 1562 fol. 250 cedula 30.3.1658, A1.23 1519 fol. 213 cedula 10.3.1660.

34. AGI AG 133 Fiscal 6.5.1663.

35. Vázquez de Espinosa, *Compendium,* 252.

36. Borah and Cook, *Aboriginal Population,* 91; Gibson, *Aztecs,* 311.

37. See chap. 3 n. 29.

38. Gibson, *Aztecs,* 309.

39. See chap. 5.

40. See chap. 9.

41. AGI AG 50 Venegas de los Ríos 13.11.1566.

42. AGCA A1.23 1515 fol. 231 cedula 28.5.1630.

43. AGI JU 328 fols. 281–304 Ordinances of Dr. Barros for Granada 1563, AG 9 Dr. Villalobos 15.5.1573, AG 10 President of the Audiencia 4.4.1596, AG 25 Testimonio . . . 1672 (Vecino of Granada 14.3.1671).

44. See fig. 7 and chap. 8.

45. AGI CO 988 Cargo de tributos 1562, AG 966 census 1581.

46. AGI AG 54 Memorial of the Procurador of Nicaragua 1574; Herrera, *Historia general* 9 dec. 4 lib. 8 cap. 7:127–28; Ponce, *Relación breve,* 351; López de Velasco, *Geografía,* 329; Vázquez de Espinosa, *Compendium,* 250, 252. There were between 100 to 200 cacao beans to a real. For the species of fruit trees cultivated see chap. 3.

47. See chap. 8 and AGI AG 162, CDI 5:552–29 and RAHM CM A/115 fols. 73–76v. Bishop Carrasco (probably 1550s), AG 181 Bishop of Nicaragua 15.7.1683; MacLeod, *Spanish Central America,* 72.

48. AGCA A1.30 252 1910 Residencia on Don Cristóbal de Torres 1651.

49. AGI AG 128 Libro de tasaciones 1548 and see chap. 6; AGCA A3.16 147 999 tasaciones 1676–96, A3.16 146 989 tasaciones 1704.

50. Vázquez de Espinosa, *Compendium,* 262.

51. AGI AG 966 census 1581.

52. See chap. 9 and AGI AG 50 Venegas de los Ríos 15.6.1584; AGCA A1.23 1517 10027 fols. 207–208 cedula 12.12.1609; AGI AG 40 Testimonio . . . 1631, AG 25 Testimonio . . . 1672.

53. AGI AG 128 Relación y forma . . . n.d. (but in the 1570s). See chap. 9.

54. *Recopilación,* 2 lib. 6 tít. 1 ley 22:194 17.12.1551.

55. AGCA A1.38 258 1955 Ordinances for the reform of estancias de ganado 1608.

56. AGCA A1.38 4778 41245 Ordenanzas 21.10.1683.

57. AGI AG 133 20.4.1663, Fiscal 6.5.1663.

58. For example, AGI AG 257 Corregimiento of Sutiaba 1705; AGCA A1.30 213 1726 Complaints against the corregidor of Sutiaba 1718.

59. Ponce, *Relación breve,* 373–74; *Recopilación,* 2 lib. 6 tít. 1 ley 33:197 19.7.1568.

60. For example, AGCA A1.23 1514 fol. 132 cedula 26.5.1609; AGI AG 131 1640.

61. See chap. 9 and AGI AG 50 Venegas de los Ríos 15.6.1564.

62. For references to the exploitation of these products see chap. 9.

63. Herrera, *Historia general,* 9 dec. 4 lib. 8 cap. 7:128; López de Velasco, *Geografía,* 328; Vázquez de Espinosa, *Compendium,* 253.

64. *Recopilación,* 2 lib. 6 tít. 1 ley 31: 196 17.9.1501.

65. Herrera, *Historia general,* 9 dec. 4 lib. 8 cap. 7: 127; Alcedo, *Diccionario,* 3: 321; López de Velasco, *Geografía,* 320–21; Serrano y Sanz, *Relaciones históricas,* 468 (Pineda 1594); Vázquez de Espinosa, *Compendium,* 248, 251, 259.

66. AGI AG 181 Bishop of Nicaragua 15.7.1683; Alcedo, *Diccionario,* 3: 331; Juarros, *Statistical and Commercial History,* 72.

67. AGI AG 40 Lara de Córdova 27.7.1604; AGCA A3.16 146 989 tasaciones 1704.

68. For evidence of these crafts see AGI AG 10 Venegas de los Ríos, n.d., AG 50 Venegas de los Ríos 15.6.1564, AG 162 Bishop of Nicaragua 6.4.1679, AG 44 Cabildo of Granada 1695; Herrera, *Historia general,* 9 dec. 4 lib. 8 cap. 7: 126.

69. Herrera, *Historia general,* 9 dec. 4 lib. 8 cap. 7: 126.

70. AGCA A1.38 4778 41425 Ordenanzas 21.10.1683; *Recopilación,* 2 lib. 8 tít. 13 ley 24: 503 31.8.1600; Puga, *Provisiones,* fol. 184 2.3.1552.

71. See chap. 9.

72. *Recopilación,* 2 lib. 6 tít. 3 ley 23: 212 21.11.1600; AGCA A1.23 1516 fol. 47 cedula 28.3.1632; Vázquez de Espinosa, *Compendium,* 252, 260.

73. AGI AG 162 Información . . . 20.8.1651.

74. *Recopilación,* 2 lib. 6 tít. 5 ley 18: 230 17.7.1572.

75. Ibid., ley 3: 202 6.11.1528, 26.10.1541, 8.2.1588, tít. 7 ley 10: 247. 8.7.1577; AGI AG 128 Relación y forma . . ., n.d.

76. AGI AG 250 Ordenanzas 28.6.1568, AG 965 Archdean of León, n.d.

77. Molina Agrüello, "Gobernaciones," 119. Gibson notes this practice in the Valley of Mexico (Gibson, *Aztecs,* 167–68).

78. For example, Antonio Roque, a moreno and *vecino* of Nueva Segovia, was made governor of the Indians he had "conquered" in the mountains (AGI AG 390 cedula 13.10.1709; Molina Argüello, "Gobernaciones." 119–20).

79. AGI AG 128 Relación y forma . . ., n.d.

80. AGI JU 330 Sentences of Palacio 1580.

81. Gibson, *Aztecs,* 156.

82. AGI AG 52 Lic. Cavallón 27.2.1555.

83. *Recopilación,* 2 lib. 6 tít. 3 ley 15: 210 10.10.1618. See AGI AG 29 28.7.1685 for an account of the number of alcaldes and regidores appointed in each village in Nicaragua.

84. *Recopilación,* 2 lib. 6 tít. 3 ley 17: 211 11.8.1563.

85. ANCR CC 3728 Bishop of Nicaragua 1.11.1711; AGCA A3.16 497 3819 Tribute debts 1718.

86. For example, AGCA A1.23 1582 10226 fol. 25 cedula 17.1.1707.

87. *Recopilación,* 2 lib. 6 tít. 3 leyes 6 and 7: 208–209 both 10.10.1618. Probably in the 1570s Indian sacristans and flutists were required to pay tribute (AGI AG 167 Dean of León, n.d.), but a later document maintained that they and the fiscals were exempt from tribute (AGCA A3.16 150 1043 Teniente 21.12.1768).

88. See chap. 15 for ownership of houses, cattle, horses, and oxen.

89. AGI AG 128 Relación y forma . . ., n.d.; *Recopilación,* 2 lib. 6 tít. 1 ley 4: 190 13.7.1530, ley 5: 190 7.12.1551.

90. *Recopilación,* 2 lib. 6 tít. 1 ley 2: 190 19.10.1514.

91. There were many laws to this effect, for example, *Recopilación,* 2 lib. 6 tít. 3 ley 21:212 2.5.1563 to 12.7.1600.

92. AGCA A3.16 147 999 tasaciones 1676–96.

93. This proposition is supported by evidence from the *padrones* of Quesalquaque and Posolteguilla in 1719, which provide information on marriages for individual barrios. It shows that the percentages of marriages in which one person was from another barrio were 85.2 percent and 45.7 percent respectively, but the percentage of marriages in which one person was from another village only 41.3 percent and 40.2 percent, respectively, which are lower than those recorded as marrying out of their villages in the east in 1676–96. The closer correspondence between the two percentages for Posolteguilla is probably a function of the smaller number of barrios—three as opposed to eight in Quesalquaque (AGCA A3.16 498 3826 Padrón of Posolteguilla 9.9.1719, A3.16 497 3822 Padrón of Queslaquaque 15.9.1719).

94. The percentages of those marrying out of their villages or barrios, 1685–1719, were as follows: 1685–86: Mesoamerican zone (villages of El Viejo, Chinandega, Quesalquaque, and Posolteguilla), 59.8 percent; South American zone (villages of Jinotega, Linagüina, Teustepet, and Boaco), 55.5 percent; 1717–19: Mesoamerican zone (same villages), 70.5 percent; South American zone (same villages), 59.3 percent. The date of the figure for Posolteguilla, 1658–86, is actually 1676, and data are unavailable for one barrio of Chinandega for 1686 (AGCA A3.16 147 999 tasaciones 1676–96, A3.16 1605 26438 Padrones of El Viejo, Chinandega and Chichigalpa 1718, A3.16 497 3824 and 3826 Padrones of Quesalquaque and Posolteguilla 1719, A3.16 497 3817 Padrón of Jinotega and Linagüina 1717, A3.16 497 3821 Padrón of Boaco 1719, A3.16 497 3823 Padrón of Teustepet 1718).

95. AGI AG 966 census 1581. For the jurisdiction of Granada of 3,943 adults, 3,554 were married, 229 were widows or widowers, and 103 were single. The rest were unclassified. The same percentage cannot be calculated for León because the information on widows and widowers is incomplete.

96. AGCA A3.16 147 tasaciones 1676–96. Of a total of 4,760 adults, 3,502 were married, 435 were widows or widowers, and 823 were single.

97. AGI AG 966 census 1581. Part of the variation in the ratios stems from the fact that children were inconsistently enumerated, particularly in the east. The figures for the separate jurisdictions are: León (excluding Posoltega and Chichigalpa for which the numbers of children are not given), 0.75; Chontales (León), 0.63; Chontales (Granada), 0.76; Nueva Segovia, 0.75; Sebaco, 1.40.

98. The adult-child ratios for 1717–19 were: Mesoamerican zone: Posolteguilla, 0.48; Quesalquaque, 0.49; South American zone: Teustepet, 0.31; Boaco, 0.29; Jinotega, 0.29, and Linagüina, 0.27 (for sources see n. 94 above).

99. See chap. 12.

100. AGI AG 128 Relación y forma . . . n.d.; AGCA A1.30 255 1932 Visita of Jinotega 21.2.1663, A1.38 4778 41245 Ordenanzas 21.10.1683.

101. AGCA A3.16 495 3773 Padrón of Diriamba 1661, A3.16 495 3778 Padrones of Posoltega 1663 and 1676.

102. AGI AG 966 census 1581.

103. AGCA A1.23 1512 fol. 378 cedula 24.5.1571.

104. Ibid.; AGCA A1.38 4778 41245 Ordenanzas 21.10.1683.

105. Lutz, "Santiago de Guatemala."

106. AGCA A1.12 77 630 Cabildo of Granada 29.7.1689.
107. AGI AG 9 and CDI 24:513–57 Lic. López 9.6.1550, AG 50 Venegas de los Ríos 15.6.1564, AG 50 Venegas de los Ríos 13.11.1566, AG 162 Bishop of Nicaragua 15.2.1591, AG 181 Bishop of Nicaragua 15.7.1683; AGCA A1.12 32 300 Autos hechos . . . 1714; AGI AG 362 1715.
108. AGI AG 162 Bishop of Nicaragua 15.2.1591.
109. AGI AG 20 Memorial of regular clergy 1.2.1659; Nolasco Pérez, *Mercedarias,* 119, 122.
110. AIG AG 167 Memorial de los curatos 1.10.1663.
111. AGI AG 966 census 1581, AG 181 Bishop of Nicaragua 15.7.1683; AGCA A1.12 32 300 1715.
112. AGI AG 162 Información . . . 1560; *CDHCR,* 7:112–43 Información . . . de Juan Romo 1564.
113. AGI AG 222 Audiencia 7.9.1712.
114. *Recopilación,* 1 lib. 1 tít. 13 ley 7:96 2.12.1578, lib. 1 tít. 18 ley 10:158 11.6.1594, lib. 1 tít. 7 ley 43:67 16.8.1642.
115. AGI AG 40 Memorial . . . 1631.
116. See chap. 9.
117. AGI AG 29 Navia Bolaños 12.11.1684.
118. Gibson, *Aztecs,* 127.
120. *CDHCR,* 7:112–43 Información . . . de Juan Romo 1564; AGI AG 133 20.4.1663.

CHAPTER 11

1. AGI AG 966 census 1581; AGCA A3.16 147 999 tasaciones 1676–96.
2. AGI AG 21 Frasso 25 and 26.11.1663.
3. AGI AG 966 census 1581; AGCA A3.16 147 999 tasaciones 1676–96.
4. AGCA A3.16 496 3803 Pueblo of Poteca 1703.
5. AGI AG 44 Cabildo of Nueva Segovia 23.1.1663.
6. AGCA A3.16 496 3803 Pueblo of Poteca 1703; *CDHCN,* 1–12 Audiencia 26.7.1704, 12–63 Bishop Garret 30.11.1711, Fiscal 5.6.1713; AGI AG 303 Expediente sobre la conquista de los indios Zambos Mosquitos 1718; Denevan, *Upland Pine Forests,* 290–91; Floyd, *Anglo-Spanish Struggle,* 63–66.
7. AGI AG 44 Cabildo of Nueva Segovia 23.1.1663; ANH P3 L102 Fiscal 15.11.1679, L104 14.11.1679; AGCA A1.12 78 646 Captain of Sebaco, n.d., A3.16 520 4114 Cura of Sebaco 30.5.1705.
8. AGI AG 43 cedula 19.7.1653; ANH P3 L102 Fiscal 15.11.1679, L104 14.11.1679.
9. See chap. 10 and AGCA A3.1 520 4110 Sigueyra, vecino of Nueva Segovia 18.3.1586, A3.16 491 3726 Morillo, vecino of Granada 1631, A3.1 520 4102 Pueblo de Santísima Trinidad 10.1.1673, A3.12 491 3729 Indians of Condega and Telpaneca 8.5.1696.
10. AGCA A1.30 210 1714 Complaints against the corredigor of Chontales 1623, A1.30 210 1715 Charges against the corregidor of Chontales 1623, A3.16 491 3726 Morillo, vecino of Granada 31.1.1631; AGI AG 162 Bishop of Nicaragua 14.7.1647, AG 21 Frasso 25 and 26.11.1663; AGCA A3.16 491 3727 Vecinos of Nueva Segovia 2.11.1669; AGI AG 44 Vecinos of Nueva Segovia 1674, AG 162 Bishop of Nicaragua 6.4.1679; AGCA A3.12 491 3729 Indians of Condega and Telpaneca 8.5.1696.

11. AGCA A1.23 1517 10072 fols. 207–208 cedula 12.12.1649.

12. AGCA A1.30 255 1932 Visita of Jinotega 21.2.1663, A1.12 77 623 Pueblos of Sebaco 31.1.1614, Testimonio . . . 13.4.1627, A3.12 491 3729 Indians of Condega and Telpaneca 8.5.1696.

13. AGCA A3.16 146 986 Padrón of Boaco 17.5.1701.

14. AGI AG 966 census 1581.

15. AGI AG 162 Bishop of Nicaragua 6.4.1679, AG 21 Frasso 25 and 26.11. 1663; AGCA A3.16 146 986 Padrón of Boaco 17.4.1701.

16. *CDHCN*, 131–34 Town of Nueva Segovia 24.10.1664; AGI AG 44 Vecino of Nueva Segovia 1674, AG 162 Bishop of Nicaragua 6.4.1679, AG 44 Cabildo of Granada 1695; AGCA A3.12 491 3729 Indians of Condega and Telpaneca 8.5.1696.

17. For example, AGCA A1.30 255 1932 Visita of Jinotega 21.2.1663.

18. AGCA A1.44 448 2955 cedula 17.4.1619, A1.30 210 1714 Complaints against the corregidor of Chontales 1623, A1.30 210 1715 Charges against the corregidor of Chontales 1623; AGI 162 Bishop of Nicaragua 6.4.1679.

19. AGI AG 21 Frasso 25 and 26.11.1663, AG 44 Cabildo of Granada 1695.

20. For the privileges of caciques see chap. 10.

21. AGCA A1.30 255 1932 Visita of Jinotega 21.2.1663. In Telpaneqilla in 1671 the average was 4.1 (AGCA A3.16 190 1921 Padrón of Telpanequilla 21.12.1671).

22. The number of adults per household in Jinotega in 1717 was 2.18, or 2.08 if absentees are excluded (AGCA A3.16 487 3817 Padrón of Jinotega 12.10.1717). Corresponding figures for other villages are: Linagüina, 1717, 2.64 (2.48); Teustepet, 1718, 4.01 (3.18); and Boaco, 1719, 2.74 (2.56) (AGCA A3.16 497 3817, 1717, 3823, 1718, and 3821, 1718, respectively).

23. AGCA A3.16 147 999 tasaciones 1676–96. See also chap. 10 and n. 93.

24. Boaco had 8.4 percent absent; Linagüina, 7.7 percent; and Jinotega, 4.4 percent (sources as in n. 22).

25. AGI AG 966 census 1581. These figures are likely to have been higher because of the underenumeration of children, particularly in the east (see chap. 12; sources as in n. 22).

26. AGI AG 167 Dean of León 20.2.1573.

27. See chap. 10.

28. For descriptions of the economy of the Indians prior to missionization see n. 34.

29. AGCA A1.23 1525 10080 fol. 254 cedula 15.9.1713.

30. AGCA A1.12 5802 48962 Fr. Albuquerque 1608; AGCA A1.23 1514 fol. 147 cedula 29.8.1609, A1.12 78 646 Captain of Sebaco, n.d.

31. AGCA A1.12 78 646 Captain of Sebaco, n.d.

32. AGI AG 223 Fr. de la Concepción 13.1.1699.

33. See chap. 4; AGCA A1.12 78 646 Captain of Sebaco, n.d.

34. For a description of the economy of Indian groups inhabiting the area outside Spanish control and the way that it influenced the settlement pattern see AGI AG 174 Mercedarian missionaries 15.8.1608, AG 12 Dr. Criado de Castilla 30.11.1608, AG 223 Fr. de la Concepción 13.1.1699, AG 371 Fr. Ximénez 9.9.1748; Vázquez, *Crónica*, 4: 114.

35. AGI AG 371 Fr. Ximénez 9.9.1748.

36. AGCA A1.12 5802 48962 Fr. Albuquerque 1608, A1.12 78 646 Captain of Sebaco, n.d.; AGI AG 371 Fr. Ximénez 9.9.1748.

37. Holm, "Creole English," 178–81. See also chap. 2.

38. *CDHCN,* 1–12 Audiencia 26.7.1704, 63–77 Consulta de Consejo of Indias 8.7.1739; AGI AG 299 Bishop of Nicaragua 30.11.1711.

39. AGI AG 299 Bishop of Nicaragua 30.11.1711. See chap. 2.

40. AGI AG 299 Bishop of Nicaragua 30.11.1711; M. W., "Mosqueto Indian," 300–301; Raveneau de Lussan, *Voyage into the South Seas,* 285–87; Dampier, *New Voyage,* 15.

41. M. W., "Mosqueto Indian," 301; *CDHCN,* 12–63 Aranzibia 14.1.1715.

42. AGI AG 223 Fr. de la Concepción 13.1.1699.

43. AGI AG 223 Fr. de la Concepción 13.1.1699, AG 229 Testimony of five Indians . . . 1710 (18.10.1707); *CDHCN,* 12–63 Fiscal 5.6.1713, Aranzibia 14.1.1715; AGI AG 300 Informe de Consejo de Indias 25.2.1714; M. W., "Mosqueto Indian," 308, 310; Esquemeling, *Buccaneers,* 114, 235; Raveneau de Lussan, *Voyage into the South Seas,* 285.

44. AGI AG 300 Informe de Consejo de Indias 25.2.1714.

45. M. W., "Mosqueto Indian," 310.

46. Raveneau de Lussan, *Buccaneers,* 285.

47. AGI AG 299 Testimony of five Indians . . . 1710 (18.10.1707). See also *CDHCN,* 12–63 Aranzibia 14.1.1715, which records that they did not possess "crías de animales."

48. AGI AG 223 Fr. de la Concepción 13.1.1699; *CDHCN,* 12–63 Fiscal 5.6.1713, Aranzibia 14.1.1715; Vázquez, *Crónica,* 4:81.

49. AGI AG 301 Governor of Costa Rica 15.12.1721.

50. There are many references to this trade; for example: AGI AG 223 Fr. de la Concepción 13.1.1699; *CDHCN,* 12–63 Fiscal 5.6.1713; AGI AG 300 Informe de Consejo de Indias 25.2.1714; M. W., "Mosqueto Indian," 300; Vázquez, *Crónica,* 4:81.

51. AGI AG 299 Bishop of Nicaragua 30.11.1711; *CDHCN,* 12–63 Aranzibia 14.1.1715; Sloane, *Voyage to the Islands,* lxxvii; M. W., "Mosqueto Indian," 309.

52. M. W., "Mosqueto Indian," 309.

53. Dampier, *New Voyage,* 16.

54. Helms, "Matrilocality"; Helms, *Asang,* 24–27; Helms and Loveland, *Frontier Adaptations,* 14.

55. *CDHCN,* 12–63 Aranzibia 14.1.1715.

56. AGI AG 299 Bishop of Nicaragua 30.11.1711.

57. AGI AG 301 Governor of Costa Rica 15.12.1721.

58. M. W., "Mosqueto Indian," 301, 307; Esquemeling, *Buccaneers,* 234; Dampier, *New Voyage,* 17.

59. Conzemius, *Ethnographical Survey,* 101.

60. M. W., "Mosqueto Indian," 302; Floyd, *Anglo-Spanish Struggle,* 62; Helms, "Cultural Ecology," 78.

61. AGI AG 299 Bishop of Nicaragua 30.11.1711, AG 302 Testimony 1725 (Vecino of Olancho 21.6.1718); Floyd, *Anglo-Spanish Struggle,* 62–64.

62. M. W., "Mosqueto Indian," 306–307; Roberts, *Narrative of Voyages,* 100, 116; Floyd, *Anglo-Spanish Struggle,* 67.

63. M. W., "Mosqueto Indian," 301, 306–307; Dampier, *New Voyage,* 17; Helms, *Asang,* 20.

64. M. W., "Mosqueto Indian," 305, 307; Dampier, *New Voyage,* 16; Floyd, *Anglo-Spanish Struggle,* 66; Holm, "Creole English," 176.

65. *CDHCN,* 1–12 Audiencia 26.1.1704; AGI AG 299 Bishop of Nicaragua 30.11.1711, AG 301 Governor of Costa Rica 15.12.1721.

66. M. W., "Mosqueto Indian," 309; Esquemeling, *Buccaneers,* 235–37; Dampier, *New Voyage,* 16.

CHAPTER 12

1. AGI AG 8 Fr. de la Torre 22.5.1553.

2. AGI IG 857 Juan de Estrada, n.d. Sherman suggests that the letter may have been written in the 1550s (Sherman, *Forced Native Labor,* 347).

3. AGI AG 167 Dean of León, n.d. The breakdown for the jurisdictions is: León, 2,400; Granada, 3,000; Sebaco, 300; Nueva Segovia, 600; and Nicoya, 450.

4. MacLeod, *Spanish Central America,* 53, 139.

5. AGI AG 162 Bishop of Nicaragua 12.1.1578.

6. AGI AG 55 Moreno 8.1.1578.

7. AGI AG 162 Bishop of Nicaragua 12.1.1578.

8. See chap. 8.

9. López de Velasco, *Geografía,* 318–26. Sherman wrongly assumes that Velasco's figures refer to the 1570s; the decline that he notes in fact occurred within half the time he suggests (Sherman, *Forced Native Labor,* 5–6, 353).

10. AGI AG 966 census 1581.

11. The average rate of decline has been calculated using Cook and Borah's co-efficient of population movement (ω) (See Cook and Borah, *Essays,* 1:89–91); where p_1 and t_1 are the initial population and date, and p_2 and t_2 the later population and date.

$$\omega = \frac{\dfrac{p_2 - p_1}{t_2 - t_1} \times 100}{\sqrt{p_1 p_2}}$$

12. AGI AG 40 Córdova y Guzmán 29.6.1607; AGCA A1.23 1517 fols. 207–208 cedula 12.12.1649.

13. AGI CO 986 Oficiales reales 10.11.1652.

14. AGI AG 13 Sánchez Araque 26.1.1613; AGCA A1.23 1514 fols. 232–35 cedula 24.1.1613. Of this number 11 were described as "infieles" and 110 were tributary Indians who had just come out of the mountains.

15. The tributary population declined from 1,645 in 1581 to 1,274 in 1621. (AGI AG 966 census 1581; AGCA A1.30 210 1713 Residencia on the corregidor of Realejo 1621).

16. AGI AG 21 Frasso 25.11.1663, AG 40 Certificación sacada de los libros reales . . . 2.1.1674.

17. AGCA A3.16 495 3781 Contador of Nicaragua 29.11.1676.

18. AGI AG 29 Navia Bolaños 28.7.1685; AGCA A3.16 147 999 tasaciones 1676–96.

19. MacLeod (*Spanish Central America,* 53) gives the total number of tributary Indians from Navia Bolaños's account as 4,716, but it is not clear how he obtained this figure. Also, a note on the enclosing cover to the letter, also written by Navia Bolaños, indicates that there were 17,245 "indios tributarios enteros casados viudos solteras solteros y lavoríos" (AGI AG 29 7.6.1686).

20. The evidence from five villages between 1685–86 and 1718 is as follows:

Tributary Indians	1685–86	1694–96	1718	Percent change 1685–1694–96	Percent change 1694–1718
Mesoamerican zone					
El Viejo	440	390	604	−11.4	+54.9
Chinandega	261	251	448	− 0.4	+78.5
South American zone					
Matagalpa	340	370	432	+ 8.8	+16.8
Jinotega	165	143	183	−13.3	+20.0
Teustepet	122	126	92	+ 3.3	−27.0

Sources: AGCA A3.16 147 999 tasaciones 1676–96, A3.16 1605 26438–39 tasaciones 1718.

21. *Padrón* of Diriamba (1663), 1:2.3 (101:228) AGCA A3.16 495 3773 11.3.1663; *padrón* of Posoltega (1663), 1:2.3 (167:389) AGCA A3.16 495 3778 5.4.1663; *padrón* of Posolteguilla (1676) 1:2.9 (95:272) AGCA A3.16 495 3778 17.1.1676; *padrón* of Posolteguilla (1719) 1:2.0 (338:673) AGCA A3.16 498 3826 9.9.1719; *padrón* of Quesalquaque (1719) 1:2.5 (290:732) AGCA A3.16 3822 15.9.1719.

22. *Padrones* of Teustepet (1718) 1:2.2 (132:289) AGCA A3.16 497 3823 20.4.1718; *padrón* of Boaco (1718) 1:2.0 (321:627) AGCA A3.16 497 3821 24.3.1718; *padrón* of Jinotega (1717) 1:2.1 (180:383) AGCA A3.16 497 3817 12.10.1717; *padrón* of Linagüina (1717) 1:3.0 (44:132) AGCA A3.16 497 3817 12.10.1717.

23. AGI AG 29 Navia Bolaños 28.7.1685. For barrios in Nueva Segovia see chap. 11 and AGI AG 43 Arbieto 19.7.1653.

24. See chap. 9 and AGI AG 371 Fr. Ximénez 9.9.1748.

25. See chap. 17.

26. AGI AG 183 Frs. Ovalle and Guevara 4.3.1681.

27. Esquemeling, *Buccaneers,* 234.

28. AGI AG 300 Informe de Consejo de Indias 25.2.1714 but the document includes a testimony given in 1707.

29. AGI AG 299 Bishop of Nicaragua 30.11.1711, AG 302 Santaella Malgarejo 3.4.1715.

30. An average multiplication factor of 2.5 is taken from the range of 1:2.0 to 1:2.9. In calculating the average rate of decline (ω), the date of the *tasaciones* made between 1676 and 1686 is taken as 1686 because most of the *tasaciones* were made at that date.

31. AGI AG 55 Arias Riquel 4.3.1580.

32. AGI AG 29 Navia Bolaños 12.11.1684.

33. AGCA A1.23 1517 fols. 207–208 cedula 12.12.1649.

34. AGI AG 162 Bishop of Nicaragua 6.4.1679.

35. MacLeod, *Spanish Central America,* 98–100; Veblen, "Native Population Decline," 497–98.

36. See chap. 7 and Ashburn, *Ranks of Death,* 81, 95–96; MacLeod, *Spanish Central America,* 8–9. Ashburn notes that typhus is generally associated with poverty where inadequate housing, clothing, and sanitation encourage the spread of disease by lice and rats. In hot, moist coastal regions where little

clothing is worn and washing can occur frequently, the disease is unlikely to spread. By contrast, in cold, dry uplands, where water is scarce and bathing and washing of clothes occur less frequently, unhygenic conditions are fostered which encourage the spread of disease.

37. MacLeod, *Spanish Central America,* 98–100; Veblen, "Native Population Decline," 490–91, 498; Lovell, 'Land Settlement," 247.

38. AGI AG 55 Moreno 8.1.1578.

39. Thiel, "Población de la República de Costa Rica," 89.

40. *CDHCN,* 92–112 Dr. Criado de Castilla 30.11.1608.

41. AGI AG 64 Miners of Honduras 1617.

42. AGCA A3.16 83 1187 Cura of Nicoya 21.3.1676 (Costa Rica), A3.16 495 3781 Contador of Nicaragua 29.11.1676; AGI AG 43 Cabildo of León 23.11.1677, AG 162 Bishop of Nicaragua 6.4.1679.

43. AGI AG 223 and AG 297 Fr. de la Concepción 13.1.1699.

44. AGCA A1.23 1582 10266 fol. 137 cedula 11.5.1717, A3.16 497 3818 Padrón of Teustepet 26.4.1718.

45. AGI AG 25 Testimonio . . . 1672.

46. AGI AG 50 Oficiales reales 15.3.1586; Ayón, *Historia de Nicaragua,* 2:13.

47. For example, AGI AG 25 Testimonio . . . 1672.

48. AGCA A1.12 32 268 Priests of El Viejo 19.8.1629.

49. For example, AGCA A1.30 255 1932 Visita of Jinotega 21.2.1663.

50. AGCA A1.12 77 623 Pueblos of Sebaco 31.1.1614, 13.4.1627.

51. AGI AG 43 Arbieto 19.7.1653; AGCA A1.23 1518 fol. 211 cedula 17.3. 1657.

52. Most of the slaves were introduced under individual licenses (See AGI AG 386 to 402 for cedulas permitting the introduction of generally two to eight slaves). Two large shipments arrived at Trujillo, one in 1581 (200 slaves) (AGI AG 10 President of the Audiencia 24.3.1581) and another in 1607 (150 slaves) (AGI AG 12 Dr. Criado de Castilla 15.5.1607).

53. AGI AG 40 Cabildo of León 7.9.1635.

54. AGI AG 40 Pueblo of Masaya 10.3.1607, AG 40 real provisión 12.2.1609.

55. A cedula to this effect was issued for Honduras (AGI AG 39 n.d.), and it seems likely that it would have applied to the whole audiencia.

56. AGI AG 24 List of men and arms in the Reino de Guatemala 4.10.1662.

57. AGCA A3.37 74 1058–60 Licenses to take mules to Panama 1710–19 (Costa Rica section), A3.37 167 1173 Request for licences to take mules to Panama 1707.

CHAPTER 13

1. Floyd, *Anglo-Spanish Struggle,* 61.

2. Ibid., 81–82, 167.

3. ANH UC real orden 19.5.1787.

4. Sorsby, "Spanish Colonization," 149 n. 14.

5. AHNM Estado 4227 31.10.1787; AGI AG 828 Families from Asturias 15.2.1788; Floyd, *Anglo-Spanish Struggle,* 168–71; Sorsby, "Spanish Colonization," 145–52.

6. AGI AG 448 President of the Audiencia 23.11.1737, AG 558 Account of the corregimientos of Nicaragua 26.9.1776.

7. Lynch, *Spanish Colonial Administration,* 46.

8. Haring, *Spanish Empire,* 134.

9. Wortman, "Bourbon Reforms," 236.

10. Wortman, "Government Revenue," 274. The percentage decline for Nicaragua was higher than that for Central America as a whole, which was 32 percent.

11. AGI AG 950 Bishop Morel 8.9.1752, AG 535 On the establishment of the Villa of Rivas 1778.

12. AGI AG 535 On the establishment of the Villa of Rivas 1778 (27.2.1782), AG 940 Memorial of the life of Don Hurtado y Plaza 15.11.1783.

13. AGI AG 535 On the establishment of the villa of Rivas 1778; AGCA A3.1 15 324 fol. 16 cedula 19.9.1783.

14. Figures for the corregimiento of Realejo in 1740 show that by then more Spaniards (174) were living in El Viejo than in Realejo (160), which had formerly been an Indian town (AGCA A1.17 210 5014 Visita of the corregimiento of Realejo 1740).

15. AGI AG 950 Bishop Morel 8.9.1752.

16. AGI AG 362 Bishop of Nicaragua 2.6.1746, AG 950 Bishop Morel 8.9.1752; *BAGG,* 2:479–86 Larria 15.11.1765, Díaz de Corcuera 26.9.1766; AGI AG 558 Governor of Nicaragua 26.9.1766, Account of the corregimientos of Nicaragua 26.9.1776.

17. Marure, *Bosquejo de las revoluciones* 1:6–9; Wortman, "Government Revenue," 264, 279.

18. Thompson, "Narración de una visita oficial," 191–229.

19. *CDHCN,* 96–136 Díaz Navarro 30.11.1758.

20. AGI AG 950 Bishop Morel 8.9.1752.

21. AGCA A1.38 2646 22150 Resumen general de las familias . . . 7.5.1804. The number of Spanish and Ladino families living in Indian villages was 7,976; in valleys and haciendas, 3,273; in towns and *reducciones,* 2,458. The account is incomplete since it does not include the town of Nicaragua.

22. AGCA A1.45 445 2935 Querella contra los vecinos de Cacaolistagua 1769. This document gives the assets of 17 small holdings in the valley of San Juan Cacaolistagua, listing all the crops grown by them, as well as the agricultural equipment they possessed.

23. AGI AG 264 Ventas y composiciones de tierras 1743.

24. *CDHCR,* 9:187–205 Informe on the Zambos-Mosquitos 16.2.1731; *BAGG,* 2:479–86 Larria 15.11.1785; Radell, "Historical Geography," 150–56.

25. Radell, "Historical Geography," 155–56.

26. AGCA A3.3 37 333 Ugarte, hacendado of León 27.3.1787.

27. *CDHCR,* 9:476–90 Estadística de los haciendas de Nicoya 1751; *CDHCR,* 10:7–10 Informes sobre el corregimiento de Nicoya 15.11.1765; AGCA A3.6 409 8383 Owners of haciendas in Nicoya 1775; ANCR CC 3741 Owners of haciendas in Nicoya 9.7.1778; Cabrera, *Guanacaste,* 345. In 1785, 20 hatos and haciendas were owned by vecinos of Nicaragua, 86 by local people and 6 by *cofradías* (ANCR CC 3544 Los hateros . . . 1785).

28. For example, the taxes on the export of cotton were removed in 1786 (AGI AG 472 real orden 14.3.1786).

29. AGCA A3.5 1105 20007 fol. 188 cedula 4.3.1792, A1.23 1542 fol. 215v. and A1.38 1745 11,716 reales ordenes 15.11.1803.

30. AGI AG 656 N273 fol. 197 Gaçeta de Guatemala 23.8.1802, AG 452 Relación de las providencias enconómicas . . . 3.1.1804; Salvatierra, *Historia de Centro América* 2: 13.

31. AGCA A1.53 482 3211 Visita de los obrajes de León 1724; AGI AG 950 Bishop Morel 8.9.1752; AGCA A1.53 459 3005 Vecino of the town of Nicaragua 20.7.1793, A1.45 446 2938 Larrabe contra los indios de Chinandega 1799, A1.73 478 3172 Fiscal 25.6.1799, A3.23 159 1139 Cuentas de las cantidades 1800; Thompson, "Narración de una visita oficial," 191–229 (1825).

32. AGCA A1.53 482 3211 Visita de los obrajes de León 1724. For examples of Indians being employed in indigo cultivation see AGCA A1.30 222 1763 Charges against the corregidor of Sutiaba 1774, A1.30 222 1766 Complaints against the corregidor of Realejo 26.2.1774, A1.30 252 1909 Complaints against the teniente of Masaya 27.8.1779.

33. Woodward, *Class Privilege and Economic Development*, 4–9.

34. Smith, "Indigo Production," 193.

35. This tax on indigo had previously been used to pay for the construction of Fort Omoa (AGCA A1.23 4624 fol. 104 cedula 12.2.1760, A1.23 1528 fol. 509 cedula 12.12.1764.

36. Smith, "Indigo Production," 206.

37. Ibid., 208.

38. AGI AG 668 Cosecheros habilitados . . . 30.9.1801. This figure was considerably higher than the income from indigo taxes paid between 1783 and 1792, which amounted to 8,283 pesos (AGI AG 668 Derechos cobrados en el Monte Pío 16.4.1793).

39. AGCA A1.1 2209 15778 fol. 8 real orden 25.7.1792. For prices of indigo see Rubio Sánchez, "El Añil," 333–36.

40. AGCA A1.5 51 1275 fol. 4 real orden 20.5.1817.

41. Salvatierra, *Historia de Centro América,* 2: 200.

42. Smith, "Indigo Production," 209–10.

43. AGCA A1.23 1542 fol. 214, 215v. reales ordenes 15.11.1803.

44. For trends in indigo production see Wortman, "Government Revenue," 257–64.

45. AGCA A3.23 159 1138–39 Cuentas de las cantidades . . . 1797–1818. The figures for production are calculated on the basis of the four-peso tax and are therefore only a rough guide:

Year	Production, pounds	Year	Production, pounds	Year	Production, pounds
1797	40,270.5	1809	21,025 (to April only)	1814	1,350
1798	49,031	1810	14,274	1815	3,317
1799	41,328 (to June only)	1811	1,185	1816	NA
1800– 1807	NA	1812	3,455	1817	1,859
1808	24,872	1813	NA	1818	600

The above figures can be compared with those given for the audiencia by Smith, "Indigo Production," 197, 199 n. 55.

46. Salvatierra, *Historia de Centro América*, 2:205.

47. *CDHCR*, 9:374–86 Relación de la Laguna de Nicaragua 1745; AGI AG 950 Bishop Morel 8.9.1752; *CDHCN*, 96–136 Díaz Navarro 30.11.1758; Juarros, *Statistical and Commercial History*, 68; Thompson, "Narración de una visita oficial," 191–229 (1825).

48. AGI AG 950 Bishop Morel 8.9.1752, *CDHCR*, 9:524–28 12.5.1757.

49. AGCA A1.12 78 644 21.2.1769; Wortman, "Government Revenue," 262.

50. Salvatierra, *Historia de Central América*, 2:36.

51. AGI AG 362 Bishop of Nicaragua 28.7.1746; *BAGG* 7:157—75 20.1. 1800.

52. Salvatierra, *Historia de Centro América*, 2:35–36; Radell, "Historical Geography," 167.

53. AGI AG 950 Bishop Morel 8.9.1752; AGCA A1.45 445 2935 Querella contra los vecinos de Cacaolistagua 4.11.1769, A1.45 445 2936 Complaints of the villages of Sutiaba 6.5.1773; *BAGG*, 2:479–82 Larria 15.11.1765; AGCA A3.16 246 4912 Intendant of Nicaragua 20.7.1793, A1.45 446 2938 Larrabe contra los indios de Chinandega 1799; *BAGG*, 7:157–75 3.1.1800.

54. *BAGG*, 7:157–75 20.1.1800. Exports of sugar were worth 5,000 pesos compared to the total value of exports, which was 391,000 pesos.

55. See discussion earlier in this chapter.

56. Salvatierra, *Historia de Centro América* 2:167; Haring, *Spanish Empire*, 275–76; Floyd, *Anglo-Spanish Struggle*, 120; Fallas, *Factoría de tabacos*, 37–44.

57. Fallas, *Factoría de tabacos*, 163–69; Wortman, "Bourbon Reforms," 228.

58. AGI AG 777 Juan del Barrio 3.6.1784, Quintana 5.9.1786; *CDHCR*, 10:193–211 Sobre la reducción de las siembras de tabaco 13.4.1787, 13.9. 1787, *CDHCR*, 10:254–56 Real Junta Superior de Hacienda 27.3.1792, *CDHCR*, 10:448–57 Diputación provincial . . . 23.3.1814, 512–15 Consejo de Indias 14.6.1817; Fallas, *Factoría de tabacos*, 99.

59. *CDHCR*, 9:524–28 12.5.1757.

60. AGCA A1.17 210 5014 Visita of the corregimiento of Realejo 1740.

61. AGCA A3.3 37 733 Ugarte, hacendado of León 27.3.1787.

62. AGI AG 656 N76 fols. 225–27 Gaçeta de Guatemala 1798.

63. AGCA A3.3 37 733 Ugarte, hacendado de León 27.3.1787; Radell, "Historical Geography," 154–55.

64. AGCA A1.1 2 61 Account of the village of Aramecina 9.6.1821; Radell, "Historical Geography," 150.

65. AGI AG 362 Bishop of Nicaragua 28.7.1746.

66. AGCA A3.3 2537 37171 El síndico procurador general de Guatemala 23.1.1775.

67. AGCA A1.17 2335 17508 Información rendida . . . por Díaz Navarro 1744; *CDHCN*, 96–136 Díaz Navarro 30.11.1758; *CDHCR*, 10:7–10 Informes sobre el corregimiento de Nicoya 15.11.1765; AGCA A3.37 1061–62 Licences to take mules to Panama 1721 and 1777.

68. Salvatierra, *Historia de Centro América*, 2:211.

69. AGCA A3.3 39 777 El común de hacendados de Granada 22.10.1794.

70. AGCA A3.3 38 745 Audiencia 10.11.1791. A total of 7,311 had been sold for 4½ to 6 pesos and 12,886 for 6 to 9 pesos.

71. AGCA A3.3 40 791 Estado general que manifiesta el número de ganados 7.2.1791, A3.3 40 790 Juez of the feria of Jalpatagua 1795.

72. For example, AGCA A3.3 39 769 Vecino of Granada 21.12.1798.

73. Registered losses at the annual cattle fair 1792–98 were as follows:

Year	Total leaving haciendas	Number				Total Arriving at fair	Percent of loss
		Lost	Died	Used	Sold		
1792	24,054					16,814	30.1
1793	22,914	1,126	1,397	—	3,772	16,619	27.5
1795	33,817	518	7,298	255	2,812	21,132	37.5
1796	25,529	562	5,622	207	2,472	16,396	35.8
1797	10,159	111	2,503	96	1,363	6,089	40.1
1798	9,814	306	709	93	1,974	6,659	32.1

Sources: 1792: AGCA A3.3 38 760; 1793: AGCA A3.3 39 768; 1795: AGCA A3.3 40 791; 1796: AGCA A3.3 2446 35830; 1797: AGCA A3.3 45 805; 1798: AGCA A3.3 2367 34946.

74. AGCA A3.3 37 733 Ugarte, hacendado of León 27.3.1787 (Guatemala), A3.3 38 745 Cabildo of León 23.10.1791.

75. AGCA A3.3 38 748 Fiscal 7.1.1791.

76. AGCA A3.3 39 777 El común de hacendados de Granada 22.10.1794.

77. AGI AG 669 17.10.1791.

78. AGCA 3.3 40 780 6.12.1794.

79. AGCA A3.3 38 748 Fiscal 7.1.1791, A3.3 45 805 Plano que representa la feria de ganados 9.1.1798.

80. Salvatierra, *Historia de Centro América,* 2: 211.

81. AGCA A3.2 505 3914 Fiscal 21.4.1739, A3.9 482 3651 Miners of León 1740, Priest of Masaya 13.8.1744, Priest of Sutiaba 5.9.1744.

82. AGCA A3.9 483 3653 Sargento Mayor de las Milicias 27.10.1772, A3.17 1719 27698 28.8.1789; Floyd ("Bourbon Palliatives," 116, 118, 122) refers to AGI AG 729 Instrucción e inspección de las minas del Peñon 15.10.1777, Captain General 9.9.1780, real orden 23.2.1784.

83. AGCA A3.2 157 1121 Quintos 1772. Figures for other dates are: 1745: 68 marks; 1768, 53 marks; 1770, 19 marks; 1774, 74 marks; 1777, 75 marks; 1785, 44 marks (AGCA A3.2 157 1118–19, 1121–23 Quintos 1745 to 1777, A3.2 453 3430 1768, A3.2 454 3446 1785).

84. AGI AG Jefe político of Nicaragua 4.6.1814; Salvatierra, *Historia de Centro América,* 2: 212. The ores were said to yield 2¼ to 2½ marks of silver per arroba.

85. For pearl production see *CDHCN,* 96–136 Díaz Navarro 30.11.1758; *BAGG,* 2: 479–86 Larria 15.11.1765, Díaz de Corcuera 26.9.1766; *CDHCR,* 10: 7–10 Informe sobre el Corregimiento de Nicoya 15.11.1765; ANCR Guatemala 384 González 25.2.1774; *BAGG,* 7: 157–75 3.1.1800, 20.1.1800; *CDHCR,* 10: 292–94 Informe de Salvador sobre las pesquerías de perlas 23.2.1803; Thompson, "Narración de una visita oficial," 191–229 (1825).

86. MNM Bª-XI-Cª-B-nº1 Hodgson and Hodgson 1782; AHNM Estado 4227 Fuertes 24.6.1784.

87. *BAGG,* 7: 157–75 20.1.1800. Much of the wood was exported to Peru

(AGI AG 558 Account of the corregimientos of Nicaragua 26.9.1776; Thompson, "Narración de una visita oficial," 191–229 [1825]; Radell, "Historical Geography," 121).

88. In 1725 at a wharf near Granada were built three vessels destined for Portobello and Cartagena (AGCA A3.16 503 3889 20.2.1775).

89. Radell, "Historical Geography," 121; Radell and Parsons, "Realejo," 310.

90. Radell, "Historical Geography," 119; Radell and Parsons, "Realejo," 309; Thompson, "Narración de una visita oficial," 191–229 (1825). Cockburn (*Journey Overland,* 118) noted that ships were also built for Acapulco, as well as Peru.

91. AGCA A1.17 210 5014 Visita of the corregimiento of Realejo 1740; AGI AG 950 Bishop Morel 8.9.1752; Radell, "Historical Geography," 121.

92. Radell, "Historical Geography," 212; Radell and Parsons, "Realejo," 311. Between 1782 and 1789 only four ships called at Realejo to purchase indigo, wood, and pitch (AGI AG 456 Governor of Nicaragua 23.12.1789).

93. See chap. 14 and *BAGG,* 2:479–86 Larria 15.11.1765, Díaz de Corcuera 26.9.1766.

94. *BAGG,* 7:157–75 20.1.1800.

95. AGI AG 362 Bishop of Nicaragua 28.7.1746; *BAGG,* 2:479–86 Larria 15.11.1765, Díaz de Corcuera 26.9.1766; AGI AG 456 Governor of Nicaragua 23.12.1789.

96. PRO CO 123/1 fols. 185–88 no author, n.d.; Floyd, *Anglo-Spanish Struggle,* 68–69.

97. For the location of English settlements see AGCA A1.12 117 2473 Cap. Yarrince 18.9.1759; SHM Plano 5185 Sig. D-13-37 Clapp 2.9.1771; AGI AG 665 and *CDHCN,* 198–205 Diario de Antonio Gastelu 11.7.1776; MNM Bª-XI-Cª-B-nº-1 Hodgson and Hodgson 1782.

98. PRO CO 123/1 fols. 55–79 Hodgson 1757.

99. MNM Bª-XI-Cª-B-nº-1 Hodgson and Hodgson 1782; PRO CO 123/3 fols. 185–88 no author, n.d.; White, *The Case of the Agent,* 47.

100. AHNM Estado 4227 Fuertes 24.6.1784; Edwards, "British Settlements," 5:211.

101. MNM Bª-XI-Cª-B-nº-1 Hodgson and Hodgson 1782; Floyd, *Anglo-Spanish Struggle,* 58.

102. AGI AG 665 and *CDHCN,* 198–205 Diario de Antonio Gastelu 11.7.1776; BM Add. 12,431 fol. 202 Request for information from Capt. Kimberley, no date; MNM Bª-XI-Cª-B-nº-1 Hodgson and Hodgson 1782; Long, *History of Jamaica,* 1:318.

103. PRO CO 123/5 fols. 194–97 Return of the inhabitants of the Mosquito Coast 20.10.1787, CO 123/6 fols. 82–85 Embarkations from the Mosquito Coast 1787.

104. Floyd, *Anglo-Spanish Struggle,* 162–82.

CHAPTER 14

1. AGCA A3.16 255 5730 14.8.1811.
2. AGI AG 259 cedula 27.9.1721; Haring, *Spanish Empire,* 67.

3. AGCA A1.23 2595 fol. 253v. decreto 13.3.1811, A1.23 1543 fol. 85 cedula 24.11.1815 to pay from 1.1.1816; Salvatierra, *Historia de Centro América*, 2:159.

4. AGI AG 230 Contador 27.9.1734.

5. For Matagalpa see AGCA A3.16 146 993 tasaciones 1753, A3.16 149 1036 tasaciones 1753; for Sutiaba, Telica, Quesalquaque, and Posoltega see A3.16 499 38430–33 tasaciones 27.7.1735.

6. AGCA A3.16 500 3852 Governor of Nicaragua 14.5.1740.

7. AGCA A3.16 146 993 tasaciones 1753, A3.16 149 1036 tasaciones 1753. New *tasaciones* were ordered for Nueva Segovia in 1741 and were made in 1743 (AGCA A3.16 500 3856 Teniente of Nueva Segovia 6.6.1741, A3.16 498 3829, 3853, 3854, 3859, 3860 Padrones for Tepesomoto, Totogalpa, Mozonte, Comalteca, and Yalagüina). Another count was ordered in 1750 (AGCA A3.16 501 3869 Audiencia 19.2.1750).

8. AGCA A3.16 2325 34320 Libro de tasaciones 1757 and 1761 for the whole area, A3.16 503 3899 and 3891 tasaciones for Granada 1757, A3.16 149 1027 tasaciones for León 1757, A3.16 149 1029 tasaciones for Realejo 1757 and for Sebaco A3.16 149 1034 1755.

9. AGI AG 560 15.1.1771.

10. AGI AG 545 Don Gerónimo de la Vega 1.7.1767.

11. AGCA A3.16 500 3852 Governor of Nicaragua 14.5.1740.

12. AGI AG 560 Testimonio de la real cédula despachada 1778.

13. AGI AG 560 15.1.1771, 26.6.1771, Testimonio de la real cédula despachada 1778, Instruction for the enumeration . . . 7.7.1767, cedula 7.12. 1776, Contador general 23.4.1781.

14. Enumerations made 1788–92 give figures for the *tasación* of 1793 and another count in 1795–98 for the *tasación* of 1799 (AGCA A3.16 246 4912 Estado que manifiesta los partidos . . . 20.7.1793, A3.16 153 1101 Estado que manifiesta el número de tributarios 3.6.1793 and 19.9.1799). For later enumerations see AGCA A3.16 255 5730 8.7.1806 (Guatemala); *BAGG*, 3:217–25 Estado de los curatos 8.7.1806; AGCA A3.16 153 1103 *tasaciones* 1811, A3.16 152 1073–97 tasaciones 1816–17.

15. AGCA A3.16 255 5730 14.8.1811; Salvatierra, *Historia de Centro América*, 2:157.

16. AGCA A3.16 2327 34374 Instructions to curas 30.10.1805.

17. Ibid.; A3.16 196 2064 1806 (Honduras).

18. Many cases are to be found in the following *legajos:* AGCA A3.16 494–95, 503–504, 520.

19. AGCA A3.16 2327 34374 Instructions to curas 30.10.1805.

20. AGI AG 236 Audiencia 30.4.1755; AGCA A1.23 1528 fol. 121 cedula 13.9.1754, A1.23 1528 fol. 161 cedula 11.12.1756.

21. AGI AG 239 Testimonio . . . 1758; AGCA A1.23 1528 fol. 247 cedula 24.5.1759; Zavala, *Instituciones coloniales,* 91–94.

22. AGCA A1.23 1529 fol. 138 Crown approves an *auto* of 10.2.1763 to this effect in 22.8.1767.

23. AGI AG 230 President of the Audiencia 15.11.1736; AGCA A3.9 482 3651 Cabildo of León 29.8.1742, A3.16 502 3880 26.3.1752; AGI AG 545 Don Gerónimo de la Vega 1.7.1767; AGCA A1.30 252 1909 Complaints against the *teniente* of Masaya 1779; AGI AG 743 King to the Audiencia 6.9.1788, 10.7.

1793; AGCA A1.23 1532 fol. 600 cedula 11.3.1790, A1.23 1532 fol. 695 cedula 21.10.1790.

24. AGCA A3.16 150 1044 Corregidor of Sebaco and Chontales 5.5.1769; MNM 570 fols. 263–79 Descripción de Realejo, n.d.

25. AGCA A1.30 252 1909 Complaints against the *teniente* of Masaya 1779.

26. AGCA A3.16 246 4912 Estado que manifiesta los partidos 20.7.1793 in reply to a cedula requesting information about the level of tribute payment (27.7.1787).

27. Martínez Peláez, *Patria del criollo*, 252, 689, n.73.

28. AGCA A3.16 153 1103 tasaciones 1811. Figures for 1816–17 show the same characteristic spread (AGCA A3.16 152 1073–97).

29. For problems over tribute collection see: AGCA A3.16 499 3846 Cabildo of Yalagüina 1739, A1.12 78 644 30.8.1768, A1.12 53 470 Corregidor of Sutiaba 27.2.1774.

30. AGCA A1.21 481 3202 Corregidor of Sebaco and Chontales 20.12.1755.

31. For tribute arrears of some villages in Nicaragua see AGCA 3.16 149 1036 1709–50.

32. AGCA A3.16 500 3856 *Teniente* of Nueva Segovia 6.6.1741 gives arrears for the villages of Mozonte, Totogalpa, Yalagüina, and Litelpaneca, 1725–38.

33. For example, AGCA A3.17 148 1017 Pueblo of Nicaragua 1732, A3.16 500 3852 Governor of Nicaragua 14.5.1740.

34. AGI AG 251 Treasurer of Nicaragua 29.5.1727; AGCA A1.23 1526 fol. 255 cedula 11.3.1730; ANCR Cartago 382 Fiscal 20.11.1734; AGI AG cedula 25.5.1737; AGCA A3.16 502 3880 26.3.1752.

35. Gibson, *Aztecs*, 205, 392.

36. AGCA A3.16 500 3849 and 3850 Ayudante and escribano publico of Granada 27.10.1739, 10.9.1739.

37. AGCA A3.16 500 3848 Padrón of Totogalpa 23.4.1741.

38. AGCA A3.16 195 2037 1799.

39. AGCA A3.16 502 3881 6.7.1752, A3.16 246 4912 Estado que manifiesta los partidos 20.7.1793.

40. AGCA A3.16 246 4912 Estado que manifiesta los partidos 20.7.1793.

41. AGCA A1.23 1538 fol. 136 real ordén 9.11.1812.

42. AGCA A1.11 60 501 Razón de los nuevos establecimientos 26.4.1773.

43. AGCA A1.30 220 1756 Village of El Viejo 28.8.1768, A1.30 222 1763 Charges against the corregidor of Sutiaba 1774, A1.23 1530 fol. 400 cedula 11.9.1776.

44. AGCA A1.11 60 501 Razón de los nuevos establecimientos 26.4.1773, A1.17 4683 40392 1773, A3.9 174 1685 Alcalde Mayor of Tegucigalpa 31.5.1777 (Honduras), A3.16 246 4912 Estado que manifiesta los partidos 20.7.1793.

45. AGCA A3.9 174 1685 22.7.1777.

46. For example, AGCA A3.16 498 3833 Pueblo of Quesalquaque 4.12.1725; AGI AG 545 Testimonio . . . sobre las extorciones del corregidor de Sutiaba 1761, Don Geronimo de la Vega 1.7.1767; AGCA A1.30 219 1751 Complaints against the corregidor of Sutiaba 8.11.1768, A1.11 60 501 Razón de los nuevos establecimientos 26.4.1773, A1.11 51 454 *Raciones* paid to priests 1774; AGI AG 558 Account of the corregimientos of Nicaragua 26.9.1776; AGCA A1.11 56 474 Village of Lovigüisca 18.1.1780; AGI AG 572 Cabildo of Granada 24.4.1785; AGCA A1.30 251 1908 Complaints against the *subdelegado* of Matagalpa 7.3. 1810.

47. AGI AG 572 Cabildo of Granada 24.4.1785.

48. For example, AGCA A1.11 53 466 Complaints against the *cura* of El Viejo 1769, A1.23 1529 fol. 598 cedula 3.9.1770, A1.11 51 454 *Raciones* paid to priests 1774, A1.11 51 455 Indians of Matagalpa 1785.

49. AGCA A1.17 4683 40392 Testimony in favor of the corregidor of Sutiaba 1773.

50. AGCA A1.23 1538 10093 fol. 136 cedula 9.11.1812.

51. For example, AGCA A1.30 232 1818 Complaints against the Governor of Nicaragua 1748.

52. AGCA A1.11 60 501 Razón de los nuevos establecimientos 26.4.1773, A1.17 4683 40392 Testimony in favor of the corregidor of Sutiaba 1773.

53. AGCA A1.30 219 1751 Complaints against the corregidor of Sutiaba 8.11.1768; AGI AG 558 Account of the corregimientos of Nicaragua 26.9.1776.

54. For accounts of the *repartimiento de hilados* see AGCA A3.16 498 3833 Village of Quesalquaque 4.12.1725, A1.30 248 1891 Cobradores de Totogalpa 1739; AGI AG 545 Testimonio . . . contra el corregidor de Sutiaba 1761; AGCA A1.30 219 1751 Complaints against the corregidor of Sutiaba 8.11.1768, A1.30 220 1756 Village of El Viejo 1769, A1.11 60 501 Razón de los nuevos establecimientos 26.4.1773, A1.11 54 471 Pueblo of Sutiaba 1774; AGI AG 536 Bishop of Nicaragua 26.2.1774, AG 558 Account of the corregimientos of Nicaragua 26.9.1776.

55. AGCA A1.30 239 2569 cedula 25.1.1789 (Honduras).

56. *CDHCR,* 10:7–10 Informes sobre el corregimiento de Nicoya 15.11. 1765; ANCR Guatemala 327 Interrogatorio . . . contra el corregidor de Nicoya 1761, ANCR Guatemala 498 Complaints against the corregidor of Nicoya 14.7.1785; *CDHCR,* 10:292–94 Informe de Don Salvador sobre las pesquerías de perlas 23.2.1803; Gerhard, "Shellfish Dye," 180–81.

57. ANCR 453 Guatemala Complaints against the corregidor of Nicoya 1781.

58. For example, AGCA A3.16 498 3833 Village of Quesalquaque 4.12.1725; ANCR Guatemala 327 Cura of Nicoya 19.5.1760; AGI AG 545 Testimonio . . . contra el corregidor de Sutiaba 1761, AG 536 Bishop of Nicaragua 26.2.1774, AG 558 Account of the corregimientos of Nicaragua 26.9.1776; AGCA A1.30 227 1791 Charges against the corregidor of El Viejo 1794.

59. See chap. 10 and AGI AG 545 Testimonio . . . contra el corregidor de Sutiaba 1761; AGCA A1.30 219 1751 Complaints against the corregidor of Sutiaba 8.11.1768; AGI AG 545 Don Gerónimo de la Vega 1.7.1767, AG 572 Cabildo of Granada 24.4.1785, AG 743 King to Audiencia 11.3.1790.

60. AGCA A1.30 230 1809 Complaints against the Governor of Nicaragua 16.1.1725.

61. AGCA A3.16 498 3833 Village of Quesalquaque 4.12.1725. See also AGI AG 545 Testimonio . . . contra el corregidor of Sutiaba 1761.

62. Floyd, *Anglo-Spanish Struggle,* 88–95.

63. AGI AG 371 Fr. Ximénez 9.9.1748.

64. AGCA A1.12 77 634 Pueblo of Matagalpa 7.3.1730.

65. AGCA A1.12 117 2472 Consulta de Fr. Ortiz 1768; AGI AG 962 Informe on the Colegio de Propaganda Fide 23.12.1782, AG 963 On the Matagalpan missions 22.11.1813; Peralta, *Límites de Costa Rica,* 226–31 3.7.1815.

66. AGI AG 940 Memorial of the life of Don Hurtado y Plaza 15.11.1783; AGCA A1.1 118 2489 Instancia presentada por el Fiscal 23.9.1801.

67. AGCA A1.12 117 2472 Consulta de Fr. Ortiz 1768; AGI AG 962 Informe

on the Colegio de Propaganda Fide 23.12.1782; Peralta, *Limites de Costa Rica*, 226–31 3.7.1815.

68. AGI AG 950 Bishop Morel 8.9.1752.

69. AGCA A3.16 501 3870 Pueblo of Boaco 1.5.1750; AGI AG 950 Bishop Morel 8.9.1752, AG 449 Corregidor of Sebaco and Chontales 20.11.1757; AGCA A1.12 117 2472 Consulta de Fr. Ortiz 1758; *BAGG*, 6: 237–51 Bishop of Nicaragua 22.5.1790; Peralta, *Límites de Costa Rica*, 226–31 3.7.1815; Floyd, *Anglo-Spanish Struggle*, 95–99.

70. AGCA A1.12 334 7057 cedula 9.5.1747, A1.12 117 2472 Consulta de Fr. Ortiz 1768 cedula 30.11.1756.

71. AGI AG 371 Fr. Ximénez 9.9.1748, Frs. Guerra and Aguilar 1.6.1750.

72. AGCA A1.12 117 2474 Fr. Orosco 20.12.1768, A1.1 118 2489 Instancia presentada por el Fiscal 23.9.1801.

73. *BAGG*, 6: 237–51 Bishop of Nicaragua 22.5.1790.

74. AGCA A1.12 50 494 Informe relativo a que 47 indios caribes . . . 1768, A1.1 118 2489 Instancia presentada por el Fiscal 23.9.1801.

75. AGCA A1.1 118 2489 Instancia presentada por el Fiscal 23.9.1801.

76. AGCA A1.12 50 494 Informe relativo a que 47 indios caribes . . . 1768, A1.1 119 2486 Sobre haber salido . . . 47 indios caribes 1768.

77. AGCA A1.1 119 2486 Sobre haber salido . . . 47 indios caribes 1768, A1.1 118 2489 Instancia presentada por el Fiscal 23.9.1801.

78. AGCA A1.1 118 2489 Instancia presentada por el Fiscal 23.9.1801.

79. AGI AG 963 Fr. Ramón Roxas 22.11.1813; Peralta, *Límites de Costa Rica*, 226–31 3.7.1815.

80. AGI IG 1525 Misioneros Apostólicos de Propaganda Fide 7.1.1813, AG 962 Fiscal 19.5.1815.

81. AGCA A1.12 78 641 19.1.1770; *BAGG*, 6: 237–51 Bishop of Nicaragua 22.5.1790; AGI AG 963 Jefe político de Nicaragua 4.6.1814.

82. ANCR CC 5290 Bishop of Nicaragua 3.7.1815; AGI AG 962 Fiscal 19.5.1815.

CHAPTER 15

1. AGCA A3.16 152 1073–74 and 1092 tasaciones 1816.

2. AGCA A1.12 78 644 11.8.1768.

3. AGI AG 535 Vecinos of the valley of Rivas 5.11.1778.

4. *Recopilación*, 2 lib. 6 tít. 7 ley 12: 192 3.11.1536.

5. AGCA A1.12 78 644 11.8.1768; ANCR CC 321 Corredigor of Nicoya 12.6.1772; AGI AG 575 Juan de Ayssa 20.1.1778.

6. AGI AG 950 Bishop Morel 8.9.1752; AGCA A1.17 210 5014 Visita of the corregimiento of Realejo 1740; AGI AG 234 Bishop of Nicaragua 2.6.1746; *BAGG*, 2: 463–86 Larria 15.11.1765, Díaz de Corcuera 26.9.1766; AGI AG 558 Governor of Nicaragua 17.4.1776; *BAGG*, 7: 157–75 20.1.1800.

7. AGI AG 558 Governor of Nicaragua 17.4.1776.

8. *BAGG*, 7: 157–75 20.1.1800.

9. AGCA A1.10.1 2646 22150 Resumen general de las familias . . . 7.5.1804.

10. AGI AG 950 Bishop Morel 8.9.1752; AGCA A3.16 502 3882 25.9.1754.

11. AGI AG 950 Bishop Morel 8.9.1752. For a detailed description of the village of Chinandega see MNM 570 fols. 263–79 Descripción de Realejo, n.d.

12. AGCA A1.17 210 5114 Visita of the corregimiento of Realejo 1740.

13. Ibid. In fact, the size of Spanish households is likely to have been even higher, since more individuals in this group owned houses that were probably rented to nonwhites:

Village	Spaniards		Mixed Races		Indians	
	No. Houses	Population	No. Houses	Population	No. Houses	Population
Realejo	12	60	70	348	1	7
Chinandega	6	23	72	260	137	525
Chichigalpa	3	16	21	94	39	118
El Viejo	39	174	105	415	178	674
Total	60	273	268	1,117	355	1,324
Average household size		4.6		5.2		3.7

The racial character of the household is defined according to the racial status of the head of household.

14. For example, ANCR CC 3737 Información seguida ante el corregidor de Nicoya 4.5.1774; AGCA A3.12 491 3736 Hacendado of Sutiaba 31.8.1772, A1.45 3345 Pueblo de San Jorge de Nicaragua 14.6.1793, A1.45 446 2938 Larrabe contra los indios de Chinandega 1799, A1.45 446 2939 Indians of the village of Masaya 1807.

15. AGCA A1.45 445 2936 Villages of Sutiaba 6.5.1773.

16. AGCA A1.23 1528 fol. 125 cedula 15.10.1754; Ots Capdequí, *España en América,* 85–86.

17. AGCA A1.45 445 2936 Fiscal 1778.

18. AGI AG 627 Apuntamientos sobre la agricultura, Larrazábal 20.10.1810; Martínez Peláez, *Patria del criollo,* 170–71.

19. AGCA A1.23 1538 fol. 136 decreto 9.12.1812, A1.23 1543 fol. 407 real orden 29.4.1820.

20. AGCA A1.30 216 1738 Complaints against the corregidor of Sutiaba 1753, A1.45 445 2936 Villages of Sutiaba 6.5.1773.

21. AGCA A1.73 477 3157 Tribute of the villages of Matagalpa 1785, A1.73 478 3176 Pueblo of Camoapa 1804, A3.16 246 4912 Estado que manifiesta los partidos 20.7.1793.

22. In Nicoya the *caja* was kept in the house of the corregidor so that the Indians had no knowledge of the money that went in and out (ANCR Guatemala 453 Complaints against the corregidor of Nicoya 1781).

23. The total value of community funds in Nicaragua was: 1791: 21,243 pesos 3 reals; 1801, 55,533 pesos 3¼ reals; 1819: 80,694 pesos ¼ real (AGCA A3.4 168 1176 Fondos de comunidad 1791–1819).

24. AGCA A1.23 1531 fol. 336 cedula 5.11.1782; Gibson, *Aztecs,* 215.

25. AGCA A1.73 477 3160 Pueblo of El Viejo 5.5.1791.

26. The community funds in Nicaragua in 1801 were as follows:

Jurisdiction	Number of *cajas*	Funds pesos	reals	Average funds (pesos)	Percent of total funds
León	11	21,441	6	1,949	38.6
Granada	22	22,995	0	1,043	41.3
Nueva Segovia	5	4,419	4	884	8.0
Sebaco	12	6,717	1½	560	12.1
Total	50	55,533	3½	1,111	100.0

Source: AGCA A3.4 168 1176 Fondos de comunidad 1801.

27. AGCA A1.45 484 3316 Principal of Theoteguilla 1741, A3.16 246 4912 Estado que manifiesta los partidos . . . 20.7.1793.

28. For examples of loans see AGCA A3.4 168 1176 Fondos de comunidad 1791–1803, 1817.

29. In 1799 the period of loans was extended by two years because crops were attacked by a plague of locusts (AGCA A1.73 478 3172 Fiscal 25.6.1799).

30. AGCA A1.73 478 3162 Fiscal 3.10.1791.

31. AGCA A1.73 478 3164 Governor of Nicaragua 23.1.1793, Fiscal 7.2.1793.

32. AGCA A1.1 262 5763 fol. 1 cedula 23.6.1815, A1.77 91 1056 17.1.1818 (Honduras, but the order was applied to the entire audiencia).

33. ANCR CC 498 Cofradías of Nicoya 1788–1825; AGCA A3.3 40 785 1795 (Guatemala).

34. *CDHCR*, 9:476–90 Estadística de los haciendas de Nicoya 1751; AGCA A1.12 119 2489 Pueblo of San Ramón 14.2.1767.

35. ANCR CC 497 Cofradías of Nicoya 1784–1800, Guatemala 441 Corregidor of Nicoya 27.1.1781; Gibson, *Aztecs*, 130.

36. AGCA A1.11 60 501 Razón de los nuevos establecimientos. . . 26.4.1773.

37. For example, ANCR Guatemala 441 Corregidor of Nicoya 27.1.1787; AGCA A1.11 53 466 Complaints against the cura of El Viejo 1769.

38. AGI AG 252 Media anatas paid on lands 1713–33 and AG 264 Ventas y composiciones de tierras 1748–1751.

39. For example, AGCA A1.30 220 1756 Complaints against the corregidor of El Viejo 28.8.1768; AGI AG 536 Bishop of Nicaragua 26.2.1774; ANCR Guatemala 498 Complaints against the corregidor of Nicoya 14.7.1785.

40. AGCA A1.30 220 1756 Complaints against the corregidor of El Viejo 28.8.1768.

41. AGCA A1.17 2335 17508 Información rendida por Díaz Navarro 19.1. 1744, A3.16 83 1190 Corregidor of Nicoya 13.2.1745 (Costa Rica), A3.16 501 3869 Fiscal 30.9.1751, A3.9 174 1685 Alcalde Mayor of Tegucigalpa 1777 (Honduras), A1.73 478 3169 23.6.1797.

42. AGCA A3.16 499 3847 Village of Managua 1722, A3.16 148 1017 Pueblo of Nicaragua 1732; AGI AG 656 N31 f.247 Gaçeta de Guatemala 4.9.1797, N267 fol. 174 12.7.1801, N331 fol. 439 November, 1803.

43. AGI AG 656 N267 fol. 174 Gaçeta de Guatemala 12.7.1802.

44. AGCA A3.9 482 3651 Cabildo of León 29.8.1742; AGI AG 545 Don Gerónimo de la Vega 1.7.1767; AGCA A1.30 252 1909 Complaints against the

teniente of Masaya 1779; AGI AG 743 King to Audiencia 6.9.1788, AG 656 N89 fol. 321 Gaçeta de Guatemala 26.11.1798.

45. AGI AG 656 N300 f.95 Gaçeta de Guatemala 25.4.1803.

46. AGCA A1.17 210 5014 Visita of the corregimiento of Realejo 1740; AGI AG 950 Bishop Morel 8.9.1752; AGCA A3.16 503 3892 Corregidor of Sutiaba 30.3.1764, A1.45 445 2936 Villages of Sutiaba 6.5.1773, A1.1 118 2482 Bishop of Nicaragua 23.6.1778, A1.45 446 2939 Pueblo of Masaya 1807; MNM 570 fols. 263–79 Descripción de Realejo, n.d.

47. AGI AG 656 N273 fol. 197 Gaçeta de Guatemala 23.8.1802.

48. MNM 570 fols. 263–79 Descripción de Realejo, n.d.

49. AGCA A1.17 210 5014 Visita of the corregimiento of Realejo 1740.

50. AGCA A1.73 478 3169 1797.

51. ANCR Guatemala 369 Pueblo of Nicoya 12.8.1769.

52. AGCA A1.45 485 3345 Pueblo of San Jorge de Nicaragua 14.6.1793; AGI AG 656 N89 fol. 321 Gaçeta de Guatemala 26.11.1798.

53. AGCA A1.11 53 466 Complaints against the cura of El Viejo 1769; ANCR Guatemala 441 Corregidor of Nicoya 27.1.1781; AGCA A1.11 476 3152 1781; ANCR Guatemala 917 18.9.1803.

54. AGI AG 940 Memorial of the life of Don Hurtado y Plaza 15.11.1783; Juarros, *Statistical and Commercial History,* 66.

55. AGCA A1.17 2335 17308 Información rendida por Díaz Navarro 19.1. 1744; ANCR Guatemala 327 Cura of Nicoya 19.5.1760; *CDHCR,* 10:7–10 Informes sobre el corregimiento de Nicoya 15.11.1765; ANCR Guatemala 453 Indians of Nicoya 1781; AGI AG 940 Memorial of the life of Don Hurtado y Plaza 15.11.1783; *CDHCR,* 10:292–94 Informe de Salvador sobre las pesquerias de perlas 23.2.1803; Juarros, *Statistical and Commercial History,* 72.

56. *BAGG,* 2:479–88 Larria 15.11.1765; AGI AG 572 Cabildo of Granada 24.4.1785.

57. *CDHCN,* 96–136 Díaz Navarro 30.11.1758; AGI AG 572 Cabildo of Granada 24.4.1785.

58. AGI AG 743 King to Audiencia 6.9.1788, 10.7.1793.

59. For example, AGCA A1.30 222 1766 Complaints against the corregidor of Realejo 26.2.1774.

60. *BAGG,* 7:157–75 20.1.1800.

61. For example: AGCA A3.16 498 3833 Pueblo of Quesalquaque 4.12.1725, A3.9 482 3651 Cabildo of León 29.8.1742, A1.30 216 1743 Complaints against the corregidor of Sutiaba 1759; AGI AG 558 Account of the corregimientos of Nicaragua 26.9.1766; AGCA A1.30 216 1766 and A1.30 1530 fol. 400 cedula 26.2.1774, A1.30 252 1909 Complaints against the teniente of Masaya 27.8. 1779; AGI AG 572 and A1.23 1532 fol. 602 cedula 24.4.1785; AGI AG 743 King to Audiencia 6.9.1788, 10.7.1793; AGCA A1.23 1532 fol. 600 cedula 11.3.1790; AGI IG 1525 Anguiano 14.5.1797.

62. AGCA A3.16 498 3828 1727; *CDHCN,* 96–136 Díaz Navarro 30. 11.1758.

63. AGCA A1.30 230 1809 Residencia on the Governor of Nicaragua 16.1. 1725, A3.16 498 3833 Pueblo of Quesalquaque 4.12.1725, A3.9 482 3651 Cabildo of León 29.8.1742; AGI AG 362 Bishop of Nicaragua 28.7.1746; AGCA A1.30 232 1818 1748.

64. AGI AG 950 Bishop Morel 8.9.1752.

65. AGCA A1.23 1529 fol. 598 cedula 30.9.1770, A1.23 1530 fol. 400 cedula 11.9.1776.

66. AGCA A3.17 148 1017 Pueblo of Nicaragua 1732, A3.16 500 3852 14.5.1740, A3.16 246 4912 Estado que manifiesta los partidos . . . 20.7.1793.

67. Martínez Peláez, *Patria del Criollo,* 525.

68. For sources for 1676–86 see chap. 10; AGCA A3.16 149 1027 and 1029 tasaciones 1759. In nine villages in the jurisdiction of León, 531 men married within the same barrio, 758 within the same village, and 143 out of the village. There were 49 other marriages.

69. AGCA A3.16 503 3891 tasaciones 1759. Of a total of 869 males in Nindirí, Masaya, and Managua, 342 married women from their own villages.

70. AGCA A3.16 149 1027 and 1029 tasaciones 1759, A3.16 503 3891 tasaciones 1759.

71. AGCA A1.30 219 1751 Complaints against the corregidor of Sutiaba 8.11.1768.

72. AGCA A3.16 194 2030 28.2.1797 (Honduras).

73. AGCA A1.23 2590 21161 cedula 7.4.1798.

74. AGCA A3.16 152 1092 padrones 1817. In 1759 only 5 of 1,481 married males in the jurisdiction of León were married to *libres* or ladinos, and only 3 of 869 in the villages of Nindirí, Masaya, and Managua (AGCA A3.16 149 1027 and 1029 tasaciones 1759).

75. AGCA A1.17 210 5014 Visita of the corregimiento of Realejo 1740:

Village	Families	Adults	Children	Family size	Adult-child ratio
Chinandega	176	309	216	3.0	1 : 0.70
Chichigalpa	41	74	44	2.9	1 : 0.59
El Viejo	207	374	298	3.3	1 : 0.80
Total	424	757	558	3.1	1 : 0.74

76. For example, in 1757 10.5 percent of the children of Sutiaba were classified as orphans (AGCA A3.16 502 3875 Padrón of Sutiaba 12.10.1757).

77. See chap. 16.

78. AGI AG 362 Rentas eclesiásticas 30.8.1723; AGCA A1.17 210 5014 Visita of the corregimiento of Realejo 1740, A1.18 211 5025 Relación histórica . . . 1740; AGI AG 950 Bishop Morel 8.9.1752; BNM 2676 fols. 404–406 Account of Mercedarian convents 1791.

79. AGI AG 371 Fr. Ximénez 9.9.1748.

80. AGI AG 362 Bishop of Nicaragua 2.6.1746.

CHAPTER 16

1. AGCA A3.16 501 3870 Pueblo of Boaco 1.5.1750, A1.12 50 507 Pueblo of Boaco 8.1.1768 (Honduras); *BAGG,* 5:214–36 Informe relativo a que 47 indios caribes 1768; *BAGG,* 6:237–51 Bishop of Nicaragua 22.6.1790; Floyd, *Anglo-Spanish Struggle,* 95–101, 115, 173.

2. For 1777 see chap. 17; *BAGG*, 3: 217–20 Estado de los curatos 8.7.1806.

3. AGCA A1.12 77 633 Corregidor of Sebaco and Chontales 16.9.1726.

4. AGCA A3.16 500 3856 Teniente of Nueva Segovia 6.6.1741, A3.16 498 3829, A3.16 500 3853–54, 3859–60 Padrones of Tepesomoto, Totogalpa, Mozonte, Comalteca and Yalagüina 1741, A3.16 501 3865 Comandante of Nueva Segovia 20.7.1742.

5. AGCA A3.16 499 3846 Pueblo of Yalagüina 5.8.1739.

6. AGI AG 950 Bishop Morel 8.9.1752; *BAGG*, 2: 479–86 Larria 15.11.1765, Díaz de Corcuera 26.9.1766, *BAGG*, 7: 157–75 20.1.1800.

7. AGCA A1.12 2817 24864 Rector of Nueva Segovia 24.6.1752.

8. AGI AG 950 Bishop Morel 8.9.1752.

9. Ibid.

10. *BAGG*, 1: 46–48 Relación geográfica del partido de Chontales y Sebaco 25.8.1740.

11. AGCA A1.73 478 3169 1797.

12. AGCA A3.4 168 1176 Fondos de comunidad 1801.

13. *BAGG*, 1: 46–48 Relación geográfica del partido de Chontales y Sebaco 25.8.1740; *BAGG* 2: 479–82 Larria 15.11.1765.

14. AGCA A3.3 40 785 and 787 1795.

15. Floyd, *Anglo-Spanish Struggle*, 61.

16. ACGA A1.30 226 1786 Residencia on the corregidor of Matagalpa 1788.

17. AGCA A1.12 77 633 Corregidor of Chontales and Sebaco 16.9.1726, A1.23 1585 10229 fol. 313 cedula 16.10.1726.

18. For sources see n. 4 and AGCA A3.16 502 3871–88 Padrones of nine villages in Sebaco and Chontales 1755. For 1676–96 see chap. 10.

19. For sources see n. 4 and AGCA A3.16 502 3871–88 Padrones of nine villages in Sebaco and Chontales 1755. Of 1,376 couples, 192 had one partner descibes as 'libre.'

20. For sources see n. 4.

21. AGCA A3.16 500 3855 Padrón of lavoríos of Nueva Segovia 1741 and sources in n. 4.

22. AGCA A1.12 2817 24864 Rector of Nueva Segovia 24.6.1752.

23. AGCA A1.1 118 2489 and *BAGG*, 7: 119–45 Instancia presentada por el Fiscal 23.9.1801.

24. AGCA A1.12 119 2489 Inventory of the mission of San Ramón 14.2.1767.

25. AGCA A1.23 1529 fols. 532–44 cedula 18.5.1773.

26. AGCA A1.12 117 2473 Yarrince 18.9.1759; *BAGG*, 5: 214–36 Informe relativo a que 47 indios caribes . . . 5.8.1768; Floyd, *Anglo-Spanish Struggle*, 88, 90–91.

27. AGCA A1.12 117 2473 Yarrince 18.9.1759.

28. AGCA A1.12 77 635 1731; AGI AG 371 Fr. Ximénez 9.9.1748, AG 449 Corregidor of Sebaco and Chontales 20.11.1757, AG 940 Memorial of the life of Don Hurtado y Plaza 15.11.1783; Wickham, *Journey Among the Woolwa*, 169.

29. AGI AG 940 Memorial of the life of Don Hurtado y Plaza 15.11.1783; Roberts, *Narrative of Voyages*, 104.

30. AGCA A1.12 134 1504 13.12.1722 (Honduras); AGI AG 501 Anguiano 10.5.1804; Long, *History of Jamaica* 1: 323, 326–27; Henderson, *British Settlement*, 190; Roberts, *Narrative of Voyages*, 100; Floyd, *Anglo-Spanish Struggle*, 66–67.

31. AGCA A1.23 1529 fols. 532–44 cedula 18.5.1773; AGI AG 371 Fr. Ximénez 9.9.1748.

32. AGI AG 371 Fr. Ximénez 9.9.1748.

33. AGCA A1.24 1529 fols. 532–44 cedula 18.5.1773.

34. AGI AG 371 Fr. Ximénez 9.9.1748; Wickham, "Notes on the Soumoo," 205.

35. AGI AG 371 Fr. Ximénez 9.9.1748.

36. Wickham, "Notes on the Soumoo," 205.

37. Ibid.; Heath, "Miskuto Grammar," 48; Conzemius, *Ethnographical Survey*, 126–28.

38. *CDHCN*, 63–77 Consulta de Consejo de Indias 8.7.1739; AGCA A1.17 335 7088 and *CDHCN*, 78–96 Rivera 23.11.1742.

39. AGCA A1.17 4501 38303 Porta Costas 1.8.1790.

40. AGI AG 228 Lic. de Ererra 29.4.1725; AGCA A1.17 335 7088 and *CDHCN*, 78–96 Rivera 23.11.1742, A1.17 4501 38303 Porta Costas 1.8.1790; *BAGG*, 7: 157–75 5.3.1800.

41. MNM Bª-XI-Cª-B-nº-1 Hodgson and Hodgson 1782; AGCA A1.17 4501 38303 Porta Costas 1.8.1790, A1.1 118 2484 and *BAGG*, 6: 171-92 Aprobando el gasto . . . en la fundación del pueblo de San Juan 27.6.1790. Two other maps show the dispersion of the Zambo-Mosquito in small settlements along the coast: Mapa Ideal Particular de la Provincia de Nicaragua y sus Corregimientos, n.d. (MNM) and Razón de los establecimientos que hay desde el escudo de Veraguas hasta Onduras by John Clapp 2.9.1771 (SHM Plano 5185 Sig. D-13-37).

42. *CDHCN*, 63–77 Consulta de Consejo de Indias 8.7.1739.

43. White, *Case of the Agent*, 51.

44. PRO CO 123/1 fols. 55–79 Hodgson 1757; MNM Bª-XI-Cª-B-nº-1 Hodgson and Hodgson 1782; AGCA A1.1 118 2484 Aprobando el gasto . . . en la fundación del pueblo de San Juan 27.6.1790, A1.17 4501 38303 Porta Costas 1.8.1790; Henderson, *British Settlement*, 180; Roberts, *Narrative of Voyages*, 115, 128–30, 142; Young, *Residence on the Mosquito Shore*, 107–108.

45. PRO CO 123/1 fols. 55–79 Hodgson 1757; AGCA A1.17 4501 38303 Porta Costas 1.8.1790; *BAGG*, 7: 157–75 5.2.1800; Henderson, *British Settlement*, 180; Roberts, *Narrative of Voyages*, 119–21, 156.

46. See chap. 5.

47. Henderson, *British Settlement*, 180–81; Roberts, *Narrative of Voyages*, 150; Young, *Residence on the Mosquito Shore*, 102–105.

48. AGI AG 302 8.7.1739; AGCA A1.12 117 2473 Yarrince 18.8.1759; AGI AG 665 and *CDHCN*, 198–205 Diario de Antonio Gastelu 11.7.1776; AGCA A1.17 4501 38303 Porta Costas 1.8.1790; *BAGG*, 7: 157–75 5.3.1800; Roberts, *Narrative of Voyages*, 108, 116–18; Young, *Residence on the Mosquito Shore*, 82; Peralta, *Límites de Costa Rica*, 46 (25.6.1737); Floyd, *Anglo-Spanish Struggle*, 58, 60–61.

49. Henderson, *British Settlement*, 190.

50. *CDHCN*, 63–77 Consulta de Consejo de Indias 8.7.1739; Floyd, *Anglo-Spanish Struggle*, 62.

51. Henderson, *British Settlement*, 183.

52. BM Add. 17,566 fol. 169 Relación de las poblaciones 19.1.1746; PRO CO 123/1 fols. 55–79 Hodgson 1757; AGI AG 665 Diario de Antonio Gastelu 11.7.1776; Edwards, "British Settlements," 5: 210. Goods valued at 2,000 pesos were given to the king annually for distribution to the Zambo-Mosquito.

53. Floyd, *Anglo-Spanish Struggle*, 123–25, 172–82.
54. BM Add. 17,566 fol. 169 Relación de las poblaciones 19.1.1746; AGCA A1.12 117 2473 Yarrince 18.9.1759; MNM Bª-XI-Cª-B-nº-1 Hodgson and Hodgson 1782.
55. Henderson, *British Settlement*, 146, 182.
56. PRO CO 123/1 fols. 55–79 Hodgson 1757.
57. *CDHCN*, 44–66 25.8.1793; Henderson, *British Settlement*, 185–86; Helms, "Cultural Ecology," 79.
58. Roberts, *Narrative of Voyages*, 116–18.
59. Henderson, *British Settlement*, 183; Strangeways, *Sketch of the Mosquito Shore*, 330–31; Young, *Residence of the Mosquito Shore*, 48; Helms, *Asang*, 22–23.
60. Henderson, *British Settlement*, 187; Strangeways, *Sketch of the Mosquito Shore*, 331.
61. Strangeways, *Sketch of the Mosquito Shore*, 331–33.
62. Henderson, *British Settlement*, 186; Strangeways, *Sketch of the Mosquito Shore*, 331–33.
63. PRO CO 123/1 fols. 55–79 Hodgson 1757; Serrano y Sanz, *Relaciones historicas*, 285–328; Henderson, *British Settlement of Honduras*, 186–87.
64. PRO CO 123/1 fols. 55–79 Hodgson 1757.

CHAPTER 17

1. The tributary population of the villages of Sutiaba, Posoltega, and Quesalquaque increased from 2,314 to 2,877 (AGCA A3.16 147 999 tasaciones 1686, A3.16 499 3840–43 tasaciones 1735).
2. AGCA A3.16 147 999 tasaciones 1686, A1.17 210 5014 Visita of the corregimiento of Realejo 1740:

Village	Tributary Indians, 1686	Adults, 1740	Children, 1740	Families, 1740	Family Size	Adult-Child ratio
Chinandega	186	309	216	176	3.0	1 : 0.70
Chichigalpa	160	74	44	41	2.9	1 : 0.59
El Viejo	440	374	298	207	3.3	1 : 0.80

3. The increase was from 489 in 1676–86 to 599 in 1741 (AGCA A3.16 147 999 tasaciones 1676–96, A3.16 498 3829, 500 3853–54, 3859–60 Padrones of villages in Nueva Segovia 1741).
4. *BAGG*, 1:46–48 Relación geográfica del partido de Chontales y Sebaco, Posada 1740.
5. The increase in the male tributary population was from 495 in 1685 to 704 in 1755 (AGCA A3.16 147 999 1676–86, A3.16 149 1034 1759 and A3.16 502 3871–73, 3884–88 Padrones of 9 villages in Sebaco and Chontales 1755).
6. AGI AG 234 and 362 Bishop of Nicaragua 2.6.1746.
7. AGI AG 950 Bishop Morel 8.9.1752.
8. AGCA A3.16 147 999 tasaciones 1676–86, A3.16 149 1027 and 1029 tasaciones 1759, A3.16 503 3891 and 3899 tasaciones 1759. In the jurisdiction of

León the male tributary population increased from 1,770 to 2,041 and in Granada from 2,370 to 4,719.

9. AGI AG 560 cedula 8.11.1765. See chap. 14.

10. AGI AG 560 15.11.1771.

11. AGI AG 560 1777.

12. On November 10, 1776, the crown ordered the compilation of censuses for all Spanish overseas territories. Orders were sent to the secular and ecclesiastical authorities to the effect that they were to make separate counts. Each census was to include the number of inhabitants classified by sex, marital status, and race. The intention was that censuses should be taken annually, but the time-consuming process made the task impossible. Unfortunately, the returns for Nicaragua have not survived (Browning, "Observations on the 1776 Census," 5–13).

13. AGCA A3.9 174 1685 1776 (Honduras).

14. AGCA A3.16 153 1101 Estado que manifiesta el número de tributarios . . . 3.6.1793, 19.12.1794, 19.9.1799.

15. These are also the figures given for that date in AGCA A3.16 151 1058–59 1776–77.

16. AGCA A3.29 1749 28130 Extracto del número de personas . . . capaces de tomar bulas de Santa Cruzada 1778; AGI AG 562 Estado de las bulas de Santa Cruzada 23.7.1779.

17. In a comparison of the figures of those who purchased indulgences with the total population included in the 1776 census, the former account for only 56 percent (AGI figures) and 63 percent (AGCA figures) of the total population.

18. AGI AG 656 vol. 6 N256: 100 Gaçeta de Guatemala 26.4.1802; Juarros, *Statistical and Commercial History,* 497. Mariano Mendez suggests that the figure of 103,943 was calculated from the population of some villages for 1778 added to others for 1795 (Peralta, *Límites de Costa Rica,* 241–72, reference to p. 248). This could very well be the case.

19. AGI AG 656 vol. 6 N286: 301 Gaçeta de Guatemala 22.11.1802.

20. AGI AG 627 Apuntamientos sobre la agricultura . . . Larrazábal 20.10.1810.

21. AGCA A1.11 76 620 no author, n.d.

22. *BAGG,* 7: 157–75 ca. 1800; Squier, *Notes on Central America,* 45.

23. Squier, *Notes on Central America,* 45. This census appears to have been used as a basis for the creation of constituencies for elections to the *diputación provincial* (Peralta, *Costa de Mosquitos,* 545–52 13.12.1820). Peralta gives a detailed breakdown of the figures region by region, although those for Nueva Segovia are clearly estimates.

24. Squier, *Notes on Central America,* 46.

25. AGI AG 558 Governor of Nicaragua 17.5.1776; AGCA A3.16 151 1101 Estado que manifiesta el número de tributarios . . . 3.6.1783.

26. AGCA A3.16 153 1100 and 1101 Estado que manifiesta el número de tributarios . . . 19.9.1799, A3.16 152 1092 Padrones 1816–17.

27. AGCA A3.16 150 1039 Padrón of Tepesomoto 15.12.1796, A3.16 153 1072 Padrón of Mozonte 3.8.1796.

28. See table 15 and ANCR Guatemala 315 Padrón of Nicoya 13.12.1760.

29. Thiel, "Población de la República de Costa Rica," 80, 92.

30. Number of lavoríos in the 1720s and 1730s:

Jurisdiction	1726	1728	1731	1733
León		189	218	
Granada	112			112
Sebaco (Chontales)	16			16

Sources: 1726: AGCA A3.16 148 1012; 1728: AGCA A3.16 148 1013; 1731: AGCA A3.16 148 1016; 1733: AGCA A3.16 520 4155.

These figures include female tributaries. Although there are no separate accounts of the *lavorío* population of Nueva Segovia, an inspection of the padrones of five villages in 1741 reveals that there was an equally small number of *lavóríos*—27 compared to 599 tributary Indians—i.e., 4.3 percent of the total male tributary population (AGCA A3.16 498 3829, 500 3853–54, 3859–60 Padrones of villages in Nueva Segovia 1741).

31. AGCA A3.16 246 4912 Estado que manifiesta los partidos . . . 20.7. 1793. That the figures refer to 1777 is clear if they are compared to those in AGCA A3.16 153 1101 Estado que manifiesta el número de tributarios . . . 3.6.1793, 19.12.1794. The total tributary population of Sebaco is slightly different in the two documents: 2,484 in the former and 2,499 in the latter.

32. AGCA A3.16 153 1101 tasaciones 1811, A3.16 152 1073–97 tasaciones 1816–17.

33. AGCA A3.16 152 1092 padrones 1816–17.

34. AGI AG 371 Fr. Ximénez 9.9.1748.

35. AGI A1.17 210 5018 Corregidor of Sebaco and Chontales 8.7.1743.

36. AGI AG 449 Corregidor of Sebaco and Chontales 20.11.1757.

37. Conzemius, "Miskito and Sumu Languages," 58.

38. AGCA A1.12 118 2487 Manzanares 13.4.1798; Conzemius, "Jicaques of Honduras," 163.

39. Roberts, *Narrative of Voyages*, 100.

40. The dates used for the calculation of the rates of decline are 1686 and 1806 since these are the dates for which the information relating to the tributary population is most detailed and most nearly complete.

41. AGCA A3.9 482 3651 Vicar of Posoltega 13.8.1744, 5.9.1744; ANCR Guatemala 327 Cura of Nicoya 19.5.1760; AGCA A1.12 78 644 30.8.1768; AGI AG 743 Auto of Fiscal 16.6.1779.

42. Floyd, *Anglo-Spanish Struggle*, 66–67.

43. AGCA A3.16 501 3870 Pueblo of Boaco 1.5.1750; AGI AG 950 Bishop Morel 8.9.1752, AG 449 Corregidor of Sebaco and Chontales 20.11.1757; AGCA A1.12 117 2472 Consulta de Fr. Ortiz 1768; Floyd, *Anglo-Spanish Struggle*, 95–99.

44. Solano Pérez-Lila, "Población indígena de Guatemala," 313; Veblen, "Native Population Decline," 498.

45. AGCA A3.16.3 513 5373 22.6.1739, A3.16.3 513 5376 2.3.1743 (Both Honduras).

46. AGI AG 251 Betancurt 29.5.1727; AGCA A1.23 1526 fol. 225 cedulas 29.5.1727, 11.3.1730, A1.23 1586 fols. 83 and 239 cedulas 30.1.1728, A1.23 1586 fol. 434 cedula 9.12.1728.

47. Veblen, "Native Population Decline," 498.

48. AGCA A1.23 1586 fols. 83 and 239 cedulas 30.1.1728, A3.16 497 3821 Padrón of Boaco 24.3.1718, 3823 Padrón of Teustepet 20.4.1718.

49. Veblen, "Native Population Decline," 498.

50. AGCA A3.16 148 1017 Pueblo of Nicaragua 1732, A1.23 1589 fol. 169 cedula 23.5.1733; AGI AG 230 Contador de cuentas reales 27.9.1734.

51. AGCA A3.16 500 3858 Corregidor of Matagalpa 20.5.1743, A3.16 83 1190 Cura of Nicoya 13.2.1745.

52. AGCA A3.16 503 3900 22.9.1751; ANCR CC 5290 Bishop of Nicaragua 3.7.1815.

53. AGCA A3.16 501 3869 Rector of Nueva Segovia 12.12.1749, Villages of Nueva Segovia 30.9.1751; Ashburn, *Ranks of Death,* 149–54.

54. AGCA A3.12 186 1886 Villages of Nueva Segovia 11.4.1753, 14.4.1753, 15.4.1753, A1.12 117 2474 Autos relativo a las misiones de Paraka y Pantasma 1769.

55. AGCA A3.16 503 3901 and 3902 Number of Indians dead as a result of an epidemic of "*viruelas*" 11.10.1782, 31.1.1783. The figures for 1777 are taken from AGCA A3.16 153 1101, and, as indicated in the discussion of the Indian population, the figures for the jurisdiction of León probably refer to 1759.

56. AGI AG 472 Estado de las siembras 15.9.1786; AGCA A1.45 385 3509 Pueblo of Catacamas 8.2.1788 (Honduras).

57. AGCA A3.16 152 1073 Matrículas for Matagalpa 26.12.1816.

58. AGCA A1.26 199 1639 Fiscal 7.9.1801.

59. AGCA A1.46 107 1315 20.9.1809 (Honduras).

60. AGI CO 815 Razón de las ciudades . . . 1683 and AG 29 Navia Bolaños 28.7.1685; AGCA A3.29 1749 Extracto del número de personas . . . capaces de tomar bulas de Santa Cruzada 6.6.1778.

61. AGCA A1.53 482 3211 Visita de obrajes de León 1723.

62. AGI AG 627 Apuntamientos sobre la agricultura . . . Larrazábal 20.10. 1810.

63. *CDHCN,* 96–136 Díaz Navarro 30.11.1758.

64. Ibid.; AGCA A3.16 150 1044 Corregidor of Sebaco and Chontales 5.5.1769.

65. *BAGG,* 7: 157–75 20.1.1800.

66. AGCA A3.29 1749 28130 Extracto del número de personas . . . capaces de tomar bulas de Santa Cruzada 6.6.1778.

67. SHM Plano 5185 Sig. D-13-37 Razón de los establecimientos 2.9.1771; MNM Bª-XI-Cª-B-nº-1 Hodgson and Hodgson 1782; AGCA A1.17 4501 38303 Porta Costas 1.8.1790.

68. BRP MA 279 fol. 192 Relación de las poblaciones que tienen los ingleses 19.1.1746.

69. Henderson, *British Settlement,* 146.

CHAPTER 18

1. Radell, "Indian Slave Trade," 76; Denevan, ed., *Native Population,* 291.

2. Cook and Borah's figures for the decline of the Indian population in Central Mexico until 1548 give a depopulation ratio of 4.4:1 (the actual figures are 27,650,000 on the eve of the Spanish conquest to 6,300,000 in 1548) (Cook and

Borah, *Essays,* 1:115). Depopulation ratios for the Chibcha are: for Tunja (1537 to 1564), 1.4.:1 (232,407 at the time of Spanish conquest to 168,440 in 1564) (Friede, "Tunja," 13), and for the Sabana de Bogotá (1537 to 1592–95), 2.2:1 (120,000 to 160,000 at conquest to 62,791 [excluding the city of Bogotá] in 1592–95) (Villamarin and Villamarin, *Indian Labor,* 83–84). The degree of decline was slightly less in the Central Andean highlands, where between 1525 and 1571 the Indian population declined from 4,641,200 to 1,349,190, a depopulation ratio of 3.4:1 (Smith, "Depopulation of the Central Andes," 459).

3. Dobyns, "Estimating Aboriginal American Population," 414–15.

4. AGCA A3.29 1749 28130 Extracto del número de personas . . . capaces de tomar bulas de Santa Cruzada 6.6.1778.

Bibliography

ARCHIVAL SOURCES

Although few colonial documents exist in Nicaragua owing to natural disasters and political upheavals, sufficient documents are available in the archives of Spain and Central America to make the study of Nicaraguan colonial history a rewarding task. The most important archives for this study were the Archivo General de Indias, in Seville, and the Archivo General de Centro América in Guatemala City. The Archivo General de Indias (AGI) is particularly important for the sixteenth century, for which few documents have survived in Central America. The most important sections researched for this study were the Audiencia de Guatemala, Patronato, Justicia and Contaduría. Many of the documents from the AGI for the period 1522 to 1550 have been published in a seventeen-volume collection, the Colección Somoza (CS). The Archivo General de Centro América (AGCA) contains important documents of a more local character dating from the midsixteenth century onwards. The archive is well catalogued, although there may be some difficulty finding a number of documents owing to their disturbance during the earthquake in 1976. The most important section used was that dealing with Nicaragua, although some documents in the Guatemala, Honduras, and Costa Rica sections yielded additional information, in the latter two sections about Nueva Segovia and Nicoya, respectively. Similarly, the Archivo Nacional de Historia, (ANH) in Tegucigalpa, and the Archivo Nacional (ANCR), in San José, provided details about the same two areas. The Archivo Nacional de Historia contains many unclassified documents, and research there tends to be time-consuming, though not unrewarding; the Archivo Nacional, however, is well catalogued.

A number of other archives in Spain yielded valuable information. The most important was the Real Academia de la Historia (RAHM), in Madrid, and in particular its Colección Muñoz. All the other archives, including the Biblioteca Nacional, the Biblioteca del Palacio Real, the Archivo Histórico Nacional, the Museo Naval, and the Servicio Histórico Militar, contained a small number of relevant documents, most of which were geographical descriptions of the area. Essential for the history of the Mosquito Coast were documents contained in the British Museum (BM) and the Public Record Office (Colonial Office) (PRO), in London.

Apart from the Colección Somoza already mentioned, there are a number of collections of published documents of varying degrees of usefulness. The *Colección de documentos referentes a la historia colonial de Nicaragua*, published in 1921 to commemorate the centenary of independence, contains a number of seventeenth- and eighteenth-century documents, but they are poorly transcribed and should be used with caution. The most valuable collection of published documents is the eleven-volume *Boletín del Archivo del Gobierno,* now the Archivo General de Centro América. For Nicoya the *Colección de documentos para la historia de Costa Rica* was useful, particularly for the eighteenth century. Various volumes published by Peralta at the end of the nineteenth century contain transcripts of documents contained in the AGI referring mainly to the Mosquito Coast and Costa Rica. The *Relaciones históricas y geográficas* published by Serrano y Sanz also contains useful material on eastern Nicaragua. As for most studies of early colonial history, the two Spanish collections of unedited documents (CDI and CDIU) contained a few essential documents for the early sixteenth century.

PUBLISHED WORKS

To establish the nature and distribution of Indian cultures at the time of the Spanish conquest, the following accounts were invaluable: Andagoya, Benzoni, Herrera, López de Gómara, López de Velasco, Martyr, Oviedo, Ponce and Torquemada. None of these accounts covers the eastern part of the country, and the earliest descriptions of the area are to be found in the seventeenth-century travel accounts of Dampier, Raveneau de Lussan, Exquemelin, and M. W. The early Central American histories by Fuentes y Guzmán, Remesal, and Vázquez also constituted important sources of information for the early history of the area.

Alcedo, A. de. 1786–89. *Diccionario geográfico-histórico de las Indias Occidentales ó América.* 5 vols. Madrid: Manuel González.
Alvarez Rubiano, P. 1954. *Pedrarias Dávila.* Madrid: Consejo Superior de Investigaciones Científicas, Instituto Gonzalo Fernández de Oviedo.
Andagoya, P. de. 1865. *The Narrative of Pascual de Andagoya.* Edited by C. R. Markham. Hakluyt Society Publications, 1st ser., vol. 34. London: T. Richards.
Anon. 1778. *The Present State of the West Indies.* London: R. Baldwin.
Anon. 1845. *Bericht über das Mosquitoland.* Berlin: Verlag von Alexander Duncker.
Anon. 1885. "Report on the Mosquito Country." In *The Kemble Papers.* 2:419–31. Collections of the New York Historical Society for the Year 1884. New York.
Ashburn, P. M. 1947. *The Ranks of Death: A Medical History of the Conquest of America.* New York: Coward-McCann.
Ayón, T. 1882–89. *Historia de Nicaragua desde los tiempos mas remotos hasta el año 1852.* 3 vols. Granada: El Centro-Americano.
Ball, A. P. 1977. "Measles." In G. M. Howe, ed. *A World Geography of Human Diseases.* Pp. 237–54. London and New York: Academic Press.
Bancroft, H. H. 1886. *The Native Races of the Pacific States.* 2 vols. San Francisco: A. L. Bancroft.
Barón Castro, R. 1942. *La población de El Salvador.* Madrid: Consejo Superior de Investigaciones Científicas, Instituto Gonzalo Fernández de Oviedo.

Bartlett, A. S., E. S. Barghoorn, and R. Berger. 1969. "Fossil Maize from Panama." *Science* 165:389–90.

Bataillon, M. 1953. "Las Casas et le Licencié Cerrato." *Bulletin Hispanique* 55:79–87.

Baudez, C. F. 1967. *Recherches archéologiques dans la Vallée du Tempisque, Guanacaste, Costa Rica.* Travaux et Memoires de l'Institut des Hautes Etudes de l'Amérique Latine, no. 18. Paris.

————. 1970. *Central America.* London: Barrie and Jenkins.

————, and M. D. Coe. "Archaeological Sequences in Northwestern Costa Rica." *Proceedings, 34th International Congress of Americanists* (Vienna), pp. 366–73.

Bell, C. N. 1899. *Tangweera: Life and Adventures Among Gentle Savages.* London: Arnold.

Benedict, R. 1943. "Two Patterns of Indian Acculturation." *American Anthropologist* 45:207–12.

Benzoni, G. 1967. *La historia del Nuevo Mundo.* Biblioteca de la Academia Nacional de la Historia, no. 86. Caracas.

Bergmann, J. F. 1969. "The Distribution of Cacao and Its Cultivation in Pre-Columbian America." *Annals of the Association of American Geographers* 59:85–96.

Black, F. L. 1975. "Infectious Diseases in Primitive Societies." *Science* 187:515–18.

Borah, W. 1951. *New Spain's Century of Depression.* Ibero-Americana, vol. 35. Berkeley and Los Angeles: University of California.

————. 1954a. "Race and Class in Mexico." *Pacific Historical Review* 23:331–42.

————. 1954b. *Early Colonial Trade and Navigation Between Mexico and Peru.* Ibero-Americana, vol. 38. Berkeley and Los Angeles: University of California.

————. 1964. "America as Model: The Demographic Impact of European Expansion upon the Non-European World." *Proceedings, 35th International Congress of Americanists* (Mexico) 3:379–87.

————, and S. F. Cook. 1960. *The Population of Central Mexico in 1548.* Ibero-Americana, vol. 43. Berkeley and Los Angeles: University of California.

————, and ————. 1963. *The Aboriginal Population of Central Mexico on the Eve of Spanish Conquest.* Ibero-Americana, vol. 45. Berkeley and Los Angeles: University of California.

Bovallius, C. 1886. *Nicaraguan Antiquities.* Stockholm: Sällskapet für Antropologi och Geografi.

Brasseur de Bourbourg, M. L'A. 1857–59. *Histoire de nations civilisées du Méxique et de l'Amérique-Centrale.* 2 vols. Paris: A. Bertrand.

Brinton, D. G. 1891. *The American Race.* New York: N. D. C. Hodges.

————. 1895. "The Matagalpan Linguistic Stock of Central America." *Proceedings of the American Philosophical Society* 34:403–15.

Brown, A. W. A. 1977. "Yellow Fever, Dengue and Dengue Haemorrhagic Fever." In G. M. Howe, ed. *A World Geography of Human Diseases.* Pp. 217–317. London and New York: Academic Press.

Browning, D. 1974. "Preliminary Comments on the 1776 Census of the Spanish Empire." *Bulletin of the Society for Latin American Studies* 25:5–13.

Bruman, H. 1948. "The Culture History of Mexican Vanilla." *HAHR* 28: 360–76.

Bustamante, M. E. 1982. "La fiebre amarilla en México y su origen en América." In E. Florescano and E. Malvido, eds. *Ensayos sobre la historia de las epidemias en Mexico.* 1:19–35. Mexico: Instituto Mexicano de Seguro Social.

Cabrera, V. M. 1924. *Guanacaste: Libro conmemorativo del centenario de la incorporación del partido de Nicoya a Costa Rica.* San José: Lines.

Cámara Barbachano, F. 1964. "El mestizaje en México." *Revista de Indias* 24:27–85.

Campbell, L., and T. Kaufman. 1976. "A Linguistic Look at the Olmecs." *American Antiquity* 41:80–89.

Carneiro, R. L. 1956. "Slash and Burn Agriculture: A Closer Look at Its Implications for Settlement Patterns." In A. F. Wallace, ed. *Men and Cultures.* Selected Papers of the 5th Congress of Anthropological and Ethnological Sciences. Pp. 229–34.

Caso, A. 1948. "Definición del indio y lo indio." *America Indigena* 8: 239–47.

Chagnon, N. 1967. "Yanomamö Social Organization and Warfare." In Fried, M. Harris and R. Murphy, eds. *War.* Pp. 109–59. New York: Natural History Press.

Chamberlain, R. S. 1939. *Castilian Backgrounds of the Repartimiento-Encomienda.* Carnegie Institution of Washington Publication 509. Washington, D.C.

———. 1953. *The Conquest and Colonization of Honduras, 1502–1550.* Carnegie Institution of Washington Publication 598. Washington, D.C.

Chapman, A. 1957. "Port of Trade Enclaves in Aztec and Maya Civilizations." In K. Polanyi, C. M. Arensberg and H. W. Pearson, eds. *Trade and Market in Early Empires.* Pp. 114–53. New York: Free Press.

———. 1958. "An Historical Analysis of the Tropical Forest Tribes on the Southern Border of Mesoamerica." Ph.D. diss., Columbia University.

———. 1960. *Los Nicarao y los Chorotega según las fuentes históricas.* Serie historia y geografía, vol. 4. San José: Universidad de Costa Rica.

Chaunu, P. 1955–59. *Séville et l'Atlantique.* 8 vols. Paris: Colin.

Chevalier, F. 1963. *Land and Society in Colonial Mexico.* Berkeley and Los Angeles: University of California Press.

Clark, G., and M. Haswell. 1966. *The Economics of Subsistence Agriculture.* London: Macmillan.

Cobo, B. 1956. *Obras.* 2 vols. Biblioteca de Autores Españoles, nos. 91, 92. Madrid: Ediciones Atlas.

Cockburn, J. 1735. *A Journey Overland, from the Gulf of Honduras to the Great South Sea.* London: C. Rivington.

Coe, M. D. 1962a. "Costa Rican Archaeology and Mesoamerica." *Southwestern Journal of Anthropology* 18:170–83.

————. 1962b. Preliminary Report on Archaeological Investigations in Coastal Guanacaste, Costa Rica. *"Proceedings, 34th International Congress of Americanists* (Vienna), pp. 358–65.

Collier, A. 1964. "The American Mediterranean." In *HMAI*, 1: 122–42.

Collinson, J. 1870. "The Indians of the Mosquito Territory." *Anthropological Society of London Memoirs* 3: 148–56.

Colmenares, G. 1969. *Encomienda y población en la provincia de Pamplona (1549–1650)* Bogotá: Universidad de los Andes, Departamento de Historia.

Colón, H. 1947. *Vida del Almirante Don Cristóbal Colón.* Biblioteca Americana, Cronistas de Indias. Mexico: Fondo de Cultura Económica.

Conzemius, E. 1921–23. "The Jicaques of Honduras." *International Journal of American Linguistics* 2: 163–70.

————. 1927. "Die Rama-Indianer von Nicaragua." *Zeitschrift für Ethnologie* 59: 291–362.

————. 1929. "Notes on the Miskito and Sumu Languages of Eastern Nicaragua and Honduras." *International Journal of American Linguistics* 5: 57–115.

————. 1932. *Ethnographical Survey of the Miskito and Sumu Indians of Honduras and Nicaragua.* Smithsonian Institution, Bureau of American Ethnology Bulletin 106. Washington, D.C.

Cook, N. D. 1965. "La población indígena en el Peru colonial." *Anuario del Instituto de Investigaciones Históricas* (Universidad del Litoral, Rosario) 8: 73–110.

————. 1981. *Demographic Collapse: Indian Peru, 1520–1620.* Cambridge: Cambridge University Press.

Cook, O. F. 1909. *Vegetation Affected by Agriculture in Central America.* U.S. Department of Agriculture, Bureau of Plant Industry Bulletin 145. Washington, D.C.

Cook, S. F. 1945. "Demographic Consequences of European Contact with Primitive Peoples." *Annals of the American Academy of Political and Social Sciences* 237: 107–11.

————, and W. Borah. 1960. *The Indian Population of Central Mexico.* Ibero-Americana, vol. 44. Berkeley and Los Angeles: University of California.

————, and ————. 1968. *The Population of Mixteca Alta, 1520–1960.* Ibero-Americana, vol. 50. Berkeley and Los Angeles: University of California.

————, and ————. 1971–79. *Essays in Population History: Mexico and the Caribbean.* 3 vols. Berkeley and Los Angeles: University of California Press.

Cooper, J. M. 1942. "Areal and Temporal Aspects of South American Culture." *Primitive Man* (Catholic Anthropological Conference, Washington, D.C.) 15 (1–2): 1–38.

Cotheal, A. I. 1848. "A Grammatical Sketch of the Languages Spoken by the Indians of the Mosquito Shore." *Transactions of the American Ethnological Society* 2: 235–64.

Craig, A. K. 1966. *Geography of Fishing in British Honduras and Adjacent Coastal Waters.* Coastal Studies Series, vol. 14. Baton Rouge: Louisiana State University.

Crosby, A. W. 1967. "Conquistador y Pestilencia: The First New World Pandemic and the Fall of the Great Indian Empires." *HAHR* 47:321–37.

————. 1972. *The Columbian Exchange: Biological and Cultural Consequences of 1492.* Westport, Conn.: Greenwood Press.

————. 1976. "Virgin Soil Epidemics as a Factor in the Aboriginal Depopulation in America." *William and Mary Quarterly* 33:289–99.

Cruikshank, E. A. 1935. *The Life of Sir Henry Morgan.* Toronto: Macmillan Company of Canada.

Dampier, W. 1937. *A New Voyage Round the World.* London: A. & C. Black.

Denevan, W. M. 1961. *The Upland Pine Forest of Nicaragua: A Study in Plant Geography.* University of California Publications in Geography, vol. 12, no. 4. Berkeley and Los Angeles.

————. 1966. *The Aboriginal Cultural Geography of the Llanos de Mojos of Bolivia.* Ibero-Americana, vol. 48. Berkeley and Los Angeles: University of California.

————, ed. 1976. *The Native Population of the Americas in 1492.* Madison: University of Wisconsin Press.

Deutschmann, Z. 1961. "The Ecology of Smallpox." In J. May, ed. *Studies in Disease Ecology,* Pp. 1–13. New York: Hafner Publishing Co.

Díaz de la Calle, J. 1646. *Memorial y noticias sacras y reales del imperio de las Indias Occidentales.* Madrid.

Dixon, C. W. 1962. *Smallpox.* London: Churchill.

Dobyns, H. F. 1963. "An Outline of Andean Epidemic History. *Bulletin of the History of Medicine* 37:493–515.

————. 1966. "Estimating Aboriginal American Population." *Current Anthropology* 7:395–449.

————. 1976. *Native American Historical Demography: A Critical Bibliography.* Bloomington and London: Indiana University Press.

Duffy, J. 1972. *Epidemics in Colonial America.* Port Washington, N.Y. and London: Kennikat.

Dunn, F. L. 1965. "On the Antiquity of Malaria in the Western Hemisphere." *Human Biology* 37:385–93.

Edwards, B. 1819. "Some Account of the British Settlements on the Mosquito Shore." In *The History, Civil and Commercial of the British West Indies.* 5th ed. 5 vols. 5:202–14. London.

Esquemeling, J. 1924. *The Buccaneers of America.* Translated by W. S. Stallybrass. London: Routledge & Sons.

Fallas, M. A. 1972. *La factoría de tabacos.* San José: Editorial Costa Rica.

Floyd, T. S. 1961. "Bourbon Palliatives and the Central American Mining Industry, 1765–1800." *The Americas* 18:103–25.

————. 1967. *The Anglo-Spanish Struggle for Mosquitia.* Albuquerque: University of New Mexico Press.

Frank, A. G. 1979. *Mexican Agriculture, 1521–1630: Transformation of the Mode of Production.* Cambridge: Cambridge University Press.

Friede, J. 1953. *Los Andakí, 1538–1947: Historia de la acculturación de una triba selvática.* Mexico and Buenos Aires: Fondo de Cultura Económica.

———. 1963. *Los Quimbayas bajo la dominación española: Estudio documental (1539–1810).* Bogotá: Banco de la República.

———. 1965. "Algunas consideraciones sobre la evolución demográfica en la provincia de Tunja." *Anuario Colombiano de Historia Social y de la Cultura* 2 (3): 5–19.

Fröebel, J. 1859. *Seven Years' Travel in Central America, Northern Mexico and the Far West of the United States.* London: R. Bentley.

Fuentes y Guzmán, F. A. 1932–33. *Historia de Guatemala: Recordación Florida.* Biblioteca "Goathemala" de la Sociedad de Geografía e Historia. Vols. 6–8. Guatemala.

Gage, T. 1928. *The English-American: A New Survey of the West Indies, 1648.* London: Routledge & Sons.

Gámez, J. D. 1939. *Historia de la Costa de Mosquitos (hasta 1894).* Managua: Talleres Nacionales.

García Peláez, F. de P. 1943–44. *Memorias para la historia del antiguo reino de Guatemala.* 3 vols. Guatemala: Tip. Nacional.

Gerhard, P. 1964. "Shellfish Dye in America." *Proceedings, 35th International Congress of Americanists* (Mexico City) 3: 177–91.

———. 1972. "Colonial New Spain, 1519–1786: Historical Notes on the Evolution of the Minor Political Jurisdictions." In *HMAI,* 12: 63–137.

Gibson, C. 1955. "The Transformation of the Indian Community in New Spain." *Journal of World History* 2: 581–607.

———. 1964. *The Aztecs Under Spanish Rule.* Stanford: Stanford University Press.

Ginsberg, M. 1968. *Essays in Sociology and Social Philosophy.* Harmondsworth: Penguin.

González, E. R., and R. Mellafe. 1965. "La función de la familia en la historia social hispano-americana colonial." *Anuario del Instituto de Investigaciones Históricas* (Universidad del Litoral, Rosario) 8: 57–71.

Grieshaber, E. P. 1979. "Hacienda-Indian Community Relations and Indian Acculturation: An Historiographical Essay." *LARR* 14: 107–28.

Haberland, W. 1975. "Further Archaeological Evidence for the Nicarao and Pipil Migrations in Central America." *Proceedings, 41st International Congress of Americanists* (Mexico) 1: 551–59.

Hanke, L. 1949. *The Spanish Struggle for Justice in the Conquest of America.* Philadelphia: University of Pennsylvania Press.

Haring, C. H. 1910. *The Buccaneers in the West Indies in the XVII Century.* London: Methuen.

———. 1963. *The Spanish Empire in America.* New York: Harbinger Books.

Harris, D. R. 1969. Agricultural Systems, Ecosystems and the Origins of Agriculture. In P. J. Ucko and G. W. Dimbleby, eds. *The Domestication and Exploitation of Plants and Animals.* Pp. 3–15. London: Duckworth.

Harris, M. 1964. *Patterns of Race in the Americas.* New York: Walker.

Harrower, D. F. 1925. "Rama, Mosquito, and Sumu of Nicaragua." *Indian Notes and Monographs* 2, no. 1. New York: Museum of the American Indian, Heye Foundation.

Harshberger, J. W. 1911. *Phytogeographic Survey of North America.* Leipzig: W. Engelmann.

Hartman, C. V. 1907. *Archaeological Researches on the Pacific Coast of Costa Rica.* Pittsburgh Carnegie Museum Memoirs 3, no. 1. Pittsburgh.

Healy, P. F. 1976. "Los Chorotega y Nicarao: Evidencia arqueológica de Rivas, Nicaragua." In *Las Fronteras de Mesoamérica.* 2 vols. Mesa Redonda XIV de la Sociedad Mexicana de Antropología (Mexico). 2: 257–66.

———. 1980. *Archaeology of the Rivas Region, Nicaragua.* Waterloo, Ont.: Wilfrid Laurier University Press.

Heath, G. R. 1913. "Notes on the Miskuto Grammar and on Other Indian Languages of Eastern Nicaragua." *American Anthropologist* 15: 48–62.

Helms, M. W. 1969. "The Cultural Ecology of a Colonial Tribe." *Ethnology* 8: 76–84.

———. 1970. "Matrilocality, Social Solidarity, and Culture Contact." *Southwestern Journal of Anthropology* 26: 197–212.

———. 1971. *Asang: Adaptations to Culture Contact in a Miskito Community* Gainesville: University of Florida Press.

———. 1976. *Middle America: A Culture History of Heartlands and Frontiers.* Englewood Cliffs, N.J.: Prentice-Hall.

———. 1978. "Coastal Adaptations as Contact Phenomena Among the Miskito and Cuna Indians of Lower Central America." In B. L. Stark and B. Voorhies, eds. *Prehistoric Coastal Adaptations: The Economy and Ecology of Maritime Middle America.* Pp. 121–49. New York: Academic Press.

———, and F. O. Loveland, eds. 1976. *Frontier Adaptations in Lower Central America.* Philadelphia: Institute for the Study of Human Issues.

Henderson, Capt. G. 1809. *An Account of the British Settlement of Honduras . . . to Which Are Added Sketches of the Manners and Customs of the 'Mosquito Indians.* London: C. R. Baldwin.

Herrera y Tordesillas, A. de. 1934. *Historia general de los hechos de los castellanos en las islas i tierra firme del Mar Océano.* 17 vols. Madrid: Real Academia de la Historia.

Hershey, O. H. 1912. "Geological Reconnaissance in Northeastern Nicaragua." *Bulletin of the Geological Society of America* 23: 493–516.

Holm, J. 1978. "The Creole English of Nicaragua's Miskito Coast: Its Sociolinguistic History and a Comparative Study of Its Lexicon and Syntax." Ph.D. diss., University of London

Howe, G. M. ed. 1977. *A World Geography of Human Diseases.* New York and London: Academic Press.

Hubbs, C. L., and G. I. Roden. 1964. "Oceanography and Marine Life Along the Pacific Coast." In *HMAI,* 1: 143–86.

Incer, J. 1970. *Nueva geografía de Nicaragua.* Managua: Editorial Recalde.

Israel, J. I. 1975. *Race, Class and Politics in Colonial Mexico, 1610–1670.* Oxford: Oxford University Press.

Jacobs, W. R. 1974. The Tip of the Iceberg: Pre-Columbian Indian Demography and Some Implications for Revisionism. *William and Mary Quarterly* 3d ser., 31: 123–32.

Jaramillo Uribe, J. 1964. La población indígena de Colombia en el momento de la conquista y sus transformaciones posteriores. *Anuario Colombiano de Historia Social y de la Cultura* 1, no. 2: 239–93.

Jiménez Moreno, W. 1959. *Síntesis de la historia pre-tolteca de Mesoamérica esplendor del Mexico antiguo.* 2 vols. Mexico: Centro de Investigaciones Antropológicas.

———. 1961. El mestizaje y la transculturación en Mexiamérica. In *El mestizaje en la historia de Ibero-América.* Mexico D. F.: Instituto Panamericano de Geografía e Historia, Comisión de Historia.

Johnson, F. 1940. The Linguistic Map of Mexico and Central America. In *The Maya and Their Neighbors.* Pp. 88–114. New York: D. Appleton Century.

———. 1948a. "Central American Cultures." In *HSAI,* 4: 43–68.

———. 1948b. "The Post-Conquest Ethnology of Central America." In *HSAI,* 4: 199–204.

Juarros, D. 1823. *A Statistical and Commercial History of the Kingdom of Guatemala.* Translated by J. Baily. London.

Kaufman, T. 1974. "Mesoamerican Indian Languages." *Encyclopedia Britannica.* 15th ed. 11: 954–63. Chicago: Benton.

Keith, R. G. 1976. *Conquest and Agrarian Change: The Emergence of the Hacienda System on the Peruvian Coast.* Cambridge, Mass: Harvard University Press.

Kirchhoff, P. 1943. "Mesoamerica." *Acta Americana* 1: 92–107.

———. 1948. "The Caribbean Lowland Tribes: The Mosquito, Sumo, Paya and Jicaque." In *HSAI,* 4: 219–29.

Konetske, R. 1945. "Legislación sobre inmigración de extranjeros en América durante la época colonial." *Revista de sociología,* nos. 11–12: 269–99.

Kroeber, A. L. 1939. *Cultural and Natural Areas of Native North America.* University of California Publications in Archaeology and Ethnology no. 38. Berkeley and Los Angeles.

Kubler, G. 1952. *The Indian Caste of Peru, 1795–1940.* Smithsonian Institution, Institute of Anthropology, Publication 14. Washington, D.C.

Landero, Fr. M. 1935. "Los Taoajkas ó Sumos del Patuca y Wampú." *Anthropos* 30: 33–50.

Lange, F. W. 1971a. "Culture History of the Sapoa River Valley, Costa Rica." Ph.D. diss., University of Wisconsin.

———. 1971b. "Northwestern Costa Rica: Pre-Columbian Circum-Caribbean Affiliations." *Folk* 13: 43–64.

———. 1978. "Coastal Settlement in Northwestern Costa Rica." In B. L. Stark and B. Voorhies, eds. *Prehistoric Coastal Adaptations: The Economy and Ecology of Maritime Middle America.* Pp. 101–19. New York: Academic Press.

Las Casas, B. de. 1812 *Breve relación de la destrucción de las Indias.* London: Schulze and Dean.

———. 1957–58. *Obras escogidas.* 5 vols. Biblioteca de Autores Españoles, nos. 95–96, 105–106, 110. Madrid: Ediciones Atlas.

Lathrap, D. W. 1970. *The Upper Amazon*. London: Thames and Hudson.

Lauer, W. 1959. "Klimatische und Planzengeographie Grundzüge Zentralamerikas." *Erdkunde* 12: 344–54.

Lee, R. L. 1948. "Cochineal Production and Trade in New Spain to 1600." *The Americas* 4: 449–73.

Leeds, A. 1961. "Yaruro Incipient Tropical Forest Horticulture: Possibilities and Limits." In J. Wilbert, ed. *The Evolution of Horticultural Systems in Native South America: Causes and Consequences*. Antropológica Supplement 2, pp. 13–46. Caracas.

Lehmann, W. 1920. *Zentral-Amerika*. 2 vols. Berlin: Dietrich Reimer.

León-Portilla, M. 1959. *La filosofía náhuatl*. Mexico: Universidad Autónoma de Mexico, Instituto de Historia.

———. *Religión de los Nicarao*. Instituto de Investigaciones Históricas, Serie Cultura Náhuatl, Monografías, no. 12. Mexico: Universidad Nacional Autónoma de Mexico.

Levy, P. 1873. *Notas geográficas y económicas sobre la República de Nicaragua*. Paris: Librería Española de E. Denné Schmitz.

Límites. 1905. *Límites entre Honduras y Nicaragua*. Madrid: Idamor Moreno.

Linares, O., P. D. Sheets, and E. J. Rosenthal. 1975. Prehistoric Agriculture in Tropical Highlands. *Science* 187: 137–45.

Long, E. 1774. *A History of Jamaica . . . an Account of the Mosquito Shore*. 3 vols. London: T. Lowndes.

López de Gómara, F. 1918. *Hispania Victrix: Historia general de las Indias*. Historiadores primitivos de Indias, vol. 1, Biblioteca de Autores Españoles, no. 22. Madrid: Imp. Los Sucesores de Hernando.

López de Velasco, J. 1894. *Geografía y descripción universal de las Indias*. Madrid: Tip. Fortanet for Real Academia de la Historia.

Lothrop, S. K. 1926. *Pottery of Costa Rica and Nicaragua*. 2 vols. Contributions from the Museum of the American Indian, Heye Foundation, no. 8. New York.

———. 1940. "South America as Seen from Middle America." In *The Maya and Their Neighbors*. Pp. 417–29. New York: D. Appleton Century.

———. 1966. "Archaeology of Lower Central America." In *HMAI*, 4: 180–208.

Loveland, F. O. 1976. "Tapirs and Manatees: Cosmological Categories and Social Process Among Rama Indians of Eastern Nicaragua." In M. W. Helms and F. O. Loveland, eds. *Frontier Adaptations in Lower Central America*. Pp. 67–83. Philadelphia: Institute for Human Issues.

Lovell, W. G. 1980. Land and Settlement in the Cuchumatan Highlands (1550–1821): A Study in the Historical Geography of Northwestern Guatemala." Ph.D. diss., University of Alberta.

Lozoya, M. de. 1920. *Vida del Segoviano Rodrigo de Contreras, gobernador de Nicaragua (1534–1544)*. Biblioteca de Historia Hispano-Americana. Toledo: Imp. de la Editorial Toledana.

Lutz, C. 1976. "Santiago de Guatemala, 1541–1773: The Socio-Demographic History of a Spanish American Colonial City." 2 vols. Ph.D. diss., University of Wisconsin.

———. 1981. "Population Change in the Quinizalapa Valley, Guatemala, 1530–1770." In D. J. Robinson, ed. *Studies in Spanish American Population History.* Pp. 175–94. Boulder, Colo.: Westview Press.

Lynch, J. C. 1958. *Spanish Colonial Administration, 1782–1810: The Intendant System in the Viceroyalty of Rio de la Plata.* University of London Historical Studies, no. 5. London: Athlone.

McBryde, F. W. 1940. "Influenza in America During the Sixteenth Century (Guatemala: 1523, 1559–62, 1576)." *Bulletin of the History of Medicine* 8: 296–302.

MacLeod, M. J. 1973. *Spanish Central America: A Socioeconomic History, 1520–1720.* Berkeley and Los Angeles: University of California Press.

McNeill, W. H. 1976. *Plagues and Peoples.* Oxford: Basil Blackwell.

Magnus, R. W. 1974. "The Prehistory of the Miskito Coast of Nicaragua: A Study in Cultural Relationships." Ph.D. diss., Yale University.

———. 1975. "The Prehistoric Cultural Relationships of the Miskito Coast." *Proceedings, 41st International Congress of Americanists* (Mexico City) 1: 568–78.

———. 1976. "La costa atlántica de Nicaragua." *Vínculos* 2: 67–74.

———. 1978. "The Prehistoric and Modern Subsistence Patterns of the Atlantic Coast of Nicaragua: A Comparison." In B. L. Stark and B. Voorhies, eds. *Prehistoric Coastal Adaptations: The Economy and Ecology of Maritime Middle America.* Pp. 61–80. New York: Academic Press.

Malvido, E. 1982. "Efectos de las epidemias y hambrunas en la población colonial de Mexico." In E. Florescano and E. Malvido, eds. *Ensayos sobre la historia de las epidemias en Mexico.* 1: 179–91. Mexico: Instituto Mexicano de Seguro Social.

Mangelsdorf, P. C., R. S. MacNeish, and G. R. Willey. 1964. "Origins of Agriculture." In *HMAI*, 1: 427–45.

Manson-Bahr, P. H. 1948. *Manson's Tropical Diseases.* London: Cassel.

Martínez Peláez, S. 1975. *La patria del criollo.* San José, Costa Rica: Editorial Universitaria Centroamericana.

Martyr D'Anghera, P. H. 1912. *De orbe novo.* Edited by F. MacNutt. 2 vols. London and New York: Knickerbocker Press.

Marure, A. 1913. *Bosquejo de las revoluciones de Centro-América desde 1811 hasta 1834.* 2 vols. Paris: Ch. Bouret.

Mason, J. A. 1940. "The Native Languages of Middle America." In *The Maya and Their Neighbors.* Pp. 52–87. New York: D. Appleton Century.

Mason, P. 1970. *Patterns of Dominance.* Oxford: Oxford University Press.

Matson, G. A., and J. Swanson. 1963. "Distribution of Hereditary Blood Antigens Among Indians in Middle America: V, In Nicaragua." *American Journal of Physical Anthropology* 21: 545–49.

Melendez, C. 1977. *Costa Rica: Tierra y poblamento en la colonia.* San José: Editorial Costa Rica.

Millon, R. F. 1955. "Trade, Tree Cultivation, and the Development of Private Property in Land." *American Anthropologist* 57: 698–712.

Miranda, J. 1952. *El tributo indígena en la Nueva España durante el siglo XVI*. Mexico: Fondo de Cultura Económica.

———. 1963. "La población indígena de Mexico en el siglo XVII." *Historia mexicana* 48: 182–89.

Molina Argüello, C. 1949. *El gobernador de Nicaragua en el siglo XVI: Contribución al estudio de la historia del derecho nicaraguense*. Sevilla: Escuela de Estudios Hispanoamericanos.

———. 1960. "Gobernaciones, alcaldías mayores and corregimientos en el reino de Guatemala." *AEA* 17: 105–32.

———. 1972. "Comunidades y territorialidad en las jurisdicciones." In *Memoria del primer congreso venezolano de historia*. Pp. 445–56. Caracas: Academia Nacional de Historia.

Moreno, L. 1938. "Los extranjeros y el ejercicio del comercio en Indias." *ASGH* 14: 441–54.

Moreno Navarro, I. 1973. *Los cuadros de mestizaje americano: Estudio antropológico del mestizaje*. Madrid: Ediciones Porrua.

Morison, S. E. 1942. *Admiral of the Ocean Sea: A Life of Christopher Columbus*. London: Oxford University Press.

Motolinía, T. 1970. *Memoriales e historia de los indios de Nueva España*. Biblioteca de Autores Españoles, no. 240. Madrid: Real Academia de la Historia.

Newson, L. A. 1976. *Aboriginal and Spanish Colonial Trinidad: A Study in Culture Contact*. London and New York: Academic Press.

———. 1978. "The Law of Cultural Dominance and the Colonial Experience." In D. Green, M. Hazelgrove and M. Spriggs, eds. *British Archaeological Reports (Supplementary)*, no. 47 (2): 75–87. *Social Organization and Settlement*.

———. 1982. "The Dopopulation of Nicaragua in the Sixteenth Century." *JLAS* 14: 253–86.

———. "Indian Population Patterns in Colonial Spanish America." *LARR*, 20 no. 3: 41–74.

Newton, A. P. 1914. *The Colonizing Activities of the English Puritans*. New Haven, Conn.: Yale University Press.

Nietschmann, B. 1972. "Hunting and Fishing Focus Among the Miskito Indians, Eastern Nicaragua." *Human Ecology* 1: 41–67.

———. 1973. *Between Land and Water: The Subsistence Ecology of the Miskito Indians, Eastern Nicaragua*. London and New York: Seminar Press.

Nolasco Pérez, P. 1966. *Historia de las mercedarias en América*. Madrid: Revista "Estudios."

Ots Capdequí, J. M. 1959. *España en América: El régimen de las tierras en la época colonial*. Mexico: Fondo de Cultura Económica.

Oviedo y Valdés, G. Fernández de. 1959. *Historia general y natural de las Indias, islas y tierra firme del Mar Océano*. 5 vols. Biblioteca de Autores Españoles, nos. 117–121. Madrid: Ediciones Atlas.

Palerm, A. 1967. "Agricultural Systems and Food Patterns." In *HMAI*, 6: 26–52.

Palmer, M. G. 1945. *Through Unknown Nicaragua*. London: Jarrolds.

Pardo, J. J. 1944. *Efemérides de la Antigua Guatemala, 1541–1779.* Guatemala: Unión Tipográfica.

Parsons, J. J. 1955. "The Miskito Pine Savannas of Nicaragua and Honduras." *Annals of the Association of American Geographers* 45: 36–63.

———. 1962. *The Green Turtle and Man.* Gainesville: University of Florida Press.

Paso y Trocoso, F. de 1940. *Epistolario de Nueva España.* 16 vols. Madrid: Antigua Librería Robredo de José Porrua e Hijos.

Patiño, V. M. 1963–69. *Plantas cultivadas y animales domésticos en América equinoccial.* vol. 1, *Frutales* (1963); vol. 2, *Plantas alimenticias* (1964); vol. 3, *Plantas medicinales* (1965); vol. 4, *Plantas introducidos* (1969). Calí, Colombia: Imprenta Departmental.

Pendleton R. L. 1943. "General Soil Conditions in Central America." *Proceedings of the Soil Science Society of America* 8: 403–407.

Peralta, M. de 1882. *El río de San Juan de Nicaragua: Derechos de sus ribereños las Repúblicas de Costa Rica y Nicaragua según los documentos históricos.* Madrid.

———. 1883. *Costa Rica, Nicaragua y Panama en el siglo XVI: Su Historia y sus límites.* Madrid: Librería de M. Murillo; Paris: Librería de J. I. Ferrer.

———. 1890. *Límites de Costa Rica y Colombia.* Madrid.

———. 1898. *Costa Rica y Costa de Mosquitos: Documentos para la historia de la jurisdicción territorial de Costa Rica y Colombia.* Paris: Imp. Lahure.

Phelan, J. H. 1967. *The Kingdom of Quito in the Seventeenth Century.* Madison: University of Wisconsin Press.

Pim, B., and B. Seeman. 1869. *Dottings on the Roadside in Panama, Nicaragua and Mosquito.* London: Chapman and Hall.

Pitt-Rivers, J. 1967. "Race, Colour, and Class in Central America and the Andes." *Daedalus* 96: 542–59.

Pollitzer, R. 1954. *Plague.* World Health Organization Monograph Series, no. 22. Geneva: WHO.

Ponce, Fr. A. 1873. *Relación breve y verdadera de algunas cosas que sucedieron al Padre Fray Alonso Ponce en las provinicas de Nueva España.* 2 vols. Madrid: Imp. Viuda de Calero.

Portig, W. H. 1965. "Central American Rainfall." *Geographical Review* 55: 68–90.

Puga, V. de 1945. *Provisiones, cédulas, instrucciones para el gobierno de la Nueva España.* Madrid: Ediciones Cultura Hispánica.

Purseglove, J. W. 1968. *Tropical Crops: Dicotyledons.* 2 vols. London: Longmans.

Radell, D. R. 1969. "Historical Geography of Western Nicaragua: The Spheres of Influence of León, Granada and Managua, 1519–1965." Ph.D. diss., University of California.

———. 1976. "The Indian Slave Trade and Population of Nicaragua During the Sixteenth Century." In W. M. Denevan, ed. *The Native Population of the Americas in 1492.* Pp. 67–76. Madison: University of Wisconsin Press.

———, and J. J. Parsons. "Realejo—A Forgotten Colonial Port and Ship-building Centre in Nicaragua." *HAHR* 51: 295–312.

Raveneau de Lussan, S. de 1930. *Journal of a Voyage into the South Seas in 1684 and the Following Years with the Filibusters.* Translated by M. E. Wilbur. Cleveland: A. H. Clark.

Recopilación de las leyes de los reynos de las indias. 1943. 3 vols. Madrid: Gráficas Ultra.

Richardson, F. B. 1940. "Non-Maya Monumental Sculpture of Central America." In *The Maya and Their Neighbors.* New York: D. Appleton Century.

Rivet, P., P. Stresser-Péan, and C. Loukotka. 1952. "Langues du México et de l'Amérique." In A. Meillet & M. Cohen, eds. *Les langues du monde.* Pp. 1069–97. Paris: Centre National de la Recherche Scientifique.

Roberts, O. W. 1827. *Narrative of Voyages and Excursions on the East Coast and in the Interior of Central America.* Edinburgh: Constable.

Roberts, R. J., and E. M. Irving. *Mineral Deposits of Central America.* U.S. Geological Survey Bulletin 1034. Washington, D.C.

Rodríguez Becerra, S. 1977. *Encomienda y conquista: Los inicios de la colonización en Guatemala.* Sevilla: Universidad de Sevilla.

Rosenblat, A. 1954. *La población indígena y el mestizaje en América.* Buenos Aires: Editorial Nova.

Roys, R. L. 1943. *The Indian Background of Colonial Yucatan.* Carnegie Institution of Washington Publication 548. Washington, D.C.; reprint, Norman: University of Oklahoma Press, 1972.

Rubio Sánchez, M. 1952. "El Añil ó xiquilite." *ASGH* 26: 313–49.

Saco, J. A. 1932. *Historia de la esclavitud de los indios en el Nuevo Mundo.* 2 vols. Colección de Libros Cubanos, vols. 18, 19. Havana: Cultural S. A.

Sahlins, M. D., and E. R. Service. 1960. *Evolution and Culture.* Ann Arbor: University of Michigan Press.

Salvatierra, S. 1939. *Contribución a la historia de Centro América.* 2 vols. Managua, Nacaragua: Tip. Progreso-Managua.

Sánchez-Albornoz, N. A. 1974. *The Population of Latin America: A History.* Berkeley and Los Angeles: University of California Press.

Sangster, G. 1977. "Diarrhoeal Diseases." In G. M. Howe, ed. *A World Geography of Human Diseases.* 145–74. London and New York: Academic Press.

Sapper, K. 1924. "Die Zahl und die Volkdichte der Indianischen Bevölkerung in Amerika." *Proceedings, 21st International Congress of Americanists* (The Hague) 1: 95–104.

Sauer, C. O. 1950. "Cultivated Plants of South and Central America." In *HSAI,* 5: 487–543.

———. 1952. *Agricultural Origins and Dispersals.* New York: American Geographical Society.

———. 1966. *The Early Spanish Main.* Berkeley and Los Angeles: University of California Press.

Schuchert, C. 1935. *Historical Geology of the Antillean-Caribbean Region.* London: Wiley.

Segraves, B. A. 1974. "Ecological Generalization and Structural Transformation of Sociocultural Systems." *American Anthropologist* 76:530–52.

Serrano y Sanz, M. 1908. *Relaciones históricas y geográficas de América Central*. Colección de libros y documentos referentes a la historia de América, vol. 8. Madrid: Librería General de V. Suarez.

Service, E. R. 1955. "Indian-European Relations in Colonial Latin America." *American Anthropologist* 57:411–25.

Shea, D. E. 1976. "A Defense of Small Population Estimates for the Central Andes." In Denevan, ed., *The Native Population of the Americas in 1492*. Pp. 157–80. Madison: University of Wisconsin Press.

Sherman, W. L. 1967. "Indian Slavery in Spanish Guatemala." Ph.D. diss., University of New Mexico.

———. 1971. "Indian Slavery and the Cerrato Reforms." *HAHR*, 51: 25–50.

———. 1979. *Forced Native Labor in Sixteenth-Century Central America*. Lincoln and London: University of Nebraska Press.

Shrewsbury, J. F. 1970. *A History of Bubonic Plague in the British Isles*. Cambridge: Cambridge University Press.

Simpson, L. B. 1940. *Studies in the Administration of New Spain IV: The Emancipation of the Indian Slaves and the Resettlement of the Freedmen, 1548–53*. Ibero-Americana vol. 16. Berkeley and Los Angeles: University of California.

Slicher Van Bath, B. 1979. "Economic Diversification in Spanish America around 1600: Centres, Intermediate Zones and Peripheries." *Jahrbuch für Geschichte von Staat, Wirtschaft und Gesellschaft Lateinamerikas* 16:53–95.

Sloane, H. 1707. *A Voyage to the Islands of Madera, Barbados, Nieves, S. Christophers and Jamaica*. 2 vols. London.

Smith, C. T. 1970. "Depopulation of the Central Andes in the Sixteenth Century." *Current Anthropology* 11:453–64.

Smith, R. S. 1959. "Indigo Production and Trade in Colonial Guatemala." *HAHR* 39:181–211.

Smole, W. J. 1980. "*Musa* Cultivation in Pre-Columbian South America." In W. V. Davidson and J. J. Parsons, eds. *Historical Geography of Latin America: Papers in Honor of R. C. West*. Pp. 47–50. *Geoscience and Man*, vol. 21. Baton Rouge: Louisiana State University.

Snarskis, M. J. 1976. "Stratigraphic Excavations in the Eastern Lowlands of Costa Rica." *American Antiquity* 41:342–53.

Solano Pérez-Lila, F. de. 1969. "La población indígena de Guatemala (1492–1800)." *AEA* 26:279–355.

Sorsby, W. S. 1972. "Spanish Colonization of the Mosquito Coast, 1787–1800. *Revista de Historia de America*, nos. 73–74, pp. 145–53.

Squier, E. G. 1852. *Nicaragua: Its People, Scenery, Monuments and the Proposed Interoceanic Canal*. New York: Appleton.

———. 1853. "Archaeology and Ethnology of Nicaragua." *Transactions of the American Ethnological Society* 3, pt. 1.

———. 1855a. Nicaragua: An Exploration from Ocean to Ocean." *Harper's New Monthly Magazine* 11:744–63.

———. 1855b. *Notes on Central America*. New York: Harper and Brothers.

————. 1891. *Adventures on the Mosquito Shore.* New York: Worthington.

Stanislawski, D. 1983. *The Transformation of Nicaragua, 1519–1548.* Ibero-Americana vol. 54. Berkeley and Los Angeles: University of California.

Stevens, R. L. 1964. "The Soils of Middle America and Their Relation to Indian Peoples and Cultures." In *HMAI,* 1: 265–315.

Steward, J. H. 1955. *Theory of Culture Change: The Methodology of Multilinear Evolution.* Urbana, Chicago, and London: University of Illinois Press.

————, ed. 1946. *The Marginal Tribes. HSAI,* 1.

————, ed. 1948. *The Circum-Caribbean Tribes. HSAI,* 4.

————, ed. 1949. *The Comparative Ethnology of South American Indians. HSAI,* 5.

Steward, J. H., and Faron, L. C. 1959. *Native Peoples of South America.* New York: McGraw-Hill.

Stone, D. Z. 1949. "Los grupos mexicanos en la América Central y su importancia." *Antropología e Historia de Guatemala* 1: 43–47.

————. 1957. *The Archaeology of Central and Southern Honduras.* Papers of the Peabody Museum, vol. 49, no. 3. Cambridge, Mass.: Harvard University.

————. 1959. "The Eastern Frontier of Mesoamerica." *Mitteilungen aus dem Museum für Volkerkunde im Hamburg* 25: 118–21.

————. 1966. "Synthesis of Lower Central American Ethnohistory." In *HMAI,* 4: 209–33.

————. 1968. "Nahuat Traits on the Sula Plain, Northwestern Honduras." *Proceedings, 38th International Congress of Americanists* (Stuttgart-München) 1: 531–36.

————. 1972. *Pre-Columbian Man Finds Central America.* Cambridge, Mass.: Peabody Museum Press.

Stout, P. F. 1859. *Nicaragua: Past, Present, and Future.* Philadelphia.

Strangeways, T. 1882. *Sketch of the Mosquito Shore, Including the Territory of the Poyais.* Edinburgh.

Strong, W. D. 1948. "The Archaeology of Costa Rica and Nicaragua." In *HSAI,* 4: 121–42.

Stuart, L. C. 1964. "Fauna of Middle America." In *HMAI,* 1: 315–62.

Swann, M. M. 1980. "The Demographic Impact of Disease and Famine in Late Colonial Northern Mexico." W. V. Davidson and J. J. Parsons, eds. *Historical Geography in Latin America: Papers in Honor of R. C. West.* Pp. 97–109. *Geoscience and Man,* vol. 21. Baton Rouge: Louisiana State University.

Tannenbaum, F. 1943. "Discussion of Acculturation Studies in Latin America: Some Needs and Problems." *American Anthropologist* 45: 204–206.

Taylor, B. W. 1963. "An Outline of the Vegetation of Nicaragua." *Journal of Ecology* 51: 27–54.

Termer, F. 1935. "La habitación rural en la América del Centro, a través de los tiempos." *ASGH* 11: 391–409.

Thiel, B. A. 1967. "Monografía de la población de la República de Costa Rica en el siglo XIX. *Revista de estudios y estadísticas,* no. 8, Serie Demográfica. San José: Dirección General de Estadística y Censos, Ministerio de Industria y Comercio.

Thompson, G. A. 1927. "Narración de una visita oficial a Guatemala de Mexico en el año 1825. *ASGH* 3: 101–229.

Thompson, J. F. S. 1948. *An Archaeological Reconnaisance in the Cotzumalhua Region, Escuintla, Guatemala.* Carnegie Institution of Washington Publication 574. Washington, D.C.

———. 1956. "Notes on the Use of Cacao in Middle America. *Notes on Middle American Archaeology and Ethnology* 128: 95–116.

———. 1967. "The Maya Central Area at the Time of Spanish Conquest and Later: A Problem in Demography." *Proceedings of the Royal Anthropological Institute of Great Britain and Northern Ireland for 1966,* pp. 23–37.

Torquemada. Fr. J. de 1723. *Monarquía indiana.* 3 vols. Madrid: Nicolas Rodríguez.

Trigueros, R. 1954. Las defensas estratégicas del río de San Juan de Nicaragua. *AEA* 11: 413–513.

Vallejo, A. R. 1938. *Historia documentada de los límites entre la República de Honduras y las de Nicaragua, El Salvador y Guatemala.* New York.

Vázquez, F. 1937–44. *Crónica de la provincia del Santísimo Nombre de Jesús de Guatemala.* 4 vols. Biblioteca "Goathemala," vols. 14–17. Guatemala: Sociedad de Geografía e Historia.

Vázquez de Espinosa, A. 1942. *Compendium and Description of the West Indies.* Smithsonian Institution of Washington, Miscellaneous Collections, vol. 102. Washington, D.C.

Veblen, T. T. 1977. "Native Population Decline in Totonicapán, Guatemala. *Annals of the Association of American Geographers* 67: 484–99.

Vellard, J. 1956. "Causas biológicas de la disaparición de los indios americanos." *Boletín del Instituto Riva-Aguero* 2: 77–93.

Villamarin, J. A. and J. E. Villamarin. *Indian Labor in Mainland Colonial Spanish America.* Newark: University of Delaware.

Vivó Escoto, J. A. 1964. "Weather and Climate of Mexico and Central America." In *HMAI,* 1: 187–215.

Von Hagen, V. W. 1943. "The Jicaque (Torrupan) Indians of Honduras." *Indian Notes and Monographs,* no. 53. New York: Museum of the American Indian, Heye Foundation.

W., M. 1752. "The Mosqueto Indian and His Golden River." In A. Churchill, ed. *A Collection of Voyages and Travels.* 6: 297–312. London: T. Osborne.

Wagley, C. 1951. "Cultural Influences on Population: A Comparison of Two Tupí Tribes." *Revista do Museu Paulista* 5: 95–104.

Wagner, P. L. 1958. *Nicoya: A Cultural Geography.* University of California Publications in Geography, vol. 12: 195–250.

———. 1964. "Natural Vegetation of Middle America." In *HMAI,* 1: 363–83.

West, R. C. 1959. "The Mining Economy of Honduras in the Colonial Period." *Proceedings, 33d International Congress of Americanists* (Costa Rica) 2: 767–77.

West, R. C. 1964. "Surface Configuration and Associated Geology of Middle America." In *HMAI*, 1: 33–83.

————, and J. P. Augelli. *Middle America: Its Lands and Its Peoples*. Englewood Cliffs, N.J.: Prentice-Hall.

White, R. 1793. *The Case of the Agent to the Settlers on the Coast of Yucatan and the Late Settlers on the Mosquito Shore*. London: T. Cadell.

Wickham, H. A. 1869. "Notes on a Journey Among the Woolwa and Miskito Indians." *Proceedings of the Royal Geographical Society* 13: 58–63.

————. 1872. *A Journey Among the Woolwa or Soumoo Indians of Central America*. London.

————. 1895. "Notes on the Soumoo or Woolwa Indians of Blewfields River, Mosquito Territory." *Journal of the Anthropological Institute* 24: 198–208.

Willey, G. R. 1966. *An Introduction to American Archaeology*. Vol. 1, *North America*. Englewood-Cliffs, N.J.: Prentice-Hall.

Wolf, E. 1959. *Sons of the Shaking Earth*. Chicago and London: University of Chicago Press.

Wood, C. S. 1975. "New Evidence for a Late Introduction of Malaria into the New World." *Current Anthropology* 16: 93–104.

Woodward, R. L. 1966. *Class Privilege and Economic Development: The Consulado de Comercio of Guatemala, 1793–1871*. James Sprunt Studies in History and Political Science, vol. 48. Chapel Hill: University of North Carolina Press.

Wortman, M. 1975a. "Government Revenue and Economic Trends in Central America, 1787–1819." *HAHR* 55: 251–86.

————. 1975b. "Bourbon Reforms in Central America, 1750–1786." *The Americas* 31: 222–38.

Young, T. 1842. *Narrative of a Residence on the Mosquito Shore During the Years 1839, 1840, 1841*. London: Smith, Elder.

Zavala, S. 1943. *New Viewpoints on the Spanish Colonization of America*. Philadephia: University of Pennsylvania Press.

————. 1967. *Contribución a la historia de las instituciones coloniales en Guatemala*. Guatemala: Editorial Universitaria.

Zinsser, H. 1960. *Rats, Lice, and History*. New York: Bantam.

Zorita, A. de. 1965. *The Lords of New Spain*. London: Phoenix House.

PUBLISHED MAPS

Comisión de Límites. 1929. *Cartografía de la América Central*. Guatemala Tip. Nac.

Edwards, B. 1793. "A New Map of the West Indies for the History of the British Colonies." In Vol. 1 of *The History, Civil and Commercial of the British Colonies in the West Indies*. 2 vols. London.

Jeffreys, T. 1775. "The Bay of Honduras." Map 10 in *The West Indian Atlas or a General Description of the West Indies*. London.

Pinkerton, J. 1818. "Spanish Dominions in North America. Southern Part." Map 45 in *A Modern Atlas*, directed and supervised by J. Pinkerton, drawn by L. Herbert. Philadephia: T. Dobson & Sons.

Squier, E. G. 1855. Map in *Notes on Central America*. New York and London.

Strangeways, T. 1822. "A Map of Mosquitia and the Territory of the Poyais with Adjacent Countries." In *Sketch of the Mosquito Shore*. Edinburgh.

Tanner, H. S. 1822. "Map of North America Constructed According to the Latest Information." In *A New American Atlas*. Philadelphia.

Thompson. 1816. Map 13 in *Atlas to Thompson's Alcedo or Dictionary of America and the West Indies*, by A. Arrowsmith. London.

Vandermaelen, P. 1827 "Partie du Guatemala." Plate 72 in *Atlas Universal de Geographie*. Brussels: H. Ode.

Index

Aboriginal culture, sources for: 24, 26, 48, 64, 353n., 354n., 430
Aboriginal population: 48, 84–88, 335–37, 374n., 375n.; of Latin America, 5, 8; of Central America, 84–85, 374n.
Acapulco, Mexico: 129, 147, 264, 412n.
Achiote: 52, 140
Administrative structure: 127–29, 255–57
Age structure, in missions: 200
Agoutis: 44, 47, 72, 307
Agriculture, commercial: development of, 91, 127, 131–32, 171, 174, 270, 283, 341; capital for, 91, 261; profits from, 91–92, 278; nature of, 107, 131–32, 144, 260; promotion of, 257, 261, 291; *see also* Labor
Agriculture, Indian: in pre-Columbian times, 43, 49–53, 61, 64–72, 335; in colonial period, 173–80, 195–96, 202–203, 287–95, 302–303, 307, 309; in missions, 198–99, 305
Aguarcha (mission): 281
Aguila, Antonio de (Recollect friar): 281
Aguilar, Joseph de (Franciscan friar): 282
Aguirre, Miguel de (Franciscan friar): 281
Alarcón, Diego (Mercedarian friar): 168
Alboawinneys: 205
Albuquerque, Juan de (Mercedarian friar): 69, 167
Alcabala: 181, 261, 272
Alcaldes, Indian: 114, 183–84, 292, 297; *see also* officials, Indian
Alcaldes mayores: duties of, 128, 142–43, 154, 191, 273–74, 276, 394n.; exactions by, 128, 165–66, 246, 256; and Indian tribute, 154, 273–74, 276; salaries of, 256
Alfara, Juan Baptista de (Franciscan friar): 281
Alfereces: 184
Alguaciles: 184, 297
Almojarifazgo: see taxes
Alvarado, Pedro de (conquistador): 94
Anahuac: 31
Andagoya, Pascual de (chronicler): 24, 63, 353n.

Andes: 5, 12, 337, 427n.
Anil: *see* indigo
Animals: 43–44, 46, 53, 72; hunted, 72, 181, 307, 309; *see also under individual species*
Annonas: *see* soursops; sweetsops
Anteaters: 47
Apastepeque, El Salvador: 262–63
Archaeological evidence: 18, 24, 28, 32, 36, 53–54, 60, 64, 69, 71–75, 77, 309, 361n.
Argentina: 5, 12–13, 337
Armada de Barlovento: 152
Armadillos: 44, 53, 307
Ashburn, P. M.: 119, 406n.
Atlantic region: physical geography of, 41–42, 45–47; land use of, 375n.
Attacks: by Zambo-Mosquito, 40, 80, 194, 201, 203–205, 256, 259, 281, 301, 306–307, 326; by English, 148, 281
Attacks, by Indians: on mines, 94, 106, 117; on towns, 94, 162–63, 194, 306; on missions, 167; on Indian villages, 194–95
Audiencia de los Confines: 95, 98
Avocadoes: 52, 260, 294
Aztecs: *see* Nahuatl

Bananas: 67, 69, 117, 203, 260, 294, 368n.
Bands: 12–13, 341
Baptisms: 86, 375n.
Barbecho (system of cultivation): 50, 87
Bark cloth: 55, 65, 76–77, 80, 196
Barón Castro, R.: 384n.
Barrientos, Francisco de (royal official): 78
Barros, Dr. Manuel (governor): 154, 158
Basketry: 55, 77, 295
Baudez, C. F.: 24–25
Bawihka: 27, 34–35, 39; *see also* Sumu
Bay Islands: 92, 255, 359n.
Bay of Fonseca: 28, 31, 92, 265
Beans: in pre-Columbian times, 43, 50–51, 71; as tribute, 99, 101, 179, 196, 275; in colonial period, 112, 144, 179, 196, 203, 260, 293, 305

449